MEDIA LAW

Media law is a fast-developing area of scholarship that raises many high-profile and controversial questions. Recent issues include the use of privacy injunctions, the regulation of the press, the political power of media moguls, mass leaks of government information, and the responsibility of the digital media to prevent the spread of extreme content and fake news. This study looks at these issues and the key debates in media law. The book includes chapters examining the protection of personal rights to reputation and privacy, the administration of justice, the role of government censorship, the protection of the newsgathering process, the regulation of the media and the impact of digital communications. The analysis is grounded in an account of media freedom that looks at the important democratic functions performed by the media and journalism. Examining various key themes, this study shows how those functions continue to evolve in a changing political culture and also how the media are subject to a range of legal and informal constraints. The book asks whether the law strikes the right balance in protecting media freedom while preventing the abuse of media power, and considers the future of media law in the digital era. It is essential reading for students and scholars of media law alike.

Media Law

Jacob Rowbottom

·HART·

OXFORD · LONDON · NEW YORK · NEW DELHI · SYDNEY

HART PUBLISHING

Bloomsbury Publishing Plc

Kemp House, Chawley Park, Cumnor Hill, Oxford, OX2 9PH, UK

1385 Broadway, New York, NY 10018, USA

29 Earlsfort Terrace, Dublin 2, Ireland

HART PUBLISHING, the Hart/Stag logo, BLOOMSBURY and the Diana logo are
trademarks of Bloomsbury Publishing Plc

First published in Great Britain 2018

Reprinted 2020, 2021

A catalogue record for this book is available from the British Library.

Library of Congress Cataloging-in-Publication data

Names: Rowbottom, Jacob, author.

Title: Media law / Jacob Rowbottom.

Description: Oxford, UK : Hart Publishing, 2018.

Identifiers: LCCN 2018017518 (print) | LCCN 2018017749 (ebook) |
ISBN 9781782256663 (Epub) | ISBN 9781782256656 (pbk. : alk. paper)

Subjects: LCSH: Mass media—Law and legislation—Great Britain. |
Press law—Great Britain. | Freedom of expression—Great Britain.

Classification: LCC KD2870 (ebook) | LCC KD2870 .R69 2018 (print) |
DDC 343.4109/9—dc23

LC record available at https://lccn.loc.gov/2018017518

ISBN: PB: 978-1-78225-665-6
          ePDF: 978-1-78225-664-9
          ePub: 978-1-78225-666-3

Typeset by Compuscript Ltd, Shannon
Printed and bound in Great Britain by CPI Group (UK) Ltd, Croydon CR0 4YY

To find out more about our authors and books visit www.hartpublishing.co.uk.
Here you will find extracts, author information, details of forthcoming events
and the option to sign up for our newsletters.

For Maya and Alys

Preface

What is media law? Is it just a term to describe an eclectic collection of laws that journalists and editors are most likely to encounter in the course of their profession? The view taken in this book is that the study of media law is not simply a tour of bits of tort law, crime and regulation that impact on publishers and have little else in common. Instead, media law is developing as a discipline that has certain key themes and issues that bring increasing unity to different areas of law.

When looking at various areas of law from a media law perspective, similar questions are encountered. In particular, scholars often look at the impact of the law on media freedom, whether the law enables or hinders the media in performing its important functions, and whether the law restrains the abuse of media power. As the following chapters will show, various areas of law are shaped by similar considerations and challenged by the same developments in the media landscape. Consequently, different areas of law are increasingly taking a more consistent approach to certain issues affecting the media. These developments reflect the influence of the European Convention on Human Rights, which requires the diverse areas of law to be interpreted in accordance with Article 10's protection of freedom of expression (along with other fundamental rights). While differences remain among the various causes of action, framing the legal issues as part of media law can shape the analysis of the law and its future development.

Writing a book about media law at this time is a challenging task, given that the area is fast moving and subject to constant change. Traditionally, media law referred to the various provisions that regulated newspapers and broadcasters. As will be shown, media law now governs a wide variety of communications ranging from those of powerful organisations to individual speakers, and much in between. The approach taken here will focus on the mass media institutions (old and new), but will also consider how the framework of media law can accommodate the rights and responsibilities expected of the other actors communicating with the world at large.

Another challenge comes from the changes in the industry. It is common to hear people bemoaning the decline of parts of the traditional media. There is much to this, and it is not clear how far the traditional business models can continue to support the levels of media activity thought to be healthy in a democracy. Many newspapers find themselves under intense economic pressure and have to cut back on activities and staff. The arguments in this book frequently refer to the issue of media power at a time when certain parts of the media see that power as coming under challenge.

This book does not take such a gloomy view for the future prospects of news production and does not consign the concern with the power of the media to the history books. Instead, it will be argued that significant changes are taking place, but these changes to some degree represent a shift in communicative power between media institutions, rather than a demise of media power itself. While the media is just one element in a broader system of mass communication, it is nonetheless a powerful actor that performs a set of important functions. While no one can accurately predict what will happen, the approach taken in this book will assume that the distinct role of the media (in whatever format) will remain in the UK for the foreseeable future.

The following chapters aim to provide an overview of the key issues and debates in media law. The aim is not to provide a comprehensive account of all the laws or a manual for those litigating a case, but to introduce the reader to the main fault lines and trends. Of course, some parts will engage in an examination of the detail, but this will be to illustrate the central features and debates. In approaching this task, the analysis taken in the following chapters rests on a particular view about the role of the media. In particular, it will be argued that a central goal for media law is to address concerns about the power of the media and to make it accountable. The book also takes the view that media freedom is primarily justified by its service to the audience and public in a democratic society. This approach will be explained in Chapter 1.

The organisation of this book is slightly different from other media law texts, and features several lengthy chapters dealing with multiple legal issues. For example, defamation law and privacy are taken together as personal rights. Similarly, the law of contempt of court and reporting court proceedings are also taken together in the same chapter. By grouping the issues in this way, it is hoped that the various common issues and themes (as well as the differences) will be apparent to the reader. The first chapter will look at media freedom, and Chapters 2, 3 and 4 will look at several key areas of media liability—the protection of personal rights, the administration of justice and the role of censorship. In Chapter 5, the discussion will move away from issues of liability to the protection of the newsgathering process. Media regulation, ownership and plurality will be considered in Chapter 6. Chapter 7 will then look at the issues posed by the digital media. While various issues raised by the changes in digital communications will be considered throughout the book, there are enough specific issues that warrant separate consideration. Finally, the book has a short conclusion, which will discuss some of the key themes and trends across all the various areas of law.

The arguments and ideas in this book have formed as I have taught Media Law courses for over a decade, first at Cambridge University and then at Oxford University. I have benefited greatly from the discussions with both colleagues and students on those courses. Many books and articles have been of great assistance, both in teaching the course and in forming the views expressed in the following chapters. I am particularly indebted to E Barendt, *Freedom of Speech*, 2nd edn (Oxford, Oxford University Press, 2005), H Fenwick and G Phillipson, *Media Freedom under the Human Rights Act* (Oxford, Oxford University Press, 2007) and G Robertson and A Nicol, *Media Law* (London, Sweet and Maxwell, 2007). Particular thanks are also due to the following, who kindly read through draft chapters of this book and discussed the various issues: Michael Birnhack, Oliver Butler, Ian Cram, Richard Danbury, David Erdos, Tom Gibbons, Alisdair Gillespie, Andrew Kenyon, Uta Kohl, Nicole Moreham, David Rowbottom, Judith Townend and Paul Wragg. Thanks are also due to the staff at Hart Publishing, including Bill Asquith, Roberta Bassi, Rosamund Jubber, Francesca Sancarlo, and Linda Staniford and to Maria Skrzypiec. Finally, and not least, many thanks to Lucia, Maya and Alys for their patience and support.

January 2018

Contents

Table of Cases

European Union

Hong Kong

Regulatory decisions

Tribunal decisions

United States of America

Table of Legislation

Table of Statutes

Table of Statutory Instruments etc

Table of EU and International Material

1

Media Freedom

I. Introduction

The concept of media freedom lies at the heart of media law. In each area where the law regulates media activity, a key question is whether the measure is compatible with media freedom. That will be a central theme for the later chapters that look at the substantive areas of law. The question for this chapter is what media freedom means and demands. This includes considering why the media warrants protection that is not afforded to every other type of activity or institution. Another question is what it means to say that a measure violates media freedom? It might be thought that any legal intervention limits media freedom, but in practice many areas of law regulate the media in ways that raise no concern (for example, a newspaper cannot violate sex discrimination laws in its employment practices). Some legal interventions may even enhance media freedom. The challenge lies in identifying those measures that are permissible and those that strike at the heart of media freedom. Addressing these issues requires some understanding of what the media should ideally do and why its functions are important.

To add to the challenges, the concept of media freedom is used as a powerful rhetorical tool. The imposition of a privacy injunction is often greeted with a declaration in newspapers that it marks the end of press freedom.[1] In the aftermath of the Leveson Inquiry into the culture, practice and ethics of the press, steps taken to introduce a system for the official recognition of self-regulatory bodies were said by some newspapers to be the 'death warrant'[2] and 'the death knell for 300 years of Press freedom'.[3] A quick review of the history books shows that the media has not enjoyed unbroken freedom for 300 years and that it has faced far more serious threats in the past. It is important to step back from the rhetoric and identify when such appeals to media freedom are mere strategic slogans and when the concerns should be taken seriously.

---

[1] T Wells, 'The day free speech drowned in a paddling pool of olive oil' *The Sun* (20 May 2016).
[2] Editorial, 'A dark day for freedom' *Daily Mirror* (31 October 2013).
[3] E Ashton, 'Ministers win fight on Press Charter' *The Sun* (31 October 2013.)

In this chapter, it will be argued that the reason why media freedom is valued rests on a particular vision about what the media should do. In particular, the media should ideally hold power to account, inform people and provide a platform for speakers. It will also be argued that the reasons for valuing media freedom explain why limits on certain activities may be permissible. Laws requiring broadcasters to cover political matters with impartiality are sometimes justified as serving the goals that underpin media freedom by increasing the diversity of viewpoints heard. That example divides opinion, but highlights a tension in which the importance of the media can point to the need for both freedom and restraint.[4] The point sounds like a contradiction in terms, but can be easily explained. Media freedom is important *because* the media is powerful. A powerful set of media institutions has the capacity to expose abuses of power and inform the audience on a scale not found with most other speakers. The other side of the coin is that the media can hurt reputations, mislead and suppress information.[5] Media power calls for some mechanisms to make the media accountable and provide redress for abuses. Later chapters will show that much of media law is a delicate balancing act between these concerns.

This chapter will first place the concept of media freedom in its historical context and look at the way that right is protected in law. After that introduction, the discussion will look at why media freedom is justified and argue that it has a separate foundation to individual freedom of expression. Two key factors will be discussed: the institutional nature of the media, and its communicative power. It will then be argued that media freedom is valued instrumentally for its service to the public, and the key functions of the media in providing that service will be outlined. After that, the chapter will argue not only that media freedom is valued for different reasons than freedom of expression, but also that the content of the right is distinct. The final parts of the chapter will look at two key problems in applying the concept of media freedom: how 'media' institutions are distinguished from other speakers, and what constitutes an interference with media freedom. Many of the issues discussed will recur in later chapters, and the current chapter will provide a framework to evaluate the substance of media law.

II. Historical Background

To get a sense of why media freedom is such a powerful rhetorical concept and given high status in the political culture, it is important to see how the concept developed historically. The first arguments for media freedom emerged as a reaction against

---

[4] See also J Oster, *Media Freedom as a Fundamental Right* (Cambridge, Cambridge University Press, 2015) 34–35.
[5] ibid, 33.

state-imposed controls on the use of the printing press, which explains why the concept is often referred to as 'press freedom'. During the Tudor period, a system of press licensing was established and such controls were sustained until the end of the seventeenth century.[6] The system of licensing restricted the use of the printing press to those with official authorisation and thereby imposed a 'prior restraint' (as the control was applied before publication). The earlier arguments for press freedom were a criticism of licensing, most famously in John Milton's essay *Areopagitica*, and often defined press freedom in terms of an absence of prior restraints. Under that early view, any penalties imposed *after* publication did not engage press freedom.

When the system of licensing finally lapsed at the end of the seventeenth century, the press continued to be subject to a number of other controls, such as the law of seditious libel. The state also held powers to investigate such crimes, including powers to search premises and seize belongings, which were used to harass and intimidate publishers that were critical of government. Consequently, the arguments for press freedom were developed to target the law of sedition and the use of the investigatory tools. During the eighteenth century, it became recognised that press freedom requires more than just an absence of state licencing and campaigners took significant risks to assert this demand for freedom. The famous case of *Entick v Carrington* is now remembered for upholding the rule of law, but was an important milestone in the campaign for 'liberty of the press' that curbed the use of broad search warrants against writers and publishers.[7]

As well as reacting to the types of control being imposed by government, the arguments for media freedom also owe much to the political and constitutional culture of the time. In the late eighteenth century, writers were starting to identify a constitutional role for the press in checking the powers of government, which fit with the concerns about abuse of power and corruption that were prevalent during that period.[8] As the UK began its transition into a more democratic system of government, an ideal of the press as a 'fourth estate' developed, in which newspapers were said to protect and represent the interests of the people.[9] As the electorate expanded, media freedom was defended as a means to educate the public on political issues.[10] As will be seen in later chapters, these ideas may have been formulated in a different political culture, but continue to have considerable force in contemporary debate.

The classic arguments for press freedom often presented a romanticised view of the media, as crusaders battling a corrupt and overbearing government. The older arguments were made as a response to severe penalties against publishers, so it is understandable that those accounts appear libertarian in orientation. The romanticised view

---

[6] For background see F Siebert, *Freedom of the Press in England, 1476–1776: The Rise and Decline of Government Control* (Urbana, University of Illinois Press, 1952).

[7] See J Rowbottom, '*Entick and Carrington*, the Propaganda Wars and Liberty of the Press' in A Tomkins and P Scott (eds), *Entick v Carrington: 250 Years of the Rule of Law* (Oxford, Hart, 2015).

[8] JL de Lolme, *The Constitution of England* (London, Spilsbury and Kearsley, 1775); J Bentham, *On the Liberty of the Press and Public Discussion* (London, W Hone, 1821).

[9] WT Stead, 'Government by Journalism' (1886) 49 *The Contemporary Review* 653.

[10] See M Hampton, *Visions of the Press in Britain, 1850–1950* (Urbana, University of Illinois Press, 2004).

of the press is less fashionable in an age where journalists suffer a lack of trust and are blamed for a range of problems. The classic narrative, however, helps to understand the ideal of media freedom and its role in the self-image of media professionals. Press freedom as a concept has evolved and changed with the political system, yet the basic ideal has proved to be enduring.

The narrative of the press 'winning' its freedom in battles against oppressive government controls should not be taken at face value.[11] The arguments for press freedom were not dreamed up by detached idealists, but were often used as rhetoric bound up in the politics of the day. Different political factions relied on their own writers to propagate the merits or evils of the press when it suited their strategic interests. Moreover, in some cases the lifting of controls may not have been a simple 'victory' for the press, but may have had more to do with the control being inconvenient for the government or hard to enforce.[12] Consequently, when one restriction was lifted, the government often found other controls to manage the press. That remains true today, with contemporary governments often declining to use legal powers to censor and impose liability, and instead resorting to techniques of news management and other forms of information control. For this reason, the trajectory has not been one of ever-increasing media freedom. Instead, the nature of the constraints change and evolve.

The classic narrative that frames press freedom solely in terms of protection from state oppression has more limited application in the current media environment. Media publishers now include very large corporations that wield considerable communicative power and have the potential to influence government, as well as hold it to account. The concept of media freedom has evolved to reflect this change. During the twentieth century, the concerns about media power led to a shift in thinking, with new accounts of media freedom emphasising the need for 'social responsibility'.[13] The evolution was most clearly recognised with the emergence of the broadcast media, which was subject to an intricate regulatory system. That social responsibility or 'public service' model was also a product of its time, as in the mid-twentieth century many large industries became subject to detailed regulations to promote certain social goals. That approach sits at odds with the hostility to the state under the classic version of press freedom developed in the eighteenth and nineteenth centuries. Many of the debates about media law reflect the division between these different visions of media freedom. The concept of media freedom is complex, with various actors advancing different arguments depending on the political and constitutional culture. Now, the question is whether the concept of media freedom needs to evolve further to accommodate the changes in the digital era.

To understand the meaning of media freedom in the current political culture and communicative environment, this chapter will examine the main justifications for the right, how it is protected in law and what constitutes an interference. The discussion will present a particular view of media freedom being justified in serving the needs

---

[11] For criticism see J Curran and J Seaton, *Power Without Responsibility*, 7th edn (London, Routledge, 2009) Part 1.

[12] Siebert (n 6) 4, refers to press licensing lapsing on account of it being too 'cumbersome' to operate.

[13] F Siebert, T Peterson and W Schramm, *Four Theories of the Press* (Urbana, University of Illinois Press, 1956).

of audience and stressing certain democratic functions. While this account of media freedom was developed as a critique of the earlier 'libertarian' view that demanded an absence of state interference,[14] it now has considerable support in the UK academic literature (though not a consensus)[15] and can explain the current interpretation of freedom of expression in the domestic courts and the European Court of Human Rights. Before looking at the normative justifications for this account of media freedom, the next section will briefly outline the changing ways the right is protected in domestic law.

III. The Protection of Media Freedom in UK Law

Britain is sometimes said to have a proud tradition of respecting free speech.[16] Whether such pride is warranted is a matter for debate, given that the country has also had its traditions of censorship and secrecy. However, the way in which free speech and media freedom are protected in law has changed significantly in recent decades. Traditionally, media freedom and freedom of speech in the UK were residual liberties, in which persons were free to act where there was no legal restriction. Under this approach, the Victorian scholar AV Dicey explained that freedom of the press was protected through the operation of the rule of law, in which publishers were to be 'subject only to the ordinary law of the land'.[17] If that requirement were followed, publishers would not be subject to a system of licensing or prior restraints that restrict individual liberty without first showing a violation of the law. To Dicey, liberty of the press was not a specific right in the modern sense, but rather a consequence of equality before the law and the absence of penalties imposed by government discretion. That approach offered little protection where a post-publication penalty was imposed by statute. To guard against legislative interference, free speech was dependent upon political support from within Parliament rather than the courts.

The courts gradually came to recognise both freedom of speech and media freedom as rights protected in the common law. This common law right could shape the

---

[14] T Gibbons, 'Free Speech, Communication and the State' in M Amos, J Harrison and L Woods (eds), *Freedom of Expression and the Media* (Leiden, Martinus Nijhoff, 2012) 22.

[15] For various works in this tradition see E Barendt, *Freedom of Speech* (Oxford, Oxford University Press, 2005); H Fenwick and G Phillipson, *Media Freedom under the Human Rights Act* (Oxford, Oxford University Press, 2006); Gibbons (n 14); O O'Neill, 'The Rights of Journalism and the Needs of Audiences' in J Lewis and P Crick (eds), *Media Law and Ethics in the 21st Century* (Palgrave, 2014); Oster (n 4); J Rowbottom, *Democracy Distorted* (Cambridge, Cambridge University Press, 2010) Ch 7. For a criticism of this general approach, see P Wragg, 'The legitimacy of press regulation' (2015) *Public Law* 290.

[16] *A-G v Guardian Newspapers Ltd (No 2)* [1990] 1 AC 109 at 283; Watkins J in *Verrall v Great Yarmouth Borough Council* [1981] QB 202 at 205; AV Dicey, *Introduction to the Study of the Law of the Constitution*, 8th edn (London, Macmillan, 1915) 152.

[17] Dicey, ibid, 152–55.

development of legal doctrines and was relied on to prevent public bodies bringing actions in defamation law.[18] Similarly, the common law right allowed the courts to interpret statutes in ways that avoided interferences with media freedom unless authorised by express words or necessary implication.[19] That did not prevent Parliament from restricting expression and media freedom, but at least required the legislature to 'squarely confront what it is doing and accept the political cost'.[20]

The Human Rights Act 1998 incorporates the European Convention on Human Rights (ECHR) and thereby brings Article 10, which provides for the protection of the 'right to freedom of expression', into the domestic law. Consequently, media freedom and freedom of expression are no longer residual liberties. The 1998 Act requires courts to go as far as possible to interpret statutes compatibly with the right.[21] If a statute cannot be interpreted compatibly, then the court has the power to issue a declaration of incompatibility, but not to invalidate the statute.[22] Public bodies are also under an obligation to act compatibly with Convention rights.[23] For example, any actions undertaken by the public body that regulates broadcasting, Ofcom, that violate Article 10 will be unlawful. While there are limits to the protection offered, the system under the 1998 Act has allowed the courts to develop their own jurisprudence on media freedom, which shall be elaborated in later chapters.

The protection of media freedom and freedom of speech is not absolute under Article 10 and restrictions are permissible if prescribed by law, serve one of a number of legitimate aims listed in Article 10(2) and are necessary in a democratic society. In applying that provision, there is a presumption in favour of the right and any competing interests should be narrowly construed.[24] In discussions of the legal protection for freedom of speech and media freedom, the qualified protection under Article 10 is often compared with the US First Amendment, which simply provides that 'Congress shall make no law [...] abridging the freedom of speech, or of the press'. Unlike Article 10, the lack of an explicit balancing mechanism in the US Constitution thereby gives very strong protection to expression rights. The First Amendment thereby places more pressure on the US courts to define what is 'speech', the 'press' or an 'abridgement' to provide a control mechanism.

Another significant difference is that the US First Amendment explicitly refers to 'the press' in addition to speech. Article 10 refers only to 'the right to freedom of expression'.[25] The protection of the media is nonetheless recognised as an aspect of the Article 10 right and any restriction must be subject to careful scrutiny.[26] What this means in practice will depend on how the court interprets media freedom and determines what weight to assign to the right. As will be seen in later chapters, this generally

---

[18] *Derbyshire County Council v Times Newspapers Ltd* [1993] AC 534.
[19] *R v Secretary of State for the Home Department, ex p Simms* [2000] 2 AC 115.
[20] ibid, 131.
[21] Human Rights Act 1998, s 3.
[22] ibid, s 4.
[23] ibid, s 6.
[24] *Sunday Times v UK* (1979–80) 2 EHRR 245 at [65].
[25] The only explicit reference to the media in the text provides that Article 10 'shall not prevent States from requiring the licensing of broadcasting, television or cinema enterprises'.
[26] *Bergens Tidende v Norway*, App no 26132/95 (2001) 31 EHRR 16 at [56].

depends on the context, with the court taking into account a range of factors. Given the overlap of media rights and individual speech rights in the text of Article 10, it is common to see the terms 'freedom of expression' or 'freedom of speech' being used interchangeably with media freedom. In many cases little will turn on the distinction. However, that does not mean that the two are the same and it will be argued in the following section that media freedom is valued for different reasons than the speech of an individual and that the content of the right is sometimes distinct from that of individual expression.

IV. Why Media Freedom is Different from Freedom of Expression

Before looking at the content of the right to media freedom, it is first important to look at the reasons for protecting the right. It will be argued here that media freedom has a separate foundation to individual freedom of expression. Freedom of speech is partly justified by focusing on the position of the speaker, in terms of individual self-expression and the autonomy to choose what to say.[27] By contrast, media freedom is justified largely in terms of its service to the public, to the audience and to other speakers. As Lord Justice Laws said, the 'journalist enjoys no heightened protection for his own sake, but only for the sake of his readers or his audience.'[28] Two key reasons explain why media freedom is valued for different reasons than individual freedom of expression: that the media is usually an institution and that it holds significant power.

A. An Institutional Speaker

The mass media is an institution and not a human being.[29] In many cases, a media entity is a large organisation composed of various departments and people performing different functions, and subject to various internal hierarchies. The final output of a media entity will be the product of an interaction of various different components, such as multiple reporters, photographers, headline writers and editors.[30] Given this institutional complexity, the arguments for freedom of expression that rest on certain human interests are less forceful in the case of the media. For example, free speech is

---

[27] See Barendt (n 15) 23–30, contrasting the interests of the speaker with those of the audience and public.

[28] *R (on the application of Miranda) v Secretary of State for the Home Department* [2014] EWHC 255 (Admin), [2014] 3 All ER 447 at [46].

[29] J Lichtenberg, 'Foundations and limits of freedom of the press' in J Lichtenberg (ed), *Democracy and the Mass Media* (Cambridge, Cambridge University Press, 1990) 106.

[30] Barendt (n 15) 417.

often justified as an aspect of individual autonomy, in which people are free to speak their minds and engage with others. Another speaker-based justification is that freedom of expression helps to facilitate self-fulfilment, by allowing for self-expression and the development of one's personality. These arguments, however, do not justify media freedom because, as the Leveson Report noted, 'press organisations are not human beings with a personal need to be able to self-express.'[31] The state is not under an obligation to respect a media organisation's status as a human being by allowing it to speak up for itself.

Similarly, individual freedom of expression is often justified as a form of democratic participation.[32] Allowing a person to freely express an opinion reflects the person's inclusion in the democratic process and is a basic political right similar to voting or writing to an MP. Under this view, freedom of speech is valued as a way of allowing people to influence democratic decisions and know that they have been heard. However, a media institution is not a citizen in a democracy and does not have the same interest in participation. Again, the argument runs that media freedom is not justified by the speaker-based democratic justifications. This line of argument is focused on the traditional mass media, namely newspapers and broadcasters. A citizen journalist self-publishing on the internet is a type of media that operates outside of the traditional institutions. Such a lone reporter will sometimes rely on both individual expression rights and media freedom rights. That such overlap can occur does not undermine the conceptual distinction between the two rights. The central point is that the professional institutions that constitute 'the media' (as typically understood) do not have the same interest as an individual exercising the right to freedom of expression.

A response to these arguments is that while a media institution is not a human being itself, it is composed of individuals that each have their own speech rights. However, the difficulty with this response is that the people working within the media speak on behalf of the institution, rather than in their own right. An analogy can be drawn with a teacher, who does not purport to exercise his or her own self-expression when speaking in the classroom.[33] Instead, the teacher executes the task required by their employment contract. Similarly, the person working in the media is constrained by the rules and conditions of his or her employment. An editor can instruct journalists about the types of story to be prioritised and slants to be taken. Most institutions are established to pursue a certain set of goals that constrain their speech-related choices. The argument runs that when a media institution speaks, it does not simply express the personal views of those people working for it. Of course, the views of the reporter or columnist will often correspond with the editorial line in the paper and no instruction will be required. That, however, does not turn the expression in the institutional setting into the individual's freedom of speech, just as a teacher's agreement with a syllabus does not change the status of that expression. The journalist or columnist is present because he or she fits with the objectives of the media company.

---

[31] Leveson LJ, *An Inquiry into the Culture, Practice and Ethics of the Press: Report* (HC 780, 2012) p 62.

[32] See J Weinstein, 'Participatory Democracy as the Central Value of American Free Speech Doctrine' (2011) 97 *Virginia Law Review* 491.

[33] On the distinct rights of those working in education, see R Post, *Democracy, Expertise and Academic Freedom* (New Haven, Yale University Press, 2012).

Under this view, the institutional speech is not an exercise of 'intellectual free will', but is made to serve the goals of that particular institution.[34]

Even if the media institution does not reflect the personal speech rights of the journalist, the argument that such institutions are separate may be challenged on the basis that media speech reflects the personal speech right of the person setting the terms and goals of the institution, to whom the journalist is responsible. If a dominant proprietor or editor determines a newspaper's content, then it could be argued that it is the exercise of that person's expression rights.[35] Under this view, there are human decisions behind the media institution, and the speech of the institution represents the views of those people.

One response to this argument is that when media institutions are commercial institutions, the decisions are not the free choices of even those leading the organisations. Shareholder companies are structured in a way to limit the discretion of its officials and make sure that decisions are made in the interests of the company. More broadly, any for-profit company will be constrained by economic incentives. Along these lines, Ed Baker argued that speech by a company does not reflect the 'freely chosen expression of the speaker'[36] but is driven by the demands of the market and need to maximise profit. On this view 'the enterprise's profit calculations determine the content, form, and frequency of its commercial speech.'[37] The argument can then be applied to those media entities that are commercially owned. So, a newspaper columnist may choose to write a shock-driven diatribe (with or without any belief in the merits of the argument) to maximise the number of eyeballs on the employer's website. On this view, the difference with the commercial media is not simply that it is an institution, but that '[m]arket determination breaks the connection between commercial speech and individual choice.'[38]

The focus on commercial institutions is, however, too narrow. The state-owned media and charity-owned media may not be constrained by commercial pressures, but are subject to their own institutional constraints and objectives. Again, the head of a charity or public broadcaster does not use the institution's resources as a vehicle for his or her self-expression and its communications are to serve the goals of the institution. The commercial media provides a useful example of how institutional constraints can work, but the point can apply more broadly beyond market pressures.

The arguments so far advanced will not apply to all types of institutional expression. The point can be illustrated with membership interest groups, which are institutions with an internal hierarchy and decision-making process that often represent the views of its members. Such a group can be seen as an agent that is exercising human self-expression rights on behalf of its members.[39] The application of the speech right to representative institutions will still be slightly different than with individual speakers, as the employees of the organisation are still constrained. The example shows that

---

[34] See R Bezanson, 'Institutional Speech' (1995) 80 *Iowa Law Review* 735.
[35] See the discussion in A Koltay, 'The concept of media freedom today: new media, new editors and the traditional approach of the law' (2015) 7 *Journal of Media Law* 36, 50.
[36] CE Baker, *Human Liberty and Freedom of Speech* (Cambridge, Cambridge University Press, 1989) 197.
[37] ibid, 201.
[38] ibid, 224.
[39] Bezanson (n 34) 745–50 refers to this as traceability.

some types of institutional expression can engage speaker-based interests. However, that will not normally apply to a media institution, which is not a representative membership organisation.

Sometimes media companies claim to be acting as a type of interest group, in so far as the content represents the views and interests of its audience. However, the market pressure to maximise sales does not turn the media organisation into a representative of its consumers. There are many reasons why a consumer will choose a particular media product that do not signal approval of the editorial content. For example, a person might buy a paper because it is cheap, has a special offer, or to discover what other people are thinking. Even if the consumer does like what is being said in a newspaper or television programme, that does not mean that the media body speaks on that person's behalf. In any event, commercial pressures do not always make the media responsive to consumers and may lead it to respond to the needs of advertisers. The commercial media is not a pressure group and cannot rely on the representation of its audience to claim a speaker-based interest.

While there is much appeal in arguments that distinguish the media as an institution, there are significant limits in the arguments above as a basis for a separate justification for media freedom. First, there is a danger in overstating the controls imposed by commercial pressures or other institutional goals. Even with commercial pressures, the editor or journalist may retain considerable discretion in deciding what messages to advance in the editorial content.[40] There may be areas where advertisers and the audience are neutral, allowing the editor to choose a slant free from such pressure. Even where the market imposes a pressure to support a particular side in a political debate, the editor is still free to choose the specific details or tone of the content. The desire to maximise profit or serve any other goal is a significant constraint on the institutional media, but does not dictate the editorial line of a newspaper in every case.

Secondly, it is not clear why commercial and institutional constraints are singled out to distinguish the media. If the true motives of speakers are examined to decide whether expressive acts are true statements of a person's belief or values, then much speech is vulnerable to being viewed as 'unfree'. Speech is often constrained by social pressures or professional interests. A person may choose not to express a particular view for fear of offending friends or colleagues, or may publicly express support for a viewpoint that he or she privately disagrees with. To require the exercise of unencumbered free will as a condition for a speaker-based justification to apply would be too demanding. The argument needs to be modified so that there is something about the formalised and consistent institutional constraints that is more significant than the informal social pressures that influence a person's expressive choices.

Finally, the focus on the institutional setting of the speech does not capture all the reasons why speaker-based interests are thought to have less force for the media. Imagine that a wealthy media mogul decides to subsidise a newspaper and shield it from commercial pressures on the condition that he could have final say on all editorial decisions. In such a case, the newspaper would retain its institutional form, but

---

[40] See Rowbottom, *Democracy Distorted* (n 15) 179. Baker (n 36) 228, notes this point, but argues that it is not sufficient to engage liberty interests in corporate speech.

would function as the mouthpiece of the owner. Think of such a newspaper as equivalent to an interest group with the proprietor as its only member. Many commentators would regard such a situation as the clearest example of an abuse of media freedom, rather than an act of self-expression to be celebrated. The reason for distinguishing the media lies not only with the institutional form, but also with concerns about communicative power, which will be the focus of the following section.

B. Media Power

Singling out media institutions as distinct from individual speakers is intuitively appealing. However, the appeal of that distinct treatment rests on the fact that media institutions generally hold significant communicative power. Focusing on the institutional or commercial nature of the large media entity provides a formal criterion that aims to make a clean division between media freedom and individual speech, but the underlying concern is often with power. That explains why a media company that is bankrolled and directed by an oligarch is not a celebrated example of individual self-expression. Along these lines, Onora O'Neill has argued that while self-expression is particularly important part of freedom of speech, the approach is different when looking at powerful organisations:

> The communication of the powerful can shape and influence, improve and damage others' lives, and in democracies we have long since taken steps to regulate the communication of most powerful organisations.[41]

The point is not just that the mass media is a set of institutions, but that those institutions are powerful.

The argument begs the question what is meant by media power? A large media organisation cannot coerce people into doing something they do not wish to do. In one influential account, Manuel Castells argues that communication is a form of power that operates through the 'construction of meaning'.[42] For example, several decades ago, drink driving was not widely condemned and was even seen as a positive trait in so far as it reflected an ability to hold your drink.[43] A sustained campaign, however, has changed attitudes and a heavy stigma now attaches to such conduct. The social meaning of drink driving has changed over time, partly as a result of a communicative strategy. Power, on Castells' view, lies not just in getting people to do things through coercion, but can be achieved through shaping social meanings.[44] Communicative power is not limited to the ability to get people to *do* certain things. The power of the media lies in being able to shape public opinion more broadly. This can have an impact on politics, in influencing voting decisions or the topics for political discussion.

---

[41] O'Neill (n 15) 41.
[42] M Castells, *Communication Power* (Oxford, Oxford University Press, 2009) 10.
[43] See L Lessig, 'The Regulation of Social Meaning' (1995) 62 *University of Chicago Law Review* 943 for a range of examples discussing this type of regulation.
[44] Castells (n 42) 10.

The power also has an impact on social lives, influencing how others perceive people. The later chapters will show how the different parts of media law are concerned with the various areas of life that the media can influence.

The power to shape public opinion should not be viewed in crude terms of 'thought control' or direct instruction to the public. Much social science research carried out to investigate the impact of media coverage has concluded that the direct effects of the media are minimal. The research on media effects has shown how mass communications influence audiences not by telling people what to think, but through effects such as framing, priming and agenda-setting. With agenda setting, the 'influence is on the salience, the importance or prominence, of issues and other topics in the news, not on attitudes and opinions'.[45] So a choice to run stories on crime may cause people to think about that issue more frequently and make it into a topic for political discussion. The media can sometimes be said to have an agenda-setting effect on political leaders, in which elected officials respond to issues that have been given a high profile in the news.[46] Priming is the way that issues high on the agenda shape the criteria for making choices.[47] Again, a repeated emphasis on issues of crime may lead people to focus on law and order policies when evaluating the performance of the government. The term framing is sometimes used to refer 'to the way in which opinions about an issue can be altered by emphasising or de-emphasising particular facets of that issue.'[48] On this account, if a newspaper runs a story on immigration, it could emphasise the role played by incoming labour in providing various public services, or it could emphasise the issue in terms of jobs going to foreign workers. The presentation frames the terms of the debate and can influence the direction of opinion. The term 'framing' is also used in a narrower sense to mean the effects based solely on the presentation of equivalent information.[49] A classic example is choosing whether to present a risk in terms of possible losses or gains, which can influence whether a person has a positive or negative response.[50] Effects such as agenda setting, priming and framing show how the power of communications can be subtle, and does not simply operate in the direct way sometimes associated with the old fears about propaganda.

So far, the argument is that communicative resources provide a source of power. That alone does not explain why the communicative power of the media should be treated differently from that of individual speakers. The most common explanation is that with the modern media, communicative resources are concentrated in the hands of a small number of owners, editors and other content producers. Producing professional mass media content on a regular basis has traditionally had high start-up costs and further costs in the dissemination and marketing of content. That concern was

[45] M McCombs, 'The Agenda-Setting Function of the Press' in G Overholser, KH Jamieson, *Institutions of American Democracy: The Press* (Oxford, Oxford University Press, 2005) 158.

[46] S Iyengar, 'A Typology of Media Effects' in K Kenski and K Jamieson (eds), *The Oxford Handbook of Political Communication* (Oxford, Oxford University Press, 2017).

[47] ibid.

[48] S Iyengar, 'The State of Media Effects Research' in J Curran (ed), *Mass Media and Society*, 5th edn (London, Bloomsbury, 2010) 279.

[49] See discussion in M Cacciatore, DA Scheufele and S Iyengar, 'The End of Framing as we Know it ... and the Future of Media Effects' (2016) 19 *Mass Communication and Society* 7.

[50] See D Kahneman and A Tversky, 'Choices, Values and Frames' (1984) 39 *American Psychologist* 341.

reflected in AJ Liebling's famous remark that freedom of the press is guaranteed only to those who own one.[51] The economics of the media therefore restricts the exercise of media freedom in practice to a small number of people. There is no reason to privilege the self-expression or participation rights of a select number, where most other people have no similar opportunity to speak in such a forum.

The limit of media power to a small number is not solely based on the economics of publishing and also reflects a basic division of labour. Not everyone can track leading public issues and assess the evidence due to limits of time and expertise. The media therefore develops the resources and expertise to carry out this function and alert the public. As Sonja West explains, the media are 'repeat player specialists'.[52] The allocation of that function gives the media both its public importance and its power. While local media today is rarely thought of as powerful, similar points can apply in so far as it provides a focal point for local attention, has the resources to research what is happening locally, attend court, and has on-going relations with local police and government. That local level power explains why there is often concern about the lack of competition or diversity in some local news sources.

The communicative power of the mass media means that it is a gatekeeper that decides which ideas will most likely be heard or placed high on the political agenda. A media organisation might decide not to carry stories that promote certain viewpoints or that are sympathetic to certain groups. In such a case, the decision of the media can undermine free speech in so far as it stops important views being heard. When acting in such a way, media institutions can become a type of censor. On this view, the power of the mass media means it is not like any other speaker, but *is* the forum in which competing views play out.[53]

The arguments above explain why the justifications for individual freedom of expression do not have the same force in relation to powerful media institutions. Freedom of speech is normally seen as a matter of personal autonomy and self-fulfilment. However, there is no reason why either of those interests require concentrated powers to communicate on a wide scale. As already noted, the concentrated power of the media has the potential to curtail the autonomy and self-fulfilment of others. Freedom of expression is also frequently justified in the name of a democracy. However, the norm in a democracy is one of equality, in which citizens have an *equal opportunity* to influence collective decisions. The mass media, in reaching a large audience on a regular basis, will necessarily have disproportionate opportunities to influence political opinion. However, nobody seeks the elimination of the mass media through the levelling of all speech opportunities. Instead the unequal power of the media is reconciled with political equality by ensuring that it functions to serve the interest of the audience and public, which will be outlined below.

Those concerns with communicative power also explain why the argument that free speech aids the discovery of the truth applies differently with the mass media. The classic truth argument for free speech runs that if ideas can be freely expressed, then the process of scrutiny and debate will allow the best ideas and arguments to

---

[51] AJ Liebling, *The Press* (New York, Ballatine, 1964) 30–31.
[52] S West, 'Press Exceptionalism' (2014) 127 *Harvard Law Review* 2434, 2445.
[53] Lichtenberg (n 29) 123.

be identified. While the media can serve this function by providing a platform and evaluating credible arguments, the power of the media can also be used to distort the process. The gatekeeping function of the media means that certain ideas may gain an undue advantage in the marketplace of ideas because they happen to be favoured by a particular media owner or editor. The power of the media means that the marketplace does not function on a level playing field.[54] Consequently, it may be important to provide mechanisms in which the choices of the media can be contested and challenged in order to facilitate the discovery of the truth.

The arguments based on media power advanced above are open to challenge in the light of the developments in digital communications. In particular, the costs of entry for publishers have declined significantly in the digital era, as have the costs of distribution. When user-generated content became a mass phenomenon, people were quick to point out that everyone had become their own media outlet.[55] People can write on whatever topics they want and have the potential to reach a wide audience. Accordingly, there is now a question of whether the media continues to hold significant communicative power beyond that held by individual speakers.

While the media system remains in transition, it is argued here that it would be premature to consign concerns about media power to history.[56] Many people can speak and make their thoughts available to the public at large, but that is not the same as a media institution which provides comprehensive and authoritative coverage across a wide range of areas, or produces high quality dramas, comedies or reality shows. The production of significant quantities of high quality and diverse media content on a regular basis normally requires significant expertise, resources and manpower. News organisations still need to cultivate sources and invest in the processes of research and investigation. As Eli Noam points out, when the expense of producing the content is coupled with the relatively low cost of reproducing another copy to each audience member (especially on the digital media), there is an economy of scale that works to the advantage of large companies and can generate a level of concentration.[57] The digital media may even increase some costs, such as digital marketing or the acquisition of data about audiences that helps the content reach a wide audience.

The trend is also supported by the economics of attention. A number of studies have shown that a small number of sites tend to gain a disproportionate amount of attention in the digital media, and that there is a long tail of sites that get much fewer views—called a 'power-law' distribution.[58] That explains why certain large organisations have become more rather than less powerful in the digital era. *The Guardian* and *New York Times* are no longer geographically limited, but have become brands with a

---

[54] S Ingber, 'The marketplace of ideas: A legitimizing myth' (1984) *Duke Law Journal* 1.

[55] D Gillmor, *We the Media* (Sebastopol, CA, O'Reilly, 2004).

[56] For example, the Competition and Markets Authority recently found that traditional media institutions continue to have political influence and are a main source of news in the UK, see Competition and Markets Authority, *Anticipated Acquisition by 21st Century Fox, Inc of Sky Plc: Provisional Findings Report* (23 January 2018).

[57] E Noam, *Media Ownership and Concentration in America* (Oxford, Oxford University Press, 2009) 36.

[58] The trend was identified over a decade ago, see M Hindman, *The Myth of Digital Democracy* (Princeton University Press, 2008) and discussion in J Rowbottom, 'Media Freedom and Political Debate in the Digital Era' (2006) 69 *Modern Law Review* 489. See also J Webster, *The Marketplace of Attention* (Cambridge Mass., MIT Press, 2014), discussing how various forces mean 'cultural consumption across all forms of media remains surprisingly concentrated', 19.

global audience. Once that audience has been established and gains a reputation, then audiences are likely to come back. Not every traditional media outlet will be so fortunate and an established newspaper may be superseded by a popular website. However, such a development may represent a change in the elite, in which a web-based media company takes the place of a print-based publisher.

An even bigger change comes with the presence of the giant tech firms that provide a type of media service in organising and providing access to the content found online. Companies such as Google and Facebook may not produce media content in same way as a newspaper, but perform a gatekeeping function that wields significant power on a global scale and which also tends to be concentrated in the hands of a small number of companies. That power is increased by the data collected about users, which can be used to tailor and target services to maximise the company's impact and command of attention. The types of media company and activity that have access to a mass audience are evolving, but there remain sets of institutions that wield significant communicative power. This is not to overlook the significant changes resulting from digital communications. The relationship between the media and audience is changing, with greater input and scrutiny from the readers. It will be noted later that drawing the line between the media and other speakers is no easy task, but that issue of definition should not be mistaken for a level playing field.

The argument so far is that media freedom is justified for different reasons than individual freedom of speech. However, the discussion has not set out a positive case for protecting media freedom. It is argued here that the central reason for valuing media freedom is instrumental, namely that a free media will serve the interests of the audience and the public more generally. Along such lines, Lichtenberg emphasises an instrumental justification for press freedom that is 'contingent on the degree to which it promotes certain values at the core of our interest in freedom of expression generally.'[59] Under this view, not everything done by the media engages media freedom. Tearing down a person's name with scant evidence would constitute an abuse of media power, rather than an exercise of its freedom. By contrast, when the media engages in serious and careful reporting of a matter of general interest, its freedom will be of strongest importance, as it serves the interest of the audience. This account of media freedom is reflected in the European Court of Human Rights statements that Article 10 comes with various 'duties and responsibilities', which can require the media to act in accordance with professional ethics in order to benefit from the strongest protection.[60] The justification for media freedom is therefore conditional.

This explains why the argument is not against media power, but rather to ensure the power is exercised responsibly and in accordance with democratic values. A powerful media is necessary for a number of reasons: to bring audiences together; to facilitate communication among citizens in the same political system; and to be able to challenge the government—all of which promote the values underpinning freedom of expression.[61] By contrast, a small media may be easily bullied and would not have the

---

[59] Lichtenberg (n 29) 104.
[60] See *Bladet Tromsø v Norway*, App no 21980/93 (2000) 29 EHRR 125 and *Stoll v Switzerland*, App no 69698/01 (2008) 47 EHRR 59.
[61] Gibbons (n 14) 36.

resources to investigate important issues. For this reason, in many systems the state provides support for the media in order to maintain the power of certain institutions. The power of the media is, however, worthy of protection only in so far as such freedom enables certain functions to be performed.

C. Non-instrumental Arguments for Media Freedom

Before considering the functions of the media further, an objection to the instrumental account of media freedom should be considered. Ronald Dworkin has warned that instrumental justifications for media freedom amount to mere policy arguments that invite the rights of the media to be balanced with other competing interests.[62] The argument runs that if media freedom is valued for serving the interests of the audience, the media may be restricted where it is thought to be in the audience's interest. For this reason, he argues that the rights of the media should be assimilated with the human right to expression. The argument was advanced in the USA, where individual expression tends to be afforded stronger protection. The argument has less appeal in the United Kingdom, where the expression rights of individuals can be balanced with competing interests in any event. However, a more general issue with Dworkin's argument is that it assumes other competing interests should not qualify media freedom. That still begs the question why the media should enjoy such strong protection in the first place.

One line of argument that could support Dworkin's view is that media freedom should be protected to respect the autonomy of the audience. The argument runs that if media freedom is restricted because it is feared the content will lead audience members to have false beliefs or behave in a way that is harmful, then the restriction shows a lack of respect to the audience as rational autonomous agents.[63] According to this view, responsibility for consequent action lies with the listener, not with the speaker. That justification can apply to both freedom of expression and media freedom, in so far as it looks at *why* the government chooses to restrict content.

There are many areas of media law where this principle will not come into play. For example, if the legislature provides that newspapers include a 'conscience clause' in journalists' contracts (so that reporters cannot be required to act in ways considered unethical), that would not show a lack of respect for the audience. Privacy law arguably does not engage this principle in so far as it does not rest on a concern about people having false beliefs or acting in a way that is harmful. With privacy, the disclosure of the information is the harm itself.

The argument based on audience autonomy is strongest where liability is attached to the publication of particular content on the basis that it will change a person's views or beliefs in a way that is harmful. The censorship offences considered in Chapter 4 provide the best examples. If the government prohibits the publication of state secrets

---

[62] R Dworkin, *A Matter of Principle* (Oxford, Clarendon Press, 1985) 385–86.
[63] T Scanlon, 'A Theory of Freedom of Expression' (1972) 1 *Philosophy & Public Affairs* 204, 213.

to protect itself from embarrassment or for fear of criticism, that restriction infringes audience autonomy. However, some state secrecy laws raise no such problem, such as where the prohibition is to stop foreign countries seeing information that would reveal confidential sources. While Thomas Scanlon, who set out a powerful case for audience autonomy, argued that the principle applies with equal force to all types of expression,[64] there are certain areas where the interests of audience autonomy are more forceful. For example, censoring political information can be particularly objectionable, as showing respect for each person equally as autonomous agents is a key element of democratic citizenship.

There are reasons to be sceptical of this argument. The case for audience autonomy assumes that the media and other content providers can influence beliefs through the provision of *reasons*, while in practice such influence can arise through more subtle effects such as framing, as outlined earlier. There may also be cases where the people wish government to protect them from certain types of message. If the audience mandates a restriction, then it may be compatible with audience autonomy.[65] That can be more pressing still where the media is concerned, as its power and authority mean that citizens can plausibly ask for channels of accountability and the prevention of abuse of communicative power. The argument to respect audience autonomy could also have far-reaching consequences.[66] Such an argument would object to a ban on cigarette advertising, which has been widely accepted and upheld in the courts.[67] Whatever theoretical appeal it may have, the audience autonomy argument does not fit with the practice of freedom of expression in the UK and Europe. The argument therefore cannot be taken as an absolute and does not defeat an instrumental justification for media freedom. However, it provides an important consideration in determining how the interests of the audience are served and for evaluating restrictions on content in media law.

V. The Functions of the Media

So far, the argument has been that media freedom is valued not because it serves the interests of the media as a speaker, but because it serves the public interest more generally. The media can promote the values associated with freedom of speech by educating the audience, promoting awareness of different cultures, providing entertainment, and so on. The most commonly stated reason for protecting media freedom, which

---

[64] ibid, 223.
[65] See R Amdur, 'Scanlon on Freedom of Expression' (1980) 9 *Philosophy and Public Affairs* 287.
[66] Which led Scanlon to move away from this account of expression in a later work: see T Scanlon, 'Freedom of Expression and Categories of Expression' (1979) 40 *University of Pittsburgh Law Review* 519.
[67] Barendt (n 15) 17.

elevates that right to its constitutional status, is the important role played by the media in a democracy. Two democratic functions assigned to the media recur in the literature on media freedom and the Article 10 jurisprudence. The first is the role of the media in 'imparting information and ideas' and the second is in acting as a 'public watchdog'.[68] In addition to those two well-established functions, two more functions are of increasing importance in the digital era: providing a platform to other speakers, and 'curating' the mass of content that can be found in the digital media. Each will be considered below.

A. Imparting Information and Ideas

In imparting information and ideas, the media is seen to facilitate opinion formation and decision-making among the public. While the free expression of individuals also plays an important role in opinion formation,[69] the media performs a special function given its capacity to collect, filter, verify, package and disseminate information. The point was underlined by Lord Bingham in *McCartan Turkington Breen v Times Newspapers*, stating that in order to 'participate in the public life of their society' people rely on the media to be 'alerted to and informed about matters which call or may call for consideration and action.'[70] Similarly, in its landmark ruling in *Lingens v Austria*, the European Court of Human Rights stated that '[f]reedom of the press furthermore affords the public one of the best means of discovering and forming an opinion of the ideas and attitudes of political leaders.'[71] Under this view, the media is an accessible source for information, which members of the public may use to develop their own views and arguments.

The function of the media in informing people seems self-evident, but there are varying interpretations of this function that make different demands of the media and the public. At its most demanding, the informational function suggests that the media provides accurate, in-depth and analytical coverage, to which members of the public will pay attention, assess and then form their judgment accordingly. The more demanding version of this view points to an ideal in which the media enables people to become 'informed citizens' with an understanding of public affairs.[72] Such arguments are often influenced by the work of Jurgen Habermas, stressing the role of rational-critical debate in the process of the formation of public opinion, which is then transmitted to government through formal processes such as elections.[73] Under such an account, individuals engaging in rational and reasoned debate should be as well informed as possible.[74]

---

[68] *Observer v UK*, App no 13585/88 (1991) 14 EHRR 153 at [59].

[69] For the classic democracy-based justification for freedom of expression that looks at the benefit to the audience, see A Meiklejohn, *Free Speech and Its Relation of Self-Government* (New York, Harper, 1948).

[70] *McCartan Turkington Breen v Times Newspapers* [2001] 2 AC 277, 290–91.

[71] *Lingens v Austria* (1986) 8 EHRR 407 at [42].

[72] For discussion of this model of citizenship, see the concluding chapter of M Schudson, *The Good Citizen* (New York, The Free Press, 1998).

[73] J Habermas, *Between Facts and Norms* (Cambridge, Polity, 1996) 356 and 382.

[74] See also J Mansbridge et al, 'A systemic approach to deliberative democracy' in J Parkinson and J Mansbridge (eds), *Deliberative Systems* (Cambridge, Cambridge University Press, 2012) 20, J Fishkin, *When People Speak* (Oxford, Oxford University Press, 2009) 33.

The account can seem unrealistic and takes an idealistic view of citizens and the media. Most people lack the time, motivation or cognitive capacity to form opinions on public matters through such a rational process of debate. Moreover, the idea of the media providing sober briefings on political matters and policy analysis seems a far cry from what the media actually does.[75] In later work, Habermas accepts that there are limits to what the media can do in facilitating informed debate, but still sees an important role for the media in the overall system that aids the formation of public opinion.[76] Even when the realities are accepted, the demanding version is still often taken to be an ideal and provides the basis for evaluating the media. Under that view, the modern media is often criticised for its focus on sensationalism, preoccupation with strategy and personality, and attention to matters of marginal public importance. The implication is that the media should be doing more to inform the public in a way that is serious and in depth. While the demanding version of the informational function may be unrealistic, some critics argue that media standards should be improved to move closer to the ideal.

The informative function of the media can be modified into an account that is less demanding. On this account, it is accepted that media content will simplify and that the public lack the time, inclination and expertise to make a thorough assessment of all the relevant information. The content provided by the media can nonetheless perform a valuable function, in so far as it sends a signal about matters of public importance and allows the public to rely on shortcuts to process information quickly. A newspaper story detailing a politician's social circle may appear trivial, but can provide a cue that enables the assessment of the person's character.[77] The argument runs that the media does not facilitate a high-minded reasoning process, but enables the public as a whole to make reliable collective assessments.[78] This modified version of the argument means that some of the sensationalist or personality-driven coverage should not be dismissed as lacking in value to the audience. It is not, however, a free-for-all argument and still requires the media to engage with matters of public importance with accuracy and seriousness. However, it does not impose unrealistic expectations about the levels of political information among citizens or the quality of media coverage.

B. The Watchdog Function

The second function assigned to the media is to act as a 'public watchdog'. Under this function, the media have a role in holding the government and other powerful institutions to account. The argument runs that the media exposes corruption and abuse of power, and forces those in office to explain their actions. The power of the mass

---

[75] See J Parkinson, 'Rickety Bridges: Using the Media in Deliberative Democracy' (2006) 36 *British Journal of Political Science* 175.

[76] J Habermas, 'Political Communication in Media Society: Does Democracy Still Enjoy an Epistemic Dimension?' (2006) 16 *Communication Theory* 411, 415.

[77] See S Popkin, *The Reasoning Voter* (Chicago, University of Chicago Press, 1991).

[78] B Page and R Shapiro, *The Rational Public: Fifty Years of Trends in Americans' Policy Preferences* (Chicago, University of Chicago Press, 1991).

media is therefore justified as a force that checks other centres of power. The argument is incredibly popular and is frequently asserted by the media (especially in response to calls for stronger media laws). The media thereby uses the watchdog argument to legitimate its own power and claims that it is acting on behalf of the public.

The idea of the media acting as a watchdog has a long-standing pre-democratic pedigree. During the eighteenth century, the idea developed that the press could supplement the checks and balances among the formal institutions of government to guard against abuse of power.[79] That further developed into the quasi-constitutional function of the press, acting as a fourth estate. The ideal remains powerful, with the defining image of the modern watchdog function reflected in the Watergate scandal, in which the journalist is presented as a crusader uncovering the abuse of high-level power. In the aftermath of Watergate, US Supreme Court Justice Potter Stewart put forward a strong version of this argument, in which the primary purpose of the constitutional protection of the press is 'to create a fourth institution outside the Government as an additional check on the three official branches.'[80] Today, the reporting of numerous political and corporate scandals in the media continues to be justified by the watchdog role.

The watchdog argument stresses the importance of the media being separate from government. The argument claims that whenever government pursues an action that might regulate or gain leverage over the press, alarm bells should ring. If government has the power to punish the media, then abuses of power are more likely to go undetected. However, a sharp division between government and the media is not realistic. The media and government are in a relationship of mutual dependence. The media needs access to government officials and information, while the government relies on the media for publicity. The watchdog function does not therefore demand a complete separation, but requires protection from attempts to *dominate* the media or to engage in collusion concerning the direction of reporting. To avoid dominance or bullying, it is important that the media remains powerful and that it has some protection from the possible channels of pressure.[81]

Another key aspect of the watchdog function is that it is relatively undemanding of citizens. The watchdog argument does not ask the media to educate people, nor does it ask citizens to be attentive and knowledgeable of public affairs. It requires the media to watch government, process the information for the public and then sound an alarm in the event of any foul play. The media thereby tells the public when their attention is required. The watchdog function requires only that some of the people are listening to the alarm in order for the deterrent effect to work.[82] The role for the media as a public watchdog is also rooted in an implicit mistrust of government, in which abuse of power is often suspected and government actors require constant monitoring. Given the high levels of cynicism and mistrust in modern politics, it is unsurprising that the argument remains salient.

[79] de Lolme (n 8).
[80] P Stewart, 'Or of the Press' (1975) 26 *Hastings Law Journal* 631.
[81] See J Rowbottom, 'Leveson, press freedom and the watchdogs' (2013) 21 *Renewal* 57.
[82] M Schudson, *Why Democracies Need an Unlovable Press* (Cambridge, Polity, 2008) 14.

C. Providing a Platform and Curating Content

Another key function for the media is the provision of a platform for other individual speakers. Such a function is closely connected with the provision of information, as by allowing other people to speak, the public become informed about the range of views in society and the intensity with which they are held. The provision of access to speakers has long been an element of the media's functions. For example, newspapers have accepted letters from readers. In previous decades, there have been experiments with public access television, though these earlier forms of access required considerable moderation from the media body. However, the primary function of the media was traditionally to present its own summary of events and perspectives, and access was at the discretion of the editor and limited due to shortages of space.

In the digital era, the media does not have the same constraints of space and thereby can provide more opportunities to engage with the public. The most obvious example is the role of user comments underneath media articles on a website. The change should not, however, be overstated. The main function of the media generally lies in the provision of its own content. Not everyone can appear on a popular television programme or write a newspaper article. Even where the media provides a platform for others, that will not normally give the individual speaker the same level of prominence as the media body's own content. That is unsurprising, as the provision of a platform supplements the more traditional media functions, rather than replaces them. While it is valuable to hear what others think, many people will still gain greatest value in accessing the professionally produced content. The position is a little different with digital intermediaries that do not produce their own content, but host that produced by others. The provision of the platform to various speakers provides a core element of what an intermediary company does, which can be regarded as a distinct type of media activity.[83]

The provision of a platform function is more closely aligned with freedom of expression than the other functions of the media, as the media company is facilitating the expression of others. Those individuals using the platform may not be subject to institutional constraints or wield power. More broadly, the provision of the platform may have greatest value for the speaker rather than for the audience receiving that content. However, the important point is that the media providing the platform does not itself hold an expressive interest as a speaker. The role of the host is valued only in so far as it serves the interests of the speakers using the platform or the members of the audience receiving the content.

Another key function of the media that is especially prominent in the digital era is curation. Given the mass of content that is made available to the public, people need some way to navigate the material. There are various ways that the media can perform this role. When producing edited content, the journalist can draw on various digital sources, help to summarise the diversity of views and direct others to where such content can be found through links. It is common to hear news reporters summarising the reaction on Twitter to various events. More broadly, the media can help people

---

[83] *Magyar Tartalomszolgaltatok Egyesulete v Hungary*, App no 22947/13 (2016) 42 BHRC 52 at [79].

to find what they are looking for. Such functions are most obviously performed by digital intermediaries, whether through providing a search engine, by allowing users to recommend content or through other methods of aggregation.

The platform and curation roles are complementary. The provision of the platform helps more people to express themselves and publish, while the curation function helps audience members sift through that content. There are, however, some tensions. While providing a platform serves the speech interests of the individual user, the curation function is clearly aiming to serve the interests of the audience. When a media company or digital intermediary provides a platform, it will also provide some mechanism to prioritise the content made available. The difficult question is how that decision should be made. A traditional news organisation might see this simply as an exercise of editorial freedom, in selecting certain views for promotion. The digital intermediary may, however, operate in a different way and rank content based on popularity or relevance rather than according to traditional news values. There are also questions as to whether certain speakers should be denied a platform in certain circumstances. Such denial of access may arguably serve the interests of the public in certain cases, but limits the extent to which the free speech interests of the individual speakers are served.

There are other arguments for media freedom, but the informational and watchdog functions are two key themes that are commonly advanced in the literature. The platform and curation roles are also becoming increasingly important in relation to the digital media. These functions are often associated with the 'liberal' account of the media, which is sometimes criticised as legitimating the power of the media with reference to lofty ideals, when in practice it provides cover for publishers to pursue profits and avoid any rigorous accountability for the harms it may cause. Moreover, there are many occasions where the media fails to perform these functions and sometimes can misinform and mislead. The democratic functions should not provide cover to evade responsibility, but provide a standard for evaluation. The media is thereby protected on the condition that its power is used in pursuit of these functions. Ultimately, media law is about getting the balance right, so that media entities can perform their important functions outlined above, while curbing the opportunities for that power to be abused.

D. Democratic Functions—Which Democracy?

So far the discussion has referred to a number of democratic functions. Such discussion may give a misleading impression that there is a clear agreement about what the media must do to serve the needs of a democracy. There are various theories of democracy, which have different expectations of citizens, and will consequently have differing views about how the media can best serve the public.[84] For example, a 'minimalist' democrat, that sees little role for citizens beyond voting in periodic elections, will not expect the media to make members of the public well informed on public issues.[85]

---

[84] For discussion of the way the media can perform functions in various models of democracy, see CE Baker, *Media, Markets and Democracy* (Cambridge, Cambridge University Press, 2002) and C Christians et al, *Normative Theories of the Media* (Urbana, University of Illinois Press, 2009) 102.

[85] J Schumpeter, *Capitalism, Socialism and Democracy*, 5th edn (London, Routledge, 1976).

Instead, the minimalist democrat will tend to stress the watchdog function, in which the media acts on behalf of the public.[86] By contrast, those theories at the other end of the spectrum, which seek to maximise the participation of citizens, may assign a bigger role for the media in providing a platform for others. Other theories may characterise democracy as a competition of interests, which may then expect the media to represent and mobilise key groups in society.[87] That account of democracy may value a partisan media that engages in robust advocacy. By contrast, a deliberative theory of democracy stresses the role of reasoned discussion in the process of collective decision-making.[88] A deliberative democrat will therefore tend to emphasise the role of the media in informing the public and in facilitating debate among different sections of society.[89] The examples above are not exhaustive, and there are many other perspectives on what democracy requires.

It is easy to make much of these various differences and argue that there is no such thing as general 'democratic functions' of the media. There are important differences between the theories and each will pull in slightly different directions. However, most democratic theories will broadly accept the types of function assigned to the media discussed above, even if there are differences in emphasis. Any theory of democracy will assign some role to the media in informing the public on some matters and acting as a watchdog (even if there are differences in how the public use that information). To analyse many of the practical questions of media freedom, a fairly simplistic model of democracy can be employed that does not require a clear choice to be made between the competing theories. A rough and ready approximation of how a democracy works is for the most part sufficient for us to identify the key role of the media in the political system and the reasons for valuing media freedom.

In practical terms, it is important to remember that no political system fully reflects a coherent theory of democracy and the UK political system has evolved pragmatically. This means that most systems will have practices that reflect different democratic models. A system that has institutions reflecting a mixture of democratic theories offers a number of advantages, with the strengths of one offsetting the disadvantages of other.[90] The benefits of such a mixture will be important when looking at the multiple systems of media regulation discussed in Chapter 6. Each theory of democracy contributes something to our understanding of an effective democracy, and it is important to learn from the various insights even if we do not subscribe to any particular theory in its entirety.

While the argument here does not track a particular democratic theory, it will be argued in later chapters that changes in political culture and the practice of democracy have important implications for media law. At its most obvious, the traditional culture of deference and secrecy has given way to a culture that prioritises transparency and

---

[86] V Blasi, 'Checking Value in First Amendment Theory' (1977) 2(3) *Journal of the American Bar Foundation* 521, 542 connecting the watchdog role with minimal democracy.

[87] See Christians et al (n 84) 98 and Baker, *Media, Markets and Democracy* (n 84) 177.

[88] J Cohen, 'Democracy and Liberty' in J Elster (ed), *Deliberative Democracy* (Cambridge, Cambridge University Press, 1998) 186.

[89] Mansbridge et al (n 74) 20. See also the 'public journalism movement' in the USA, J Rosen, *Getting the Connections Right: Public Journalism and the Troubles in the Press* (New York, Twentieth Century Fund, 1996).

[90] See Baker, *Media, Markets and Democracy* (n 84) for an account of 'complex democracy'.

open debate on matters of general importance (or at least claims to). While that change has taken place over a number of decades, in more recent years there has been a further shift away from political activity within formal democratic institutions, such as political parties and parliamentary politics.[91] The new politics may envision little hope for the informed citizen and can be hostile to experts. This is sometimes labelled as a 'post-representative' account of a democracy and sees many actors outside of formal politics, such as NGOs or more loosely connected networks of activists, performing important democratic functions. Under this view, the democratic system can be seen as more chaotic, in which unelected and self-appointed representatives speak on behalf of others.[92] This change can have significant implications for the way concepts such as the 'public interest' or 'public figures' are understood. While such changes mean that the authority of the media is under challenge from various alternative sources of information, there is a significant role for the media in such a system to fill the gaps left by the decline of other democratic institutions, to monitor those in power and highlight injustice.[93] The extent to which such changes describe what is happening to democracy in the UK is open to debate and the formal institutions of representation remain important. The point for present purposes is that the practice of democracy is not static and consequently the functions of the media in a democracy continue to evolve.

VI. How is Media Freedom Protected?

The argument advanced so far has been that media freedom is justified instrumentally by its capacity to perform certain democratic functions that serve audiences, speakers and the public. While media freedom has a different theoretical foundation from freedom of speech, that does not mean that the two rights will necessarily be different in content.[94] Accordingly, the various differences in the reasons for protecting media freedom outlined above may be accepted, but the legal right itself could be much the same as that held by the individual.[95] That approach was the tradition in the UK and in *A-G v Guardian Newspapers (No 2)*, Sir John Donaldson MR stated that:

> it is important to remember why the press occupies this crucial position. It is not because of any special wisdom, interest or status enjoyed by proprietors, editors or journalists. It is

---

[91] For example, see the 'monitorial' model of democracy in J Keane, *Democracy and Media Decadence* (Cambridge, Cambridge University Press, 2013).

[92] ibid.

[93] See J Zaller, 'A New Standard of News Quality: Burglar Alarms for the Monitorial Citizen' (2003) 20 *Political Communication* 109 and Keane (n 91) 241.

[94] Baker, *Human Liberty and Freedom of Speech* (n 36) 234.

[95] See Barendt (n 15) 419 on treating media freedom as equivalent to freedom of expression.

because the media are the eyes and ears of the general public. They act on behalf of the general public. Their right to know and their right to publish is neither more nor less than that of the general public. Indeed it is that of the general public for whom they are trustees.[96]

Importantly, Donaldson MR accepted that the rights of the media are protected for different reasons than freedom of expression, namely acting for the benefit of the general public. However, he reasoned that because the media is a 'trustee' of the public, the content of the media freedom rights is the same as that of the rights held by individual members of the public.

The problem with Donaldson MR's formulation is that it does not explain any mechanism that bestows such status as a trustee on the press or guards against abuse of trust. That account does not factor in the specific ways that the media can serve the public and is blind to the differences in power.[97] To give the same right to a media organisation that is given to an individual would simply entrench its power to amplify its views and exercise disproportionate influence over the political system. There are occasions where media organisations should be subject to regulations that would not be appropriate in relation to an individual speaker.[98] For example, broadcasters in the UK are subject to requirements to cover matters of political controversy with 'due impartiality', a requirement that would be unthinkable in relation to individual expression. Conversely, the media is sometimes entitled to greater protection than individual speakers, which includes the protection of journalists' sources and access to certain types of information. An approach that treats freedom of speech and media freedom identically would not be able to account for such differences.[99]

Despite the inability to accommodate special privileges for the media under such identical treatment, many media institutions may nonetheless see considerable appeal in holding the same rights as individual speakers. While special protection for the media appears to help it act as a public watchdog, one criticism is that such protection weaves the media into the fabric of the state, and thereby undermines the very independence that lies at the heart of the fourth estate.[100] This has practical implications too, as any benefits granted to the media can be used as leverage. The government may use threats to limit a benefit or cut a subsidy as a tool to influence media coverage.

These concerns may explain why media representatives are sometimes reluctant to accept special protection that at face value seems to be beneficial. For example, media representatives were critical of proposals to make liability for contempt of court in relation to internet archives conditional on receiving prior warning from the Attorney General.[101] The concern lay in the fact that liability would turn on the direction of a government officer. Some parts of the industry were wary about accepting special protection in relation to police search powers under the Police and Criminal Evidence Act 1984, for fear that differentiation from the ordinary citizen might in the

---

[96] *A-G v Guardian Newspapers Ltd (No 2)* (n 16) 183.
[97] Fenwick and Phillipson (n 15) 21.
[98] See Fenwick and Phillipson, ibid, 27, describing a 'variable geometry' model for media freedom that allows for distinct privileges and responsibilities.
[99] Barendt (n 15) 420.
[100] A Hutchinson, 'Moles and Steel Papers' (1981) 44 *Modern Law Review* 320, 324.
[101] See Ch 3.

long term weaken the position of the media.[102] Most parts of the newspaper industry have rejected a system of self-regulation that offers potential shields for legal costs, for fear that any system of regulation with an element of state support would undermine the independence of the press.[103]

A rejection of special protection may reflect a strategic decision that the media has less to risk by having the same protection as an individual than by accepting special privileges. Under this view, the media can protect itself through its political power, rather than through special legal rights and privileges. Along these lines, a prosecutor or litigant will have to think carefully before bringing an action against the media, for fear that it may result in adverse publicity. Attempts to censor the media often result in a public backlash against the government. That potential can sometimes offer more protection to the media than a legal guarantee. Consequently, even if the media had identical legal rights to an individual, it would in practice be treated differently as a consequence of media power. The idea underlying the argument is that a media institution can fend for itself, needs no separate protection and should exist outside the formal constitutional system. The point should not be overstated and the press has on a number of occasions accepted some special privileges, which will be considered in later chapters, and thereby does not demand identical treatment. In any event, the argument is not convincing. Whatever appeal it may have for the media, it is less compelling from the perspective of the public, as the protection secured in practice through the political power of the media may not be aligned with the service to the audience and wider public. A media institution may rely on its political power to avoid its democratic functions and responsibilities.

While Donaldson MR's approach represents the tradition in the UK, the law has since moved away from treating media freedom and individual speech as identical. In *Commissioner of Police of the Metropolis v Times Newspapers Ltd*, the High Court endorsed Lord Donaldson's approach and stated that there 'is no special Convention right for proprietors, editors or journalists.'[104] However, Tugendhat J then stated that 'there is a distinction between different types of speech, and different roles that people may play, which is not captured by Lord Donaldson's statement of the law.'[105] In particular, the 'activity of journalism' may be subject to some special protection, which indicates a shift away from Donaldson MR's thinking and shows that different considerations may come into play when looking at journalism as opposed to other speech activities. The Court of Appeal in *Marine A* similarly said that the law has 'evolved' since Lord Donaldson's statement in which 'those who inform public debate on matters of public interest as journalists (whether in the print, broadcasting or internet media) are accorded a special position, given the role of journalism in enabling proper and effective participation in a democratic society.'[106] The statements show that the media is not treated identically to an individual speaker in practice.

---

[102] G Robertson and A Nicol, *Media Law*, 5th edn (London, Sweet and Maxwell, 2007) 340.
[103] See Ch 6.
[104] *Commissioner of Police of the Metropolis v Times Newspapers Ltd* [2011] EWHC 2705 (QB), [2014] EMLR 1 at [127].
[105] ibid [129].
[106] *R v Marine A* [2013] EWCA Crim 2367, [2014] 1 WLR 3326 at [56].

This, however, begs the question of how media speech is identified and distinguished from other types of speech.

VII. What is the Media?

If media freedom has distinct content, then the key question is who benefits from the protection and is subject to any additional responsibilities? In other words, what is the media? To answer that question, a distinction can be drawn between institutional and functional definitions of the media.[107]

A. Institutional Definitions

Under an institutional definition of the media, particular types of speaker are identified as media bodies and then subject to a separate scheme of rights protection.[108] That is recognised in Justice Stewart's famous argument that treats the media as analogous to a branch of government under the separation of powers, which therefore requires the identification of media institutions to be protected from government interference.[109] The media is then institutionally defined in much the same way as the executive, judiciary and legislature.

One objection to distinguishing the media to offer enhanced or more limited protection is that a scheme of differential rights amounts to discrimination based on the identity of the speaker.[110] The approach may also be seen as elitist, in so far as special privileges are afforded to a type of institution. The earlier discussion explained that these objections are misguided and the differentiation of media freedom is partly based on its institutional nature. The media is also singled out for special treatment as a way of addressing concerns about communicative power while recognising that it performs important functions in a democratic society. Rather than amounting to an *unfair* discriminatory application of the right to expression, the media simply holds a

---

[107] I take the distinction between institutional and functional definitions of the media from R Danbury 'The Full Liberty of Public Writers: Special Treatment of Journalism in English Law' (DPhil thesis, University of Oxford, 2014). A distinction between 'functional' approaches and 'institutional protection' is also drawn in J Oster, 'Theory and Doctrine of "Media Freedom" as a Legal Concept' (2013) 5 *Journal of Media Law* 57. The functional definition is also used in I Shapiro, 'Why Democracies need a Functional Definition of Journalism now more than ever' (2014) 15 *Journalism Studies* 555. I use the terminology of functional and institutional definitions to draw on Barendt's second and third perspectives on media freedom, see (n 15) 420–2, to which the following discussion is also indebted.

[108] See discussion in Barendt, ibid.

[109] Stewart (n 80) 633.

[110] In relation to distinctions based on corporate identity, see *Citizens United v FEC* 558 US 310 (2010) at 346 and 350. See also Barendt (n 15) 421 and Oster (n 4) 25–26. For a response to such criticisms in the US, see F Schauer, 'Towards an Institutional First Amendment' (2005) 89 *Minnesota Law Review* 1256.

different type of right. By analogy, a school is not the holder of classic speech rights when performing its function as an educator, and the curriculum can be regulated. That is a form of differential treatment based on institutional status and function, which is not regarded as unfair. The same can be said of the media, and the different treatment of that class of speaker is not an invitation for the state to discriminate between viewpoints.

A more common and compelling objection is that it is hard to identify particular speakers as media institutions. There has always been a blurred boundary between the media and other speakers. For example, should a person handing out leaflets be viewed as the media in its role in providing information? However, prior to the digital era, in many cases it was relatively straightforward to identify a media institution. It was clear which entities were engaged in broadcasting and held a licence. Similarly, a definition of a newspaper could be drawn—based of the scale of distribution across a region, the frequency of publication and nature of the content—even if it lacked sharp boundaries.[111] Given the developments in digital communications, identifying the media has become a bigger challenge. The point was summarised by Tugendhat J in *Commissioner of Police of the Metropolis v Times Newspapers Ltd*:

> In the past, in order to communicate with the public at large, it was necessary to have access to the costly equipment associated with printing on paper, or broadcasting through radio and television. It was therefore possible in most cases to identify the activity of journalism with the activities of those who were engaged professionally as proprietors, editors, broadcasters and journalists. What the internet has done is to enable any member of the public to communicate directly with the rest of the public at large at almost no cost. So the difference today is that the activity of journalism can in practice be carried on by amateurs who do not need professional publishers or broadcasters, and it is in fact carried on by amateurs in that way to an increasing extent.[112]

Both individual speakers and the media to some degree rely on the same digital technology and distribution on the internet, which makes the two harder to separate. In the European Court of Human Rights, Judges Sajo and Vucinic went as far as to say that the distinction between journalists and other speakers is 'rapidly disappearing.'[113] The discussion of media power earlier explained why the distinction has not collapsed and it is a mistake to assume that the digital media creates a level playing field. Digital communications are now more like a spectrum of different content producers rather than a rigid division between sectors. At one end of the spectrum are individual speakers posting their own messages and at the other there are still large media organisations that employ people to produce content or facilitate the publication of other people's content. There is much in between, such as amateur websites covering a niche area or small-scale news providers with a handful of employees. Some interest groups produce digital publications that shape public debate. There are also loose networks of individuals that contribute to particular forums or act in concert to produce content. The difficulty lies in identifying which institutions have significant communicative power and can be expected to perform certain democratic functions.

---

[111] For example, a newspaper was defined in the Newspaper Libel and Registration Act 1881, s 1 (most of the provisions have since been repealed).

[112] *Commissioner of Police of the Metropolis v Times Newspapers Ltd* (n 104) [130].

[113] *Youth Initiative for Human Rights v Serbia* (no 48135/06) (2013) 36 BHRC 687.

While it is difficult, identifying media institutions is not impossible in the digital era. For example, under the Criminal Practice Directions, accredited journalists enjoy a stronger presumption of access to certain documents in court.[114] Accreditation can be demonstrated by showing a press card, which a person can apply for if they work professionally in the media and their work involves 'the gathering, transport or processing of information or images for publication in broadcast electronic or written media'.[115] The Crime and Courts Act 2013, s 41 was enacted as part of a scheme to provide incentives to 'relevant publishers' to join a newspaper self-regulator. That provision defines a relevant publisher as someone 'who, in the course of a business [...], publishes news-related material (a) which is written by different authors, and (b) which is to any extent subject to editorial control.' Similarly, in competition law, if a special regime of merger controls applies to newspapers and broadcasters, that also assumes those types of media institution can be identified.[116] There are various examples and each will have its own flaws, but each shows that it is possible to find criteria to separate media institutions for the purposes of certain media laws.[117] While it raises the usual problems in deciding where to draw the line, that problem is not unique to the definition of the media.[118]

B. Functional Definitions

While it is possible to define the media in institutional terms, an alternative objection is that it may not be desirable to limit media freedom in such a way. The benefits of media freedom could be extended to all those that produce journalistic content and meet the responsibilities assigned to the media. Under this view, if the main concern with media freedom is to serve the interests of the audience, then the issue is how far the speaker is serving those interests, rather than the status of the speaker. The focus on media institutions may also seem out of step with current trends, as media functions are more fluid and can be performed by a number of individuals and amateurs, and not just designated media bodies. For this reason, a functional definition of the media is often preferred in the cases and literature.

A functional definition looks at what the speaker is doing to decide if media freedom rights apply.[119] In the *Marine A* decision mentioned earlier, it was noted that the protection of media freedom is afforded to 'journalistic activity' rather than to a distinct institution.[120] Under this approach, media freedom is to be respected whenever the speaker is acting in accordance with the democratic functions of providing information and ideas, acting as a public watchdog or providing a platform. The media is therefore defined by a set of products or processes that we associate with journalism.

---

[114] Criminal Practice Directions [2015] EWCA Crim 1567, 5B.26–30.
[115] See www.ukpresscardauthority.co.uk (last accessed 17 January 2018). The criteria includes 'internet-based services'. See also the discussion in Danbury (n 107).
[116] For example, The Enterprise Act 2002, s 58 has a provision referring to 'newspaper' mergers.
[117] See West (n 52) 2458–62, Koltay (n 35) 48–49, Oster (n 4) Ch 2.
[118] See also Oster (n 4) 27.
[119] See Oster (n 107). Barendt endorses such an approach in his 'third perspective' on media freedom, (n 15) 421–24.
[120] *R v Marine A* (n 106).

For this reason, the Strasbourg Court has recognised that an NGO performing a watchdog function benefits from the heightened protection for media freedom.[121] Similarly, the public interest defence in the Defamation Act 2013 and the protection of journalists' sources are open to anyone, as long as they meet the required conditions. So as long as the duties and responsibilities associated with journalism are met, then any speaker can receive heightened protection. This also means that media institutions will not receive automatic protection and will have to show that their activities fulfil the criteria for journalism. Opening up media freedom in this way does not collapse the distinction between media freedom and freedom of expression. Not everything a person says falls within media freedom; instead the expression only qualifies for protection when it is part of a journalistic activity.

The functional approach is not as simple as it may first appear and can potentially be as elitist as the institutional approach. While the functional approach claims to protect anyone engaged in the activity of journalism, that begs the question of how 'journalism' is defined. This is no less difficult a question than defining the media as an institution. In practice, journalistic activity tends to be defined by reference to the products and processes associated with the traditional mass media. Content is more likely to be protected as journalism if it concerns a matter of public interest and been through a process that meets the professional and ethical standards expected of journalists, such as verification and fact-checking. While the functional protection of media freedom can apply to anyone, if the standards are defined with reference to traditional media organisations, then those organisations are most likely to fulfil those standards. For this reason, the difference between institutional and functional definitions may not be as significant in practice as it may first seem.

A functional definition also risks conflating issues of media freedom and individual freedom of speech that were distinguished earlier. Where individual freedom of speech and media freedom perform similar democratic functions, such as informing the audience, there is a case for offering heightened protection to both. However, the individual or non-media body will also hold interests in freedom of speech that are not held by media institutions. With a functional approach, there is a risk of losing sight of this difference and generalising the expectations of media institutions to all speakers, even where non-media functions are performed. For example, in *Medžlis Islamske Zajednice Brčko v Bosnia and Herzegovina*, the Grand Chamber of the European Court Human Rights stated that an NGO, as a social watchdog, was expected to follow the duties and responsibilities of a journalist even when it made allegations in a private letter to a state authority (as opposed to publishing the content to the world at large).[122] Such missteps are not inevitable under a functional definition, but it is important to be aware of such risks when developing the standards under Article 10.

Both the institutional and functional definitions of the media have shortcomings. There is, however, a role for both, and the appropriate definition will depend on what question is being asked. If the question is whether the media should be subject to a specific regulatory regime or have privileged access to certain types of information, then it makes sense to specify the type of institution. For example, publishers will

---

[121] *Steel v UK*, App no 68416/01 (2005) 41 EHRR 22 at [89].
[122] *Medžlis Islamske Zajednice Brčko v Bosnia and Herzegovina*, App no 17224/11 (2017). Compare the dissent of Judge Sajo.

need to know whether they are subject to a particular regulatory system in advance. Similarly, the purpose of providing special media access to the family courts would be defeated if anyone could claim to be the media and attend sensitive family cases. By contrast, if the question is whether a publisher should have a defence to a particular cause of action, then it makes sense to take a functional definition, so that anyone fulfilling journalistic standards can benefit. On the latter questions, the court can apply the functional definition on a case-by-case basis. The combination means that the institutional approach will help to identify those core institutions that are clearly recognisable as media entities, while the functional approach recognises the fluidity in the communicative environment and allows for the protection of journalistic activity that takes place outside established media institutions. The two approaches can also be combined, so that certain protections might only be available to media institutions when performing certain types of journalistic function.

Whether an institutional or functional approach is taken, the definition of the media is not static. As the means by which people communicate and the practices of the media change, so too does our understanding of what the media is. Thirty years ago, the term 'media' was generally used to describe either mass printed material, such as newspapers and magazines, or broadcasters. Now the digital media has transformed the ways in which people can communicate. In the light of this change, there are now multiple media sectors. Some digital intermediary companies primarily provide a platform to speakers and do not promote messages based on the news values of a newspaper editor. Social media companies and search engines do not engage in traditional journalism, but they help organise and distribute the mass of information. The provision of those platforms and the selection of content through algorithms is increasingly recognised as a type of media function. Consequently, this develops how we understand what a media institution or activity looks like.[123] There are also a range of responsibilities and expectations that are gradually being applied to such companies, which will be considered further in Chapter 7. For present purposes, the point is that the yardstick by which we define the media and its processes continues to evolve.

VIII. Interferences with Media Freedom

The final question to consider is what constitutes an interference with media freedom and what the media should be protected from. When discussing media freedom, it is most common to have state censorship in mind. At the start of this chapter, it was

---

[123] While this shows how the definition of the media evolves, it continues to reflect the practices of certain professional institutions, and the difficulties identified with a functional definition discussed earlier can still arise.

noted that the earlier theories of media freedom were a reaction against a system of state licensing. Licensing was a particularly objectionable prior restraint as it allowed a government official to restrict the speaker before publication. Along these lines, Blackstone saw press freedom as the right of a person 'to lay what sentiments he pleases before the public', but not to protect that person from post-publication penalties.[124] The arguments that primarily focused on licensing were generalised to include concerns about judicially imposed prior restraints. The suspicion of prior restraints is especially forceful where the measure restricts content before any legal wrong has been established, such as a pre-trial injunction. Prior restraints can be particularly damaging for the media, where the content may soon go stale and even a temporary injunction may thwart the main reason for publication.[125] For this reason, the courts will rarely grant a pre-trial injunction in defamation cases[126] and the European Court of Human Rights has also warned that prior restraints 'call for the most careful scrutiny on the part of the Court'.[127]

In the USA, the Supreme Court has taken a robust stance with a strong rule that state-imposed prior restraints are presumptively invalid.[128] While the UK and European jurisprudence expresses caution about such restrictions, there is no strict rule forbidding prior restraints. Several types of prior restraints are widely accepted in the UK, such as privacy injunctions and cinema licensing.[129] Moreover, not all prior restraints are equally problematic.[130] A narrowly-drafted order that has been contested in court may raise concerns about media freedom, but not of the same magnitude as a control resting on administrative discretion.[131] The issue for media freedom will depend on the type of restraint. In recent years increasing concern has been expressed about new forms of prior restraint being imposed through techniques such as the blocking of internet content by digital intermediaries, which stops material being accessed without a determination of its legality and with decisions being made by a private company. There is no hard and fast rule against prior restraints, but the use of such measures remains a live issue in media law.

The concern with prior restraints should not obscure the problems with post-publication penalties.[132] A punishment—whether a fine, damages, criminal or regulatory sanction—all constitute an interference with the freedom of the media. A post-publication penalty can have a significant chilling effect on expression. If the penalty is particularly harsh, if the procedure for defending the publication is complex or if the law is vague, then publishers may simply choose not to publish and thereby avoid the risk of legal proceedings. The self-censorship caused by such a chilling effect

---

[124] W Blackstone, *Commentaries on the Laws of England, A Facsimile of the First Edition of 1765–1769* (Chicago, University of Chicago Press, 1979), also noting that if a person 'publishes what is improper, mischievous, or illegal, he must take the consequence of his own temerity'.

[125] *Observer v UK* (n 68).

[126] *Bonnard v Perryman* [1891] 2 Ch 269.

[127] *Observer v UK* (n 68).

[128] See *New York Times v United States* 403 US 713 (1971).

[129] See Barendt, *Freedom of Speech* (n 15) Ch 4.

[130] ibid, 118.

[131] See the dissent of Justice Butler in *Near v Minnesota ex rel Olson* 283 US 697 (1931), and the discussion in I Cram, *A Virtue Less Cloistered* (Oxford, Hart, 2002) 130.

[132] Barendt, *Freedom of Speech* (n 15) 118–21.

may be worse for media freedom than some prior restraints in so far as the issue is not tested by a court at any stage.

Both prior restraints and post-publication penalties provide formal measures that are at least scrutinised by the system of human rights protection, which imposes a burden on government to show that a restriction serves a recognised legal interest and is necessary. As will be seen in later chapters, the government sometimes resorts to more subtle techniques of censorship. Government can make veiled threats to the media, seek to restrict access to certain events or information, refuse to cooperate with the media outlet in future, or publicly criticise the media entity. As such methods do not rely on an open and formal exercise of public power, the techniques of control are hard to challenge in courts as a violation of a fundamental right. However, it is important to recognise that such techniques used by government can be a challenge to media freedom, and to look for mechanisms to guard against such pressures.

The state is not the only threat to media freedom, and challenges can come from private actors. Some media entities may depend on the infrastructure owned by private companies to disseminate their content. A digital intermediary has the power to block content, push content lower down the search rankings or suppress certain stories on the list of trending issues. The intermediary can decide which media bodies to promote and make more visible. Such private intermediaries, however, are not required to respect the rights of others and there are arguments that such choices are an aspect of the intermediaries' editorial autonomy. However, as with a powerful media organisation, there are increasing demands to make digital gatekeepers subject to some form of accountability for their decisions. Such demands reflect the view that intermediaries are developing into a new type of media company that exercise a distinct type of communicative power.

Pressure can come from other types of private actor. The pressure from advertisers to carry or not carry certain content may be seen to inhibit media freedom. Again, such pressures are hard to guard against, as the media entity is not entitled to advertising revenue. A company is free to withdraw its advertising. More complex still are claims of internal private censorship. The power of a newspaper mogul to put pressure on journalists or editors to spike a story can be seen to undermine media freedom. However, some would argue that such pressure is simply a legitimate consequence of the hierarchy and management within the media company rather than a matter of fundamental rights.

The challenge in relation to private censorship lies with identifying those pressures that are legitimate and those that are a threat to media freedom. One answer to this question is that private censorship occurs when a concentration of private power seeks to subvert the journalist or media from performing its democratic function in accordance with professional norms. A letter from an individual to a newspaper complaining about its coverage and threatening to stop buying it is not censorship. By contrast, a large company's threat to withdraw advertising if certain content is published can be seen as private censorship in so far as a single entity has the power to impose significant adverse consequences in response to media coverage. This view sees media freedom not simply as an absence of state interference, but as the autonomy of the journalist and editor to act according their professional judgement. Media freedom requires independence from the state and the various centres of power, including the market.

The protection from private censorship often requires some positive state action to regulate the private actors. Laws requiring access to the infrastructure of communication on fair terms provides one example.[133] The law does not simply restrict the media, but can insulate it from other external pressures. Measures to support professional standards may reinforce the autonomy of journalism. Freedom of information laws can arguably make the media less dependent on insider sources for certain information. A state-imposed condition prior to a media merger, requiring editorial appointments to be made by a board independent of the proprietor, may uphold editorial autonomy. Some types of media law can work to uphold rather than restrict media freedom. Consequently, it is important to recognise that while state action can be a threat to media freedom, it is not the sole threat and nor does every state measure pose a risk of censorship.

IX. Conclusion

The discussion started out showing that media freedom is not the same as freedom of speech. The justification for media freedom does not rest on the same human values that typically support freedom of expression. The primary reasons for this differentiation are based on the fact that media bodies are institutions and wield considerable communicative power. Accordingly, much of media law is about constraining the abuse of media power, making that power accountable and harnessing the power for socially useful purposes.

The protection of media freedom is thereby conditional on the media serving the interests of the public, namely the key democratic functions. While some basic democratic functions of the media have been outlined, the specific ways these functions are performed will be taken up in later chapters. The various functions assigned to the media have evolved both with the political system and communications environment. Along these lines, the watchdog function of the press was articulated before the UK became democratic. As the country moved to a mass democratic system, the media began to perform a role in informing the public to equip them as citizens and democratic participants. Both the political culture and technology has developed to provide greater direct participation by individuals. Accordingly, the media (broadly defined to include digital intermediaries) now performs a function both in providing a platform for speakers and in curating the mass of content found online.

The changes in technology also mean that the media has been undergoing a period of rapid change. Facing stiff competition from the online publishers and declining revenues, many of the old models of journalism appear to be under threat. There is a

---

[133] See *Centro Europa 7 SRL and Di Stefano v Italy*, App no 38433/09 (2012) 32 BHRC 417 at [133], *Animal Defenders International v United Kingdom*, App no 48876/08 (2013) 57 EHRR 21.

constant stream of stories about established media bodies having to make cuts to their departments and a decline in local news sources. For all the talk of formal media institutions, looser networks of individuals can also perform some journalistic functions. A group blog written by specialists may not have a formal staff or any training, but can be a valuable source of information. There is an ongoing debate about whether the media will retain the institutional form that is prevalent today and whether the power of the traditional institutions will wane.

In the medium term, despite all the changes, some parts of the media landscape from the pre-internet era are likely to continue to perform an important function. The UK market can still support a significant number of national newspapers and the public service broadcasters remain a key source of news. In the longer term, it is hard to predict what will happen. If more newspapers or news providers close, that might enhance the power of those media institutions that survive. In other words, if the market can support a smaller number of papers and television channels, those entities will face less competition and wield greater influence. Moreover, the old media elites may be replaced by a new elite group of companies. This has already been witnessed with the growth of the tech giants such as Apple, Google, Facebook and Amazon. Collectively they wield a power that the press barons of a century ago could only envy. Digital media is disrupting many traditional models and practices, but so far there remains an elite set of media-related companies that have considerable communicative power. While the discussion focuses on the national elites and international actors, these arguments can also apply where power is exercised by the local media and specialised publications that also have a type of elite status and special function within the relevant field.

The argument in this chapter has been that a powerful set of institutions providing content on a regular basis to a large audience has been both necessary and a possible threat to the operation of the UK's democracy. With this background, the following chapters will examine the substance of media law, looking at whether the law successfully constrains the abuse of traditional media power and how it is responding to the developments in digital communications. At the same time, the impact of the law on media freedom will be a key theme. It is important to be alert to the risk that media laws can be vulnerable to abuse by those in positions of power and used to censor. The discussion will also show how the role of public opinion has evolved in the current political culture, which demands a greater role for citizens in the evaluation and scrutiny of public matters. The various developments in political culture, media business models and technology are collectively changing the expectations and demands made of the media. While these changes continue at rapid pace, there remains a consistent role for the media in serving the public and performing a set of functions that are vital to the health of a democracy.

2

Personal Rights: Reputation and Privacy

I. Introduction

This chapter will consider the protection of the two personal rights that are most prominent in discussions of media law: reputation and privacy. Reputation has long been protected in the law of defamation and for much of the last century has been one of the major legal risks for the media. By contrast, a right to privacy is a relative newcomer in media law, with the English courts denying a free-standing right to protect private information prior to the Human Rights Act 1998.

There are differences in the content of the two rights. The law of defamation attaches liability to false statements, while privacy is largely concerned with true facts. The law of defamation provides damages as a remedy, while privacy is primarily protected through an injunction. Despite these differences, there are sufficient similarities to deal with these two rights together. Both are concerned with personal rights that are protected in private law, rather than protecting the public as a whole. Both defamation and privacy laws seek to curb the abuse of media power and both protect rights under Article 8 of the European Convention on Human Rights (ECHR). More broadly, both areas of law look at similar issues in weighing personal rights with the interest of the public in receiving the information. While examining the differences, this chapter will highlight a number of common themes in the two areas of law.

The chapter will begin by outlining the interests protected and the main elements for liability in defamation law. The same issues will then be considered in relation to the protection of private information. Having set out the main issues for liability, the chapter will examine the method for protecting media freedom in these areas of law. The discussion will then briefly discuss some other areas of law protecting related personal interests. The final section will discuss some of the main remedies available to protect the personal rights.

II. Defamation Law

The law of defamation seeks to protect a person's reputation. The basic rule is that a speaker is prima facie liable if he or she makes a statement to a third party that refers to the claimant, which causes or is likely to cause serious harm to the claimant's reputation. The harm at the centre of the tort concerns the way a person is seen in the eyes of others. Protecting this interest in law raises a number of difficult questions. The court will first need to decide what the statement means and what effect that meaning has on the claimant's reputation. There is also the question of how serious the damage to reputation has to be before it can trigger liability in tort law, and whether any evidence is necessary to demonstrate that level of damage. Once these questions are resolved, there are further difficulties in ensuring that the legal protection of reputation does not inhibit freedom of expression.

The law of defamation has had a long history in England and Wales, both in tort law and criminal law. Libel was a criminal offence on account of 'its supposed tendency to arouse angry passion, provoke revenge, and thus endanger the public peace'.[1] Given that the goal was to protect the peace (rather than the rights of the individual concerned), the truth of the statement was initially no defence in the criminal law—the maxim went 'The greater the truth, the greater the libel'.[2] That position changed and truth became a defence in criminal cases in 1843.[3] By contrast, in civil libel actions (protecting the personal rights of the individual) the truth of the statement provided a defence long before 1843, on the basis that 'the law will not permit a man to recover damages in respect of an injury to a character which he either does not, or ought not, to possess'.[4] Both the civil and criminal libel actions were heard before a jury, and to be judged by one's peers was regarded as an important protection for speakers.[5] During the twentieth century, the number of prosecutions in criminal libel declined, and the crime was finally abolished in 2009.[6] The civil law of defamation has remained a significant restriction on the media, although it has been subject to major reforms in the Defamation Act 2013.

Prior to the reforms enacted in 2013, the civil law of defamation achieved considerable notoriety. The law had a number of features—such as a presumption of damage,

---

[1] *R v Holbrook* (1878) 4 QBD 42 at 46. For background on the history of criminal libel, see Faulks J (chair), *Report of the Committee on Defamation* (Cmnd 5909, 1975) Ch 16.

[2] The statement is often attributed to Lord Mansfield.

[3] Libel Act 1843, s 6 (subsequently repealed by the Coroners and Justice Act 2009).

[4] *M'Pherson v Daniels* (1829) 10 Barnewall and Cresswell 263, 272.

[5] Fox's Libel Act 1792 confirmed this position in criminal libel, following the opposing views in the *Seven Bishops' Case* (1688) 3 Mod Rep 212, 87 ER 136. While that Act applied to criminal trials, the position was the same in civil cases: *The Capital and Counties Bank v Henty* (1882) 7 App Cas 741, 775. See also *Cook v Telegraph* [2011] EWHC 763 (QB) at [94].

[6] Coroners and Justice Act 2009, s 73.

a reverse burden of proof and limited defences—that gave claimants an advantage in the process and left the law open to abuse by those with the resources to hire lawyers. Accordingly, Tony Weir once wrote that the law of defamation

> protects the wicked such as Robert Maxwell from the disclosure of their misdeeds. It induces the greedy to sue and tempts them to tamper with the evidence.[7]

There are many examples of such abuse of the tort. Lord Archer received half a million pounds in damages in 1987 after suing a newspaper for publishing a story alleging that he had slept with a prostitute.[8] Over a decade later, Archer was found to have committed perjury in the libel trial and was sentenced to four years in prison. More generally, the pro-claimant tilt in the law of defamation was seen to have a chilling effect. A journalist writing about a person known to be litigious had to tread carefully. In some cases, it was simply not worth the risk and some stories were never published. The volume of work generated by this area of law meant that libel law became a field of expertise that sustained numerous legal careers.[9] While the old law was subject to a number of criticisms, steps have been taken to strike a fresh balance with freedom of expression, including a public interest defence, the limitation of damages and a requirement of serious harm before an action can be brought.

While the reforms are welcome, few people think that the media (or anyone else) should have the unfettered freedom to tear down a person's reputation without any form of redress. The law of libel continues to have an important function and the law has to perform a difficult balancing act. Before looking at the workings of defamation law, it is first worth considering why the law seeks to protect reputation in the first place. To address that question, the following section will look at arguments based on dignity, on reputation as a resource, and on securing the conditions for the fair evaluation of a person's character.

A. Why Protect Reputation?

A person's reputation rests on how he or she is seen by others. A reputation is enjoyed when a person is part of a community and interacts with others on a regular basis. A person stranded on a desert island may not suffer attacks on character, but nobody would say that person enjoys a good reputation.[10] No person is, however, entitled to demand that others hold a particular opinion of him or herself.[11] When viewed as one's esteem in the eyes of others, it is hard to see reputation as a personal interest held by the individual.[12] Moreover, a reputation can be used to influence choices, such

---

[7] T Weir, *A Casebook on Tort*, 10th edn (London, Sweet and Maxwell, 2004) 523.
[8] For background on this case, see *R v Archer* [2002] EWCA Crim 1996, [2003] 1 Cr App R (S) 86.
[9] For comparison with the US, see R Weaver, 'Defamation and democracy' in A Kenyon (ed), *Comparative Defamation and Privacy Law* (Cambridge, Cambridge University Press, 2016) 93.
[10] The example is often used in privacy law, see C Fried, 'Privacy' (1968) 77 *Yale Law Journal* 475.
[11] T Gibbons, 'Defamation Reconsidered' (1996) 16 *Oxford Journal of Legal Studies* 587, 593.
[12] ibid, 592.

as whether to believe a person or choose to employ that person. Consequently, there is a strong argument that a person's good name should be open to challenge if someone believes it is undeserved or needs to be reassessed.[13] For example, a newspaper report may show that a person with a reputation for generosity is really mean spirited and self-centred. Reputations need to develop and change as people acquire new information and adjust their assessment of others.

For these reasons, there are some important qualifications in defamation law. The law does not protect an undeserved reputation and there is no objection when the attack is based on true facts. Defamation law protects reputations only where the statement is false. However, the law does not intervene in every case where an assessment of reputation is based on falsities. The law of defamation only steps in where a statement *lowers* a person's reputation. That does not mean false statements that put a person in a good light are harmless. A positive reputation that is based on untrue facts can have costs for other people, such as hiring the wrong person, voting for an incompetent candidate or befriending a dishonest person. The audience has an interest in receiving true information, but that is not the main concern in defamation law.[14] Unless some other legal control applies, a good (but underserved) reputation can only be challenged through corrective statements made by others.[15]

One way to justify the protection of reputation from a negative false attack is to reformulate the harm so that it does not simply relate to one's esteem in the eyes of others, but engages other personal interests.[16] Along these lines, reputation is often described as being a central aspect of a person's dignity.[17] In an influential article, Robert Post explains how an attack on reputation can harm a person's status and inclusion within a community. On this view, the aspect of dignity that defamation law protects is 'the respect (and self-respect) that arises from full membership in society'.[18] When the defamatory statement is published to a third party, the audience has to choose whether to accept that statement and view that person as unworthy of being treated with the respect that is normally afforded to a member of the community.[19] The function of defamation law is to 'police' those deviations from the community's rules of respect.[20] The argument values reputation not because a good name is itself intrinsically worthy of protection, but because it instrumentally serves a broader interest in personal dignity.[21] The argument moves the concern of the law away from how other people evaluate the claimant (an external element) to how it impacts on the 'private self' (an internal element), such as 'our own sense of intrinsic self-worth'.[22]

---

[13] ibid, 595–96.

[14] ibid, 597.

[15] Although that corrective statement may itself be subject to a claim in libel, in so far as it lowers the existing reputation.

[16] See L McNamara, *Defamation and Reputation* (Oxford, Oxford University Press, 2007) Ch 2.

[17] *Reynolds v Times Newspapers Ltd* [2001] 2 AC 127, 200 (HL).

[18] R Post, 'The Social Foundation of Defamation Law: Reputation and the Constitution' (1986) 74 *California Law Review* 691, 711.

[19] ibid, 711.

[20] ibid, 710.

[21] A Ripstein, *Private Wrongs* (Cambridge, Mass, Harvard University Press, 2016) 196–97. See also E Barendt, 'What is the Point of Libel Law?' (1999) 52 *Current Legal Problems* 110, 117.

[22] Post (n 18) 710.

Locating the harm within the self is seen to provide a more compelling case for legal intervention, than if the harm is solely explained in terms of how the person is seen by others.

A common criticism of dignity as a rationale lies in the vagueness of the concept.[23] The concept offers little guidance on practical questions as to when reputation deserves protection and how it should be set against other rights and interests. Dignity can sometimes be invoked as a label to justify legal intervention. David Feldman has argued that not all aspects of a person's dignity are worthy of legal protection, stating that while defamation 'sometimes incidentally protects dignity, it is often dignity and self worth of the worst sort: self-importance and pomposity'.[24] Moreover, while the focus on a personal interest may bolster the case for legal intervention, it fails to reflect the damage that a defamatory statement causes to the interaction and engagement with others.[25] Dignity captures an important dimension to reputation, but there are other aspects that can make it worthy of protection.

Reputation can also be viewed as a type of resource that shapes how a person's actions are interpreted, and can open or close various opportunities to engage with others. A resource-based account of reputation is easily explained in the commercial context. A building company will want a reputation for safety and efficiency if it is to get more contracts. Reputation will also be important for professionals for similar reasons. A doctor with a reputation for competence is more likely to be promoted and progress in his or her career. Social opportunities will often depend on reputation. A person known for being trustworthy and loyal will have different social prospects from a person known for being two-faced. Reputation can also be a political resource that enables a person to influence collective decisions and mobilise others.[26] Most obviously, a politician's reputation is important for voters to make an assessment in an election. The reputation of a participant in political debate has an impact on whether that person is likely to be believed. It is to be hoped that a reputation for integrity or expertise will make a person more persuasive. Even if that is not the case, a reputation provides people with a shortcut in assessing arguments. Some speakers might have a reputation for being straight talkers, for being tough, or honest.

A false attack on a reputation can devalue a person's resources to engage in various activities. The view that reputation should be valued as a type of resource does not rest on showing that an attack on reputation actually causes any social isolation, political failure or professional losses. An attack on reputation is an attempt to diminish the resources that provide an *opportunity* to engage with others in certain ways. The impact is on the resource itself, rather than on the way it is used. The resource-based view is therefore consistent with an action in defamation arising even where a person has suffered no form of exclusion or lack of influence in practice.

Simply that a reputation is a resource does not provide a reason for legal protection. One possible argument for protection is that the way the resource is acquired

---

[23] For discussion in the context of defamation, see A Mullis and A Scott, 'The swing of the pendulum: reputation, expression and the re-centring of English libel law' (2012) 63 *Northern Ireland Legal Quarterly* 27, 37–39 and E Barendt, 'What is the Point of Libel Law?' (n 21).

[24] D Feldman, 'Human dignity as a legal value: Part 2' (2000) *Public Law* 61, 75.

[25] See D Howarth, 'Libel: Its Purpose and Reform' (2011) 74 *Modern Law Review* 845, 853.

[26] J Thompson, *Political Scandal: Power and Visibility in the Media Age* (Cambridge, Polity, 2000) 246.

warrants safeguards from its unfair depletion. Along these lines, Robert Post has identified a strand of thought that views 'reputation as property' that is acquired through one's efforts and labour.[27] The unjustified attack thereby deprives the person of something they have worked hard to secure. The comparison with property is not always helpful, especially as it tends to invoke an understanding of reputation in economic or monetary terms. Moreover, not every reputation will have been acquired through one's own efforts and labour, and in other cases a person's efforts may go unrecognised by the community. The reputation enjoyed can arise through certain matters of chance, such as when a person's conduct attracts attention and which factors happen to be taken into account when assessing his or her character. The law of defamation, however, sidesteps these issues by assuming that an existing reputation is worthy of protection from false attack. That still does not explain why such an assumption should be made.[28]

Another reason for protecting reputation as a resource focuses on the value of the activities that it facilitates. Earlier, it was noted that a reputation plays an important role in forming relationships. Along these lines, David Howarth advances an account in which reputation is valued because 'it helps us to form and maintain social bonds', and notes that 'all human beings have an interest in the formation and maintenance of social relationships'.[29] Under this view, the exclusion caused by the defamatory statement harms the person through exclusion and ostracisation.[30] Similarly, if reputation is a resource that can be used in the exercise of political power, then an attack on reputation can lead to a person's political participation being devalued or to that person being excluded.

All of the arguments so far do not seek to provide absolute protection for reputation, but merely aim to ensure that these interests are not harmed without due cause. This leads to a more general argument for legal protection that does not focus on the impact on personal dignity, self-esteem or activities, but demands that any social judgement of a person should take place on fair terms, namely that challenges to reputation should be based on correct facts. Along these lines, Arthur Ripstein argues that defamation protects a 'basic right to have no wrong attributed to you that you did not do'.[31] Such a line of argument is supported in dicta from the courts that the 'law recognises in every man a right to have the estimation in which he stands in the opinion of others unaffected by false statements to his discredit'.[32] This line of argument gets to heart of the concern to explain why statements that are false and lower people in the eyes of others are intrinsically wrong.[33] Thomas Gibbons explains that the argument does not treat reputation as an interest worthy of protection in itself, but is about the conditions on which people evaluate others and in which reputations are formed.[34]

---

[27] Post, 'The Social Foundation of Defamation Law' (n 18) 694.
[28] McNamara (n 16) 42.
[29] Howarth (n 25) 849.
[30] ibid.
[31] Ripstein (n 21) 192. See also Gibbons (n 11).
[32] *Scott v Sampson* (1882) 8 QBD 491.
[33] Ripstein (n 21) 199, which explains why the tort is limited to negative statements.
[34] Gibbons (n 11).

While securing fair terms is an appealing rationale for defamation, it does not explain why this wrong requires legal intervention. Normally in social relations, the expectation is that false statements will be rebutted through counter-speech. While there is a risk that an attack on reputation may be false or unjustified, the classic free speech argument is that people should hear all sides of the story and decide for themselves whether an attack is warranted or not. That is not the approach taken in defamation law. When a claim is brought in defamation, the matter is removed from public debate and the court is called on to settle the matter.[35]

The legal intervention can sometimes be explained in terms of 'market failure'. A reputation is valuable to a person for all reasons outlined above, but cannot be expected to fend for itself in the 'marketplace of ideas' and the normal processes of self-correction in public debate. A market failure may flow from the asymmetries in communicative power, which means that in some cases the speaker making the attack has more chance of being heard. The mass media is in a strong position to cause damage to a person's reputation and there is limited scope for an individual to reverse that damage through communications of their own. Some newspapers also enjoy a degree of authority, which will make an allegation almost a matter of public record. As such, a defamatory statement in the media does more than merely contribute to a discussion of the merits of conduct, but dominates that view of the person. The law may therefore intervene to prevent a person suffering undue negative effects as a result of an abuse of an asymmetry of communicative power.

Even where asymmetries of communicative power are not present, the law of defamation will still not allow the dispute to play out in the marketplace of ideas. One reason lies in the way that people process information. In particular, a negative statement is more likely to command greater attention, be shared as gossip and remembered. A correction may be less interesting and newsworthy. 'Politician in Corruption Scandal' makes a better headline than 'Politician is Honest After All'. Social scientists have also noted a pattern known as 'negativity bias', in which people are more likely to pay attention to negative stories and be convinced by such material.[36] While the law has not relied on such social science research, it reflects the age-old adage that 'mud sticks'. For this reason, attacks on reputation can be particularly harmful. A lifetime of good deeds and citizenship can soon be forgotten once an allegation of some misconduct is made. Defamation can provide a way to counteract such biases in the way people process information.[37]

The discussion has explored how a defamatory statement can be an affront to a person's dignity, it can devalue a resource that sets the terms on which we interact with others, and the usual processes of political debate may be insufficient to correct the harms of some false allegations. None of the explanations, taken alone, provides a complete rationale for defamation law, but each tells us something about why reputation is thought to warrant legal protection. How well defamation law serves these goals is another question, and the discussion below will show how the law can have

---

[35] Post, 'The Social Foundation of Defamation Law' (n 18) 712.
[36] For a discussion of such biases in relation to political information, see S Soroka, *Negativity in Democratic Politics* (Cambridge, Cambridge University Press, 2014).
[37] See K Craik, *Reputation: A Network Interpretation* (Oxford, Oxford University Press, 2009) 148.

unintended consequences (such as the chilling of legitimate expression). The arguments for protecting reputation also need to be set against the case for media freedom, discussed in Chapter 1. Before looking at those tensions in the substance of the law, it is first important to note the impact of Article 8 of the ECHR in this area.

B. Article 8

Reputation is now afforded some protection not only in the domestic law, but also under the ECHR. Reputation is listed as an interest under Article 10(2) that can sometimes justify an interference with freedom of expression. If reputation is a mere interest, then it should be narrowly construed and any doubts when striking a balance with Article 10 should be resolved in favour of the expression right.[38] However, in *Radio France*, the Strasbourg Court found that reputation is not merely a competing interest, but is 'one of the rights guaranteed by Article 8 of the Convention', which protects the right to respect for 'private and family life'.[39] Later decisions qualified that position by providing that Article 8 is engaged only when the attack on reputation is serious enough to undermine 'personal integrity'.[40] That reasoning suggests that Article 8 is concerned with the effect on the defamed person and not with the loss of esteem suffered as a result of the 'external evaluation' of the person.[41] However, other cases have not separated reputation in such a way and have stated that to engage Article 8 'an attack on a person's reputation must attain a certain level of seriousness and in a manner causing prejudice to personal enjoyment of the right to respect for private life'.[42] Under either approach, when an attack is less serious, reputation will be treated merely as a competing interest and there will be an assumption in favour of the expression right when conducting any balance. However, where the attack on reputation is more serious and Article 8 becomes engaged, the right to reputation enjoys equal status with freedom of expression and media freedom. The result is a confusing scheme in which it is often unclear when a reputation should be weighed as a fundamental right or a mere competing interest. To add to the confusion, even the threshold of seriousness requirement has not been consistently followed in later Strasbourg decisions.[43]

The recognition that reputation can be protected under Article 8 (in some cases at least) is significant because the state is sometimes under an obligation to take positive steps to protect that right.[44] A positive obligation means that controls on false

---

[38] See *Reynolds* (n 17).

[39] *Radio France v France*, App no 53984/00 (2005) 40 EHRR 29 at [31].

[40] *Karako v Hungary*, App no 39311/05 (2011) 52 EHRR 36. For a contrasting reading of the cases, see *Guardian News and Media Ltd, Re HM Treasury v Ahmed* [2010] UKSC 1, [2010] 2 AC 697 at [39]–[42].

[41] *Karako*, ibid, [23].

[42] *Axel Springer v Germany*, App no 39954/08 (2012) 55 EHRR 6 at [83]. The court also noted that the concept of private life covers 'physical and psychological integrity'; *Delfi v Estonia*, App no 64569/09 (2016) 62 EHRR 6 at [137].

[43] T Aplin and J Bosland, 'The Uncertain Landscape of Article 8 of the ECHR: The Protection of Reputation as a Fundamental Right?' in Kenyon, *Comparative Defamation and Privacy Law* (n 9) 280.

[44] *Pihl v Sweden*, App no 74742/14 (7 February 2017) at [26].

statements about a person are not only *permissible* under the ECHR, but are some-times *mandatory*. The domestic law needs to be designed in a way that can accom-modate some Article 8-based claims to protect reputation, though under the ECHR signatory states enjoy a margin of appreciation in deciding on the means to fulfil that positive obligation.[45] By attaching liability to publications, defamation law provides a way to protect Article 8 rights from interference by other private actors.

C. Elements of Liability in Defamation Law

Having set out the arguments for protecting reputation, the discussion will now turn to the substance of the law to examine how protection is provided in practice. In order to bring an action in defamation law, the claimant has to establish several elements: that there was a publication to a third party; that the publication referred to the claim-ant; that the statement had a defamatory meaning; and that the statement caused or is likely to cause serious damage to the claimant's reputation.

i. Publication

The law of defamation attaches liability to the 'publication' of a statement to a third party. Consequently, it does not apply to a letter sent only to the claimant, as that would have no impact on the person's good name in the eyes of others. Publication can include a wide range of formats beyond the traditional media, such as the spoken word,[46] private communications in a letter to a third party and messages on social media. A wide range of actors in the chain of dissemination can also be classed as publishers, ranging from the editor and author, to those involved in the printing and distribution of content. Despite the broad definition of a publication, the mass media is likely to be a repeat player in this area and defamation is traditionally seen as a media tort. This can be explained as the media is in the business of publishing content, has a high profile and relatively deep pockets. That high visibility means people will be aware of what is said about them in the media and will care if any negative statements are made. However, defamation has never been exclusively about media content, and in recent years there have been a number of high-profile cases relating to internet and social media publications, which continue to increase.[47]

    The definition of a publication casts a wide net for potential defendants and can generate hardship for those playing a minor role in the chain of publication (sometimes referred to as 'secondary publishers'). A distributor or printer, for example, will normally have little responsibility for the content of the publication. However, there are a number of safeguards and defences that limit the scope for liability. The Defamation Act 2013 provides that an action should not be brought

---

[45] *Tamiz v United Kingdom*, App no 3877/14 (19 September 2017) at [78].
[46] Though the spoken word constitutes a slander rather than a libel.
[47] For example, see *Monroe v Hopkins* [2017] EWHC 433 (QB), [2017] 4 WLR 68.

against a secondary publisher unless it is not reasonably practical for an action to be brought against the 'author, editor or publisher' (sometimes known as 'primary publishers').[48] Even when an action against a secondary publisher can be brought, a defence is available to persons that are not the 'author, editor or publisher', that took reasonable care and did not know or have reason to believe that they were contributing to a defamatory publication.[49] Those provisions will help protect distributors and other intermediaries, but will offer no defence for newspapers and broadcasters that clearly fall into the category of a primary publisher.

ii. Meaning

Once publication is shown, the next issue is to determine the meaning of the statement and whether it referred to the claimant. Many statements are open to multiple interpretations, with some being defamatory and some not. Moreover, there may be multiple interpretations of a statement that have different defamatory meanings. If a newspaper alleges that a politician is corrupt, then that can mean the person has behaved unethically or it could mean the person has acted unlawfully. If the publisher wants to defend the claim by arguing that the statement is true, then he or she needs to know which meaning has to be proven to defeat the claim.

The way the court deals with this problem is to pick a single meaning of the statement from the perspective of a reasonable person (the 'natural and ordinary meaning' under the 'single meaning rule').[50] The publisher will then have to defend the single meaning decided by the court. For example, if the defendant wants to run the truth defence, then it must provide evidence to prove that single meaning. The point is illustrated by the common scenario in which a newspaper or broadcaster reports that someone is subject to a criminal investigation. The court has identified three meanings that can be attributed to such statements that a person is under investigation: (1) that the person is guilty of wrongdoing; (2) that there are reasonable grounds to suspect the person is guilty of the wrong; or (3) that there are reasonable grounds for investigating whether the person has committed the wrong.[51] The court will then choose one of those interpretations of the statement as the single meaning. Accordingly, the court has devised rules about the types of evidence that will be required to prove the truth of each these meanings. The single meaning rule thereby provides a case management function that helps to define the issues in the litigation.

The single meaning rule has long been regarded as 'artificial', given that most statements will be open to multiple interpretations.[52] In *Ajinomoto Sweeteners* the court declined to follow the rule in relation to the tort of malicious falsehood.[53]

---

[48] Defamation Act 2013, s 10.
[49] Defamation Act 1996, s 1.
[50] *Slim v Daily Telegraph* [1968] 2 QB 157, 172–73; *Jeynes v News Magazines Ltd* [2008] EWCA Civ 130 at [14].
[51] *Chase v News Group Newspapers Ltd* [2002] EWCA Civ 1772, [2003] EMLR 11 at [45].
[52] *Slim* (n 50) 172.
[53] *Ajinomoto Sweeteners Europe SAS v Asda Stores Ltd* [2010] EWCA Civ 609, [2011] QB 497.

Sedley LJ said the 'rule is productive of injustice', in which actual injury to reputation goes unremedied simply because the reasonable reader would have understood it to have a less defamatory meaning.[54] Rimer LJ stated that applying the rule was a matter of luck, in which the selected meaning tips the balance in favour of one of the parties, in a way that does not realistically reflect how the audience understood the statement.[55] Andrew Scott has argued that the rule should be abandoned in defamation law, and favours a system in which publishers narrow down the meanings they wish to defend by offering public retractions and corrections in relation to those meanings that they are unwilling to support.[56] Such an approach would take the case management functions of the single meaning rule outside of the courts, and the parties would determine the meaning of the statement (for the purposes of litigation) through their public statements.

In addition to the single meaning based on the 'natural and ordinary' understanding of a statement, there can also be an 'innuendo' meaning. The meaning of a statement can change if the audience has knowledge of additional facts. To give a basic example, if a news report says that a person is a member of a political organisation, that statement is harmless enough. However, if some people know that the political organisation has strong links to terrorist and extremist groups, then the meaning of the statement changes and can have a defamatory imputation.[57] The defamatory meaning that follows from the additional knowledge is known as the 'innuendo'.

The determination of the meaning can have a decisive effect on libel proceedings. At the early stages of litigation, the claimants will often argue that the statement makes a more serious allegation (which will be harder for the defendant to prove and raise the prospect of higher damages), while the defendant will claim the statement had a less serious meaning.[58] As a result, the court can hold preliminary hearings on the meaning in advance of the full trial. Once the meaning is decided, both the claimant and defendant will be in a position to evaluate the likely success of their argument and decide whether to maintain their position or settle the case. Such hearings can allow some cases to be dealt with efficiently, yet there is also a risk that it adds to the complexity of defamation and increases the potential for satellite litigation to escalate legal costs.[59]

As will be clear from the discussion so far, the meaning of a statement is not determined by the intention of the publisher. The publisher could make a statement with one meaning intended, but the court could decide that it means something else. The publisher therefore faces a level of unpredictability, as it is not known at the time of publication what meaning will be attributed to the statement. Moreover, there is no requirement that the publisher intend to refer to the claimant. In the famous case

---

[54] ibid, [33]–[34].

[55] ibid, [43].

[56] A Scott, '*Ceci n'est pas une pipe*: the autopoietic inanity of the single meaning rule' in Kenyon (n 9).

[57] If the extrinsic facts are a matter of general knowledge, then the meaning would be pleaded as part of the natural and ordinary meaning rather than the innuendo.

[58] See discussion in Scott (n 56) 44–45 and G Robertson and A Nicol, *Media Law*, 5th edn (London, Sweet and Maxwell, 2007) 145.

[59] Robertson and Nicol, ibid, 107.

of *Hulton v Jones*, the claimant was able to recover damages in relation to an article referring to a fictional character sharing the claimant's unusual name.[60] The law can operate harshly if a person can be liable for consequences that were unintended and where the publisher is not at fault. In a study of the history of libel law, Paul Mitchell explains the adoption of a strict liability standard as a response to concerns about growing media power at the turn of the twentieth century, as well a reflection of the judicial disapproval of the style reporting in the popular press.[61] However, as will be shown, a number of factors have gradually softened the strictness of liability and incorporated negligence standards in relation to certain elements of the tort.[62]

iii. Is the Statement Defamatory?

The law of defamation attaches liability only to those statements that lower a reputation in the eyes of right-thinking people. A person might enjoy a reputation in the criminal community for being a skilled chemist producing illegal narcotics, which that person deeply values. However, a statement that damages that reputation would not be protected in the law, because a right-thinking person would not hold an illegal narcotics producer in high esteem.[63] As Gibbons points out, such an approach rejects certain standards (such as the values of the criminal fraternity) for evaluating a person's conduct.[64] The court thereby holds considerable power in deciding what standards right-thinking people should apply.

The identification of the appropriate standard to determine how a person should be evaluated points to a broader function of defamation law. Robert Post argues that the law of defamation is not just about protecting individual interests, but maintains 'community identity' by affirming what sorts of conduct are worthy of respect.[65] So in an action for defamation following an accusation of corruption, the court reaffirms the position that corrupt actions are contrary to the rules of that community. That communitarian aspect, however, puts defamation law into tension with a liberal account of freedom of expression that rejects 'the maintenance of community cohesion' as a basis for controls on speech.[66] Under such a view, the standards of a community should remain open to revision and challenge through a process of free speech, rather than legally enforced by the state.

When considering the appropriate standards for evaluating conduct, the courts can still allow space for pluralism in values. In many areas, there will be a grey area where an activity will lower a person's reputation in the eyes of one group of people, but not others. A statement that a person is an atheist may lower that person's reputation in

---

[60] *Hulton v Jones* [1910] AC 20.

[61] P Mitchell, *The Making of Modern Defamation Law* (Oxford, Hart, 2005) at 120–21.

[62] For an account of how negligence standards 'infiltrated' defamation law prior to the 2013 reforms, see E Descheemaeker, 'Protecting Reputation: Defamation and Negligence' (2009) 29 *Oxford Journal of Legal Studies* 603, 625–40.

[63] *Byrne v Deane* [1937] 1 KB 818.

[64] Gibbons, 'Defamation Reconsidered' (n 11) 592–93.

[65] Post, 'The Social Foundation of Defamation Law' (n 18) 714 and 737–38.

[66] ibid, 734.

the eyes of a religious organisation, but one would not say that it lowers the reputation in the eyes of right-thinking people more generally. However, if that statement was made about someone who claims to be a devout Christian, then an argument can be made that the false statement is defamatory in so far as it implies a level of hypocrisy. By taking this step, the court can look at the statement in its context and differentiate between particular individuals, the community to which they belong and the reputation they hold.

iv. Damage

To say that a statement is defamatory means that it is likely to have a particular effect on the mind of the audience (by lowering the person in their estimation). The right to reputation could thereby raise questions of media effects, namely whether it is possible to prove that a statement is likely to have such an impact. Prior to the Defamation Act 2013, the court avoided such issues by placing itself in the position of the reasonable person and asking how it would react to the statement. Once the court decided the statement would *tend* to have the effect of lowering a person's estimation in the eyes of the reasonable person, the traditional rule was to presume that the defamatory statement caused actionable damage.[67] As a result, a person could bring an action against a publisher even if he or she could not prove that any harm had been suffered as a consequence of the defamatory statement.

The rule was sometimes justified on the basis that the imputation of wrongdoing or of other discreditable conduct is the principal injury and that the effects (such as loss of social and professional opportunities) are consequent losses. The presumption of damage was thereby seen to reflect the role of defamation as vindicating a person's reputation.[68] Another justification for the presumption of damage was more pragmatic, on the basis that it is difficult for a claimant to prove the various ways that a statement had an effect on the audience and the extent to which it had circulated.[69] While such evidence could be relevant in assessing the level of damages, it was thought to be too demanding to require proof of injury as a condition for bringing a claim. Against these justifications, the presumption of damage was subject to criticism in so far as it contributed to the pro-claimant advantages that were prominent prior to 2013.

Before the 2013 reforms, there were already some safeguards in place to prevent actions being brought for negligible damage to reputation. In *Thornton*, Tugendhat J ruled that a libel action is not actionable unless it 'substantially affects' the claimant's reputation or has a tendency to do so.[70] In addition to that threshold, if there is very little at stake in a claim, for example where a statement is seen by a handful of people,

---

[67] By contrast, slander required proof of damage.

[68] J Varuhas, 'The Concept of "Vindication" in the Law of Torts: Rights, Interests and Damages' (2014) 34 *Oxford Journal of Legal Studies* 253, 278.

[69] *Ley v Hamilton* (1935) 153 LT 384 at 386. For criticism, see Barendt, 'What is the Point of Libel Law?' (n 21) 123–24.

[70] *Thornton v Telegraph Media Group Ltd* [2010] EWHC 1414 (QB), [2011] 1 WLR 1985 at [96].

then it could be deemed an abuse of process to demand that the court spend its time and resources hearing such a claim.[71] While that might deny the claimant the right to vindicate his or her name, in such a case the award of damages is likely to be small, so any vindication would be minimal in any event.[72]

Section 1 of the Defamation Act 2013 changed the common law rule by providing that a 'statement is not defamatory unless its publication has caused or is likely to cause serious harm to the reputation of the claimant'.[73] There are competing interpretations on whether this marks a radical departure from the earlier common law rule or is merely an evolution from *Thornton*. In *Lachaux*, Warby J in the High Court took the more radical view and found s 1 to mean 'that libel is no longer actionable without proof of damage' and the presumption of damage no longer stands.[74] Under this view, the question is no longer whether a statement *tends* to harm a reputation, but whether it has or is likely to do so on the balance of probabilities.[75] However, this did not mean that concrete evidence had to be brought in every case, as the seriousness of the harm could be inferred from the circumstances of the publication.[76] Even this more radical approach thereby avoids some of the difficulties in ascertaining the effects of the media in relation to a specific publication. In particular, the courts would look at the nature of the allegation, where it was published and the people it was published to. While numbers were not decisive for such an inference, Dingemans J in *Sobrinho* stated that 'Mass media publications of very serious defamatory allegations are likely to render the need for evidence of serious harm unnecessary'.[77]

In the Court of Appeal in *Lachaux*, Davis LJ found the effects of s 1 to be less radical. Davis LJ stated that s 1 did not abolish the presumption of damage in libel cases, but merely raised the threshold to a standard of seriousness for that damage to be actionable.[78] Davis LJ warned that claimants would be in a difficult position if they were required to adduce 'tangible evidence to support an assertion of harm to reputation (an intangible matter)'.[79] That reflects the traditional view that to require proof of a causal effect on the audience would be to set an impossible task and that the harm to reputation is actionable regardless of consequent losses. Under this approach, publication in the mass media is also likely to be a factor in deciding whether the seriousness threshold has been met.[80] The practical difference of the Court of Appeal's approach in *Lachaux* lies in the greater willingness to infer significant damage, stating that if the meaning of the statement 'is evaluated as seriously defamatory it will ordinarily then be proper to draw an inference of serious reputational harm'.[81] Under that reading, s 1 does not mark a far-reaching liberalisation of the law, but is a device to 'weed out' trivial claims. The interpretation will no doubt be the subject of further litigation.

---

[71] *Jameel (Yousef) v Dow Jones & Co Inc* [2005] EWCA Civ 75, [2005] QB 946 at [54].
[72] ibid, [49].
[73] Defamation Act 2013, s 1.
[74] *Lachaux v Independent Print Ltd* [2015] EWHC 2242 (QB), [2016] QB 402 at [60].
[75] ibid, [65].
[76] ibid. See also *Cooke v MGN* [2014] EWHC 2831 (QB), [2015] 1 WLR 895 at [43].
[77] *Sobrinho v Impresa Publishing* [2016] EWHC 66 (QB), [2016] EMLR 12 at [47].
[78] *Lachaux v Independent Print Ltd* [2017] EWCA Civ 1334.
[79] ibid, [72].
[80] ibid, [65].
[81] ibid, [82].

The Defamation Act 2013 also introduces a special regime for for-profit companies, by providing that a 'body that trades for profit' must show that 'serious financial loss' was caused, or is likely to be caused, by the statement.[82] That requirement reflects the fact that companies do not have any personal feelings or suffer a loss to dignity.[83] This might be thought to impose a difficult threshold to meet for the reasons stated earlier, that it can be hard to demonstrate that a publication influenced or is likely to influence a person's behaviour to the detriment of the claimant. However, to assess such a loss, the court will look at the circumstances surrounding the case, such as the place and extent of publication, the extent to which the company relies on publicity to attract business, the likely impact of the statement on a potential customer and whether any business had been lost.[84] By looking at the circumstances of the case to determine the impact of a statement, the court will avoid an impossible-to-meet standard of causation. Moreover, the effects of a statement may be easier to establish when the damage is viewed in economic terms. Requiring some evidence (whether documentary or an expert witness) pointing to a financial loss, or potential loss, caused by the defamatory publication nonetheless imposes an additional hurdle for corporate claimants.[85] That approach aims to strike the balance in favour of freedom of expression where a corporate, as opposed to human, interest in reputation is at stake.

v. Repetition

Liability for a defamatory statement does not just attach to the original author of a statement, but also extends to those who repeat the statement. As a consequence, the prima facie rule is that if a newspaper interviews someone and the person makes a defamatory statement in the course of that interview, then the newspaper publishing the interview can also become a target for liability. Similarly, a publisher can be liable for reporting accusations made by another person. If a newspaper repeats an allegation made by an opposition politician (outside of Parliament) that the Prime Minister is corrupt, then the newspaper will have to prove the truth of the allegation of corruption, and not the mere fact that someone else made that comment. Similarly, users of the social media that repeat such allegations could become targets for liability (as long as the threshold of seriousness is met).

Liability for repetition can strike at the heart of the function of the media in reporting the details of disputes and statements of others.[86] The fact that a person is making an allegation may be newsworthy in itself and the media may not be well placed to verify the truth of a statement made by someone else. However, the newsworthiness

---

[82] Defamation Act 2013, s 1(2). The Court of Appeal in *Lachaux* did not decide whether that part of the provision changes the presumption of damage, at [82].

[83] JA Weir 'Local Authority v. Critical Ratepayer—A Suit in *Defamation*' (1972) 30 *Cambridge Law Journal* 238 at 240. The European Court of Human Rights has left open the question 'whether the reputation of a company falls under the notion of private life under Article 8(1)', *Firma Edv Fur Sie v Germany*, App no 32783/08 (2 September 2014) at [23]. It remains to be seen whether such a position would leave the financial loss requirement open to challenge.

[84] See *Brett Wilson LLP v Person(s) Unknown* [2015] EWHC 2628 (QB), [2016] 4 WLR 69 at [28]–[30].

[85] See *Undre v Harrow LBC* [2016] EWHC 931 (QB), [2017] EMLR 3.

[86] For the importance of this function see *Jersild v Denmark*, App no 15890/8 (1995) 19 EHRR 1.

of the allegation does not mean a publisher should escape liability if it provides a platform for others to tear down a person's name. To guard against such effects and the risk of liability, a publisher reporting a defamatory statement should ensure that the article as a whole does not carry a defamatory meaning, for example by contextualising the reported comments and including any denials of the allegations.[87]

Further protection for publishers is provided under s 4 of the Defamation Act 2013, which states that when relying on the public interest defence, publishers are not expected to verify the truth of a statement that is repeated as part of an 'accurate and impartial account of a dispute to which the claimant was a party'. The provision is limited only to repetitions that relate to an account of a *dispute*. In its application, a key issue will be whether the dispute was reported with a sufficient level of impartiality. The central aspect of an impartial report is that it does not endorse or embellish the defamatory statement.[88] Simply that a person reports the dispute with a level of humour should not be sufficient to fall outside the defence.[89] However, the defence represents a limited exception to the general rule that publishers are liable for repetition.

D. Costs and Litigation

The complexity of defamation law means that it can be a costly area to litigate. Before a case comes to trial, there can be multiple hearings to determine the meaning of the statement, whether the claim is an abuse of process and whether certain defences can be run. Significant costs can be run up, even if the case does not come to a full trial. The issues are significant for the media, as it is likely to be a repeat player and can potentially face multiple libel actions in a year. The costs can also facilitate the abuse of the law to chill expression. A person that lacks the resources to defend a libel claim (or face the risk of losing) is more likely to cave in to demands in a letter from a wealthy person threatening a legal action, regardless of the merits of the claim. The legal costs also raise an obvious point about access to justice for claimants. The substance of the law offers little protection to reputation if few people can afford to enforce their legal rights. The legal costs have contributed to the view of libel being primarily a rich person's game.

An attempt to address the problem was introduced in 1999 through conditional fee agreements, in which a claimant pays no legal fee if they lose. However, if the claimant wins, then the lawyers are entitled to an additional 'success fee' on top of the ordinary legal fees, which the unsuccessful defendant would normally be expected to pay. The imposition of a large costs award can contribute to a chilling effect and inhibit media reporting. An order requiring the *Daily Mirror* to pay Naomi Campbell's success fee and insurance premiums in a privacy claim was found to violate Article 10

---

[87] Robertson and Nicol (n 58) 144.
[88] *Galloway v Telegraph Group Ltd* [2006] EWCA Civ 17, [2006] EMLR 11 (on the pre-2013 common law reportage defence).
[89] *Roberts v Gable* [2007] EWCA Civ 721, [2008] QB 502 (on the pre-2013 defence).

as a disproportionate measure.[90] While Campbell had been awarded £3,500 in damages in the privacy action, the *Mirror* was ordered to pay over £1 million for her legal fees. At the time of writing, there is a question mark as to whether awarding the recovery of success fees and insurance premiums under conditional fee agreements will be assumed to violate Article 10 in privacy and libel cases.[91] Possible alternatives to that scheme include a system of fixed legal costs, to stop lawyers' fees becoming disproportionate to the damages at stake. The challenge lies in devising a system that secures access to justice and representation in complex proceedings, while not imposing the risk of very large costs awards on either party.

Very few cases now make it to full trial so the highest legal costs are normally avoided. Procedures such as the offer to make amends under the Defamation Act 1996 provide an incentive for an early settlement.[92] There are also safeguards in the case management powers of the court to prevent excessive legal costs being run up.[93] The system of press self-regulation under the Royal Charter was designed to incentivise the use of arbitrations to hear media law claims and thereby significantly reduce the legal costs compared with a court.[94] However, the costs incentives under the Charter scheme have not been brought into force and at present the decision to fight a libel claim is still laden with financial risk. That risk and the consequent chilling effect means the impact of defamation law on the media cannot be judged by the number of court cases alone. Much takes place outside the court, either with stories never being published or cases being settled. The substance of the law and procedures for litigation will determine how that risk is assessed and will impact on what gets published.

Until recently, defamation law was an exceptional area where a private law claim was heard before a jury. That increased the complexity of proceedings further as issues of fact for the jury had to be separated from those of law, and the lawyers had to argue a case before a jury that had not been given the opportunity to read about the case in advance.[95] The Defamation Act 2013 sought to address this concern by establishing a presumption that a judge alone will hear the case. There is some irony that free speech and media freedom campaigners advocated the removal of the jury. The right to a jury trial in libel was something advocates of press freedom fought to secure two centuries ago. Lord Denning once described the right to a jury in libel as of the 'highest constitutional importance'.[96] To be judged by one's peers was seen to provide a safeguard against any judicial partiality, especially where the publisher had criticised government. However, the reformers in 2013 had come to see the jury trial as a costly safeguard and trial before a judge was regarded as a more efficient alternative.

---

[90] *MGN Ltd v UK*, App no 39401/04 (2011) 53 EHRR 5.

[91] *Times v Flood* [2017] UKSC 33, [2017] 1 WLR 1415 in which the Supreme Court declined to determine whether *MGN v UK* (n 90) establishes a general rule against the award of success fees and insurance premiums.

[92] Defamation Act 1996, ss 2–4.

[93] See for example, Civil Procedure Rules 1998, r 44.3(2)(a). See *Times v Flood* (2017) (n 91) at [9].

[94] See Ch 6.

[95] See *Yeo v Times* [2014] EWHC 2853 (QB), [2015] 1 WLR 971 at [67]. See also A Kenyon, '*Lange* and *Reynolds* Qualified Privilege: Australian and English Law and Practice' (2004) 28 *Melbourne University Law Review* 406, 426, in relation to the *Reynolds* defence.

[96] *Rothermere v Times Newspapers* [1973] 1 WLR 448, 452.

E. Defences

Once the claimant has established publication, defamatory meaning and serious harm, it is then for the publisher to establish a defence. Three defences have played a central role and will be considered below: truth, honest opinion and privilege. The public interest defence raises broader issues and will be considered later.

i. Truth

As the discussion noted earlier, defamation law does not protect an undeserved reputation, and liability attaches to *false* attacks on reputation. For this reason, s 2 of the Defamation Act 2013 provides that the defendant is not liable if the defamatory statement is shown to be substantially true. The 'truth' defence thereby applies a reverse burden of proof, in which a defamatory statement is assumed to be false unless the defendant shows otherwise. A finding in favour of the claimant on the truth defence means that the defendant has failed to rebut the presumption of falsity. Defamation law thereby provides limited vindication for reputation in so far as the court finds an allegation to be unproven, rather than false.[97]

The reverse burden has long been criticised for chilling the media and shielding undeserved reputations from correction. For example, Tony Weir wrote:

> This absurd reversal of the normal burden of proof encourages claimants to sue even if they know that what the defendant said was perfectly correct ... .[98]

Despite such a criticism, the reverse burden of proof has been found to be compatible with Article 10.[99] The reverse burden is sometimes defended as an application of the presumption of innocence. Earlier it was noted that Arthur Ripstein saw defamation as a basic right not to have allegations of wrongdoing made against you. When viewed in these terms, Ripstein argues that the rule in defamation applies the normal burden of proof, that a person should be assumed to be innocent of an alleged wrong unless the speaker can prove the wrongdoing.[100] Despite its obvious appeal, the argument does not explain why a principle normally applied to state actors should be applied to private speakers. There is clearly good reason for the presumption of innocence to apply when the state uses its coercive powers to impose a penalty or award compensation. Those reasons do not explain why such a presumption should be transposed into everyday social relations and legally enforced.

The argument can be modified so that the 'innocent until proven guilty' principle is applied where a powerful body makes the allegation. Along these lines, Sir David Eady defended the reverse burden as a reflection of the 'awesome power of the press' to inflict damage on a person's name, and asked why such powerful institutions should

---

[97] S Deakin, A Johnston and B Markesinis, *Markesinis and Deakin's Tort Law*, 7th edn (Oxford, Oxford University Press, 2013) 662.

[98] T Weir, *Tort Law* (Oxford, Oxford University Press, 2002) 168.

[99] *McVicar v UK*, App no 46311/99 (2002) 35 EHRR 22 at [83]–[87].

[100] Ripstein (n 21) 204.

benefit from an assumption that 'their allegations, however serious, are true?'[101] This argument reflects the earlier explanation of defamation law as a guard against abuse of media power. Accordingly, it is the power of the media to damage a name that invokes the 'innocent until proven guilty' principle and it is reasonable to expect the media to take on the risk of any inaccuracies. While a convincing rationale for some cases, that argument does not explain the imposition of the reverse burden in non-media cases.

The defence encourages journalists to be diligent, maintain a paper trail and to check stories with multiple sources. However, proving the truth of a defamatory meaning on the balance of probabilities can be challenging.[102] For serious investigative reporting, the risk of an error is significant, especially where the journalist undertakes painstaking research into areas where there is usually a lack of transparency. The reporter will have to rely on various tools of newsgathering, such as insider sources, and piece together various bits of evidence. Difficulties in proving the truth of a statement also arise where a journalist relies on a confidential source, who is unwilling to support the story in open court. In some cases, the evidence necessary to prove the truth of the statement may not be admissible in court. A further difficulty will arise where a statement is found to have a defamatory meaning that was not intended by the publisher, as a publisher will not have taken steps to verify or keep paperwork on the unintended meaning. In such cases, a defendant will have a strong incentive to settle the case once the meaning has been determined. The limits of the truth defence explain why there is a need for further protection under the public interest defence, which will be considered later.

The defence of truth sometimes requires the court to adjudicate on matters that normally lie outside the court's remit and expertise. For example, in *Cruddas v Calvert*, the court had to decide whether a politician had acted corruptly, in the sense of breaching political ethics.[103] To determine that issue the court distinguished between political fundraising practices that are legitimate and those that are unethical. Such matters of ethics are normally decided through politics rather than law, yet the context of the defamation claim meant the court had to resolve the matter. The same is true if a publication attacks the credibility of scientific research or scholarship, and the publisher argues that the allegation is true. The judge will then have to make a determination about whether the allegations relating to such matters of academic expertise are proven. In *Singh*, Lord Judge warned of the dangers of the court becoming an 'Orwellian ministry of truth' if it were to adjudicate on statements of scientific opinion.[104] However, he acknowledged that if a person makes a claim of 'verifiable fact', then the truth defence 'ineluctably casts the court in the role of historian or investigative journalist'.[105] By bringing the defamation claim, the claimant takes an

---

[101] D Eady, 'Defamation: Some Recent Developments and Non-Developments' in M Saville and R Susskind (eds), *Essays in Honour of Sir Brian Neil: the Quintessential Judge* (London, Lexis Nexis, 2003) 155.
[102] See Robertson and Nicol (n 58) 145.
[103] *Cruddas v Calvert* [2015] EWCA Civ 171, [2015] EMLR 16. See J Rowbottom, 'Corruption, transparency, and reputation: the role of publicity in regulating political donations' (2016) 75 *Cambridge Law Journal* 398.
[104] *British Chiropractic Association v Singh* [2010] EWCA Civ 350, [2011] 1 WLR 133 at [22].
[105] ibid, [23].

issue out of the normal forums for determining the truth (such as political debate or a scientific journal), and asks the court to make an authoritative ruling.[106]

ii. Honest Opinion

The defence of honest opinion, under s 3 of the Defamation Act 2013, provides considerable protection for people making statements of comment or opinion. There are a number of reasons why a statement of opinion warrants strong protection. At its most basic, free speech requires that people say what they think and express an evaluation of events. As Lord Denning once explained, if 'a citizen is troubled by things going wrong, he should be free to "write to the newspaper": and the newspaper should be free to publish his letter'.[107] Statements of opinion are a channel for self-expression and can be connected with the autonomy and self-fulfilment arguments for freedom of expression. While a media company does not have its own interest in self-expression, there are good reasons for it to carry the self-expression of others. For example, the publication of opinion has an informative value, in letting people know what others think, with what intensity, and provides a forum for debate.

More fundamentally, the European Court of Human Rights has distinguished between statements of fact that are verifiable, and statements of value judgment. To require a defendant to prove the truth of a statement of opinion would be to impose an impossible burden.[108] A separate defence for opinion and comment is therefore necessary to fulfil the obligations under Article 10. Another key difference is that statements of comment based on known true facts are assessable, so the audience can take it or leave it, and are invited to engage with the statement critically.[109] By contrast, a bare statement of fact claims to be authoritative.

There are a number of conditions that attach to the defence of honest opinion. First, the defendant has to show that the statement was one of opinion, as opposed to one of fact. In assessing this issue, the court will normally look at the article alone rather than assuming that the reader has background knowledge.[110] Under the old case law, it was said that a statement is a comment if it was 'something which is or can reasonably be inferred to be a deduction, inference, conclusion, criticism, remark, observation'.[111] So a simple statement that 'the chef poisoned his customers' with no further detail could be a statement of fact alleging some gross negligence or a deliberate act causing injury to customers. By contrast, in a statement that 'the chef poisoned his customers with an ill-judged combination of prawn and chocolate flavoured ice cream' the same words are more likely to be understood as a metaphor expressing an opinion based on poor culinary choices, rather than a direct allegation of injury.

---

[106] See Post, 'The Social Foundation of Defamation Law' (n 18) 712.
[107] *Slim* (n 50) 170.
[108] *Lingens v Austria* (1986) 8 EHRR 407 at [46].
[109] See *Joseph v Spiller* [2010] UKSC 53, [2011] 1 AC 852, expressing some scepticism about the rationale, at [100]–[101].
[110] *Telnikoff v Matusevitch* [1992] 2 AC 343.
[111] *Clarke v Norton* [1910] VLR 494, Cussen J, 499, cited in *Branson v Bower* [2001] EWCA Civ 791, [2002] EMLR 32 at [12].

While the 2013 Act names the defence 'honest opinion', the Explanatory Notes provide that a statement can be treated as one of opinion if it is inference from facts.[112] One question is whether a *statement of fact* inferred from other facts can constitute an *opinion* that is protected under the defence. For example, imagine that a newspaper reports that a company director knew about allegations of sexual harassment against members of staff because: (a) rumours were rife within the company; and (b) he had attended an event where an incident of harassment took place. The allegation of knowledge would normally be one of fact. However, it is an allegation that is inferred from the facts (a) and (b), which are both true. The question then is whether the allegation of knowledge could qualify as an opinion for the purposes of honest opinion, on the basis that it is an inference. The answer will partly depend on which of the rationales for the defence outlined above is emphasised. On one view, if the statement can be verified, then there is no hardship or impossible burden in treating it as fact and requiring the defendant to rely on truth as the primary defence. A contrasting argument is that as long as it is clear to the reader that the statement is an inference from other facts, then the readers can assess the statement for themselves and the matter can be treated as opinion.[113]

Once a statement is established to be one of opinion, there are a number of other conditions the defendant must meet. The statement must indicate 'the basis of the opinion'.[114] The statement must also be one that an honest person could have held on the basis of 'any fact which existed at the time the statement complained of was published' or 'anything asserted to be a fact' contained in a privileged statement published before the statement.[115] The defence is broad in so far as it allows a publisher to rely on facts he or she did not know of at the time of publication to show an honest person could have held the opinion.[116] However, *Gatley on Libel* notes that the provision may have more limited protection for social media, where people often make comments based on statements of fact made by others.[117] If the facts stated by others are untrue or not covered by privilege, then the social media user will not have the honest opinion defence.[118] Finally, the defence is lost if the defendant was shown not to hold the view in the statement, which is central to the opinion being 'honest'.[119] While the defence can raise some difficult questions on application, it is a relatively broad defence that plays a central role in protecting freedom of expression.

---

[112] Defamation Act 2013, Explanatory Notes, at [21].

[113] For a convincing argument in support of this approach see J Bosland, A Kenyon and S Walker, 'Protecting Inferences of Fact in Defamation Law: Fair Comment and Honest Opinion' (2015) 74 *Cambridge Law Journal* 234. While the Explanatory Notes to the Defamation Act 2013 seem to envisage this approach too ('an inference of fact is a form of opinion'), the authors argue that the case law has been more ambivalent, 237.

[114] Defamation Act 2013, s 3(3).

[115] ibid, s 3(4).

[116] The facts only have to exist at the time of publication rather than be known at that time.

[117] A Mullis and R Parkes (eds), *Gatley on Libel and Slander*, 12th edn (London, Sweet and Maxwell, 2013) at [12.23].

[118] ibid, emphasising the challenges in establishing that such facts were privileged or protected under the public interest defence. See *Joseph v Spiller* (n 109) at [99] and [131], warning about the danger of the defence not protecting many social media comments.

[119] Defamation Act 2013, s 3(5).

iii. Privilege

Privilege offers a series of defences to publishers regardless of whether the statement is true or false, or fact or opinion. The rationale for the defence is that on certain occasions, the freedom to speak (and to hear the speech of others) is particularly important and should not be inhibited by the possibility of a legal action. Some types of privilege provide an absolute defence, which means that a statement on the protected occasion cannot found liability in defamation. Most obviously, statements in parliamentary proceedings benefit from absolute privilege, given the need for full and frank exchanges.[120] If a defamation action required the courts to scrutinise and assess the truth of statements made in Parliament, it would lead to problems of the separation of powers.

The preclusion of liability under absolute privilege can have harsh effects. In one notable case, an MP referred to a person as a 'neighbour from hell' in a parliamentary debate on housing policy, giving the person's name and address, and detailing a number of complaints about her and her family. These comments were reported in newspapers and the named person was subsequently subjected to abuse. Despite the effect of these comments, the person discussed was unable to bring a defamation action, and the individual was left only with more limited means of redress through internal parliamentary procedures.[121] Absolute privilege can also be found in a limited number of other settings, such as judicial proceedings or in complaints made to the police to initiate an investigation or statements made in the course of an investigation.[122] Again, these are areas where the free flow of information is particularly important.

The other type of privilege is 'qualified privilege', in which the defence can be defeated by showing that the statement was made with malice.[123] Under statute, qualified privilege includes the protection of statements in scientific or academic journals,[124] and fair and accurate reports of a public meeting.[125] Under the common law, the classic test for qualified privilege is to ask whether the publisher has an interest or a duty to make the statement to the recipient and whether the recipient has a corresponding duty or interest to receive it.[126] Consequently, a person writing a reference to a prospective employer is protected under qualified privilege because there is a duty to be full and frank, including details of any shortcomings of the candidate. The defence has also been applied to certain communications between employer and employees about the affairs of the business,[127] and replies to an attack.[128]

---

[120] See *Ex parte Watson* [1869] QB 573 on the effects of Article 9 of the Bill of Rights of 1688.

[121] See *A v UK* (2003) 36 EHRR 51.

[122] See *Taylor v Director of the Serious Fraud Office* [1999] 2 AC 177 and *Westcott v Westcott* [2008] EWCA Civ 818, [2009] QB 407.

[123] *Horrocks v Lowe* [1975] AC 135.

[124] Defamation Act 2013.

[125] Defamation Act 1996, s 12.

[126] *Adam v Ward* [1917] AC 309. See the discussion in *Gatley on Libel* (n 117) at [14.9]–[14.18].

[127] *Hunt v Great Northern Railway Co* [1891] 2 QB 189.

[128] *Turner v MGM* [1950] 1 All ER 449, and *Watts v Times Newspapers* [1997] QB 650.

The duty/interest test for qualified privilege is difficult for the media to fulfil because it is rare that a publisher is under a duty to speak to the world at large. For example, if a newspaper detects wrongdoing, then the argument runs that the duty only extends to contacting the relevant authorities, rather than the general public.[129] Under this view, the authorities charged with investigating the issue are the appropriate recipients of such content and it is not for the public and press to monitor and assess such allegations of wrongdoing. Traditionally, a duty to communicate to the public could be found only in exceptional circumstances, for example where a suspected terrorist is at large and might be thought to pose a risk to the public.[130] The traditional approach to qualified privilege therefore provided limited protection to the media. The approach also reflected a more limited view of what the public is entitled to know. The unsatisfactory nature of this defence became apparent when the libel laws were in some cases used to curb criticism in the media. The response to such concerns was to stretch the duty/interest test to allow some reporting to the world at large on matters of public interest. The widened version of qualified privilege is now recognised as a separate public interest defence, which will be considered below.

F. Taking Stock

Nobody argues that a reputation should go unprotected and the presence of some checks on false statements about a person is an important element of media accountability. The body of law that was dominant in the twentieth century was widely criticised for creating a tilt in favour of claimants. The problem lay not only in the substance of the law, but also in the potential legal costs involved (as well as the time and energy involved in defending an action), which was seen to create a chilling effect on journalism. The law has since been modified to address some of the pro-claimant features, for example by raising the threshold of harm under the Defamation Act 2013, s 1. However, some of the key elements are still present, such as the reverse burden of proof. While the long libel trial is no longer a prominent feature in public life, there is still significant litigation, particularly in fleshing out the interpretation of the 2013 Act. More broadly, as elements of the law remain uncertain, there is still much scope for the law to chill publications and for threatening letters to deter journalists from pursuing certain stories. In such circumstances, much will depend on the media company, its resources and whether it is willing to support its journalists in taking risks. Defamation has changed in recent years and there has been a rebalance that attempts to give greater emphasis to media freedom. However, defamation still remains a significant tool that can be used to hold publishers to account and abused to apply pressure on them.

---

[129] See Ripstein (n 21) 224, citing the Scottish case of *Couper v Balfour* [1914] SC 139 requiring the statement to be published to the proper authority.
[130] *Blackshaw v Lord* [1984] QB 1 at 27.

III. Privacy

The various reforms in defamation law have rebalanced the legal protection of reputation and media freedom. While that has helped to address some of the biggest concerns for the media, the law of privacy has been in the ascendency for the last two decades. This development has taken place against a background of widespread concerns about intrusive reporting by various parts of the media, alongside numerous calls for legal reforms. In contrast with defamation, privacy law restricts the publication of true statements about a person. If a newspaper publishes an article correctly stating that a person is suffering from a terminal illness, nobody is being misinformed. However, if the person did not want the illness to become public knowledge, a gross invasion of privacy has occurred. The question is why should people be restricted from making true statements? Often we hear people say that the media should not publish information about private lives because the public has no interest in receiving such details. However, the lack of a public interest does not provide a positive reason for the law to intervene to restrict publication. The following section will first look at the reasons for protecting privacy, and after that the legal protection of private information will be considered.

A. What is Privacy?

There are many different ways an action can be said to interfere with a person's right to privacy. In the media context, the most common concern is with the disclosure of information about a person that can be considered private (known as 'informational privacy'). A breach of privacy can also arise when someone's personal space is invaded, for example through unwanted touching or intrusion into the home (which we can refer to as 'physical privacy'). The media can infringe this type of privacy through its newsgathering activities, such as the paparazzi camping outside a person's house and using long lens cameras to take detailed images. Finally, the monitoring and surveillance of a person can violate privacy, even when the activities being watched are not particularly sensitive. A recurring debate is whether there is such a thing as a unified concept of privacy to cover all these types of interference, or whether the term just describes lots of distinct interests (such as rights to property, person, image and information). The discussion below will primarily focus on informational privacy, but it will be shown later how laws designed to protect information are sometimes interpreted to cover other privacy interests.

i. Defining Privacy

A starting point is to ask what is meant by privacy and why it is worth protecting. A famous article by Warren and Brandeis described privacy as the 'right to be let alone'.[131] While that phrase captures an important element, a number of scholars have elaborated to give the concept of privacy a more concrete meaning. According to one line of argument, privacy can be defined in terms of 'access' to the person. Ruth Gavison followed such an approach and identified three types of access that lead to a loss of privacy (which track the types of interference listed above): (1) access to information about a person; (2) attention to a person; and (3) physical access or contact with a person.[132] Gavison argued that the idea of 'access' provides some unity to these different aspects of privacy. There are limits to this approach, as making loud noises outside a person's home, for example, would not invade a person's privacy, as it would not involve access to a person or information about that person.[133] Gavison aimed to provide a 'neutral' definition that identifies when a loss of privacy occurs, but does not seek to answer the normative question of whether that loss warrants a legal remedy. According to her view, there can be a loss of privacy (in descriptive terms) even if a person consents to the sharing of information,[134] and the question of consent is relevant to the normative question of whether the privacy interest should be protected.

Several scholars have adapted accounts of privacy based on access to accommodate the issues of choice and consent in the definition (and thereby address the normative questions). Nicole Moreham defines privacy as 'freedom from unwanted access',[135] which would exclude consensual sharing of personal information. A further variation is provided in Kirsty Hughes' account of a loss of privacy in terms of the penetration of barriers that a person has imposed.[136] In her view, a barrier can include physical restrictions (such as a garden fence), behavioural signals (for example, a choice to use a public toilet signals a desire not to be observed) and normative rules (such as social rules which dictate that people do not ask about your salary).[137] Under that approach, the right to privacy is understood as 'a right to respect' for the barriers that are imposed to prevent access.[138]

Another understanding of privacy focuses on 'control' rather than 'access'. In the opening page of his landmark study on privacy, Alan Westin describes the concept in terms of control, as 'the claim of individuals, groups, or institutions to determine for themselves when, how, and to what extent information about them is communicated to others'.[139] Similarly, Charles Fried describes privacy as 'the control we have over information about ourselves'.[140] More recently, Andrei Marmor has discussed privacy as being 'grounded in people's interest in having a reasonable measure of control over the ways in which they can present themselves (and what is theirs) to others'.[141]

---

[131] S Warren and L Brandeis, 'The Right to Privacy' (1890) 4 *Harvard Law Review* 193.
[132] R Gavison, 'Privacy and the Limits of Law' (1980) 89 *Yale Law Journal* 421.
[133] ibid, 437.
[134] ibid, 424.
[135] N Moreham, 'Privacy in the common law: a doctrinal and theoretical analysis' (2005) 121 *Law Quarterly Review* 628, 636.
[136] K Hughes, 'A Behavioural Understanding of Privacy and its Implications for Privacy Law' (2012) 75 *Modern Law Review* 806.
[137] ibid, 812–13.
[138] ibid, 810.
[139] A Westin, *Privacy and Freedom* (New York, Atheneum, 1967, reprinted Ig Publishing, 2015) 5.
[140] Fried, 'Privacy' (n 10) 482.
[141] A Marmor, 'What is the Right to Privacy' (2015) 43 *Philosophy and Public Affairs* 3, 3–4.

The workings of this approach will depend on what is meant by control. For example, when a person shares information with friends, it can be seen as an exercise of control in so far as the individual decides what information to disclose and who to share it with.[142] If a person was required to withhold information from all people at all times, that person would not be in control. However, when a person shares information with a friend, they can also be seen as giving up control in so far as the recipients are placed in a position where it is possible to forward that information to others.[143] For this reason, Moreham argues that the control-based accounts of privacy fail to fully capture the privacy interest, as the further sharing of information will result in a loss of privacy even though the individual had given up control.[144] One response is to adapt the meaning of control to cover such cases. Along these lines, when information is shared with a friend, it is imparted on the understanding that a social rule requires the recipient not to share it with others. The sharing comes with conditions attached and thereby takes place in a controlled environment, which is breached if the recipient passes the information on to others.[145] Under this view, the sharing of information alone need not be taken to abandon control.

A number of scholars have noted that while the different conceptions capture important dimensions of privacy, none can explain the interest fully. Looking at a broad array of privacy interests in the US, Daniel Solove favours a pragmatic approach that 'conceptualizes privacy within particular contexts' rather than providing a comprehensive and abstract definition.[146] In an important contribution, Helen Nissenbaum provides an account of privacy as 'contextual integrity', which amounts to 'a right to appropriate flow of personal information'.[147] Under this view, what flow of information is appropriate will depend on the actors involved, the type of information and any controls or expectations on the further transmission of such information.[148] The emphasis on context fits with our willingness to share medical information in the context of a doctor's appointment, but not at a social occasion.[149] The emphasis on context captures the complexity of privacy and avoids a rigid division between the public and private. It does not, however, explain what degree of privacy any particular context demands. The existing practices and expectations relating to privacy are taken as the starting point and adapted in new situations.[150]

Privacy is therefore hard to define in a way that fully captures our instincts about what is private, while not being over-inclusive. There is a vast literature on the subject,

---

[142] M Birnhack, 'A Quest for a Theory of Privacy: Context and Control' (2011) 51 *Jurimetrics* 447.

[143] Moreham, 'Privacy in the common law' (n 135) 639.

[144] Moreham ibid. See discussion in R Wacks, *Privacy and Media Freedom* (Oxford, Oxford University Press, 2013) 20.

[145] See Birnhack (n 142).

[146] D Solove, 'Conceptualizing Privacy' (2002) 90 *California Law Review* 1078, 1129, looking at privacy interests not only in relation to information, but also to physical spaces and the body.

[147] H Nissenbaum, *Privacy in Context: Technology, Policy and the Integrity of Social Life* (Stanford University Press, 2010) 127. Nissenbaum's approach can incorporate elements of both the control and access accounts of privacy, as either could be relevant in different contexts.

[148] ibid, 141–46.

[149] ibid, 146.

[150] ibid. See also the pragmatic approach in Solove (n 146) 1154.

and the discussion here is not exhaustive. None of these attempts to conceptualise privacy provide concrete answers to issues of application, but instead provide a basic orientation in thinking about privacy. Even if the issues of conceptualisation can be settled, there is a further question of why privacy is valuable and worthy of protection, which will be discussed below with reference to informational privacy.

ii. The Value of Privacy

There are a number of reasons why private information is regarded as worth protecting. Sometimes privacy is taken to be an element of individual autonomy and dignity.[151] Under this view, the public disclosure of private information deprives a person of the choice about what to share and with whom, and someone else imposes a choice on the person. The invasion of privacy represents a loss of autonomy in so far as the person becomes less able to present him or herself to the world on his or her own terms. Making that choice for another person also shows a lack of respect by failing to treat the person as 'morally responsible for their own decisions', and thereby amounts to an affront to personal dignity.[152] Along such lines, Edward Bloustein wrote over 50 years ago that media disclosures can 'destroy individual dignity and integrity and emasculate individual freedom and independence'.[153] Such concerns for human dignity provide a powerful explanation of the value of privacy interests. However, that value does not mean that all privacy interests warrant legal protection.[154] Moreover, the dignity-based arguments are vague, and do not aim to identify what information should be considered private or what level of protection should be afforded.

Another reason to value privacy is that it allows people to engage in certain activities without criticism or scrutiny. As Gavison states, 'privacy permits individuals to do what they would not do without it for fear of an unpleasant or hostile reaction from others'.[155] For example, the House of Lords found that the publication of photographs of the model Naomi Campbell leaving a Narcotics Anonymous meeting and providing details of her treatment was a violation of her privacy rights. One of the reasons advanced by the court was that the unwanted publicity would deter her from seeking treatment for drug use.[156] Similarly, people may be deterred from participating in a protest, if they know that photographs of the event will be disseminated and that they will be publicly criticised for their conduct or potentially added to a blacklist. Neil Richards takes the argument a stage further, noting that surveillance

---

[151] See Lord Hoffmann in *Campbell v Mirror Group Newspapers* [2004] UKHL 22, [2004] 2 AC 45 at [50]–[51].

[152] S Benn, 'Privacy, Freedom, and Respect For Persons' in J Pennock and J Chapman (eds), *Privacy* (New York, Atherton Press, 1971) 6–8.

[153] E Bloustein, 'Privacy as an Aspect of Human Dignity: An Answer to Dean Prosser' (1964) 39 *New York University Law Review* 962, 971.

[154] Benn (n 152) 13.

[155] Gavison (n 132) 451.

[156] *Campbell* (n 151) at [81] and [165].

of people's reading habits and communications can inhibit the freedom to develop new ideas.[157]

The example in *Campbell* provides an easy case, as there are strong policy reasons for encouraging people to pursue drug treatment. In cases where it is generally accepted that the conduct should be discouraged, such as throwing litter in the street or criminal activities, the case for privacy is weaker. In such examples, the scrutiny of conduct and criticism facilitated by the lack of privacy is a mechanism for the enforcement of social rules and laws. Many activities, however, occupy a grey area which are neither to be encouraged nor discouraged in the eyes of the law or society. A decision to have cosmetic surgery may have few costs or benefits to society, but is still regarded as private. To treat such an activity as private is not to say that the activity is desirable, but that it is a matter of individual choice, which might be hindered if the information was made public.[158] Privacy can therefore be valued as promoting freedom of action in certain spheres, which is closely connected with the dignity and autonomy arguments made above. Along these lines, David Feldman has explained, privacy protects those activities that 'should be regarded as being irrelevant to the esteem in which a person is held'.[159] On this view, by protecting a person's privacy, the law removes the ability of others to enforce their intolerance of certain conduct through social censure.[160] As will be seen in the discussion of media stories about sexual activities, there is considerable disagreement about what aspects of a person's life are legitimate targets of criticism and which aspects are matters of purely personal choice that are irrelevant to the esteem in which the person is held.[161]

Private information can also be seen as a currency or resource that people choose to share to engage in certain activities or pursue certain interests. Along these lines, Fried describes private information as 'moral capital' that enables people to build relationships of 'love, friendship and trust'.[162] Sharing information is a way to show that the discloser trusts the recipient. Fried writes that 'intimacy is the sharing of information about one's actions, beliefs, or emotions which one does not share with all, and which one has the right not to share with anyone'.[163] That intimacy is destroyed if another person can disclose the relevant information, as the subject of the disclosure no longer has the choice to share information as a way of building trust.[164] Fried, however, notes that there have to be balances struck with other goals and that only some things need to be private to provide some moral capital to be traded. Which things are classed as private in any society will depend on convention and the types of information that are most valued.[165] The argument therefore does not seek to define what is protected as

---

[157] N Richards, *Intellectual Privacy* (Oxford, Oxford University Press, 2015).
[158] See also Gavison (n 132) 451.
[159] D Feldman, 'Secrecy, Dignity, or Autonomy? Views of Privacy as a Civil Liberty' (1994) 47 *Current Legal Problems* 41, 57.
[160] ibid.
[161] Gavison (n 132) 451 asking 'whether it is appropriate for privacy to permit individuals to escape responsibility for their actions, wishes, and opinions'.
[162] Fried (n 10) 'Privacy'.
[163] ibid, 484.
[164] ibid, 485.
[165] ibid, 487.

private, but explains why those types of information that are considered private are worth protecting.

Some arguments justify the protection of privacy as a way to shield people from other types of harm. Sometimes a disclosure will result in a disproportionate social response. For example, disclosure of certain information may be likely to lead to harassment or ostracism. Large political donations are normally publicly disclosed, but in some systems an exemption may be provided where transparency would be likely to provoke violence or some other severe consequences.[166] The case for maintaining secrecy in such cases is not primarily about privacy, but instead is a means to prevent certain harsh social consequences.

The argument about disproportionate consequences rests on the possibility that the disclosure of private information will have an effect on the behaviour of the audience. However, with most of the arguments for privacy, the concern is not with how the audience will react to the content. The harm is rooted in the act of publication of the information, the lack of respect shown to the individual and the consequent inhibition of action. By framing the harm in this way, the law of privacy thereby avoids the issues of the direct effects of the media on the audience.

The discussion here has identified several key arguments that are often used to justify the legal protection of privacy. These arguments all leave open questions about the scope of privacy rights and the types of information to be protected. There are limits to what types of information should be considered private, and a privacy interest may be outweighed by a competing interest. More generally, a right to privacy needs to accommodate the fact that nobody has, or should have, absolute control over the way they are seen, and a public persona is something negotiated with other members of the public. If a person presents himself in one way to the public, another person may wish to challenge that version of events. Such difficult questions are faced by the courts when adjudicating on privacy claims, and some examples will be provided below. Before looking at the approach in law, it is first worth noting the special problems posed by intrusion and disclosure in the mass media.

iii. Privacy and Media Power

While there are good reasons for respecting private life, the law cannot guard against every invasion of privacy. The law should not regulate the social gossip that forms part of our everyday relationships, even though it frequently touches on private matters. Instead, some decisions need to be made about the types of disclosure that need legal restriction and on this issue the power of the media is a relevant factor.[167] References

---

[166] For example, in Northern Ireland political donations were initially not subject to the same transparency requirements as the rest of the UK, due to the sensitive political situation. The position has since been changed under the Northern Ireland (Miscellaneous Provisions) Act 2014. For discussion of related issues in the US see *Brown v Socialist Workers '74 Campaign Committee (Ohio)* 459 US 87 (1982).

[167] The discussion in this section draws on J Rowbottom, 'A landmark at a turning point: Campbell and the use of privacy law to constrain media power' (2015) 7 *Journal of Media Law* 170.

to media power have been made on a number of occasions to justify the legal protection of private information. Warren and Brandeis' seminal article complained of newspapers 'overstepping in every direction the obvious bounds of propriety and of decency'.[168] Over a century later, in *Lenah Game Meats*, Kirby J in the High Court of Australia stated:

> The power of modern media, so important for the freedoms enjoyed in Australia, can sometimes be abused. When that happens, the courts are often the only institutions in our society with the power and the will to provide protection and redress to those who are gravely harmed.[169]

Similarly, the case for a privacy law in England and Wales has developed in the context of debates about press ethics, including the reports by David Calcutt in the early 1990s and the Leveson Report in 2012.[170] The laws regulating privacy may be general in application, but (like libel) they have developed with the mass media paradigm in mind.

Newspapers and broadcasters are not the only powerful institutions that can interfere with privacy rights. Digital intermediaries that gather vast amounts of data provide another obvious example. Moreover, mass dissemination is not necessary for a major infringement of privacy rights.[171] Sending an intimate photograph to a person's employer is a serious infringement, without the sender holding disproportionate power. However, mass dissemination in the media makes it more likely that the information will reach the people that the individual wants to keep it secret from. As Lord Neuberger stated, a 'story in a newspaper has greater influence, credibility and reach, as well as greater potential for intrusion, than the same story on the internet'.[172] As a rule of thumb, publication in the mass media can be expected to cause serious damage to privacy rights.

The imbalance of communicative power is also an important factor because it is difficult for an ordinary individual to reply to or contextualise an intrusive disclosure made in the pages of a national newspaper. A newspaper exposure may come to define a person in the public eye, particularly where that person has no pre-existing public profile. The individual affected may feel powerless to counter media publicity and neutralise the effects of the disclosure. Furthermore, unlike the sharing of information among friends, the relationship with the media may not be ongoing and does not entail the reciprocal exchange of information. If two people share private information with one another and one of those people then shares an item of that information more

---

[168] Warren and Brandeis (n 131) 196. See discussion in Richards (n 157) 16–20.

[169] *Australian Broadcasting Corp v Lenah Game Meats Pty Ltd* [2001] HCA 63 at [183].

[170] D Calcutt, *Report of the Committee on Privacy and Related Matters* (Cm 1102, 1990) (Calcutt Committee), Lord Justice Leveson, *An Inquiry into the Culture, Practices and Ethics of the Press: Report* (HC 780, 2012).

[171] See R Post, 'The Social Foundations of Privacy: Community and Self in the Common Law Tort' (1989) 77 *California Law Review* 957, 989–90.

[172] *PJS v News Group Newspapers Ltd* [2016] UKSC 26, [2016] AC 1081 at [69]. See discussion in J Rowbottom, 'Holding back the tide: privacy injunctions and the digital media' (2017) 133 *Law Quarterly Review* 177.

widely, then that is likely to lead to a loss of the friendship. There is also a kind of 'mutual deterrent' that can discourage the further circulation of information, as if one person discloses private information about a friend, then the friend may disclose private information about that person in retaliation. These factors will not be present in the case of a media disclosure, where the media company is not a friend of the person reported on and does not share its own private information with that person. The law of privacy may be justified as a way to redress the unequal power of the media.

The media will also come in for special attention given that it is in the business of publishing information about people and has the resources for gathering information about any person and any aspect of their life. This not only gives media institutions considerable power to interfere with privacy, but also means that there is an implied threat. For example, politicians may be wary of offending the tabloid press for fear of becoming targets of a media investigation, even if such an intrusion never finally happens. Privacy laws may thereby be seen as a way to 'de-fang' media institutions of a potent source of power and influence.

B. Privacy in England and Wales

i. Development of a Privacy Action

In domestic law, there is no general right to privacy.[173] That, however, does not mean that privacy is offered no legal protection. The traditional approach to privacy protection has been piecemeal, with a number of causes of action protecting various aspects of privacy. These actions include breach of confidence, malicious falsehood, harassment, nuisance and defamation. The traditional way of thinking was that all these causes added up to a more complete protection of privacy in the aggregate. Critics of this approach noted that gaps existed between the various causes of action, which left some victims of intrusion without a remedy. The inadequacy of the law prior to the Human Rights Act 1998 was highlighted in *Kaye*, in which two newspaper reporters entered the hospital room of a seriously injured actor and conducted an interview without his consent.[174] Despite the clear ethical wrongdoing, the court was unable to offer full protection to Kaye.[175]

The law developed and by the 1990s breach confidence became the primary means to secure the legal protection of private information. The law of breach of confidence offers legal protection in relation to information that is: (1) confidential; (2) imparted on the condition of confidentiality; and (3) put to an unauthorised use to the detriment of the claimant.[176] The second factor listed meant that there would normally be

---

[173] *Wainwright v Home Office* [2003] UKHL 53, [2004] 2 AC 406.
[174] *Kaye v Robertson* [1991] FSR 62.
[175] His claim succeeded only in malicious falsehood.
[176] *Coco v Clarke* [1969] RPC 41 at 47.

a relationship—professional or personal—between the claimant and the recipient of the information that generated the obligation of confidence. For example, a doctor receives information from a patient on the understanding that it should go no further. These requirements were gradually loosened and the courts showed an increasing willingness to *imply* an obligation of confidence even where there was no pre-existing relationship between the parties.[177] For example, a person finding a diary labelled 'top secret' in the street could be under an *implied* obligation of confidence despite having never met the writer.[178] Under that approach, an editor or journalist could become bound by an obligation if he or she *should* have known that the information was confidential. The obligation could thereby attach to a newspaper editor who commissions a photographer to snoop on a celebrity at a private swimming pool, knowing that it is an activity that is supposed to be private. The loosening of the requirements thereby provided greater scope for the doctrine to be used to restrain the media.

A catalyst for further change came with the Human Rights Act 1998, which incorporated a right to private and family life under Article 8. While that right can only be directly asserted against public authorities, the Strasbourg jurisprudence provides that public bodies are under a positive obligation to take steps to secure privacy rights.[179] Consequently, the courts have developed the law of confidence in a way to protect Article 8 rights in cases between two private parties.[180] Perhaps the strongest statement came from Buxton LJ in *McKennitt v Ash*, in which he said that Articles 8 and 10 'are the very content of the domestic tort'.[181] While the extent of this duty on the courts is uncertain, it is clear that Article 8 has had an indirect impact on claims between individuals and media institutions. So, while the common law offers no general right to privacy, Article 8 comes close to providing such protection.

The framework for the law was settled in the landmark decision of *Campbell v MGN*, in which Lord Nicholls stated that privacy claims should be pursued under a new action of 'misuse of private information', rather than accommodated by stretching the law of confidence. That step was more than a matter of labelling and changed the nature of the action. Lord Hoffmann noted that breach of confidence 'traditionally fastens on the conscience of one party to enforce equitable duties which arise out of his relationship with the other'.[182] By contrast privacy is about 'the protection of human autonomy and dignity—the right to control the dissemination of information about one's private life and the right to the esteem and respect of other people'.[183]

---

[177] In *Douglas v Hello* [2001] QB 967, Brooke LJ at [71] stated that the obligation could be implied where the claimant takes steps to make clear that no photographs are to be taken. For discussion of this development see R Mulheron, 'A Potential Framework for Privacy?' (2006) 69 *Modern Law Review* 679, 687–88; T Aplin, 'The Development of the Action for Breach of Confidence in a Post-HRA Era' (2007) *Intellectual Property Quarterly* 19; H Fenwick and G Phillipson, *Media Freedom under the Human Rights Act* (Oxford, Oxford University Press, 2006) 730, citing *Creation Records v News Group Newspapers* [1997] EMLR 444 and *Shelley Films v Rex Features* [1994] EMLR 134 as examples of an implied obligation.

[178] *A-G v Guardian Newspapers (No 2)* [1990] 1 AC 109, 281.

[179] *X and Y v Netherlands*, App no 8978/80 (1985) 8 EHRR 235, [23]; *Von Hannover v Germany (No 2)*, App nos 40660/08 and 60641/08 (2012) 55 EHRR 15 at [98].

[180] *Campbell* (n 151) at [132]–[133]; *Douglas v Hello (No 3)* [2005] EWCA Civ 595, [2006] QB 125 at [53].

[181] *McKennitt v Ash* [2006] EWCA Civ 1714, [2008] QB 73 at [11].

[182] Lord Hoffmann in *Campbell* (n 151) at [44].

[183] ibid, [51].

The cause of action of misuse of private information therefore has a different focus from breach of confidence and places privacy interests centre stage.

ii. Reasonable Expectations

In its reformulation of the law in *Campbell*, the House of Lords provided a two-stage test for misuse of private information: (1) whether the information falls 'within the sphere of the complainant's private or family life'; and if so (2) whether the privacy right outweighs the right to freedom of expression (the balancing stage).[184] In relation to the first stage, the court normally asks whether the claimant had a 'reasonable expectation of privacy'.[185] The test appears somewhat circular, as it states that something is private when you can reasonably expect it to be private. The test is objective, as it is what you could *reasonably* expect rather than what you *actually* expect. The reference to an 'expectation' can also be misleading.[186] For example, there might be occasions where a reasonable person expects a celebrity's friend to sell a story to the press, but such a sale would still be an invasion of privacy. As Moreham points out, it is better to think of the test as asking whether a person had a reasonable *desire* for privacy.[187]

When considering an Article 8 claim against a public authority, Lord Kerr argued that the presence of the reasonable expectation should not be the sole test to determine whether privacy rights are engaged, and should instead be treated as a factor for the court to consider.[188] Under Lord Kerr's approach, the court should consider other contextual factors, such as the age of the claimant and the use to which the information will be put. Barendt supports a similar position in relation to misuse of private information, arguing that the reasonable expectation test adds very little to the court's analysis, amounts to a 'ritual incantation' and often confuses the question of whether Article 8 is engaged with whether it can be overridden by free speech considerations.[189]

Despite the criticisms, the reasonable expectation test has been dominant in deciding whether the privacy right is engaged. Lord Toulson in *JR38* argued that the various contextual factors mentioned by Lord Kerr could in any event be taken into account to determine whether a reasonable expectation exists.[190] That is reflected by the approach taken in *Murray*, in which Clarke MR stated that the following factors are relevant in deciding whether there is a reasonable expectation of privacy:

the attributes of the claimant, the nature of the activity in which the claimant was engaged, the place at which it was happening, the nature and purpose of the intrusion, the absence of

---

[184] Lord Nicholls in *Campbell* (n 151) at [20].
[185] ibid, [21] and Baroness Hale at [134]. Compare Lord Hope's 'substantial offence' test at [92].
[186] Moreham, 'Privacy in the common law' (n 135) 647.
[187] ibid, 648.
[188] *JR38's Application for Judicial Review* [2015] UKSC 42 at [39] and [53]. Lord Kerr made these arguments in a case concerning the direct application of Article 8 to the actions of a public authority, as opposed to a misuse of private information claim.
[189] E Barendt, '"A reasonable expectation of privacy": a coherent or redundant concept?' in Kenyon (n 9) at 114, and 'Problems with the "reasonable expectation of privacy" test' (2016) 8 *Journal of Media Law* 129.
[190] *JR38's Application for Judicial Review* (n 188) at [98].

consent and whether it was known or could be inferred, the effect on the claimant and the circumstances in which and the purposes for which the information came into the hands of the publisher.[191]

In looking at the attributes of the claimant, the courts have regularly held that a child's expectation of privacy is more easily triggered and given greater weight.[192] Of course, that does not mean the child's interests are a trump card, and the courts should be wary of claimants asserting the rights of a child as a way to protect their own privacy.

On the purpose of the disclosure, the courts have little tolerance for cases where private information is supplied to the media to blackmail or put undue pressure on a person.[193] The method by which information is acquired can also be significant.[194] A person being secretly filmed is deceived into thinking the activity is private and cannot be taken to consent to the capture of the information.[195] Again, this is not a trump card and covert acquisition does not by itself transform mundane information into private data. Moreover, secret filming and recordings are often key methods used by the media to gather important stories, and will sometimes be justified at the balancing stage. These factors show that even if the reasonable expectation test does amount to something of a conclusory label, it provides considerable flexibility and allows for a range of factors to be taken into account.

Under both the reasonable expectation test and Lord Kerr's proposed alternative, the engagement of the privacy right is fact sensitive and determined on a case-by-case basis. Inevitably, some of these factors are relevant not only to the question of whether the right is engaged, but also to what weight should be assigned to the right in the balancing stage. Consequently, the analysis in the two stages of the *Campbell* formula will often overlap. The following sections will outline some of the key factors that the court examines to decide if the privacy right is engaged, starting with the nature of the information, the form of the information, voluntary and involuntary past disclosures, and the location of the activity in question.

iii. Nature of the Activity and Information

There are some types of information that are assumed to be private without the need for any further enquiry. For example, a person's health or financial records will normally be private,[196] reflecting the contemporary social rules that attach significance to medical and financial information.[197] As the identification of private information draws on contemporary social standards, the designation of certain information as being core to privacy will change over time.

---

[191] *Murray v Express Newspapers* [2008] EWCA Civ 446, [2009] Ch 481 at [36].
[192] ibid.
[193] See *ZAM v CFW* [2013] EWHC 662 (QB), [2013] EMLR 27.
[194] *TRK v ICM* [2016] EWHC 2810 (QB) at [18]–[19].
[195] Benn (n 152) 10–11.
[196] *Campbell* (n 151) at [145].
[197] For example, see Fried (n 10) 487, discussing the role of convention in identifying private areas. See also the discussion in Post, 'Social Foundations of Privacy' (n 171).

The point is illustrated by debates about whether all sexual activity should be regarded as private. The area generates controversy, as people have different views on the morality of certain sexual activity. The status of such information is also important to certain sections of the media, where stories about people's sex lives have been a core part of their appeal to a broad audience. For a long time, the court has found that in certain contexts information about sexual activity is private. In the famous case of *Argyll v Argyll*, the court held that the doctrine of confidence could apply to certain private information shared between a married couple.[198]

While the court was protective of information shared within the context of a marriage, in *A v B* Lord Woolf found that in the case of a short-term relationship, the expectation of privacy is weak at best.[199] As a result, a newspaper was free to publish a 'kiss and tell' story detailing a footballer's short-term affairs with two women. Under Lord Woolf's approach, the court treated sexual activity on a spectrum in which a strong expectation of privacy arises in relation to a marriage, while at the other end of the spectrum lie short-term affairs, one night stands and encounters with prostitutes, which receive weaker protection.[200] On this view, a short-term relationship is more open to public criticism. The decision was criticised on the ground that the length of a relationship is not relevant to assessing the private nature of the information.[201] The decision can also be criticised on the grounds that the law should not discriminate between different lifestyles and treat the choice to be in a short-term sexual relationship as less worthy of protection.

The decision in *A v B* contrasts with the later decision in *CC v AB*, in which Eady J warned that the courts should not judge the moral worth of a person's sexual relationship to determine whether the information is protected by law or not.[202] On this view, an expectation of privacy could attach to extra-marital affairs or, as applied by the same judge in *Mosley*, to BDSM activities with five women.[203] While *A v B* was criticised for its moral evaluation, the reverse argument was put forward by a newspaper editor that criticised Eady J in *Mosley* for taking an 'amoral' position in relation to the status of different relationships.[204] The 'amoral' position of the court, however, reflects the view discussed earlier that such activities are matters for individual choice and should not be subject to pressure in the form of mass media publicity. While the *A v B* and *CC v AB* judgments show contrasting values about the status of the information, the view of Eady J is now the dominant approach and in most cases information relating to sexual activity will be considered private.[205]

Information about sexual activity provides one example of changing standards. Another example concerns information about a person subject to criminal investigation (but not charged). There is an argument that when the allegations are serious,

[198] *Argyll v Argyll* [1967] Ch 302.
[199] *A v B* [2002] EWCA Civ 337, [2003] QB 195.
[200] See also *Theakston v MGN* [2002] EWHC 137 (QB), [2002] EMLR 22 where the photos were protected, but not the written information.
[201] Aplin (n 177) 30.
[202] *CC v AB* [2006] EWHC 3083 (QB), [2007] EMLR 11 at [25].
[203] *Mosley v News Group Newspapers* [2008] EWHC 1777 (QB), [2008] EMLR 20 at [127]–[130].
[204] See Paul Dacre's Hugh Cudlipp Lecture at the London College of Communication, 22 January 2007.
[205] However, traces of Lord Woolf's approach to shorter term relationships can still be found in some cases, see *YXB v TNO* [2015] EWHC 826 (QB) at [61].

publicising the fact of an arrest can be particularly disruptive and have stigmatising effects on the individual.[206] However, there are also arguments that the activities of the police and authorities should be open to public scrutiny and that the public can be informed. In practice, the court will tend to assess the expectation of privacy in relation to an arrest without charge based on a range factors including the seriousness of the charge, the impact of the publicity and the circumstances in which the information became available.[207] Such investigations are another area where the understanding of private information continues to evolve.

iv. Photographs

The form of the information is a relevant factor when deciding whether an expectation of privacy exists and whether the intrusion is proportionate. In particular, the courts have held that photographs are more likely to be intrusive. For example, even where the publication of the fact of a relationship or of medical treatment is permitted, the inclusion of a photograph showing a private act may go too far in interfering in private life.[208] Lord Phillips in *Douglas v Hello* commented that photographs enable the audience 'to act as a spectator, in some circumstances voyeur would be the more appropriate noun, of whatever it is that the photograph depicts'.[209] Accordingly a picture shows exactly how a person appeared on a particular occasion and what expression he or she had, in a way that would be difficult to convey in words.[210]

Under the current domestic law, the publication of a photograph does not automatically engage the expectation of privacy. In *Campbell*, Lord Hoffmann indicated that to be private, the image must either display an activity in private place, or at least show a person 'in a situation of humiliation or severe embarrassment'.[211] In other words, the photograph must contain some private or sensitive information. The position in *Campbell* is in tension with some statements from the European Court of Human Rights. In *Reklos v Greece*, the Strasbourg Court found the state to be in violation of Article 8 for failing to provide a remedy after a photographer took a photo of a newly born baby in hospital without the prior consent of the parents.[212] In so far as the photograph was taken in private place, the finding that Article 8 was engaged is consistent with Lord Hoffmann in *Campbell*. However, the Court went further:

> A person's image constitutes one of the chief attributes of his or her personality, as it reveals the person's unique characteristics and distinguishes the person from his or her peers. The right to the protection of one's image is thus one of the essential components of personal

---

[206] See *Hannon v News Group Newspapers* [2014] EWHC 1580 (Ch), [2015] EMLR 1 [82]–[104]; *ZXC v Bloomberg* [2017] EWHC 328 (QB), [2017] EMLR 21, and N Moreham and M Warby (eds), *Tugendhat and Christie: The Law of Privacy and the Media* (Oxford, Oxford University Press, 2016) 236–37.

[207] ibid. Compare the majority and dissent on the public's relationship with the presumption of innocence in *Khuja v Times Newspapers Ltd* [2017] UKSC 49, [2017] 3 WLR 351.

[208] *Campbell* (n 151); Fenwick and Phillipson (n 177) 784.

[209] *Douglas v Hello* (n 180) at [83].

[210] *Douglas v Hello* (n 177) at [165] (in the decision on the interim injunction).

[211] *Campbell* (n 151) at [75].

[212] *Reklos v Greece*, App no 1234/05 (2009) 27 BHRC 420.

development and presupposes the right to control the use of that image. While in most cases the right to control such use involves the possibility for an individual to refuse publication of his or her image, it also covers the individual's right to object to the recording, conservation and reproduction of the image by another person. As a person's image is one of the characteristics attached to his or her personality, its effective protection presupposes, in principle and in circumstances such as those of the present case (see para 37, above), obtaining the consent of the person concerned at the time the picture is taken and not simply if and when it is published. Otherwise an essential attribute of personality would be retained in the hands of a third party and the person concerned would have no control over any subsequent use of the image.[213]

The Strasbourg Court has since endorsed that reasoning[214] and the remarks have been cited with approval in the UK.[215] As Kirsty Hughes notes, there is some ambiguity in about how far the principle in *Reklos* goes, and the decision is open to broad and narrow interpretations.[216] At its broadest, the reasoning suggests that in principle the *capture* of an image of a person without consent engages Article 8, at least where the person does not knowingly or accidentally leave himself or herself open to the possibility of being photographed.[217] Alternatively, the principle could be explained with reference to the facts of the case, as it concerned the image of newborn child without parental consent—which will normally be regarded as a private moment.[218] Despite the uncertainties in the reach of Article 8, the discussion will show that the courts have moved beyond Lord Hoffmann's focus on embarrassing images and have expanded the tort to cover photographs that depict relatively innocuous activities.[219]

v. *Voluntary Disclosure*

The general rule in breach of confidence is that the confidential quality of the information is destroyed once the information is in the public domain.[220] That much makes sense, as we cannot describe something that is widely known as secret or confidential. An interest in *privacy*, however, is not automatically destroyed following publicity. In *Douglas v Hello*, Lord Phillips gave an example of a photograph surreptitiously taken of a person naked by a private swimming pool, and stated that even where an image has been widely viewed, the re-publication of photographs can still constitute an intrusion.[221] Despite this, there are circumstances where information is so widely known that it can no longer be considered private. The difficult question is when the circumstances and extent of publicity will work to weaken the expectation of privacy.

---

[213] ibid at [40].
[214] *Couderc v France*, App no 40454/07 [2016] EMLR 19 at [85].
[215] *Weller v Associated Newspapers* [2015] EWCA Civ 1176, [2016] 1 WLR 1541 at [28].
[216] See K Hughes, 'Photographs in Public Places and Privacy' (2009) 2 *Journal of Media Law* 159, 164–65.
[217] *Reklos* (n 212) [37]. For support in the domestic court, see Lord Kerr in *JR38* (n 188) at [41]. See Hughes, ibid.
[218] *Mahmood v BBC* [2014] EHWC 4207 (QB) at [10]; Hughes (n 216).
[219] *Murray* (n 191); *Weller* (n 215).
[220] *A-G v Guardian (No 2)* (n 178) 282.
[221] *Douglas v Hello* (n 180) at [105].

To address this question, it is important to consider how the information became publicly available. A person that voluntarily shares information and puts it into circulation gives up a degree of control. However, simply because information has been shared with one party does not mean the person consents to its sharing with others. Sometimes the sharing is subject to an understanding that it will go no further, and the discussion earlier noted that such conditions are an element of the individual's control of the information. Along these lines, the fact that the Prince of Wales shared a journal marked 'confidential' with up to 75 people could not be taken to mean that he consented to the content of the journal being published in a national newspaper.[222] On this view, privacy rights allow the person to decide *what* information is to be shared and *with whom* it is to be shared. The need to protect people's ability to take on different roles in different contexts, suggests that information can be shared with one group (such as family) without implicitly sharing it with others (such as colleagues).[223] This analysis was taken a stage further by Buxton LJ in *McKennitt*, stating that if 'information is my private property, it is for me to decide how much of it should be published'.[224] That explains why a person has the option to selectively disclose information, but may go too far in making an analogy with property. An individual clearly has some rights over personal information, but that does not mean exclusive control over what can be said on the subject.

The consent of the individual can, however, be inferred from the circumstances. If a person is particularly relaxed about sharing information with a large number of people, then there must come a point where he or she cannot expect the matter to remain private. If a person posts photographs of him or herself on social media with no privacy setting, then that is likely to weaken an expectation of privacy in relation to that information. However, to decide whether such consent should be implied requires a closer look at the context, such as the number of people the information was initially shared with, the number of people likely to see it and the presence of any efforts to restrict the flow of the information. A person who makes information publicly accessible but which is normally seen by only a handful of people, is not obviously consenting to the content being shared with the world at large in the mass media. The point is important, as the culling of information and images from social media is a common practice in the mass media. Those who find themselves thrust into the public eye will often have old social media comments turn up in the newspapers.

A variation of voluntary disclosure arises where the individual does not disclose the specific item of information, but puts a 'zone' of his or her life into the public eye. In such circumstances, it might be argued that the claimant has a lower expectation of privacy. The argument was greeted with scepticism in *McKennitt v Ash*, where the fact that a folk singer had spoken about the death of her fiancé in an interview to promote a charity was not to be taken as an invitation for her former friend to publicly comment on the singer's private life. For the reasons stated above, Buxton LJ concluded that such an argument 'completely undermines that reasonable expectation

---

[222] *Prince of Wales v Associated Newspapers* [2006] EWCA Civ 1776, [2008] Ch 57.
[223] Nissenbaum (n 147) Ch 7.
[224] *McKennitt* (n 181) at [55].

of privacy'.[225] Buxton LJ's point has been followed in subsequent cases, with judges sometimes referring to 'that discredited zone argument'.[226]

However, the 'zone' argument should not be so easily dismissed, and if a person puts certain aspects of their life into public view, then that can sometimes invite comment. Along these lines, the European Court of Human Rights has stated that the 'conduct of the person concerned prior to publication of the report' is a relevant factor in deciding whether privacy is infringed.[227] Such past conduct can include publicity in relation to the 'zone' of the person's life, though the court will consider the circumstances to take a more 'tailored' approach to this question.[228] Along these lines, it is important to consider whether the decision to make the 'zone' public was truly voluntary or whether a person felt compelled to disclose an aspect of their life. A person may make certain disclosures by virtue of their profession. Actors and musicians may be required to talk about aspects of their lives to promote their work.[229] By contrast, a truly free choice to put an area of one's life into the public eye can reduce the expectation of privacy. Such publicising of an area of one's life sits between the voluntary disclosure of the specific information and the general courting of publicity. The fact that a zone of a person's life has been voluntarily made public alone may not be sufficient to defeat a privacy claim, but nor is the matter irrelevant.

vi. Previous Disclosures by Third Parties

So far, the discussion has focused on the effect of voluntary disclosures by the claimant. A further issue is whether an unwanted disclosure by a third party that puts a matter into the public domain weakens the expectation of privacy. For an unwanted disclosure to destroy any future privacy rights in relation to that information is particularly harsh on the individual concerned. While such information may no longer be secret or confidential as a result of disclosures, re-publication can still be an intrusion that causes significant distress to the individual concerned. While the violation of privacy caused by republication is most obvious in relation to photographs, the principle can also apply to written text wherever further access to the information will cause some additional harm.[230]

The issue has arisen in a number of cases where the court has to decide whether an injunction restraining publication should be imposed or discharged in situations where the information is widely available on the digital media. In the famous case of *Mosley*, the claimant sought an injunction to restrain the publication of photographs and video of his sado-masochistic activities. Unfortunately for Mosley, within a day of the publication, the footage had been viewed 1.4 million times and copied by numerous other websites. Eady J reluctantly declined to grant an injunction on the ground that

---

[225] ibid.
[226] *Rocknroll v News Group Newspapers Ltd* [2013] EWHC 24 (Ch) at [19].
[227] *Axel Springer* (n 42) at [92]. See *AAA v Associated Newspapers Ltd* [2013] EWCA Civ 554 at [101].
[228] *GYH v Persons Unknown* [2017] EWHC 3360 (QB) at [33].
[229] See *X v Persons Unknown* [2006] EWHC 2783 (QB), [2007] EMLR 10.
[230] *PJS* (n 172).

any attempt to restrain publication was futile. Eady J warned that the courts should not act like a modern-day King Canute attempting to hold back the tide and stated that the material had 'entered the public domain to the extent that there is, in practical terms, no longer anything which the law can protect'.[231] This ruling did not prevent Mosley from pursuing the initial publisher for damages or from seeking the removal of the material by internet intermediaries, but did prevent a pre-trial injunction.

Mosley is an exceptional case where the claimant was particularly unlucky. In *PJS*, the Supreme Court declined to discharge an injunction restricting the reporting of a celebrity's 'three-way' sexual encounter with two men, despite widespread publicity abroad and on the digital media.[232] A significant part of the Supreme Court's reasoning was that the internet publicity took place after a pre-trial injunction had been awarded, while in *Mosley* the publicity took place prior to the application for an injunction. As a result, *PJS* could be distinguished from *Mosley*, as there were additional rule of law considerations in protecting an existing injunction. However, even without that factor, the courts will normally be reluctant to find that internet publications by others destroy the privacy right. Moreover, the court will take into account where republication is likely to take place. If content is widely available on the digital media, fresh publication in the mass media can cause additional harm in so far as the information is brought to a new and wider audience.[233] The press complains that this means it cannot report on what is being widely discussed elsewhere. However, a decision to discharge the court order would concede the limited use of injunctions in the internet age and an inability of the court to prevent further breaches of privacy.

The cases considered so far concern interim injunctions and the question is partly about the effectiveness of the remedy. A remaining question is whether a person can be liable for damages for publishing private information that is already well known. For example, imagine that a newspaper publishes private information and an injunction restricting publication is declined because of exceptional widespread publicity. Would a person who subsequently repeats the private information on the social media be liable in damages? The issue goes to the question of whether publicity truly destroys the interest in privacy. Such a legal action seems unlikely, but could arise where a person wishes to 'clean up' all traces of a story in the aftermath of the exposure. In such circumstances, again, the context of the case is significant and courts should look at the power of the particular publisher and nature of the publication to determine whether any additional harm to the privacy interests has occurred.

vii. Privacy and Public Places

The place of an activity is another factor considered when deciding if there is an expectation of privacy. There are some places where a person will have an obvious expectation of privacy, such as a home or a hospital room. The issues are more complex when a person claims that an expectation of privacy has been violated by the

---

[231] *Mosley v News Group Newspapers Ltd* [2008] EWHC 687 (QB) at [36].
[232] *PJS* (n 172).
[233] ibid.

sharing of information about an activity that took place in public. When acting in a public setting, a person implicitly consents to sharing some information with people in the vicinity, even though they are not trusted friends or confidantes.[234] Little weight can be placed on such implicit consent where a person has no alternative but to use a public place to engage in a private activity. A person visiting an abortion clinic, for example, may have to use publicly accessible roads and pavements to access the facility.[235] That does not signal a decision to share the information about that treatment with the rest of the world.

An expectation of privacy may also depend on the public place in question and whether a person is likely to be observed in that area (and by whom).[236] Some places may be crowded and busy all the time. A footballer who chooses to conduct an affair in various well-attended nightspots will be more likely to invite public scrutiny. By contrast, the same cannot be said if the activity takes place in a remote part of the countryside that is accessible to anyone but rarely visited. Moreover, some spaces are neither fully private nor public. If a person visits a gym that is open only to members, the person agrees to be observed by other members using that facility (which may be a considerable number), but not the world at large. Accordingly, the courts should take into account not just the fact that a place is open to public, but also how widely used the space is in practice.[237]

In determining whether there is an expectation of privacy in a public place, many of the factors mentioned earlier will come together in an overall assessment. Accordingly, the courts give some weight to the method by which information is captured. If a person is photographed using a long lens camera or recorded using a hidden microphone, the individual is not implicitly consenting to the sharing of that information. The person has no knowledge of the recording and it cannot be taken to be one of the normal incidents that flow from being in a public place.[238]

The nature of the activity of the claimant in the public place or the type of information being acquired is also important to the assessment.[239] In *Campbell*, Baroness Hale famously commented that a photograph of a person going out for a pint of milk does not engage an expectation of privacy.[240] By contrast, a person had an expectation that footage of a suicide attempt in a town centre would not be broadcast on television.[241] By drawing a distinction between everyday activities and situations of 'humiliation and severe embarrassment', the court in *Campbell* attempted to limit the protection of privacy in public places by taking a relatively narrow definition of activities that will generate 'private information' in such settings.

Subsequent decisions have extended the reach of the law to cover a broader range of activities in public places. In particular, in *Von Hannover v Germany*, the Strasbourg

---

[234] *Kinloch v HM Advocate* [2012] UKSC 62, [2013] 2 AC 93 at [19].
[235] See N Moreham, 'Privacy in public places' (2006) 65 *Cambridge Law Journal* 606, 626.
[236] *Murray* (n 191) at [36]. Moreham, 'Privacy in public places' (n 235) 621–23.
[237] Moreham, ibid.
[238] Feldman (n 159) 60.
[239] *Weller* (n 215) at [61].
[240] *Campbell* (n 151) at 154. See also *John v Associated Newspapers Ltd* [2006] EWHC 1611 (QB), [2006] EMLR 27.
[241] *Peck v UK*, App no 44647/98 (2003) 36 EHRR 41.

Court found that photographs of Princess Caroline of Monaco engaged her Article 8 rights, even though there was nothing embarrassing or humiliating in the images.[242] The Princess was frequently followed by paparazzi photographers and the images published showed her engaged in activities including shopping, horse riding, sitting at a restaurant and canoeing. The domestic courts have also moved away from the stricter limits in *Campbell* and applied misuse of private information to photographs in public places that do not contain anything sensitive. In *Murray*, the court refused to rule out an argument that JK Rowling's infant son had an expectation of privacy when photographed in the street with his parents.[243] In *Weller*, the Court of Appeal upheld a finding that the publication on the *Daily Mail* website of photographs of a musician with his children shopping and in a café in Los Angeles violated the expectation of privacy.[244] In both cases, the fact that the claims were brought by the children was significant, especially as young children cannot be taken to have consented to any incidental publicity. The court in *Weller* also emphasised that a family outing is an activity that lies at the heart of Article 8's protection of family life.[245] Consequently, a walk with one's children is not the same as Baroness Hale's trip for a bottle of milk. The court thereby continues to focus on the nature of the activity, but it is no longer limited to the humiliating and embarrassing activities. The cases thereby represent an expansion on what can be considered private information, extending to relatively innocuous details.

There are several factors that can explain these developments. The first relates to intrusive methods used to gather the information. Along these lines, the decision of the European Court of Human Rights in *Von Hannover* could be explained by a desire to protect people from harassment by the paparazzi.[246] While such methods can raise Article 8 issues, there are problems in applying the domestic law of misuse of private information to offer such protection. Earlier, it was noted that the way information is acquired is relevant to determining whether it is private. However, that relevance arises where the information in question is prima facie private and the method of capture goes to the question of whether consent to sharing the information can be implied from the circumstances (which explains why such consent is harder to imply where a long lens camera is used). If a case such as *Von Hannover* is explained in terms of harassment, then the method of gathering the information is not simply an issue of implied consent, and is instead the central focus of the protection. There may be good reason to curb the activities of the paparazzi harassing celebrities, but the concern is not with the unwanted publication of private facts

---

[242] *Von Hannover v Germany*, App no 59320/00 (2005) 40 EHRR 1.

[243] *Murray* (n 191).

[244] *Weller* (n 215).

[245] ibid, [61].

[246] See Fenwick and Phillipson (n 177) 681–83, and 768. The domestic courts have found that the approach taken in *Von Hannover* is not dependent on an element of harassment, see *Murray v Express Newspapers plc* [2007] EWHC 1908 (Ch), [2007] EMLR 583 at [46]–[47] and *McKennitt* (n 181) at [41]. However, the Court of Appeal in *Murray* (n 191) accepted that the campaign of harassment was 'part of the context in which the decision was made' at [59].

(protecting the right to *informational privacy*), it is with other aspects of the privacy right.[247] Instead, laws of harassment may provide more appropriate protection for such types of intrusion.

The decisions in *Murray* and *Weller* can also be explained by the court's focus on how the information will be used (which relates to the 'misuse' aspect of the tort). For example, those people who witness events in a public place are normally free to tell others what they have seen. However, the court in *Murray* noted that different considerations apply if the information is acquired for publication in a national newspaper. While it may be reasonable to expect people in public places to be photographed as part of a general street scene, one could reasonably expect not to be the focus of an image for a national newspaper when going for a walk to the shops.[248] Accordingly, the information contained in the photograph is not self-evidently private, but the publicity given to the activity and the direction of attention on the claimant can render the publication an invasion of privacy. These cases are perhaps less concerned with the protection of private facts (as traditionally understood) and more with ensuring that certain activities or areas of life are not subject to persistent monitoring and mass exposure, recognising the detrimental impact of media publicity on those areas of life.

There is every reason to sympathise with the experiences of the Wellers and Murrays, and to protect a wider range of information from mass media disclosures. The extension of misuse of private information can, however, put the doctrine under some strain. There is a danger that courts will be tempted to stretch the definition of private information to cover relatively innocuous details to address the concerns with media publicity. Once established, the risk is that such a wide understanding of private information will become the norm and applied more widely to non-media cases that do not pose a risk of mass publicity. Moreover, as noted, the nature of the interest at stake in media cases is sometimes ambiguous, as it involves intrusion caused by acquiring the information (through long lens cameras) and the persistent presence of the press following the person (concerning surveillance and attention), as opposed to informational privacy.[249] The privacy interests at stake may go beyond the publication of private facts that was the initial concern in *Campbell*. For some of the broader privacy interests, the issues may be better addressed through laws specifically tailored to combat harassment or the methods of newsgathering, as opposed to a private facts tort.

viii. Misuse of Information

The discussion above has shown how the expectation of privacy varies depending on the use or misuse of the information in question. The 'misuse' of information has primarily referred to the unwanted *publication* of private facts. However, the tort

---

[247] See discussion in Hughes, 'Photographs in Public Places and Privacy'(n 216) 162.

[248] *Murray* (n 191) at [50].

[249] N Moreham, 'Beyond information: physical privacy in English law' (2014) 73 *Cambridge Law Journal* 350.

may also be expanding by looking at other ways the information can be misused. In particular, the courts have hinted that the *capture* of private information may itself constitute a misuse. In the breach of confidence case, *Tchenguiz*, Lord Neuberger stated that:

> it would be a breach of confidence for a defendant, without the authority of the claimant, to examine, or to make, retain, or supply copies to a third party of, a document whose contents are, and were (or ought to have been) appreciated by the defendant to be, confidential to the claimant.[250]

While not central to the final decision in that case, the dicta states that accessing or recording certain types of private information can constitute a breach of confidence, regardless of whether it is subsequently disclosed.

The line of argument has also been developed in relation to misuse of private information. Moreham highlights dicta suggesting that the capture of sensitive information can engage Article 8 and argues that the law could be extended to protect other aspects of privacy beyond information.[251] For example, in *CTB*, Eady J stated that privacy is about *intrusion*, as well as information.[252] In *Gulati*, the court awarded Alan Yentob £85,000 for the interception of phone messages, even though no personal information about him was included in the newspaper publication.[253] While the case concerned damages and provides no direct authority for an extension of the law, the reasoning of the court seems supportive of such a development. In the Chancery Division, Mann J appeared to view 'misappropriation' of private information as a form of misuse under the tort.[254]

Extending the tort of misuse to attach liability to the misappropriation, capture or examination of information (as opposed to publication) raises many difficult questions. A person can capture and examine private information in ways that are otherwise lawful. For example, if a membership list of a political party is disclosed on a leakers' website, does a person 'misappropriate' that information by downloading the database? Similarly, do people who search the social media to find out the identity of a celebrity protected under a privacy injunction also engage in an act of misappropriation? The case for expanding the law to the capture and examination of information aims at curbing the more intrusive forms of newsgathering such as phone hacking, but the effects would go far beyond media practices and could potentially even regulate the conduct of the audience. If mere examination without publication becomes a tort, then some other conditions are needed to limit the scope for liability.[255]

---

[250] *Tchenguiz v Imerman* [2010] EWCA Civ 908, [2011] Fam 116 at [69].

[251] Moreham, 'Beyond information' (n 249). See also the discussion in M Tilbury, 'Privacy: Common Law or Human Right?' in N Witzleb, D Lindsay, M Paterson and S Rodrick (eds), *Emerging Challenges in Privacy Law* (Cambridge, Cambridge University Press, 2014).

[252] *CTB v News Group Newspapers Ltd* [2011] EWHC 1326 (QB) at [23]. However, the statement was made in relation to the issue of re-publication of known facts, rather than expanding the tort to guard against intrusion more generally.

[253] *Gulati v MGN* [2015] EWCA Civ 1291, [2017] QB 149.

[254] *Gulati v MGN* [2015] EWHC 1482 (Ch), [2016] FSR 12 at [143].

[255] See N Moreham, 'A Conceptual Framework for the New Zealand Tort of Intrusion' (2016) 47 *Victoria University of Wellington Law Review* 283.

For example, the court might have to specify the types of information that a person has an expectation not to have examined. Alternatively, the law could restrict the tort to the access of information through unlawful means (such as hacking). These are just possibilities, but illustrate the problems and complexities of expanding the private information tort.

The test of misuse of private information was developed primarily to deal with unwanted publicity, often with the mass media in mind. However, this publicity is only one type of threat to privacy. In the era of big data, it is well known that what might cause an invasion of privacy is not the disclosure of a single item of information, but the aggregation of lots of items of information none of which are sensitive when viewed in isolation. For example, if one person takes a photograph of an individual as a part of a street scene, then there is no threat to privacy. However, if lots of street scene images are accumulated, enabling the audience to track the movements of an individual over the course of day, then greater privacy issues arise. Misuse of private information could be developed so that a person has a reasonable expectation that others will not compile significant data about a person's movements. However, such a development would represent a further expansion of the types of information that are considered to be private. Further difficulties arise where the invasion of privacy is not caused by any single agent disclosing information, but where lots of people disclose individual items of information (for example on social media)—none of which can be considered private in isolation, but which collectively represent an intrusion when all the information is available to the audience. In such circumstances, there may be no individual that breaches the expectation of privacy for the purposes of the tort. These are the challenges facing privacy in the digital era. However, the tort of misuse of private information is likely to provide limited protection in such cases. The threats to privacy may be better dealt with under other causes of action, such as data protection or by placing responsibilities on digital intermediaries.

ix. Taking Stock

The law regulating private information has grown considerably in the last two decades. The law has developed to fill some important gaps and provide a means to address abuses of media power. When looking at the terms and basic framework for misuse of private information, it is hard to take issue with these developments. However, the developments have generated considerable controversy, and newspapers complain about the threat to press freedom. Some of the arguments are self-serving, but others raise valid concerns. The question of whether there is a reasonable expectation of privacy is of considerable importance, as once it is established, the issue moves to the question of the public interest and the defendant will have to provide some reasons to justify the publication. While addressing genuine problems in relation to media reporting, there is a danger that courts will be tempted to allow Article 8 to be triggered more easily (for example, by finding an expectation of privacy in relation to a wider range of information or to the capture of information), which takes the misuse tort away from its focus on the publication of private facts. If the threshold is lowered, there is greater scope for the law to be used strategically to inhibit critical media reporting. The question is whether such consequences can be avoided through the protection of media freedom at the balancing stage.

C. The Balancing Stage

Once the court is satisfied that an expectation of privacy is engaged, the second stage for the court is to balance the Article 8 rights with Article 10. In this task, the courts have stated that neither right enjoys presumptive priority.[256] In weighing the two rights, the court will look at the strength of the privacy right and the Article 10 rights. The difficulty with the 'balancing' test is that there is no simple formula or calculus to determine what weight should be assigned to either right in this process.

In *Axel Springer*, the European Court of Human Rights sought to give greater structure by providing a set of criteria for striking the balance.[257] The factors to be considered by the court are: (1) whether the disclosure is a contribution to a debate of general interest; (2) how well known the subject of the disclosure is; (3) the past conduct of the claimant and whether publicity had been sought; (4) the method of obtaining the information; (5) the content, form and consequences of the publication; and (6) the severity of the sanction imposed. The approach provides a structure for analysis, although many of these factors restate the criteria either for an expectation of privacy or for media freedom. The latter considerations will be considered in the following section.

The approach taken avoids bright line or mechanistic rules that can have arbitrary cut-offs, and instead forces the court to engage with the central substantive question. The difficulty with such context sensitivity is that the court will resort to forms of ad hoc balancing, which can make the law inconsistent and difficult to predict.[258] To address this, the court will build up certain rules of thumb to indicate the weighting to be given to certain factors, but that does not amount to a guarantee that a particular balance will be struck.[259] Such a fact-sensitive approach also renders first instance judges vulnerable to being swayed by their sympathy for the claimant, who provides evidence to the court of the harm and distress caused by the disclosure.[260] An appellate court will also be reluctant to overturn the first instance court's assessment of where the balance lies, which is an 'evaluative judgment based on certain findings of fact'.[261] Consequently, much lies in the hands of the judge hearing the facts of the case.

---

[256] *In re S (a child)* [2004] UKHL 47, [2005] 1 AC 593.
[257] *Axel Springer v Germany* (n 42).
[258] *Weller* (n 215) at [58].
[259] For a contrary view, that the courts often take a more rigid categories-based approach, see P Wragg, 'The Legitimacy of Press Regulation' (2015) *Public Law* 290, 299–303.
[260] See Hoffmann LJ in *R v Central Independent Television plc* [1994] Fam 192, 202.
[261] *Weller* (n 215) at [57].

IV. The Public Interest

When looking at the elements for any media law liability, the courts will take into account freedom of expression and media freedom. The heightened threshold for 'serious harm' in defamation is one example of how the protection of expression rights can be incorporated into the law. Once the elements of liability are established, then there will normally be a process for the court to weigh media freedom with the personal right more generally. In privacy, this arises in the balancing stage, and in defamation law there is a specific public interest defence. Before looking at the specific ways these rights are balanced in those two causes of action, the discussion will set out some common features in the way that Article 10 and media freedom are analysed by the courts.

A. Political Speech and Matters of General Interest

A central factor in determining the weight to be assigned to expression rights and media freedom is the extent to which the publication contributes to a debate on a matter of general interest.[262] In particular, both domestic courts and the Strasbourg Court have stressed that heightened protection is to be afforded to political speech.[263] In *Campbell v MGN*, Baroness Hale stated:

> There are undoubtedly different types of speech, just as there are different types of private information, some of which are more deserving of protection in a democratic society than others. Top of the list is political speech. The free exchange of information and ideas on matters relevant to the organisation of the economic, social and political life of the country is crucial to any democracy. Without this, it can scarcely be called a democracy at all.[264]

By referring to 'the organisation of the economic, social and political life of the country' Baroness Hale offers a broad definition of political expression. At the other end of the spectrum, the court will grant relatively limited protection to gratuitous insults, pornography and hate speech, which is deemed to be of 'low value' to the audience. Sitting in between the two extremes are commercial and artistic expression, which receive an intermediate level of protection. The approach of the court reflects the audience-based justification for media freedom discussed in Chapter 1, in which the media serves the audience with the information and ideas necessary for opinion formation and holds power to account.

---

[262] *Cumpana v Romania*, App no 33348/96 (2005) 41 EHRR 14 at [93]; *Von Hannover* (2005) (n 242) at [63].
[263] See *Lingens* (n 108).
[264] *Campbell* (n 151) 45 at [148].

There are difficulties in defining the categories of speech. For example, artistic speech can make a political point by satirising a public figure. Hate speech can sometimes be used in a political context, for an example where an extreme political party has a racist campaign slogan. Gossip may be intrusive and unpleasant, but it can serve certain social functions and contribute to the formation of social rules.[265] The courts recognise such overlaps and will take into account various factors in deciding how strong the protection should be. The approach is nonetheless controversial, as it means the court assesses the value of speech, rather than leaving audiences to decide for themselves.

The heightened protection required for political speech was recognised before the Human Right Act 1998. In *Derbyshire CC v Times Newspapers*, the House of Lords ruled that government bodies cannot bring an action in libel, reasoning that to allow such institutions to sue for libel would be 'contrary to the public interest' and place 'an undesirable fetter on freedom of speech'.[266] Government bodies 'should be open to uninhibited public criticism'.[267] Accordingly, people are free to state outright falsities about government without any risk of liability. The priority for expression in such cases is relatively straightforward, as the government has no pressing interest in protecting its own reputation. When a publication is on a matter of general interest, but relates to a specific individual, then the balance changes as the personal rights are engaged. Exactly how this balance should be struck will vary according to a number of circumstances, which will be considered below.

B. Personal Rights and the Public Interest

A starting point when striking a balance between personal rights and the public interest is to look at the status of the individual involved. In the landmark decision in *Lingens v Austria*, the Strasbourg Court stated that the 'limits of acceptable criticism are accordingly wider as regards a politician as such than as regards a private individual'.[268] The question is why politicians should be treated any differently from private individuals at all.

A simple argument for the lower protection of the rights of a public figure is based on consent and runs that the politician 'knowingly lays himself open to close scrutiny of his every word and deed'.[269] This approach views the rough treatment from the press as part of the rules of the game, with the politician having partially waived rights to reputation and privacy by voluntarily entering politics. The argument is convenient, but it is not clear what level of criticism the politician consents to. While robust scrutiny must be accepted, by entering politics the individual does not consent to the publication of outright falsities or the exposure of deeply personal facts. The argument

---

[265] See D Zimmerman, 'Requiem for a Heavyweight: A Farewell to Warren and Brandeis's Privacy Tort' (1983) 68 *Cornell Law Review* 291.
[266] *Derbyshire CC v Times Newspapers* [1993] AC 534.
[267] ibid, 547.
[268] *Lingens* (n 108) at [42].
[269] ibid.

based on consent is also less forceful for those public figures that did not know that they would be in the public eye. The senior civil servant or company executive may not foresee media publicity as a part of their job, and consent is harder to infer.

The central reason for the limitation of personal rights is less to do with consent, and instead represents a prioritisation of the discussion of matters of general interest. For example, a report of a major failure in government policy may suggest a level of incompetence by the individual responsible for that area of policy. In such cases, the impact on the personal rights is a side effect of general political discussion. The actions of a public official can also be a matter of general interest in its own right. The most obvious example arises where the politician stands for election and the electorate needs to assess the candidates, including fitness for office and past conduct. In *AAA*, the public had an interest in knowing that Boris Johnson's extramarital affair resulted in the conception of a child, in so far as it showed the politician's 'reckless behaviour'.[270] The character, temperament and trustworthiness of an elected official is important, given the considerable discretion of the official to make and influence decisions on our behalf.

The discussion of a politician's personality may also be a way that the public can exercise a degree of control over government.[271] Modern democracies rarely work according to the ideals in which highly-informed citizens deliberate on substantive issues and then transmit their views to elected officials. Instead, attention is focused on the role of political leaders, who rely on image and representations in the media to persuade the public. Robust criticism can provide a way to puncture the representations being made by those in office and express anger in relation to an official's actions. An attack on reputation may simply be one of the sanctions that the citizen can wield to keep the politician vigilant and responsive between elections.[272] The requirement for politicians to tolerate greater criticism and the consequent weakening of personal right can thereby be understood as a transfer of power, in which the public has greater scope to define the political leader and challenge the existing image.

Even if the above arguments for public figures to tolerate criticism and scrutiny fail, there is still a negative case for media freedom based on the dangers of legal powers being misused. Actions in libel and privacy can be threatened to silence critics. The threat of being taken to court, running the risks of litigation, as well as the costs and stresses discussed earlier, will be enough to persuade some people not to make certain statements critical of a politician, even if they firmly believe such matters to be true and of public importance. Imposing some limit on a public figure's ability to enforce personal rights provides a safeguard against the abuse of the law to inhibit criticism.

---

[270] *AAA* (n 227) at [43]. This is particularly important if we understand an election as a process of choosing elites, rather than providing a mandate, where an assessment of the individual politician is a central task for citizens.

[271] See J Green, *The Eyes of the People: Democracy in an Age of Spectatorship* (Oxford, Oxford University Press, 2010) 129–30, emphasising the people's 'control of the means of publicity' as a key democratic constraint on political leaders.

[272] See J Keane, *Democracy and Media Decadence* (Cambridge, Cambridge University Press, 2013) 103–104, on the role and benefits of a culture of 'muckraking'.

There are of course limits to these arguments. While some celebrate the ridicule and attack of political figures as a realistic mechanism of democratic control, others worry that it debases political culture. An environment of unchecked and fierce criticism can produce a culture where mistrust is the norm and where political engagement declines.[273]

Aside from the impact on political culture, there is the human interest in the personal rights that needs to be accounted for. Long ago, Lord Diplock commented that 'every man, whether he is in public life or not, is entitled not to have lies told about him'.[274] More recently, in *Lindon v France*, in a concurring opinion, Judge Loucaides stated that reputation 'is a sacred value for every person including politicians' and should not be 'at the mercy of the mass media or other persons dealing with politics'.[275] In *Couderc*, the Grand Chamber of the European Court of Human Rights stressed that public figures are entitled to respect, stating that

> the fact that an individual belongs to the category of public figures cannot in any way, even in the case of persons exercising official functions, authorise the media to violate the professional and ethical principles which must govern their actions, or legitimise intrusions into private life.[276]

These concerns are supported by the reports of politicians being subject to extreme forms of abuse on the internet, often directed towards female politicians.[277] If leeway is granted to criticise political actors, that should not mean carte blanche to make blatantly false statements and engage in gross intrusions into private lives.

Finally, if the weakening of the politician's personal rights is a transfer of power, then it is important to ask whom the power is really being transferred to. While it might be described as a transfer to the 'people', in practice those who hold greater communicative resources will exercise that power. In that sense, protecting the right to make some defamatory and intrusive statements will empower the media, providing greater leverage over politicians. The need to keep media power accountable therefore explains why the public interest defences in defamation and privacy are not absolute, but are conditional on good conduct and the performance of the democratic functions in accordance with professional ethics.

i. Who is a Public Figure?

The discussion so far has looked at the elected official as the main example of the public figure, but there is a debate about how far the category of a public figure should extend. The category has been held to include those working in close proximity to a politician or holding a senior government post. The courts have found that a press officer for a senior politician, who was also in a relationship with that politician, was

---

[273] See M Flinders, *Defending Politics* (Oxford, Oxford University Press, 2012) 44–46.
[274] *Silkin v Beaverbrook Newspapers Ltd* [1958] 1 WLR 743, 746.
[275] *Lindon v France*, App no 21279/02 (2008) 46 EHRR 35.
[276] *Couderc* (n 214) at [123].
[277] See Committee on Standards in Public Life, *Intimidation in Public Life* (Cm 9543, 2017).

not a private figure.[278] Those occupying senior roles in non-governmental powerful organisations have also been found to be public figures. For example, the head of large bank was treated as a public figure, thereby triggering a public interest in knowing the fact of an extra-marital affair.[279] That approach can be justified in so far as those private actors wield considerable power or play important social roles, which need to be scrutinised and held to account.

Broader still is the question of whether a celebrity should be regarded as a public figure. The law has oscillated in taking relatively broad and narrow views of the public figure in various decisions. In an early privacy case, Lord Woolf reasoned that a professional footballer must 'accept that his actions will be more closely scrutinised by the media'.[280] The gist of the argument runs that a role model becomes a quasi-public figure, who implicitly holds him or herself out to a higher standard of conduct. The public therefore has a right to know when these standards have not been met.

A contrasting approach was taken in *McKennitt v Ash*, where Buxton LJ distinguished voluntary role models, such as clergymen and headteachers (who hold themselves out to a higher standard of conduct) from involuntary role models, such as a professional footballer or musician who happens to be skilled in an area that attracts public admiration.[281] However, Buxton LJ's distinction appears counterintuitive. An exposé of a primary school headteacher's private life in a national newspaper may be a more obvious abuse of media power than a story about an internationally famous musician. The former may enjoy no prior public profile and have fewer resources to contextualise or rebut the statement.

There is also a difficult question of determining when a person holds him or herself out to higher standard of conduct and voluntarily becomes a role model, and what level of scrutiny this justifies. As with the position of politicians discussed above, the category may have less to do with the celebrity's consent and voluntary choice, and instead reflects a convenient shorthand for a conclusion that certain positions should be subject to public scrutiny. In *Ferdinand*, the court found that the captain of the England football team was in such a position. That holding moved away from the rigid formulation in *McKennitt* and found that there are some positions in professional sport where the individual takes on a public role. The category of public figure can be interpreted in an expansive fashion to include a number of celebrities.

Similar shifts have taken place within the Article 10 jurisprudence. In the landmark decision of *Von Hannover* in 2004, the Strasbourg Court emphasised Princess Caroline of Monaco's lack of official duties in concluding that disclosures about her personal life did not contribute to a debate on a matter of general interest, despite her position in the public eye.[282] By contrast, in the *Von Hannover* decision of the Grand Chamber in 2012, finding no violation of Article 8, the Court stressed that Princess Caroline and

---

[278] *Trimingham v Associated Newspapers Ltd* [2012] EWHC 1296 (QB), [2012] 4 All ER 717 at [249]. See E Barendt, 'Carina Trimingham v Associated Newspapers: A Right to Ridicule?' (2012) 4 *Journal of Media Law* 309.

[279] *Goodwin v News Group Newspapers Ltd* [2011] EWHC 1437 (QB), [2011] EMLR 27.

[280] *A v B* (n 199).

[281] *McKennitt* (n 181) at [65].

[282] *Von Hannover* (2005) (n 242).

her husband were 'undeniably very well known' and could not be described as 'ordinary private individuals'.[283] The difficulty in defining a public figure makes it likely that the pendulum will continue to swing between narrow and broad approaches, with each move seeking to correct the shortcomings of the previous approach.

While not occupying the same position as holders of official power, the public role of celebrities should not be dismissed. Celebrity is a cultural resource, in which a person attracts attention simply for being that person.[284] That can have an effect in shaping the cultural discourse in a broad sense. The lives of the celebrity can help set the standards by which society judges people. A realistic picture of the celebrity, including their various character flaws, may also make people more tolerant of the shortcomings of others. For example, if a celebrity reveals a history of mental health problems, then that can help to changes attitudes on the issue. More broadly, celebrity can be converted into political capital. The most obvious example is the election of Donald Trump, who for years enjoyed media coverage as a celebrity businessman. The coverage, while not uncritical, helped to generate a level of goodwill that would not normally be given to a career politician. The audience had been conditioned to accept Trump's brash talk and gaffes as part of his celebrity persona. The goodwill, acceptance and cultural capital acquired by Trump could then be deployed in the political sphere.

The example of Trump is not isolated. There are numerous examples of celebrities using their status to focus attention on various causes. Many recent contributions to democratic theory have stressed the importance of public life outside the formal democratic institutions, which can include the work of 'unelected representatives' that advance particular issues and causes.[285] While the definition of a public figure should not become so broad as to be meaningless, it is also important to understand how the public and private are increasingly blurred and that the significance of celebrity is not limited to the sphere of entertainment.

Finally, when discussing either public figures or the public interest, it is not clear what constitutes the 'public'. There is no neat, unified public in which attention is focused on the same people. While there are national and international figures, there are also many smaller scale publics and niche communities, which have their own role models and figures that are important to their own members, but to few other people. For example, a person may have legendary status among the gamer community, but may be unlikely to be recognised by most people in the street. This has always been the case, but the digital media has greatly facilitated the formation of communities around various interests across geographical boundaries. For the court, such matters are likely to be a question of degree. Prominence and leadership in one area of life is something the court can consider, but it is unlikely to put the person on a par with a figure that is nationally recognisable.

---

[283] *Von Hannover v Germany* (2012) (n 179) at [120].
[284] For discussion of celebrity from a legal perspective, see D Rolph, *Reputation, Celebrity and Defamation Law* (Aldershot, Ashgate, 2008).
[285] Keane (n 272) 55–64.

ii. An Economic Public Interest?

On many occasions, the court has made clear that what is in the public interest is not to be equated with what the public is interested in.[286] The European Court of Human Rights has similarly stated that 'the public interest cannot be reduced to the public's thirst for information about the private life of others, or to the reader's wish for sensationalism or even voyeurism'.[287] While that much is well established, a variation of the argument emerged in *A v B*, in which Lord Woolf stated that the court 'must not ignore the fact that if newspapers do not publish information which the public are interested in, there will be fewer newspapers published, which will not be in the public interest'.[288] The point has been repeated in later decisions,[289] suggesting that the disclosures of private facts helps to subsidise the content of the media that is important in a democracy and valuable to the audience.

The argument is far-reaching, as it appears to justify the publication of any story that will help newspapers remain profitable.[290] Even if defamatory or intrusive stories were being used to finance more socially beneficial content, the argument suggests that the individual can be required to sacrifice personal rights to sustain media enterprises. Given that the media is not permitted to distribute pirated music or film content in order to boost revenues, it is not clear why it should be free to interfere with personal rights solely to remain profitable. Along these lines, if there are genuine fears about the finances of media, one could make a case for the public subsidy of the media to facilitate the democratic functions, rather than to allow legal rights to go unprotected.[291]

Despite these problems, there are elements to the argument that should not be dismissed so quickly. Aside from profits, newspapers need to publish stories that the public is interested in to bring eyeballs to their content. This in turn allows the media to ensure that important stories reach a mass audience. By cultivating a mass audience through popular content, the media can make sure that a wide range of people receive valuable content, even where that is low priority for the audience. This factor cannot be a trump card against assertions of privacy. It is, however, an important background factor and suggests that the court should not be puritanical in the assessment of the public interest or dismissive of tabloid styles of reporting. Media freedom is not to be limited to the dry reporting of important facts, sober analysis and investigative stories, even if particular importance is assigned to those activities.

The discussion has focused on some general themes that are used to assess the weight to be given to freedom of expression and media freedom. Despite some common issues relating to the personal rights, there are different approaches to protecting

---

[286] *Lion Laboratories v Evans* [1985] QB 526.

[287] *Couderc* (n 214) at [101].

[288] *A v B* [2002] EWCA Civ 337, [2003] QB 195 at [11].

[289] See *K v News Group Newspapers* [2011] EWCA Civ 439, [2011] 1 WLR 1827 at [13]; *Campbell* (n 151) at [73] and [143].

[290] See Fenwick and Phillipson (n 177) 799.

[291] For similar points, see F Schauer, 'Uncoupling Free Speech' (1992) 92 *Columbia Law Review* 1321, and A Kenyon, 'Protecting Speech in Defamation Law: Beyond Reynolds-Style Defences' (2014) 6 *Journal of Media Law* 21, 44–45.

media freedom in defamation and privacy law, with each having its own framework for weighing the right to publish with the rights of the claimant.

C. The Public Interest Defence in Defamation Law

In defamation law, a challenge for defendants lies in establishing a public interest in the publication of an untrue statement. Lord Hobhouse expressed the point in the landmark decision in *Reynolds*:

> There is no human right to disseminate information that is not true. No public interest is served by publishing or communicating misinformation. The working of a democratic society depends on the members of that society being informed, not misinformed.[292]

On this view, false information manipulates rather than facilitates authentic opinion formation. Accountability and opinion formation require that people know what government and public figures are actually doing. On this view, the truth defence will go some way to protecting the public interest.

The public interest certainly does not extend to *dishonest* statements that knowingly misinform the public and injure the individual's reputation. However, the discussion of the truth defence earlier noted that there are several reasons why a defendant may not be able to prove the truth of a statement, even where there is no lack of honesty. If the law requires that the journalist only publish where there is certainty about the relevant facts, then there will be a strong disincentive to engage in reporting where there is a higher risk of error, but where there is a public interest. This is likely to arise where the person subject to the investigation is deliberately seeking to cover up facts and deter media scrutiny. The truth defence alone is therefore not sufficient. The case for a public interest defence is not that there is anything valuable in misinformation, but that offering some protection to publications on matters of public interest (including some erroneous statements) will facilitate a process that produces valuable and accurate content in the long term. In other words, the media and other publishers need some slack and space to breathe if they are to perform their democratic functions.

One approach to address this issue is to provide a public interest defence for statements made in good faith. This approach means a defence would be available as long as the defendant believed the statement to be true. Along such lines, the US Supreme Court in *New York Times v Sullivan* provided that where a claimant is a public figure, the claim can only succeed if there is clear and convincing evidence that the publisher knew the statement was false or had serious doubts about the accuracy of the statement.[293] The approach reflects the high priority given to expression rights in the USA. Both the courts and Parliament have resisted calls for a similar defence to be adopted in England and Wales. In *Reynolds v Times Newspapers*, the House of Lords

---

[292] *Reynolds* (n 17) 238.
[293] The standard is termed 'actual malice'. See *New York Times Co v Sullivan* 376 US 254 (1964); *St Amant v Thompson* 390 US 727 (1968); *Gertz v Robert Welch, Inc* 418 US 323 (1974).

found that such an approach would give the media a licence to publish sensational claims 'based on the slenderest of materials'.[294] Lord Hobhouse took a sceptical view of assertions of media freedom, noting that the commercial pressure on the media 'to excite the interest of readers' incentivises the tendency 'to exaggerate, distort or otherwise unfairly represent alleged facts'.[295] On this view, a good faith defence is more likely to be abused as a vehicle to meet those commercial demands than to serve the audience's needs. In any event, if the reputation interest falls within Article 8, then a good faith defence could potentially fall foul of the ECHR in failing to give sufficient weight to reputation rights.

The court took its first steps towards a more limited public interest defence in *Reynolds*, recognising an extended form of qualified privilege. The defence (known as *Reynolds* privilege) was available if the defendant could show that publication was on a matter of general interest, that the inclusion of the defamatory statement was justifiable as a contribution to the discussion of that matter, and that the defendant had met the requirements of responsible journalism. Lord Nicholls provided a non-exhaustive criteria to take into account when applying the 'responsible journalism' part of the test, including the 'seriousness of the allegation', 'the source of the information', the 'steps taken to verify the information', '[w]hether comment was sought from the plaintiff' and the 'tone of the article'.[296] The defence therefore reduced the strictness of defamation and brought the test closer to a negligence standard. The defence also sought to incentivise media compliance with professional standards and ethics.

While a clear breakthrough in the protection of media freedom, the defence in *Reynolds* had a number of shortcomings. As a form of qualified privilege, *Reynolds* used the language of the duty/interest test, which indicated a high threshold. Some judges approached the question by finding a duty to exist only where 'a publisher would be open to legitimate criticism if he failed to publish the information in question'.[297] Given that high threshold, it was unsurprising that relatively few claims succeeded in the first years of the defence. For this reason, Lord Hoffmann and Baroness Hale in *Jameel v Wall Street Journal* preferred to see *Reynolds* as a public interest defence, that is distinct from and more likely to be available to the media than the traditional defence of qualified privilege. In *Jameel* and several later judgments, the court stressed that *Reynolds* should be applied more flexibly and that the failure to fulfil one of the criteria for responsible journalism should not be fatal to the defence.[298]

The *Reynolds* test took a functional definition of the media, so the defence was available to anyone that fulfilled the conditions of responsible journalism. However, the requirements of responsible journalism followed the practices of the established mass media and were harder for other types of publisher to fulfil. Unlike a political journalist in a leading newsaper, a blogger or social media commentator should not be expected to phone up a politician for comment before making a defamatory

---

[294] *Reynolds* (n 17) 201.
[295] ibid, 219.
[296] ibid, 204–205.
[297] *Loutchansky v Times Newspapers (No 4)* [2001] EMLR 38 at [18].
[298] See *Yeo v Times Newspapers Ltd* [2015] EWHC 3375 (QB), [2017] EMLR 1.

statement. If responsible journalism is defined by what is expected of a professional journalist, then the defence will in practice be most useful to those working in the traditional media. A former editor of *The Guardian* described the 'long, drawn out, rather arduous way of processing stories' and the legal oversight that was necessary to meet the *Reynolds* standards.[299] A national newspaper may have had the resources to do this, but it was unlikely a local newspaper would too.[300] A small website or blogger was also unlikely to meet those standards or afford the legal advice. Had the issue arisen, the problem could have been avoided by applying the criteria flexibly so the standards of responsibility vary depending on the nature of the publisher.[301]

Reynolds privilege was abolished in 2013 and replaced by s 4 of the Defamation Act 2013. While the intention behind the provision was largely to codify the *Reynolds* test and follow a negligence standard,[302] the test offers a different formulation. To establish the defence, the defendant must meet the following two requirements: (1) 'the statement complained of was, or formed part of, a statement on a matter of public interest'; and (2) 'the defendant reasonably believed that publishing the statement complained of was in the public interest'. Deciding whether the content is part of a statement on a matter of public interest will be determined by applying the factors discussed earlier. The effect of the defence will largely depend on how the 'reasonable belief' standard is applied. Section 4 states that the court will look at 'all the circumstances of the case' to determine whether the belief was reasonable. In interpreting the provision, the court is likely to be influenced by the 'duties and responsibilities' under Article 10 of the European Convention, that journalists and other watchdogs 'are acting in good faith in order to provide accurate and reliable information in accordance with the ethics of journalism'.[303] The Strasbourg Court has also echoed the terminology of *Reynolds*, stating that the media is expected to meet 'the tenets of responsible journalism'.[304] That line of reasoning suggests that the court could develop a set of standards similar to those in *Reynolds* to determine what is required under the 'ethics of journalism'.

The court should avoid some of the problems with the old common law defence described above and apply the standards flexibly in ways that suit a non-professional publisher that does not have so many resources or access to legal advice.[305] In *Economou*, an early case on s 4, the court supported this approach by stating that the defence will be established only if the belief 'is one arrived at after conducting such enquiries and checks as it is reasonable to expect of the particular defendant in all the circumstances of the case'.[306] Warby J also stated that the 'enquiries and checks that can reasonably be expected must be bespoke, depending on the precise

---

[299] House of Commons, Culture, Media and Sport Select Committee, *Press standards, privacy and libel* (HC 2009–10, 362-II), evidence given on 5 May 2009 at Q897.
[300] ibid.
[301] *Economou v de Freitas* [2016] EWHC 1853 (QB), [2017] EMLR 4 at [246]. See *Grant v Torstar Corpn* [2009] SCC 61 for a similarly flexible approach in relation to Canadian law.
[302] Defamation Act 2013, Explanatory Notes at [35].
[303] *Bladet Tromsø v Norway*, App no 21980/93 (2000) 29 EHRR 125.
[304] *Bedat v Switzerland*, App no 56925/08 (2016) 63 EHRR 15 at [50].
[305] See *Delfi v Estonia* (n 42) at [113] noting how the 'duties and responsibilities' can vary according to the role the publisher.
[306] *Economou* (n 301) [241].

role that the individual plays'.[307] For example, a person that provides an interview to the media performs a role that is 'closer to that of a source or contributor than that of a journalist'[308] and is entitled to expect the media institution carrying the content to conduct some checks.[309] That approach envisages some joint responsibility between a source and the media carrying the story. The standard of care to be taken when a citizen acts alone in publishing information to the world at large has yet to be tested. It is likely that the relevant 'role' of the publisher will depend on factors including whether the publisher held themselves out to be authoritative and meeting the standards of a journalist, or whether the person was clearly an individual offering their own view.

Section 4 follows *Reynolds* and strikes a balance between reputation and media freedom according to the circumstances of each case, rather than through a bright line rule. While this approach might lead to a fairer balance on the facts of each case, there are a number of costs to such a defence. First, the defence may require the court to make additional findings of fact to determine whether the reasonable belief standard was fulfilled, which can increase the time and costs of libel litigation. Secondly, a defence that applies a case-by-case approach will lack predictability. It will sometimes be difficult for a lawyer to advise on whether the conduct of the journalist is likely to pass the public interest test. One of the benefits of the test in *New York Times v Sullivan* is the degree of certainty that a statement about a public figure will benefit from strong protection. Finally, a judge that has heard the evidence first hand of the damage to the claimant's reputation may be reluctant to allow the false statement to go without remedy.

If the s 4 test requires the court to assess the conduct of the publisher, then there is a danger that the courts will be setting the standards of good journalistic practice. It is easy for courts to prescribe ideal standards for journalists after the event, while at the time of publication journalists face tight deadlines and sometimes have to make snap decisions or face losing a story. Too close scrutiny might inhibit media freedom and undermine the choices made by the journalist. To avoid this risk, the s 4 defence provides 'the court must make such allowance for editorial judgement as it considers appropriate'. Again, that allowance will depend on the procedure taken by the publisher. If it can be shown that the editor diligently went through the necessary 'checks and enquiries' then greater respect is likely to be shown to the editorial judgment.[310] However, it is not clear what level of respect will be shown to the judgment of a citizen journalist who lacks professional training and is not expected to meet the professional standards.[311] If the provision on editorial freedom aims to protect professional expertise, then it is harder see why such leeway should be given. By contrast, if the provision is merely seen as a guard against the courts applying unrealistic standards with the benefit of hindsight, then there are stronger reasons to give a margin for individuals to speak and publish.

---

[307] ibid, [246].

[308] ibid, [242].

[309] ibid, [246]. Even where the defendant was the author of the article, the fact it was published in a national newspaper meant he was entitled to expect it to carry out some checks, [258].

[310] ibid, [240].

[311] See J Rowbottom, 'In the Shadow of Big Media: Freedom of Expression, Participation and the Production of Knowledge Online' (2014) *Public Law* 491.

D. The Public Interest and Privacy Law

In privacy cases, the court has to assess the relative weight of the claimant's right against the defendant's media freedom and expression rights. The approach is known as 'parallel analysis', in which the court will determine whether the interference with the privacy right and any restriction on the Article 10 rights are proportionate. This process is less structured than the s 4 defence in defamation and in making this assessment the court will look at the factors discussed earlier to decide whether the interference with the expectation of privacy is serious and whether there are any factors demanding heightened protection for media freedom. The status of the subject of the article, the topic of the publication, and the method by which the information was acquired are among the relevant factors.

The court will also look at different items of information disclosed and the extent to which each interferes with the right. For example, in *Campbell* the newspaper was entitled to publish the bare fact of the model's drug treatment, but the inclusion of photographs of her leaving Narcotics Anonymous and details of the treatment was a disproportionate interference with her privacy.[312] Similarly, cases disclosing the fact of a public figure's extra-marital affair may be in the public interest, but additional salacious details may be disproportionate to any public interest benefits.[313] While the test mostly requires a balance of the factors that have already been discussed, there are some specific issues that can arise in privacy cases that help to indicate where the balance lies, which are discussed in the following sections.

i. Hypocrisy

The court has held that the public has an interest in having false statements made by public figures corrected. A clear example arose in *Campbell*, in which the model had made public statements denying her previous drug use, so the *Daily Mirror* could justify the publication of the bare fact that she was being treated for drug addiction as a way of setting the record straight.[314] In *Ferdinand*, the newspaper could publish a story about a footballer's affair on the grounds that he had said in an interview that he had put his old ways behind him and was a 'reformed character'.[315] The newspaper disclosure thereby corrected a false image.[316]

Fenwick and Phillipson criticise the line of reasoning and ask what harm arises from the public being misled by a false image.[317] The argument runs that publicising a role model's misdeeds can cause greater social harm in as much as it might encourage the emulation of such conduct.[318] The point is forceful in so far as it asks what concrete

---

[312] *Campbell* (n 151).
[313] Fenwick and Phillipson (n 177) 785.
[314] *Campbell* (n 151) at [24], [82], [129].
[315] *Ferdinand v MGN Ltd* [2011] EWHC 2454 (QB).
[316] ibid, [93].
[317] Fenwick and Phillipson (n 177) 803–805.
[318] ibid, 805.

harm arises from keeping certain facts secret. However, it is also difficult to make a case for legally enforced public ignorance to allow the celebrity to continue to trade on a false image for public admiration and approval. There is a stronger case for saying that the public should not be manipulated.[319] If the public is to 'buy into' the celebrity, dedicate time to following their lives and be influenced by commercial endorsements, then the public is entitled to ask that the image not be based on falsities.

The difficulty lies in deciding when the public has been misled. In *Campbell* and *Ferdinand*, the court could look to misleading past statements by the claimants. However, if a celebrity is said to mislead the public solely by presenting a particular image, such as agreeing to be photographed with his family, can a newspaper then publish private details as a way of showing the family life to be more troubled?[320] The issue is very similar to the 'zone' argument that was discussed earlier. The question is difficult as all public personas, whether of a celebrity or not, will conceal some facts about their life. The very right to privacy requires that people be allowed to withhold certain information that is not thought to be relevant to the assessment of a person's character.[321] The ordinary selective disclosures that a person makes in everyday social relations—such as presenting an outward face of happiness to the public in times of personal difficulty—will not be sufficient to trigger a public interest in disclosure. The issue is likely to be one of degree that focuses on the extent to which the public has been misled and any overt attempts by the person to generate the false impression.

ii. Exposing Wrongdoing

Any account of the public interest in publication accepts that the media has a role in exposing wrongdoings. Courts have long held that no confidence attaches to iniquity, and a similar approach has been taken in the law of privacy. The difficult question is what type of conduct amounts to wrongdoing that justifies public exposure and censure in the media? When publishing its account of Max Mosley's sexual activities, the newspaper company argued that there is a public interest in revealing conduct that is 'immoral, depraved and to an extent adulterous'.[322] Eady J rejected this line of argument, stating that it was 'not for the state or for the media to expose sexual conduct which does not involve any significant breach of the criminal law'.[323] According to this view, the fact that a newspaper editor regards conduct as morally repugnant or wrong does not mean that the publication of private facts can be justified as exposing wrongdoing. As noted in the discussion of privacy, Eady J's approach reflects a liberal concern to allow people to pursue their own actions free from the inhibiting effects of newspaper criticism.

---

[319] ibid, 777–78.
[320] See *Theakston v MGN* [2002] EWHC 137 (QB), [2002] EMLR 22. Compare *AMC and KLJ v News Group Newspapers Ltd* [2015] EWHC 2361 (QB).
[321] Feldman, 'Secrecy, Dignity, or Autonomy?' (n 159) 57; Fenwick and Phillipson (n 177) 804. See J Rachels, 'Why Privacy is Important' (1975) 4 *Philosophy and Public Affairs* 323, 327 on the difference between selective disclosure and dishonesty.
[322] *Mosley v News Group Newspapers* (n 203) at [124].
[323] ibid.

A challenge to Eady J's view came from Tugendhat J in the *Terry* case, in which he pointed out that breaches of the criminal law cannot be a sole test for whether conduct deserves public censure. [324] He pointed out that the criminal law is not static and public disclosures can be part of the process of changing social standards. The European Court of Human Rights has also noted that matters in the public interest are not to be confined to pre-existing debates, and that there is a role for the media in putting new issues on the agenda.[325] To shut out criticism of lawful conduct poses a risk that existing standards will become entrenched and protected in law.

The freedom to discuss such matters cannot, however, mean that a disclosure is in the public interest simply because a person believes certain conduct is morally wrong. To do so would be to eliminate the protection of privacy, which aims to protect activities from criticism.[326] Moreover, to allow the mass media to engage in such criticism of specific individual behaviour is not simply to permit a contribution to a debate about social standards, but is to allow the media to enforce its view by using its powers of publicity to discourage certain conduct. For these reasons, the Supreme Court in *PJS* found that the desire to criticise conduct does not generate a freestanding public interest argument. The Supreme Court required media criticism to have some connection to a legally-recognised public interest before it can receive greater weight in the balance with privacy. Under this view, the courts should give the media some margin to decide what information the public should receive, but that margin is normally related to those areas that are regarded as being in the public interest. It is not a licence for the media to disclose any information simply because the editor or reporter disapproves of the conduct. The right to express disapproval has greater force outside the media context. Greater leeway for criticism should be shown in relation to communications between individuals, where conversations, gossip and exchanges can play a role in shaping social rules, without having such a destructive effect on privacy rights.[327]

V. The Legal Protection of Personal Rights: Miscellaneous Provisions

The torts of misuse of private information and defamation are the most high-profile media laws that protect personal rights. There are a range of other actions that also

---

[324] *Terry (previously referred to as LNS) v Persons Unknown* [2010] EWHC 119 (QB), [2010] EMLR 16 at [104].
[325] *Couderc* (n 214) at [114].
[326] P Wragg, 'A Freedom to Criticise? Evaluating the Public Interest in Celebrity Gossip after Mosley and Terry' (2010) 2 *Journal of Media Law* 295; G Phillipson, 'Press freedom, the public interest and privacy' in Kenyon (n 9); J Rowbottom, 'To punish, inform and criticize' in J Petley (ed), *Media and Public Shaming: Drawing the Boundaries of Disclosure* (London, IB Tauris, 2013).
[327] Rowbottom, 'To punish, inform and criticize', ibid.

help to protect related interests, such as malicious falsehood, nuisance and intentional infliction of emotional distress.[328] The discussion of defamation and privacy has illustrated the central themes and issues for debate, so those other torts will not be discussed here. However, it is worth noting the existence of two areas that have become of increasing importance to the media: data protection and harassment.

A. Data Protection

The law of data protection seeks to regulate the activities of those who collect and hold personal data. While it applies to a wide range of bodies, the area of law has the potential to regulate various media activities and publications. The area is now governed by the Data Protection Act 2018, which was passing through Parliament at the time of writing, and the EU General Data Protection Regulation (GDPR), which came into force in May 2018.[329]

The law of data protection covers 'personal data', which is broadly defined and includes 'any information relating to an identified or identifiable natural person', and ranges from a person's name, location and online identifier to various other aspects of a person's identity.[330] It is therefore broader than the concept of private information discussed earlier. Two concepts are key in data protection law. First, is 'processing' information, which can include 'any operation or set of operations which is performed on personal data', including the collection, recording and storing of information, as well as disclosure by transmission and making information available.[331] The other key concept is that of a 'controller' of personal data, which refers to a person that 'determines the purposes and means of the processing of personal data'.[332] A processor is therefore the person or body that engages in the activity of processing on behalf of the controller.

Under data protection law, a controller is subject to a number of obligations in relation to the processing of personal data. Personal data must be processed fairly, lawfully and in a transparent manner, and the data must be obtained for a specified lawful purpose. The processing will be lawful if it meets one of several conditions, including consent from the data subject, necessity for a task carried out in the public interest, or the pursuit of certain 'legitimate interests'.[333] Other requirements in relation to processing include that data is adequate, relevant and not excessive in relation to the purpose. The data should also be kept accurate, not held for longer than necessary, and be processed in a way that ensures its security.[334] The Regulation also includes

---

[328] *Rhodes v OPO* [2015] UKSC 32, [2016] AC 219.

[329] As the terms of the Data Protection Act 2018 had not been finalised at the time of writing, the discussion will refer to the provisions of the EU Regulation.

[330] Regulation (EU) 2016/679 of the European Parliament and of the Council of 27 April 2016 on the protection of natural persons with regard to the processing of personal data and on the free movement of such data, and repealing Directive 95/46/EC, [2016] OJ L 119 ('General Data Protection Regulation') Art 4.

[331] ibid.

[332] ibid.

[333] ibid, Art 6.

[334] ibid, Art 5.

provisions relating to automated decision-making and the practice of 'profiling', in which large datasets are used to predict various aspects of a person's life—which is a major concern about the activities of digital intermediaries.[335] In addition, controllers are required to establish various systems to ensure compliance with data protection principles, for example by designing technical and organisational measures to make sure that any processing is limited by default,[336] and that appropriate records are kept of processing activities.[337]

More stringent obligations are applied in relation to certain types of sensitive personal information, including data revealing a person's 'political opinions, religious or philosophical beliefs, or trade union membership' and 'data concerning health or data concerning a natural person's sex life or sexual orientation'.[338] Such data can only be processed in limited circumstances, such as where the data subject gives consent, where the data subject 'manifestly' makes the data public, where the processing is necessary for public health, or necessary for 'archiving purposes in the public interest, scientific or historical research purposes or statistical purposes'.[339]

The GDPR and the domestic legislation also provide a number of rights for data subjects, such as rights to access personal information held about the subject and the right to the rectification of any inaccuracies.[340] The GDPR includes a 'right to erasure', which incorporates the 'right to be forgotten' that the Court of Justice of the European Union recognised and which required Google to remove certain results in response to search engine queries.[341]

While data protection law affects a wide range of businesses and institutions, the provisions can regulate the newsgathering process and the publication of information. Many things that the media does will amount to a processing of personal data. Researching a news story will often require journalists to acquire and collect information. Once a story is published, the media organisation will store research material, in case they have to defend the story in court or if there is a need to follow up the story later. To apply the full data protection obligations to the media could have an inhibiting effect on journalism. For example, a requirement to gain the consent of a subject or notify that person before processing data would frustrate attempts to carry out undercover sting operations, a key tool in the process of newsgathering.[342] Moreover, the publication of the information will amount to the processing of personal data, so data protection law could regulate media content too. The types of information given the strongest protection, such as political activity, sexual conduct or health issues, can often be of strong interest to the media and feature in some coverage.[343]

---

[335] ibid, Art 22. See R Jay, *Guide to the General Data Protection Regulation* (London, Sweet and Maxwell, 2017) 56.

[336] General Data Protection Regulation (n 330), Art 25. Similar obligations can also apply to processors, see Art 32.

[337] ibid, Art 30.

[338] ibid, Art 9.

[339] ibid.

[340] ibid, Arts 15 and 16.

[341] See Ch 7.

[342] D Erdos, 'European Union data protection law and media expression: fundamentally off balance' (2016) 65 *International Comparative Quarterly* 139, 144.

[343] *Tugendhat and Christie: The Law of Privacy and the Media* (n 206) 311.

Data protection law therefore provides a route for protecting privacy rights and for the correction and removal of inaccurate information (even where it would not be serious enough for an action in defamation). If fully applied to the media, the risk is that such obligations could also protect relatively innocuous information and deprive the public of valuable content.

To guard against such risks, a number of provisions offer some protection for media activities. The processing of personal data will be fair if done for 'legitimate interests', which has been held to include the pursuit of a 'legitimate business' and the journalistic interest in publishing information.[344] The accommodation of such interests is not absolute and will not protect intrusions that are disproportionate to those interests. In making that assessment, media freedom has to be balanced with privacy rights, which to some degree replicates the issues in the misuse of private information tort.[345]

Data protection law also includes an exemption for processing for 'journalistic purposes' in relation to some of the obligations.[346] Under the domestic Act, an exemption is available where the processing takes places with a view to the publication of journalistic material and the data controller reasonably believes that publication would be in the public interest. The exemption also requires the controller to show a reasonable belief that compliance with the relevant data protection obligation was not compatible with the purposes of journalism. The public interest does not provide a trump card, but is something that has to be weighed with the seriousness of the intrusion and whether it is a proportionate response. In requiring a *reasonable* belief (and no separate requirement of an actual public interest), the exemption leaves considerable space for editorial discretion. While there is no definition of journalism in the Regulation or Act, in one case under the old law, the court found that the exemption is potentially available to anyone that publishes content to the world at large with the necessary public interest.[347] However, the Information Commissioner's guidance on the old law points out that the exemption would not protect ordinary social media posts, which would count as a conversation rather than journalism.[348]

Breaches of data protection law can be reported to the Information Commissioner who oversees the operation of that law in the UK, and is another regulator that affects the media. In the event of a breach, the Commissioner can ask the controller to take corrective action and can issue a financial penalty where there is a failure to comply. This can provide a less expensive route than the courts to deal with certain intrusive media activity. However, when applying the journalism exemption, the Information Commissioner will take the codes of practice devised by specialist media regulators into account.[349] Such a provision aims to reduce the level of regulatory overlap and

---

[344] *Murray* [2007] in the High Court (n 246) Patten J, at [76] and Information Commissioner, *Data Protection and Journalism: A Guide for the Media* (September 2014) 41, both with reference to the old law under the Data Protection Act 1998, Sch 2.

[345] Information Commissioner, ibid, 41.

[346] General Data Protection Regulation (n 330) Art 85.

[347] *The Law Society v Kordowski* [2011] EWHC 3185 (QB), [2014] EMLR 2 at [99]. See also *Tietosuojavaltuutettu v Satakunnan Markkinapörssi Oy and Satamedia Oy* (C-73/07) [2008] ECR I-9831 [58]–[62].

[348] Information Commissioner, *Data Protection and Journalism* (n 344) 30.

[349] Data Protection Act 2018.

secure consistency, so that media regulators will remain the primary bodies that set the standards expected of journalists. Moreover, in a study of data protection in EU countries, David Erdos has found relatively limited enforcement of the duties against media bodies, to some degree reflecting a level of respect for media freedom and the presence of specialist media regulators to handle any complaints.[350] The data protection laws have nonetheless proven to be an important tool in addressing intrusive methods of reporting. The Information Commissioner's work investigating the use of private detectives by journalists helped to uncover an illegal trade in private information that was used to gather material for news stories.[351]

In addition to the regulatory route for enforcement, a failure to comply with data protection law can found a court action for damages. In relation to claims against the media, breach of data protection law is often pleaded alongside misuse of private information. In many publication cases, however, data protection has not added much to misuse of private information and will be limited where the media exemption applies. In earlier cases, the court also showed a reluctance to rely on data protection to supplement defamation law. While an action can be brought under data protection law for false and inaccurate statements about a person, Eady J in *Quinton* expressed caution before allowing the statute to provide a 'set of parallel remedies when damaging information has been published about someone, but which is neither defamatory nor malicious'.[352] He also expressed the view that it would not be necessary or proportionate for the court to order an apology or correction in relation to a publication.[353]

The stance against parallel remedies expressed in *Quinton* appears to be softening. Simon LJ, in the Court of Appeal, stated that there is no reason not to allow data protection and defamation claims to be brought together, given that both actions aim to protect different aspects of the personal right (with defamation protecting reputation and data protection being concerned with distress).[354] Moreover, some commentators have called for the journalism exemption to be more narrowly construed, which would allow the statute to be more widely enforced against the media.[355]

The area of law is likely to grow in importance more generally, given the increasing concerns about the aggregation of data through the digital media and the use of large databases. These controls will be particularly important in relation to the digital intermediaries that do not benefit from the exemption for journalism, such as search engines and social media companies, most notably with the right to be forgotten discussed in Chapter 7. As media lawyers become more familiar with data protection law in relation to intermediary claims, that might have a knock-on effect with

---

[350] D Erdos, 'Statutory regulation of professional journalism under European data protection: down but not out?' (2016) 8 *Journal of Media Law* 229.

[351] Information Commissioner, *What Price Privacy? The unlawful trade in confidential personal information* (HC 1056, 2006). See Erdos (n 350).

[352] *Quinton v Peirce* [2009] EWHC 912 (QB), [2009] FSR 17 at [87].

[353] ibid, [88].

[354] *Prince Moulay Hicham Ben Abdallah Al Alaoui of Morroco v Elaph Publishing Ltd* [2017] EWCA Civ 29, [2017] 4 WLR 28 at [42]–[43].

[355] H Tomlinson, 'The "Journalism Exemption" in the Data Protection Act: Part 1' Inforrm Blog, 28 March 2017, available at inforrm.org/2017/03/28/the-journalism-exemption-in-the-data-protection-act-part-1-the-law-hugh-tomlinson-qc/ (last accessed 18 January 2018). See also Leveson (n 170) 1082.

similar claims being made against media companies too. There are, however, dangers in this path noted above. Data protection law is potentially very expansive. That area of law was not developed with the media in mind and is unlikely to be sensitive to journalistic processes. Moreover, this area of law could potentially undermine the safeguards and standards developed in those areas of law and regulation that have developed specifically for the media. For these reasons, the exemption for journalism should continue to be applied generously.

B. Harassment

Another important protection for personal rights can be found in the Protection from Harassment Act 1997. The Act provides that a 'person must not pursue a course of conduct' that amounts to harassment of the claimant and which the defendant knows or ought to know amounts to harassment. The course of conduct means that there must be more than one single isolated episode. A person that commits harassment can be liable under both criminal law and the civil law. While the statute was enacted to target stalking and similar activities, harassment law has an obvious application in relation to certain newsgathering activities. For example, if 'paparazzi' photographers camp outside a person's house each day, that could amount to a course of conduct, which would enable the individual to seek an injunction under the Act. That cause of action is a more appropriate control than stretching the tort of misuse of private information to cover such newsgathering activities, as discussed earlier.

Less obviously, the 1997 Act has been applied beyond newsgathering activities to the publication of media content.[356] For example, if a newspaper repeatedly publishes content that ridicules or intimidates a person, that can constitute harassment. To fall within the 1997 Act, the publication must target an individual, rather than simply cause alarm and distress among the readership.[357] The scope of this provision has also been extended by a ruling that making a single article continuously available on the internet will constitute a course of conduct (as it is likely to cause upset on more than one occasion).[358]

There are a number of protections for media freedom. A course of conduct amounts to harassment only if it meets a threshold of conduct that is 'oppressive and unacceptable'.[359] The Act also provides that a course of conduct does not amount to harassment if it is reasonable in the circumstances.[360] In applying that standard to claims based on publication, the court takes into account media freedom and freedom of expression, looking at the public interest of the content. The courts also take into account whether the journalist in question acted responsibly and professionally.[361]

---

[356] *Thomas v News Group Newspaper Ltd* [2001] EWCA Civ 1233, [2002] EMLR 78.
[357] *Levi v Bates* [2015] EWCA Civ 206, [2016] QB 91 at [28], although the claimant need not be specifically targeted as long as harm to that person is direct and foreseeable.
[358] *Kordowski* (n 347) at [64].
[359] Lord Nicholls in *Majrowski v Guy's and St Thomas's NHS Trust* [2006] UKHL 34, [2007] 1 AC 224 [30].
[360] Protection from Harassment Act 1997, s 1(3).
[361] *Lisle-Mainwaring v Associated Newspapers Ltd* [2017] EWHC 543 (QB).

In *Trimingham*, Tugendhat J stated that journalistic speech will be held to be reasonable unless 'the course of conduct is so unreasonable that it is necessary (in the sense of a pressing social need) and proportionate to prohibit or sanction the speech in pursuit of one of the aims listed in art 10(2)'.[362] In that case, the court held that articles commenting on a political aide's sexual orientation and appearance did not amount to harassment.[363] By contrast, a court held that a 'persistent and unrelenting broadcasting campaign' that includes 'references to a fatwa and to Jihad in relation to a particular individual' crossed the line into harassment.[364]

In so far as it restricts intrusive newsgathering, the Act provides important protection for privacy interests. However, when applied to publications, the Act can overlap with defamation and privacy. A series of articles that are grossly insulting or ridicule an aspect of a person's life can lower a person's reputation and also cause considerable distress for the purposes of harassment. That overlap can have some significance in terms of the remedy sought, but (as will be argued below) it is important to ensure that such claims in harassment are not abused strategically to avoid the defences and protections in defamation and misuse of private information.

Earlier it was noted that the protection of privacy had traditionally been achieved in a piecemeal manner. The development of misuse of private information was seen as a move away from that traditional approach, offering a more general expansive tort that places privacy centre stage. However, those old causes of action such as nuisance and malicious falsehood did not go away, and the discussion has shown that some new causes of action have emerged in recent decades. While there are dangers of duplication and overlap, each cause of action covers different personal interests. The discussion has shown how data protection can guard against the aggregation and processing of information, while harassment guards against intrusive behaviour. Consequently, there is a case for saying that the legal landscape has changed, but privacy rights continue to be protected in piecemeal fashion through various separate torts.

VI. Remedies

As the discussion noted earlier, defamation and privacy have different histories, roots in different areas of law and protect different types of right. As a result, these causes of action have traditionally offered different remedies. The central difference has been that in defamation damages are the primary remedy, while in privacy the claimant will normally seek an injunction. The following section will outline this difference, but will

---

[362] *Trimingham* (n 278) at [53].
[363] ibid.
[364] *Shakil-Ur-Rahman v ARY Network Ltd* [2016] EWHC 3110 (QB), [2017] EMLR 10 at [114], though the claim failed as the claimant was outside of the jurisdiction at the relevant time.

also show that the differences are becoming less sharp and that there is some pressure for a closer assimilation of remedies in the two torts. The impetus for such assimilation comes from the fact that both are covered under Article 8 of the ECHR and from the overlap where both causes of action can apply on the same facts.

A. Damages

The primary remedy in defamation law is compensatory damages. Prior to the reform of defamation law in 2013, the role of juries in awarding damages could make the sums unpredictable and sometimes disproportionate. The most notable instance came in *Tolstoy*, in which the defamed individual was awarded £1.5 million in damages, which was subsequently found to violate Article 10.[365] Now that libel cases are heard before a judge, damages are more likely to be awarded on a consistent basis, and it is now said that £300,000 represents the upper limit.[366] Significant sums are still awarded to serve the vindicatory function of defamation law, as it sends a signal to the public about the seriousness of the tortious conduct. The courts also have the power to award exemplary damages where the defendant calculated that the benefit of publication would outweigh the costs of liability, but this power is used only in extreme cases.

Damages initially played a more minor role in misuse of private information, as the claimant primarily wants the court to stop publication.[367] Damages in the early years of the misuse tort were to compensate for 'distress and disappointment' and were negligible compared with the large sums awarded in some defamation cases. In *Douglas v Hello*, Michael Douglas and Catherine Zeta-Jones were awarded damages of £3,750 each for distress, and an additional £7,000 for the inconvenience of selecting the wedding photographs authorised for publication under time pressure.[368] In *Campbell*, the claimant was awarded damages totalling £3,500 (including £1,000 in aggravated damages). More recently, in *Weller* the eldest child received £5,000, while the two younger children received £2,500 each.[369] Max Mosley was awarded the relatively high sum of £60,000, but it is important to remember that the case was an extreme intrusion into the claimant's private life.[370]

A significant change came with the decision in *Gulati*, where the court awarded the victims of phone hacking damages ranging from £72,500 to £260,250 for misuse of private information.[371] The court found that damages are not limited to distress, but compensate for infringement of the right itself, namely the loss of control of the information.[372] Damages may become a more central remedy for privacy given that the proliferation of private information on the internet and social media can render injunctions less effective. If a court order cannot stop private information circulating, then courts will be more minded to make the publisher compensate the claimant.

---

[365] *Tolstoy Miloslavsky v UK*, App no 18139/9 (1995) 20 EHRR 442.
[366] *Rai v Bholowasia* [2015] EWHC 382 (QB) at [179].
[367] The foundation in equity means that claimants can also seek an account of profits.
[368] *Douglas v Hello* (n 180).
[369] *Weller* (n 215).
[370] *Mosley* (n 203).
[371] *Gulati* (n 253).
[372] ibid.

Traditionally, exemplary damages were not available for misuse of private information. The rule was part of the legacy of the action's origins in equity.[373] However, the Supreme Court has hinted that the matter could be revised in future.[374] Moreover, the Crime and Courts Act 2013, s 34 envisages some circumstances where a newspaper can be subject to exemplary damages in privacy cases.[375] A greater reliance on damages could bring the privacy tort closer to defamation.

B. Injunctions

Injunctions can be awarded as a final remedy, post-trial, in both defamation and privacy actions to stop republication of the statement. More controversial are interim injunctions, which play a central role in the protection of privacy. Given the sensitive nature of the information, the argument runs that the protection of privacy cannot wait and will be irreparably damaged by the time of a full trial.[376] The interim injunction is a good example of a prior restraint that stops material making it to the public and raises serious concerns for media freedom. By restraining publication, the claimant achieves his or her objective and the claim often does not advance to a full trial, as the initial assessment of the merits at the interim hearing gives the defendant an incentive to settle and the story may no longer be newsworthy by the time of a final ruling.[377] For these reasons, the interim decision can play a decisive role in the outcome of the litigation.

In cases that do not involve expression rights, the test for an interim injunction is whether there is a serious issue to be tried or a real prospect of success for the claimant at full trial.[378] Section 12(3) of the Human Rights Act 1998 provides that where a pre-trial injunction affects freedom of expression, a higher threshold must be met:

> No such relief is to be granted so as to restrain publication before trial unless the court is satisfied that the applicant is likely to establish that publication should not be allowed.

In *Cream Holdings*, the House of Lord found that the provision will normally require the claimant to establish that he or she is *more likely than not* to succeed at trial.[379] By raising the threshold for a pre-trial injunction, the court offers some protection against prior restraints. Such a higher threshold cannot, however, be required in all cases and the court can depart from that standard when the circumstances require. For example, a lower threshold can be applied in an urgent hearing where the judge has little time

---

[373] In *Mosley* (n 203), Eady J referred to the origins in equity and the traditional limit to tort claims (see [181] and [190]) and declined to extend exemplary damages to privacy cases as there was no authority for such a move.

[374] *PJS* (n 172) at [42] and [92].

[375] See discussion in Ch 6.

[376] Though such protection is not mandated by Art 8, *Mosley v UK*, App no 48009/08 (2011) 53 EHRR 30 at [120].

[377] See *AG v Punch* [2002] UKHL 50, [2003] 1 AC 1046 at [100]. For example, following the Supreme Court's decision in *PJS*, the parties came to a settlement, see *PJS v News Group Newspapers* [2016] EWHC 2770 (QB).

[378] *American Cyanamid v Ethicon* [1975] AC 396 (HL).

[379] *Cream Holdings Ltd v Banerjee* [2004] UKHL 44, [2005] 1 AC 253.

to hear the evidence supporting the application, or in cases where the consequences of publication on the claimant are likely to be very serious and hard to reverse.[380]

Where the matter is urgent (for example, where the claimant discovers he or she will be the subject of a newspaper exposé the following day), the process can begin with an emergency hearing over the telephone to apply for a temporary injunction until a further hearing. The matter will then come back to court days later for a fuller hearing and a chance to hear to the evidence. Normally, the respondent will be notified of the application and the hearing in court will be contested.[381] The effect of the hearing can go beyond the named parties. Under the *Spycatcher* principle, a third party will be in contempt of court if it has notice of an interim injunction but nonetheless publishes the protected information.[382] An injunction on one newspaper can thereby have the effect of binding the media as a whole.

In contrast with privacy law, an interim injunction is not normally available in defamation cases. The rule established in *Bonnard v Perryman* provides that to get a pre-trial injunction the claimant must establish that the defences will be defeated at trial.[383] The claimant therefore bears a very high threshold for an interim injunction. The rule reflects the difficulty, given the factual issues to be determined, for the court to decide whether a defamation action would succeed until it has heard all the evidence at full trial. More broadly, the rule strikes a particular balance between media freedom and reputation by limiting the claimant only to a remedy after publication.[384]

The rule in *Bonnard* was challenged in *Greene v Associated Newspapers*, in which the claimant argued that the effect of s 12(3) of the Human Rights Act 1998 is to apply the 'more likely than not' test in defamation cases and had thereby replaced the stronger assumption against prior restraints in *Bonnard*.[385] The court rejected the argument on the grounds that s 12 was designed to protect expression rights and should not be interpreted to take away the longstanding protection in defamation.[386] The court also reasoned that the different treatment in defamation and privacy is justified, as injury to reputation can be compensated with damages or by the findings at the trial.[387] With privacy, once the information has been published, the damage is done and cannot be reversed.

There are still arguments being advanced that the rule in *Bonnard* should be reconsidered. One leading text on defamation notes that the court in *Greene* did not give much consideration to the protection of reputation under Article 8, especially the fact that both rights are to be given equal weight.[388] On this view, if reputation is protected under Article 8, then it is less counterintuitive for the Human Rights Act to remove a longstanding rule that prioritises freedom of expression over other rights. However,

---

[380] ibid, [17]–[19].
[381] Human Rights Act 1998, s 12(2). See *Terry* (n 324). Though there are exceptions, for example where such notice would tip off the person and lead to conduct that would undermine the purpose of the injunction, see Master of the Rolls, *Practice Guidance: Interim Non-Disclosure Orders* [2012] 1 WLR 1003 at [21].
[382] *Attorney-General v Newspaper Publishing plc* [1988] Ch 333.
[383] *Bonnard v Perryman* [1891] 2 Ch 269.
[384] *Khuja v Times Newspapers Ltd* [2017] UKSC 49, [2017] 3 WLR 351 at [19].
[385] *Greene v Associated Newspapers* [2004] EWCA Civ 1462, [2005] QB 972.
[386] ibid, at [61].
[387] ibid, at [78].
[388] *Gatley on Libel and Slander* (n 117) at [25.22].

that might cause a complex formulation in which injunctions are more easily avail-able when the defamatory publication engages Article 8, but with the rule in *Bonnard* applying where the attack on reputation is not serious enough to engage Article 8. Moreover, if there is a move to provide similar treatment in defamation and privacy claims, this does not mean that injunctions must be more widely available in defama-tion cases. Given the limited effectiveness of injunctions and increasing awards of damages in privacy, there could be moves to limit injunctions in privacy cases and treat damages as the main remedy for both.[389]

For as long as it stands, the rule in *Bonnard* maintains a sharp distinction in rem-edies for defamation and privacy, which can lead to the strategic framing of claims in order to benefit from the desired remedy. A person seeking an injunction can attempt to bypass the rule in *Bonnard* by making a claim in privacy. In some cases, the two causes overlap, such as where a statement is false and relates to a personal matter. The courts are alert to the risks of abuse. In *McKennitt v Ash*, Buxton LJ stated that it would be an abuse of process to bring a claim in misuse of private information to avoid the rule in *Bonnard* where 'the nub of the case was a complaint of the falsity of the allegations'.[390] In *Terry*, Tugendhat J declined to grant an injunction for misuse of private information in relation to an extra-marital affair on the grounds that the claimant really wanted to protect his commercial reputation. In most cases, however, identifying the nub of the claim may not be so obvious for the court.

Similar issues arise in relation to the law of harassment, where the claimant can obtain an interim injunction. In *Merlin v Cave*, the defendant sent emails and pub-lished content on websites criticising a company's safety record.[391] Normally if a person criticises a company for their products or services, the legal remedy lies in defa-mation. However, the company sought a pre-trial injunction relying on the Protection from Harassment Act 1997. The court stated that if the claimant's concern is with rep-utation, then defamation is the normal claim for a remedy and harassment law should not be used to bypass the rule in *Bonnard*.[392] However, in cases where the course of conduct had 'additional elements of oppression, persistence or unpleasantness, which are distinct from the content of the statements', then *Bonnard* will not act as a bar to an injunction.[393] While the application for an injunction failed, the case shows how the growth of other areas of law covering similar areas can potentially provide alternative routes to an injunction.

C. Super-injunctions

Interim injunctions are controversial as a prior restraint on expression. More con-troversial is a type of restraint nicknamed a 'super-injunction'. This term refers to an injunction that stops the media not only from naming the parties in the case, but also from revealing the fact that an injunction has been issued in a particular

---

[389] See *Mosley v UK* (n 376).
[390] *McKennitt v Ash* (n 181) at [79].
[391] *Merlin v Cave* [2014] EWHC 3036 (QB), [2015] EMLR 3.
[392] ibid, [56].
[393] ibid, [40].

dispute. This type of injunction should not be confused with anonymised injunctions, which allow the fact of the injunction and surrounding details to be reported, but not the identity of certain parties. The rationale for a super-injunction is that revealing even the minimal level of information about the presence of an injunction would 'let the cat out of the bag' and allow people to piece together the story or lead to a further violation of the right. However, the use of such measures is a significant departure from the principle of open justice, in which the workings and decisions of the court are subject to public scrutiny.[394] The guidance on interim injunctions states that super-injunctions should be granted only in the 'rarest' cases and normally only for a limited time, for example to prevent publishers being tipped off before receiving notice of the order.[395]

D. Discursive Remedies

Sometimes a wrong caused by a publication can be remedied with additional publicity that sets the record straight. A remedy of that sort will not normally be appropriate for privacy law, where unwanted publicity is the essence of the wrong. Such a remedy can, however, be attractive in defamation, where the issue lies in the falsity of the statement and where the cause of action seeks to vindicate the rights of the wronged party. There is some scope for such a remedy under the Defamation Act 2013, which gives the judge the power to order the defendant to publish a summary of the judgment.[396] That, however, will not amount to a formal retraction or apology, so may limit its effectiveness for vindication. Nor does a summary of a judgment always declare where the truth lies, but simply shows certain statements have not been proven to be true. If the court disposes of a case early on in summary proceedings, then there is a power to declare a statement to be false, and order a correction and apology to be published.[397] However, that provision will apply only in those cases where no prospect of success for the defence can be identified at an early stage. The offer to make amends process under the Defamation Act 1996 also encourages the early settlement of claims where the defendant offers to make a correction and apology, and pay compensation.

The Defamation Act 2013 has been criticised for missing an opportunity to develop a bigger role for 'discursive remedies'.[398] A greater role for rights of reply, correction and apologies would avoid the high award of damages and provide a 'more speech' remedy that potentially plays a role in restoring reputation. However, in some cases it may require the court to make additional findings of fact, if it is to authoritatively conclude on where the truth lies. Andrew Kenyon has argued that such counter-publicity could play a role in defences, which would avoid the problems

---

[394] See Ch 3.

[395] See *Practice Guidance: Interim Non-Disclosure Orders* (n 381). In *Donald v Ntuli* [2010] EWCA Civ 1276, [2011] 1 WLR 294, the Court of Appeal stated that privacy interests can be adequately protected in many cases by restricting newspapers to reporting the facts contained in the judgment.

[396] Defamation Act 2013.

[397] Defamation Act 1996, s 8 and s 9.

[398] A Mullis and A Scott, 'Tilting at Windmills: the Defamation Act 2013' (2014) 77 *Modern Law Review* 87, 107–108.

of a court-ordered correction.[399] For example, the public interest defence could be made conditional on the defendant offering a right to reply, or offering a correction once the falsity is known. That would at least reduce the 'all or nothing' problems in the public interest defence, where the defeated claimant receives no remedy and suffers unwarranted damage to reputation.[400] The discursive conditions could thereby provide a means for mitigating the damage. However, if such measures were introduced, the effect may be limited in some cases. The discursive remedy gives the claimant access to an audience and thereby helps address inequalities in communicative power. However, it does not address the problem of negativity bias discussed earlier. In some cases, 'mud sticks' and a public rebuttal of the defamatory statement may work to draw attention to the allegation, rather than set the record straight.

VII. Conclusion

This chapter has focused on three central issues: the protection of reputation; the protection of private information; and the balance struck with media freedom and freedom of expression. Both reputation and privacy are personal rights. The justification for protecting those rights often relates to similar arguments based on dignity, the capacity to form relationships and engage in other activities, as well the power of the media. The discussion has shown how both torts relate to the way a person is evaluated socially. In defamation, the court identifies the appropriate standards for judging a person's conduct. In privacy, the court decides what information about a person can be made available by others to evaluate his or her character.

   In practice, a contrast is frequently drawn between defamation and privacy, in which the former has been re-balanced with the aim of offering greater protection for expression. The rebalancing of defamation can be seen as an acknowledgement of the difficulties of the earlier pro-claimant tilt and also a reflection of the current culture that offers a bigger role to public opinion. By contrast, the law of privacy is regarded as imposing a new set of legal constraints on the media, where previously there were few. The differing trajectories of privacy and defamation do not reflect any incoherence in the law. While defamation may previously have over-protected some reputations, the law previously under-protected the right to privacy. The shifts in doctrine can be understood as creating greater parity between the two interests.

   The protection of personal rights has been presented as a way of curbing some of the excesses of media power and holding the media to account. The various causes of action are, however, applicable to all publishers and not just the large institutions. A challenge for the current law is to find a way to maintain the channel of media

---

[399] Kenyon, 'Protecting Speech in Defamation Law' (n 291).
[400] ibid, 44.

accountability, but without the law disproportionately regulating everyday interactions. To guard against this, it was argued that public interest defences, for example, should be interpreted flexibly in ways that do not demand every speaker to follow the processes of the professional media. Accordingly, defences need to accommodate rights to freedom of expression that are not present with large media companies. Another challenge lies in the fact that there are other powerful institutions that can have a devastating effect on personal rights, such as the large tech companies, but against whom the publication torts seem less effective. The position of such institutions will be considered in Chapter 7.

The practice of protecting reputation and personal rights has also evolved with the changes in communications. When defamation trials were more frequent and prominent, some legal practitioners could be identified as 'libel lawyers' or 'libel silks'. Such terms are still used, but increasingly there has been a rise in firms identifying themselves as 'reputation management' specialists. The work of such firms no doubt includes the writing of letters threatening litigation, but also includes a toolkit based on a range of other services, using data protection, privacy and harassment law. In addition to legal services, such firms will often offer advice on how to improve your online profile through search engine optimisation, requests to take down digital content and the promotion of positive content. Such a shift in the profession reflects the fact that a person's name is not just impacted by a one-off newspaper splash, but also by the persistent availability and opportunities to re-circulate content online.

In much of media law, there is a question of whether the content published has an effect on and influences its audience. These issues have traditionally been sidestepped in defamation through the presumption of damage and the court determining whether the meaning of the statement is defamatory. The requirement to show serious harm under the Defamation Act 2013 potentially changed that, but the court seems willing to infer damage if the defamatory statement is serious enough and thereby avoid the need for evidence of media effects. In privacy, the publication itself and the impact on the individual is the cause of damage, rather than the effect on the general audience.

The approach of the courts in handling claims of media freedom is different in privacy and defamation. The former takes a general balancing approach, while the latter considers the reasonable belief of the publisher. However, both take an approach that is fact sensitive taking into account multiple factors. The absence of bright line rules might avoid injustice through arbitrary cut-offs, but also means that the law is less predictable, and that determined and well-resourced parties may have an incentive to litigate a claim, while others may settle to avoid the risk of loss.

Both privacy and defamation also highlight the difficulties in identifying the scope of public interest arguments. The blurring of the public and private is a recurring theme in many areas of law, and this is true for media law too. The public interest is not simply limited to the scrutiny of formal government institutions, but expands to a range of privately-owned bodies. The discussion also noted the prominent role played by personality and celebrity in contemporary culture, which can give an individual's public profile a wider significance.

The discussion highlights a key fault-line in media law that reflects two features in the current culture. On the one hand, the political culture makes increasing demands for transparency, accountability and robust criticism in all walks of life. This ranges not only from newspaper exposés, but also to eruptions of scrutiny and shaming on the social media. Such demands generate a pressure for freedom of expression to prevail over rights to reputation and privacy in an increasing number of cases. On the other hand, the increased weight given to individual rights such as privacy shows that the law cannot be understood as simply moving towards greater liberty of speech or media freedom. Instead, the controls change over time and follow contemporary values. The rise of privacy and the shielding from social criticism reflects a society that has greater emphasis on individual autonomy, freedom of choice and pluralism in lifestyle. Such values suggest that there are parts of a person's life that are not appropriate for public scrutiny.

Both sides of the contemporary culture have their merits, but are open to abuse. Libel and privacy can sometimes be invoked to shield people from legitimate criticism. The public interest is sometimes asserted to justify publications that make little contribution to public debate and merely boost sales. The tension between these aspects of the contemporary culture helps to explain the simultaneous expansion of public interest arguments and growth of Article 8 of the ECHR. The tension can also be seen in the extent to which the media demands greater freedom to hold power to account, but is subject to restraint to hold its own power in check. The personal rights discussed in this chapter are focal point in media law in managing this tension in a society that values transparency and robust debate, while also placing considerable weight on the dignity and autonomy of those individuals that are subject to media attention.

3

The Media and the System of Justice

I. Introduction

This chapter looks at the reporting of the system of justice. Two themes will be discussed. The first is the potential for the media to undermine the administration of justice, for example when media coverage influences a jury or discourages witnesses to a crime from coming forward. The second theme concerns the ability of the media to report what is happening in court. Both engage the freedom of the media to discuss and scrutinise the workings of the legal process. However, the two issues have important differences. With contempt of court, the law seeks to stop the media influencing jurors, witnesses and parties to the legal proceedings. Here the concern is with the media bringing external influences to bear on the legal process. By contrast, when reporting court proceedings, the concern relates to the media relaying matters inside the courtroom to the outside world. In such cases, the court aims to stop the media from reporting certain information that is private, sensitive or would undermine the administration of justice.

Within these areas, there has been a level of ambivalence about the role of public opinion and the media. The freedom to scrutinise the workings of the system of justice and criminal investigations has long been recognised. However, that was once matched with concerns that the free expression of public opinion could amount to 'trial by media' that usurps the court and would undermine the dignity and authority of the judiciary. Now those concerns have largely receded (at least as a basis for legal restriction) and the legal system often relies on publicity to inform the public in ways that can bolster the authority of the court. Restrictions on the media are now largely premised on the need to protect the administration of justice and the rights of those involved.

As with media law in general, the digital media poses a number of challenges. While the legal doctrines have developed with the mass media in mind, individual users are now able to post comments that may jeopardise a fair trial or reveal sensitive information about the proceedings. To guard against this, a range of responses can be taken. Individuals posting content on the social media can be prosecuted under various laws.

The recipients of the content can also have some responsibility, for example with special controls being imposed on jurors. Despite these developments, the law continues to recognise the importance of the mass media, by expecting higher standards of care and by granting media institutions special access to the courts.

The chapter will first examine the legal controls imposed on the media in the law of contempt of court (known as 'contempt by publication'). The discussion will then look at the open justice principle and the limits on the reporting of the courts. Aside from the legal controls, a major challenge to the coverage of the legal system comes from the fact that many media institutions now pay less attention to the courts at the local level, unless there is an element of notoriety or celebrity in the case. The final parts of the chapter will consider whether there are ways to open up coverage of the courts and sustain a level of scrutiny of its processes.

II. Contempt of Court

The law of contempt of court seeks to protect the system of justice by making a publisher liable for publications that create a substantial risk that legal proceedings will be 'seriously impeded or prejudiced'. The risk is most pressing where a case is heard before a jury and publication potentially influences jurors about the merits of a case.[1] A jury should make its decision based only on material admitted to the court that both parties have had chance to test. That process could be undermined if jurors are exposed to media content expressing a conclusion about an issue in the case, or revealing evidence not admitted into court. For example, a newspaper report revealing a defendant's past conviction could make the jury more susceptible to a finding of guilt. In the most severe cases, such publicity can render the jury's verdict unsafe and lead to the quashing of a conviction. Such an outcome would cause significant hardship to the victim of the crime, and the defendant may suffer too if he or she has to go through a retrial. Aside from the impact on the individuals, there is a general social interest in ensuring the fair workings of the legal system.[2] Before looking at the way the law guards against this risk, the discussion will distinguish contempt from broader concerns with 'trial by media', will set out the different strategies for protecting the court from prejudicial coverage and consider some of the issues for media freedom.

---

[1] See Lord Bridge in *Re Lonrho plc* [1990] 2 AC 154, 209, stating that the 'possibility that a professional judge will be influenced by anything he has read about the issues in a case which he has to try is very much more remote' than with a jury. The chance of an appellate tribunal being influenced by the media was said to be even more remote.

[2] See H Fenwick and G Phillipson, *Media Freedom under the Human Rights Act* (Oxford, Oxford University Press, 2007) 247.

A. Goals and Strategies

i. Trial by Media

Media coverage of certain crimes is often criticised as 'trial by media', in which individuals are alleged in news reports to have committed offences and thereby suffer the consequent stigmatisation. The argument against trial by media runs that a person's guilt should be determined by a court and not by public opinion. On this view, the courts' determination of issues should influence the public's interpretation of events.[3] Trial by media is also seen to be unfair, given that newspapers and broadcasters are not constrained by the rules of evidence or regulated by any procedural safeguards. Such complaints reflect a concern with media power, namely that the media should not use its communicative resources to select and interpret evidence, and publicise its own conclusions on alleged transgressions of the law. Despite the potential for unfairness, the process of media publicity can sometimes reveal facts that were not considered in the trial, which can help the public to scrutinise legal decisions.

While the current law of contempt does not attempt to deal with trial by media (in the broad sense of being judged in the coverage), the old common law of contempt was used to guard against that concern in the famous *Sunday Times* case, resulting in a decision that had significant repercussions for media freedom.[4] The facts of the case arose from the newspaper's campaign for the victims of the drug Thalidomide that started in 1967 and continued into the 1970s. While the drug company was settling a negligence claim with the victims and applying pressure to accept a relatively low compensation payment, *The Sunday Times* published an article arguing that the company should make a more generous offer.[5] The newspaper proposed to publish another article criticising the testing and marketing of Thalidomide, after which the Attorney-General obtained an injunction to restrain publication on the grounds that it would be a contempt of court.

The House of Lords upheld the injunction and stated that the old common law of contempt requires that legal disputes are not 'prejudged' in the national press. Lord Diplock stated that holding a litigant up to 'public obloquy' could hinder access to the courts by discouraging people from pursuing their legal rights.[6] He also warned of the danger of media discussion usurping the function of the court by making its own determination of the legal dispute.[7] Lord Reid spoke of the dangers of 'trial by media', which would generate 'disrespect for the processes of the law' and would be unfavourable to 'unpopular people and unpopular causes'.[8] The decision therefore envisaged a division of labour in which the courts are the sole institution to decide

---

[3] Along these lines, the protection of reports of court proceedings as privileged in defamation law reflects the court's authoritative determination of the issues.

[4] *A-G v Times Newspapers Ltd* [1974] AC 273 (HL).

[5] See H Evans, *My Paper Chase* (London, Little Brown, 2009) 325.

[6] *A-G v Times Newspapers Ltd* (n 4) 313. Lord Diplock also stated that the published article about the low settlement offer amounted to a contempt, 312.

[7] ibid, 310.

[8] ibid, 300.

what the existing law demands and how it should be interpreted.[9] If *The Sunday Times* thought the system of compensation was inadequate, then the appropriate response, Lord Diplock thought, was to lobby Parliament to change the law relating to compensation, rather than 'vilifying individual litigants'.[10] The reasoning reflects a view that public opinion should be channelled towards the elected institutions for formal representation, rather than placing pressure on other centres of power. The point can be compared to earlier attitudes seen elsewhere in media law, for example where courts have said that allegations of misconduct should be reported to the appropriate authorities rather than to the world at large.[11] As a result of this holding, *The Sunday Times* was unable to publish its full investigation into the testing and marketing of Thalidomide until the injunction was finally discharged in 1976.

The European Court of Human Rights found that the injunction violated Article 10 of the European Convention on Human Rights (ECHR). The Strasbourg Court thought the article did not pose any risk of 'trial by media' as it was 'couched in moderate terms'.[12] The Court stated that 'courts cannot operate in a vacuum' and, while the courts are the final arbiter of legal disputes, 'this does not mean that there can be no prior discussion of disputes elsewhere'.[13] The Court thereby envisaged a broader role for public opinion in engaging with the system of justice. The Strasbourg Court also found that the domestic court failed to give priority to freedom of expression, especially as the proposed article was on a matter of 'undisputed public concern' in discussing the 'question of where responsibility for a tragedy of this kind actually lies', and the role of the press was not limited to discussing the general principles away from specific cases.[14] The law was subsequently changed in 1981 as a response to that ruling.

Whatever the misgivings about trial by media, the current law of contempt of court does not aim to stop the public forming its own judgment about a particular person or their actions. While Lord Diplock stated that, under the current law, 'trial by the media, is not to be permitted in this country',[15] the guard is limited and seeks to preserve the integrity of the legal system and ensure that publicity does not interfere with formal legal proceedings. The development therefore reflects a shift in the role of public opinion, accepting that members of the public have a right to form their own views on a particular case. Most of the time, the formal legal process and public opinion work in parallel.

There may be considerable sympathy for those individuals that are widely reported in the media to be subject to a police investigation. The fact that a person is subject to

---

[9] For a similar reading of the case see Lord Coulsfield in *Megrahi v Times Newspapers Ltd* (2000) JC 22, 36.

[10] *A-G v Times Newspapers Ltd* (n 4).

[11] For example, *Blackshaw v Lord* [1984] QB 1, 41 suggested that there would rarely be a duty or interest to publish to the world at large. In *R v Shayler* [2002] UKHL 11, [2003] 1 AC 247, the court found that a security service employee concerned about misconduct could make a complaint through the official channels, rather than publish the allegation to the world at large.

[12] *Sunday Times v UK*, App no 6538/74 (1979–80) 2 EHRR 245 at [63].

[13] ibid, [65].

[14] ibid, [66].

[15] *A-G v English* [1983] 1 AC 116, Lord Diplock at 141–42.

an investigation may have a stigmatising effect,[16] especially with certain types of crime. Such concerns about the stigmatising effects of publicity surrounding an investigation or prosecution are better addressed through other controls such as defamation, misuse of private information, anonymity rules or the regulation of police communications. Along these lines, some public figures that have experienced such adverse publicity have called for those investigated for certain sexual offences not to be publicly named until charged, in order to ensure that reputations are not unduly damaged.[17] More broadly, the fact that a person is under investigation will sometimes be protected as private information, although this depends on the circumstances and whether there is a countervailing public interest.[18] The law of defamation also offers some protection against trial by media, but only where the claims made are untrue. However, in *Flood*, Lord Dyson commented that even unproven allegations are likely to be protected under the public interest defence when the claim relates to professional misconduct in the performance of a public function.[19] Those comments point to a broader role for public opinion to assess allegations, even where the publication engages with a private law right. Trial by media remains a concern, but even those areas of law protecting private rights such as defamation and privacy leave room for media freedom and the potential public interest in publication.

ii. Deterrents and Safeguards

By imposing a post-publication penalty, the law of contempt aims to deter the media from publishing prejudicial content, and to incentivise more responsible reporting.[20] In some cases, an injunction is imposed to protect the administration of justice, though such cases are the exception rather than the norm.[21] There are, however, alternatives to penalties on the media that do not seek to deter prejudicial coverage, but instead aim to minimise the effects of the publicity on the course of justice.[22] Courts can impose internal safeguards including: an instruction from the judge to the jury to ignore media coverage; vetting jurors to check for exposure to prejudicial content; staying the hearing until the effects of the media coverage have died down; and relocation of a trial to an area where there has been less exposure to the prejudicial

---

[16] Though it is frequently said in court that the public are not unduly suspicious and can distinguish a report of an investigation from an allegation of guilt, see Lord Rodger in *Ahmed v HM Treasury* [2010] UKSC 1, [2010] 2 AC 697 at [60]. See also *Lewis v Daily Telegraph Ltd* [1964] AC 234, 286 and the discussion in *Khuja v Times Newspapers Ltd* [2017] UKSC 49, [2017] 3 WLR 351.

[17] 'Paul Gambaccini, Sir Cliff Richard and Nigel Evans unite to protect those accused of sex assaults' *The Daily Telegraph* (3 July 2016).

[18] See *ZXC v Bloomberg LP* [2017] EWHC 328 (QB).

[19] *Flood v Times Newspapers Ltd* [2012] UKSC 11, [2012] 2 AC 273, Lord Dyson at [195].

[20] *A-G v English* (n 15) 141 'The public policy that underlies the strict liability rule in contempt of court is deterrence'.

[21] *A-G v Random House Group Ltd* [2009] EWHC 1727 (QB), noting that the use of injunctions will be rare.

[22] See Fenwick and Phillipson (n 2) 177–78 contrasting different strategies for countering effects of media publicity.

media coverage.[23] The central benefit of this strategy is that it protects the administration of justice without inhibiting media freedom. However, the strategy transfers responsibility for the effects of media coverage to the court and may impose considerable costs. For example, elaborate jury vetting procedures will take up the court's time. A stay on proceedings can cause hardship to all the parties involved, delay justice and maybe affect the quality of the evidence before the court. Most drastic of all, discharging a jury and ordering a retrial once proceedings have commenced imposes a significant cost on the courts, the parties and the witnesses. Furthermore, some internal controls may not succeed in limiting the effects of prejudicial content. If a national newspaper puts prejudicial material into wide circulation, then it may be hard to arrange the trial in a way that eliminates the risk of the jury being influenced. Despite the costs and shortcomings, such internal safeguards are used in addition to the liability imposed on the media.

iii. Media Freedom

At first sight, the control of potentially prejudicial material may be thought to pose relatively few issues for media freedom. A restriction to prevent the media influencing the legal process is a temporary measure as the potential prejudice to a court's decision only arises *before* that decision is made. Once a jury has given its verdict, the law of contempt normally allows the media to publish what it wants. Moreover, assertions of the media acting to inform and educate the audience may be received with some scepticism where the reporting of crime is sensationalist and aiming solely to maximise sales. The press baron Lord Northcliffe's motto was 'Get me a murder a day', which had more to do with circulations and sales than a sense of public service.[24] In any event, the compelling interest in protecting the legal process may outweigh the freedom to report investigations.[25]

Despite the various reservations, there are good reasons why the media should be free to publish information about criminal investigations prior to the conclusion of proceedings. Media reports can help scrutinise a police investigation and sometimes challenge the way those investigations are being conducted. If media reporting is postponed until the end of the proceedings, then the story may no longer be newsworthy and the media will have no incentive to publish at all. There is also a general interest for the public to know what is happening in the justice system. The discussion of the *Sunday Times* investigations into Thalidomide illustrated how the reporting of legal proceedings can relate to matters of general importance, in which there are

---

[23] ibid, 177–78. See the dissent of Judge Yudkivska in *Bedat v Switzerland*, App no 56925/08 (2016) 63 EHRR 15 advocating greater use of such measures. For the role of internal measures in the US and the contrast with the UK, see J Brandwood, 'You Say "Fair Trial" and I Say "Free Press"' (2000) 75 *NYU Law Review* 1412.

[24] See K Williams, *Get Me a Murder a Day: the History of Mass Communication in Britain* (London, Arnold, 1998).

[25] Along such lines, interferences with Art 10 are permitted when necessary to maintain the 'the authority and impartiality of the judiciary'. See *Worm v Austria*, App no 22714/93 (1998) 25 EHRR 454 and *Bedat v Switzerland* (n 23) at [55].

strong interests in media freedom. What is necessary, then, is to strike a balance that permits the reporting of crime and other legal cases, but which does not jeopardise the fairness of the proceedings.

The reporting of police investigations and subsequent prosecutions is not solely about the media checking government and other powerful actors, but may work to further the goals of government. Media reports about a crime can aid police investigations by encouraging witnesses to come forward.[26] Sometimes the government may wish to have certain investigations publicised in order to be seen to be doing something about a crime or issue. Naming an individual suspect and providing details of an alleged crime may also show that certain government law enforcement powers are necessary.[27] As a result, various disclosures may be tolerated, encouraged and even facilitated by government bodies as a way to control the flow of information and pursue their objectives. An awareness of such dynamics is important to our understanding of what happens in this area of law, and simple stories of watchdogs versus censors should be resisted.

In the past, there were concerns about the strategic reliance on contempt laws to evade other protections for media freedom.[28] For example, when defamation cases were heard by a jury, the law of contempt of court could restrict reports of defamation proceedings that could influence jurors prior to the trial. The law of contempt then provided a way around the rule in *Bonnard v Perryman*, which imposes a high threshold for a pre-trial injunction in defamation.[29] The concern was that by starting proceedings in defamation law, a repetition of or comment on the defamatory statement in the media could amount to a contempt.[30] That gave rise to the 'gagging' writ, which could achieve the effect of an injunction in preventing repetition of the defamatory statement, without meeting the high threshold required by *Bonnard*. Prior to the Contempt of Court Act 1981, the courts were wary of such uses of the law and stated that the fact that libel proceedings had been initiated did not preclude media discussion of the case, as not every such publication posed a risk of prejudice to the proceedings.[31] However, now that defamation cases are heard by a judge, such an abuse of process is unlikely to arise. Nonetheless, the old risk of gagging writs shows how various areas of media law are interconnected and litigants can sometimes use one area of law strategically to find routes around the limits of another.

The discussion has shown how the law of contempt serves a number of important goals, but raises significant issues for media freedom. The Contempt of Court Act 1981 attempts to strike a balance with these competing considerations. The legislation was enacted following a number of the proposals to reform the old common law of

---

[26] *Re A (A Child) (Application for Reporting Restrictions)* [2011] EWHC 1764 (Fam), [2012] 1 FLR 239 at [69].

[27] Fenwick and Phillipson (n 2) 255–56.

[28] For background see G Robertson and A Nicol. *Robertson and Nicol on Media Law*, 5th edn (London, Sweet and Maxwell, 2007) 434.

[29] See Ch 2 for discussion.

[30] *A-G v News Group Newspapers Ltd* [1987] QB 1, 8 (CA).

[31] *Thomson v Times Newspapers Ltd* [1969] 1 WLR 1236, 1240 (CA). For discussion see P Londono, D Eady and ATH Smith, *Arlidge, Eady and Smith on Contempt*, 5th edn (London, Sweet and Maxwell, 2017) at [4-370]–[4-375].

contempt in the 1970s, and the central catalyst for action was the Strasbourg Court's decision in *Sunday Times*. The Act was said to have brought about 'a permanent shift in the balance of public interest away from the protection of the administration of justice and in favour of freedom of speech'.[32] The following sections will outline the main issues in the law of contempt and show how the law has been interpreted to give considerable latitude for media reporting (which itself has been a source of criticism).

B. The Contempt of Court Act 1981 and Strict Liability

i. *The Scope of Strict Liability*

The primary control to prevent media coverage influencing the legal process is found in the Contempt of Court Act 1981. Under s 2 of the Act, it is a contempt to make a publication that 'creates a substantial risk that the course of justice in the proceedings in question will be seriously impeded or prejudiced'. The main sanction for contempt against the media is a fine. The court also has the power to impose a custodial sentence, although the last time an editor was imprisoned for contempt was in 1949. The publisher does not need to intend to create any prejudice to the course of justice to commit a contempt and the Act creates a strict liability offence to maximise the deterrent effect. There are a number of limits on the scope of the strict liability rule, which give the 1981 Act its liberalising effect. The risk of prejudice must occur to 'particular legal proceedings', as opposed to undermining the administration of justice across a range of cases.[33] Accordingly, an article stating that witnesses in sexual offence trials are likely to be ridiculed and humiliated by the defence counsel may arguably discourage witnesses coming forward generally, but does not prejudice particular legal proceedings and will not fall within the strict liability rule.

The strict liability rule is limited to publications while legal proceedings are 'active'.[34] Active proceedings are defined in Schedule 1 to the Act, but for present purposes the most important part is that criminal proceedings are active once a person is arrested or a warrant for arrest has been issued, and cease to be active once a trial is complete or the prosecution is discontinued.[35] The active proceedings rule ensures that strict liability is applied only for a limited period of time. If proceedings are not active, then any contempt of court proceedings must be pursued under the common law, which requires a showing of intent to impede or prejudice the administration of justice.[36] The approach shows a compromise, in which outside of the active period, the balance lies in favour of media freedom. Within the active period, greater weight is given to the administration of justice. However, as will be seen, even while proceedings are active there is still ample room for media freedom.

---

[32] *A-G v Newspaper Publishing plc* [1988] Ch 333, 382 (CA).
[33] Contempt of Court Act 1981, s 1.
[34] ibid, s 2(3).
[35] Where a warrant for arrest is issued, but no further steps are taken, then the proceedings will cease to be active after 12 months, see Sch 1, para 11.
[36] Contempt of Court Act 1981, s 6(c).

The strict liability rule does not specifically target the media, but applies to publications 'addressed to the public at large or any section of the public'.[37] An email to a juror would therefore not constitute a statutory contempt, as it is addressed to a specific individual rather than a section of the public. Instead, such a communication would have to be prosecuted as an intentional contempt under the common law. The requirement of publication to the public means that the rule is typically applied to the professional media more than other publishers. However, the ability for people to publish to the world at large via the digital media vastly increases the scope of contempt of court to apply to statements made by non-media speakers. The extent to which the strict liability rule applies to the digital media depends on whether the message is to a section of the public or is a private communication. This raises difficult questions of application, such as whether a message on the social media sent to a large group of friends or followers (and which is likely to be forwarded to others) is a public or private communication for the purposes of the Act? When facing such a question, a court is likely to consider the context, nature and circulation of the publication.[38]

The strictness of the rule is also limited by the provision that a publisher will not be guilty of contempt, if he 'does not know and has no reason to suspect that relevant proceedings are active'.[39] The clause does not provide an easy escape route for a journalist, as the court has stated that journalists are expected to show 'a high standard of care before they are in a position to avail themselves of that defence'.[40] To rely on the provision, the reporter will normally have to show that they asked the relevant authority if any proceedings are active.[41] The standards of a professional journalist should not be expected of every individual commenting on a criminal investigation on the social media. When posting comments and messages relating to such a matter, an individual would not normally enquire with the authorities to check the status of the proceedings. The provision should therefore offer some protection for individual speakers outside of the professional media from being found liable for inadvertently committing a contempt.

In another defence, a distributor will not be liable if, having taken all reasonable care, he or she does not know the publication contained the prejudicial content and 'has no reason to suspect that it is likely to do so'.[42] A newsagent or company distributing the publication will normally have a defence under this provision. As with other areas of media law, the provision seeks to make sure that a broad definition of a publisher does not make the law over-inclusive and punish those that bear no responsibility for the prejudice. The provision may also provide further scope for internet intermediaries to avoid liability, over and above the general protections offered to those providing services as a conduit, cache or host of digital content.[43] Consequently, while the strict

---

[37] ibid, s 2(1).

[38] *Arlidge, Eady and Smith on Contempt* (n 31) at [4.63]. The Law Commission, *Contempt of Court (1): Juror Misconduct and Internet Publications* (Law Com No 340, 2013) at [2.45] concluded that the issue is best decided on a case-by-case basis.

[39] Contempt of Court Act 1981, s 3.

[40] *R v Duffy; A-G v News Group Newspapers Ltd* (unreported, 9 February 1996). See also *Arlidge, Eady and Smith on Contempt* (n 31) at [4-283]–[4-287].

[41] *R v Duffy*, ibid.

[42] Contempt of Court Act 1981, s 3(2).

[43] The specific provisions relating to internet intermediaries are discussed in Ch 7.

liability rule applies to all publications, the various provisions allow for the different treatment of different types of publisher. In practice, the differentiation allows the liability to reflect the levels of power and responsibility assigned to the particular publisher, and the different expressive interests at stake.

ii. Substantial Risk of Prejudicing or Impeding the Course of Justice

The test for contempt of court lies in s 2(2) of the 1981 Act, which provides that the strict liability rule applies only where a publication creates a substantial risk that proceedings will be seriously impeded or prejudiced. As the law aims to deter the *risk* of prejudice or impediment at the time of publication, the fact that the publication did not cause any *actual* prejudice or impediment to a trial is not relevant to whether it is a contempt.[44] Furthermore, a contempt can arise even when an active investigation is abandoned before it comes to trial. In such a case, a publisher will not know at the time of publication whether the matter would come to trial or not.

While the most common form of contempt concerns material that could influence a potential juror, the strict liability rule applies to publications that can impede the course of justice in other ways. This can arise where the publication applies pressure that could alter the conduct of a party or witness in the course of litigation.[45] An attempt to pressure a litigant to settle a claim or a defendant to plead a particular way can thereby amount to a contempt. After the arrest of Christopher Jefferies on suspicion of the murder of Joanna Yates in late 2010, several newspapers published articles vilifying Jefferies and attacking his character. Jefferies was subsequently released without charge and was completely innocent. The newspaper articles 'monstering' Jefferies were nonetheless in contempt partly because the negative stories may have stopped people from coming forward to say positive things about Jefferies' character.[46]

The main cases concerning the media tend to relate to publicity about a crime that could taint the integrity of the jury's decision. In such cases, when deciding if the risk to the course of justice is 'substantial' or whether the prejudice or impediment is 'serious', Schiemann LJ stated that the court should consider the following factors: (1) 'the likelihood of the publication coming to the attention of a potential juror'; (2) 'the likely impact of the publication on an ordinary reader at the time of publication'; and (3) 'the residual impact of the publication on a notional juror at the time of trial'.[47] Each of these factors will be considered in turn.

When looking at whether the publication is likely to come to the attention of the juror, the court will take into account both where the publication was disseminated and how widely.[48] As Parker LJ noted, a local newspaper in Devon is unlikely to

---

[44] *A-G v English* (n 15), Lord Diplock at 141–42.
[45] *A-G v Unger* [1998] 1 Cr App R 308, 315.
[46] *A-G v MGN Ltd* [2011] EWHC 2074 (Admin), [2012] 1 WLR 2408.
[47] *A-G v MGN Ltd* [1997] EMLR 284. See also *A-G v English* (n 15) 141–42; *A-G v News Group Newspapers Ltd* (n 30). See also the discussion in Fenwick and Phillipson (n 2) 259–66.
[48] *A-G v MGN Ltd*, ibid, 290.

come to the attention of the juror in Newcastle.[49] By contrast, a publication in the national mainstream media is more likely to come to the attention of a juror in any part of the country. Accordingly, a television production company was found to be in contempt of court for comments asserting the guilt of two defendants that were made in the course of a popular quiz show with an audience of over six million people, even though the comments were broadcast six months prior to the trial.[50] Similarly, in 2011, two newspaper companies were found in contempt after a photograph showing the defendant in a murder trial posing with a gun was published by mistake on the website of two national newspapers.[51] The photograph was made available for a number of hours, and the court placed significant weight on the broad readership of those papers, along with the power of the visual image, in deciding that there was a significant risk.[52]

In determining the likely impact of the publication, if seen by the juror, the court will look at both the content and its presentation.[53] If the information relates to a central issue that is being contested in the trial then it will be more likely to pose a risk of prejudice. Where witnesses are being asked to identify an offender in the trial, a newspaper report naming the defendant and publishing a photograph will be likely to cause prejudice.[54] Revealing a defendant's prior conviction may be particularly prejudicial, as such evidence is admissible in court only if certain criteria are fulfilled (which the media cannot determine in advance of the judge's decision).[55] A particularly sensational report is also more likely to get attention and be remembered by a juror.[56] More surprisingly, the fact that prejudicial information is contained in a serious and authoritative publication can also point to a contempt, as the information is less likely to be taken with a pinch of salt or written off as gossip.[57] In this respect, the law does not privilege the broadsheet press, but simply reflects the potential influence of the content. Ultimately, there are no hard and fast rules. The impact rests on the nature of the article and how the content relates to the issues to be determined at the trial.

Finally, in looking at the residual impact of the publication at the time of the trial, the court will look at the closeness of the publication to the date of the court proceedings.[58] If publication takes place far in advance of the hearing, then the courts are more willing to assume that any prejudicial impact will have faded by the time the trial takes place and that the evidence at the trial will take precedence in the minds of the jurors (known as the 'fade factor').[59] By contrast, a publication taking place at the time of the trial is far more likely to have an impact on the juror at the relevant time.[60] Empirical research conducted by Cheryl Thomas found some support for this

---

49 *A-G v News Group Newspapers Ltd* (n 30) 17.
50 *A-G v Hat Trick Productions Ltd* [1997] EMLR 76.
51 *A-G v Associated Newspapers Ltd* [2011] EWHC 418 (Admin), [2011] 1 WLR 2097.
52 ibid, [36] and [41].
53 *A-G v MGN Ltd* (1997) (n 47) 290.
54 Robertson and Nicol (n 28) 422.
55 See Criminal Justice Act 2003, s 101.
56 See *A-G v Morgan* [1998] EMLR 294.
57 *A-G v Condé Nast Publications Ltd* [2015] EWHC 3322 (Admin).
58 *A-G v MGN Ltd* (1997) (n 47) 291.
59 *A-G v News Group Newspapers Ltd* (n 30).
60 *A-G v Condé Nast Publications Ltd* (n 57).

assumption, noting that jurors are far more likely to recall the information published at the time of the trial.[61] However, Thomas also noted that that there was some recall of earlier media coverage in relation to high-profile cases.[62] Reliance on the fade factor means that while the strict liability rule applies as soon as proceedings are active, in practice the rule is likely to restrain publication for a limited period of time closer to the trial.

The questions of time and location of the publication are more complex in the context of internet publications. Most news publications are now available online to a national or international audience and transcend geographical boundaries. Publications on the digital media can be accessed immediately before or during a trial, even if the article was initially published at a much earlier date. If a publication is deemed to be a continuous act or takes place each time an article is accessed, then the contempt of court restrictions could apply to material published over a longer time period and in any geographical area.[63] Moreover, once something is published online, the publisher loses control of its circulation, with the potential for the content to be shared and copied.[64] It is, however, important not to overstate the risk. The court should still take into account time and location when assessing the *likelihood* of the content being viewed. The website of the local newspaper in Devon is still very unlikely to be viewed by anyone in Newcastle, unless they have a connection with the area or are looking up specific information. Similarly, in most cases it is unlikely that a potential juror will be reading through archived newspaper reports of criminal convictions from several years earlier. The dangers will arise when individuals are actively searching out content relating to a specific individual or crime, or where the content is linked to a current story. Such problems can be partly addressed by imposing responsibilities on the juror, which will be discussed below.

iii. Aggregate Effects of Media Coverage

In applying the strict liability rule, each publication is judged individually and will be found in contempt if it increases the risk of prejudice.[65] Looking at the contribution made by the individual publication makes sense given that contempt imposes criminal liability. However, the rule has been criticised, as if a newspaper publishes an article that does not in itself raise the risk of prejudice, but contributes to an environment that jeopardises a fair trial, then no contempt will be committed. In *A-G v MGN*, a trial for an assault was stayed as a result of prejudicial media coverage.[66] The incident

---

[61]   C Thomas, *Are Juries Fair* (Ministry of Justice, 2010), 41.

[62]   ibid.

[63]   See *HM Advocate v Beggs (No 2)* 2002 SLT 139, 2001 SCCR 879, finding that publication under Scottish law takes place throughout the period that the article is available. See also *R v Harwood*, Southwark Crown Court (20 July 2012) at [37].

[64]   *A-G v Associated Newspapers Ltd* (2011) (n 51) at [54].

[65]   *A-G v MGN Ltd* (1997) (n 47). However, if the same person is responsible for more than one publication, then the collective effect of the publications for which he is responsible can be considered, *A-G v MGN Ltd* (2011) (n 46) at [20].

[66]   *A-G v MGN Ltd* (1997) (n 47).

generated considerable media attention on account of the involvement of a well-known actress and her boyfriend. However, no contempt was committed by the five newspapers that reported the incident in 'typical graphic tabloid style' while the proceedings were active. The court reasoned that the actions of the newspapers were to be judged separately to assess the risk of prejudice 'in the light of the saturation publicity given over previous months'.[67] The newspapers therefore did not add any significant risk of prejudice that was not already in existence.

The criticism of this approach is that it fails to deter media reporting that contributes to the collective prejudicial effects.[68] With high-profile criminal proceedings, a newspaper or broadcaster might feel a strong competitive pressure to include the latest details about a crime, or otherwise lose an audience. As ATH Smith commented at the time of the decision, 'it is incredibly difficult to say of any particular publication, judged as it must be against the "feeding frenzy" that the press can generate, that it has created a "serious risk of substantial prejudice"'.[69] The point should not be overstated, as Schiemann LJ added that the mere fact that 'there is already some risk of prejudice does not prevent a finding that the latest publication has created a further risk'.[70] The publication of particularly damning facts at the time of trial, even if already in the public domain, may still be a contempt on account of the additional risk generated by the further publicity.[71]

The principle in *A-G v MGN* could have wider application in relation to internet publications. For example, imagine the prior criminal convictions of a defendant had been published by a freely-available news source long before proceedings were active. At the time of the trial, a person repeats the content on the social media, which is subsequently shared by a large number of other users. Even if no single act of publication will cause a significant risk of prejudice given the small audience for each social media message, the aggregate effects of all the publicity might have considerable impact on the trial. If the principle taken in *MGN* is applied in this context, the law of contempt offers little restraint. To be clear, it is not desirable to apply the law of contempt to every individual that forwards a piece of prejudicial information. However, the example shows the limits for contempt of court to address this type of problem. The problem is just one illustration of the challenges in combatting harms that are caused where lots of publications 'pollute' the informational environment, but none causes significant harm alone. The law developed to constrain large media publications, and is less well suited to tackling such de-centralised and uncoordinated causes of harm from multiple publishers. To deal with this problem it seems likely that controls on digital intermediaries will be increasingly important, which will be discussed further below.

---

[67]   ibid, 294.

[68]   Proposals were initially made to reverse the effect of the decision (National Heritage Select Committee, Second Report of the 1996–97 Session, *Press Activity Affecting Court Cases* (HC 1996–97 86) at xi.) but were never implemented and the principle in *MGN* has since been affirmed in the courts. See *A-G v MGN Ltd* (2011) (n 46) at [19]–[20].

[69]   ATH Smith, 'Contempt, Free Press and Fair Trial: A "Permanent Shift"?' (1997) 56 *CLJ* 467.

[70]   *A-G v MGN Ltd* (1997) (n 47) 289.

[71]   *A-G v Condé Nast Publications Ltd* (n 57).

iv. Contempt and Grounds for a Stay or Appeal

As noted earlier, there are other steps that can be taken to protect the administration of justice from publicity. If a publication causes prejudice to proceedings, trials can be stayed or in extreme cases convictions quashed as unsafe. One question is how the level of prejudice required for a stay or the quashing of a conviction relates to that required for a contempt? In *Birmingham Post*, Simon Brown LJ stated, in the context of a publication at the time of trial, that the decision to stay or allow an appeal is normally 'highly likely to be a telling pointer' that the publication is a contempt.[72] The two situations do not, however, necessarily overlap. The proceedings in *A-G v MGN* discussed above were stayed due to the aggregate effects of coverage without a finding that any publisher was in contempt of court. The example shows that there can be a stay of proceedings or an appeal against conviction without there being a contempt of court. There can also be a contempt of court without a stay of proceedings or an appeal. Simon Brown LJ stated that 's 2(2) postulates a lesser degree of prejudice than is required to make good an appeal against conviction' or for a stay.[73] Consequently, this means that the level of prejudice required for a contempt is that which would 'create a *seriously arguable* ground of appeal', as opposed to a *successful* ground of appeal.[74]

The different standards show how the court can reach different conclusions on the question of a stay or appeal and on a contempt. However, the different conclusions on the two issues can give an impression of the courts 'speaking with two voices' in which the vulnerability of the jury to media publicity is a basis for finding a contempt, but an application for a stay or appeal is rejected on the grounds that the safeguards are effective and juries are sufficiently robust for a fair trial to go ahead.[75] The difference in approach can be explained, as a stay or appeal serves a different purpose than the law of contempt. The stay or appeal is primarily about ensuring that the defendant receives a fair trial in practice. When deciding whether to grant a stay, the judge has to consider the real danger to the trial, the effects of any alternative measures and the costs of the stay.[76] By contrast, contempt of court is about deterring a risk of prejudice, regardless of whether that risk eventuates. The lower level of prejudice therefore fits with the deterrent goal for contempt.[77]

v. Impact of the Internet

As with other areas of media law, internet publications pose a number of challenges. Earlier, it was noted that under a continuous publication rule, each time content is accessed there will be a fresh publication.[78] Under such an approach, s 2(2) can apply

---

[72] *A-G v Birmingham Post and Mail Ltd* [1999] 1 WLR 361, 371.

[73] ibid, 370.

[74] ibid, 370; *A-G v MGN Ltd* (2011) (n 46) at [28].

[75] *A-G v Unger* (n 45).

[76] *A-G v Birmingham Post and Mail Ltd* (n 72) 370–71.

[77] See also Fenwick and Phillipson (n 2) 266.

[78] See *HM Advocate v Beggs (No 2)* (n 63) and *Harwood* (n 63). For discussion see Law Commission, *Juror Misconduct and Internet Publications* (n 38) Ch 2.

to content in online archives that was initially published before proceedings were active, but remain accessible to the public after proceedings have been initiated. The application of contempt laws to newspaper archives could lead to media publishers becoming the unwitting publisher of prejudicial material. Section 3 provides a defence where the publisher did not know or had no reason to suspect that proceedings were active. However, there is a good chance that a large media organisation will know of any investigations or proceedings, and may even be reporting on them.[79] While knowing about the active proceedings, the news organisation may not go to the trouble of cross-checking its archive for any potentially prejudicial material.

The Law Commission proposed a system to protect the media in such cases, in which there would be no contempt in relation to archives unless the publisher had received notice from the Attorney-General that prejudicial content relating to active proceedings is accessible.[80] The proposal was dropped following a critical reaction from media representatives, particularly in relation to the prospect of a government officer having the legal power to tell the media to remove content.[81] The media appeared to be more willing to face the risk of liability than face direction from a government official. The media representatives' preference for the status quo may, however, be explained by the fact that the risk of successful proceedings for contempt in relation to archive material seems relatively unlikely in practice.

The risk of online material prejudicing a trial can also come from the activities of jurors. A significant risk is that jurors, having been selected, will go online and begin to search for content relevant to the case. Jurors are warned not to undertake their own research, and such research may constitute a common law contempt.[82] A juror was convicted for common law contempt and imprisoned for six months after going online to look up legal terms and information about the case she was sitting on, finding details concerning a prior conviction of the defendant.[83] One juror, having been selected for a trial concerning a child sex offence even went on to the social media to announce his predisposition by stating 'Woooow I wasn't expecting to be in a jury Deciding a paedophile's fate, I've always wanted to Fuck up a paedophile & now I'm within the law!'.[84] The juror was sentenced to two months in prison.

While the common law of contempt provides a control on such conduct, statutory controls were enacted to make it an offence for a juror 'to research the case during the trial period'.[85] The offence covers research not just about the events in the case, but also about the judges, the lawyers, the law itself or court procedure.[86] It is also an offence to share such research with other jury members. The statute provides that no offence is committed if the juror needs that information for reasons not connected

---

[79] Law Commission, ibid, [2.77] and [2.127].
[80] ibid, [2.152].
[81] Dominic Grieve MP, HC Deb 30 June 2014, vol 583, col 41WS.
[82] There are, however, some uncertainties in common law contempt, such as whether the contempt is committed by conducting the research or by virtue of breaking the judge's direction: Law Commission, *Juror Misconduct and Internet Publications* (n 38) at [3.13].
[83] *A-G v Dallas* [2012] EWHC 156 (Admin), [2012] 1 WLR 991.
[84] *A-G v Davey and Beard* [2013] EWHC 2317 (Admin), [2014] 1 Cr App R 1.
[85] Juries Act 1974, s 20A (as amended by Criminal Justice and Courts Act 2015).
[86] ibid.

with the case.[87] These developments represent a broader trend in the law sometimes shifting its focus away from the publisher who disseminates the content, to the individual user that accesses it. However, these controls only go so far and cannot deal with any risk of prejudice caused by content viewed by the juror prior to selection for the jury. Furthermore, a juror cannot be held responsible for content that is stumbled on. For example, content that is prejudicial may be automatically linked to a current article on a related topic that contains non-prejudicial material. In other cases, a person may send the relevant article to a juror without knowing that the person is hearing that case. Rather than imposing liability, Ian Cram prefers alternatives measures, such as questioning jurors to identify and filter out those most likely to engage in online research, or giving jurors greater freedom to ask questions of the judge to address their concerns.[88] Whichever measures are taken to promote juror responsibility, there is still a role for controls on the publisher to reduce the risk of a juror seeing prejudicial content that he or she cannot filter out.

In addition to the harm arising from the media's own material, there is also a danger of the media being held responsible for comments posted by others on its website. This can pose considerable risk in the case of a high-profile and emotive criminal trial, where members of the public have strong views. In such circumstances, the media can be expected to moderate and often disable any user comments. While that inhibits the use of the media as a forum for discussion, comments posing a risk of prejudice are predictable in relation to many areas of criminal reporting. In one case, the court ordered a media organisation not to include any reports of a trial on its Facebook page and to disable comments.[89] In the same case, Facebook was also directed to remove pages that attracted prejudicial comments in relation to the trial.[90] Finally, the Court of Appeal warned that the individual users could be liable for any prejudicial comments posted.[91] While liability for publications on the digital media will be discussed more broadly in Chapter 7, the approach reflects a strategy that potentially targets all links in the chain of communication.

vi. Bringing Proceedings

Contempt of court proceedings under the 1981 Act require the Attorney-General's consent or the motion of a court.[92] In practice, much is left to the policy of the Attorney-General to determine how strictly contempt laws will be enforced. While in the 2000s there was much commentary about the sparing use of contempt laws,[93] some high-profile proceedings have reasserted this area of law.[94] However, the law

---

[87] ibid, s 20A(6).
[88] I Cram, *Citizen Journalists: Newer Media, Republican Moments and the Constitution* (Cheltenham, Edward Elgar, 2015) 169.
[89] *R v F* [2016] EWCA Crim 12, [2016] 2 Cr App R 13 at [44].
[90] ibid, [42].
[91] ibid, [43].
[92] Contempt of Court Act 1981, s 7.
[93] See B Woffinden, 'Treating Contempt with Contempt' (2007) 18 *British Journalism Review* 5.
[94] *A-G v MGN* (2011) (n 46).

is still invoked relatively rarely given the frequency with which the media publishes content that could fall within the strict liability rule. As with other areas of media law, controls are exercised at an informal level. The Attorney-General will sometimes offer warnings to the media in relation to high-profile cases, requesting it to show caution in its reporting.[95] Such statements can only be advisory and the media can choose to run the risk of a prosecution if it does not share the Attorney-General's assessment.[96] However, if the newspapers do not heed a warning, then a prosecution is more likely to be brought for contempt and the failure to heed the warning could be an aggravating factor when imposing a penalty.[97]

The Attorney-General's consent might be thought to provide some safeguard for media freedom by requiring authorisation at the highest level prior to a prosecution. However, the provision is the source of controversy in so far as it hands the power to a politician.[98] The government has an interest in controlling the flow of information and the power can be used for political advantage, for example by taking a permissive stance where media reporting advances the goals of the government. Fenwick and Phillipson warn that the Attorney-General can face a conflict of interest when potentially prejudicial reporting of a criminal investigation serves the government's interests, for example in making a case for strengthening police powers or even just raising the profile of an issue.[99] This power also gives the politician some potential leverage over the media, which could be used sparingly to foster good relations with the media or enforced to punish critics.[100] However, the government's discretion is constrained by its desire not to appear biased and by the possibility of the court bringing contempt proceedings on its motion, or staying a trial. The overall picture is that the law of contempt is generally enforced sparingly, rather than selectively enforced in a biased way. However, to eradicate suspicion, the power to initiate proceedings could be handed to a more independent officer.[101]

vii. Discussion of Matters of Public Interest

A key element in making the 1981 Act compliant with Article 10 of the ECHR is the provision under s 5 that a publisher will not be in contempt of court if any prejudice or impediment to particular legal proceedings is incidental to the good faith discussion of public affairs or matters of general public interest.[102] Where the prejudice is incidental, the provision prioritises the public interest in publication over the interest in the administration of justice that is potentially prejudiced. Whether the prejudice is

---

[95] ibid, at [4]; 'Old Bailey prepares for marathon trial over News of the World hacking claims' *The Guardian*, 28 October 2013; 'Police shootings: media warned over coverage after arrest of Dale Cregan' *The Guardian*, 19 September 2012.

[96] Robertson and Nicol (n 28) 422.

[97] *A-G v MGN Ltd* (2011) (n 46). See also *A-G v Express Newspapers* [2004] EWHC 2859 (Admin), [2005] EMLR 13.

[98] Fenwick and Phillipson (n 2) 254–57.

[99] ibid.

[100] ibid.

[101] ibid, 257.

[102] See the Contempt of Court Act 1981, s 5.

deemed sufficiently incidental will depend on the nature of the topic under discussion and its connection with the legal proceedings. In the leading case of *English*, a newspaper published an article expressing support for a pro-life candidate in a by-election and was strongly critical of the practice of doctors allowing severely disabled babies to die of starvation. The article was published on the third day of a trial of a doctor for murder by causing the death through starvation of a three-day old baby with Down's Syndrome.[103] The article did not mention the trial, but risked prejudicing the proceedings as it related to an issue in the trial by suggesting that such practices were common among paediatricians. However, the prejudice was incidental to the discussion of the important issue and the by-election, and no contempt was found. By contrast, if the article refers to details that are more 'closely related' to a particular set of proceedings (such as referring to the defendants or a particular locality), then it will be less likely to be incidental and the administration of justice will prevail over the public interest in discussion.[104] In *TVS*, the court noted that it is difficult to formulate a clearer test and that applying the provision 'is largely a matter of first impression'.[105] While the protection under s 5 is important, the interpretation of the strict liability rule under s 2(2) and the small number of prosecutions means there is considerable leeway for media coverage, and reliance on s 5 is rarely necessary in practice.

C. Intentional Contempt

In those cases where the statutory strict liability rule does not apply—such as where the publication is made to a specific individual (as opposed to the general public or a section of the public) or where proceedings are not active—publication can still be regulated by the common law of contempt.[106] Some courts have indicated that the threshold for common law contempt is met where the publication poses a 'real risk' of prejudicing or impeding the administration of justice, rather than the higher 'substantial risk' threshold in the 1981 Act.[107] Moreover, the common law of contempt does not require the level of prejudice to be 'serious'. A significant limit is that contempt under the common law does not impose a standard of strict liability. The mens rea requires the Attorney-General to fulfil the additional hurdle of proving that the publisher had the necessary specific intent, which will be difficult to establish when proceedings are not yet active (and where the publisher does not know if proceedings will be initiated).[108] Despite these limits, there is some scope for the common law to interfere with media freedom (in theory at least) in relation to serious investigative journalism, in which a reporter uncovers a crime and hands its file to the police in the hope that it will trigger

---

[103] *A-G v English* [1983] 1 AC 116.
[104] *A-G v TVS Television Ltd* (1989) Times, 7 July, in which a programme included a photograph of the defendant, albeit with his faced blacked out.
[105] ibid.
[106] Contempt of Court Act 1981, s 6(c), which provides that the Act does not displace liability at common law for conduct intended to prejudice or impede the administration of justice.
[107] *A-G v News Group Newspapers plc* [1989] QB 110; Robertson and Nicol (n 28) 439.
[108] *A-G v Sport Newspapers Ltd* [1991] 1 WLR 1194.

a prosecution. The reporting of the media body's own investigation will not be neutral about the case, as it is making the allegation about a crime. However, such coverage could pose a real risk of influencing a potential juror. Liability in such circumstances would be out of step with other areas of media law, in which the disclosure of criminal activity is normally accepted to be a matter of general interest. For this reason, in *Sport Newspapers*, Hodgson J proposed to limit the common law offence to where proceedings are pending, so that it applies for a shorter period.[109] While the status of the comments is uncertain, Hodgson J's remarks represent an attempt to carve out some protection for media freedom. In any event, such a prosecution in relation to a serious investigative report seems unlikely given the hurdle in establishing the mens rea, the general prosecution policy and the constraints imposed by Article 10.

D. Media Effects and Power

Contempt of court raises familiar questions of whether the media has an effect on the audience. The law asks about the likely influence of the media on a juror's decision.[110] The issue is not whether the media coverage secures a particular result, but whether it will play on the mind of the notional juror at all or taint the process of decision-making. When the publication includes types of information that the juror simply should not know and is likely to remember, such as a prior conviction not admitted as evidence in the proceedings, then the tainting effect can be assumed. The line is harder to draw where, for example, the prejudice arises from the sensational tone of the coverage. The strictness of the law of contempt will therefore depend on the extent to which the juror is deemed to be susceptible to external influence. In recent years, there have been assumptions that the juror is more robust and that proceedings at trial will help to insulate the decision from external influences. On this view, the trial provides a counterweight to any power of the media, and is thought to focus the mind of the jurors on the evidence that has been subject to scrutiny in court. In particular, the trial judge will provide a direction to the jury telling them to ignore what they have seen in the media.[111] However, the robustness ascribed to the jurors is to some degree a matter of faith.

While the assumptions in the current law take a more sceptical view of media effects, there are various ways the media can influence the system of justice that are hard to constrain in a legal rule. The influence of the media at stake in contempt is concerned with reports directly dealing with issues specific to a trial. However, the potential influence of the media can often be subtle, through its framing, agenda-setting or priming effects.[112] The way a juror understands a case is likely to be shaped by the frames and perspectives seen in the general media coverage long before proceedings or a trial are

---

[109] ibid.

[110] The discussion relates to the 'prejudice' limb of contempt, as opposed to an 'impediment' caused by pressuring witnesses.

[111] In *A-G v Guardian Newspapers Ltd* [1999] EMLR 904, Sedley LJ stated that threshold under s 2(2) will be met only when the risk of prejudice persists after such a direction from the judge.

[112] See Ch 1.

under way. When presenting a case to a court, a lawyer may rely on narratives prevalent in the media portrayal of crime. For example, a young man prosecuted for reckless driving may be characterised as a 'boy racer'. The images and stories in the media may make certain narratives about a case more likely to appeal to a juror. That provides an example of the broad ways in which the media has the power to influence aspects of the justice system. However, that broader influence is not the issue in contempt of court, which is concerned with reports about particular proceedings.

E. Concluding Thoughts

The discussion has shown a change in the law of the contempt. The *Sunday Times* case showed the breadth of the earlier law and the concerns with 'trial by media' and pre-judgment in the press. Like several other major media law statutes, the Contempt of Court Act 1981 attempted to strike a fresh balance by curbing the earlier restrictions and replacing it with a more tailored law that would be more credible, while imposing a significant control on publications falling within its terms.[113] Alongside other criminal publication offences, the statute has not been enforced as widely as its terms might suggest. For some time, it seemed to receive relatively minimal respect from certain parts of the press, who published sensationalist stories in relation to criminal investigations. The law still provides a significant control as it can be used to punish the more extreme risks to a fair trial. However, much of the liberalisation in this area of law stems from a belief that the media has limited effects and that the process of a court hearing is likely to correct any possible risks of prejudice. Rather than pursuing the media, the recent steps taken in relation to material on the internet have emphasised the greater responsibility of jurors as potential viewers of the content.

III. Open Justice

The principle of open justice requires that legal proceedings are conducted transparently and in public view. The default position is that members of the public can sit in on court proceedings and speak about what happened after. Open justice has long been regarded as a fundamental constitutional principle, which over a century ago Lord Shaw stated had received 'a constant and most watchful respect' since the end of the Stuart era.[114] That remark was made in the landmark case of *Scott v Scott*,

---

[113] The Obscene Publications Act 1959 and Official Secrets Act 1989 were similarly presented as liberalising statutes.
[114] Lord Shaw in *Scott v Scott* [1913] AC 417 at 477; Toulson LJ in *Guardian News and Media Ltd v City of Westminster Magistrates' Court* [2012] EWCA Civ 420, [2013] QB 618 at [2].

in which Mrs Scott applied for a declaration that her marriage was void as a result of Mr Scott's impotence. The proceedings took place in camera and Mrs Scott subsequently sent a written transcript of the court proceedings to three people, including Mr Scott's father and sister, in order to defend her character and reputation.[115] Mr Scott asked the court to commit Mrs Scott and her solicitor for contempt for distributing details of a hearing in camera and for an injunction to prevent further dissemination. The House of Lords declined to restrict publication, finding that the judge had neither the power to hear the proceedings in camera nor to restrict reports of the trial after the proceedings had come to a conclusion. In the ruling, Lord Shaw described the open administration of justice as a 'constitutional right', rather than a matter of judicial discretion.[116] While leaving open the scope for some limitations of the principle, the case stands as a strong statement that justice is to be administered in public. The principle now receives further support from Article 6 of the ECHR, which requires that 'everyone is entitled to a fair and public hearing' in relation to their 'civil rights and obligations or of any criminal charge'.[117]

To elaborate on what open justice requires, Lord Diplock usefully divided the principle into two main elements: (1) that proceedings are 'held in open court to which the press and public are admitted'; and (2) the freedom to publish 'fair and accurate reports of proceedings that have taken place in court'.[118] The first element, at its most basic, is a right to sit in the public gallery and hear what is happening in court. The requirements of open justice have evolved to match developments in the way cases are heard. When more and more arguments and evidence are submitted on paper rather than spoken in court, the public will often need access to court documents to make sense of the proceedings. Consequently, the courts have taken a number of steps to allow the public to see the relevant paperwork, with skeleton arguments being made available and access granted to documents that are part of the evidence in court.[119] The principle is not absolute and where there are countervailing reasons, such as a risk of harm to others, the court will conduct a proportionality analysis to decide whether to decline access to the documents.[120] While these developments are important, there are still improvements that could be made. Complaints are sometimes made that it is hard to know in advance what cases will be heard in certain courts.[121] That might well

---

[115] *Scott v Scott* ibid. The phrase 'in camera' is used to refer to proceedings held in private, from which the public is excluded. See *Clibbery v Allan* [2002] EWCA Civ 45, [2002] Fam 261 at [17]–[20].

[116] *Scott v Scott* (n 114) 477.

[117] The Convention has not, however, superseded the common law, and in most cases the common law principles are the central focus of the court's analysis: *Kennedy v The Charity Commission* [2014] UKSC 20, [2015] AC 455.

[118] *A-G v Leveller Magazine Ltd* [1979] AC 440, 450.

[119] On skeleton arguments, see *Gio Personal Investment Services Ltd v Liverpool and London Steamship Protection and Indemnity Association Ltd* [1999] 1 WLR 984 and *R v Howell* [2003] EWCA Crim 486. In civil cases, the courts have recognised a right to access documents submitted to the court to be read as evidence, *Barings plc (in liquidation) v Coopers & Lybrand (a firm)* [2000] 1 WLR 2353. In criminal proceedings, documents placed before a judge and referred to in the course of proceedings should be accessible, *Guardian News and Media Ltd v City of Westminster Magistrates' Court* (n 114) at [85]. See now the Criminal Practice Directions [2015] EWCA Crim 1567, 5B.

[120] *Guardian News and Media Ltd v City of Westminster Magistrates' Court* (n 114) at [85].

[121] See J Townend, 'Positive Free Speech and Public Access to Courts' in A Kenyon and A Scott (eds), *Positive Free Speech: Rationales, Methods and Implications* (Oxford, Hart, 2018).

have much to do with the sheer volume of cases that the courts (especially magistrates) have to deal with at relatively short notice, but some means for the public to check what is happening in advance would be a useful starting point if the courts are to be freely monitored by any interested person.

The strong status assigned to open justice stands in contrast to the tradition of secrecy found in relation to other areas of government.[122] The principle also stands in contrast to the traditional view of media freedom and freedom of speech as *negative* rights against state interference. Open justice amounts to a *positive* obligation on the state to facilitate media reporting and newsgathering by providing access to the hearing and documents. While the domestic courts have traditionally been slower to recognise claims that freedom of expression and media freedom require a right to information, the right of access to the courts is an exception to that general approach.[123]

The other key element of open justice is the right to report court proceedings. The general rule is that the media is free to publish whatever has been said in open court, subject to any reporting restrictions. In contrast to the positive rights of access, the right to report fits with the traditional understanding of media freedom, in allowing the publication of the information acquired without legal obstacle.

Both aspects of open justice assign an important role for the media to convey events to those outside the courtroom. In *A v BBC*, Lord Reed stated that as 'the media are the conduit through which most members of the public receive information about court proceedings, it follows that the principle of open justice is inextricably linked to the freedom of the media to report on court proceedings'.[124] In *Binyam Mohamed*, it was noted that '[i]n reality very few citizens can scrutinise the judicial process: that scrutiny is performed by the media, whether newspapers or television, acting on behalf of the body of citizens'.[125] While anyone can take advantage of open justice, the media is in a strong position to make use of those rights. One reason is practical, as the media representatives will have the time, expertise and resources necessary to follow what is happening in court. In addition to the practical advantages, the media also has some legal benefits. Where access to the courts is limited and requires permission, an application by a representative of the media to attend will be given considerable weight and, as will be seen, accredited journalists have a privileged position in gaining access to some court hearings.[126] Like the classic justifications for media freedom, the open justice principle relies on the media to serve the interests of the public. One question that will be considered later is what happens to open justice if the leading media entities decide that court reporting is no longer profitable.

---

[122] See J Jaconelli, *Open Justice: A Critique of the Public Trial* (Oxford, Oxford University Press, 2002) for the contrast.

[123] *Independent Newspapers v A* [2010] EWCA Civ 343, [2010] 1 WLR 2262. Open justice is particularly important as a route for access, given that court documents are exempt from the Freedom of Information Act 2000, under s 32.

[124] *A v BBC* [2014] UKSC 25, [2015] AC 588.

[125] *R (on the application of Mohamed) v Secretary of State for Foreign and Commonwealth Affairs* [2010] EWCA Civ 158, [2011] QB 218 at [38].

[126] Toulson LJ in *Guardian News* (n 114) noted that the case for access is particularly strong where the documents are sought for a serious journalistic purpose.

A. Arguments for Open Justice

i. Public Scrutiny and Criticism

The central justification for open justice advanced by the court is that it is necessary for the attainment of justice. Under this view, transparency allows for the monitoring of the judicial process. The argument is much like the watchdog argument for press freedom. In *Scott*, Lord Shaw cited Bentham's words that '[p]ublicity is the very soul of justice' and 'guards against improbity'.[127] In his book, *The Road to Justice*, Lord Denning wrote of the beneficial effects of publicity:

> The judge will be careful to see that the trial is fairly and properly conducted if he realises that any unfairness or impropriety on his part will be noted by those in court and may be reported in the press. He will be more anxious to give a correct decision if he knows that his reasons must justify themselves at the bar of public opinion.[128]

More recently, Toulson LJ stated in *Guardian News and Media Ltd v City of Westminster Magistrates' Court* that the rule of law must be 'policed' through 'the transparency of the legal process'.[129] Along similar lines, it is said that publicity means 'every judge sitting in judgment is on trial'.[130] The main argument advanced for open justice is that publicity creates some mechanism of accountability, that the mechanism will deter judicial error and impropriety, and will thereby sustain public confidence in the judicial system. Publicising the outcomes of a case can also contribute to public confidence in the system in knowing that offenders are treated appropriately and proportionately. While open justice has long had legal recognition, Lord Sumption has stated that its 'significance has if anything increased in an age which attaches growing importance to the public accountability of public officers and institutions and to the availability of information about the performance of their functions'.[131]

The arguments that open justice allows greater scrutiny, accountability and confidence in the courts rest on a number of assumptions, which are questionable in practice. First, it is not clear that the media and public are likely to detect judicial improbity or bias. As Jaconelli notes, the strongest objection to an unfair or biased decision is most likely come from the parties to the litigation themselves, who are well versed in the facts of the case and scrutinise the issues closely.[132] Nonetheless the prospect of scrutiny and the possibility of such defects being uncovered by the media provide a guard against poor judicial conduct and is preferable to secrecy.

---

[127] *Scott v Scott* (n 114) 476–77.
[128] AT Denning, *The Road to Justice* (London, Stevens and Sons, 1955) 64.
[129] See also Lord Toulson in *Kennedy v The Charity Commission* (n 117), 'In a democracy, where power depends on the consent of the people governed, the answer must lie in the transparency of the legal process. Open justice lets in the light and allows the public to scrutinise the workings of the law, for better or for worse'.
[130] *R (on the application of Mohamed) v Secretary of State for Foreign and Commonwealth Affairs* (n 125) at [38].
[131] *Khuja* (n 16) at [13].
[132] Jaconelli (n 122) 35–37.

The idea that transparency will promote public confidence seems self-evident, but is also more questionable on closer inspection. While secret trials cause suspicion, openness does not eliminate such mistrust. The argument for transparency assumes that people will be reassured by the apparent lack of bias and high standards in the courtroom. However, publicity can provide reasons for doubting that high standards are being met. If the media are to police the judicial process, then journalists will need to sound the alarm when they believe something is going wrong in the system. This means that people should be free to speak if they suspect some foul play even if it turns out that such suspicion is misplaced. In *Harman*, Lord Scarman stated that the scrutiny of the administration of justice 'serves no purpose unless it is accompanied by the rights of free speech, ie the right publicly to report, to discuss, to comment, to criticise, to impart and to receive ideas and information on the matters subjected to scrutiny'.[133] However, scrutiny and criticism can undermine public confidence in the system of justice and the authority of the courts. If people hear allegations of judicial bias or incompetence, then the justice system may be viewed unfavourably.

For the open justice principle to have its policing effects, the argument assumes that there is a relationship between public opinion and the courts. This is what Lord Denning referred to when he talked of judges having to 'justify themselves at the bar of public opinion'. However, beyond such general statements, it is not clear what form of accountability to the public is envisaged in the open justice principle. The courts are not directly accountable as elected branches of government are.[134] The courts are designed to be insulated from, rather than responsive to, public opinion. The chain of accountability is likely to be more indirect. For example, publicity about the courts can generate political pressure on the democratic branches of government to enact some legal reform.

As noted above, the commitment to public scrutiny and criticism also stands in tension with protecting the court's authority. At one time, the authority of the court was legally protected under the old common law offence of 'scandalising the court', in which the 'scurrilous abuse of a judge' and 'unwarranted attacks upon the integrity or impartiality of a judge or court' would be in contempt of court.[135] In the earliest cases on scandalising the court, it was suggested that the offence would be committed even where the criticism of the court was deserved.[136] In so far as that earlier approach sought to maintain the confidence of the court by suppressing even honest statements, it reflected a view that a court was entitled to respect and authority on account of its status.

Attitudes gradually changed over time to take a more permissive stance in relation to criticism. In *Blackburn (No 2)*, the Court of Appeal rejected an application to find the Conservative MP (and future Lord Chancellor) Quentin Hogg in contempt for ridiculing the court,[137] with Lord Denning stating 'We do not fear criticism, nor do we

---

[133] *Harman v Secretary of State for the Home Department* [1983] 1 AC 280, 316.

[134] Jaconelli (n 122).

[135] *Arlidge, Eady and Smith on Contempt* (n 31) at [5-213].

[136] Law Commission, *Contempt of Court: Scandalising the Court* (Law Com No 335, 2012) at [25], citing *R v Almon* (1765) Wilm 243.

[137] *R v Commissioner of Police of the Metropolis, ex p Blackburn (No 2)* [1968] 2 QB 150.

resent it'.[138] In *Harris*, Munby J explained how this development reflected a broader change in the political culture:

> Society has in large part lost its previous habit of deferential respect. Much of what might well, even in the comparatively recent past, have been considered by the judges to be scurrilous abuse of themselves or their brethren has today, as it seems to me, to be recognised as amounting to no more than acceptable if trenchant criticism.[139]

Consequently, the offence did not prohibit criticism that was 'expressed in the more robust, colourful or intemperate language of the tabloid press or even in language which is crude, insulting and vulgar'.[140] Judges were expected to be able to take such criticisms in their stride. Munby J even commented that most criticism is 'healthy'.[141] In 1985, Lord Diplock described the offence of scandalising the court as 'virtually obsolescent'[142] and it was finally abolished in 2013 following recommendations of the Law Commission. As with changes in contempt of court since the *Sunday Times* case discussed earlier, the history of the offence illustrates the shifting attitude to legal institutions, which no longer need to be shielded from public opinion. By permitting greater criticism, the abolition of the offence complements the rationale for open justice.

Even without using the criminal law to protect the courts from attack, an ambivalence towards public criticism of the courts remains. The tension between scrutiny and confidence was illustrated in the 1980s when television journalists revealed a number of miscarriages of justice in the BBC programme *Rough Justice*. While exposing miscarriages of justice is a part of the media's watchdog function and a matter of public interest, some judges condemned such investigations. This time, Lord Denning took a position that contrasted sharply with his earlier celebrations of open justice and scrutiny, stating:

> after a decision has been given by judge and jury, the media must not go round trying to get what they call 'fresh evidence' so as to show, if they can, the decision was wrong. That is undermining our system of Justice altogether.[143]

When asked whether this meant that the perceived integrity of the judicial system was more important than the fate of an innocent person, Lord Denning replied 'Certainly' and added that the integrity of the system is 'one of the foundations of our society'.[144] In a parliamentary debate, Lord Denning said that errors in the system should be corrected through the internal processes of appeal, rather than through review in the media.[145] Review in the media, he thought, was as objectionable as trial by media. In that view, challenges were best dealt with by the formal institutions charged with the

---

[138]   ibid.

[139]   *Harris v Harris* [2001] 2 FLR 895 at [372].

[140]   ibid, [372].

[141]   ibid.

[142]   *Secretary of State for Defence v Guardian Newspapers* [1985] AC 339 at 347. As early as 1941, Justice Frankfurter, in the US, stated the offence had 'long since been disavowed in England' and had 'never found lodgment here'. See *Bridges v California* 314 US 252 (1941) at 287.

[143]   Lord Denning in a BBC interview, rebroadcast in 'Retrial by TV: The Rise and Fall of Rough Justice', *Timeshift*, April 2011.

[144]   ibid.

[145]   HL Deb 09 April 1986, vol 473, col 289.

relevant task. However, Lord Denning's objection is misplaced, as 'trial by media' is not directly comparable with the public scrutiny of a judicial decision. While both may discuss the possible guilt of a party, the latter focuses on the conduct of a public body that should be an object for public attention.

Even in the current political climate, where politicians are seen to be fair game for the harshest styles of newspaper reporting, reservations are still expressed when courts are subject to strong criticism. The *Daily Mail's* front page declaration that three High Court judges were 'Enemies of the People' following a Brexit-related ruling caused much concern about the rule of law being undermined.[146] Such reporting may not be fair or sensible, but what is striking is that the media was criticised on the basis that the reporting could undermine the status of the institution. Public criticism is still seen to create special problems for the judiciary.

The ambivalence about the relationship between public opinion and the courts is also found in the Article 10 jurisprudence. While the domestic law no longer criminalises the 'scandalising' of the court, the Strasbourg jurisprudence leaves it open for the state to impose some controls on statements attacking the judiciary. Under Article 10(2) expression can be subject to restrictions that serve the legitimate aim of 'maintaining the authority and impartiality of the judiciary'.[147] The European Court of Human Rights has noted the tension in dealing with criticisms of the judiciary. On the one hand, the Court has recognised the importance of the media checking whether the judges are 'discharging their heavy responsibilities in a manner that is in conformity with the aim which is the basis of the task entrusted to them'.[148] At the same time, a court 'must enjoy public confidence if it is to be successful in carrying out its duties',[149] and judges do not normally defend themselves from public attacks. The need to protect confidence in an institution means that the Court will engage in a slightly different balancing exercise for criticism of judges than with the criticism of politicians.[150]

In deciding where the balance lies, much depends on whether a statement is characterised as a fair criticism of the court or as an unproven attack on the judges. Some decisions of the Strasbourg Court have been criticised for being too willing to take the latter view.[151] In *Barford v Denmark*, the European Court of Human Rights found that a criminal conviction for questioning the impartiality of two lay judges that worked for the government did not violate Article 10. The Court reasoned that the statement was 'not a criticism of the reasoning' of the court nor was it a criticism of the composition of the court, but an unproven personal attack on the judges.[152] In *Prager*, a journalist was convicted in defamation law after publishing an article claiming the members of a Vienna Court regularly acted unfairly and harshly towards defendants.[153] The Court found the conviction did not violate Article 10 on the grounds that it amounted

---

[146] See 'Enemies of the People' *Daily Mail* (4 November 2016) and Lord Neuberger in an interview with BBC Radio Four's Today Programme (16 February 2017).
[147] Art 10(2).
[148] *Prager and Oberschlick v Austria* (1996) 21 EHRR 1 at [34].
[149] ibid.
[150] Compare with criticism of politicians in Ch 2.
[151] See discussion in I Cram, *A Virtue Less Cloistered* (Oxford, Hart, 2002) 175–78.
[152] *Barfod v Denmark* (1991) 13 EHRR 493 at [35].
[153] *Prager and Oberschlick v Austria* (n 148).

to unfounded attack. However, the decisions have not all been in one direction and the Court has been more willing to protect expression where it is based on thorough research, made in good faith, is a statement of opinion and contributes to a debate of public interest.[154] The determination is fact sensitive, but the Article 10 jurisprudence leaves considerable scope for controlling attacks on the court.[155]

The stance of the earlier decisions that shielded the judiciary sit uneasily with the prevailing political culture. In the current climate, no public institution is *entitled* to the public's confidence. Instead, confidence is something that is earned and established in the course of public debate, which requires criticism to be freely aired.[156] In so far as there are fears that criticism might undermine public confidence in the courts, the current strategy for averting such an effect seems to involve greater reliance on public relations than on legal restriction. Like other major institutions, the courts now place less emphasis on forms of censorship and publisher liability, and take a more proactive role in shaping public opinion and the understanding of their work through their communications and relations with the media, which will be discussed later.

ii. Informational Functions

Open justice is not just about improving the functioning of the justice system, but also has an informational value. By reporting on the court processes, the media helps to inform the public on the workings of the system of justice and the judiciary. In addition, some cases may reveal something important about society in general. In *Harman*, Lord Scarman stated that 'trials will sometimes expose matters of public interest worthy of discussion other than the judicial task of doing justice between the parties in the particular case'.[157] A judicial hearing about a racist attack may reveal details about the prevalence of certain attitudes and social problems, for example.

Court proceedings also provide an important source of information for journalists. The evidence disclosed in court is on oath and will often help journalists look behind the public relations gloss in official government communications. By observing the process, the journalist may encounter evidence and documents that would not otherwise come to light. This can provide the basis for further investigations and also help in verifying stories already under investigation.[158] Such access can sometimes raise strategic considerations for litigants. For example, proceedings may be brought with the hope that certain information will be revealed in court, while in other cases parties may avoid litigation to prevent certain information being accessed. Of course, aiding newsgathering cannot be the central reason for open justice, and in *Binyam Mohamed*

---

[154] *De Haes v Belgium*, App no 19983/92 (1998) 25 EHRR 1.

[155] Many of the cases before the Strasbourg Court are concerned with individual defamation claims, see Law Commission, *Contempt of Court: Scandalising the Court, A Consultation Paper* (Law Com CP 207, 2012) at [49].

[156] See *Derbyshire CC v Times Newspapers* [1993] AC 534, [1993] 2 WLR 449, showing that the protection of the reputation of a public institution is not itself a reason for restricting speech.

[157] *Harman* (n 133) 316. See also Fenwick and Phillipson (n 2) 169–70.

[158] See the evidence discussed by the Joint Committee on Human Rights, *Twenty Fourth Report of the Session of 2010–12, The Justice and Security Green Paper* (2012 HL 286, HC 1777) at [199].

it was said that 'the courts do not function in order to provide the media with copy, or to provide ammunition for the media'.[159] However, the evidence in court proceedings can play an important role in the newsgathering process, and this should not be overlooked when weighing up the competing interests.

iii. Furthering the Goals of the Legal System

Open justice can also have a very different type of public information value, in so far as it tells the public about the possible consequences of their actions. The reporting of court proceedings means that people are alert to the types of conduct that will attract prosecution or a civil claim. In addition to the warning function, the courts in England and Wales have noted 'the valuable deterrent effect that the identification of those guilty of at least serious crimes may have on others'.[160] More controversially, the publicity can be seen as an informal element of punishment following a criminal conviction.[161] Such publicity will only be effective for certain types of crime, and in some circles a criminal conviction may even work as a badge of honour. However, in so far as publicity is desirable, both the deterrent and punitive functions rely on the media to carry details of the conviction. For example, the *Manchester Evening News* website has a monthly report titled 'Locked Up' providing a photograph of those recently convicted and summary of the crime. Many crime reports in the press also use language associated with shaming, with certain types of criminal often labelled as a 'fiend' or 'monster'. The approach is controversial, as the stigma attached to certain types of crime may be disproportionate to the gravity of the offence and undermine the goals of rehabilitation. In some countries the identities of convicted criminals are not routinely publicised and such identification is not required under Article 6 of the ECHR.[162] However, in the UK, naming a convicted defendant is 'a normal consequence of his crime'.[163] This function of publicity is problematic in so far as it gives an informal punitive function to the media and public opinion, while the courts are supposed to determine what sort of sanction is appropriate.[164] For as much as judges frown upon 'trial by media', the system relies on the media to assist in the deterrent effects of post-trial publicity.

Practices of naming and shaming criminals stand in contrast to the classic arguments that the media acts as a check on the state. Instead, the media advances the work of the state by encouraging greater compliance with the law. Of course, this is

---

[159] *R (on the application of Mohamed) v Secretary of State for Foreign and Commonwealth Affairs* (n 125) at [242].

[160] Hooper LJ in *R (on the application of Y) v Aylesbury Crown Court* [2012] EWHC 1140 (Admin), [2012] Crim LR 893 at [44].

[161] See Jaconelli (n 122) 273. J Spencer, 'Naming and Shaming Young Offenders' (2000) 59 *Cambridge Law Journal* 466–68. For discussion of these issues see J Rowbottom, 'To Punish, Inform and Criticise' in J Petley (ed), *Media and Public Shaming* (London, IB Taurus, 2013).

[162] See J Jacobs and E Larrauri, 'Are criminal convictions a public matter? The USA and Spain' (2012) 14 *Punishment and Society* 3, contrasting the limits in Spain with the freedom to publish in the USA.

[163] *R (on the application of Trinity Mirror Plc) v Croydon Crown Court* [2008] EWCA Crim 50, [2008] QB 770.

[164] *R (on the application of Ellis) v Chief Constable of Essex* [2003] EWHC 1321 (Admin), [2003] 2 FLR 566 at [30].

something the media has done in practice for a long time, not just through the reporting of the legal proceedings, but also through the various narratives of crime reporting in general.[165] However, the reporting of legal proceedings is not unwanted publicity that the government is required to tolerate, but for much of the time is a tool for social control that aids the state.

B. Limits on Open Justice

The court can impose limits on access to the courts under its own inherent jurisdiction.[166] While the decision in *Scott* offers a strong statement in favour of open justice, Lord Haldane accepted that cases involving wards of court and 'lunatics' were exceptions to the principle.[167] Lord Haldane also stated that the open justice principle could be limited where necessary for the attainment of justice.[168] On this view, restrictions may be necessary in cases concerning trade secrets, in which publicity would destroy the subject matter of the proceedings.[169] In *Leveller*, Lord Diplock stated that as the rationale for the principle is to serve justice, it can be overridden when the interests of justice so require.[170] Where the courts impose a limit on open justice under their own inherent jurisdiction, the restriction must be 'to no more than the extent that the court reasonably believes it to be necessary in order to serve the ends of justice'.[171] Anyone seeking to displace the general rule thereby faces a heavy burden. In *Scott v Scott*, Lord Shaw stated that the mere 'fear of giving evidence in public' alone is not a reason for conducting the hearing away from the public, even if it would deter people from bringing proceedings.[172] However, the exceptions are flexible and have expanded to offer greater protection for litigants in some cases. In *A v BBC*, Lord Reed explained that the exceptions are not closed and 'open justice may change in response to changes in society and in the administration of justice'.[173] For example, in some cases the principle may need to be departed from to protect 'a party or witness whose safety may be endangered or who may suffer commercial ruin if his identity becomes known' or 'where the decision turns on intimate medical evidence'.[174] In such a case, a departure from the principle would be necessary to prevent painful and humiliating disclosures of personal information, as long as there is no countervailing public interest.[175]

In addition to the inherent jurisdiction of the courts, the rights under the ECHR also provide a basis for departing from open justice.[176] The terms of Article 6 provide

---

[165] See C Greer and R Reiner, 'Mediated Mayhem: Media, Crime, Criminal Justice' in M Maguire, R Morgan, and R Reiner, *The Oxford Handbook of Criminology* (Oxford, Oxford University Press, 2012).

[166] Though in *Khuja* (n 16) at [18], Lord Sumption stated that the inherent jurisdiction powers relate to access and do not extend to reporting restrictions.

[167] *Scott v Scott* (n 114) 437.

[168] ibid, 438. For criticism, see Lord Halsbury, 442–43.

[169] See Lord Shaw *Scott v Scott*, ibid, 482–83.

[170] *A-G v Leveller Magazine Ltd* (n 118) 450.

[171] ibid, 450.

[172] Lord Shaw in *Scott v Scott* (n 114) 484–85.

[173] *A v BBC* (n 124) at [40].

[174] ibid, at [41].

[175] ibid.

[176] *In re S (a child)* [2004] UKHL 47, [2005] 1 AC 593 at [23].

a set of interests that can justify the exclusion of the public and the press where necessary.[177] Other Convention rights can also qualify the open justice principle. For example, in a case dealing with privacy or where publicity may expose a person to a risk of torture in their home country, the courts may be required to limit access to and reporting of the trial in order to protect Article 3 and 8 rights.[178] Along these lines the ECHR may offer greater scope for open justice to be balanced with other competing rights than under the common law.[179] Further limits to open justice are imposed by statute. The statutory restrictions are automatic for certain classes of cases, while in other types of case the judge has a statutory discretion to limit access or reporting.

Where the court has a discretionary power (whether under inherent jurisdiction, statute or in applying the ECHR), the judge will normally enter into a type of balancing exercise to decide whether to limit access to the court, impose restrictions on the reporting of proceedings, or lift such restrictions. In striking the balance, the courts will weigh up a number of issues, such as the public interest in knowing the information, the watchdog function of the media and the harm that could flow from publicity.

i. Types of Restriction: Access and Reporting

To decide if a limit on open justice is proportionate or not, the court will look at the type of restriction. A restriction on access to the courts, preventing people sitting in on a case and seeing the supporting documents, is a significant curtailment of the principle and will require a strong justification. Open justice is not all or nothing, and restrictions can be imposed on access to parts of a hearing, while allowing access to other parts. Another type of control is a restriction on the reporting of what happened in open court or key facts about the case. The reporting restrictions allow the media to attend the hearing and gather information that is relevant to its investigations, even if it cannot directly say what has happened. The impact of reporting restrictions should not be underestimated, as it amounts to a prior restraint on expression. Lord Sumption has stated that restricting the reporting of a case that has been seen and heard amounts to 'direct censorship'.[180]

A common limit on open justice is to withhold the identity of a person in the proceedings or restrict the reporting of that person's identity (or both). In *A v BBC*, the Supreme Court upheld a decision not to disclose the identity of an individual that was to be deported following his conviction for a sex offence, as revealing such information would have posed a risk of serious harm and ill-treatment in his country of origin.[181] The practice is also common in privacy cases, for obvious reasons. An anonymity order is less restrictive than a denial of access to the court, and many of the benefits of open justice (such as scrutiny) can be secured even if the public are not informed of

---

[177] Art 6 of the ECHR provides: 'the press and public may be excluded from all or part of the trial in the interests of morals, public order or national security in a democratic society, where the interests of juveniles or the protection of the private life of the parties so require, or to the extent strictly necessary in the opinion of the court in special circumstances where publicity would prejudice the interests of justice'.

[178] Lord Neuberger, *Bank Mellat v HM Treasury (No 1)* [2013] UKSC 38, [2014] AC 700 at [2].

[179] See Robertson and Nicol (n 28) 15–18.

[180] *Khuja* (n 16) at [16].

[181] *A v BBC* (n 124).

the names of the parties.[182] However, an anonymity order can still have a significant impact on media freedom. In *Ahmed*, Lord Rodger noted that the media will need to identify individuals in order to give stories a personal angle that is more appealing to the potential audience.[183] He also warned against the use of restrictions on the assumption that the media should report a story 'in some austere, abstract form, devoid of much of its human interest'.[184] The issue is not simply about making a story more interesting for the audience. Information about a person's identity can be crucial to the understanding and interpretation of events, by helping to contextualise the facts of a case in a way that is difficult when referring to a person by a letter.

The Supreme Court in *Khuja* had to consider whether to allow the media to report the name of a person that had once been arrested in relation to a crime (without any charge), but who had been mentioned in open court proceedings to which he was not a party. The claimant argued that such disclosure of his arrest would interfere with the right to a private and family life. In the earlier case of *Ahmed*, Lord Rodger had found that publishing the name of a person subject to an investigation or charge would not normally pose a risk that justifies a restriction on publication, and stated that 'the law proceeds on the basis that most members of the public understand that, even when charged with an offence, you are innocent unless and until proved guilty in a court of law'.[185] That approach ascribes a level of sophistication to the audience and assumes they will not jump to a conclusion that a person is guilty. In *Khuja*, Lord Sumption accepted that the public may misinterpret information, but found that such risks were inherent in open justice and did not justify a restriction on reporting.[186] In his view, the public are simply entitled to know some details. In a dissent in the same case, Lord Kerr and Lord Wilson rejected an approach that ascribes the desired level of sophistication to the audience, and focused on the reality that publicity can harm individual rights and undermine the presumption of innocence.[187] The dissenters drew on past examples to show the devastating effect that media publicity can have, and stressed the problems with trial by media, although the concern was framed in terms of the protection of individual rights rather than the authority of the court.[188] Neither the majority nor dissenters expressed their view in absolute terms and they recognised that a different balance may be warranted depending on circumstances. Nonetheless the different approaches reveal contrasting views on the right of the public to receive information and the effect of the media disclosures on the public, which are recurring debates in media law.

A court decision that a certain matter should not be disclosed in open court does not mean the media is automatically prohibited from reporting the information. However, the media publication of withheld material would undermine the court's decision not to reveal the information in the first place. This issue arises where, for

---

[182] *R (on the application of C) v Secretary of State for Justice (Media Lawyers Association intervening)* [2016] UKSC 2, [2016] 1 WLR 444 at [18].
[183] *Ahmed v HM Treasury* (n 16) at [63].
[184] ibid.
[185] ibid, [66].
[186] *Khuja* (n 16) at [34]. See also Lord Rodger in *Ahmed*, ibid, at [60].
[187] *Khuja*, ibid, [55].
[188] ibid, [49].

example, the court withholds the name of a witness in a hearing, but a journalist none-theless finds out who that person is and wishes to reveal the identity in a report about the proceedings. Prior to 1981, there was some uncertainty as to whether the court had the power to prohibit the publication of such material. In 1974, the Phillimore Committee noted this uncertainty in relation to a case where two blackmail victims had been named in a publication, and recommended the introduction of a statutory power to prohibit the publication of such information.[189] That recommendation was followed with the enactment of s 11 of the Contempt of Court Act 1981, which pro-vides that where the court has the power to withhold a name or other matter from the public, an order can be made prohibiting the publication of the information in con-nection with the proceedings. The provision does not give the court any new power to withhold information, but where there is such a power in existence, the court may also issue an order to restrain publication.[190]

Another important power is under s 12 of the Administration of Justice Act 1960, which provides that it is a contempt to publish details relating to certain specified types of private proceedings.[191] The provision seeks to ensure that media reporting does not undermine the purpose of excluding the public from the hearing in various types of sensitive case. In other areas, the regulation of media reporting also comes from spe-cific statutory provisions dealing with that category of case.

ii. Prejudice to Hearings by Reporting the Courts

Where a hearing is held in open court, the reporting of the case can come into tension with contempt of court law if the facts revealed at a trial will prejudice the outcome of another set of proceedings. For example, two people may be tried separately in rela-tion to crimes arising from the same set of facts. This could arise if two people commit a burglary and in the course of that crime one of the individuals kills someone. One defendant may be charged with murder and the other with burglary, dealt with in sepa-rate trials, but concerning the same events. If one of these cases is heard earlier, then the conclusions of the court could prejudice the decision of the later trial. Normally open justice is protected by the provision that publishers will not be guilty of contempt under the strict liability rule for 'a fair and accurate report of legal proceedings held in public, published contemporaneously and in good faith'.[192] However, where there is a substantial risk of prejudice to any future legal proceedings, the court may issue an order postponing the publication of the report.[193] That approach has the advantage of providing some clarity for the media on occasions where there are multiple hearings

---

[189] Phillimore LJ (Chairman), Report of the Committee on Contempt of Court (Cmnd 5794, 1974) at [141], fn 72, referring to *R v Socialist Worker Printers & Publishers Ltd, ex p Attorney General* [1975] QB 637.

[190] *Ahmed v HM Treasury* (n 16) at [31].

[191] The provision applies to private hearings relating to certain issues of childcare, mental health, national security, confidential research and also where the court has prohibited information relating to the private proceedings.

[192] Contempt of Court Act 1981, s 4(1).

[193] ibid, s 4(2).

relating to the same facts or people. However, such measures are also prior restraints and can attract controversy. While the court looks at the same factors as for the strict liability rule in contempt (such as the robustness of jurors) when deciding if there is a substantial risk, the court also has to decide whether such a 'drastic' measure is necessary and consider the public interest in allowing publication.[194] While there have in the past been concerns about courts being too willing to impose such orders,[195] more recent guidance has stressed that such powers should be used as a 'last resort'.[196]

C. Restrictions: Three Examples

There are specific rules regulating access to the courts and reporting, which vary according to the type of court and issue at stake. The rules are numerous and detailed, but several key areas will be discussed briefly to illustrate the methods and difficulties of limiting open justice.[197]

i. National Security

If a court hearing concerns an issue or evidence that raises national security issues, then some restriction on open justice will be necessary. Details of ongoing covert operations or information revealing the identity of security service sources cannot be freely provided in open court. The inherent jurisdiction of the court allows for open justice to be balanced with competing factors and, where necessary, proceedings can be held in camera for the protection of national security.[198] The court will permit this where, for example, an open hearing would undermine the administration of justice by deterring the prosecution of a case.[199] There are also statutory provisions that allow for limits on public access. Where prosecutions are brought under the Official Secrets Acts, the court can exclude the public (or parts of the public) from any part of the hearing if evidence or statements in court would jeopardise national safety, although the passing of the sentence takes place in public.[200] The publicity at sentencing thereby allows for the deterrent and punitive effects discussed earlier, even where the public are not to know of the details of the hearing.

Where a hearing takes place in private for national security reasons, any reporting of the events in court will be a contempt of court under the Administration of

---

[194] *R (on the application of Telegraph Group plc) v Sherwood* [2001] EWCA Crim 1075, [2001] 1 WLR 1983 at [22]. Unlike s 2 of the Contempt of Court Act 1981, s 4 does not require the prejudice to be 'serious'.

[195] *Ex p News Group Newspapers* (1999) *Times*, 21 May 1999.

[196] *R (on the application of Press Association) v Cambridge Crown Court* [2012] EWCA Crim 2434, [2013] 1 WLR 1979 at [13].

[197] In discussing these issues, I have benefited from the useful overview in E Barendt, J Bosland, R Craufurd Smith and L Hitchens, *Media Law: Text, Cases and Materials* (Harlow, Pearson, 2014) Ch 13.

[198] See P Scott, 'An Inherent Jurisdiction to Protect the Public Interest' (2016) 27 *King's Law Journal* 259, 269. See the Civil Procedure Rules 1998, Part 39.2.

[199] *Guardian News and Media Ltd v Incedal* [2014] EWCA Crim 1861, [2015] 1 Cr App R 4 at [17].

[200] Official Secrets Act 1920, s 8(4) and Official Secrets Act 1989, s 11(4).

Justice Act 1960, s 12(1)(c). Where the proceedings do not take place in private, but information is withheld from the court, publishing the withheld information could be subject to a reporting restriction under the Contempt of Court Act 1981, s 11.[201] On occasions the courts have allowed accredited journalists to attend parts of private hearings relating to security issues, while excluding the public and imposing reporting restrictions.[202] While that allows the process to be observed, the imposition of reporting restrictions means that public accountability primarily lies in the hands of the formal political channels, for example through the Intelligence and Security Committee of Parliament.[203]

While there are obvious reasons for restrictions on open justice in cases that raise security issues, the controls can be a source of controversy. This is not least because claims of government secrecy that underpin certain legal proceedings are often viewed with suspicion for the reasons set out in Chapter 4. Controls restricting the reporting of court hearings relating to the government's attempts to suppress information or punish the source of leaked information are therefore likely to be viewed in a similar light. For example, in *R v Times Newspapers*, the proceedings in court concerned the prosecution of a civil servant for the leak of a letter containing details of a meeting between Tony Blair and George Bush in 2004 discussing the war in Iraq.[204] To some, the leak of the letter was an act in the public interest in so far as it aimed to inform the public about the war. The prosecution was criticised as an attempt to protect government interests, as opposed to national security.[205] The fact the civil servant was prosecuted for the leak can be seen to add a further public interest element, in seeing how the legal process deals with such matters and ensuring fair proceedings. The court imposed a reporting restriction under the Contempt of Court Act 1981, s 11, prohibiting publications 'in connection with these proceedings' revealing the content of the letter.[206] While the order was limited and sought only to protect the administration of justice,[207] it can be seen to compound the problem by adding another layer of control to preserve secrecy, where the government's underlying legal right is thought by some not to deserve protection.[208] The underlying problem, however, lies with the over-protection of official information, rather than with the powers of the court to protect its proceedings.

A more extreme restriction on open justice can be found in closed material proceedings, which allows the government to rely on evidence that is not disclosed in open court or to the other party to the proceedings. There are obvious reasons why in some

---

[201] *R v Times Newspapers* [2007] EWCA Crim 1925, [2008] 1 WLR 234.

[202] *Incedal* (2014) (n 199). However, the court has warned that the presence of journalists can pose challenges for the management of the trial, *Guardian News and Media v Incedal* [2016] EWCA Crim 11, [2016] 1 WLR 1767 at [66].

[203] *Incedal* (2016) ibid, at [75].

[204] *R v Times Newspapers* (2007) (n 201).

[205] See R Norton Taylor, 'For their eyes only' *The Guardian* (13 October 2006), and 'Two convicted in trial over leaked Bush-Blair memo' *The Guardian* (10 May 2007).

[206] The Court of Appeal overturned a broader order that had been imposed by the trial judge that prohibited publication of material in relation to the proceedings that 'might reveal' the protected information, *R v Times Newspapers* (2007) (n 201) at [33].

[207] ibid, [34]–[35].

[208] See discussion in K Ewing, *Bonfire of the Liberties* (Oxford, Oxford University Press, 2010) 162.

cases it may be undesirable to disclose sensitive evidence to a member of a terrorist network, but still proceed with a legal action or defence.[209] A key difference with other restrictions on open justice is that in a closed material procedure the other party cannot attend the parts of the court hearing dealing with the secret evidence and therefore does not have the chance to challenge the evidence directly. Instead, a special advocate represents the other party. The restriction is such an extreme limit on a fair procedure that it cannot be established under the court's inherent jurisdiction and can only be authorised by statute.[210] The procedure was first used in the UK in relation to immigration and terrorism cases, and has more recently been extended in civil claims.[211] While the central criticism of the procedure relates to the limitation of natural justice, closed material proceedings also represent a significant restriction on media freedom, as the hearing and evidence remains secret. The lack of public scrutiny, alongside the defendant's procedural disadvantages, heightens the risks to the quality of the decision-making process and public confidence that open justice is supposed to secure.

ii. Family Law

Family law proceedings are normally heard in private.[212] The need for secrecy in some family law cases is obvious, as such proceedings will often involve highly personal private information. In many cases children will be involved, so the privacy interests may be more sensitive and there will be concerns about publicity harming the well-being of the child. A child may also be particularly uncomfortable giving full and frank evidence knowing that a journalist may report on the proceedings.[213]

The perceived secrecy of the family courts has led to criticisms about a lack of transparency, public knowledge and accountability.[214] However, in recent years, steps have been taken to secure greater public confidence by making the process more transparent. Under guidelines from 2014, the courts are now more likely to publish judgments in family law cases.[215] While the family courts are normally closed to members of the public, representatives of the media are usually allowed to attend the proceedings.[216] This default right to attend applies only to accredited members of the press, which shows how certain media institutions enjoy rights not held by the general public.[217] An application can be made to exclude media representatives, for example where

---

[209] While the law of public interest immunity allows for the non-disclosure of sensitive information, the effect is that neither party can rely on the withheld evidence. Accordingly, where crucial evidence is of such sensitivity, the government may not proceed with its case (or parts of it).

[210] *Al Rawi v Security Services* [2011] UKSC 34, [2012] 1 AC 531.

[211] Justice and Security Act 2013, ss 6–14.

[212] See Family Procedure Rules 2010, SI 2010/2955, r 27.10 in relation to the High Court and Family Court; in relation to appeals, see Domestic and Appellate Proceedings (Restriction of Publicity) Act 1968, s 1.

[213] *Re X (Disclosure of Information)* [2001] 2 FLR 440 at [24]. Barendt, Bosland, Craufurd-Smith and Hitchens (n 197) 637.

[214] *Re X (A Child) (Residence and Contact: Rights of Media Attendance)* [2009] EWHC 1728 (Fam), [2009] EMLR 26 at [32]–[33].

[215] Practice Guidance Issued by the President of the Division, *Transparency in the Family Courts: Publication of Judgments* [2014] 1 WLR 230.

[216] Family Procedure Rules 2010, r 27.11.

[217] See discussion in Ch 1.

necessary 'in the interests of any child' concerned or connected with the proceedings, for the safety of a party, witness or connected person, for the orderly conduct of proceedings, or where 'justice will otherwise be impeded or prejudiced'.[218]

While the media will normally have the right to attend the family court, there is no general right to access documents filed in family court proceedings and an application has to be made to the court for such access.[219] The journalists sitting in on family proceedings are often subject to reporting restrictions. In particular, the Administration of Justice Act 1960 prohibits the publication of documents filed or accounts of what happened in front of a judge in certain types of private hearing, but does not restrict an account of the nature of the dispute or certain bare facts.[220] The provision also means that a parent in such proceedings cannot tell a journalist what happened in court even on a confidential basis, which is a significant restriction on the parties' freedom to speak.[221] In addition, children involved in certain proceedings dealing with powers under the Children Act 1989 or the Adoption and Children Act 2002 are not to be publicly identified.[222] As well as the automatic restrictions on reporting, the judge will often have the discretion to relax or increase the reporting restrictions, in which case the judge will undertake a balancing exercise examining the competing interests.[223]

The right of the media to attend family cases demonstrates a level of trust that journalists will respect the reporting restrictions and not leak any details. While that approach represents differential treatment based on the status of the speaker, there are good reasons for providing such a privilege to the established media. Such entities are located within the jurisdiction and will be known to the relevant authorities, making it easier to enforce the restrictions in the event of a breach. As repeat players in the process, the established media will also want to secure a reputation for respecting the restrictions in order to continue gaining access in future. By contrast, there may be stronger concerns that a blogger based overseas does not have as strong incentive for following the restrictions.[224] The professional journalist is also more likely to have an understanding about the types of information that can be reported under the restrictions and thereby avoid inadvertent disclosures.

The court will undertake a balancing exercise to decide whether to exclude the media, to allow access to documents, or impose or lift reporting restrictions. In any of these exercises, the courts will weigh the interests in privacy and the rights of the child with the arguments for open justice. In approaching the balancing exercise, the courts recognise that there is a general public interest in people knowing what is happening in court that will be present in most cases.[225] However, as with privacy cases, the weight

---

[218] Family Procedure Rules 2010, r 27.11(3).

[219] Family Procedure Rules, Practice Direction 29.12. See G Millar and A Scott, *Newsgathering: Law Regulation and the Public Interest* (Oxford, Oxford University Press, 2016) 236–40.

[220] Administration of Justice Act 1960, s 12. See *Re B* [2004] EWHC 411 (Fam), [2004] 2 FLR 142 at [82].

[221] M Hanna, 'Irreconcilable Differences: The Attempts to Increase Media Coverage of Family Courts in England and Wales' (2012) 4 *Journal of Media Law* 274, 278.

[222] Children Act 1989, s 97.

[223] *Re Webster (A Child)* [2006] EWHC 2733 (Fam), [2007] EMLR 7 at [53].

[224] *Re X (A Child)* (n 214) at [66]–[67]. Though Hanna argues that the misconduct of the foreign media should not lead to the exclusion of all media, Hanna (n 221) 293.

[225] *Spencer v Spencer* [2009] EWHC 1529 (Fam), [2009] EMLR 25.

attached to media freedom will be variable. Simply that the family in question is in the public eye does not make the case a matter of public interest.[226] The court will also consider whether the measure is proportionate. For example, an order to exclude the media from the whole hearing is the most drastic measure, and in many cases it will be more proportionate to exclude the media either from a part of a hearing or apply reporting restrictions.[227]

Stronger arguments for transparency come into play when a public body is involved in the case.[228] For example, a decision to take a child into care is a far-reaching intervention into family life that should be subject to checks and accountability mechanisms.[229] The free speech rights of the parents, who may wish to talk about their treatment at the hands of the state, are also stake.[230] Particular weight to transparency will be given where there is an allegation of a miscarriage of justice.[231] A reporting restriction cannot be imposed for fear that a local authority will be subject to unfair criticism.[232] Where the actions of the public body are in question, there is a public interest in knowing about the case.

Given the limits on reporting, there is a question as to whether journalists will have any reason to attend family proceedings. Holman J once commented in the family court that to 'permit the presence of accredited journalists, but then tightly to restrict what they can report, creates a mere illusion of transparency'.[233] However, some value may be obtained in attending the hearing and acquiring background knowledge about the family courts. By allowing the media to comment on the nature of the case, they are 'enabled to exercise a role of "watchdog" on the part of the public at large and to observe family justice at work for the purpose of informed comment upon its workings and the behaviour of its judges', even if 'they are unable to report in their newspapers or programmes the identity of the parties or the details of the evidence which are likely to catch the eye and engage the interest of the average reader or viewer'.[234] Moreover, a journalist that has witnessed the proceedings will be better placed to challenge any reporting restrictions that are imposed.

Despite these factors, there is some force in Holman J's criticism and journalists have a limited return on time spent observing the family courts, so media attendance will be reserved for the more exceptional cases.[235] However, the legal restrictions are not the only explanation for limited reporting of the courts' proceedings. The decision not to report most family cases may have more to do with the news values and limited budgets of the media than with legal controls. One judge noted that the interest in the

---

[226] ibid.

[227] ibid at [60].

[228] *Re Webster (A Child)* (n 223) at [74].

[229] *Re B* (2004) (n 223); *Re B* [2007] EWHC 1622 (Fam), [2008] 1 FLR 482 at [18].

[230] See *Re Webster (A Child)* (n 223) at [100].

[231] ibid, at [99].

[232] *Re B* [2007] EWHC 1622 (Fam), [2008] 1 FLR 482.

[233] *Fields v Fields* [2015] EWHC 1670 (Fam) at [3].

[234] *Re X (A Child)* (2009) (n 214) at [38]. See also *DL v SL* [2015] EWHC 2621 (Fam), [2016] 1 WLR 1259 at [1].

[235] Hanna (n 221) 279. See also *Re Al Hilli (Reporting Restrictions)* [2013] EWHC 2190 (Fam), [2014] 1 FLR 403 at [28].

workings of family courts tends to arise when the case affects a celebrity, but otherwise the press galleries in courts remain quiet.[236]

iii. Children in Criminal Proceedings

In criminal proceedings, the normal rule is that the public and the media can access the hearing and name the individuals involved. However, in addition to the inherent powers of the court to restrict access, there are statutory powers to exclude the public to protect children in criminal cases. In proceedings for offences 'against, or any conduct contrary to, decency or morality', the court can exclude persons from the court where a child or young person is called as a witness.[237] However, that provision is not to be used to 'authorise the exclusion of bona fide representatives of a newspaper or news agency'.[238] The court also has the power under the Youth Justice and Criminal Evidence Act 1999 to exclude people from the court when a child (or vulnerable person) gives evidence in a sexual offences case or where there are reasonable grounds for believing a person will, or will seek to, intimidate the witness.[239] If the order to exclude under the 1999 Act includes members of the media, then the media organisations can collectively nominate a representative to remain in court for the proceedings. That ensures that one person from the media is at least in a position to challenge the reporting restrictions. While those rules regulate young persons in the ordinary court, in the youth court the usual assumptions about open justice are reversed and the default rule is that proceedings are closed to the public. However, an exception is made for 'bona fide representatives of newspapers or news agencies', who are permitted to attend.[240] In all these examples, the accredited media professionals enjoy a privilege not enjoyed by the general public.

The main controls to protect children come in the form of reporting restrictions.[241] When criminal proceedings take place in the youth court, automatic reporting restrictions are applied that prohibit the publication of any matter that is likely to lead to the identification of a child 'concerned in the proceedings' (a defendant, victim or witness).[242] Where it is in the public interest to do so, the judge can dispense with the reporting restrictions in relation to a child that has been convicted of an offence (and thereby allow identification of the defendant).[243] Outside the youth courts, the presumption is that criminal proceedings in the Crown Court and magistrates' court can be reported, unless stated otherwise. The judge has the power to impose reporting restrictions on the identity of a victim, defendant or witness for as long as that person

---

[236] *Spencer v Spencer* (n 225) at [64].

[237] Children and Young Persons Act 1933, s 37.

[238] ibid.

[239] Youth Justice and Criminal Evidence Act 1999, s 25.

[240] Children and Young Persons Act 1933, s 47.

[241] For a useful summary, see *Reporting Restrictions in the Criminal Courts*, April 2015 (Judicial College) and Barendt, Bosland, Craufurd-Smith and Hitchens (n 197) 633–36.

[242] Children and Young Persons Act 1933, s 49. The restriction applies only for as long as the person is under the age of 18.

[243] ibid, s 49(4A).

is below the age of 18.[244] The special restrictions on open justice in cases involving children are sometimes explained by a need to protect minors from the traumatic effects of publicity and scrutiny. Along these lines, Moore-Bick LJ stated that the restrictions preventing the identification of victims, witnesses and defendants under 18 aim to 'to protect children and young persons who are caught up in legal proceedings from the adverse effects of publicity to which they might otherwise be exposed'.[245]

When deciding whether to apply or lift a reporting restriction, the courts will balance the long-term interests of the child with the public's right to know. Here the courts can consider the potential impact of publicity on a person's welfare, rehabilitation and future prospects.[246] Against this, there may be an interest for the public to know about crimes taking place around them, as well as the interest in open justice in order to detect any faults in the legal process. The workings of the balancing process can be seen where the court has the power to allow the identity of a child defendant to be reported. In *Cornick*, the court named a 16-year-old that had been convicted of murdering a schoolteacher.[247] The case for allowing reporting was strengthened by the public interest in debating matters concerning school security, which would be better informed by the identification of the defendant.[248] The court also took into account the seriousness of the crime and the fact that much information was already public. More controversially, the court considered the role of naming the defendant in deterring others from similar crimes. Coulson J stated that while '[i]ll-informed commentators may scoff', those involved in the criminal justice system know 'that deterrence will almost always be a factor in the naming of those involved in offences such as this'.[249]

While Coulson J is right to point out that such factors are common in the balancing exercise, it is important to ask why such a detail will have an additional deterrent effect given that the media will normally be able to report the facts of the crime and the conviction, even when it cannot name the defendant. One explanation is that naming a person makes the decision more memorable and will have a stronger deterrent effect by gaining more attention. An alternative explanation is that naming a defendant adds to the deterrent by subjecting the convicted criminal to unwanted publicity. The latter consideration, however, stands in sharp contrast to earlier statements made by Lord Bingham that there is no role for 'naming and shaming' when deciding whether to allow a young defendant's name to be reported.[250] Lord Bingham stated that such publicity is not a part of the punishment. The conflicting statements reflect the controversy discussed earlier about whether publicity should be considered an informal

---

[244] Youth Justice and Criminal Evidence Act 1999, s 45. However, s 39 of the Children and Young Persons Act 1933 applies to civil and family proceedings, at the time of writing. The restrictions do not protect the identity of a defendant once he or she has turned 18. However, the judge can impose a lifelong anonymity order for victims and witnesses that continue to apply after they have reached 18, under s 45A of the 1999 Act.

[245] *R (on the application of JC) v Central Criminal Court* [2014] EWCA Civ 1777, [2015] 1 WLR 2865 at [50].

[246] For criticism, see Cram, *A Virtue Less Cloistered* (n 151) 135–37.

[247] *R v Cornick* [2014] EWHC 3623 (QB), [2015] EMLR 9. See also see *R v Winchester Crown Court* [2000] 1 Crim App R 11.

[248] *Cornick*, ibid, at [26].

[249] ibid, at [27].

[250] *McKerry v Teesdale & Wear Valley Justices* (2000) 164 JP 355.

element of the sanction at all, and the concerns about the negative effects of publicity are heightened where the defendant is under 18.

In some exceptional cases, lifelong anonymity orders for defendants have been issued under the Human Rights Act 1998, where necessary to protect the right to life, the prohibition of torture and respect for private and family life. In those few cases, the courts refer to the threat of publicity to rehabilitation, but the lifelong protection is granted only in the most extreme cases where publicity would have a devastating effect and potentially put the life of the offender at risk.[251] Such powers are not limited to children, but the case for anonymity will often be stronger where the defendant is a child.

D. Filming the Courts

Securing a fundamental right to attend and report on court proceedings is an important element of media freedom. However, for the various benefits to flow, the right has to be exercised in practice. In other words, journalists need to show up in court, write up what they saw and publish it. Court reporting has declined in recent years. News budgets have been squeezed, while covering the courts can be costly and offer lower returns to the media. This is not to say that it has died, but that newspapers are likely to invest in reporting only in certain types of case, where a party is well-known or where the facts will generate interest. The point is a symptom of a broader trend, in which intense financial and commercial pressures have impacted on some public interest functions of the media.

There are a number of measures that can help to address this, such as the use of audio-visual media in the court, to allow people to view the process directly rather than relying on reporters. Traditionally, the English courts have not been receptive to any audio or visual recording for public distribution. No photographs can be taken or sketches drawn of a person inside the courtroom during proceedings, under the Criminal Justice Act 1925, s 41. The rationale for the provision is to stop defendants and witnesses being 'pilloried'.[252] As one court put it:

> Justice could not be properly administered if judges or witnesses suffered the pressures, embarrassment and discomfort of being photographed whilst playing their particular role in court with the expectation that every sign, mood, mannerism or observation should later be displayed on the public media.[253]

The provision does not prohibit a person attending the proceedings and drawing a sketch from memory after the event, which explains the use of the distinctive style of drawing that often accompanies television news coverage of a trial. There is a case for change and for photographs to be authorised on certain occasions to promote the public understanding of the courts, as long as it would not undermine the administration

---

[251] See discussion in *A (A Protected Party) v Persons Unknown* [2016] EWHC 3295 (Ch), [2017] EMLR 11.
[252] Jaconelli, *Open Justice* (n 122) 315.
[253] *In re St Andrew's Heddington* [1978] Fam 121, 125.

of justice.[254] However, unauthorised photographs taken using mobile devices in court and posted on the social media are a growing problem. Such photographs can be used to intimidate, ridicule and identify those involved in a case on a particularly stressful occasion, and publication on social media can invite others to comment. To combat this problem, the taking of such 'trophy' photographs has been prosecuted as a common law contempt rather than as a summary offence under s 41, on the grounds that the penalty of imprisonment under contempt is more appropriate and reflects the seriousness of the conduct.[255]

Televising courts raises a wider range of issues beyond the question of photography. Many warn of the danger of the courts becoming a 'media circus', in which lawyers have to play to both the jury and the wider public. However, Joseph Jaconelli notes that the strength of the arguments for or against televising the courts depends on the type of case and the person being filmed.[256] He argues that televising may have little impact on the judge, but could have significant detrimental effects on a defendant in a criminal trial, both in increasing the levels of stress at the time of the trial (whatever the outcome) and undermining the scope for rehabilitation if convicted.[257] In any event, such publicity is accepted for judges and witnesses in some of the major public inquiries. For example, the Leveson Inquiry into press ethics was live streamed and much footage repeated on television news. The potential for televising some court cases is illustrated by the experience in Scotland, where a number of proceedings have been filmed.[258]

The position in England and Wales is beginning to change and there have been a number of experiments for limited broadcasting of court proceedings. Most notably, proceedings in the Supreme Court are excluded from the ban on photographs and sketches.[259] The Supreme Court streams its proceedings live on its website and also has its own YouTube channel. The hearings are also streamed on the *Sky News* website and some are made available via the BBC iPlayer. The filming of the Supreme Court can be seen as part of a broader step to make the top court more accessible. Not only are Supreme Court judgments made available on the Court's website, but a press summary is also provided, which makes the issues and reasoning of the Court clearer to the lay person. Judges on the Supreme Court give public talks and sometimes give interviews to discuss the work of the court. The Court does not attempt to preserve confidence in its workings by punishing critics that 'scandalise' the court, but seeks to engage with the public directly through its own communications.

Steps have been taken to film some proceedings in other courts. Since 2013, lawyer's submissions and judgments in certain types of case in the Court of Appeal can be

---

[254] See Crime and Courts Act 2013, s 32.

[255] *Solicitor General v Cox* [2016] EWHC 1241 (QB), [2016] 2 Cr App R 15 at [17] and [31].

[256] Jaconelli, *Open Justice* (n 122) 351.

[257] ibid, 351, stating that 'the effect of the camera is likely to prove neutral' on the conduct of the judge, and finding a stronger case for some filming of civil cases.

[258] Lord Hope issued the Television in the Courts Notice, 6 August 1992, permitting proceedings in the Court of Session and High Court of Justiciary to be televised. A further Notice was issued by Lord Hamilton on 23 January 2012. In 2013, Channel Four broadcast a two hour documentary called *The Murder Trial* using footage from court proceedings.

[259] Criminal Justice Act 1925, s 41(2).

recorded and broadcast, if the specified conditions are met.[260] In 2016, the government conducted a pilot to film the judge's sentencing remarks in certain Crown Court cases, though the footage in the pilot was not for broadcast.[261] The move to put cameras into the courtrooms is seen to be the next stage of the open justice principle. At a time when people can readily access information and footage from Parliament online, there is a strong expectation for the courts to cater to the needs of the contemporary communicative environment. Putting a human face to the judges is also an important part of public relations.

However, there are limits to what such direct access can achieve. Even if the televising or live streaming of certain court hearings became routine practice, most members of the public will lack the time to sit through hours of legal argument. Without legal training or expertise, some rulings and arguments may prove difficult to follow. Those watching at home may not have access to the documents that are sometimes necessary to know what is going on. Furthermore, those parts of the proceedings that go unfilmed, such as witness evidence, may still leave aspects of the process seeming mysterious. There are clear benefits in making some footage accessible where it does not otherwise jeopardise the integrity of the proceedings. However, it is no substitute for court reporting by the media, which gives the public an abbreviated, accessible and digested account of the proceedings.

E. Live Text-based Communications and Citizen Reporters

Another method of making court proceedings more accessible is the use of live text-based communications, such as Twitter, in the courtroom to relay events to the world at large as they happen. To use such technology, a member of the public should normally ask the court for permission to activate a mobile phone or laptop in the courtroom in order to send live messages.[262] In deciding whether to grant permission, the judge will consider the impact of such messages on the administration of justice. By contrast, a representative of the media or 'legal commentator' may use the live text-based service without permission, reflecting a level of trust given to the professional journalist to know what sort of communication may interfere with the legal process. The use of such technology is permitted where the proceedings are open to the public and in those parts of the proceedings where there are no reporting restrictions. The use of live text-based communications allows for established legal journalists and amateur commentators to reach audiences in a different way, which may generate some interest.

There are hopes that amateur reporters—whether on Twitter or publishing longer reports on blogs—will fill some gaps left as a result of the decline in court reporting in the mainstream media. However, the coverage is likely to be limited to those cases that attract the dedicated amateur. Much will also depend on the expertise of the person relaying events on the digital media to follow the proceedings, ensure that any restrictions on reporting are honoured and be in a position to challenge any restrictions that

---

[260] Court of Appeal (Recording and Broadcasting) Order 2013, SI 2013/2786.
[261] Crown Court (Recording) Order 2016, SI 2016/612.
[262] See Lord Judge, *Practice Guidance: The Use of Live Text-Based Forms of Communications (Including Twitter) From Court for the Purposes of Fair and Accurate Reporting* [2012] 1 WLR 12.

are imposed. In addition, there are also questions as to whether the amateur should benefit from some of the privileges afforded to professional journalists in accessing the courts. As noted, accredited journalists are at an advantage in securing access to certain court documents and types of hearing. Under the current rules, accreditation is available only to media professionals, but not amateur reporters. While it would be difficult to have a completely open door to anyone that wishes to publish a report on family or youth court proceedings (for fear that any restrictions might be breached), the rules could be developed to provide similar rights of access to those non-professionals with a track record of responsible reporting and level of knowledge about court proceedings.

F. Alternatives to Hearings in Court

The open justice principle potentially applies to bodies other than the courts. That is the implication of comments made in *Guardian News*, in particular by Toulson LJ (as he then was), stating that open justice applies 'to all tribunals exercising the judicial power of the State'.[263] In the Supreme Court, Lord Toulson returned to the issue in *Kennedy* and stated that the 'considerations which underlie the open justice principle in relation to judicial proceedings apply also to those charged by Parliament with responsibility for conducting quasi-judicial inquiries and hearings'.[264] Accordingly, he thought that the Charity Commission could be subject to certain elements of the principle, as could some other regulatory bodies. However, Lord Toulson argued that the expansion of open justice was subject to a degree of flexibility and that the 'practical operation may vary according to the nature of the work of a particular judicial body'.[265] Such an approach would make the open justice principle similar to natural justice in administrative law, in that it applies to a wider range of decisions, but with the demands of the principle varying widely according to the context.

Lord Toulson's view was not shared by all the judges in *Kennedy*, with Lord Carnwath arguing that bodies like the Charity Commission were not performing quasi-judicial functions. Instead, Lord Carnwath believed that any moves towards transparency were better dealt with under freedom of information laws. The debate reflects one of the challenges with the fragmentation of power away from traditional state institutions, and in assigning adjudicatory functions to various agencies and regulators. The dilemma is how far those bodies should be subject to the same principles as the court, or whether subjecting such bodies to court-like obligations would undermine the purposes of delegating the function in the first place. If the latter view is taken, there are dangers of open justice becoming marginalised and some proceedings relating to legal rights taking place away from public view.

The problem is also illustrated by moves to encourage people to use alternatives to the courts, such as arbitration. The reasons for such a move are strong, providing a less expensive route to justice that will be more efficient and accessible for most citizens.

---

[263] *Guardian News and Media Ltd v City of Westminster Magistrates' Court* (n 114) at [70].
[264] *Kennedy v The Charity Commission* (n 117) at [124].
[265] ibid, [115]. Consequently, there is no obligation for a body such as the Charity Commission to conduct hearings in public.

Arbitration hearings, however, take place behind closed doors and are not open to journalists. Lord Neuberger has called for greater openness in relation to arbitrations on the grounds that public scrutiny is a strong pressure on a judge 'to get the law right'.[266] An improvement in the levels of transparency could include the publication of the awards made by arbitrators, but that does not come close to attaining open justice. However, an arbitrator does not have the same constitutional status as a court and owes its authority to an agreement by the parties. While scrutiny of its functions is important, the arbitrator does not have the same reason to communicate with the public and declare principles of law as would be expected of a branch of the state.

Another move to improve access to justice, online dispute resolution, could also have implications for open justice. Advocates of such systems cite the dispute resolution mechanisms on *Ebay*, as an example of how claims can be resolved online.[267] Reforms could include a system for certain categories of case to be heard digitally in which papers are submitted and reviewed online by caseworkers, who provide a channel for mediation and negotiation. If there is no agreement between parties, then the case could go to a formal determination by a judge, who reads papers and submissions that are sent in electronically. In some cases, conversations over the telephone may aid the gathering of evidence by the judge. The approach therefore allows justice to take place outside of the courtroom. Where the evidence needs further testing, the judge could call for an oral hearing (or arrange for a hearing using a video conference facilities).[268] An online system for relatively low value civil law claims (referred to as an 'online solutions court') is already being developed.[269] In 2017, the government proposed a system of online convictions for low-level crimes, in which the defendants can review the evidence against them and, if pleading guilty, accept the penalty online.[270] At present, a similar system of online pleading is used in relation to certain road traffic offences, and pilots for online hearings are being conducted in relation to certain types of proceeding. If those projects are a success, online justice is likely to be a growth area.

The difficult question is how a system of online justice would fit within the open justice principle. The government has promised to maintain a system in which victims, witnesses, and the public have access to case listings and case outcomes when appropriate.[271] There may, however, be much that is lost if the journalist looks only at documents and is not able to see the parties in person, which can be an important aspect of understanding a case and the way to present it. At the other extreme, there are dangers in the publicity being over-inclusive. If a system of online justice was designed to maximise transparency and put relevant documents and communications online,

[266] Lord Neuberger, 'Arbitration and the Rule of Law', speech to the Chartered Institute of Arbitrators Centenary Celebration, Hong Kong (15 March 2015).

[267] See Online Dispute Resolution Advisory Group, *Online Dispute Resolution: For Low Value Civil Claims* (Civil Justice Council, February 2015).

[268] Ministry of Justice, *Transforming our justice system: summary of reforms and consultations* (Cm 9321, 2016) 4.

[269] See Briggs LJ, *Civil Court Structure Review: Final Report* (Judiciary of England and Wales, 2016).

[270] *Transforming our justice system* (2016) (n 268) 7.

[271] Ministry of Justice, *Transforming our justice system: assisted digital strategy, automatic online conviction and statutory standard penalty, and panel composition in tribunals. Government response* (Cm 9391, 2017) 10.

the public would potentially see those cases which the media would normally take no interest in or see no public interest in reporting.[272] At present, the editorial values of the media act as a filter that would be lost if case information was uniformly placed online. A system of transparency for online justice may achieve greater uniformity, but that might result in too much publicity in some cases and not enough in others. There are possibilities that sit between the two extremes, such as requiring members of the public to register and apply for access to documentation or transcripts.[273] A video or telephone hearing could be open to observation only to those in a special booth in a court building, which restricts any recordings of the proceedings.[274] Such steps could impose some barriers that replicate some of the existing filters on publicity. At present, the experiments in online decision-making are only for low-level crime and small value claims, so media reporting is unlikely to be an issue. The challenges to open justice are likely to become more pressing if online court systems are adopted more widely in the future.

The difficulty in all these examples is in providing a route for justice that is cheaper and more efficient than the court, but that does not cut corners and reduce the quality of the decisions. As more alternatives are utilised, ways to accommodate open justice need to be developed or else the principle will become marginalised in a system of justice that increasingly takes place outside of the courts.

IV. Conclusion

This chapter has looked at the role of the media in reporting legal proceedings, both in the run up to court hearings and in reporting what is said in court. Both relate to important elements of media freedom, in being able to monitor the use of the state's coercive powers and its related machinery, and more generally in informing the public about what is happening in the system of justice. Media coverage can, however, undermine other important competing interests. Most obviously, there are dangers of coverage jeopardising a fair trial. The proceedings may also relate to sensitive matters that require some protection from publicity. The law therefore aims to strike a balance between these various goals, and the balance struck helps to reveal the priorities in the legal system.

Media law has arguably become less protective of the legal process and offers broader protection for media freedom. The old concerns about 'trial by media' and

---

[272] P Gibbs, 'How can justice be "seen to be done" in an online system?' Inforrm (14 February 2017), available at https://inforrm.wordpress.com/2017/02/14/how-can-justice-be-seen-to-be-done-in-an-online-system-penelope-gibbs/ (last accessed 24 January 2018).
[273] Briggs LJ, *Civil Courts Structure Review: Interim Review* (Judiciary of England and Wales, 2015) 45.
[274] ibid.

prejudgment of legal issues in the press reflected a view that matters in legal proceedings should be left to the courts and that there was less of a role for the public to interpret the events prior to court hearings. Similarly, the courts had an ambivalent view about their decisions being subject to public scrutiny. As evidence of a change in culture, the old restrictions on scandalising the court no longer apply and instead the courts seek to maintain their authority through more pro-active public relations methods rather than censorship—a trend seen with many other institutions. The law of contempt is now more narrowly focused on matters that could unduly influence a jury, a litigant or witness. The current approach allows for the public to form its own view, so long as there is no interference with other legal interests. While the law is less protective of judges and the authority of the court, it remains protective of the interests at stake in the legal process and there are significant exceptions to open justice.

Controls on reporting courts and police investigations can also form a secondary battle in broader disputes about what the media can publish. If a person brings an action in privacy or if criminal proceedings are brought to protect national security, there will sometimes be a secondary dispute about whether the details of the proceedings can be reported. Sometimes the secondary disputes involve the strategic use of arguments about media law on both sides. For example, if a piece of information is subject to a privacy action, media institutions may argue that the fact that legal proceedings are taking place provides a public interest in revealing details about the case (so the public know what the courts are doing).[275] The other side of the coin is that a reporting restriction can provide an additional control on the media to prevent information being reported, even where there is an arguable public interest (for example, where a whistleblower discloses important information and is subsequently prosecuted). In these cases, the primary dispute is about a separate legal interest, such as privacy or secrecy, but arguments surrounding open justice or the protection of the administration of justice become used as tools to support the position on either side.

In reporting on the system of justice, the media does not just act as a check on the state, but to some degree acts as the state's publicist. Reporting on an investigation can promote a view that the authorities are taking action in relation to an issue or encourage others to aid an investigation. The reporting of proceedings in court can stand as a warning to others about possible consequences of an action, and the publicity attracted by a criminal conviction can be an informal element of the punishment. Publicity in the media is not solely a means to scrutinise public bodies, but is used by government as a tool to further its goals.

The discussion has also shown some of the challenges posed by the digital media. If the court cannot stop the flow of information online, then it will look to other stages in the process of publication and dissemination. In relation to contempt of court, there is a renewed emphasis on regulating the conduct of the potential audience for information, namely the juror, rather than the publisher. With open justice, the courts

---

[275] For example, newspapers have argued that a privacy injunction should be discharged on the grounds that the publication of the private information would contribute to a debate about privacy injunctions. The argument was rejected, see *PJS v News Group Newspapers* [2016] EWCA Civ 393, [2016] Fam Law 962 at [31].

sometimes limit access to sensitive hearings only to accredited professional journalists. That control seeks to permit some level of transparency, but relies on the responsibility of professional journalists to observe reporting restrictions in order to stop the information making it online in the first place.

Both areas of law have, however, a slightly different focus in relation to the power and impact of the media. The law of contempt fits with the more traditional publication offences, where the rationale is to deter the dissemination of content that could have certain effects on the reader. The current approach of the courts reflects a view that media coverage will mostly have a minimal effect and that jurors are more robust in resisting media influence. By contrast, the restrictions on reporting the courts' proceedings are similar to the law of privacy in so far as the disclosure of certain sensitive information itself is thought to be the harm.

Both contempt of court and the reporting of proceedings touch on the ability of the media to scrutinise government and inform the public about important matters. However, it is also an area where the interests of the media in building an audience or boosting profits are clear to see. A major crime story is likely to generate considerable sales, so the media will have a significant interest in pushing the boundaries of the law as far as possible. However, where the case is not gossip-worthy, shocking or scandalous, there are increasing dangers in the media turning a blind eye to events. Reporting legal proceedings requires time and expertise, which may not be justified economically if it does not produce a sensational story. Consequently, one of the biggest threats to open justice may not be from legal restrictions but from the economic incentives that reduce the level of court reporting. That provides a major ongoing challenge in ensuring that open justice is not just protected on paper, but is a right that is regularly exercised in practice.

4

Censorship, Obscenity and Secrecy

I. Introduction

Censorship is a loaded term that has long carried pejorative connotations of authoritarian and paternalist government. The anti-democratic nature of censorship and the association with totalitarianism was underlined by Lord Bridge in *Spycatcher*:

> Freedom of speech is always the first casualty under a totalitarian regime. Such a regime cannot afford to allow the free circulation of information and ideas among its citizens. Censorship is the indispensable tool to regulate what the public may and what they may not know.[1]

There is, however, a danger in invoking the term 'censorship' to discredit any restriction on publication that a person does not like. Moreover, few people demand absolute protection of freedom of speech or media freedom. Most people accept that there are some types of sexual or violent content that should be restricted and that state secrets cannot be freely circulated. A central difficulty lies in identifying when a restriction on media content crosses the line and becomes oppressive censorship?

A starting point is to take a definition of censorship as the imposition of a control on expression aiming to stop people receiving certain content or messages on the basis that an authority decides that it would be bad for those people (a paternalist approach) or that it goes against the interests or wishes of the authority (an authoritarian approach).[2] The most objectionable types of censorship also tend to contain a high level of discretion so that the authority can selectively apply a standard to curtail speech which it opposes or of which it disapproves.

To explore the issue of state censorship, this chapter will focus on two areas: the law relating to obscene content; and government secrecy. The two areas are very different, but provide useful case studies because: (i) both have a long history in the UK; (ii) people generally accept the need for some controls in both areas; and (iii) both have been criticised as forms of censorship. This chapter will identify the rationale

---

[1] *A-G v Guardian Newspapers Ltd (No 1)* [1987] 1 WLR 1248 (HL).
[2] See the discussion of non-instrumental arguments for audience autonomy in Ch 1.

underpinning obscenity and secrecy laws, examine the techniques employed to regulate the content and how those techniques have evolved. From this, the chapter will identify some general trends and patterns in the methods of censorship. The discussion will show that heavy-handed use of censorship powers is often counter-productive, generates considerable backlash and mobilises opposition. It will be shown how the classic publication offences in obscenity and secrecy law are not the primary tools used by government, but support a broader system of formal and informal methods of managing the flow of information. To identify these trends, the discussion will first look at laws regulating obscene and pornographic publications, and then turn to government secrecy. Finally, controls on terrorism-related content will be briefly discussed to show how similar controls are being applied in related areas.

II. Obscene, Indecent and Pornographic Content

This section will look at the controls targeting obscene, indecent and pornographic content. A longstanding control in this area is the law of obscenity, which imposes criminal liability on publishers of content that would 'deprave and corrupt' the likely reader and grants police powers to seize such material. The law is best known for a number of high-profile prosecutions in the 1960s, 70s and 80s that targeted works of literature, pornography and so-called 'video nasties'. However, the law regulating sexually explicit and violent content is a combination of different types of control. The laws include the regulation of film and video, and the criminalisation of the possession of indecent images of children and extreme pornography.[3] The discussion will show how the law has gradually moved away from a reliance on the older broadly-worded publication offences, and instead relies on a combination of laws targeting more specific content and informal controls. As a result, the area provides a useful case study in the changing techniques for control. Before looking at the substance of the law, the following section will provide a summary of the arguments advanced for regulating obscene and pornographic content.

A. Why Restrict Obscene, Indecent and Pornographic Content?

There are various reasons why legal controls are imposed on content that is deemed to be obscene, indecent or pornographic. There is a vast literature about the case for restricting or permitting pornography, and similar debates about the depictions of

---

[3] While the discussion refers to video, those regulations have since been applied to other formats for sale, such as DVD.

violence in the media. As will be seen below, some of the arguments for restricting pornography are different from those focusing on obscenity more generally. In this brief space, it would be impossible to do justice to the various strands of argument and their subtle variations. What follows is a discussion of the types of argument commonly advanced to justify the restriction of sexual and extreme violent content, and the key fault lines that recur in the debates about such material.[4]

The first type of argument can be labelled 'moralistic' and runs that it is morally wrong to publish and view certain types of content. This should be distinguished from the types of moral argument that could be said to underpin most content controls. For example, it is morally wrong to commercially publish (for entertainment purposes) footage of someone being violently sexually assaulted, and most people would accept that the state has a right to ban such material. However, such a ban need not rest on a *moralistic* reason, as the restriction can be justified on the basis that the content relates to an actual injury to the individual in the footage. By contrast, a moralist argument asserts that disapproval of the content provides a free-standing reason to restrict content regardless of any other harm.[5] Along these lines, an argument runs that a restriction on obscene publications is justified in order to 'protect the moral consensus' in society and prevent 'social and moral disintegration'.[6] As a proponent of this view, Lord Devlin commented that 'morality is something that is essential to the well-being of a nation, and to the healthy life of the community', and that the law of obscenity targets the person that 'seeks by his writing to corrupt that fundamental sense of morality'.[7] By connecting the case for restriction to the consequences on the well-being of the nation, Devlin's argument was cast in terms stronger than mere moral disapproval of conduct and indicated that a broader harm to society was at stake. In his well-known critique of Devlin's argument, HLA Hart argued that the potential for immoral acts to threaten the disintegration of society was unsupported by evidence.[8] Instead, Hart argued that such claims merely disguised the true nature of Devlin's position, which sought to justify the punishment of conduct solely on the ground that it is considered to be immoral. There is scope to rely on moralistic arguments to restrict expression under the ECHR, in so far as Article 10(2) provides for the protection of morals.[9] However, the legal moralist argument is at odds with a liberal pluralistic society that seeks to accommodate a range of moral views.[10] In a liberal society, the prevailing moral views should be open to revision and challenge, and the dominant viewpoint should not be preserved through legal control.[11]

---

[4] The identification of the various strands of argument presented here owes much to the useful discussion in D Feldman, *Civil Liberties and Human Rights in England and Wales*, 2nd edn (Oxford, Oxford University Press, 2002) Ch 16.

[5] B Williams (Chair), *Report of the Committee on Obscenity and Film Censorship* (Cmnd 7772, 1979) 52 ('Williams Report').

[6] ibid, 51.

[7] G Robertson, *Obscenity* (London, Weidenfeld and Nicolson, 1979) 48, citing CH Rolph, *The Trial of Lady Chatterley: Regina v Penguin Books Ltd* (Harmonsworth, Penguin, 1961).

[8] HLA Hart, *Law, Liberty and Morality* (Oxford, Oxford University Press, 1963) 55.

[9] *Handyside v United Kingdom* (1979–80) 1 EHRR 737.

[10] See Feldman (n 4) 923.

[11] Williams Report (n 5) 52.

Given this tension with current liberal values, the moralist arguments tend to be associated with the older uses of obscenity law and the famous cases, including *Lady Chatterley's Lover*, *Last Exit to Brooklyn* and *Oz Magazine*, or the campaign against video nasties in the 1980s.[12] Those cases are more significant as cultural milestones than as legal precedents, as the publicity surrounding the trials helped to change attitudes towards the law, turned public opinion against the moralist justifications, and promoted a liberal culture in relation to certain sexual and violent content. The ultimate success of the publishers in that cultural change means that there is a tendency to look back on the older obscenity cases with a combination of shock and amusement. The liberal narrative runs that the obscenity prosecutions were a last gasp from moralist authorities attempting to impose their standards, only to be outwitted by younger publishers that pushed the boundaries. As evidence of the cultural change, literary works that were subject to prosecution are now celebrated and thought of as classics. Some of the video nasties prosecuted in the 1980s are now sold in boxed sets commemorating banned films. Overtly moralist arguments now tend to evoke that earlier era and the case for control is often cast in other terms. However, moralist arguments have not entirely gone away and can still be detected in some parts of the law.

A second argument for the restriction of obscene, indecent and pornographic material is that certain types of content should be restricted to prevent offence to the audience. There are a number of problems with relying on offence as a reason for banning the publication of certain content. One danger is that an offence-based standard for restriction would reduce the content permitted for publication to the level of the most easily offended or least tolerant.[13] Such a concern could be addressed if an objective standard of offence to a 'reasonable person' is applied. However, an objective standard could still have a disproportionate impact on material that is unpopular or challenges prevailing views. In any event, offence-based standards are inconsistent with the principle that freedom to speech should not be limited only to that which people wish to hear. While Article 10 permits the protection of morals, the Strasbourg Court in *Handyside* stated that freedom of expression extends to information and ideas that 'offend, shock or disturb'. As Sedley LJ stated in *Redmond-Bate*, 'Freedom only to speak inoffensively was not worth having'.[14]

Despite these concerns, offence can provide a basis for restriction in certain circumstances.[15] While offence caused (in Feinberg's words) by the 'bare knowledge' that content is being viewed by others in private will not be sufficient to support a restriction, some measures may be justified to protect people from offence that they cannot reasonably avoid.[16] Along these lines, offence may not justify an outright ban on publication, but it can be advanced as a reason for imposing some regulations to prevent unwanted exposure to offensive content. Sexually explicit material may be permissible in certain art galleries or a licensed sex shop, but can be prohibited from display on a public billboard.[17] In another example, under the Ofcom Code, television

---

[12] See *R v Penguin Books Ltd* [1961] Crim LR 176; *R v Anderson* [1972] 1 QB 304 and *R v Calder and Boyars* [1969] 1 QB 151.

[13] Feldman (n 4) 928.

[14] *Redmond-Bate v Director of Public Prosecutions* (1999) 163 JP 789.

[15] See J Feinberg, *Offense to Others* (Oxford, Oxford University Press, 1988).

[16] ibid, 93–94.

[17] Indecent Displays (Control) Act 1981.

broadcasters are required not to cause 'undue offence'.[18] The measures do not stop people accessing content elsewhere if that is what they want to see, but regulates its exposure to a wider audience. Even these controls are controversial, as in a democracy there are times when people need to be confronted with controversial and challenging content.[19] More broadly, a person should not be prevented from speaking in a public place simply because others find the content offensive.[20] While restrictions on the availability of content in certain contexts may sometimes be necessary, such policies also need to be approached with care.

A third type of argument for restricting obscene and pornographic content rests on the injury or types of harm it can cause to people. A version of the argument runs that content can be prohibited where people have been harmed or exploited in the course of production.[21] That argument provides a convincing reason for prohibiting images of sexual activity involving children or real scenes of sexual violence. The argument attracts considerable support in so far as the publication in question is linked to an actual injury, and its restriction is thereby based on a more concrete type of harm.[22] However, the reach of the argument is not limited to material where a person is forced into certain acts against his or her will. Even where a person agrees to participate in the making of a pornographic image, that consent may not be meaningful if the person is subject to undue pressure and intimidation. More broadly, as West explains, the consent may not be meaningful where a person's economic and social circumstances mean that there are no reasonable alternatives to earn money.[23] While taking a realist approach to questions of consent, this rationale for the prohibition of certain pornography becomes more controversial, as not every person involved in the production will suffer such exploitation.[24] The challenges in defining and identifying exploitation means the direct link between the content and the harm caused to those in the course of production is therefore not as clear cut or narrow as it may first appear. However, the argument is still limited to depictions of real people and does not apply to images that are clearly fabricated.

While the direct link to individual injury makes the strongest argument for restricting obscene content, a broader argument is that obscene content has an indirect link to certain types of harm and damage. The most basic way of framing the issue is to look at whether content encourages the reader to commit certain acts that are harmful to others. This is a particularly controversial issue and numerous empirical studies have been conducted to assess the impact of pornography on behaviour.[25] The findings of such studies are heavily contested on both sides. This controversy is unsurprising and

---

[18] The Ofcom Broadcasting Code (April 2017) s 2.
[19] *R (on the application of ProLife Alliance) v BBC* [2003] UKHL 23, [2004] 1 AC 185, Lord Scott at [98].
[20] See E Barendt, *Freedom of Speech*, 2nd edn (Oxford, Oxford University Press, 2005) 386.
[21] C West, 'Pornography and Censorship', *The Stanford Encyclopedia of Philosophy* (Fall 2013 Edition), Edward N Zalta (ed), available at https://plato.stanford.edu/archives/fall2013/entries/pornography-censorship/ (last accessed 24 January 2018).
[22] Williams Report (n 5) 131 at [10.5].
[23] West (n 21).
[24] ibid.
[25] For example, debates often refer to the evidence heard by the Meese Commission, see Attorney-General's Commission on Pornography, *Final Report* (US Department of Justice, 1986).

goes back to the general issue of media effects on the audience. While the evidence is mixed and contested, that is not enough for the argument to be dismissed. To demand concrete empirical evidence demonstrating an effect on people's thought processes and consequent conduct is to set an impossibly high threshold. The question of media effects should not be dismissed by attacking 'straw man' questions of causation, such as whether pornography turns people into rapists, and so on.

The indirect effects of the content can be subtle in shaping the prevailing culture. The criticism therefore runs that repeated exposure to scenes of sexual violence can normalise such behaviour and trivialise the seriousness of such offences. As Gail Dines writes, the mass of pornography in circulation creates 'a world that is at best inhospitable to women, and at worst dangerous to their physical and emotional well being'.[26] Such arguments move away from concerns about *obscenity* and focus specifically on *pornography* as reinforcing a culture in which women are subordinate. Along these lines, Catherine MacKinnon argues that the harm in pornography is not simply to the individuals involved in the production or to the victims of any crime that may be encouraged, but instead constitutes a harm to women as a group.[27] In MacKinnon's view, pornography 'fuses the dominance and submission with the social construction of male and female'.[28] Under this argument, the pornographic image constructs how women are seen and does so in a way that de-humanises and institutionalises the subordination of women.[29] This argument fits with the account of media effects outlined in Chapter 1, in which communications are a form of power through the 'construction of meaning'. Rae Langton has also argued that pornography amounts to a form subordination because it is 'verdictive speech that ranks women as sex objects, and, second, exercitive speech that legitimates sexual violence'.[30] While the publishers of pornography tend not to have the same political power as the mainstream media, Langton argues that the publishers nonetheless have an authoritative voice in certain settings, such as when people view pornography to learn more about legitimate sexual activities.[31]

A culture where pornographic images are pervasive and easily accessible is sometimes said to have a 'silencing' effect on people. Taken literally, a silencing effect can arise when the display of obscene or pornographic content generates a hostile and intimidating environment in which certain people are uncomfortable speaking out.[32] However, Langton points out that pornography can silence people by generating conditions that deprive statements from carrying force and authority. Langton gives the example of a book detailing the cruel treatment and suffering that had taken place in the pornography industry.[33] While the book was written to criticise the industry, it was included in a catalogue of pornographic books for sale. In that example, the protest against pornography was deprived of its force by being treated as a form of sexual entertainment alongside the adult titles it sought to condemn. As pornography

---

[26] G Dines, *Pornland: How Porn Has Hijacked Our Sexuality* (Boston, Beacon Press, 2010) 85.
[27] C MacKinnon, 'Not a Moral Issue' (1984) 2 *Yale Law & Policy Review* 321, 338.
[28] ibid, 326.
[29] ibid, 326 and 340.
[30] R Langton, 'Speech Acts and Unspeakable Acts' (1993) 22 *Philosophy & Public Affairs* 293 at 307–308.
[31] ibid, 312.
[32] For criticism see R Dworkin, *Freedom's Law* (Oxford, Oxford University Press, 1996) 232.
[33] Langton (n 30) 322.

is thought to deprive people of a meaningful opportunity to express themselves, the argument runs that controls on pornographic expression may enhance rather than restrict freedom of expression.

A problem with arguments relying on the indirect harms caused by pornographic content lies in the difficulty in generalising about pornography, as the term refers to a wide range of material. This can range from professionally produced films, amateur content, communication on websites, and can cater to a range of different audiences and lifestyles.[34] Some of the content may be seen to have positive benefits in allowing people to challenge the dominant views about sex and speak out for minority lifestyles. There are strands of feminist writing that defend pornography as sexual expression, arguing that it has no fixed harmful meaning and can be open to competing interpretations.[35] Even if any harmful effects on the audience can be proven, that might not be true for all types of material that can be classed as pornographic. The challenge for lawyers is then to design a system that targets content that is potentially harmful, without unduly restricting people's legitimate preferences and lifestyle choices. Even if content is harmful in any of the ways outlined above, that does not mean content should be legally prohibited by legislation, as there are a number of other issues, such as the difficulty in drafting the control and the potential impact on other rights and interests.

The arguments concerning pornography may seem a far cry from the issues facing the traditional media. However, in the digital era, pornography is no longer confined to adult stores and top shelves at the periphery of media consumption. The production and dissemination of pornographic content is an industry, in which some companies and intermediaries make significant profits and attract more traffic than some traditional media sites.[36] The type of content that audiences become accustomed to seeing also has the potential to influence content on the mainstream media. The availability of pornographic content may shape audience expectations and the standards of the community, which in turn may increase the level of sexual and violent content that audiences will accept on television, cinema and leading websites. As this process shifts the centre of gravity in the standards of popular culture, the mainstream media can then work to reinforce the culture that raises the various concerns discussed above.

As with all areas of media law, any steps to control content can raise issues under Article 10 of the European Convention on Human Rights (ECHR). However, obscene content typically raises few free speech issues under the current jurisprudence. There is a debate about whether pornography should qualify for protection as expression at all. In the US, content deemed to be obscene under the constitutional standard is not protected under the First Amendment.[37] Under Article 10 of the ECHR, the courts tend not to draw a bright line that excludes obscene content from its protection, but gives such content little weight against other interests. In *Miss Behavin'*, Baroness Hale

---

[34] See discussion in L Green, 'Pornographies' (2000) *The Journal of Political Philosophy* 27. See also Feldman (n 4) 927.

[35] See B Crawford, 'Toward a Third-Wave Feminist Legal Theory: Young Women, Pornography and the Praxis of Pleasure' (2007) 14 *University of Michigan Journal of Gender & Law* 99.

[36] See S Tarrant, *The Pornography Industry* (Oxford, Oxford University Press, 2016) 42–44.

[37] *Miller v California* 413 US 15 (1973), though pornography that does not fall foul of that standard may be constitutionally protected.

stated that '[p]ornography comes well below celebrity gossip in the hierarchy of speech which deserves the protection of the law.'[38] Under this view, obscene or pornographic content does little to inform the public and deserves relatively minimal protection. However, there are also reasons not to be dismissive of the expression rights at stake with obscenity laws. There are dangers that the laws can be used to silence unpopular or minority views. Works thought to be corrupting may simply challenge current standards. Works of literature now regarded as of artistic value have been subject to obscenity prosecutions in the past. As noted above, it is also difficult to generalise about pornographic speech as a category. Content relating to sexual activities may reflect a person's lifestyle choices, and the right to a private life may be at stake. Article 10 gives the court considerable scope to regulate this area, but issues relating to the rights freedom of expression and media freedom can still be present.

B. Obscene Publications Law

i. Background

While there are various laws regulating obscene and indecent publications, the best known control can be found in the criminal law of obscenity. The law of obscenity has its origins in the common law offence of obscene libel, which was established in a 1727 decision concerning publications titled *The Nun in her Smock* and *The Art of Flogging*.[39] The offence grew in significance during the Victorian era, with a number of investigations and private prosecutions being brought by the voluntary organisation, the Society for the Suppression of Vice.[40] The increased use of the common law offence failed to stop the trade in obscene publications during the nineteenth century, as the risk of prosecution was not enough to deter some sellers and publishers.[41] To address this shortcoming, Lord Campbell introduced the Obscene Publications Act of 1857 to supplement the common law offence by providing the police with powers of search and seizure. This meant that obscene publications were not just subject to post-publication sanction, but also to a prior restraint that enabled materials to be removed and destroyed before sale.[42]

An exercise of the powers under the 1857 Act led to the famous decision of *R v Hicklin*. In that case, a publication that criticised Popish practices and promoted the goals of the Protestant Electoral Union was seized, on the basis that it included details of what was said in confession in the Catholic church. The significance of the decision in *Hicklin* lies in Lord Cockburn's formulation that a publication is obscene if it tends to 'deprave and corrupt those whose minds are open to such immoral

---

[38] *Belfast City Council v Miss Behavin' Ltd* [2007] UKHL 19, [2007] 1 WLR 1420 at [38].

[39] *King v Curl* (1727) 1 Barn KB 29.

[40] MJD Roberts, 'Making Victorian morals? The society for the suppression of vice and its critics, 1802–1886' (1984) 21 *Historical Studies* 157.

[41] C Manchester. 'Lord Campbell's act: England's first obscenity statute' (1988) 9 *The Journal of Legal History* 223.

[42] ibid, 227.

influences, and into whose hands a publication of this sort may fall'.[43] While that legal framework remained in place for nearly a century, a number of high-profile cases targeting literary works led to demands to liberalise the law and to the enactment of the Obscene Publications Act 1959.

ii. The Main Provisions

The Obscene Publications Act 1959 provides, under s 2, that it is an offence to publish an obscene article (whether or not for gain) or to possess an obscene article with a view to publishing it for gain.[44] The Act attaches liability to the publisher, so the possession of obscene material for private viewing does not fall under the offence. As with other areas of law, the Act takes a broad definition of a publication to include the distribution, circulation, sale and giving of an article, as well as the transmission of data and showing 'matter to be looked at'.[45] With this broad definition, the offence can be used to target a range of actors in the chain of dissemination. The offence has, for example, been used against those selling obscene content in adult shops.[46] However, s 2 provides some protection for 'innocent dissemination', stating that a person will not be convicted if he had not examined the article and had no reasonable cause to suspect the article was obscene.[47]

In addition to the criminal offences relating to publication, s 3 grants significant powers to magistrates to issue warrants for constables to search for obscene articles being kept for publication for gain and to seize such material. A warrant need not name the items to be seized and the police thereby have considerable power to remove any articles reasonably believed to fall in that category.[48] Once seized, the magistrate has the power to order the forfeiture of the material. The power can operate as a prior restraint on expression that stops content going into circulation. However, the occupier of the searched premises, the owner or the maker of the material should have the opportunity to make a case against forfeiture.[49]

iii. Defining Obscenity

A particularly challenging issue in this area of law is deciding what sort of material is obscene. Section 1 defines obscene material as that which will 'deprave and corrupt persons who are likely, having regard to all relevant circumstances, to read, see or hear the matter contained or embodied in it'. The provision does not attempt to define

---

[43] *R v Hicklin* (1868) LR 3 QB 360.

[44] See also the Obscene Publications Act 1964. For practical purposes, the statutory offence rendered the common law of obscene libel obsolete, see s 4(4) of the 1959 Act. However, the common law offence was finally abolished under the Coroners and Justice Act 2009.

[45] Obscene Publications Act 1959, s 1(3).

[46] For example, see *DPP v Jordan* [1977] AC 699.

[47] Obscene Publications Act 1959, s 2(5).

[48] ibid, s 3(1), Robertson (n 7) 87–89. If any articles are seized during a raid, the police also have broad powers to seize any documents found in the premises that 'relate to a trade or business carried on at the premises', s 3(2).

[49] Obscene Publications Act 1959, s 3(3)–(4).

what obscene content looks like and instead focuses on the effect of the article on the likely reader. The deprave and corrupt standard is primarily concerned with 'the influence on the mind' as opposed to the behaviour of the reader.[50] The rationale of the statute is therefore not that the content will turn law abiding people into murderers or rapists and does not rely on an assumed causal link between the material and people's conduct.

The 1959 Act takes the term 'deprave and corrupt' from the Victorian *Hicklin* test,[51] but seeks to liberalise the law. One liberalising effect is that the deprave and corrupt standard is applied to the article 'as a whole' and not solely to the offending passages.[52] A book or film should be assessed by its overall context, so a moral ending to a story can arguably provide an antidote to any scenes of sex and violence.[53] However, there are also difficulties in determining what is meant by an article 'as a whole'. Individual magazine articles have been judged as separate items, rather than as components in a magazine judged as a whole.[54] That begs the question of how a website should be judged? Should a webpage be judged in isolation, in the context of the whole website, or in relation to any linked content? The answer will depend on the website, how it is organised and the way people access it.

Defining obscenity in terms of the deprave and corrupt effect means that the law is not primarily concerned with shielding the audience from material deemed to be offensive. In fact, the deprave and corrupt standard seems more concerned with the opposite effect, namely that a person viewing the material will actually like what they see and want to see more of it. This feature of the test leads to the 'aversion argument', where the content in question is more likely to repulse than corrupt the likely reader, and so is not obscene.[55] The repulsion may be such that it discourages any deviant thoughts and reinforces a person's moral character. The result is the counter-intuitive position that, in theory at least, the content most likely to offend the reader will arguably fall outside the definition of obscene material. Whatever the theory, in practice it has not stopped juries finding extreme content to be obscene.

The deprave and corrupt standard has the advantage of being flexible. The term 'corrupt' means a deviation from an accepted standard, which will change over time. Consequently, the effect on the mind of the reader is determined as a question of fact applying contemporary standards. The flexibility of the test also means that the Act can be applied to a wide range of content and not just to the most obvious cases of pornographic material. For example, in *A and BC Chewing Gum*, a set of cards targeted at children depicting scenes from the Second World War (including a torture chamber and a beheading) were found to be capable of being obscene by the Divisional Court.[56] A publication detailing how to use illegal drugs was also found to be capable of being obscene.[57] In 2007, the powers under s 3 were used to seize and destroy a T-shirt with

---

[50] *DPP v Whyte* [1972] AC 849, 863.
[51] *Hicklin* (n 43) 371.
[52] Obscene Publications Act 1959, s 1(1).
[53] Compare *Charleston v News Group Newspapers* [1995] 2 AC 65 in relation to defamation.
[54] *Anderson* (n 12); Robertson (n 7) 62.
[55] *Anderson* (n 12).
[56] *DPP v A and BC Chewing Gum Ltd* [1968] 1 QB 159.
[57] *R v Skirving* [1985] QB 819.

the words 'Gunchester' from a shop in Manchester.[58] Consequently, the Act is not simply about pornography or content that will perpetuate sexist attitudes, but can apply to other types of content deemed to be corrupting.[59]

The deprave and corrupt standard is subject to a number of criticisms. With the flexibility of the test comes a level of vagueness and uncertainty. The courts have stated that the term means something stronger than 'being led astray morally', but have not gone beyond that.[60] In *Calder and Boyars*, Salmon LJ stated that the statute provides the test 'in plain English' and 'it is rarely necessary and often unwise for the judge to attempt to improve upon or re-define the definition'.[61] The court has also held that the jury should apply the standard to the particular publication before them, and that it is 'not relevant' that similar obscene content is in circulation elsewhere without attracting prosecution.[62] Furthermore, the fact the law does not deem an item to be obscene in itself, but instead looks at the circumstances of publication in the light of contemporary standards, means that different juries are entitled to come to different conclusions about the same content. A decision to acquit a defendant in relation to a publication to a particular audience or part of the country does not provide a final ruling on the legality of the particular content. As a result, the Act provides much scope for inconsistency and uncertainty in the law.

In addition to the uncertainty for publishers, the deprave and corrupt standard gives the jury a difficult task in assessing the impact of the material on the mind of a person or hypothetical person. The likelihood is that a jury will form a view about the content, the context of its publication and whether it is socially acceptable, and then reason backwards to make an assumption about the effect on the mind of the reader.[63] Given the difficulties of the standard, in 1972 Lord Wilberforce expressed 'serious doubts whether the Act will continue to be workable in this way, or whether it will produce tolerable results'.[64]

A more fundamental objection to the 'deprave and corrupt' standard concerns its underlying rationale. Joel Feinberg argued that the deprave and corrupt test reflects a combination of 'moralism and paternalism'—the classic hallmarks of censorship.[65] It is moralistic in so far as 'lustful states of mind' are thought to be 'inherent evils whether or not they issue in harmful conduct'.[66] The paternalism can be seen in the fact that the law seeks to protect individuals from moral 'harm to their characters', regardless of whether those people have 'voluntarily run the risk of corruption'.[67] That a person is prevented from being depraved or corrupted even if they are perfectly happy with that outcome sits uncomfortably with the liberal view that adults are responsible moral agents, who decide for themselves what to read.

---

[58] '"Depraved" gun T-shirts banned' *Manchester Evening News* (1 September 2007).

[59] H Fenwick and G Phillipson, *Media Freedom under the Human Rights Act* (Oxford, Oxford University Press, 2007) 424.

[60] *Knuller v DPP* [1973] AC 435 at 456.

[61] *Calder and Boyars* (n 12) 168.

[62] *R v Elliott* [1996] 1 Cr App R 432, citing *R v Reiter* [1954] 2 QB 16.

[63] Williams Report (n 5) 10 at [2.6], citing Lord Wilberforce in *Whyte* (n 50).

[64] *Whyte* (n 50) 862.

[65] Feinberg (n 15) 172, discussing the test in *Hicklin*.

[66] ibid.

[67] ibid.

For these reasons, there have been calls to replace the test with a legal formulation that better articulates the harm of pornography and other extreme content. There have been steps in this direction, for example in controls on extreme pornography. The challenge lies in drafting a provision that captures the necessary harmful content and is not ridden with loopholes, quickly outdated and in constant need of amendment. Attempts to provide a more precise alternative are fraught with difficulty and the lack of an obvious alternative formulation means the deprave and corrupt test remains in place as a flexible catch-all offence.[68]

iv. The Likely Reader

The Obscene Publications Act 1959 liberalised the law by providing that an article is obscene only if it depraves and corrupts the 'likely' reader, whereas the earlier law had applied the standard to a person 'into whose hands a publication of this sort may fall'.[69] The current law therefore allows the court to consider the likelihood of the material being seen by a particular audience, which will then determine the standard to be applied. Lord Wilberforce described the law as taking a 'relative conception of obscenity', in which an 'article cannot be considered as obscene in itself: it can only be so in relation to its likely readers'.[70] Accordingly, Lord Wilberforce added that 'to apply different tests to teenagers, members of men's clubs or men in various occupations or localities would be a matter of common sense'.[71] Content is not to be judged at the 'the level of something that is suitable for a fourteen-year-old school girl' unless that happens to be the likely readership.[72] While the deprave and corrupt standard varies according to the likely reader, that does not mean a person cannot be further depraved and corrupted if he or she has already been exposed to obscene content. The offence can therefore be committed where the likely readers of material are, in the words of one magistrates' court, 'inadequate, pathetic, dirty minded men, seeking cheap thrills'.[73]

To apply the standard, the court has to determine who the likely audience is for the material. If a person is prosecuted for publishing an article to a specific person, then there is no need to speculate about the likely reader and the question for the court is whether the material will tend to deprave and corrupt that person.[74] If the publication is to a larger group of people or if the proceedings concern the prospective publication to a number of people,[75] the court will look at the circumstances to identify the likely reader. Difficult issues arise where the material will tend to deprave and corrupt some parts of the audience, but not others. On this question, the courts have taken differing

---

[68] See Home Office, *Consultation: On the possession of extreme pornographic material* (August 2005).
[69] *Hicklin* (n 43).
[70] *Whyte* (n 50) 860.
[71] ibid, 863.
[72] See *R v Martin Secker & Warburg* [1954] 1 WLR 1138, in which Stable J took steps towards a more liberal interpretation of the common law of obscene libel.
[73] See also Lord Cross in *Whyte* (n 50) 862, citing the finding of the justices.
[74] *R v Clayton and Halsey* [1963] 1 QB 163.
[75] The 'possession for gain' offence under s 2 and forfeiture proceedings under s 3 will normally look at the potential circulation to a wider number of readers.

views. In *R v Calder and Boyars,* the court found that where a publication is to a large group, it will only be obscene if it depraves and corrupts a 'significant proportion' of the likely audience.[76] However, in *DPP v Whyte*, Lord Pearson preferred a de minimis standard in which the courts ask if the material would tend to deprave and corrupt more than a 'really negligible' proportion of the audience.[77] Either formulation provides an important safeguard by ensuring the deprave and corrupt test is not applied to the standards of the most vulnerable audience member. A publisher that restricts access to those above a certain age, while never watertight as a control, can thereby reduce the chance that a small child is counted as part of the likely audience.

Where the publication is on the internet, it can be hard to determine who is likely to see the material. In *Perrin*, it was found that where content is freely available on the internet without any system of age verification, then vulnerable young people can be among the likely readers.[78] The Court of Appeal also found that a direction to the jury asking whether a significant proportion or negligible number of viewers would be corrupted would, in that type of case, only complicate the law and that the jury should simply be asked if 'there is a likelihood of vulnerable persons seeing the material'.[79] If the approach in *Perrin* is taken in relation to all freely accessible internet publications, then it could undo the liberalising goal of the 1959 Act by judging all content by the standards of the child. However, the decision need not have this effect and the court should take into account the circumstances and likely reach of the website to consider the likelihood of the material being seen by a child.[80]

v. *Privacy*

A publication can take place when one person shows, gives or lends content to another on a non-commercial basis. That was an intended effect of the Act to cover cases where, for example, a person shows a pornographic magazine to a child. The principle is of more general application and could apply when a person shows obscene content to a friend or partner in his or her own home. By potentially criminalising communications between consenting adults in a private setting, the Act has been criticised for showing little respect for rights to privacy and sexual freedom.[81] Prior to the digital media, the risk of such communications between consenting adults being detected was low. However, in 2012 the Act was applied in *GS* to a conversation via an internet chat service 'concerning incestuous, sadistic paedophile sex acts on young and very young children'.[82] While the case provokes little sympathy for the defendant, the decision takes the application of the Act one step further in so far as the words of a conversation between consenting adults was a publication attracting criminal liability.

---

[76] *Calder and Boyars* (n 12).
[77] *Whyte* (n 50) 866.
[78] *R v Perrin* [2002] EWCA Crim 747 at [22]. The court found that content behind a paywall was unlikely to deprave and corrupt the likely reader, as it would be judged by the standards of an adult.
[79] ibid, at [30].
[80] A Gillespie, *Child Pornography: Law and Policy* (London, Routledge, 2011) 152–53.
[81] See Robertson (n 7) 74, citing Justice Marshall in *Stanley v Georgia* 394 US 557 (1969), 565.
[82] *R v GS* [2012] EWCA Crim 398, [2012] 1 WLR 3368.

The case provides a reminder that in the digital era, more conversations are recorded and can constitute a publication that falls within the ambit of media laws.[83]

vi. Who Decides?

Whoever gets to decide whether material will deprave and corrupt the likely reader will draw the boundaries on the sort of content deemed fit for publication. For the s 2 offence, the application of the deprave and corrupt standard is a question of fact. Where the case goes to the Crown Court, the question is in the hands of the jury, as representatives of the 'the ordinary man'.[84] As the jurors are assumed to be well placed to judge moral standards, expert evidence cannot normally be provided to the court on the question of whether a publication is obscene.[85] The search, seizure and forfeiture powers under s 3 give the police and magistrates broad powers to decide whether content is obscene. In the past, there have been concerns about the corrupt use of those powers, for example where the police seek payment from adult shops or distributors, and for the powers to be used against unfavoured minorities.[86] The discretionary power raises the danger of selective use, which is another key problem of censorship.

The s 3 power should not be used strategically to censor publications and avoid the cost and uncertainty of a criminal prosecution. To guard against that risk, a person subject to s 3 proceedings can in effect request that the matter be dealt with under a criminal prosecution under s 2 by expressing an intention to continue publishing the material, and the publisher will thereby have a right to defend the publication before a jury.[87] Whether a publisher would wish to take the risk of a criminal prosecution will depend on the particular issue and principle at stake. In most cases, it is easy to imagine that a person would accept forfeiture and desist in publishing the material to avoid the risk of a criminal conviction.

vii. Public Good Defence

A further way the 1959 Act liberalised the law of obscenity was the inclusion of a public good defence. Section 4 of the Act provides a defence for articles that are 'justified as being for the public good on the ground that it is in the interests of science, literature, art or learning, or of other objects of general concern'. Putting this question at the defence stage may seem a little strange in so far as it accepts that the publication inflicts some legally recognised harm, but nonetheless permits the publication for the

---

[83] See discussion in Ch 7.

[84] *Jordan* (n 46).

[85] See *Anderson* (n 12). An exception to that rule applies when the jury 'cannot be expected to understand the likely impact of the material upon its members without assistance'. For example, expert evidence may be admitted to explain the impact of the content on a particular class of people, such as children. See *Jordan* (n 46).

[86] Robertson (n 7) 82.

[87] The Solicitor General gave an undertaking to that effect in 1964, see *Britton v DPP* (1996) for discussion. See also Obscene Publications Act 1959, s 3(3A).

sake of the public good.[88] Critics argue that the protection of the public good should be incorporated as an element in the definition of obscenity, so that publications that serve the public good are not deemed to deprave and corrupt in the first place.[89]

The public good defence helps to ensure that the Act does not unduly interfere with certain types of expression that are deemed to be of value. The experience with the Act, however, highlights the practical difficulties in drawing appropriate boundaries between different categories of speech, such as the artistic and the pornographic. On this question, expert evidence can be brought before the jury to show that a publication serves one of the interests listed in the statute. That has caused some obscenity trials to attract considerable media attention, with the defence calling a number of experts to comment on the cultural or artistic value of the work. The approach has also seen defendants advance broader arguments for pornographic material to be treated as serving the public good. In *Jordan*, the defence argued that pornography might serve the public good by providing some therapeutic value in so far as it allowed the readers to 'relieve their sexual tensions'.[90] The House of Lords rejected that argument, finding that such an effect was really concerned with the prior question of whether the content would deprave and corrupt, rather than whether the publication was in the public good. The court added that 'objects of general concern' should be interpreted narrowly to refer to objects with a 'degree of similarity to those mentioned' in the section.[91]

viii. Taking Stock

The terms of the Obscene Publications Act and the various judicial formulations make the statute look like a draconian restriction on content that threatens criminal liability whenever prevailing moral standards are challenged. That, however, is not the reality of the Act today. The statistics show that the Act is used sparingly. In 2014, only 10 people were convicted under the Obscene Publications Act and in 2015 the figure was just 2.[92] That does not mean the Act is unimportant, as the prosecutions that do take place can have significant implications for those involved. Moreover, the scope of the Act is still being given an expansive interpretation to deal with new circumstances, as was seen in the *GS* case discussed earlier.

There are several reasons why reliance on the Act has declined. First, contemporary standards have changed over time and juries have become more tolerant of material that would previously have attracted prosecution.[93] Along with the changing standards, prosecutors have also changed their policies. Earlier, the policy had been to tolerate nudity, but not hardcore pornography.[94] As will be explained below, the tendency

---

[88] Williams Report (n 5) 15 at [2.19].
[89] Robertson (n 7) 161–66.
[90] *Jordan* (n 46).
[91] ibid. See also *A-G's Reference (No 3 of 1977)* [1978] 3 All ER 1166, rejecting an argument that the magazines in question could serve the public good by contributing to sex education. The 'purposes of learning' is taken to refer to the 'product of scholarship'.
[92] HC Deb 28 March 2017, vol 624, col W68914.
[93] G Robertson and A Nicol, *Media Law*, 5th edn (London, Sweet and Maxwell, 2007) 213–15.
[94] ibid.

now is for prosecutors to target images of child abuse and extreme pornography, which are controlled under separate statutes. More broadly, a number of general offences in other statutes, such as s 127 of the Communications Act 2003, regulate the dissemination of grossly offensive, obscene and indecent material via digital communications. In addition, there are regulatory systems in place for certain types of media content. For all these reasons, there is now less need to invoke the provisions of the Obscene Publications Act.

These developments show how the techniques for controlling content are evolving in the current media environment. The next sections will look at some of the other controls on obscene and pornographic content, and will begin by looking at the role of special regulatory bodies for video and cinema.

C. Cinema and Film

The Obscene Publications Acts now pose relatively minimal risk to the mainstream media. However, cinema, video and on-demand content are subject to a separate set of regulations that seek to address some of the issues relating to obscenity law.[95] Starting with films, cinemas are licensed by local authorities, which can attach conditions to the licences.[96] Cinemas are normally required under the licence conditions to follow the classification guidelines provided by the British Board of Film Classification (BBFC). Local authorities are also required by law to include a condition that children are not admitted to see a film that has not been deemed suitable for the age group by the classification body or licencing authority.[97]

The BBFC was established in 1912 by the film industry and has become the main regulator of cinema.[98] The BBFC is a private company financed by fees charged for its services, and its senior appointments are made by the company's Council of Management. Under this arrangement, the BBFC staff review works submitted for cinema release to decide whether to certify the film and, if so, decide what classification to award it. In this process, the BBFC can advise on any cuts or changes in order to attain a particular classification. The local authority retains discretion and can impose its own classification rather than follow the BBFC. In some cases, the local authority will impose more liberal standards to allow younger people to view a particular film or to allow parents accompanied with babies to watch certain films targeted at adults.[99] In other cases, local authorities have prohibited the showing of a film that has been certified by the BBFC. However, in most cases, the decisions of the BBFC tend to be followed.

The relationship between the system of film classification and the criminal law was the subject of uncertainty. Cinema was initially exempt from the Obscene Publications Acts, on the grounds that cinema already had its system of censorship and an extra

---

[95] Television and radio are subject to more general regulations, which include provisions on undue offence, see Ch 6 on broadcast regulations.

[96] Licensing Act 2003, s 1. And Sch 1, defining 'regulated entertainment'.

[97] ibid, s 20.

[98] See *R v Greater London Council, ex p Blackburn* [1976] 3 All ER 184 at 187; *Mills v London County Council* [1925] 1 KB 213.

[99] See 'Babies could watch 18-rated movies due to loophole' *The Daily Telegraph* (29 May 2017).

criminal control was unnecessary.[100] However, when some cinemas were permitted to show films with stronger sexual content, the common law offence of indecency was relied upon and applied to cinema. In 1973, when the BBFC refused to certify a film titled 'More about the Language of Love', the Greater London Council exercised its discretion to allow the film to be shown in cinemas. The exhibitors of the film were subsequently convicted of outraging public decency and in *ex p Blackburn*, the Court of Appeal found that it was unlawful for the GLC to have approved the showing of a film that is contrary to the law of indecency.[101] Given the lower threshold for the offence of indecency, the film industry preferred to be within the remit of the 1959 Act.[102] In 1977, the law was amended so that cinema was subject to the Obscene Publications Acts, but not the law of indecency. That reform clarified the position, but means that the criminal law runs in parallel with the regulatory framework, and BBFC certification does not provide immunity from prosecution under the Act.

The regulation of film was soon further complicated by the arrival of video. The ability to watch films in the home meant that there was greater concern about content suitable only for adults falling into the hands of children. In response to these concerns, the police and prosecutors mounted a campaign in the early 1980s against various films described as 'video nasties', accompanied by many scare-mongering stories in the national press. During this period, the Director of Public Prosecutions drew up a list of potentially obscene titles to guide the authorities, which included films such as *Driller Killer* and *The Evil Dead*.[103]

The episode highlighted the problems of the Obscene Publications Act applying different standards to alternate formats. While some of the video titles had never been released in the cinema, others on the list had been granted a certificate by the BBFC for cinema viewing. As a result, the retailers and distributors were placed in a difficult position, as they may not have had chance to review the titles and to check for any obscene content. For those seeking to restrict the circulation of the 'video nasties', the reliance on the Obscene Publications Act was unsatisfactory, as a prosecution or forfeiture proceedings led to a delay, during which the content would be freely available.[104] Furthermore, the prosecutions were producing inconsistent results. For example, a video shop that was prosecuted for selling a number of 'video nasties', including *The Evil Dead* (which had been granted a certificate by the BBFC), was acquitted by a jury in Leeds in 1984.[105] However, a video dealer was fined £1,800 by magistrates in Weatherby for possessing videos for gain including *The Evil Dead*.[106] Such inconsistencies reflect the approach in obscenity law, whereby a finding of fact in

---

[100] Williams Report (n 5) 45 at [4.29].

[101] *Blackburn* (n 98). See discussion in Robertson (n 7) 264–65.

[102] Williams Report (n 5) 171. In *R v Stanley* [1965] 2 QB 327, 333, Lord Parker noted the lower threshold for indecency, stating the 'words "indecent or obscene" convey one idea, namely, offending against the recognised standards of propriety, indecent being at the lower end of the scale and obscene at the upper end of the scale.'

[103] For the list, see J Petley, *Video and Film Censorship in Modern Britain* (Edinburgh, Edinburgh University Press, 2011) 213–15.

[104] Graham Bright MP in the Second Reading, HC Deb 11 November 1983 vol 48, col 522.

[105] 'Doubts remain after "obscene" video test case' *The Guardian* (26 May 1984).

[106] The defendant, however, pleaded guilty, so the issue was not tested before the magistrates, '"Obscene" video is an 18-certificate film' *The Guardian* (26 January 1984).

one case does not bind another court and where the action is brought against the publisher in a particular context, rather than finding the content itself to be obscene.[107]

The uncertainties in the law were unsatisfactory for both sides of the debate, but the campaigners against the video nasties sought to resolve this inconsistency through a stricter control, which led to the enactment of the Video Recordings Act 1984.[108] Under the Act, it is an offence to: (1) supply a video work (which includes DVD and Blu-ray formats) or have in one's possession for the purposes of supply a video work that has not been certified by the designated body; or (2) supply a video work in breach of any classification. Under the Act, the Home Secretary has the power to designate a body to certify video releases and that function has been performed by the BBFC. As a result, the industry self-regulatory body took on a statutory function. The Act aimed to simplify the law, so that retailers would not be expected to review the content of what they sold and could rely on the certification decisions of the BBFC.[109] Under the arrangement, the decisions of the BBFC to refuse classification or impose an age restriction can be challenged before the Video Appeals Committee (VAC).[110]

Under the 1984 Act, the BBFC is to approach the classification decision having 'special regard' for the likelihood of the work being viewed in the home.[111] This means that a stricter standard may sometimes be applied to video and DVDs than to cinema, as the age restrictions are harder to enforce in relation to home viewing and the viewer can watch scenes in isolation from the rest of the film.[112] A subsequent amendment also provides that the classification body must have special regard to 'any harm that may be caused to potential viewers or, through their behaviour, to society by the manner in which the work deals with' criminal behaviour, illegal drugs, violent conduct, 'horrific behaviours or incidents' or 'human sexual activity'.[113] The provision is therefore distinct from the Obscene Publications Act in so far as it refers to 'harm' flowing from the content and thereby raises some of the difficult questions discussed earlier about whether media content influences behaviour.

Under the system, the BBFC is not to classify a video that falls foul of any criminal law controls.[114] While that aims to provide some consistency, the difficulty is that the provisions of the Obscene Publications Act 1959 are open to interpretation. Accordingly, the BBFC might take a view that a work does not fall foul of the criminal law, but prosecutors might take a differing view. However, when the Video Recordings Act was being passed, the government hoped the use of the Obscene Publications Act in relation to certified titles would be reduced to a minimum,[115] and greater communication between the BBFC and the DPP would provide consistency in standards.[116] Ultimately, while there is no immunity, certification by the BBFC

---

[107] Williams Report (n 5) 36 at [4.5].

[108] In 2009, it was found that the Video Recordings Act 1984 failed to comply with a procedural requirement in EU law. The Video Recordings Act 2010 rectified this error.

[109] See David Mellor in the Second Reading, HC Deb 11 November 1983 vol 48, col 557.

[110] Video Recordings Act 1984, s 4(3).

[111] ibid, s 4.

[112] BBFC, *How does classification work?*, www.bbfc.co.uk/what-classification/how-does-classification-work, (last accessed 6 January 2018), noting that a stricter application is relatively rare.

[113] Video Recordings Act 1984, s 4A.

[114] *R v Video Appeals Committee of the British Board of Film Classification, ex p British Board of Film Classification* [2000] EMLR 850 at [6].

[115] HC Deb 11 November 1983 vol 48, col 560.

[116] HC Deb 11 November 1983 vol 48, col 561.

renders the prospects of a prosecution in relation to the film very unlikely. In practice, this means that juries and magistrates are not the main arbiter of what can be shown on video or in the cinema, and that the setting of standards primarily rests with an industry body.[117]

Despite the attempt to tighten up the law, the new system paved the way for a further liberalisation in the late 1990s. At that time, government ministers and the BBFC became concerned that prohibited content was widely available on the black market. It was thought that if stronger content could be brought within the system of regulation through more liberal standards, then it would allow the regulator to negotiate cuts to certain scenes and would reduce the demand for black market material. In 1997, the BBFC proposed a strategy that would grant R18 certificates to a wider range of titles, and the restrictions would focus on more extreme violent and sadistic content.[118] A junior Home Office minister in the Conservative government informally approved the strategy.[119] The new guidelines for classification allowed for some shots of penetration, and a film called *The Pyramid* was granted an R18 certificate, which would not have been permissible under the old rules.[120]

By this time, the government had changed and the Home Office, now under the Labour government, were reported as saying that the BBFC's policy change was an 'unacceptable, unilateral decision'.[121] The BBFC thereby came under considerable political pressure concerning the liberalisation of standards.[122] The police and customs authorities also expressed concern that some of the material being classified would be found to be obscene in the courts.[123] As a result, the new policy was suspended in late 1997. The following year, the BBFC devised new guidelines that permitted videos of 'real sexual activity' under the R18 classification as long as it was not violent and was legal.[124] The new rules permitted erections to be shown, but not 'clear sight of penetration, oral, vaginal or anal, or of masturbation', and scenes of ejaculation were not to be included.[125] Applying these guidelines, the BBFC refused to classify a film called *Makin' Whoopee*, on the grounds that it included 'extremely explicit' scenes including 'many close-up shots of penetration'.[126] The decision was subject to an appeal before the VAC and the hearing focused on whether the video was obscene. While the BBFC and Customs & Excise thought that the video was obscene, the VAC concluded that it was not.[127]

The tensions between the BBFC and its appeal body continued, and the Board refused to grant an R18 classification to a number of titles (with names including

---

[117] Robertson and Nicol (n 93) 817.

[118] R Duval, 'The Last Days of the Board' in E Lamberti (ed), *Behind the Scenes at the BBFC* (London, British Film Institute, 2012) 147. An R18 certificate permits the work to be shown in specially licensed cinemas and sold in licensed sex shops.

[119] ibid.

[120] *Video Appeals Committee* (n 114) at [16]. Though Petley notes that even the new liberal regime imposed significant limits, see Petley (n 103) 137–38.

[121] *The Sunday Times* (23 November 1997).

[122] See Petley (n 103) and BBC, Panorama, *Porn Wars* (broadcast on 2 November 1998).

[123] *Video Appeals Committee* (n 114).

[124] ibid, at [18].

[125] ibid, at [18].

[126] ibid, at [16].

[127] ibid, at [16].

Horny Catbabe, *Nympho Nurse Nancy* and *Office Tarts*). Again, the Video Appeals Committee reversed the decision and granted an R18 certificate to those titles. The VAC's decision was centred on the terms of the Video Recordings Act 1984, s 4A rather than the obscenity standard. The Committee reasoned that there was insufficient evidence to demonstrate the number of children that may be harmed or the extent of such harm.[128] Consequently, the VAC concluded that the risk of the material being viewed by and causing harm to children was insignificant. By contrast the BBFC argued that a precautionary approach should be taken to children's wellbeing and that until evidence was available, the certificate should be withheld.[129] The BBFC challenged the decision of the VAC in judicial review proceedings. In those proceedings, the court upheld the VAC's decision, concluding that the body had applied the right criteria under s 4A and that the finding of an insignificant risk to children was not irrational.[130] The decision dealt a blow to those seeking to restrict the availability of stronger sexual content. The decision forced the BBFC to devise a new set of classification guidelines, which permitted the sale of hardcore material.[131]

The episode shows how a change in standards and the types of material generally available was not brought about by Parliament or politicians.[132] Instead it was the product of a number of regulatory decisions, with relatively little public input. The episode also illustrates how controls introduced to address the deficiencies in the criminal law can have unintended consequences. While the BBFC and Video Appeals Committee are often seen as part of the system of censorship, their actions in the late 1990s contributed to an overall liberalisation of standards. Once the films had been certified by the BBFC, the prospects for a criminal prosecution were remote. So while the regulator will consider the criminal law standards, the conversation is two-way and the regulatory system can also influence the understanding of the criminal law.

Whatever the merits of the process of change, the liberalisation of standards is a more realistic response to sexual content in the age of the internet. While the regulator was initially concerned about the black market for videos in the late 1990s, the subsequent growth of digital communications has increased the channels for the distribution of pornographic and other extreme content. An attempt to return to the standards that were applied to cinema and video in the 1980s would have little credibility at a time when far more extreme content is being circulated with relative ease online. Any worries about video for retail were soon eclipsed by concerns about the internet, which remains the primary focus for public debate and policy makers.

D. Digital Media

The types of content that were heavily restricted and difficult to get hold of in the 1980s are now relatively easy for anyone to access in the comfort of their home.

---

[128] See Petley (n 103) 146.

[129] *Video Appeals Committee* (n 114) at [38].

[130] ibid, at [47].

[131] Petley (n 103) 154.

[132] For Petley, the BBFC's initial retraction of the more liberal policy demonstrates how the regulator can be subject to political pressure when it steps out of line with the government's favoured view. See Petley (n 103) 157.

While some commentators dismiss concerns about this development as a knee jerk panic that is found with each new technology for communication, others argue that the extremity of the content easily available to the public at large means the problem is of a different magnitude to anything that went before. Most people accept the need for some kinds of control on what can be accessed via the digital media, and the debate tends to focus on the nature and extent of the controls. The digital media also poses considerable challenges in designing measures that are effective, while remaining proportionate and not restricting adults who want to access lawful content. To assess this, the various techniques of controlling obscene content online will be outlined.

i. Targeting the Publisher

The first strategy is simply to apply the existing criminal law of obscenity to the digital media. Under the broad definition of a publication under the Obscene Publications Act, content is published within the jurisdiction when accessed on a computer in England and Wales, even when hosted overseas.[133] The decision in *GS* showed that the Obscene Publications Act 1959 can cover private messages on the digital media. The Act provides a broad offence to catch various types of extreme content. There are, however, limits to this strategy and there are obvious difficulties in enforcing the law when the publisher is either unknown or based overseas.[134] While the Obscene Publications Act 1959 remains a potential source of liability, it is playing a relatively limited role in regulating internet content.

The issue is not just the proliferation of unlawful content, and there are concerns about the ease with which lawful adult content can be accessed by children with internet access. One strategy to address this problem is to bring parts of the digital media into the existing media regulation framework. For example, some video-on-demand services submit content to the BBFC on a voluntary basis to receive an age rating, which can provide a useful way for the service to guide and inform consumers.[135] More formally, rules analogous to the film and video classification scheme are applied to certain audio-visual content on the digital media. Under amendments made to the Communications Act 2003, a UK based video-on-demand service must not contain material that the BBFC has deemed not suitable for classification or which it is reasonable to expect that the BBFC would not grant a classification were it submitted as a video.[136] The Act also provides that video-on-demand services should not include material that has been issued for an R18 certificate or could reasonably be expected to receive an R18 certificate if it were submitted, unless the material is 'made available in a manner which secures that persons under the age of 18 will not normally see or hear it'.[137] As a result, the video-on-demand services providing R18 content will need to develop an age verification system. While Ofcom rather than the BBFC

---

[133] *Perrin* (n 78).
[134] See Ch 7.
[135] BBFC, *Annual Report and Accounts 2016* (2017) 14.
[136] Known as 'prohibited material': Communications Act 2003, s 368E. For discussion of the video on-demand regulations more generally see Ch 6.
[137] Known as 'specially restricted material': Communications Act 2003, s 368E.

enforces these provisions, the BBFC classification guidelines are taken into account when deciding if the content would be prohibited or granted an R18 certificate.

The extension of certain BBFC standards to such digital services was justified as closing a gap in the law by applying comparable standards to video on-demand, video and cinema.[138] However, the changes to the law provoked considerable controversy and were criticised as a form of censorship.[139] The criticisms of this law show how new forms of media allow the old boundaries to be pushed and change the expectations about what is acceptable. The internet initially provided a route around the existing standards for content on television, film or DVD and was largely free of regulatory controls. That initial freedom thereby allowed audiences to become accustomed to more extreme content and for new businesses to be formed around that demand. As a result, an attempt to reassert controls found on other formats became viewed as a clampdown and an oppressive control on internet content.

Despite the controversy, the on-demand provisions have limited effect as they apply only to those services that provide audio-visual content that are comparable to television and that are based in the UK.[140] The rules on video on-demand do not aim to restrict adult content generally, but seek to secure fair competition by applying some equivalent standards for television and television-like services over the internet. Much of the content on the internet will be organised in a very different way from television, with various combinations of video, written articles, photos, user comments and discussion. In 2016, Ofcom ruled that a website specialising in spanking fetishes, which featured video alongside still images and text, did not have a principal purpose comparable to or in competition with linear television services and so was not subject to the video on-demand rules.[141]

A broader regulatory response to the issues of online material can be found in the Digital Economy Act 2017, which requires those making pornography available on a commercial basis to provide a way to ensure that lawful adult material is not accessible to those under 18.[142] Under the Act, pornography is defined as content that has or would receive an R18 certificate by the BBFC or that was produced solely or principally for the purpose of sexual arousal (other than extreme pornography).[143] The enforcement of the provision is assigned to the BBFC, which will give the industry body another statutory function. While a site that makes adult content available to children could already be liable under the Obscene Publications Act 1959,[144] the age verification scheme shows another move away from the criminal law of obscenity towards a regulatory system.

---

[138] The regulations also clarified what had been an interim position under the previous law.

[139] See 'Porn Regulation in the UK', *Independent* (6 December 2014).

[140] However, other EU countries may have equivalent regulations under the Audio Visual Media Services Directive, Directive 2010/13/EU of the European Parliament and of the Council of 10 March 2010 on the coordination of certain provisions laid down by law, regulation or administrative action in Member States concerning the provision of audiovisual media services [2010] OJ L 95/1.

[141] Ofcom Broadcast and On-Demand Bulletin, *Appeal by Pandora Blake about the service 'Dreams of Spanking'* (6 June 2016).

[142] Digital Economy Act 2017, s 14. For the equivalent provision for video-on-demand, see Communications Act 2003, s 368E.

[143] Digital Economy Act 2017, s 15. The part of the definition relating to content made for the purpose of sexual arousal applies where the film or material has or would receive an 18 certificate or be deemed unsuitable for classification.

[144] *Perrin* (n 78); *R v Waddon* (6 April 2000, unreported), CA (Crim Div).

Those in breach of the age verification obligation can be subject to an enforcement notice and subject to a financial penalty.[145] The Act also allows the regulator to give a notice to 'ancillary service providers' and payment service providers (such as a credit card company) of any people using its services that make adult content available without the age verification system, or that make extreme pornography available in the UK.[146] The internet service provider can be required by the notice to take steps to prevent the content being made available, for example through blocking sites.[147] The provisions show how intermediaries are increasingly seen as a source of control and subject to new responsibilities as their role in the flow of information is recognised. To some degree, the Act appears to apply to the digital media the same standards expected of a newsagent selling adult magazines or a cinema providing access to adult films. However, there is a question of what steps websites will have to take to establish an effective age verification mechanism, such as credit card details or cross checking on the electoral register. The requirement may thereby result in a loss of anonymity for the viewer, which could deter people from accessing lawful adult content.

Formal regulation is not the only type of control that can be imposed on the digital media and sometimes forms of self-regulation or co-regulation are adopted. In relation to the digital media, this can be seen with the Internet Watch Foundation (IWF) which provides services for the reporting and detection of indecent images of children. Various internet companies use a list locating illegal content compiled by the IWF, along with their own algorithms, to block such images. In relation to content that is not unlawful, the leading broadband providers have agreed to require subscribers to make a choice whether to apply filters for adult content.[148] That provides another method of preventing children accessing content that is suitable for adults only, but one that is pursued through company terms rather than through law. Such blocking measures have provoked controversies and will be considered more generally in Chapter 7.

ii. Unlawful Content: Targeting the Viewer

While the Obscene Publications Act and other traditional controls target the *publisher* of the content, the last two decades have seen a greater reliance on controls that target the *viewer* of content. This move reflects a view that even if the authorities cannot do much to stop content being supplied either by those overseas or acting anonymously, they can stem the demand for such content within the jurisdiction. The move reflects the greater power of digital media audiences to select content, but assigns responsibility to the audience for any consequences or harms that flow from those choices. To turn to the possessor of material is, however, a serious step that can have implications

---

[145] Digital Economy Act 2017, s 19.

[146] ibid, s 21.

[147] ibid, s 23. The section also provides that such requirements may 'have the effect of preventing persons in the United Kingdom from being able to access material other than the offending material', which envisages a level of over-inclusiveness. The level of over-inclusiveness is relevant to the compliance with Art 10, see Ch 7.

[148] See Ofcom, *Report on Internet Safety Measures* (2015).

for privacy and arguably freedom of thought. It is a step that should be taken only in relation to the most serious harms.

a. Images of Children

The strategy of targeting the audience has been employed in relation to indecent photographs of children. The *taking* of an indecent image of a child has been a criminal offence since 1978 under the Protection of Children Act. The statute was amended in 1994 to include the *making* of such an image. While those provisions targeted the publisher understood in the traditional sense, the Criminal Justice Act 1988 took the first step in criminalising the *possession* of indecent photographs of a child. There are several rationales for imposing special criminal liability on the possession of such images.[149] The first draws a connection between the possession and the production of the image. By possessing such images a person can contribute to a demand in production, which can then stimulate further abuse of children in making the images.[150] A second argument is that the content influences behaviour and makes the viewer more likely to commit an act of abuse.[151] A third argument makes a connection between possession and child abuse, as such images can themselves be used as a tool in grooming children (for example in suggesting to children that certain practices are normal). A fourth argument is that the viewing of certain types of photograph may be regarded as inflicting or perpetuating the injury suffered by the child in the image.[152] Finally, there is a view that the possession of such content is morally wrong and deserves to be punished.

There are limits to these rationales. While an image can be a tool in grooming, not every possessor of images will use it in that way and the problem could be addressed through specific grooming offences.[153] Furthermore, not every possessor will stimulate demand for further production of the content, as that will surely depend on the way the image was produced and how the person came to possess the material. There are also the obvious debates about media effects discussed earlier and whether the content influences the mind and conduct of the viewer. However, the harms are regarded as so serious that the law imposes a general blanket rule against possession with very limited exceptions.

The offence under the 1988 Act requires the prosecution to show that the image is indecent, that it is of a child and that the defendant had that image in his or her

---

[149] For discussion of the rationales outlined here see Gillespie (n 80) 33–39 and S Ost, *Child Pornography and Sexual Grooming* (Cambridge, Cambridge University Press, 2009) 118.

[150] When announcing the intention of criminalising possession, the then Home Secretary stated that 'it would be justified to criminalise simple possession in the hope of stamping out this degrading trade'. Douglas Hurd, HC Deb 18 January 1988, vol 125, col 689. See also Ost, ibid, for criticism.

[151] The Minister of State at the time of the enactment, John Patten, stated to the press that a criminal measure was necessary partly because the material 'fed the instincts which gave rise to sexual abuse': 'New penalty to curb child porn' *The Guardian* (1 March 1988).

[152] See also *R v Beaney* [2004] EWCA Crim 449, [2004] 2 Cr App R (S) 82, emphasising the psychological harm.

[153] Offences related to the grooming of children can be found under the Sexual Offences Act 2003, ss 12, 14, 15 and 15A. See also Gillespie (n 80) 109.

possession.[154] The Act provides a defence for those possessing the image for a legitimate reason, although this will be construed narrowly.[155] There are defences to prevent criminalisation of inadvertent possession, for example where a person is sent the image without request and did not keep it beyond a reasonable period of time, or where the defendant did not see the image and did not suspect (or did not have any reason to suspect) that it was indecent.[156] The maximum sentence for the possession offence under the 1988 Act is five years, while the taking or making of an indecent image of a child is punishable by a maximum sentence of 10 years under the 1978 Act. That difference reflects the varying levels of culpability, as the original maker of the image bears greater responsibility for the harms caused.

The possession of the content does not just mean physical print copies of images, but applies to the data used to create an image. The offence can apply where the image is downloaded or where it is stored in the computer cache after a person has viewed it (though the commission of an offence will depend on the defendant having knowledge of the cache).[157] Even when an image is deleted, a person can still be in possession if the defendant has the technical skill or equipment to retrieve the file.[158] David Ormerod has commented that this means there is a special defence for the 'computer illiterate' who lack the skills or knowledge to retrieve deleted images.[159]

The statutory scheme was initially envisaged as a system in which the 1978 Act targeted the producer or distributor of an image, while the 1988 Act targeted possession. The relation between the two offences has become confused since a series of decisions extended the 'making' offence under the 1978 Act to include the accessing of an image on a computer. In *Atkins*, the court found that intentionally storing data from the internet on a computer constituted the 'making' of an image.[160] Later in *Jayson*, the Court of Appeal found that an image is 'made' when a person opens an email attachment with the knowledge that it contains or is likely to contain an indecent image of a child.[161] The court further reasoned that when content is viewed online, the user calls up data that assembles a fresh image on the computer screen and thereby commits the 'making' offence.[162] As a result, the 1978 Act is now also used to target the viewer of the content too, and a person accessing content online can commit both the making and possession offence.[163]

These interpretations were explained by Cranston J as a recognition of the difficulty in 'applying the law to the rapidly changing nature of the internet' and as a result the courts will interpret the statutes 'by bearing in mind the policy behind the law, which is

---

[154] *R v George Steen* [2014] EWCA Crim 1390 at [15]. See also *R v Collier* [2004] EWCA Crim 1411, [2005] 1 WLR 843.

[155] Criminal Justice Act 1988, s 160(2)(a).

[156] ibid, s 160(2).

[157] *DPP v Atkins* [2000] 1 WLR 1427.

[158] *R v Porter (Ross Warwick)* [2006] EWCA Crim 560, [2006] 1 WLR 2633; *R v Leonard* [2012] EWCA Crim 277, [2012] 2 Cr App R 12.

[159] See DC Ormerod, 'Commentary' [2006] Crim LR 748.

[160] *DPP v Atkins* (n 157).

[161] *R v Smith and Jayson* [2002] EWCA Crim 683, [2003] 1 Cr App R 13 at [19]–[20].

[162] ibid, at [33].

[163] See Ost (n 149) 60 on the 'merging' of the offences.

to choke off the demand for this type of material, which leads to the exploitation and degradation of children'.[164] While there are good reasons for prohibiting the viewing of such indecent images, the 'making' offence is arguably an inappropriate means to pursue this, given that the viewer has a different level of responsibility than the initial maker of the image. Moreover, the offence of 'making' an image under s 1 of the 1978 Act does not include a legitimate reason defence that is available for the possession offence under s 160 of the 1988 Act.[165]

Liability for the making offence is limited by the requirement that the act was 'a deliberate and intentional act with knowledge that the image made is, or is likely to be an indecent photograph or pseudo-photograph of a child'.[166] That requirement has not stopped the 'making' offence expanding to situations that can potentially include inadvertent viewing. In *Harrison*, the defendant visited an adult pornography website, but the 'making' offence was committed when a pop-up advertisement on the site included an indecent image of a child.[167] The question for the court was whether the defendant knew or was likely to know of pop-up activity on that site and that there was a likelihood that the pop-up advertisement would contain an illegal image. If a jury or magistrate is willing to assume the defendant should have known such a pop-up of an unlawful image was likely even where the site hosts adult material, then there may be a danger that the offence can be committed inadvertently by those engaging in otherwise lawful activities.[168]

A further difficulty with the making and possession offences lies in defining what is meant by an 'indecent' image. The test is objective and applies if it 'offends against recognised standards of propriety'.[169] Given that the term governs the scope of a serious offence regulating people's viewing habits, some clarity to guide behaviour is important. In most cases, this will not be an issue, but Suzanne Ost notes that there may be difficulties at the lower end of the scale.[170] This raises questions of whether nudity is sufficient or whether there must be a sexual element to the image.[171] The question is determined looking at the image alone, as opposed to the context of possession, viewing or production. The difficulty is that a picture of a child on a beach with no clothes may be regarded as harmless when taken by a family member on a holiday. However, the reaction to an identical image would be quite different if taken surreptitiously by a stranger and circulated among people with a sexual interest in children. The making and possession offences do not distinguish between these circumstances and much rests on prosecutorial policy to provide a filter and avoid over-enforcement to innocent family photographs.[172]

The broad terms of the offence can in theory apply to some forms of mainstream media. In *Neal*, a person was convicted for possessing a book containing photographs

---

[164] *R v Harrison* [2007] EWCA Crim 2976, [2008] 1 Cr App R 29 at [8].
[165] The legitimate reason defence is, however, available to the showing and distributing offences under s 1.
[166] *Smith and Jayson* (n 161).
[167] *Harrison* (n 164) at [19].
[168] See discussion in *R v George Steen* (n 154) on the need to raise this possibility with the jury. Gillespie (n 80) 125–26.
[169] *R v Stamford* [1972] 2 QB 391.
[170] Ost (n 149) 57.
[171] See *R v O'Carroll* [2002] EWCA Crim 3190, [2003] 2 Cr App R (S) 21.
[172] See discussion in Feldman (n 4) 948.

taken by the well-known photographers David Hamilton, Sally Mann and Jock Sturges, which were freely available in leading book retailers such as Amazon and Waterstones.[173] Quashing the conviction in the Court of Appeal, Richards LJ stated that it is 'very unfair' for a person to be prosecuted for possessing content that is so widely available through mainstream shops. According to this view, the publisher and retailer should be the primary target of the prosecutors' attention. The decision therefore provides some guidance to prosecutors about when to target the publisher as opposed to the recipient of the content.

b. Pseudo Photographs

The offences of possessing and making images apply not only to actual images of children, but also to 'pseudo photographs'[174] and to tracings or images 'derived from the whole or part of a photograph or pseudo-photograph'.[175] The rationale for the criminalisation of 'pseudo images' is distinct from the central justification for controlling indecent images of children, as no harm normally occurs to a child in the course of producing a pseudo image. If a real child is depicted in the pseudo image, but not abused (for example where a naked body of an adult is superimposed on the image of a child), then that can also be seen to cause harm and distress to that child.[176] However, if no real child is depicted then the harm is more questionable.[177]

The law on pseudo photographs perhaps reflects the practical difficulty for the police in not being able to distinguish pseudo images from the real and therefore takes an over-inclusive approach. That, however, does not justify a prosecution where it is known the images are manipulations rather than actual depictions. Instead, the rationale seems to be that such images either are likely to influence the reader or be used as part of the grooming process. The approach contrasts with the position in the US, where a prohibition on the possession of a 'virtual' image of 'a minor engaging in sexually explicit conduct' was found to violate the First Amendment, on the grounds that no child had been harmed in the course of production.[178] However, that ruling does not stop US authorities targeting virtual images that are deemed to be obscene under the constitutional standard, thereby falling outside the protection of the First Amendment.

c. Cartoons and Drawings

The domestic law has gone further in criminalising the possession of certain non-photographic images relating to children. The Coroners and Justice Act 2009 creates an offence of possessing a 'prohibited image' that is: (1) pornographic; (2) 'is grossly offensive, disgusting or otherwise of an obscene character'; and (3) either 'focuses solely or principally on a child's genitals or anal region' or portrays certain acts listed

---

[173] *R v Neal* [2011] EWCA Crim 461.
[174] Protection of Children Act 1978, s 1 and s 160.
[175] ibid, s 7(4A).
[176] See Ost (n 149).
[177] See A Gillespie, *Cybercrime: Key Issues and Debates* (Abingdon, Routledge, 2016) 247–49 for discussion.
[178] *Ashcroft v Free Speech Coalition* 535 US 234 (2002).

in the provision.[179] The crucial point is that the provision does not apply to photographs or pseudo photographs, but targets drawings, cartoons and computer generated images. The non-photographic image does not need to depict a child involved in the sexual activity, but can include images of certain sexual activities in the 'presence' of a child.[180] The original proposals for the offence were put forward on the basis that 'it is felt by police and children's welfare organisations that the possession and circulation of these images serves to legitimise and reinforce highly inappropriate views about children'.[181] The Home Office noted that such non-photographic images are often found alongside real images of child abuse. However, the Home Office also referred to a case where the police found only drawings and cartoons, but were unable to prosecute.[182] The trend appears to be that the authorities will sometimes discover disturbing content when raiding suspected paedophiles, find the images fall outside the existing law and will then demand new laws to cover such content.

d. Child Abuse Manuals

The Serious Crime Act 2015 provides that it is an offence 'to be in possession of any item that contains advice or guidance about abusing children sexually.'[183] The provision is significant in that it creates a possession offence in relation to written text, as opposed to images. The offence thereby sees the 'paedophile manual' as a type of information primarily to facilitate certain criminal acts, and thereby warrants strict prohibition. The publication of such material would be very likely to be prohibited under the Obscene Publications Act 1959, so the law represents another part of the shift towards the targeting of the recipient of content. Like the other possession offences, there are defences where there is a legitimate reason for possession, or where the possession of the content was inadvertent.[184] The law took its inspiration from provisions of anti-terrorism laws that prohibit the possession of bomb-making instructions (showing how various areas of control borrow from one another).[185] As with other incremental developments in this area, the legislation was put forward after reports that law enforcement bodies had discovered such content in circulation, but found it was unable to take action.[186] Despite this concern, people found with such a manual will often also be in possession of indecent images of children, so in practice the provision allows for such a person to be charged with additional offences.

e. Extreme Pornography

In 2008, an offence was enacted criminalising the possession of extreme pornography. The legislation was introduced following a high profile case in which a man was found

---

[179] Coroners and Justice Act 2009, s 62.

[180] ibid. For criticism see S Ost, 'Criminalising fabricated images of child pornography: a matter of harm or morality?' (2010) 30 *Legal Studies* 230.

[181] Home Office, *Consultation on Possession of Non-Photographic Visual Depictions of Child Sexual Abuse* (2007).

[182] ibid, 4.

[183] Serious Crime Act 2015, s 69.

[184] ibid, s 69(2).

[185] 'Paedophiles to be treated as terrorists', *The Sunday Times*, 27 April 2014.

[186] Lord Taylor, HL Deb, 16 June 2014, vol 754, col 647.

to have viewed violent pornography prior to committing a brutal murder. The government commissioned research on the effects of extreme pornography to support the case for a possession offence.[187] The legislation is significant in so far as it creates a possession offence for content not related to children.

The provision defines pornography as content 'of such a nature that it must reasonably be assumed to have been produced solely or principally for the purpose of sexual arousal'.[188] A pornographic image is 'extreme' if it 'is grossly offensive, disgusting or otherwise of an obscene character' and 'if it portrays, in an explicit and realistic way': (1) 'an act which threatens a person's life'; (2) 'an act which results, or is likely to result, in serious injury to a person's anus, breasts or genitals'; (3) 'an act which involves sexual interference with a human corpse'; or (4) 'a person performing an act of intercourse or oral sex with an animal (whether dead or alive)'.[189] The statute was subsequently amended to include explicit and realistic portrayals of non-consensual penetration in the definition of extreme pornography.[190]

The Act has been criticised from various sides of the debate. On one view, the Act is under-inclusive as it does not include depictions of acts that injure body parts other than the anus, breasts or genitals.[191] Others, however, worry that it imposes a limit on sexual freedom and could potentially criminalise the recording of lawful sexual activity between adults. While the Act provides a defence where the defendant participated in consensual activities depicted in the image (excluding bestiality images),[192] that does not apply where the image depicts others engaged in the activity. In 2012, there was criticism of the prosecution of a man for the possession images of consensual activities of fisting and urethral sounding.[193]

From this discussion, there are several points that can be made about the various criminal offences. The first is that with the proliferation of pornographic content on the internet, the law now places greater responsibility on the recipient of the content. The shift in focus raises some difficult questions and it is argued here that the responsibilities that can be expected of a possessor or viewer are distinct from those expected of a publisher. In some cases, there are concerns about the level of culpability that can be assigned to the recipient.[194] Clarity in the law is also particularly important so people know what content to avoid. While a publisher may be expected to take legal advice to clarify how a law would be applied and to negotiate risk, an individual cannot be expected to go through such an assessment before viewing content on the internet (and such an assessment will not be possible where the specific image that will appear on the screen is not known in advance). While the content at stake may raise relatively minimal issues of public interest under Article 10, in some cases there can be issues of privacy and expression rights where the extreme pornography offence is applied to consensual activities between adults. While there are compelling reasons for

[187] C Itzin, A Taket and L Kelly, *The evidence of harm to adults relating to exposure to extreme pornographic material: rapid evidence assessment* (Ministry of Justice Research Series, 2007).

[188] Criminal Justice and Immigration Act 2008, s 63.

[189] ibid, s 63(7).

[190] ibid, s 63(7A).

[191] See discussion in Gillespie (n 177) 217.

[192] Criminal Justice and Immigration Act 2008, s 66.

[193] 'Jury acquits barrister in "extreme porn" case' *The Guardian* (9 August 2012).

[194] See *R v Sharples* [2012] EWCA Crim 3144.

prohibiting the possession of certain content, such laws need to be carefully drafted and applied with caution.

The second point is that laws of possession have been a growth area. When an offence is established, there is a pressure to continually expand the reach of the law through amendments or new provisions. The law has moved from regulating the possession of indecent images of children, to tracings, cartoons and certain images depicting adults. Analogies are easily made between one type of content and another, and so arguments are formed to extend the possession offences. As a result, the law can begin to drift through such analogies without fully thinking about the rationale or possible balances to be struck.

The logic of a possession offence could be extended to other areas of law. For example, people arguably have a responsibility not to view or possess revenge pornography or sensitive private photographs. In Chapter 7, it will be argued that the expansion of legal responsibilities on the audience should be resisted save for the most extreme cases. While the issues surrounding possession offences may seem far removed from the concerns of the mainstream media, the developments are important for media lawyers in understanding the latest methods of controlling content. Obscenity related offences are often a testing ground for forms of censorship, as there will be little mainstream resistance. Once established, the use of those methods to control other types of content becomes a possibility.

E. General Conclusions on Obscenity, Indecent Images and Pornography

Obscenity law has undergone a radical transformation since the high-profile prosecutions of the 1960s, 70s and 80s, which divided opinion and signalled a cultural change. The Obscene Publications Act 1959 has declined significantly in use in recent years and seems to be employed as a general offence to catch any gaps in the law. However, the decline has not led to an abandonment of controls. The account of obscenity law has shown how controls are distributed across a number of different bodies, relying on different standards.

For the media, the risks have changed. In the 1950s and 60s, some high-profile prosecutions targeted book publishers. In the early 1980s, those distributing film and video were targeted by prosecutors. In more recent years, a mainstream media body has very little reason to worry about the criminal law of obscenity. It is hard to imagine a broadcaster, large film company, or major publisher even considering the publication of the extreme content that now attracts prosecution. However, the mainstream media is subject to a more specialist set of controls. Cinema and video are subject to the regulation of the BBFC, which can advise on making cuts to films and refuse a certificate. Television is regulated by Ofcom's standards on 'undue offence'. Many major media bodies will have informal understandings with the police, and prosecutors will generally respect the editorial autonomy of a media entity in relation to such issues. Occasionally, these systems break down (for example, on some occasions art galleries have been raided by the police), but for the most part, large media bodies and institutions are controlled through systems of regulation and mutual understanding.

The specialist regulatory schemes mean that the standards for the media are often in the hands of regulators, which apply more elaborate tests than simply asking if the material would 'deprave and corrupt' the likely reader. The trajectory looks set to increase, with the BBFC performing a role in setting standards for video-on-demand, as well as enforcing the new age verification rules for internet content. Internet intermediaries also play a role in the system of control by helping to filter illegal content and by encouraging the use of filters in relation to adult content. The system of controlling sexual (and to some degree violent) content is decentralised, and thereby applies different types of control to different sectors of the media. However, the Obscene Publications Act still underpins the publication controls, as the BBFC is not supposed to classify criminally obscene material, and those classification standards are now applied in certain controls for digital content.

The criminal law still plays a prominent role, but its focus has shifted. Police and prosecution resources are primarily targeted at enforcing laws relating to indecent images of children, but there are also a number of prosecutions for extreme pornography. The change in contemporary standards means that criminal controls focus on a narrower range of content and apply more liberal standards than in previous years. Despite the seeming liberalisation of standards, far more people are now convicted of obscenity-related offences.[195] The reason for this apparent paradox of liberalisation alongside stringent control lies in both the ease with which extreme content can be circulated via digital communications and the law targeting the viewer or possessor of the material. When the law criminalises the recipients rather than publishers, there are many more people who commit offences.

III. Government Secrecy and National Security

Much like the law of obscenity, controls on government secrecy are a patchwork of different laws, regulations and informal measures. Government secrecy has also been a focus for a change in culture, this time towards a political culture that demands more accountable and transparent government. Past attempts to silence the press and punish leakers have led to a number of notorious and embarrassing episodes for government. Such examples range from the D-Notice affair in the late 1960s, the prosecution of the journalist Duncan Campbell in the 1970s, the acquittal of Clive Ponting and the disastrous attempt to prevent the publication of the book *Spycatcher* in the 1980s. With hindsight, these cases can be seen as misguided attempts to assert authority in an era that saw a move away from the old culture of deference and a change in the relationship between citizen and state. While the law has changed since those episodes,

---

[195] See J Rowbottom, 'The transformation of obscenity law' (2018) 27(1) *Information & Communications Technology Law* 4.

there is no cause for complacency and the current law also imposes some broad controls. It is also important to recognise the valid concerns of government, especially with the ease of copying and transmitting large quantities of digital information that enable mass leaks.

The law regulating government secrecy often goes to the heart of Article 10 and the justifications for media freedom. Preventing the disclosure and publication of state information will prevent the public becoming informed about certain areas of government activity. Similarly, if journalists are to act as watchdogs and monitor public bodies, then transparency is necessary to allow government conduct to be observed and scrutinised. Restricting the release of information could allow government misconduct to go undetected. Moreover, the types of information that government seeks to withhold, while sensitive, will often relate to matters of public importance. In a democracy, there is a compelling case for government transparency, and exceptions require a strong justification.

Against these obvious arguments for media freedom are the equally obvious points that not everything relating to government can be made transparent. To disclose certain information may, in some cases, have the effect of undermining the implementation of government policy.[196] Disclosing the sites of random drink driving tests in advance would undermine the deterrent effect caused by the unpredictability of the measure. By jeopardising policies that have public approval, complete transparency can frustrate democracy. The tension is acute when looking at issues of national security. Covert operations cannot, by definition, be a matter of public knowledge. Complete transparency would assist terrorists and others that a pose a risk to security. The disclosure of information relating to the security services can also threaten the safety of agents working in the field, as well as their sources. For these reasons, there are special restrictions to prevent the unauthorised disclosure of information relating to security and other sensitive matters.

While transparency is to be expected, government secrecy need not be an affront to democracy. As Dennis Thompson points out, if the secrecy measures are publicly debated and democratically approved, then such secrecy may be seen to implement the democratic will.[197] On this view, even if certain information should not be disclosed, the general policy facilitating secrecy should be transparent. The difficulty with the reconciliation of secrecy and democracy through public approval is that it is near impossible for people to assess the merits of the case for secrecy without actually knowing the information being withheld.[198] Without full disclosure, it is hard to know whether information is being withheld to protect the national interest or to hide politically inconvenient facts. Delegating to government a discretion to prohibit any information that it regards as threatening to national security would hand over a blank cheque to those in power, which could be abused to cover up information that is embarrassing or puts the conduct of the government in a negative light.

Having identified the basic tension, the following sections will assess the balance struck between these factors under the law of confidence and the Official Secrets Act. The discussion will show that while there are a range of legal controls available to

---

[196] See D Thompson, 'Democratic Secrecy' (1999) 114 *Political Science Quarterly* 181.
[197] ibid, 185.
[198] ibid.

government, there are often risks of bad publicity when enforcing the law. The later sections will show how the government can also rely on informal controls on the media.

A. Breach of Confidence

As was seen in Chapter 2, the doctrine of breach of confidence has played a foundational role in the protection of personal privacy. However, the doctrine can also be used to protect government information. In the famous Crossman diaries case, the court held that the doctrine could, in principle at least, restrain the publication of a former Cabinet minister's diaries.[199] Lord Widgery added an important qualification that when government seeks to rely on the doctrine, it must be shown that the public interest lies in favour of restricting publication.[200] Unlike personal privacy cases, there is an assumption that the dissemination of government information should not be restrained by the doctrine unless there is a clear public interest.

The doctrine has provided the government with an important tool in controlling the circulation of information. However, that tool comes with limits and risks, as was shown in the notorious *Spycatcher* series of cases. A disgruntled former MI5 agent, Peter Wright, wrote a book called *Spycatcher*, alleging that the security services had conducted unlawful activities and plotted against a Prime Minister, and that the former head of MI5 was a Soviet agent. The book also exposed a number techniques used by the security services. As Wright was then based in Australia, the government did not rely on the Official Secrets Act 1911 and brought proceedings for breach of confidence.[201] The government also sought to restrain publication in Australia, but the application was rejected by the trial judge and on appeal.[202] While that litigation proceeded, *The Guardian* and *The Observer* published articles on the Australian court proceedings that included details of the main allegations in the book. Concerned about such disclosures in the domestic press, in July 1986 the government obtained an injunction in England and Wales to prohibit the publication of details from the book in those newspapers.[203] As was noted in Chapter 2, once an interim injunction is awarded against a named party, a third party can be in contempt of court for frustrating the order by publishing the protected information before the trial. This became known as the '*Spycatcher* principle', after the government brought proceedings for contempt of court against the *Independent* and *The Sunday Times* for publishing information covered by the injunction naming *The Guardian* and *The Observer*.[204]

The book was published in the USA in July 1987, yet weeks later a majority of the House of Lords concluded that the government still had an arguable case in breach of

---

[199] *A-G v Jonathan Cape Ltd* [1976] QB 752. However, on the facts the court declined to grant an injunction as the information was no longer sensitive given the passage of time.

[200] ibid, 771.

[201] C Moran, *Classified: Secrecy and the State in Modern Britain* (Cambridge, Cambridge University Press, 2013) 336.

[202] See *A-G (UK) v Heinemann Publishers Australia Pty Ltd* [1988] HCA 25, 165 CLR 30.

[203] See *A-G v Guardian Newspapers Ltd* (n 1).

[204] *The Sunday Times* and the *Independent* were initially fined £50,000 for contempt. The fines were reversed on appeal, but the findings of contempt against both titles were upheld. See *A-G v Times Newspapers Ltd* [1992] 1 AC 191.

confidence and that the interim injunction should remain until full trial.[205] The strategy was not a success. The free availability of the book in other jurisdictions allowed copies to be brought back to the UK or ordered, so that anyone interested could get hold of a copy with relative ease. The publicity surrounding the case only generated more interest and demand for the book.

In 1988, the House of Lords declined to impose a permanent injunction on the grounds that any damage that the publication could cause to the government had already been done by the availability of the title both outside jurisdiction and within.[206] *The Sunday Times* was still found to be in breach of confidence for its previous publication of extracts of the book and was to ordered to pay an account of profits resulting from that breach.[207] The matter did not end there. The European Court of Human Rights found the UK to be in breach of Article 10 for maintaining the interim injunction after publication in the USA. The Strasbourg Court reasoned that the international publication meant there was no interest in maintaining the secrecy of the information, and the interim injunction was really aiming to protect the reputation of and confidence in the security services, which was not a sufficient reason to justify a restriction on media freedom.[208]

The decision of the House of Lords not to issue a permanent injunction and the ECtHR's finding of a violation did not prioritise the public's right to know above concerns about national security.[209] The decision had more to do with the effects of international publications in weakening the government's interest in restraining the dissemination of the material, an issue that has intensified as a challenge to secrecy in the digital era. As discussed in relation to privacy law in Chapter 2, there is now much scope for internet publishers to place information in the public domain, particularly with dedicated sites that host government leaks. As a result, internet publications are more likely to weaken the effectiveness of an injunction.

The use of injunctions to protect government secrecy also stands in contrast to the position under the US First Amendment, where there is a strong rule against prior restraints.[210] Some observers argue that the US system facilitates greater cooperation between government and the media, as the latter have to less to fear in discussing stories with officials prior to publication. By contrast, the availability of interim injunctions can have the effect of discouraging editors from contacting government prior to publication to check whether a story jeopardises national security.[211] Making such contact with the government can alert the authorities to the story and might trigger an application for an injunction.

---

[205] *A-G v Guardian Newspapers Ltd* (n 1), Lord Bridge and Lord Oliver dissenting.

[206] *A-G v Guardian Newspapers Ltd (No 2)* [1990] 1 AC 109, 260, Lord Keith stated that 'all possible damage to the interest of the Crown has already been done by the publication of *Spycatcher* abroad and the ready availability of copies in this country'.

[207] *A-G v Guardian Newspapers Ltd*, ibid.

[208] *Sunday Times v United Kingdom (No 2)*, App no 13166/87 (1992) 14 EHRR 229.

[209] *A-G v Guardian Newspapers Ltd* (n 206) 260, Lord Keith 'I do not base this upon any balancing of public interest nor upon any considerations of freedom of the press, nor upon any possible defences of prior publication or just cause or excuse'.

[210] *New York Times v United States* 403 US 713 (1971).

[211] See evidence of Alan Rusbridger in House of Commons Home Affairs Committee, *Counter-terrorism* (30 April 2014, HC 231) Ev34.

The significance of the *Spycatcher* episode lies less in the legal principles, and more in the practical lessons. While legal remedies may be available in principle for breach of confidence, the attempt to impose direct controls on multiple publications in different jurisdictions proved to be disastrous. The episode humiliated government, generated an anti-censorship backlash and was ineffective in maintaining secrecy. The legal action merely publicised *Spycatcher* and led to more sales of the 'the book they tried to ban'. Moran writes that the episode led to a change of attitude in government and recognition that 'the return to absolute secrecy under Thatcher was irrational'.[212] Instead, Moran notes that a shift took place towards greater management of information and public relations efforts rather than outright censorship.[213]

The government has on occasion still relied on the law of confidence to restrain publications. Injunctions were sought in relation to disclosures made by former security service members David Shayler and Richard Tomlinson.[214] However, breach of confidence was not used in relation to the later disclosures made by Wikileaks or Edward Snowden, both of which had simultaneous international publications. The tool has limited effectiveness in those cases where publications are spread over multiple jurisdictions. Unlike privacy cases, the principal harm to government secrecy will often arise from the publication of information overseas, and the repetition of identical content within jurisdiction may cause limited (if any) additional harm.

B. The Official Secrets Acts

i. *Official Secrecy 1911–89*

Possibly the best-known tool for protecting government secrecy is the Official Secrets Act 1989. The statute, along with its predecessors, has embodied the culture of secrecy that traditionally surrounded British public life. Before considering the current controls, it is worth looking at the earlier Official Secrets Act of 1911, which was notorious for its far-reaching terms and was utilised in some of the key battles that helped to change the UK's political culture. Section 2 of the 1911 Act criminalised the unauthorised communication of information that had been provided in confidence by a person holding office under the Crown, or which had been obtained by virtue of being an officer, employee or contractor of the Crown.[215] Section 2 also provided that it was an offence to receive such information if the recipient knew or had grounds to know that the information was being disclosed in contravention of the Act. If material was obtained in contravention of the Act, then it was also an offence to communicate it to another without authorisation. The provisions meant that the 1911 Act could be used against a journalist both for knowingly receiving and publishing leaked information. In a high-profile case from 1958, two Oxford students were sentenced to three months

---

[212] Moran (n 201) 334.
[213] ibid, 340.
[214] See *A-G v Times Newspapers Ltd* [2001] EWCA Civ 97, [2001] 1 WLR 885 and *A-G v Punch Ltd* [2002] UKHL 50, [2003] 1 AC 1046.
[215] Official Secrets Act 1911, s 2.

in prison after publishing an article in the student magazine *Isis* detailing military monitoring activity.[216] The Act was not just concerned with national security issues. For example, s 2 was used to prosecute post office workers for supplying information that enabled a robbery of a post office van.[217]

The main criticism of the 1911 Act was that it could apply to the most minor disclosures. It was often said that the Act could criminalise the communication of the menu at the civil service canteen. Several examples support the concern with the breadth of the restrictions. In 1932, a clerk in the probate registry was sentenced to six weeks in prison for providing information to a journalist about certain wills on the same day that the information was to be officially published.[218] The son of a political leader was fined after he received Cabinet memoranda for the purpose of writing a book about his father.[219] Despite its broad terms, the Act was used relatively infrequently, and the Franks Committee found that between 1945 and 1971, 23 prosecutions had been brought under s 2.

In addition to the widely-criticised breadth of the offence, s 2 suffered from a lack of clarity as to when a disclosure was unauthorised. A briefing to the press arguably did not violate s 2, in so far as such communications are implicitly authorised as part of the senior civil servant's job.[220] However, it was difficult to know just how much discretion the official held to perform such a function. Section 2 also contained an exception where the disclosure of information was to 'a person to whom it is in the interest of the State his duty to communicate it'. In a number of cases, defendants sought to rely on this provision to argue that disclosure to the public or a newspaper was in the interests of the state on the ground that it served the public interest.

Like the law of obscenity, a series of cases formed part of a key struggle towards a change in culture. With this area of law, the shift was towards greater openness in government. The attempts by government to enforce controls led not only to some spectacular losses and own goals, but also helped to mobilise public opinion towards a change of culture. In one of the key cases from this period, *The Sunday Telegraph*, its editor, a journalist (and future MP Jonathan Aitken) and his source were prosecuted under s 2 after the newspaper published a story based on a leaked report revealing the government's secret supply of arms to Nigeria.[221] The disclosure caused considerable political embarrassment by showing that the government had provided misleading answers to Parliament. The defendants were acquitted and in his summing up to the jury, Caulfield J was critical of s 2, arguing that it should be 'pensioned off' to be replaced with a new provision that would provide more guidance for defendants to assess the risk of prosecution.[222] In 1972, the Franks Committee recommended replacing the section with a more narrowly-drawn provision focusing on security issues.[223]

---

[216] O Franks (chair), *Departmental Committee on Section 2 of the Official Secrets Act 1911* (Cmnd 5104, 1972) ('Franks Report') 117.
[217] ibid, 118.
[218] ibid, 116.
[219] ibid, 116.
[220] ibid, 19.
[221] For an account of the case, see T Grant, *Jeremy Hutchinson's Case Histories* (London, John Murray, 2015) Ch 11.
[222] Franks Report (n 216) 11.
[223] ibid.

Despite these criticisms, the provision remained in place until legislation was enacted in 1989.

In the meantime, further prosecutions showed the system coming under strain. Duncan Campbell, a journalist who had revealed government monitoring activities at GCHQ in a 1976 article in *Time Out*, was prosecuted after meeting a former military officer (along with another journalist) to discuss the monitoring of communications.[224] The proceedings generated a media furore. In the course of the committal proceedings, the identity of an unnamed prosecution witness was discovered after certain details were revealed in open court.[225] In turn, this caused embarrassment for the government, as the supposedly anonymous witness was both named in Parliament and in the press. At the trial, the journalist and the former officer were found guilty under s 2. However, the prosecutor's victory was pyrrhic and the two journalists received only conditional discharges. The prosecution only served to publicise the very story the government wanted to remain hidden and enhanced the reputation of the journalist as a serious investigator of government affairs.

Even where the judges had no sympathy for the defendant, the system continued to come under strain. In 1985, a jury famously acquitted the civil servant Clive Ponting after he was prosecuted for leaking information about the sinking of the Belgrano during the Falklands War to a Labour MP, who then shared the information with the press. Ponting relied on the terms of s 2 to argue that he was under a duty in the interests of the state to disclose the information and that the leak was therefore not unlawful. McCowan J directed the jury that the interests of the state were determined by the government of the day, as opposed to the civil servant's assessment.[226] The jury nonetheless acquitted Ponting. The episode highlighted how s 2 was out of step with public opinion, to the extent that juries would not convict a public-spirited whistleblower.

The key cases show that the 1911 Act was used on some occasions to shield the government from embarrassment and criticism. Some of the prosecutions concerned disclosures that posed no real danger to national security and were of significant public interest. As a result, the Act was viewed with suspicion and attempts to enforce the law in high-profile cases could generate a political backlash. With these lessons in mind, along with those from the *Spycatcher* cases, the government sought to overhaul the law of secrecy to provide a more precise tool that would command greater public respect.

ii. The Official Secrets Act 1989

The Official Secrets Act 1989 Act was presented as a liberalisation of the system of government secrecy. The then Home Secretary Douglas Hurd told the House of Commons that the old law was unsatisfactory because it criminalised any unauthorised disclosure of official information.[227] He argued that the new provisions would criminalise

---

[224] The Attorney-General authorised charges under the more serious offences under s 1, as well as s 2. However, the s 1 charges were later withdrawn following criticisms from the judge in the course of the trial about the oppressive nature of the prosecution. See Moran (n 201) and Grant (n 221) for an account of the case.

[225] See *A-G v Leveller Magazine Ltd* [1979] AC 440 (HL).

[226] See R Thomas, 'The British Official Secrets Acts 1911–1939 and the Ponting case' [1986] *Criminal Law Review* 491.

[227] HC Deb 29 June 1988, vol 136, col 365.

the disclosure of only a 'very small amount of information'.[228] However, the Act should not be understood simply as a move to transparency. Instead, the government wanted an official secrets law that was more realistic and more effective in controlling the release of information. When understood in these terms, the Act was about restoring the authority of government, rather than surrendering power to the public.

Rather than taking the blanket approach of its predecessor, the 1989 Act restricts particular types of information. The provisions are nonetheless far-reaching. Under s 1, a person working in the security services or notified that the Act applies to him or her, commits an offence if he or she discloses any information relating to security or intelligence that was obtained by virtue of his or her work. Importantly, the offence can be committed even if the disclosure causes no damage to national security or any other interest. The provision reflects the view that all disclosures by members of the security services are harmful to the public interest and no further evidence should be required to show this.[229] Under this provision, former MI5 employee David Shayler was jailed for six months after making disclosures to the press. In 1997, Richard Tomlinson was jailed for 12 months after sending a publisher a synopsis of a book about his career in MI6. The provision was also used to prosecute Katherine Gun after she revealed the role of the security services in eavesdropping on delegates to the UN prior to the war in Iraq, although the charges were eventually dropped. Civil servants or government contractors that do not work for the security services commit an offence under s 1 if they make disclosures relating to security or intelligence, but only if the disclosure is *damaging* to the work of the security and intelligence services, or is of information (or falls within a class of information) that is likely to cause such damage.

Sections 2 and 3 provide further offences criminalising disclosures made by government employees and contractors relating to defence and foreign relations. However, these clauses include a requirement that the disclosure is damaging. For example, s 2 provides that a Crown servant or government contractor commits an offence by making a damaging disclose of information relating to defence that was obtained through his or her position. While the damage requirement is an important limitation on the offence, it is cast in broad terms. A disclosure can be regarded as damaging if 'it endangers the interests of the United Kingdom abroad' or 'seriously obstructs the promotion or protection by the United Kingdom of those interests', or if it is likely to have those effects.[230] Looking at the wording of the statute literally, there appears to be much scope for government to assert some level of damage within those terms.[231] However, it is sometimes argued that it is difficult in practice to establish damage, even when cast in such wide terms. In particular, the government may be wary of disclosing evidence necessary to show damage, for fear that the provision of the information to other parties would exacerbate the damage already done.[232] The prosecution also has to show that the person knew or had reasonable cause to believe that the disclosure

---

[228] ibid.

[229] Home Office, *Reform of Section 2 of the Official Secrets Act 1911* (Cm 408, 1988) at [41].

[230] Official Secrets Act 1989, s 2(2)(b).

[231] See discussion in S Palmer, 'Tightening secrecy law: the Official Secrets Act 1989' (1990) *Public Law* 243, 253. Fenwick and Phillipson (n 59) 946.

[232] Law Commission, *Protection of Official Data: A Consultation Paper* (Law Com CP No 230, 2017) 80.

fell into the restricted category of information and that it would be damaging.[233] The burdens and concerns about evidence may go some way to explain the limited enforcement of the offences.

Beyond issues of national security, s 4 criminalises the disclosure of information by a Crown servant or contractor that results in a criminal offence being committed, leads to an escape from legal custody, or impedes the prevention or detection of crime or apprehension or prosecution of a suspect, or is likely to have any of those effects. While not using the terminology of damage, s 4 defines the protected information with reference to its effects and likely effects on the enforcement of the criminal law.

Sections 1–4 do not control the media directly, but target the sources that supply information to the media. The Act has been used against such sources on a number of occasions. For example, in 2007 the civil servant Derek Pasquill was charged after leaking documents to the *Observer* and *New Statesman* relating to the government's policy on extraordinary rendition and relations with Muslim groups.[234] While the prosecution was later dropped, critics argue that the law was used to punish the disclosure of embarrassing facts rather than damage to the public interest.[235] The use of the Act against sources raises the risk of a chilling effect, discussed in Chapter 5, in which sources are reluctant to come forward and report any wrongdoing or important information.

In theory, the media could be liable for inciting a breach of ss 1, 2, 3 or 4, for example where it offered money for government information. However, the Court of Appeal in *Shayler*, while not wishing to enter into such a 'minefield', noted that such a prosecution could only arise in an 'extreme case on the facts'.[236] Other provisions of the Act can have a more direct application to the media. When a person leaks information contrary to ss 1–4 of the Act, s 5 makes it an offence for the recipient of the material to disclose it, if they know or ought to have known that the information was restricted by the statute. Where the information is protected under ss 1–3, the disclosure must be damaging to fall within s 5 and the defendant must know or have reasonable cause to know that it would be damaging. The provision means that a journalist may commit an offence if he or she receives and publishes information from inside intelligence sources.

Prosecutors have threatened to invoke s 5 against the media on occasion, but such threats have not been followed through to a court hearing. In 2005, the *Daily Mirror* was threatened with s 5 proceedings after it published details thought to be from a leaked memo relating to the war in Iraq.[237] While the source of the leak was convicted under the Official Secrets Act, no action was finally taken against the newspaper. A more significant use of s 5 took place in 1999, when the provision was invoked

---

[233] *R v Keogh* [2007] EWCA Crim 528, [2007] 1 WLR 1500, placing the legal burden on the prosecution. See Law Commission, ibid, 67.

[234] 'Civil servant cleared of breaching Secrets Act over papers leak' *The Daily Telegraph* (10 January 2008).

[235] See A Bailin, 'Let's free the Official Secrets Act from its cold war freeze' *The Guardian* (22 September 2011); R Norton-Taylor, 'Secrets and lies: National security is being invoked not to protect us but to shield politicians from embarrassment' *The Guardian* (11 January 2008).

[236] *R v Shayler* [2001] EWCA Crim 1977, [2001] 1 WLR 2206 at [96].

[237] See KD Ewing, *Bonfire of the Liberties* (Oxford, Oxford University Press, 2010) 157; A Savage, *Leaks, Whistleblowing and the Public Interest* (Cheltenham, Edward Elgar, 2016) 116–17.

against the journalist Tony Geraghty, who published a book about the conflict in Northern Ireland. The book included some details of surveillance methods undertaken by the military. After the book went on sale, Geraghty was raided by the police and later charged under the Official Secrets Act, along with his military source. The charges against Geraghty and the source were later dropped, it being shown that the disclosed information was already publicly available and therefore caused no damage.[238]

In addition to these climb downs, the limited use of s 5 is recognised by the courts, with the Court of Appeal stating that 'it would only be in an exceptional case that the Attorney-General would authorise a prosecution' against the media under the provision.[239] Despite these limitations, the potential effects of the provision should not be underestimated. A threat to use s 5 can be significant when the government negotiates and liaises with the press in relation to security issues. Moreover, the provision could be used to conduct searches or other investigations that will occupy the time and resources of the journalist or media company for a period. For example, while abandoning the prosecution of Tony Geraghty might appear to be a victory for media freedom, the journalist was weighed down in the legal proceedings for several months. In another example, the police sought to rely on a potential breach of s 5 in relation to content supplied by David Shayler, to seek access to material held by *The Observer*.[240] Where there is no prosecution of journalists, s 5 can still be relied on to invoke other legal powers of investigation that can inhibit journalistic activities.

iii. A Public Interest Defence

The 1989 Act is not an outright prohibition on all disclosures. Like the 1911 Act, the 1989 Act permits disclosures made in accordance with the person's official duty.[241] The provision thereby allows information to be disclosed by civil servants to the press, when done as part of their work responsibilities. The Act contains no defence of prior publication to permit the release of information that is already in the public domain, as in the *Spycatcher* case.[242] Despite this, the damage requirements can be interpreted to permit disclosures of information that are already widely known. However, that line of argument is only available where the further disclosure causes no additional damage. In some cases, even where leaked information is in wide circulation, confirmation by an insider might add to the damage in so far as it supports the authenticity of the information.[243]

There is some scope for disclosures to be justified where necessary to avoid an 'inevitable and irreparable evil' (known as the doctrine of necessity). A defence of necessity was advanced by lawyers when Katharine Gun faced prosecution for her disclosures, on the grounds that the leak was necessary to prevent an unlawful war.

---

[238] T Geraghty, 'How the MoD's big guns backfired' *The Times* (8 February 2000).

[239] *Shayler* (Court of Appeal) (n 236) at [95].

[240] *R v Central Criminal Court, ex p Bright* [2001] 1 WLR 662.

[241] Official Secrets Act 1989, s 7.

[242] *Reform of Section 2 of the Official Secrets Act 1911* (n 229) at [62]–[64].

[243] See *R (on the application of Bancoult) v Secretary of State for Foreign and Commonwealth Affairs* [2013] EWHC 1502 (Admin), [2014] Env LR 2 at [66]–[72].

The prosecution was dropped after the CPS concluded that it was unable 'to disprove the defence of necessity to be raised on the particular facts of this case'.[244] Some commentators speculated whether the decision not to prosecute was related to a reluctance to release sensitive documents to rebut the defence.[245] However, the defence is not easily made out and imposes a high threshold for defendants to meet.[246] While in *Shayler* the Court of Appeal did not rule out such a defence in future cases,[247] the status of the defence of necessity in secrecy law is unclear and does not offer strong protection to whistleblowers.[248]

The biggest debate surrounding the 1989 Act focuses on the omission of a public interest defence. When the Act was introduced, the government argued that such a defence would undermine the clarity of the law and that the rules within the legislation determine when the public interest lies with non-disclosure.[249] The arrangements under the 1989 Act are also often justified on the grounds that permitting some disclosures that are in the public interest would undermine mutual trust among the members of the security and intelligence services, if they believed that a colleague could make their actions public.[250] The 1989 Act thereby tightens the control over certain categories of protected information. The Act is therefore less of a liberalising statute and more of a measure of drawing bright lines, which mostly tend to favour secrecy.

Under the Act, the public interest is thought to be protected by a requirement for the Attorney-General's consent prior to a prosecution.[251] While that provides an additional barrier aiming to prevent the oppressive use of the law, the position of the Attorney-General as a government officer limits the independence (or at least perceived independence) of that safeguard. The CPS also provides guidelines for prosecutions involving the media.[252] The guidelines help prosecutors determine if criminal proceedings are a proportionate response, which is a separate question from whether the disclosure itself is in the public interest.[253] The procedural safeguards do not therefore provide protection equivalent to a public interest defence.

The Act does not include the general provision found in the earlier 1911 Act, which permitted disclosures where the person has a duty 'in the interest of the State'. By omitting that clause, the 1989 Act forecloses the indirect reliance on public interest arguments in fulfilling that duty, as Ponting had in 1985. In the White Paper that preceded the 1989 Act, the government stated that any argument about the public interest should be advanced in relation to damage tests.[254] That possibility is precluded

[244] CPS Press Release, 'Statement on *R v Katharine Gun*' (26 February 2004).

[245] I Cobain, *The History Thieves* (London, Portobello, 2016) 57.

[246] Law Commission (n 232) 76–77.

[247] *Shayler* (Court of Appeal) (n 236) at [69].

[248] Law Commission (n 232) 78.

[249] *Reform of Section 2 of the Official Secrets Act 1911* (n 229) at [59]–[61].

[250] Law Commission (n 232) 170 citing Lord Nicholls in *A-G v Blake* [2001] 1 AC 268, 287.

[251] Official Secrets Act 1989, s 9.

[252] Crown Prosecution Service, *Guidelines for prosecutors on assessing the public interest in cases affecting the media* (September 2012), available at www.cps.gov.uk/legal/d_to_g/guidance_for_prosecutors_on_assessing_the_public_interest_in_cases_affecting_the_media_ (last accessed 24 January 2018). Though the guidelines remind prosecutors that there is no public interest defence.

[253] Law Commission (n 232) at 173.

[254] *Reform of Section 2 of the Official Secrets Act 1911* (n 229) at [61]. See also A Bailin, 'The Last Cold War Statute' (2008) *Criminal Law Review* 625, 627–28.

where the disclosure is made by someone in the intelligence services contrary to s 1, as the offence has no damage requirement. Even under those provisions where damage is required, the potential to bring in public interest arguments is limited at best. The question of damage is distinct from the question of whether that damage is outweighed by the public interest. Along these lines, if a civil servant reveals details of a confidential memo sent by the US embassy to the government, that disclosure could damage the willingness of the ambassador to share information in future. The fact that the public is better informed as a result of the disclosure is irrelevant to the question of whether damage has occurred. Furthermore, while some of the provisions define damage as that which 'endangers the interests of the United Kingdom abroad', that does not invite the court to consider the internal domestic benefits to the country in holding government to account. The damage requirement therefore does not perform the same function as a public interest defence.

Following the enactment of the Human Rights Act 1998, the court was asked to consider whether Article 10 requires the inclusion of a public interest defence in the case of *Shayler*.[255] In that case, the defendant was a former MI5 employee who made disclosures to the national press and claimed that he wanted to expose problems including unlawfulness, incompetence and wastefulness in the security services. The House of Lords held that the intention of Parliament not to include a public interest defence in the statute was clear. Lord Bingham stated that while a 'sweeping, blanket ban, permitting of no exceptions' would fall foul of Article 10, the Act had sufficient safeguards. The court reasoned that if a member of the security services thought any matter raised an issue of public interest, then he or she could use various official complaints procedures to alert the authorities to any misconduct or problem. These channels include contacting the staff counsellor, complaining about illegalities to the Attorney-General, Director of Public Prosecutions, or the Metropolitan Police, or complaining about misconduct and incompetence to the relevant minister or senior civil servant.[256] A person can also ask the relevant official to authorise disclosure.[257] A decision not to permit disclosure following such a request could then be the subject of an application for judicial review, including a rights-based challenge. Those safeguards, Lord Bingham concluded, were sufficient to ensure that the 'the power to withhold authorisation to publish is not abused and that proper disclosures are not stifled'.[258]

The arguments in *Shayler* reveal a basic fault-line as to whether safeguards should lie in a system of complaints that is internal to the apparatus of the state, or whether a whistleblower should have a right to go public.[259] The current law takes the former approach, assigning the responsibility to various state bodies. The decision in *Shayler* has been criticised for taking an unrealistic assessment of the effectiveness of the existing safeguards.[260] The criticism runs that the people operating the safeguards are

[255] *R v Shayler* [2002] UKHL 11, [2003] 1 AC 247.
[256] ibid, at [36]. The Law Commission notes the addition of two further safeguards, the Ethical Counsellor and, for civil servants, The Civil Service Commission. See Law Commission (n 232) 178–80.
[257] Official Secrets Act 1989, s 7. See Law Commission, ibid, 189.
[258] *Shayler* (House of Lords) (n 255) at [36].
[259] See also Fenwick and Phillipson (n 59) 942.
[260] See Savage (n 237) 60; Fenwick and Phillipson (n 59) 943.

connected with the state and have a vested interest in keeping the public in the dark about any wrongdoing or misconduct.[261] In *Shayler*, the judges were aware of such issues and Lord Hope noted that '[i]nstitutions tend to protect their own and to resist criticism from wherever it may come'.[262] Moreover, a person working within the apparatus of the state will approach questions of public interest with a different mindset than someone from the outside. A senior official in the security services or government is unlikely to authorise disclosures revealing, for example, state complicity with torture overseas. In relation to the requests to authorise the disclosure of information, a whistleblower is unlikely to go through the expense and effort of judicial review proceedings. Furthermore, the employee will fear professional setbacks for raising any complaints or requests to release information.

The Law Commission has proposed to strengthen the internal safeguards by allowing complaints to go to the Investigatory Powers Commissioner, an independent judicial office holder.[263] That approach works within the framework of *Shayler*, but seeks to increase the level of independence of the person receiving the complaint. The question of whether that Commissioner is sufficiently separate from all the institutional pressures to protect government is open to debate. Critics of the internal safeguards point to the decisions of the European Court of Human Rights holding that there can be a right to go public as a last resort where the official channels for complaints are inadequate.[264] The case for a public interest defence rests on the inadequacy of the current safeguards to address allegations of misconduct and wrongdoing.

Another criticism of the scheme under the Act is that it creates an asymmetry in which the government is free to authorise the disclosure of information that puts it in a good light or supports existing policies, but others cannot challenge that selection of information. Accordingly, a release of information about military operations may be approved if it is seen to be necessary to gain public support. A public interest defence seeks to counteract the risk of abuse and the asymmetry in the control of information by giving whistleblowers, the media and the courts the chance to contest the government's assessment of where the public interest lies.

While the deficiencies of the existing system are easy to highlight, there are challenges in putting a public interest defence into operation. The various issues can be examined from the perspective of three key actors: the leaker, the media and the courts.[265] Looking at the role of the leaker, a public interest defence may encourage individual employees to make the initial call as to whether disclosure is justified. The individual security services employee or civil servant may not have the full picture and context to make an assessment of whether disclosure will jeopardise any operations or reveal any sources. Consequently, the leaker may disclose information that is not damaging in itself, but could become damaging in conjunction with other available information.[266] Moreover, a leaker may claim to be acting in the public interest, but

[261] Savage, ibid.

[262] *Shayler* (House of Lords) (n 255) at [70].

[263] Law Commission (n 232).

[264] See *Guja v Moldova*, App no 14277/04 (2011) 53 EHRR 16.

[265] For discussion of these issues see R Sagar, *Secrets and Leaks: The Dilemma of State Secrecy* (Princeton, Princeton University Press, 2013).

[266] Law Commission (n 232) 171.

pursue his or her own agenda in opposing policies, or act maliciously. Whether a public interest defence enables such errors and abuse would depend upon the conditions or threshold required of the defendant. For example, if a good faith or reasonable belief standard is sufficient to establish the defence, then greater weight would be assigned to the leaker's initial assessment and would thereby increase the risk of disclosures being made under an erroneous evaluation of the public interest. By contrast, a requirement to establish that the actions of the whistleblower were objectively in the public interest may deter the disclosure of information given the risk of that high threshold not being met. Whichever standard is adopted, the potential encouragement of leaking should not be overstated, as the protection offered by such a defence is likely to be limited in practice. The existence of a defence does not guarantee success in court, so considerable risk still attaches to whistleblowing. More broadly, even with a shield against criminal prosecution, there are many other chilling effects (such as professional costs) that can work to deter a person from disclosing information.

Aside from the leaker, there is also the position of the media in receiving and publishing leaked information. A public interest defence would give the media a right to challenge the government's assessment of where the public interest lies. However, the same risks in allowing the leaker to assess the public interest also arise with the media. A journalist might be unaware of the risk to national security, may also have an agenda in seeking to disclose information and abuse any freedom granted under a public interest defence.[267] However, there are ways to distinguish and minimise these risks. News organisations can be expected to go through a process to determine whether content is damaging or not. Media bodies do not simply publish everything that is sent to them, and in some cases go through a process of redaction. Along these lines, a public interest defence could be developed so that the media is protected if it goes through the right process to reduce the risk of harm. One of the responsibilities could be participation in the Defence and Security Media Advisory Notices system, which will be considered below. Such an approach would fit with the 'duties and responsibilities' that support stronger Article 10 protection. Despite these possibilities, the special protection for the media has been given short shrift by the courts, with Laws LJ stating that the 'constitutional responsibility for the protection of national security lies with elected government' and not the media.[268] However, there is no need to dismiss a public interest test if appropriate conditions and responsibilities can be identified.

A public interest defence would make the courts the final arbiter of the different views advanced by the leaker, media and the government. However, there are reasons to question the ability of the courts to carry out this function. To assess the public interest claim, the court would have to hear the facts concerning the disclosure and the arguments for and against releasing the information.[269] That would raise challenges in ensuring that such information can safely be revealed before a jury. Moreover, the hearing of such matters may also require limits on open justice. The challenges are not insurmountable, but would call for careful management of the process, which in

---

[267] See Sagar (n 265) 112–13.
[268] *R (Miranda) v Secretary of State for the Home Department* [2014] EWHC 255, [2014] 1 WLR 3140 at [71].
[269] *Shayler* (House of Lords) (n 255) at [70] and [36].

practice would be likely to generate controversy. If anything, the problem with a public interest defence is that it may fail to deliver significant protection in practice, given the challenges for the defendant in persuading a court to reject the government's assessment on national security issues. Nonetheless, the prospect of disappointment does not provide an argument for having no public interest defence at all. Even if the defence is not widely used, its presence alters the balance of power and takes a card out of the government's hand, which can be an important factor when looking at negotiations between the media and government. It may also provide a strategic advantage to the leaker. For example, the government may feel reluctant to bring a prosecution because they do not want to disclose to the parties the evidence that would defeat the public interest defence.

Moreover, the case for a public interest defence is strengthened in the context of a system where the surveillance of communications means that whistleblowers have a fewer places to hide. The confidentiality of journalists' sources does not protect those leakers that are discovered from punishment, but limits the risk of discovery and thereby plays an important role in facilitating an alternative flow of information that acts as a counter to government. Surveillance changes that balance of power, and a source can now be more easily discovered through the access to communications data.[270] If there is now greater potential to identify a whistleblower through digital surveillance, that may bolster the case for a public interest defence to reduce the risk of adverse consequences upon discovery.

iv. An Assessment

The Official Secrets Act 1989 was promoted as a more proportionate replacement for the previous law. The central change made by the legislation is a narrower remit in protecting only certain categories of sensitive information. However, the looser language of the 1911 Act is omitted, to avoid any possible interpretations that permit leaks of information in the public interest. The Act focuses on defined categories of information, but tightens its grip within those categories. Accordingly, Keith Ewing writes that the 'blunderbuss' of s 2 of the 1911 Act was replaced with a 'sniper's rifle'.[271]

While narrower than its 1911 predecessor, the provisions of the 1989 Act are still couched in broad terms. The provisions under s 1 relating to members of the security services are not qualified by a damage requirement. Even in the other provisions where damage is required, the statute defines damage broadly. There is an inevitability that the terms of a security statute will be cast widely. It is not possible to identify in advance exactly those types of information that will jeopardise security. Given the gravity of the potential harm, the government will generally want to keep its options open. That does not mean the precision of the terms cannot be improved upon, but the terms of such statutes are likely to be vulnerable to an expansive interpretation and potentially misused for political purposes.

---

[270] See Ch 5.
[271] Ewing (n 237) 144.

Despite the potentially broad reach, the Official Secrets Act 1989 has not been strictly enforced.[272] One possible explanation lies with the reluctance to bring evidence to establish the necessary level of damage. Another possibility is that the government has learned lessons since *Spycatcher*. An attempt to clamp down on the media is more likely to generate a hostile political backlash against the government and may prove to be ineffectual. Government has more incentive to target the sources of the leaks, who have less means to generate negative publicity. Even that strategy risks a backlash if government is seen to be acting unfairly or if the leaker attracts considerable attention. Against this background, it can be seen that the Official Secrets Act 1989 did not alter the ability to control information in either direction, with Wilkinson writing that the Act 'did not usher in an age of greater official openness, nor did it lead to an age of greater use of the OSA by the Government'.[273] The Act does, however, have a role in structuring the relationship between government and the media. The threat of a prosecution or an investigation can feature in negotiations with the media. The potential for the enforcement of the Act may also explain why the media voluntarily participates in an informal system of regulation, which will be considered later.

C. Misconduct in Public Office

While the Official Secrets Act 1989 sought to focus on a narrow range of information, there are other laws that prosecutors can reach for to fill any gaps. The old common law offence of misconduct in public office has been used to prosecute public employees, such as police and prison officers, who disclose information to journalists. The offence is committed where the holder of a public office wilfully neglects to perform his or her duty or misconducts himself or herself in a way that is serious enough to amount to an abuse of public trust and which is done without reasonable excuse or justification.[274] Applying this test, several of the newspaper sources revealed in Operation Elveden in the aftermath of the phone hacking scandal in 2011 were convicted of the offence, in relation to payments received for the supply of information.[275] By relying on such a broad offence in response to a leak of information, there is a danger that prosecutors can bypass the limits of the official secrecy offences under the 1989 Act.[276] There are, however, some hurdles when applying the misconduct offence. In particular, the jury can consider whether the disclosure was in the public interest when deciding whether the misconduct was sufficiently serious.[277] Similarly, media freedom issues may be relevant when considering whether the conduct of the public officer was justified.

In addition to targeting sources, several journalists have been prosecuted for aiding and abetting such misconduct, or for conspiracy to commit misconduct in public office.

---

[272] Savage (n 237) 37 notes that prosecutions under the Act in general are relatively rare.
[273] N Wilkinson, *Media and Secrecy: The Official History of the United Kingdom's D-NOTICE System* (Abingdon, Routledge, 2009) 434.
[274] *R v Chapman* [2015] EWCA Crim 539, [2015] QB 883.
[275] Operation Elveden investigated links between the police and news reporters, see *R v Norman* [2016] EWCA Crim 1564, [2017] 4 WLR 16.
[276] Ewing (n 237) 165; Savage (n 237) 77.
[277] *Chapman* (n 274) at [33].

A reporter for the *Milton Keynes Citizen* accused of illegally obtaining information from a police officer was prosecuted for aiding and abetting misconduct, but the case failed after the trial judge excluded the key evidence.[278] The prosecution of journalists following Operation Elveden was not a success either, with various acquittals and in some cases abandoned prosecutions.[279] In addition to the failures in the prosecutions, the strategy has generated considerable negative publicity in the media. Several newspapers described Operation Elveden as a 'witch hunt' against journalists.[280] As with the other offences, prosecutions against the media come with significant risks of a political backlash that may deter its future usage. However, these cases show how old common law offences can be used to provide an alternative route for prosecutors to target the media and its sources.

D. Voluntary Regulation

In addition to the legal constraints to protect government secrecy, there is also a less formal channel of regulation known as the Defence and Security Media Advisory-Notice System (DSMA Notice system). The system is run by a committee composed of representatives from the government and the media. Under the system, notices are issued to the media to let it know of certain categories of information that could be damaging to national security. For example, one notice asks the media not to reveal the identity, location or contact details of those working in the security services or working on counter-terrorism.[281] If the media is considering publishing information that potentially falls within a notice, then it can contact the Secretary of the Defence and Security Media Advisory Committee, who is normally a former member of the military appointed when close to the age of retirement.[282] The Secretary is paid as a civil servant and has an office in the Ministry of Defence, but is not answerable to a departmental minister.[283] Instead, the Secretary is responsible to members of the Committee.

The system was established in 1912 and has support from the media. It provides a level of efficiency and consistency through a centralised system for clearing publications, rather than leaving journalists to negotiate with a number of agencies and officials. The DSMA Notices are not enforceable in law and are regarded by many in the media as a preferable alternative to formal legal controls.[284] Clearing a publication with the Secretary does not provide an immunity in relation to the Official Secrets Act. Decisions on prosecution are made separately, and in any event the Official Secrets Act covers non-security related matters that are outside the scope of the Committee.[285]

---

[278] 'Thames Valley police leak case against Sally Murrer thrown out' *The Guardian* (28 November 2014).
[279] Though one former journalist pleaded guilty to the charges.
[280] 'Cynical attack on a free Press' *The Sun* (16 October 2015).
[281] DSMA Notice 05, *Personnel and their Families who work in Sensitive Positions*, available at www.dsma. uk/danotices/danotice_05/index.htm (last accessed 24 January 2018).
[282] Wilkinson (n 273) 483.
[283] ibid.
[284] The Defence Advisory Notice System and the Defence Press and Broadcasting Committee, *Report of the Review* (March 2015).
[285] See Wilkinson (n 273).

For example, a leak relating to crime can fall within s 4 of the Official Secrets Act 1989, but would not raise an issue under the DSMA Notice system. However, in practice, clearance by the Secretary of the Committee in relation to a security matter makes prosecution unlikely.

The system depends on a level of trust from both the government and the media. At various times the system has come under challenge from both sides. While the system is largely supported by the industry, it is not always seen in as a positive mediator. For example, the Secretary of the Defence and Security Media Advisory Committee approached Tony Geraghty—the journalist whose work on Northern Ireland led to the prosecution discussed earlier under s 5 of the Official Secrets Act—and asked for his book manuscript to be submitted for vetting. Geraghty declined the request. In Geraghty's view, he was prosecuted under s 5 because he declined to cooperate with the DSMA Committee, and the system is not 'truly voluntary'.[286] Rather than being a friendly reminder not to make an inadvertent disclosure, one journalist described the system as having a 'hint of menace' and serving as 'a good way of closing down, or at least dampening, public debate'.[287] The voluntary system therefore has to be understood as one part of the broader framework for controlling leaked information, which includes the legal tools as an alternative.

There is a convention that information provided to the Committee will not be used as a basis for legal restraint. According to Nicholas Wilkinson's history of the DSMA Notice system, that convention has been respected.[288] However, journalists are sometimes nervous about the lack of a guarantee.[289] When *The Guardian* published stories based on Edward Snowden's leaked data, the newspaper did not initially contact the Secretary of the Committee for fear that it would trigger proceedings for an injunction.[290] While the system did not stop the publication of information based on Edward Snowden's leaks, some commentators believe it is partly responsible for the muted response to the Snowden revelations in many parts of the press.[291] If that is the case, then the system can create a pressure to stop the media reporting on certain leaked stories that are available elsewhere.

The system has also been the subject of mistrust from government and in 1967 was the centre of an episode that has been described as the 'British Watergate'.[292] At the time, the Secretary of the Committee, Colonel Lohan, had a reputation for drinking, gossiping and womanising.[293] He was also a friend of the well-known investigative journalist, Chapman Pincher, and the two regularly lunched together. Quite remarkably for a broker of government secrecy, Lohan 'leaked scoop after scoop' to Pincher

---

[286] C McCrystal, 'The sub-secret underworld of the D-Notice business' (1999) 10 *British Journalism Review* 26. The claim was denied by the Secretary of the DSMA Committee, see David Pulvertaft. 'A wrongful accusation' *Evening Standard* (12 March 1999).

[287] L Harding, *The Snowden Files* (London, Guardian Books, 2014) 311.

[288] Wilkinson (n 273) 481.

[289] ibid, 477.

[290] See The Defence Advisory Notice System and the Defence Press and Broadcasting Committee (n 284) at [15]. See also the evidence of Alan Rusbridger in House of Commons Home Affairs Committee (n 211).

[291] Cobain (n 245) 60–61.

[292] Moran (n 201) 136 and Ch 4 for a comprehensive account of the episode.

[293] ibid, 162.

during their years of friendship.[294] Before publishing a story in the *Daily Express* about the government monitoring of telegrams and cables, the journalist Pincher met with Lohan to discuss the proposed publication at an expensive French restaurant in London. There appears to have been some (possibly alcohol related) misunderstanding as to what was agreed at the meeting. Lohan believed the story would not go ahead. By contrast, Pincher left with the impression that the story would not fall foul of a D-Notice (as DSMA Notices were then called). The *Daily Express* therefore went ahead and published the story.

The events blew up into a political crisis. The Prime Minister, Harold Wilson, believing that that Lohan and Chapman were conspiring to undermine his government, was furious and argued that the story was in breach of the D-Notice. Wilson then appointed a committee chaired by Lord Radcliffe to investigate the circumstances surrounding the publication of the *Daily Express* article. Wilson's response showed that when the system of voluntary regulation fails to provide the result favoured by government, formal processes can be established to put the press under close scrutiny, in the hope that the newspaper would be subject to some form of official censure. The strategy backfired when the Radcliffe Committee cleared Pincher and Lohan, which caused celebration among the newspaper industry.[295] Wilson, however, did not accept the findings and published a White Paper stating that a D-Notice had been breached. While Wilson sought to use state resources to condemn the newspaper, the White Paper caused a significant political backlash and tarnished Wilson's relations with the press. The credibility of the D-Notice system was also undermined. The journalist Pincher emerged with an enhanced reputation as a courageous reporter who had successfully taken on the government. Subsequent reforms have avoided similar controversies, but the episode shows how the system has not always been trusted by government.

The picture of the Committee suggests a system where members of the press and government are part of a 'club' that decides what is safe to publish. As is now obvious, membership of that club is no longer necessary to publish information to the world at large. The DSMA Notice system does not apply to foreign newspapers, most blogs or content on the social media. A review of the system established in the wake of the Snowden disclosures concluded that it works well in avoiding publications that would inadvertently damage security, but does less to prevent deliberate disclosures of sensitive information, for which the criminal controls should be used.[296] The review also called for representatives from the digital media to sit on the Committee, while recognising that there are challenges in securing such participation.[297] Despite the various limits and criticisms, the Committee is likely to remain in place for the foreseeable future as a means to avoid damaging disclosures in the domestic media at least.

---

[294] C Pincher, *Dangerous to Know: A Life* (London, Biteback, 2014) 233.

[295] Lord Radcliffe, *Report of the Committee of Privacy Counsellors appointed to inquire into 'D' notice matters* (Cmnd 3309, 1967).

[296] The Defence Advisory Notice System and the Defence Press and Broadcasting Committee (n 284) at [42].

[297] ibid. They also noted that Google had participated, but withdrew in 2013 following the Edward Snowden disclosures, at [36].

E. Informal Controls

The government does not need to rely on legal measures to instil a level of discipline on the release of information. The government has its power as an employer to impose both formal and informal sanctions on potential media sources. There is a professional culture within a government department or agency that can work to reinforce these controls. Those employees leaking information that break the rules of the workplace may not only be dismissed, but can also suffer professional setbacks, such as mistrust from colleagues and limited career progression.

In his study of secrecy in the US, David Pozen argues that those workplace rules and sanctions help to maintain a level of self-regulation that protects secrecy.[298] Pozen argues the officials necessarily have the power to release some information in the course of their work and that this power is regulated by a number the informal rules and understandings about what types of information can be disclosed, when and by whom.[299] According to this view, the system of secrecy is not quite the top-down model of command and control suggested by the legal framework, but is a decentral-ised system where officials have discretion to disclose information depending on rank and role within the organisation.

Another type of informal control is exercised by government through its relation-ship with the media and by acting as a gatekeeper to certain types of information. The Freedom of Information Act 2000 provides exemptions for matters related to security, so the media will depend on government for access to documents, detail and data on certain areas of policy. The power to manage the conditions for access can be a sig-nificant tool for government. For example, in a military conflict the government may release information or grant access on terms that tend to minimise the focus on casu-alties to civilians or domestic forces and portray the opposing forces as blameworthy. Journalists may also get access to information about a conflict by being 'embedded' with the military.[300] The managed supply of information can also be used to foster good relations with the media, so that the journalist is rewarded with a story and is thereby less likely to antagonise the government. The supply of information can also be used to divert attention and potentially prevent the journalist digging for sensitive stories. Such news management techniques are subtler than censorship. A formal ban on publication or a prosecution will normally be transparent. News management can border on manipulation and should not be underestimated as a technique for control-ling the flow of information.

The above examples show how government can seek to foster good relations with the media. Alternatively, the government can cut off relations with critical journalists and give the media and its sources 'flak' when stepping out of line.[301] A source of a

---

[298] D Pozen, 'The Leaky Leviathan: Why the Government Condemns and Condones Unlawful Disclo-sures of Information' (2013) 127 *Harvard Law Review* 512.

[299] ibid. While Pozen's study looks at the USA, it is a plausible thesis in explaining the UK system too. The Franks Report found civil servants had a degree of discretion for self-authorisation to disclose informa-tion, Franks Report (n 216) 15.

[300] See Cobain (n 245) 94. See also N Davies, *Flat Earth News* (London, Chatto & Windus, 2008) Ch 6 for a range of news management techniques relating to military operations.

[301] N Chomsky and E Herman, *Manufacturing Consent: The Political Economy of the Mass Media* (London, Vintage, 1994).

leak may find themselves publicly belittled and humiliated. A well-known example occurred when Dr David Kelly was publicly named by the government as the source for the BBC of allegations about the government's case for a war in Iraq. Once his identity was known, he was subject to an aggressive line of questioning from members of the Foreign Affairs Select Committee. After that episode, parliamentary questions asked what disciplinary actions would be taken against him. Within days, Kelly took his own life.[302] While an extreme case, the episode shows how the government can use its significant communications operations to attack the credibility of a source.

F. Megaleaks in the Digital Era

A major challenge posed in the digital era is the sheer scale of data that can be copied from government and then passed on to a publisher. There is no need for a leaker to photocopy masses of documents and deliver them at a secret meeting point.[303] Hundreds of thousands of documents can be acquired in a short space of time. In recent years, the biggest stories based on leaks have come from the US intelligence services, such as the Wikileaks embassy cables and the Edward Snowden leaks about internet surveillance. These disclosures were 'megaleaks' of vast quantities of information. Government practices have also facilitated such disclosures. As digital data is often shared among a wide range of government employees to promote efficiency, there are more weak points in the chain and lower level employees now have greater opportunities to get hold of sensitive data.[304]

This mass extraction of information raises complex issues. For example, a mass data leak from a foreign government may include information relating to and supplied by the British government. The material from Edward Snowden came from US intelligence, but contained information related to activities in the UK. That was always possible under any system of leaks, but is more likely when hundreds of thousands of documents are disclosed. The mass leak can have international appeal, in so far as there will be something of interest to many countries somewhere in the data. Section 6 of the Official Secrets Act 1989 provides that it is an offence to make a damaging disclosure of information relating to security, intelligence, defence or international relations communicated in confidence by the UK to another state, which the defendant receives without authorisation from that state. That provision thereby regulates the publication of information from the UK received via leaks from other states. However, if the information is also published by media outside of the jurisdiction, then in some cases the disclosure may no longer be damaging and thereby fall outside the provision.

Publication outside of the jurisdiction has been common in the age of the 'megaleak', where several media institutions collaborate in analysing the mass data and publish the results simultaneously. If any offence is committed, the domestic authorities face

---

[302] Lord Hutton found that the naming of Kelly was not part of a dishonourable or duplicitous strategy, see Lord Hutton, *Report of the Inquiry into the Circumstances Surrounding the Death of Dr David Kelly CMG* (HC 247, 2004) at [427]. For criticism of the episode, see Ewing (n 237).

[303] See A Greenberg, *This Machine Kills Secrets* (London, Virgin, 2012).

[304] See Pozen (n 298) 631.

the problem of enforcement. One response has been to turn to intermediaries to limit any disclosures by blocking or taking down certain content. If such actions are taken informally, the measures are not subject to judicial or constitutional oversight and so may be over-inclusive and difficult to assess.[305] However, even this strategy is limited where there is a determination to republish, as the data can be copied and published on fresh unblocked sites. Moreover, once in the public domain, the information will be likely to have already fallen into the hands of foreign governments.

Finally, the megaleak poses a challenge for those that would like to see a public interest defence in the Official Secrets Act 1989. The mass leak is likely to contain a range of information, some of which is in the public interest and some of which is not. The leaker may not even know the content of all the files. The question then is how it could be determined whether the leak was in the public interest. The answer must depend on the context, looking at what information was leaked, who it was leaked to and what steps were taken prior to publication. A megaleak to an organisation that takes steps to redact sensitive and damaging information may warrant a different response to one that simply uploads all the raw data online. The example shows that in the digital era, the public interest of a disclosure is not a simple matter of assessing the value of a single news story or item of leaked information.

G. Concluding Thoughts on Secrecy

Government secrecy is a challenging area in media law, as the arguments on either side can be compelling. There is a clear need to withhold some information, in order for government to function effectively. However, there is also a clear risk that such power will be abused to save officials from embarrassment. Moreover, access to information about government is necessary for an informed public and to hold government to account.

At the start of the discussion, it was noted that the challenge is in determining where the balance lies between these competing pressures. To hand that power to government alone ignores the risk of abuse, yet there are also problems in letting leakers, the media or the courts make that call, as each may lack the knowledge to make a fair assessment.[306] While the legal position assigns responsibility to the government, in practice the system functions in a grey area in which various actors compete to claim the legitimacy to decide where the public interest lies.[307] The discussion has shown that both government and the media have various tools to advance their claims. Governments rely on a combination of liability for both leakers and publishers, powers of search and investigation, voluntary regulation and government management of publicity. At the same time, the media and other publishers have the power of publicity that can be used to generate a backlash against any attempts to censor. That power has become more potent as the political culture has changed to one where

---

[305] See Y Benkler, 'A Free Irresponsible Press: Wikileaks and the Battle over the Soul of the Networked Fourth Estate' (2011) 46 *Harvard Civil Rights-Civil Liberties Law Review* 311, 339–40.

[306] See Sagar (n 265).

[307] ibid.

openness is demanded and censorship regarded as too heavy handed. The media and leakers can also use legal proceedings as a means to publicise the government's actions or seek access to official documents. What the media can safely publish is not a matter of applying black-letter law, but is an ongoing game of pressure and counter-pressure, with each player using various resources. The terms of the law are nonetheless important, in setting the parameters for this process and the strictness of the law can strengthen the hand of government in that system in negotiations. The overall system is therefore a combination of formal rules and informal pressures that combine to provide a set of checks and balances.[308] While the functioning of this system may raise many problems, a docile press that rarely challenges the determinations of government or never carries leaks is more worrying.

The discussion above focuses on what can happen when government and the media are in conflict. However, in many instances, the interests of the media and government may overlap. Some parts of the media may have no interest in challenging the government's military actions or security interests. In such cases, the compliant media institutions can provide another source of 'flak' for those sources and publishers that do challenge the government's account. At the same time, the government may choose to tolerate some unauthorised leaks. To do so is not a concession of power, but can bolster the position of the government. Writing in the USA, Pozen argues that the government often uses leaks to provide an unofficial channel of information.[309] For example, if the government wants to send a signal, say to a foreign country, it may leak the information without wanting to make it official policy. However, if the government were to tolerate only those leaks that were planted by officials, then the audience would assume anything not prosecuted is officially approved. Consequently, Pozen argues that the toleration of planted leaks must be mixed with unapproved leaks for this system to work.[310] This shows how multiple strategic factors are considered by the government and media, and that all leaks cannot simply be explained in terms of 'losses' for the government.

IV. Terrorism

This chapter has looked at two areas for case studies into censorship. Both were chosen given the long history and the response to current challenges in the media environment. There are many other areas that can raise the issues of potential censorship. Much contemporary concern focuses on terrorist-related material, which has become widely accessible via the internet. The issue of terrorist content overlaps with secrecy

---

[308] ibid.
[309] Pozen (n 298).
[310] ibid.

laws in so far as the concern is with national security. The area also has much in common with the law of obscenity in so far as it is seeking to restrict the circulation of information produced by other people and is concerned about the effect it may have on the audience.

There are a number of criminal law offences that target terrorist content. The Terrorism Act 2006 includes an offence of direct or indirect encouragement or inducement to commit terrorist acts. The indirect encouragement offence occurs through the publication of statements that glorify the commission or preparation of terrorist acts, and infer that such conduct should be emulated.[311] While the offence generated considerable debate about freedom of expression, the restriction fits with more traditional speech crimes, in so far as it targets only the publisher or those involved in the dissemination of material.[312] The focus of the offence is on communications intended to encourage certain harmful acts, or reckless to such effects. Reports relating to terrorism in the media are unlikely to fall within the provision. In any event, a media report would be likely to benefit from a defence for statements that do not express the publisher's own views and are not endorsed by the publisher. The defence thereby fits with the Article 10 protection for the detached reporting of what others have said.[313]

The problems in curbing content from overseas has prompted the government to look to internet intermediaries to take some responsibility. The offence of disseminating content that encourages or induces acts of terrorism includes a specific process of notice and takedown for intermediaries. If the intermediary receives a notice from a police constable about the content and fails to comply with the notice within two days, the provider of an electronic service may be deemed to have endorsed the statement and can thereby become liable.[314] Rather than relying on that formal system, the government tends to rely on informal contact and voluntary cooperation with the intermediaries, to block and take down images more efficiently.[315] The strategies for blocking and removing internet content in relation to indecent images of children overseen by the Internet Watch Foundation are seen to provide a model to curb terrorist material.[316]

There are also offences that impose liability for the *possession* of certain terrorism-related material. Section 58 of the Terrorism Act 2000 provides that a person commits an offence if 'he collects or makes a record of information of a kind likely to be useful to a person committing or preparing an act of terrorism' or 'possesses a document or record containing information of that kind'. The offence can be committed by downloading material from a website. In *R v G*, Lord Rodger stated that to fall under s 58, the information 'must, of its very nature, be designed to provide practical assistance to a person committing or preparing an act of terrorism'.[317] As a result, the

---

[311] Terrorism Act 2006, s 1(3).

[312] Terrorism Act 2006, ss 1 and 2. For criticism of this offence, see E Barendt, 'Incitement to, and Glorification of, Terrorism' in I Hare and J Weinstein (eds), *Extreme Speech and Democracy* (Oxford, Oxford University Press, 2009).

[313] *Jersild v Denmark* (1995) 19 EHRR 1.

[314] Terrorism Act 2006, s 3.

[315] See Baroness Warsi, HL Deb 10 Feb 2010, vol 717, WA168. Home Office, *Memorandum to the Home Affairs Committee: Post-Legislative Scrutiny of Terrorism Act 2006* (Cm 8186, 2011) at [8.1.10].

[316] See Ch 7.

[317] *R v G* [2009] UKHL 13, [2010] 1 AC 43 at [43].

provision should not prohibit the possession of everyday items that could in theory be useful to a terrorist, such as a map of the London Underground or a plan of a shopping centre. The possession offence will most obviously apply where the information provides instructions on making a bomb, methods to secure unauthorised access to government buildings, or ways to avoid government surveillance.[318] The limitation of s 58 to information designed to provide 'practical assistance' also means that the offence does not extend to the possession of propaganda 'that simply encourages the commission of acts of terrorism'.[319] That interpretation seems to rule out the use of s 58 to criminalise the downloading of texts or videos advocating terrorist causes, in a manner analogous to the strategy taken against certain types of pornography and indecent images of children.[320] Even with such limits, the offence is still broad and can be committed where the possessor does not have a terrorist purpose. The government has also expressed a desire to strengthen the offence in relation to those who repeatedly view terrorist content.[321]

The discussion shows how there is a mixed strategy for combatting terrorism. The government makes use of the traditional publication offences, prohibits the possession of more sensitive information and involves formal and informal cooperation from intermediaries. In addition, the government uses its power to communicate to send messages to counter terrorist propaganda. The approach thereby fits with the current trends for censorship, in relying on multiple strategies that mutually support one another and assigns responsibility to different actors in the chain of communication.

V. Conclusion

This chapter has primarily focused on two classic areas of censorship. Obscenity and government secrecy deal with very different issues. Under the current Article 10 jurisprudence, obscene speech is worthy of very limited protection in so far as it makes little contribution to debates on matters of general interest. By contrast, government secrecy is widely accepted as going to the heart of media freedom and the ability of the media to hold government to account. In the context of stories about government, the media is expected to push boundaries in order to perform its core democratic function.

There are nonetheless a number of similarities between the laws of secrecy and obscenity. Both were used from the 1960s to the 1980s in a high-profile series of prosecutions that often failed to achieve the desired the goal and generated criticism. Disputes in these areas were at the heart of a cultural change. The obscenity cases

---

[318] ibid, at [45].
[319] *R v K* [2008] EWCA Crim 185 at [13].
[320] C Walker, *Terrorism and the Law* (Oxford, Oxford University Press, 2011) 220, refers to the decisions halting a trend of the offence becoming akin to a 'terrorist pornography' possession offence.
[321] Home Office, 'Law tightened to target terrorists' use of the internet' 3 October 2017.

generated a change in contemporary standards about the types of sexual or violent content that are acceptable (although such matters are still widely debated). The cases relating to government secrecy reflected a change in political culture demanding greater transparency, not trusting government to exercise its powers in the public interest and assigning a bigger role for public opinion in assessing government decisions. Those cases also showed the limits of classic censorship strategies, with the prosecution of publishers generating publicity and providing a cause around which opposing opinions could mobilise. A less heavy-handed approach helps government maintain an appearance of openness and gain greater legitimacy.[322]

The image of censorship evokes classic top-down controls, with decrees of what can or cannot be said. The trajectory of obscenity and secrecy law may give the impression of such types of control being in retreat. In both areas, newspapers and broadcasters are relatively unlikely to face prosecution. However, it would be a mistake to write off the importance of these areas of law. The discussion has shown how there is less need to enforce the criminal law in relation to the media, as specialist systems of regulation have emerged to address the various issues. The DSMA Committee provides a means to clear sensitive stories and makes prosecution less likely. In relation to obscenity law, the BBFC provides a system that reduces the risk of liability in relation to cinema, and has statutory functions to regulate video and certain digital content. In addition, the government can also rely on informal understandings to encourage restraint from the media.

Both areas of law face considerable challenges in the digital era, as a result of international and anonymous communications, and the ease with which information can be captured, shared and spread. For obscenity, this means that more extreme pornography is freely available and easily shared. The ease of capturing images on mobile phones can raise problems of revenge pornography or of children making indecent images of themselves through selfies and sexting. For secrecy, the ease of capturing and sharing has also led to the rise of the megaleak, and the mass of information that can be shared among newspapers collaborating across the globe. Consequently, the old tools for controlling information are proving to be less effective.

As a result, government has adopted new strategies for control, which involve both informal arrangements and new legal measures. These strategies often avoid targeting the media and go after individuals. In obscenity law, there is an increasing strategy to target the recipient of certain types of pornography. In relation to secrecy, the government has greater incentive to target the source of a disclosure to maximise the deterrent effects on would-be leakers. There may be good reasons to prosecute such people, not least because they are within the jurisdiction. However, this strategy is also convenient in so far as a leaker of state secrets or possessor of extreme pornography is far less likely to generate a high level of resistance than a well-funded media organisation. There is also less chance of a massive backlash in such cases (though it is not impossible). Other types of control include the takedown, filtering and blocking of content by digital intermediaries, either under formal legal obligations or through informal policies.

---

[322] Pozen (n 298) 574. See also J Ferejohn, 'Accountability and Authority: Toward a Theory of Political Accountability' in A Przeworski, S Stokes and B Manin (eds), *Democracy, Accountability, and Representation* (Cambridge, Cambridge University Press, 1999).

Prosecution of publishers is just one element among other formal and informal measures to further certain government objectives. That has always been the case. For example, in Georgian times, the government would not only prosecute its critics, but would also pay writers for favourable coverage. However, the system is evolving to deal with new problems and to fit within the current political and social culture, which means a different balance among the varying elements is being struck. In this balance, the classic publication offences relating to the media appear to play a more marginal role in comparison to the other methods, but are nonetheless important in providing the backbone to the system. The criminal and civil laws help to set the standards that influence the other forms of control. For example, the framework of obscenity shapes the work of the BBFC. Government secrecy laws may promote voluntary coopera-tion, for example with the DSMA Committee, or more broadly by maintaining good relations with government. The threat of liability for the publication has incentivised the relevant actors to devise or participate in the schemes of specialist regulation. The legal controls can also set the parameters of debate when entering into negotiations with government. When a newspaper discusses the publication of a leaked document with the government, the potential for liability is a card in the government's hands. The traditional censorship laws may rarely make it into court, but nonetheless play a role in supporting a wider system for controlling information.

5

Newsgathering

I. Introduction

This chapter will look at the ways in which the law regulates and facilitates the newsgathering process. While some areas of media law regulate the publication of content, the focus here is on the earlier stage, in which the journalist or researcher collects information that might form the basis of a future publication or broadcast. Many areas of media law will shape the newsgathering process. Privacy law can prevent journalists from using certain means to acquire information. Access to the courts and court documents provide a valuable way of discovering information. The offences under the Official Secrets Act 1989 may prevent sources from supplying information to journalists. While the impact of such controls on journalism is discussed in other chapters, this chapter will take a narrower focus on the special privileges and shields that offer legal protection for general aspects of the newsgathering process.

Newsgathering has been at the heart of some of the biggest controversies relating to media ethics. The Leveson Inquiry and the reform of press self-regulation were triggered by the revelations that certain newspapers hacked into mobile phones to acquire information.[1] Controversies about the payment of police officers and the use of private detectives by journalists raised similar concerns.[2] More broadly, the media is sometimes criticised for using subterfuge to acquire evidence for stories. While such methods can have a legitimate use, there are occasions where people are entrapped and steered into saying or doing things that they would not normally do. One of the most controversial figures in recent years is the 'Fake Sheikh' Mazher Mahmood, who would pose as an important character (such as a sheikh, film producer or businessman) to capture celebrities in various compromising activities. His defenders said that his sting operations secured results and led to various people being convicted of criminal offences.[3] However, his activities eventually resulted in his own downfall. After one of

---

[1] Leveson LJ, *An Inquiry into the Culture, Practice and Ethics of the Press: Report* (HC 780, 2012) (Leveson Report).

[2] ibid.

[3] For a relatively sympathetic account of his work, see A Marr, *My Trade: A Short History of British Journalism* (Basingstoke, Macmillan, 2004) 46–49.

his sting operations led to the prosecution of a well-known singer, the case collapsed once it was discovered that Mahmood had conspired to alter a witness statement in the proceedings. Mahmood was subsequently convicted of conspiracy to pervert the course of justice.[4] Such an example shows that the way news is acquired is as much an area of controversy and potential abuse as the content that is published.

While the newsgathering process is and should be subject to certain legal controls, there is also a need for investigations to be protected from government monitoring. This means that in some cases the media may need safeguards before the material acquired in the newsgathering process is disclosed either in court proceedings or police investigations. That provides the journalist with a space of more limited legal oversight that is not available to other people or organisations. To some, that is putting the media above the law, while to others such safeguards are essential for the independence of the media from the state. To consider these issues further, this chapter will first look at the various protections for confidential sources and material acquired in the newsgathering process. The promotion of newsgathering under freedom of information laws will then be considered. Finally, the discussion will look at the arguments for a general public interest defence for journalists.

The protection of newsgathering raises a number of questions about the scope and extent of any privileges. One question is whether bloggers, non-professional writers and digital intermediaries should benefit from the protection of sources and from police searches? Another question is how far the state should go in aiding newsgathering and whether there should be a positive obligation to provide access to information held by public authorities? While such shields and privileges would benefit the media, the various costs of such protections also need to be considered. For example, journalists' protection from police searches might be abused to frustrate criminal investigations. A right of access to government-held information imposes a significant administrative burden on public bodies. Protecting newsgathering is a cause that most people will support in the abstract, but raises difficult questions in application.

II. Protecting Journalists' Sources

Confidential sources play a central role in the newsgathering process. The European Court of Human Rights has said that the protection of journalists' confidential sources 'is one of the basic conditions for press freedom'.[5] Before looking at the protection offered to sources in law, it is worth pausing to consider why confidentiality should be valued. Anonymity is not an ideal, and disclosure of a source's identity can help the

---

[4] *R v Mazher Mahmood* (Central Criminal Court, 21 October 2016).
[5] *Goodwin v UK*, App no 17488/90 (1996) 22 EHRR 123.

reader to assess the credibility of a story.[6] The US Society of Professional Journalists' Code of Ethics provides that journalists should normally identify sources so that the public has 'as much information as possible to judge the reliability and motivations of sources'.[7] Along these lines, where the identity of a source is known, people can assess whether a person providing information has an axe to grind or is biased. While various media organisations have their own guidance about when the use of anonymous sources is appropriate, the Leveson Report recommended that the press self-regulator should encourage newspapers to be as transparent as possible about their sources.[8] The need for transparency to assess a publication should not be overstated. Even if the identity of an informant is unknown, the journalist or media publication relying on that source will have a public reputation which people can use to assess the story. There are, however, other risks with confidential sources. A source that is shielded from any public scrutiny may be more likely to provide false information and half-baked rumours. An over-reliance on anonymous sources can lead to laziness in reporting, maybe giving a report greater prominence and credibility than it deserves. For all the talk of the importance of confidential sources, such confidentiality is best seen as the exception rather than the norm for journalistic practice.

While the transparency of sources provides an ideal starting point, there are good reasons why journalists will rely on confidential sources some of the time. A source may fear that they will lose their job or be victimised in some way if they are identified in an article. This will be the case where a source provides confidential information about his or her employer, as the leaking of such information will normally be a disciplinary matter. Where the journalist researches an area that is sensitive or dangerous, such as terrorism or organised crime, a source may suffer serious repercussions and risk to life if identified.[9] Accordingly, the US Society of Professional Journalists' Code of Ethics provides that anonymity is appropriate for 'sources who may face danger, retribution or other harm, and have information that cannot be obtained elsewhere'.[10] The case for confidentiality thereby runs that what the audience loses in terms of the assessability of a particular story, it gains in the overall increase in the flow of information.

The use of inside sources is sometimes necessary to hear alternatives to official information and thereby helps the media to remain independent of powerful organisations. The US legal scholar David Anderson points out that this is especially important in an age where the government places greater emphasis on news management, as opposed to direct censorship.[11] The news management strategy means that public bodies and powerful organisations will attempt to shape public opinion through the release of information, the selection of frames and the cultivation of journalists. As an element of that strategy, confidentiality is sometimes relied upon by public officials

---

[6] For discussion of assessability more broadly, see O O'Neill, *A Question of Trust* (Cambridge, Cambridge University Press, 2002). On the dangers of source anonymity see E Barendt, *Anonymous Speech: Literature Law and Politics* (Oxford, Hart, 2016) 112–15.

[7] Revised 6 September 2014, www.spj.org/ethicscode.asp (last accessed 26 January 2018).

[8] Leveson Report (n 1) 818 and 1799. Barendt, *Anonymous Speech* (n 6) 116–18.

[9] See *Duffy v Sunday Newspapers* [2017] NIQB 71 at [89].

[10] (n 7).

[11] D Anderson, 'Confidential Sources Reconsidered' (2009) 61 *Florida Law Review* 883, 897.

to informally channel information to the media that is supportive of the government. Source anonymity can therefore be double-edged, and responsibility lies with the journalist to avoid becoming a conduit for the government. However, confidentiality is also an important tool for acquiring information from insiders, which public bodies and other organisations do not want to release. With greater emphasis on managing the flow of information, the media has more reason to rely on insider sources to counter the authorised releases, and the government has greater incentive to deter unauthorised leaks by prosecuting or disciplining the source that disclosed the information. The level of protection afforded to journalists' sources is a key factor in determining who controls the flow of information.

Despite the importance of protecting sources, there are occasions where the journalist may be under a legal obligation to break the promise of confidentiality. Sometimes a third party will have a legal interest in discovering the identity of a source. A common situation arises where an employee leaks information to a journalist, and the employer wishes to take some form of disciplinary action against the disloyal employee. If the employer does not know the identity of the disloyal employee, an application can be made to the court to require a third party to identify that person.[12]

Even where genuine legal interests are at stake, requiring a journalist to reveal a source can be damaging to media freedom. A court order requiring disclosure of a source will break the relationship between the journalist and that particular informant. The journalist may have taken considerable time to cultivate a particular insider in an institution, and will be unable to rely on that person for future information once the cover of anonymity is removed.[13] More broadly, a court order undermines the promise of confidentiality and sends a signal that other journalists may not honour such promises in the future. As Lord Dyson stated in *Miranda*, if 'journalists and their sources can have no expectation of confidentiality, they may decide against providing information on sensitive matters of public interest'.[14] The potential for compelled disclosure increases the already considerable risks to a would-be leaker, and adds to the many incentives to stay quiet. This 'chilling effect' argument is attractive to the media as it can be made in any case concerning confidential sources. The argument rests on future effects that cannot be proved or disproved at the time of the court order. As will be seen, the case for protection is thereby put forward even where the source acts with malice or dishonesty. Recognising these issues for media freedom, the current law offers a qualified shield under the Contempt of Court Act 1981, s 10, which prevents the court from ordering the disclosure of a source unless necessary to serve certain interests.

While it is common to hear discussion of a *journalist's* privilege in relation to confidential sources, the protection can be valued from different perspectives, all of which can sometimes be found to influence the courts' approach.[15] The first

---

[12] *Norwich Pharmacal Co v Customs and Excise Commissioners* [1974] AC 133.

[13] See G Robertson and A Nicol, *Media Law*, 5th edn (London, Sweet and Maxwell, 2007) 316–17.

[14] *R (on the application of Miranda) v Secretary of State for the Home Department* [2016] EWCA Civ 6, [2016] 1 WLR 1505 at [113].

[15] See discussion in J Brabyn, 'Protection Against Judicially Compelled Disclosure of the Identity of News Gatherers' Confidential Sources in Common Law Jurisdictions' (2006) 69 *Modern Law Review* 895, 904, and D Carney, 'Truth and the Unnamed Source' (2012) 4 *Journal of Media Law* 117, 142–45.

perspective is that of the source, which views the privilege as a way to protect the source from suffering the consequences that would arise from disclosure. If the sole aim of the law is to shield a person from adverse consequences following the disclosure of information, then the rationale could be relied on to demand general speaker anonymity.[16] However, the current law does not offer general protection for anonymous speakers and only guards against a journalist's compelled disclosure of a source. Moreover, the protection of journalists' sources is not a generalised shield against adverse consequences. As will be seen, the protection for sources does not restrain people from discovering the identity through alternative means. A company may discover a disloyal employee through an internal investigation, CCTV footage or via company records, and then subject that person to disciplinary proceedings. If the perspective of the source was the central rationale, then it could justify the protection from identification by voluntary disclosure by the journalist, as well as compelled disclosure. However, such a broad right has not been developed in the domestic law.[17] In a controversial example, some newspaper companies voluntarily provided the police with material identifying sources that might have received unlawful payments from its journalists.[18] Whatever the journalist promised the source, a media company may see disclosure as serving its strategic interests in maintaining good relations with the police.[19] In the case of voluntary disclosure, the source can make a complaint about the breach of professional ethics to the journalist's professional body. If there is an enforceable obligation of confidence protecting the source's identity, then that could provide a separate route to prevent voluntary disclosure. Where applicable, such a legal remedy would lie in private law, rather than as an element of media freedom that the state is under an obligation to protect. While the perspective of the source is significant in explaining why disclosure can have a chilling effect, the current principles of source protection do not aim to provide the source with a general right to avoid identification and its consequences.

The second perspective views the privilege as protecting the journalist.[20] Under this view, once a journalist accepts information from a source on the condition of confidentiality, the journalist is under a professional obligation to honour the promise. In the UK, the Editor's Code of Practice provides 'Journalists have a moral obligation to protect confidential sources of information'.[21] The obligation typically plays a strong role in the professional identity of journalists. Consequently, when faced with a court

---

[16] See R Andersen Jones, 'Rethinking Reporter's Privilege' (2013) 111 *Michigan Law Review* 1221 for an argument that the privilege is best understood in terms of anonymous speech. Similar arguments could also be made for whistleblower protection as a way to shield sources from adverse consequences. Such safeguards (which are discussed later) tend to be limited to disclosures that reveal wrongdoing. See also the discussion in Barendt (n 6) 111.

[17] In *R v Norman* [2016] EWCA Crim 1564 at [32]–[33], the court expressed some doubt as to whether Art 10 was engaged by the voluntary naming of a source.

[18] ibid.

[19] ibid, at [16].

[20] See the concurring opinion of Tatel J in *In re Grant Jury Subpoena, Judith Miller* (2000) 397 F3d 964 at 1000; and *Branzburg v Hayes* 408 US 665 (1972) at 695, noting that 'the privilege claimed is that of the reporter, not the informant'.

[21] Clause 14, www.ipso.co.uk/editors-code-of-practice/ (last accessed 26 January 2018). See also National Union of Journalists Code of Conduct, cl 7, www.nuj.org.uk/about/nuj-code (last accessed 26 January 2018).

order to disclose the identity of a source, the journalist faces a dilemma: break the professional promise of confidentiality or be in contempt of court.[22] That approach fits with the emphasis on the journalist-source relationship, but is likely to attract a limited amount of sympathy from a judge considering an application to order disclosure. The courts are charged with upholding the rule of law and have rejected broader arguments that a journalist has a right of 'conscientious objection'.[23]

A third perspective is that a privilege is not explained from the perspective of the source or journalist, but is in the wider public interest. Lord Scarman explained that 'the right of the public to be informed' distinguishes the journalistic privilege from that of a doctor or priest.[24] On this view, the protection 'is not about confidences and not about confidential communications', but is about whether the audience will be deprived of information overall.[25] So the key issue is the flow of information between the source and journalist, and ultimately to the public. Lord Scarman's approach is consistent with the instrumental account of media freedom discussed in Chapter 1 and provides a flexible rationale that can be adapted with the circumstances. However, this line of argument leaves open the question of how the interests of the public are best served, and when competing interests outweigh media freedom.

The current law reflects a particular view that the public interest is best served where disclosures are made via the media, rather than through the source directly making the material available to the public. Source protection allows the media to develop as a centre of power with a degree of autonomy from legal scrutiny of its central working practices. The 'institutional integrity' of the media is thereby protected, reflecting the classic 'fourth estate' arguments that emphasise media independence.[26] The privilege credits the media as an institution that people can turn to with some protection. The media institutions are then expected to assess the information for themselves and provide the public face for the statement, and will attract legal responsibility for what is published. That explains why disclosures to the media attract special protection that is not afforded to anonymous speech more generally.

Having set out the arguments for protecting journalists' informants, it is important to remember that the protection of confidential sources cannot be absolute. Imagine a case where a journalist interviews a serial killer who remains at large and whose identity is unknown.[27] Can there really be a case for keeping the identity of the source secret? Most people would accept not. As will be seen, the main challenges lie in drawing the boundaries and deciding when source protection is outweighed.

---

[22] Such a line of argument was advanced by the journalist in *X Ltd v Morgan Grampian (Publishers) Ltd* [1991] 1 AC 1, 9. See D Carney, 'Theoretical Underpinnings of the Protection of Journalists' Confidential Sources: Why Absolute Privilege Cannot be Justified' (2009) 1 *Journal of Media Law* 97, 106–107.

[23] *Morgan Grampian*, ibid, 49.

[24] HL Deb 10 February 1981, vol 417, col 157.

[25] HL Deb 10 February 1981, vol 417, col 158. See also *Interbrew SA v Financial Times Ltd* [2002] EWCA Civ 274, [2002] EMLR 24 at [52].

[26] C Edwin Baker, *Human Liberty and Freedom of Speech* (Cambridge, Cambridge University Press, 1989) 246.

[27] See also *Nordisk Film & TV A/S v Denmark*, App no 40485/02 (December 2005) (admissibility decision), in relation to access to material relating to an undercover news report about an organisation of paedophiles.

A. Source Protection and Media Freedom

The discussion has shown why the protection of confidential sources may be desirable, but a further question is whether it should be regarded as an element of media freedom. In *British Steel v Granada*, Lord Wilberforce argued that freedom of the press was about the 'freedom to publish without pre-censorship, subject always to the laws relating to libel, official secrets, sedition and other recognised inhibitions'.[28] Lord Wilberforce's view of media freedom is similar to Blackstone's account of prior restraints and leaves little scope for source protection.[29] Even a broader account of media freedom as protection from post-publication restraints does not explain why journalists should not be required to disclose sources. Disclosure orders do not stop the media from publishing any content, but make it more difficult for journalists to gather information and research certain stories. For these reasons, the US Supreme Court has held that the protection of sources is not mandated under the First Amendment.[30] In reaching this conclusion, Justice White noted that claims of a chilling effect are largely speculative and that it is not clear that a disclosure order would stop the flow of information.[31] Ronald Dworkin has also argued that the case for journalistic privilege is one of policy, rather than a matter of constitutional right.[32] Under this view, such protection is something that may be desirable in most cases, but it will sometimes have to give way to other interests.

By contrast, the European Court of Human Rights has found that the protection of sources is a part of the right to media freedom under Article 10 of the European Convention on Human Rights (ECHR).[33] In its landmark ruling in *Goodwin v UK*, the Strasbourg Court stated:

> Protection of journalistic sources is one of the basic conditions for press freedom [...] Without such protection, sources may be deterred from assisting the press in informing the public on matters of public interest [...] Having regard to the importance of the protection of journalistic sources for press freedom in a democratic society and the potentially chilling effect an order of source disclosure has on the exercise of that freedom, such a measure cannot be compatible with Article 10 of the Convention unless it is justified by an overriding requirement in the public interest.[34]

The protection of sources and journalistic material is one area where the Strasbourg Court has provided some of its strongest statements in support of media freedom. One reason why the European Court of Human Rights has been willing to take this more robust stance is that it values media freedom primarily as an instrumental good, which can be more easily qualified and balanced with other competing interests. While the Court declares that source protection is fundamental, this does not bind it to any particular outcome in future cases or require that source protection must trump all

---

[28] *British Steel Corpn v Granada* [1981] AC 1096, Lord Wilberforce at 1168.
[29] See Ch 1.
[30] See *Branzburg* (n 20).
[31] ibid, 693–94.
[32] R Dworkin, 'The Farber Case: Reporters and Informers' in *A Matter of Principle* (Cambridge Mass., Harvard University Press, 1985).
[33] See *Goodwin* (n 5) and *Nagla v Latvia*, App no 73469/10 (16 July 2013).
[34] *Goodwin* (n 5).

other interests. Instead, source protection is weighed up in individual cases in relation to competing goals. While the protection of sources may thereby be less far-reaching than the judicial pronouncements sometimes suggest, its recognition as an element of media freedom is still significant.

B. Source Protection in Law

The reasons for respecting the confidentiality of sources have been outlined, and the discussion will now turn to the way the law protects the identity of sources from being revealed by a court order. Prior to 1981, the law offered little protection to sources. The courts had generally not required journalists to disclose their sources through discovery in a defamation action, under the common law 'newspaper rule'.[35] The protection was sometimes explained on the grounds that the claimant does not need such information, as an action in defamation lies against the media body itself and that there is a public interest in ensuring that sources do not 'dry up'.[36] In *Clough*, the court treated the newspaper rule as an exception specific to defamation and found that a general privilege for press sources had not 'crystallised' in law.[37] The court had also held that a promise of confidentiality alone was not enough to warrant protecting a person from disclosure.[38] Instead, where there was the power to order disclosure, the courts retained a 'residual discretion' not to require the identification of a source,[39] but that was not enjoyed as a matter of right.[40] That position contrasted with the confidentiality of police sources that enjoyed stronger protection from disclosure.[41] The position in the law prior to 1981 thereby recognised the importance in protecting the flow of information to the official bodies of investigation (the police), and assigned a much weaker interest in the flow to the informal investigatory and monitoring functions of the media.

The current protection for sources is now found in statute, under s 10 of the Contempt of Court Act 1981. Non-disclosure is no longer a residual discretion and the court is under a qualified duty not to order disclosure of a source. Section 10 provides:

> No court may require a person to disclose, nor is any person guilty of contempt of court for refusing to disclose, the source of information contained in a publication for which he is responsible, unless it be established to the satisfaction of the court that disclosure is necessary in the interests of justice or national security or for the prevention of disorder or crime.

---

[35] *Hennessy v Wright* (1888) 24 QBD 445, 449. For a discussion of the position under the common law prior to 1981, see Y Cripps, *The Legal Implications of Disclosure in the Public Interest*, 2nd edn (London, Sweet and Maxwell, 1994) 254–81.

[36] Lord Denning in *British Steel Corpn v Granada* [1981] AC 1096 (CA), 1128. See also *Adam v Fisher* (1914) 30 Times Law Reports 288 and the discussion in *Lyle-Samuel v Odhams* [1920] 1 KB 135, 141–42.

[37] *A-G v Clough* [1963] 1 QB 773.

[38] *D v National Society for the Prevention of Cruelty to Children (NSPCC)* [1978] AC 171.

[39] *A-G v Mulholland* [1963] 2 QB 477.

[40] *A-G v Lundin* (1982) 75 Cr App R 90. *British Steel Corpn v Granada* (n 28). Although sometimes the protection of the media was stated in stronger terms as an immunity, see Watkins LJ in the Court of Appeal in *British Steel* (n 36) at 1139.

[41] *D v NSPCC* (n 38).

That provision gives the court no additional powers to order disclosure,[42] but imposes conditions when the court exercises an existing power.[43] Under the provision, the applicant who wants to discover the source bears the burden of establishing an exception.[44] By bolstering the protection given to sources, the legislation recognises the importance of the investigatory functions of the media and its need to acquire information.

i. Publishers and Sources

Section 10 does not grant a privilege to the media as an institution, but offers protection to any person responsible for a 'publication'. The provision therefore takes a functional definition of the media, as discussed in Chapter 1, in which the protection for media freedom rests on the journalistic activity of publishing. In many cases, it will be clear when a person is responsible for a publication, but sometimes it is less obvious. One question is whether the operator of a web forum or a digital intermediary should benefit from the provision when a person seeks a court order to disclose the identity of an anonymous poster? In *Totalise*, the court held that a website operator could not rely on s 10 in relation to comments posted anonymously by users and hosted on the site. The court held that to benefit from the protection of sources under s 10, the publisher must normally exercise some 'editorial control'.[45] Under this view, the journalist takes responsibility in deciding whether information is accurate and worth publishing, which is distinct from the automated processes of a digital intermediary. Even when a newspaper chooses not to publish something, that entails an editorial judgement. That approach arguably fits with the view of the media acting as responsible gatekeepers, who are afforded a privilege only in so far as editorial processes consider the potential harm of publication and make a decision whether to publish.

The focus on editorial processes has considerable appeal. After all, the internet host seems a far cry from the classic newsgatherer, who cultivates various sources and has a professional obligation of confidence. However, a traditional understanding of the journalistic practices is coming under pressure given the blurring between media and other types of activity. For example, the mainstream media increasingly provides a platform for user-generated content. A question therefore arises as to whether a newspaper should benefit from s 10 in relation to an anonymous comment posted in response to one of its articles. Such a comment is not a journalist's source in the traditional sense. Conversely, an online intermediary may in some cases act as the equivalent of an editor. Some leaker websites that allow people to anonymously upload documents are not detached commercial operations or services, but are ideologically committed to providing a confidential forum.[46] Some platforms may also engage in

---

[42] *Secretary of State for Defence v Guardian Newspapers Ltd* [1985] 1 AC 339, 347.

[43] For example, under *Norwich Pharmacal* (n12).

[44] P Londono, D Eady and ATH Smith, *Arlidge, Eady and Smith on Contempt*, 5th edn (London, Sweet and Maxwell, 2017) at [9.106], citing *Saunders v Punch Ltd* [1998] 1 WLR 986, 993C.

[45] *Totalise v Motley Fool* [2001] EMLR 29 at [25].

[46] For an argument that various online forums should be protected as media, see Y Benkler, 'A Free Irresponsible Press: Wikileaks and the Battle over the Soul of the Networked Fourth Estate' (2011) 46 *Harvard Civil Rights-Civil Liberties Law Review* 311.

their own editorial processes, perhaps vetting some of the submissions by users, but without going through the full processes of verification expected of a professional journalist.[47] That may not be the same as traditional journalism, but nor is it purely passive.

These factors show how the nature and form of journalistic activity is changing, and Chapter 1 argued that the provision of a platform is a media function. That does not mean all platforms should have a right to guarantee the anonymity of the speech they facilitate. If source protection were to be extended to all intermediary hosting activities, then that approach would move away from the existing view that information is to be protected when channelled through the media and would move closer to the general protection of anonymous comments. However, such a dramatic change could be avoided if the application of s 10 and the 'editorial control' test extends only to those types of intermediary and hosting service that take some responsibility for the content. This might arise where the websites invite comments on a particular topic, engage in moderation and have mechanisms for taking down certain harmful communications.

On the question of what constitutes a 'source' for the purposes of s 10, Warby J gave a broad definition of the term in *Hourani* to cover those who 'provide information to others with a view to that information being published to the public or a section of the public'.[48] In that case, it was held that a person paying another to organise public demonstrations and publish material was a 'source', even though it bore no resemblance to traditional journalism. Warby J stated that it would unsatisfactory to distinguish between different classes of person supplying information for publication.[49] Such a broad reading of the term could therefore mean that a lobbyist being paid to publish advertisements advancing certain political causes could rely on s 10 to avoid disclosing the name of a client. This seems unsatisfactory, as the example of a lobbyist is one where the interests of a democracy tend to require greater transparency, rather than anonymity.[50] One problem with offering the protection of s 10 in such an example is that a lobbyist does not perform a function equivalent to a journalist. The difference is not just with the status of the publisher, but also with the relationship with the source. The client paying a lobbyist is not a 'source' in the sense of the person supplying information that may be useful for the publisher's investigation. Instead, the client provides instructions to the publisher and sets the goals for the publication. That goes beyond the mere supply of information and the position of the client is more like an anonymous speaker. Warby J found that such factors could be relevant when balancing source protection with other competing interests. However, it is argued here that there is no need to grant such a publisher even the prima facie protection that is afforded under s 10.

---

[47] The editorial processes may also be automated using algorithms to select content and decide what articles to promote.

[48] *Hourani v Thompson* [2017] EWHC 173 (QB) at [33].

[49] ibid.

[50] Such transparency is the policy underpinning the register of consultant lobbyists under the Transparency of Lobbying, Non-Party Campaigning and Trade Union Administration Act 2014.

ii. The Exceptions: National Security, Prevention of Crime and the Interests of Justice

Section 10 provides that the court should not order a publisher to disclose the identity of a source unless the exceptions are met. In applying the provision, the court will first ask whether disclosure of the source serves any of the interests named in the provision: the prevention of crime and disorder, national security and the interests of justice. If the answer is yes, then the court will ask itself whether disclosure of the source is necessary for that purpose. If these questions are satisfied, the court is not compelled to order disclosure of the source and retains a residual discretion whether to order disclosure.[51] However, in most cases, the court's attention will be focused on the question of necessity, which will be considered below.

In interpreting s 10, the courts have given a broad interpretation to the interests of national security. In *Guardian Newspapers*, the House of Lords accepted that national security was served in identifying a civil servant who had leaked information concerning the government's plans for announcing the deployment of cruise missiles at Greenham Common.[52] While the topic was sensitive, the disclosure did not harm national security. However, the court found that national security required the identification of the source, as the leak showed that the ministry had a disloyal employee who was likely to have continuing access to information raising national security concerns. The argument ran that even if the disclosure itself is not damaging, the presence of a 'bad apple' poses a threat that warrants the disclosure of the source. The logic of the argument suggests that the interests of national security demand the disclosure of any leaker who has access to security-related information, even if the leak serves the public interest, for example by blowing the whistle on corruption.[53] The decision can be criticised for accepting a weak national security argument, when the government was really concerned with punishing a disclosure that caused political embarrassment.[54]

Another exception to the protection under s 10 is where disclosure is necessary for 'the prevention of crime'. The exception is not limited to situations where the identification of a source will assist with an investigation into a particular crime or incident, or prevents the future commission of an identifiable crime that is known to be planned.[55] If the definition was so limited, then it would be difficult for the police or investigator to meet this high burden to engage the exception. Instead, Lord Griffiths in *In Re An Inquiry* found that the 'prevention of crime' was not the same as the 'prevention of a crime'.[56] The former is wider in application. Lord Oliver similarly stated the prevention of crime means 'the detection and prosecution of crimes which are

---

[51] See *Interbrew* (n 25) at [48]; *Hourani* (n 48) at [35]; *Arlidge, Eady and Smith on Contempt* (n 44) at [9.84]–[9.86].

[52] *Secretary of State for Defence v Guardian Newspapers Ltd* [1985] AC 339.

[53] H Fenwick and G Phillipson, *Media Freedom under the Human Rights Act* (Oxford, Oxford University Press, 2006) 331.

[54] On the limited evidence in support of the government's argument, see Lord Fraser and Lord Scarman's dissents in *Guardian Newspapers* (n 52). See also K Ewing and C Gearty, *Freedom Under Thatcher* (Oxford, Clarendon Press, 1990) 142.

[55] *In Re An Inquiry Under The Company Securities (Insider Dealing) Act 1985* [1988] AC 660, Lord Griffiths, 705.

[56] ibid, 705.

shown to have been committed and where detection and prosecution could sensibly be said to act as a practical deterrent to future criminal conduct of a similar type'.[57] On this interpretation, the prevention of crime can be engaged where the investigation is into general criminal networks, and not just when there is a tip-off to the police about a planned crime. Like the interests of national security, the interpretation of the prevention of crime exception is broad.

Section 10 also allows the court to order disclosure of a source when necessary in the 'interests of justice'. That provision has been at the centre of most of the reported cases. The courts have interpreted the interests of justice to apply where a person wishes 'to exercise important legal rights and to protect themselves from serious legal wrongs whether or not resort to legal proceedings in a court of law will be necessary to attain these objectives'.[58] In other words, the interests of justice are not limited to where the applicant wishes to pursue the legal wrong in court, but are also engaged where informal action will be taken against the source. The most obvious application arises where an employer wants to find out who is leaking information, not to initiate court proceedings against the leaker, but to dismiss that person from their employment. Lord Woolf reasoned that if the interests of justice did not include such informal enforcement of legal interests, then people would be incentivised to initiate legal proceedings simply to trigger the exception in s 10.[59] The approach has, however, been criticised as giving higher to status to an employer's internal enforcement of a private right than to the public interest in source protection.[60] While there are such dangers, it is also easy to see why the court did not wish to foreclose the possibility of ordering disclosure where non-legal measures will be pursued. Once the interests under s 10 are engaged, the court will consider the necessity of disclosure, which will often be the key question.

iii. Necessity

In applying the necessity test, the courts have to strike a balance between media freedom and the competing interests. The balancing exercise varies according to the interest at stake. In *Morgan Grampian*, Lord Bridge stated that when the interests of national security and prevention of crime are engaged, 'the necessity of disclosure follows almost automatically'.[61] Such an approach is troubling, given the broad definition of those two interests, and it potentially wipes out source protection when related to issues of national security or crime. Such an interpretation would be likely to fall foul of Article 10 in so far as it appears to bypass any meaningful balancing process.[62] For these reasons, Lord Bridge's comments are better interpreted as meaning that certain interests are likely to be given considerable weight in the balancing exercise.

---

[57] ibid, Lord Oliver, 709.
[58] *Morgan Grampian* (n 22). See *Ashworth Hospital Authority v MGN Ltd* [2002] UKHL 29, [2002] 1 WLR 2033 at [49]. Compare Lord Diplock in *Secretary of State for Defence v Guardian Newspapers Ltd* [1985] AC 339, [1984] 3 WLR 986.
[59] *Ashworth Hospital Authority v MGN Ltd* (n 58) at [49].
[60] R Costigan, 'Protection of journalists' sources' (2007) *Public Law* 464, 483–84.
[61] *Morgan Grampian* (n 22) 43.
[62] D Feldman, *Civil Liberties and Human Rights in England and Wales*, 2nd edn (Oxford, Oxford University Press, 2002) 853. See also Fenwick and Phillipson (n 53) 332–34 and 340.

Some earlier decisions on the interests of justice exception treated the question of necessity as a matter of balancing two interests of equal weight, which in the event of a tie break would be resolved in favour of disclosing the source.[63] Such an approach is not compatible with the Article 10 jurisprudence given that the assumption should be in favour of the right rather than the competing interest. That approach would not be taken now, given the duty of the court under the Human Rights Act 1998 to interpret s 10 in line with the ECHR.[64] While the courts still use the terminology of balancing, it should be taken to mean the type of balancing exercise found with the proportionality test in the human rights context.

In applying the necessity test, the courts will take into account a number of factors. Of particular importance will be the harm caused by the leak. If the harm is caused to a 'minor interest in property', then that will not be sufficient to outweigh source protection.[65] The European Court of Human Rights has stated that a desire to unmask a disloyal employee alone will not be enough to establish necessity.[66] However, the presence of a 'bad apple' may still be relevant to the court's assessment when coupled with other interests. The point can be illustrated by *Ashworth*, in which the *Daily Mirror* received information about the treatment of a notorious murderer in a secure hospital.[67] The journalist did not know the original source and had received the information through an intermediary. The court ordered disclosure of the intermediary, which the hospital believed would reveal the identity of the initial source. Among the factors considered by the court was the effect of leaks to the press (and prospect of future leaks by the same source) on the trust between patients and staff, and among members of staff in a psychiatric hospital.[68] The court also took into account the fact that medical information was at stake in the case, which engaged privacy rights that are normally afforded a high level of protection. While the court looked at the context of the case in making the decision, Brabyn suggests that the court was too quick to accept that future leaks were a significant risk, and argues that the disclosures may have been a 'one-off' in relation to a particularly notorious murderer.[69]

In line with the proportionality analysis, the court will also consider whether the applicant could or should have addressed the harm caused by the leak through alternative means. In *Goodwin v UK*, the European Court of Human Rights found that an order to disclose the identity of an employee who leaked confidential information was not necessary because an injunction was already in place to prevent the information being repeated. Similarly, the court found that disclosure was unnecessary when a company had failed to hold an internal investigation to discover the source of a leak.[70] Compelling a journalist to break a professional obligation should,

---

[63] Lord Donaldson in the Court of Appeal, *X Ltd v Morgan Grampian (Publishers) Ltd* [1990] 1 All ER 616, 630. See discussion in G Nicolaou, 'The Protection of Journalists' Sources' in J Casadevall et al (eds), *Freedom of Expression—Essays in Honour of Nicolas Bratza, President of the European Court of Human Rights* (Oisterwijk, Wolf Legal Publishers, 2012).

[64] *Interbrew* (n 25) at [32]; *Ashworth Hospital Authority v MGN Ltd* (n 58) at [38].

[65] *Morgan Grampian* (n 22).

[66] *Goodwin* (n 5); *Financial Times v United Kingdom*, App no 821/03 (2010) 50 EHRR 46 at [71].

[67] *Ashworth* (n 58).

[68] ibid, at [16]–[18] and [63].

[69] Brabyn (n 15) 930.

[70] *John v Express Newspapers* [2000] 1 WLR 1931.

therefore, be a last resort reserved for cases where the applicant has no other way to identify the source.[71] The implication of that factor underlines the point made earlier that s 10 does not aim to provide general protection for a source's anonymity, but instead seeks to protect the lines of communication between the journalist and source. If the identity of the disloyal employee is discovered through an internal investigation, then s 10 offer no protection. Another significant factor that the courts will consider in deciding the issue of necessity is the means by which the information was acquired.[72] For example, if the information was acquired by breaking into a person's home or hacking their computer, that will strengthen the case for disclosure.

iv. The Public Interest

When applying s 10, the courts will consider the public interest in media freedom and the protection of confidential sources.[73] The way the public interest should be assessed in the analysis has been subject to debate. On one view, the public interest refers to the value of information provided by the source in the particular case. Along these lines, Lord Bridge stated in *Morgan Grampian* that when deciding whether to order disclosure 'the nature of the information obtained from the source' is relevant and that the 'greater the legitimate public interest in the information which the source has given to the publisher or intended publisher, the greater will be the importance of protecting the source'.[74] Lord Bridge's approach to the public interest is therefore similar to that taken in defamation and privacy law, which looks at the value to the audience of receiving the particular item of information.

That approach has generated some controversy. Section 10 is supposed to put the onus on the applicant to show that disclosure is necessary for one of the listed interests. To look at the public interest of the information obtained from the source will require the journalist to justify the value of the information received, potentially weakening the default assumption that disclosure of a source is contrary to the public interest.[75] Taking the nature of the information into account is also criticised because even when the information supplied in a particular case is of limited value to the audience, an order to disclose a source can chill other sources in the future that do have information that is of public interest. The argument runs that in the long-term, disclosure will frustrate the flow of genuinely valuable information. For this reason, an alternative view is advanced that there is a 'constant' public interest in protecting sources regardless of the nature of the information.[76]

---

[71] ibid.

[72] *Morgan Grampian* (n 22).

[73] See Lord Phillips in *Ashworth Hospital Authority v MGN Ltd* [2001] 1 WLR 515 at [90]; see also the European Court of Human Rights in *Sanoma Uitgevers BV v Netherlands*, App no 38224/03 (2010) 30 BHRC 318 at [90]–[91].

[74] *Morgan Grampian* (n 22) 44.

[75] See Costigan, 'Protection of journalists' sources' (n 60) 477–78 and *Arlidge, Eady and Smith on Contempt* (n 44) [9-164].

[76] Laws LJ, *Ashworth* in the Court of Appeal (n 73) at [101].

If the 'constant' public interest means that the court should always take into account the potential for the disclosure order to chill future sources, then it is a compelling argument. However, it is difficult to argue that the nature of the information should be disregarded completely in the necessity test. To make the point, compare the following two examples. In the first, a person working in a hospital sends a journalist medical records showing that a celebrity is suffering a serious form of mental illness. In the second example, the same person leaks medical records, but this time showing that a military officer with responsibility for the operation of a nuclear submarine is suffering from such an illness and has a record of paranoid delusions. In both cases, the hospital employee breaches the contract of employment and has invaded the privacy of the individual. The leaks in both cases cause similar harm to the individual and were acquired by committing a legal wrong. However, most people would view the two leaks differently. The difference lies not in the harm caused by the leak, but by the nature of the information, as the disclosure about the celebrity is gratuitous and serves no public interest related purpose. In such a case, the court is likely to view the source as deserving less protection and the chilling of sources with such stories may be thought to be desirable.[77] By contrast, the leak about the nuclear submarine officer has an arguable public interest, and disclosure of the source may be seen to create greater long-term impediment to the newsgathering process.

That, however, cannot be the end of the matter. The public interest can be difficult to assess in relation to the process of newsgathering, which takes place before the final news article is made available to the public. Asking whether the information is of value to the public applies a standard that is appropriate when looking at a finished media product. However, the source is not making the information public or providing a final product, but is supplying the journalist with raw material that may or may not be used. For example, a source may provide a lead on what could be an important story, but after further research the journalist may decide that there is nothing worth reporting. In so doing, there is still a compelling argument to protect the process of investigation, even though the source provided no information that was of value to the public.

The public interest of the information or lack thereof is relevant to the necessity test, but cannot be decisive. If the content of the information is not the central criteria for the public interest in some cases, the court will need to look at other factors, such as the conduct of the source and journalist to indicate where the public interest lies. Along these lines, the purpose of the source in supplying the information is one consideration the courts will look at. This can be seen from the decision in *Ackroyd (No 2)*, which arose on the same set of facts as *Ashworth*.[78] Once Ashworth Hospital knew the identity of the *Daily Mirror's* intermediary source—a journalist named Ackroyd—it sought an order to compel that journalist to disclose the identity of his initial source. In the proceedings, the judge found there was no public interest in leaking the medical information of the well-known prisoner.[79] However, in assessing the necessity for disclosure under s 10, the court took into account the fact that the source's purpose was

---

[77] Lord Phillips, *Ashworth* in the Court of Appeal, ibid, at [99].

[78] *Mersey Care NHS Trust v Ackroyd (No 2)* [2007] EWCA Civ 101, [2008] EMLR 1.

[79] Tugendhat J in *Mersey Care NHS Trust v Ackroyd (No 2)* [2006] EWHC 107 (QB) [2006] EMLR 12 at [157].

a 'misguided' attempt to act in the public interest.[80] The fact that the source had such a purpose meant he was unlikely to leak information in the future. Consequently, the court declined to order disclosure of the source.

More controversially, the Court of Appeal in *Interbrew* upheld an order to disclose the identity of a source that was alleged to have doctored a presentation concerning a proposed company takeover and leaked it to a journalist.[81] Sedley LJ looked at the source's purpose, which was not to bring any wrongdoing to the attention of the public, but rather to cause harm to the company or investing public.[82] Unsurprisingly, the decision was controversial and critics argued that even where a source has a bad purpose, an order for disclosure can send out a signal that has a chilling effect on other sources.[83] Any chilling effect could also be particularly damaging in the context of financial journalism, where the complexity of the issues means that journalists rely heavily on inside sources.[84] The European Court of Human Rights found that the order in *Interbrew* violated Article 10, in particular as the bad purpose had not been established on the facts and the domestic courts had been too willing to assume the worst of the source.[85] However, the Strasbourg Court accepted that the purpose of the source is a relevant factor in deciding whether disclosure is justified, but disagreed with domestic court's decision on the facts.

The court will also look at the conduct and record of the journalist to determine the likely effect of disclosure on the public interest both on the facts of the specific case and in the future. In *Ackroyd (No 2)*, the court noted that the journalist in question had a track record for serious reporting and had previously produced stories revealing problems at the Ashworth Hospital.[86] To force the journalist to reveal the identity of the source may have broken the relationship with informants at the hospital that had helped gather information that did have a public interest element. Under this approach, the professional standards of the journalist may be a factor in strengthening source protection.

Where a person outside the traditional media seeks to rely on s 10, the court still uses the model of the professional journalist as a comparator to decide if the publisher and source deserve protection under the necessity test.[87] In *Hourani*, Warby J stated that the interests of a citizen publisher will be given greater weight under s 10 if he or she disinterestedly engages in an independent publicity campaign 'inspired by his own

---

[80] Tugendhat J, ibid, at [157] and [188]. The point was upheld by the Court of Appeal (n 78) at [82].

[81] *Interbrew* (n 25).

[82] ibid at [55]. Sedley LJ at [42] distinguished between purpose and motive, with the latter being irrelevant to the analysis. If the source's purpose 'is to bring wrongdoing to public notice it will deserve a high degree of protection, and it will not matter—assuming that it could anyway be ascertained—whether the motive is conscience or spite'.

[83] See 'Lords refuse media appeal on order to hand over leaked papers' *The Guardian* (11 July 2002); Fenwick and Phillipson (n 53) 361.

[84] See, for example, the criticism of *Interbrew* in 'Plugging the leaks in a listing ship' *The Guardian* (12 July 2002).

[85] *Financial Times v UK* (n 66). *Interbrew* was decided on an interim application. See also *Telegraaf Media Nederland Landelijke Media BV v Netherlands*, App no 39315/06 (2012) 34 BHRC 193 at [128], where the court stated that the domestic authorities should be slow to assume the bad purpose of a source.

[86] *Mersey Care NHS Trust v Ackroyd (No 2)* (n 79) at [182]–[183] and in the Court of Appeal (n 78) at [78].

[87] See *Hourani* (n 48) at [37].

investigations and passion for justice'—the journalistic ideal—as opposed to a person who simply publishes messages for an anonymous client.[88] The reasoning in *Ackroyd* and *Hourani* shows that while s 10 can be relied upon by anyone, the court takes into account the practices and processes of the professional journalist when deciding what weight to give to the rights of the publisher. As discussed in other chapters, this example shows how functional definitions of journalism will often tend to be more easily fulfilled by established media organisations.

C. Assessment

The discussion so far shows that the court takes into account a number of factors in deciding whether to order disclosure of a source. It is hard to take issue with the general framework provided by s 10, and most people accept that the protection of sources will be qualified by competing considerations. Criticisms are often made in relation to the application of s 10 on the facts, along the lines that the courts gave too much weight to a particular factor or gave insufficient weight to media freedom. The line of criticism is also supported by the findings of the European Court of Human Rights that the domestic courts have fallen short of the level of protection required by Article 10 on more than one occasion. In *Goodwin*, the European Court of Human Rights found that the order to disclose a source in *Morgan Grampian* was disproportionate, as an interim injunction had already been granted to prevent any further harm from that particular leak. The European Court of Human Rights decision in *Goodwin* has been described as the 'high-water mark' of source protection[89] and sent a powerful signal for change to the domestic courts. Even after the enactment of the Human Rights Act 1998, the domestic court's order to disclose the source in *Interbrew* was found by the Strasbourg Court to be a violation of Article 10.

In assessing the court's record on source protection, the picture is mixed. There are plenty of grand statements underlining the importance of journalists' sources, but there are also a significant number of disclosure orders. Nobody argues for absolute protection of all sources and the assessment is fact sensitive. For that reason, it is not clear whether a decision signals a particular judicial outlook, or can simply be explained away as an exceptional case on its facts. Even the decision not to order disclosure in *Ackroyd* was a limited victory for media freedom. The decision can be explained as the delay of six years between the leak and the court hearing meant there was good chance that the source no longer worked at the hospital and there had not been any further unauthorised disclosures of medical information.[90] That factor will not be present in most cases. Those journalists seeking to protect sources may also face a challenge as the courts will naturally have sympathy for those that have suffered an arguable legal wrong and wish to pursue some form of action. The first instance judge will hear the evidence of an aggrieved party and will have limited information about

---

[88] ibid at [46].
[89] Nicolaou (n 63).
[90] Brabyn (n 15).

the source and the potential effects of disclosure.[91] Weighing an established injury to the applicant's legal interests with a more speculative harm to media freedom, it may be no surprise that courts gravitate towards disclosure in many cases. That may provide some explanation why the decisions of the court are often disappointing, despite the recognition of the media freedom issues in the reasoning.

III. Journalists' Material

A. Reasons for Protecting Journalists' Material

So far, the discussion has focused on the power of a court to demand that a journalist disclose the identity of a confidential source. A related issue concerns the ability of the authorities to access journalists' material, such as notebooks, transcripts of interviews and computer hard drives. There are obvious reasons why police and other investigators sometimes want to see such material. If a television company films a riot, the police would no doubt find it useful to access that company's footage in order to identify the rioters. Similarly, if a journalist writes a detailed study on organised crime, the police would find it useful to look at the journalist's research material to obtain intelligence on criminal activities.

While useful to official investigations, the powers of the police to access such material raise some serious concerns about media freedom. In some cases, access to the material might enable the police to identify a confidential source. That is likely in cases where the police access a journalist's notes and records. Even if that is not the main purpose of the search, the fact that it may lead to the source being discovered can have a chilling effect. Given that concern, the European Court of Human Rights in *Sanoma* held that a judge or other independent and impartial body should, prior to access, assess whether the public interest asserted by the investigators or prosecutors outweighs the interest in source protection (that may be jeopardised by such access).[92] In other words, access to journalists' material cannot be at the discretion of the investigating authorities that hold the search powers. If independent review takes place only after the material has been accessed, that 'would undermine the very essence of the right to confidentiality'.[93] The goal under Article 10 is not to secure absolute immunity for the media, but to make sure safeguards are in place to limit the government discretion and scope for abuse.

Aside from the protection of sources, there are other reasons to require judicial safeguards before journalistic material can be accessed. By taking notes and records

---

[91] S Palmer, 'Protecting journalists' sources: Section 10, Contempt of Court Act 1981' (1992) *Public Law* 61, 71. See also Fenwick and Phillipson (n 53) 382.
[92] *Sanoma Uitgevers BV* (n 73) [90]–[92].
[93] ibid [91].

away, the journalist may be unable to complete the report or article being worked on.[94] Even if a raid does not lead to court proceedings or if the investigation is abandoned, the process of seizing material and investigating a journalist imposes costs in terms of time. The potential to use these powers provides some leverage over the journalist, which may serve as a warning to the media not to investigate certain difficult areas.[95] Along these lines, even if the Official Secrets Act 1989 is not frequently enforced against the media, the power to investigate crimes under that Act can be used to make life difficult for the reporter. In *Bright*, a case relating to disclosures made to the press by a former MI5 employee, Judge LJ stated that proceedings 'directed towards the seizure of the working papers of an individual journalist, or the premises of the newspaper or television programme publishing his or her reports, or the threat of such proceedings, tends to inhibit discussion'.[96] The use of powers to investigate and seize as a means to inhibit and intimidate is not new and can be seen in *Entick v Carrington*, in which officers ransacked the homes of writers and publishers that were critical of the government.[97]

More broadly, if government authorities can easily gain access to journalistic material, there is a danger that the press will be seen as an informal researcher or investigator for the state.[98] The point is illustrated by the example of riot footage. If the police can access the raw footage taken for television news, the film crew is no longer just reporting what is happening in the world, but gathering information that is useful for the prosecution of criminals. Such assistance may be regarded as of social value and there is no breach of any promise of confidentiality by the journalist. However, such access might hinder the newsgathering process by making people wary of the media. For example, rioters may turn on the reporter if he or she is seen to gather evidence for the police.

B. Protection under the Police and Criminal Evidence Act 1984

Normally, when the police and other authorities are investigating a crime in non-media cases, an application can be made to magistrates for a warrant to enter and search premises, and to seize the relevant items.[99] The application is normally made ex parte, so the person has no opportunity to challenge the search power in advance. If this process were available in relation to journalistic research, there would be serious implications for media freedom. A power to turn up at a person's home or workplace to engage in a search of property and possessions would be a 'draconian' interference with rights to privacy and media freedom, giving the police broad discretion and

---

[94] D Feldman, 'Press Freedom and Police Access to Journalistic Material' in E Barendt (ed), *Yearbook of Media and Entertainment Law* (Oxford, Oxford University Press, 1995) 52.

[95] See, for example, the discussion of the Zircon affair in Ewing and Gearty (n 54) 146–51.

[96] *R (on the application of Bright) v Central Criminal Court* [2001] 1 WLR 662, 681.

[97] See J Rowbottom, '*Entick and Carrington*, the Propaganda Wars and Liberty of the Press' in A Tomkins and P Scott (eds), *Entick v Carrington: 250 Years of the Rule of Law* (Oxford, Hart, 2015).

[98] Feldman (n 94) 48. Brabyn (n 15) 922 makes the point in relation to journalists' sources. See also Fenwick and Phillipson (n 53) 371.

[99] Police and Criminal Evidence Act 1984, s 8.

the power to look at a wide range of materials.[100] For these reasons, the Police and Criminal Evidence Act 1984 (PACE) provides that the normal process for search and seizure does not apply to journalistic material. Instead, the police and investigators are required to apply to court for an order for the journalistic material to be produced for the police to take away, or to provide access to the material on site.[101] An order for journalistic material to be produced is less intrusive than a general search power and therefore more likely to be a proportionate measure. The application is made to a circuit judge,[102] and heard inter partes, so that the journalist has the chance to challenge the application. To support the inter partes process, the Supreme Court has held that the application cannot be supported by secret evidence, unless Parliament has provided otherwise.[103] While an order for production or access is the norm, there are some circumstances when journalistic material can be subject to search powers, such as where notice of the application for access would 'seriously prejudice the investigation'.[104]

The protection under PACE is not granted to the media as an institution, but to 'journalistic material', which is defined as 'material acquired or created for the purposes of journalism'.[105] The 'purposes of journalism' are not defined in PACE and the court appears to take a functional approach. In deciding whether the material is held for journalistic purposes, the courts will consider whether it is held for activities such as 'the collecting, writing and verifying of material for publication' and 'the editing of the material, including its selection and arrangement'.[106] That is helpful where the search relates to an identifiable media organisation and the court is seeking to distinguish its journalistic material from non-journalistic documents (such financial plans). There is, however, a prior question as to what types of person should be able to rely on the protection. The special protection of PACE should not be available to any person simply because he or she collected material for the purposes of publication on the internet. To do so, would be to blow a major hole into the powers of the police to investigate. Instead, there is a strong argument that the special privilege should be afforded only in relation to material held by people or organisations that normally meet the standards and perform the functions expected of the professional media when collecting, verifying and editing material.

---

[100] *Ernst v Belgium*, App no 33400/96 (2004) 39 EHRR 35 at [103]; Feldman (n 94) 71.

[101] PACE 1984, Sch 1, para 4.

[102] ibid, Sch 1. The Terrorism Act 2000, Sch 5 provides similar safeguards before journalistic material can be accessed for the purpose of an investigation into terrorism, but does not require the officer to show reasonable grounds for believing that an offence has been committed, does not provide for an inter partes hearing and provides less stringent protection for confidential material. See Robertson and Nicol (n 13) 664–66.

[103] *R (on the application of British Sky Broadcasting Ltd) v Central Criminal Court* [2014] UKSC 17, [2014] AC 885, applying the principle of *Al-Rawi v Security Service* [2011] UKSC 34, [2012] 1 AC 531.

[104] PACE 1984, Sch 1, paras 12 and 14.

[105] Section 13. Section 13(3) further provides: 'A person who receives material from someone who intends that the recipient shall use it for the purposes of journalism is to be taken to have acquired it for those purposes'.

[106] See *BBC v Sugar* [2012] UKSC 4, [2012] 1 WLR 439, Lord Wilson endorsing the analysis of the Tribunal at [39] and [42]. While that case concerned the application of a similar test under the Freedom of Information Act 2000, Leveson LJ stated that he saw no reason for a different approach to 'journalistic purposes' for the purposes of PACE, Leveson Report (n 1) 1497.

Where the evidence sought by the police is journalistic, PACE distinguishes two types of material. If the material is held in confidence, then it is 'excluded material' and the police will be granted access only if there are reasonable grounds for believing that the material is on the relevant premises, and that the warrant would have been granted under another power enacted before PACE.[107] If the material is not held in confidence (which would be the case with the filming of a riot in public view) then it is 'special procedure material' and the judge will only grant access if there are reasonable grounds for believing:

— an indictable offence has been committed;
— that there is special procedure material on the premises;
— that the material will be of substantial value to the relevant investigation;
— that the material will provide relevant evidence.

To show that the material will have substantial value, the authorities need to provide clear and specific evidence about what is being sought and why, and should avoid making speculative claims.[108] The process should therefore not be used for a fishing expedition to see if any offences have been committed.[109] The court must be satisfied that these conditions have been established, rather than asking whether the police officer has a rational belief that the conditions have been met.[110] In addition to these requirements, access will be granted only if alternative methods of obtaining the material have not succeeded or are 'bound to fail', and it is in the public interest to grant access to the material.[111] When deciding whether to grant access, the court will also consider the impact on media freedom, and then engage in a general balancing test with the competing interests.[112]

A number of decisions applying the provisions have been criticised in so far as the courts have tended to prioritise police investigations over the freedom of journalists.[113] As with source protection, that may reflect the general preference for the enforcement of the law over abstract rights. However, the provisions should not be dismissed, as it provides a significant hurdle before journalistic material can be accessed. There have been some important rulings, such as the decision not to grant access to footage taken by television reporters of evictions from Dale Farm, a large traveller site in Essex. In reaching that conclusion, the court took into account the danger of hostility to reporters if footage was made available to the police.[114]

---

[107] See PACE 1984, Sch 1, para 3. For criticism see Feldman (n 94) 67.

[108] *R (on the application of British Sky Broadcasting Ltd) v Chelmsford Crown Court* [2012] EWHC 1295 (Admin), [2012] 2 Cr App R 33 at [31] and [45].

[109] ibid.

[110] *Bright* (n 96) 677.

[111] PACE 1984, Sch 1, para 2(b).

[112] In *Bright* (n 96), Judge LJ and Maurice Kay LJ stated that if all the access conditions are fulfilled, the court is not bound to grant access and retains the discretion, at which point issues of media freedom will be considered. By contrast, Gibbs LJ thought media freedom issues could be considered when looking at the public interest in granting access under the final stage of the PACE test.

[113] Robertson and Nicol (n 13) 340, citing cases such as *Chief Constable of Avon and Somerset v Bristol United Press* (1986) *Independent*, 4 November and *Wyrko v Newspaper Publishing plc* (1988) *Independent*, 27 May. See also R Costigan, 'Fleet Street blues: police seizure of journalists' material' (1996) *Criminal Law Review* 231.

[114] *R (on the application of British Sky Broadcasting Ltd) v Chelmsford Crown Court* (n 108).

The protection of journalistic material gives reporters a space outside the normal areas of state control and allows the media to develop as a counterweight to government power. Like any privilege, there is a danger that the protection of journalistic material can be abused and make the investigation of criminal activities in media institutions more difficult. For example, the police complained that restrictions on access to journalistic material made it harder to investigate criminal offences alleged to have been committed by journalists, such as phone hacking.[115] Addressing these complaints, the Leveson Report recommended that the government consider amending the law so that journalistic material is only deemed to be confidential if it is held 'subject to an enforceable or lawful undertaking, restriction or obligation'.[116] The recommendation aimed to bring the protection of journalistic material into line with the protection of legal professional privilege. The proposal received considerable criticism, for fear that it would weaken the protection of sources when important information is leaked in breach of the law or a legal obligation (such as confidentiality or official secrets laws).[117] While the proposal was not enacted, a later decision indicated that communications to journalists in furtherance of a crime will not be treated as confidential and therefore not be entitled to the strongest protection as 'excluded material' under PACE.[118] However, the court added that a 'genuine whistleblower acting in the public interest' may still be protected under the provision.[119] The challenge in this area lies in defining a privilege that is not vulnerable to abuse, without inhibiting some areas of legitimate journalistic activity. If the media is given generous protection from investigation, then perhaps this requires more from the system of media regulation to oversee the conduct of reporters and editors, which at least provides an alternate route to address abuses of media power and privileges.[120]

There are a number of statutes that allow for stop and search procedures outside of PACE which do not provide the same level of protection for journalists, some of which have been found to fall short of the standards required under Article 10. In *Miranda*, the spouse of the journalist responsible for the publication of the Edward Snowden leaks was detained for nine hours and searched using powers under Schedule 7 to the Terrorism Act 2000.[121] The Court of Appeal held that the statutory powers were incompatible with Article 10 of the ECHR for failing to provide adequate safeguards in relation to searches of journalistic material. The possibility of judicially reviewing

---

[115] Leveson Report (n 1) 1486.

[116] ibid, 1498.

[117] See 'Whistleblowers and press "threatened by proposed new police powers"' *The Guardian* (13 February 2013). Leveson LJ also suggested that the Home Office consider removing the requirement that alternative methods be pursued, though he was not convinced of the need for such a change. The police complained that the requirement allows newspaper companies to defeat an application for the production of material by going through the motions to give an appearance of cooperation, so that the access conditions would not be met. See Leveson Report (n 1) 1496.

[118] *R v Norman* (n 17) at [39].

[119] ibid at [39].

[120] Leveson Report (n 1) 1486, stating that if the press are to benefit from such protections from investigation 'there must be some other way in which the press itself and the journalists who work within it can be held to account in relation to their own conduct'.

[121] *Miranda* (n 14).

the exercise of the police power was not a sufficient level of independent oversight.[122] The episode shows the danger that multiple powers to investigate crimes can sometimes leave gaps in the safeguards. Such a danger has been highlighted by the use of surveillance powers, which will be considered in the following section.

IV. Surveillance of Newsgathering Processes

The protection of journalistic sources and materials are key elements of media freedom, which protect journalists from being compelled to hand over information. However, techniques of surveillance make it is possible for the authorities to discover the identity of a source without even approaching the journalist. This is not new. For example, if a journalist met with a source in an underground car park, there was a risk of being discovered by other people present at the scene. Such a risk is inherent in the newsgathering process.

The growth of surveillance technology increases the risk of sources being caught. Such surveillance can arise through technologies such as CCTV and the retention of communications records by phone companies and broadband providers. The potential use of surveillance methods to identify sources was highlighted in a high-profile case in which the police, while investigating a leak from within the force in 2012 and 2013, accessed records held by telecommunications companies to discover who had been in contact with the relevant journalists.[123] By accessing this information, the police could discover the likely source for a story without looking at the journalist's notes or asking the journalist to name the source. At the time, access to such data was regulated under Regulation of Investigatory Powers Act 2000, which allowed information to be accessed without going through PACE and without authorisation from a court.[124] The legal framework under the Regulation of Investigatory Powers Act 2000 was thereby found to offer inadequate safeguards, and failed to meet the requirement of independent prior assessment under Article 10.[125] Judicial review of the decision to access the material after the event was not sufficient.

The system of surveillance and interception of communications has since been overhauled by the Investigatory Powers Act 2016. The Act gives certain government agencies the power to intercept communications and hack into people's electronic devices (known as 'equipment interference'). While the intelligence services and certain law

---

[122] ibid, at [113].

[123] *News Group Newspapers Ltd v Metropolitan Police Commissioner* [2015] UKIPTrib 14_176-H.

[124] For other examples, see House of Commons Home Affairs Committee, *Regulation of Investigatory Powers Act 2000* (HC 2014–15, 711).

[125] *News Group Newspapers Ltd v Metropolitan Police Commissioner* (n 123); *Sanoma Uitgevers BV* (n 73); *Telegraaf Media* (n 85).

enforcement bodies can apply to engage in 'targeted' interception and interference, the intelligence services have further powers to engage in these methods on a 'bulk' basis.[126] The scheme gives law enforcement authorities considerable power to monitor the content of people's communications. For example, the Secretary of State can issue a warrant for targeted interception when necessary in the interests of national security, the economic well-being of the United Kingdom (where relevant to the interests of national security), or for the prevention or detection of serious crime.[127] The Act requires any public authority issuing a warrant to have regard to privacy and also to the protection of sensitive information, including journalistic material and journalists' sources.[128] Where the powers are used to access confidential journalistic material or to identify a source, further safeguards are imposed, in which the person seeking access must provide a statement that the purpose of the application is to access such material. A warrant will then only be granted if it is shown that safeguards have been arranged, for example relating to the handling, retention and destruction of the material.[129] A warrant must also be approved by a Judicial Commissioner, who applies the standards of judicial review to determine whether it is necessary for one of the named purposes, and proportionate.[130] While the standards of judicial review provide a limited form of oversight, it should allow the Judicial Commissioner to consider media freedom along with any other rights at stake. As with the powers discussed in earlier sections, the effectiveness will partly depend on how the judge weighs the competing interests.

While the powers of interception described above relate to the content of a communication, there are further provisions of the Act that allow for access to 'communications data'.[131] Communications data is a term to describe records that do not reveal the content of a communication, but show who spoke to whom, at what time, and on what forum. An obvious example is a record held by a telecommunications company showing which phone numbers a person called and the length of the conversation. The Act also provides the power to require telecommunications companies to retain records of internet use for up to 12 months, which enables certain authorities to access details of which websites a person has visited. While generally less intrusive than the interception of the content of a communication, the 2016 Act allows a wider range of public authorities to access communications data for a number of purposes.[132]

Under the Act, special safeguards to protect journalists' sources are in place before the communications data can be accessed.[133] Approval from a Judicial Commissioner is

---

[126] See Investigatory Powers Act 2016, s 18, s 142(2), ss 102–107 and s 183(2). The term 'targeted' may be misleading in so far as the warrant can relate to 'a group of persons who share a common purpose or who carry on, or may carry on, a particular activity', see s 17 and s 101.

[127] ibid, s 20.

[128] ibid, s 2.

[129] On interception, see Investigatory Powers Act 2016, s 28 and s 29; in relation to equipment interference see s 113 and s 114. A different regime applies for bulk interception and equipment interference, see s 154 and s 195.

[130] ibid, s 23.

[131] ibid, s 61.

[132] ibid.

[133] Initially, obtaining the communications data in a non-media case could be authorised by a senior officer of the public authority. However, the decision of the CJEU in *Secretary of State for the Home*

required for access to communications data 'for the purpose of identifying or confirming a source of journalistic information'.[134] On such an application, the Commissioner permits access if he or she considers there were 'reasonable grounds' for considering the requirements of the Act to be satisfied.[135] In this exercise, the Judicial Commissioner will consider the public interest in protecting sources and whether there is an 'overriding public interest' to disclose the identity.[136] The provision does not require prior notification to the person or media organisation to whom the order relates, so that person will not have the opportunity to contest the application. The justification advanced for that process is that notifying a subject could undermine the relevant authority's operations (for example by alerting a suspect to the fact that he or is she is under police investigation and surveillance). However, the lack of a contested hearing means the Judicial Commissioner will not hear the perspective of the media when deciding where the public interest lies. Furthermore, the provision only applies where the *purpose* is to identify or confirm the identity of a source, rather than whether such data is likely to reveal the identity of the source. Given these limits, there are concerns that the process will not be as rigorous as PACE.

The Act has generated controversy among civil liberties groups and was described by Edward Snowden as 'the most extreme surveillance in the history of western democracy'.[137] Various aspects of the statutory scheme are the subject of ongoing legal challenges, so further changes and amendments are likely. However, defenders of the Act argue that it simply puts what was already happening in surveillance on a stronger legal footing and at least introduces some level of transparency. The legal framework in the Act is complex, but the issue shows how the threats to newsgathering are changing in the digital era. The ability for communications to be observed and retained, and for government to sweep up vast amounts of data at various points in the flow of information allows newsgathering to be monitored and used for government purposes without having to raid a home or seize a notebook. In such circumstances, it is important to extend the level of protection for media freedom that has traditionally applied to offline content to digital communications. Without sufficient protection, there is a danger that the journalists will be deprived of a space to cultivate a relationship with sources and acquire evidence.

The potential for surveillance comes not only from government.[138] Companies that harvest data, such as phone companies, broadband providers and digital intermediaries, have the means to see who journalists are contacting. Such a company may have its own interests in discovering the identity of sources, for example where the company

---

Department v Watson (C-698/15) EU:C:2016:970, [2017] QB 771 found that for some categories of case prior authorisation must be granted by an independent body. At the time of writing, the government is consulting on amending the legislation.

[134] Investigatory Powers Act 2016, s 77.

[135] ibid. The requirements of the Act for this purpose are set out in s 61.

[136] ibid, s 77.

[137] The message was posted on Twitter under the account @Snowden on 17 November 2016, at https://twitter.com/snowden/status/799371508808302596?lang=en (last accessed 26 January 2018).

[138] See discussion in R Danbury and J Townend, *Protecting Sources and Whistleblowers in the Digital Age* (London, Institute of Advanced Legal Studies, 2017).

is itself subject to critical reporting. Moreover, there may be scope for misconduct by employees in leaking such communications data to interested parties. The digital communications between journalists and sources may also be exposed where the communications service providers or users' accounts are hacked. The media organisation therefore has a responsibility to ensure its system of communication is as secure as possible. There are also various laws that prohibit the misuse of such information by private actors, such as data protection law. However, it is important to remember that digital communications rely on a chain of actors and that the protection of confidential sources is as vulnerable as the weakest link in the chain.

In so far as the security of a source's identity can never be guaranteed in the digital era, then there is a case for the stronger protection of whistleblowers from adverse consequences in the event of discovery. Some limited steps have been taken in this direction by the Public Interest Disclosure Act 1988. The Act protects whistleblowers against detrimental treatment through a right in employment law in relation to disclosures on a limited range of issues—such as revealing the commission of a criminal offence, a miscarriage of justice or damage to the environment. The provision offers protection from detriment only in the employment setting and does not prevent a source being prosecuted (where an offence has been committed) or being subject to a civil law claim.[139] The provision will only protect disclosures to a journalist as a last resort, where a complaint to an employer or other official channel is not appropriate or has been unsuccessful.[140] While the provision is important in recognising the role of whistleblowers, the protection in relation to media disclosures is limited. Moreover, even if formal adverse consequences for a source in employment are prohibited, it is harder to prevent informal reactions that make life difficult for the whistleblower, such as people being shunned socially by colleagues. Despite the limits, the protection of whistleblowers from adverse consequences may need to be further developed, as the confidentiality of journalist-source communications becomes less secure.

V. Freedom of Information

A. Freedom of Information and Media Freedom

The protection of sources and journalistic material provides a special privilege for the media, but it is ultimately about restricting state intrusion into journalistic activity. The protection of newsgathering can be taken a stage further, so that the state is under

---

[139] Employment Rights Act 1996, s 47B. See A Savage, *Leaks, Whistleblowing and the Public Interest: The Law of Unauthorised Disclosures* (Cheltenham, Edward Elgar, 2016) 153.
[140] Employment Rights Act 1996, s 43G. See also s 43H, which could permit a disclosure to the media in the event of an exceptionally serious failure.

a positive obligation to aid newsgathering. One example of such a positive obligation, seen in Chapter 3, is the right to access the courts and court documents. More broadly, arguments are made for a general right to access information held by government.

There are some obvious reasons why freedom of information laws help to further the goals associated with media freedom. As the media is expected to act as a watchdog on government, it is essential that journalists are able to access official data and documents to find out how state power is being exercised. Providing access to information can also allow the media to find out the reasons for government action, by looking at draft reports, seeing what advice was provided by officials, which officials met with lobbyists and so on. Freedom of information rights are a valuable tool for those wishing to find out more about government activities.

Freedom of information also prevents government from having too much control over the flow of information. In relation to government secrecy, it was noted that government had the power to selectively release information that puts their activities in a positive light, but can refuse to disclose that which is embarrassing.[141] Government departments have significant press relations staff, which can raise concerns about 'spin' and the manipulation of information. A right to freedom of information counters such power by forcing government to relinquish some degree of control. Freedom of information thereby represents a transfer of power from the state to the public and opens up more areas of government activity to public scrutiny. As such, freedom of information fits with the current political culture, in which citizens expect to be able to monitor public bodies and where government is not simply trusted to get on with its job.[142]

Another function for freedom of information laws is to help people to assess the performance of public and private services, which can be illustrated by the existing use of the Freedom of Information Act 2000. Requests under the Act have been used to show ambulance response times or school exclusion rates in different areas. The data revealed under freedom of information requests can also help individuals make consumer choices. Data requested from the Vehicle and Operator Services Agency was used to show the failure rate for different types of cars and vehicles in MOT tests.[143] Councils regularly reveal the results of food hygiene inspections of restaurants, a practice supported by an earlier decision of the Information Commissioner upholding a request for such data.[144]

Freedom of information laws can be seen as providing an informational subsidy to the media and other organisations. The provision of data means that public servants dedicate time to collating and finding the requested information, when normally the journalist would have to perform this task. In that way, the state can be seen as sharing some, but by no means all, of its research capacity with the public.

---

[141] See Ch 4. See also S Palmer 'Freedom of Information or Freedom From Information' in J Beatson and Y Cripps (eds), *Freedom of Expression and Freedom of Information* (Oxford, Oxford University Press, 2000) 253–54.

[142] For discussion of the culture shift in the US, see M Schudson. *The Rise of the Right to Know* (Cambridge Mass, Harvard University Press, 2015) Chs 7 and 8.

[143] 'Ford leads in MOT failures as figures are revealed' BBC News (13 January 2010), http://news.bbc.co.uk/1/hi/business/8456116.stm (last accessed 26 January 2018). See Palmer (n 141) 255 on assisting consumers.

[144] Information Commissioner, Decision Notice, Bridgend County Borough Council (9 December 2005, ref: FS50073296).

Freedom of information is *useful* for the exercise of media freedom, but that alone does not establish that access to official data is *required* as an element of that right. In its earlier jurisprudence, the European Court of Human Rights held that Article 10 requires only a right to receive information that has been made freely available by others and does not create a right to access information.[145] However, in a series of more recent cases, the Strasbourg Court has chipped away at this position and indicated that Article 10 can require a right of access to information held by government in some situations.[146] In *Magyar Helsinki Bizottsag v Hungary*, the applicant was a non-governmental organisation (NGO) that sought access to the names of public defenders in order to conduct a study into the quality of legal representation.[147] The Grand Chamber found that while earlier cases did not grant a right of access, those decisions did not rule out the presence of such a right in other circumstances.[148] The Court ruled that a denial of access engages Article 10 where 'disclosure of the information has been imposed by a judicial order' or where 'access to the information is instrumental for the individual's exercise of his or her right to freedom of expression'.[149] The latter category offered by the Court is somewhat circular. Any claim of access may be instrumental to an expression right, in so far as it enables people to receive content they would not otherwise see and provide information that will influence future statements.

To avoid the right of access expanding to cover any case where it would be useful prior to the exercise of an expression right, the Court's remarks should be interpreted to mean that a right of access will arise only when the claim of access meets certain criteria to fit with the values of Article 10. Along these lines, the Court in *Magyar Helsinki Bizottsag* provided a number of factors to determine when a claim to access information engages Article 10. The Court will look at the purpose of the request. If the purpose is to conduct research for a news article or academic study, then Article 10 is more likely to be engaged.[150] Fitting with the Article 10 jurisprudence, the Court will also be more likely to grant access if the information relates to a matter of public interest.[151] The court will also look at the role of the applicant. In particular, Article 10 is more likely to be engaged where the applicant is a journalist, academic, NGO or blogger that performs some form of social watchdog role.[152] Finally, the right of access is more likely to be applied where the information is ready and available, and does not require government to engage in any further collection.[153]

The developments in the European Court of Human Rights contrast with the position taken by the UK Supreme Court in the earlier decision in *Kennedy*, in which the domestic court rejected an argument that Article 10 includes a right to access information.[154] One reason for the UK court's more cautious stance concerns the challenges in defining the scope and application of a right of access through judicial

---

[145] *Leander v Sweden*, App no 9248/81 (1987) 9 EHRR 433.
[146] *Társaság a Szabadságjogokért v Hungary*, App no 37374/05 (2011) 53 EHRR 3 at [36].
[147] *Magyar Helsinki Bizottsag v Hungary*, App No 18030/11 (8 November 2016).
[148] ibid.
[149] ibid, [156].
[150] ibid, [159].
[151] ibid, [161].
[152] ibid, [164]–[166].
[153] ibid, [169].
[154] *Kennedy v Charity Commission* [2014] UKSC 20, [2015] AC 455 at [94].

decisions. Lord Mance warned against Article 10 becoming 'a European-wide Freedom of Information law' as it would be a 'law lacking the specific provisions and qualifications which are in practice debated and fashioned by national legislatures according to national conditions'.[155] Freedom of information laws tend to be detailed statutes setting out which bodies will be subject to their obligations, which information people will have access to, in what circumstances a request can be rejected and whether there are certain categories of information that should be exempt.[156] Under this view, such questions are better dealt with through comprehensive legislation.

Lord Mance's preference for a detailed statutory system contrasts with the approach taken by the European Court of Human Rights, which follows the case-by-case balancing exercise. In a dissent in *Kennedy*, Lord Wilson argued that a case-by-case approach, which gradually clarifies the 'contours' of the right, is not problematic and is similar to the method already taken when granting access to the courts under the open justice principle.[157] However, a general right to access information raises different issues to open justice. Freedom of information requires a wide range of authorities to establish significant administrative systems to handle requests, so there is a good reason for the basic requirements to be set out in legislation, rather than fleshed out on a case-by-case basis.

Aside from the question of definition, there is also a broader concern about the dangers of expanding Article 10 into a set of obligations that secure the best conditions for media freedom, which could be a never-ending journey. While it is important to recognise that media freedom entails some positive obligations, that does not mean the content of such rights must always be a matter for the courts. Parliament also carries responsibility for promoting and protecting media freedom. Under this view, there are compelling reasons to enact freedom of information legislation, even if not judicially mandated by Article 10. That reflects the approach under the domestic law, in which rights of access are provided for under the Freedom of Information Act 2000, the main features of which will be discussed in the following section.

B. The Freedom of Information Act 2000

The UK was slow to embrace freedom of information compared with other western democracies. Traditionally, the UK government had a culture of secrecy, which imposed significant barriers to political accountability. Richard Crossman famously described secrecy as a 'British disease'.[158] Data and documents were released at the discretion of the government, which allowed the flow of information to be directed by selective disclosure. A significant provision for the release of information was created

---

[155] ibid, at [94].
[156] See Judge Spano's dissent in *Magyar Helsinki Bizottsag* (n 147), and E Barendt, *Freedom of Speech*, 2nd edn (Oxford, Oxford University Press, 2005) 108. For discussion of these issues more generally in relation to positive rights, see J Rowbottom, 'Positive Protection for Speech and Substantive Political Equality' in A Kenyon and A Scott (eds), *Positive Free Speech: Rationales, Methods and Implications* (Oxford, Hart, 2018).
[157] *Kennedy* (n 154) at [189].
[158] See J Michael, *The Politics of Secrecy* (Harmondsworth, Penguin, 1982) 12.

under the Public Records Act 1958. Under the Act, information is made available after a lapse of time (traditionally after 30 years, but this is being reduced to 20 years),[159] when certain selected government records are transferred to the national archives. These delayed releases are valuable to researchers and historians, but are of limited use to those investigating current affairs. Even with a delay of two or three decades, the transfer to the national archives is subject to significant exceptions. The government body can retain documents after the 20-year period when, in the opinion of the person responsible, it is 'required for administrative purposes or ought to be retained for any other special reason'.[160] The provision has been used to withhold documents for national security reasons.[161] Despite a procedure for authorising such retention, critics argue that the process lacks rigour and has enabled certain government departments to keep private archives of several million files.[162] The system is sometimes viewed with suspicion, with reports of some important documents going missing.[163] Moreover, access to material held at the National Archive can be declined if it falls within an exemption under the Freedom of Information Act 2000, although some of those exemptions lapse after a specified number of years.[164] The Public Records Act was an important development towards transparency, albeit a limited one.

As part of a series of constitutional reforms introduced by the Labour government elected in 1997, the Freedom of Information Act 2000 helped to change the assumption of secrecy and provides a right to access to information held by government.[165] The Act gives any person the right to request information held by a public authority. The public authorities subject to the obligation are listed in the schedules to the 2000 Act. These include bodies that are established by statute or prerogative or by a government department, and companies that are owned by the Crown or public sector.[166] Private bodies that exercise functions of a public nature or are contracted to perform a public authority's functions can be added to the list of bodies subject to the Act.[167]

As the BBC is a product of prerogative powers and Channel 4 is created by statute, both are to subject to the Freedom of Information Act. Both therefore have a dual role: first as public authorities, subject to demands for transparency, and second as media institutions that require some level of confidentiality (in relation to research, sources and so on). The tension between the two roles is addressed by an exemption for information held for the purposes of journalism, art and literature, which seeks to ensure that the creative and newsgathering processes are protected.[168] There are, however, difficulties in identifying when material is held for journalistic purposes and

---

[159] Public Records Act 1958, s 3.

[160] ibid, s 3(4).

[161] National Archives, *Access to public records* (2015) 23.

[162] I Cobain, *The History Thieves* (London, Portobello, 2016) 150–51.

[163] 'Government admits "losing" thousands of papers from National Archives' *The Guardian* (26 December 2017).

[164] Freedom of Information Act 2000, ss 63–64; *Access to public records* (n 161) 23.

[165] For discussion of the politics surrounding the enactment, see B Worthy, *The Politics of Freedom of Information: How and Why Governments Pass Laws that Threaten their Power* (Manchester, Manchester University Press, 2017).

[166] Freedom of Information Act 2000, s 6.

[167] See, ibid, s 5. For example, this power was exercised in 2015 to bring Network Rail under the Freedom of Information Act.

[168] Freedom of Information Act 2000, Sch 1, Part VI.

when it is held for ordinary operational reasons, as the two purposes can sometimes be connected.[169]

If a public authority does not comply with the obligations under the Act, then a complaint can be made to the Information Commissioner. The decisions of the Information Commissioner can in turn be appealed to the First-tier Tribunal, and further appealed to the Upper Tribunal. The Freedom of Information Act 2000 does not impose an absolute duty to disclose data. The public authority is not under a duty to provide information when the requests are vexatious or if the expense of complying with the claim would exceed a cost threshold.[170]

More broadly, the Act contains a number of exemptions, which are divided into two broad categories. The first types are absolute exemptions, which means that if the information is of the type specified in the exemption then the request for access can be refused. Unsurprisingly, information supplied by or relating to bodies that deal with national security matters (namely security and intelligence services) are subject to an absolute exemption under s 23.[171] Section 32 provides an absolute exemption for court records. While that precludes access to court documents under the Freedom of Information Act, that does not prevent access to such documents under the open justice principle.[172] The second types of exemption are qualified, in which a request can be refused only if the information is of the type named in the exemption and where 'the public interest in maintaining the exemption outweighs the public interest in disclosing the information' (known as the public interest test).[173]

Some of the exemptions apply to information within a particular category (referred to as 'class based').[174] For example, s 37 exempts communications with certain members of the royal family. To fall within a class-based exemption, there is no requirement to show that the disclosure will cause prejudice to the named interest, although the harm of the specific disclosure may still be relevant when applying the public interest test (if the exemption is qualified). Other exemptions are 'prejudice based', which requires the public authority to show that the disclosure would either prejudice or be likely to prejudice the particular interest before the qualified exemption can be relied upon. Most of the prejudice-based exemptions are also qualified and subject to the public interest test.

The breadth of the exemptions caused controversy when the statute was enacted and were seen by some to gut the Act.[175] However, the qualified exemptions are not a simple escape route. When applying the public interest test, there is an assumption in favour of disclosure.[176] Simply establishing that a class-based qualified exemption is

---

[169] See *Sugar* (n 106).

[170] Freedom of Information Act 2000, s 12 and s 14.

[171] The security services themselves are not subject to the Act, but the provision exempts information provided by those services that are held by another public body.

[172] See *Kennedy* (n 154) and discussion in Ch 3.

[173] Freedom of Information Act 2000, s 2.

[174] See Information Commissioner's Office, *The Guide to Freedom of Information* (2017) 41.

[175] R Austin, 'The Freedom of Information Act 2000: a sheep in wolf's clothing?' in J Jowell and D Oliver (eds), *The Changing Constitution*, 5th edn (Oxford, Oxford University Press, 2004).

[176] Information Commissioner, *Public Interest Test* (2016) at [7]; *Cabinet Office v Information Commissioner* (Information Tribunal, 27/1/2009) at [34].

engaged is not sufficient to make a prima facie case for non-disclosure.[177] Instead, the public authority has to show a significant and substantial interest in withholding the information.[178] Under the public interest test, the public authority also has to show that the interest in non-disclosure corresponds with the specific interest named in the exemption being relied upon. By contrast, the public interest in disclosure is broader, so that the general gains to public information can be considered when striking the balance.[179] This means the public interest test calls for the weighing of a narrowly-specified interest for withholding the information against a broad general interest in disclosure. While the Act contains many limits, it is framed in a way that seeks to tilt the assumption in favour of the requester.

i. Exemptions and Government Secrecy

Some of the exemptions may cause particular concern for media freedom. Section 36 is a controversial provision, which exempts information that, in the reasonable opinion of a qualified person, would, or would be likely if disclosed, prejudice the effective conduct of public affairs; prejudice collective responsibility; or inhibit the free and frank provision of advice or exchange of views. Similarly, the class-based exemption under s 35 applies to information relating to the formation of government policy, ministerial communications, advice from government legal officers, and the operation of any ministerial private office. The exemption could prevent access to information that is central for understanding and assessing government policy.

The exemptions do not give public bodies a free hand to escape accountability, which can be illustrated by the experience with s 35. The Tribunal responsible for hearing appeals under the Act has provided some guidance to ensure that s 35 is not abused to shield government from criticism.[180] Greater weight is given to concerns about full and frank discussion and the adverse effects of publicity while a decision is still ongoing.[181] Once a decision has been made, the case for disclosure becomes stronger.[182] The Tribunal has also stated that s 35 primarily aims to protect civil servants from 'unjust public opprobrium', so less weight will be placed on the exemption where the information relates to the conduct or statements of a minister.[183] Furthermore, the Tribunal stated that the fear that a disclosure will lead to ill-informed criticism is not a good reason for withholding information. If the authorities are concerned about misinterpretation of

---

[177] Though some class-based exemptions are said to have an inherent weight that can be assumed once engaged, for example see legal professional privilege in *Department of Business, Enterprise and Regulatory Reform v IC & O'Brien* [2009] EWHC 164 (QB).

[178] *Office of Government Commerce v Information Commissioner* [2008] EWHC 774 (Admin), [2010] QB 98.

[179] *Hogan v Oxford City Council* (17 October 2006) EA/2005/0026, EA/2005/0030 at [60]; *Department of Health v Information Commissioner*, EA/2013/0087 (26 March 2013) at [48].

[180] *Department of Education and Skills (DfES) v Information Commissioner and the Evening Standard* (Information Tribunal, 19 February 2007) at [75].

[181] *Department for Work & Pensions v Information Commissioner* (Information Tribunal, 5 March 2007).

[182] Freedom of Information Act 2000, s 35(2) specifically removes the exemption for statistical information once the decision has been taken.

[183] *Department of Education and Skills* (n 180).

the information disclosed, the primary solution is to 'inform and educate' the public so that they do not make such unfair criticisms.[184] Applying these principles, the Tribunal has ordered the release of information at high levels of government, including Cabinet papers that have traditionally been at the heart of the culture of secrecy. The Tribunal's interpretation of s 35 has come in for criticism, with the government-established Independent Commission on Freedom of Information arguing that a chilling effect on frank discussion can be caused by publicity arising once a decision has been made and calling for s 35 to be amended to ensure that the exemption has broader application.[185] So far, that call has not been taken up and no legislative change has been made to s 35.

ii. The Ministerial Veto

In addition to the various exemptions to protect public bodies and other interests, the Freedom of Information Act 2000 also includes a ministerial veto. This provides that a minister can block the disclosure of information held by a government department covered by a qualified exemption, if there has been a ruling that the public interest lies in favour of disclosure by the Information Commissioner or the Tribunal. The veto has been used on several occasions.[186] However, the potential usage was narrowed in the decision of the Supreme Court in *Evans.*[187] The case concerned a request to several government departments to release letters received from the Prince of Wales that discussed various areas of government policy. The departments declined to disclose the correspondence on the grounds that it was exempt.[188] The Upper Tribunal, however, ordered the disclosure of much of the correspondence and rejected the reliance on the exemptions.[189] Following that ruling, the government exercised the veto to prevent the information being released. The Supreme Court found that the use of the veto was unlawful and could not be used simply where the minister disagrees with the Tribunal decision.[190] Lord Neuberger stated that a minister could only use the power to override an Upper Tribunal decision where there had been a material change of circumstances (for example where there is new evidence) or where the decision to release the information was demonstrably flawed.[191] Lord Mance also thought the minister had

---

[184] ibid.

[185] Independent Commission on Freedom of Information, *Report* (Cabinet Office, 2016) 27–28. The Commission also called for s 35 to be amended to provide greater protection for internal communications relating to government policy, 25.

[186] Veto certificates, under s 53 of the Freedom of Information Act 2000, have been issued on: 24 February 2009 (minutes of Cabinet meetings where the Attorney-General's legal advice on military action against Iraq was discussed); 10 December 2009 (minutes of the Cabinet Sub-Committee on Devolution to Scotland, Wales and the Regions); 8 February 2012 (minutes of the Cabinet Sub-Committee on Devolution to Scotland, Wales and the Regions); 8 May 2012 (in relation to the NHS transitional risk register); 31 July 2012 (minutes of Cabinet meetings at which the Attorney-General's advice on military action against Iraq was discussed); 16 October 2012 (correspondence from Prince Charles); 30 January 2014 (a review of HS2).

[187] *R (on the application of Evans) v A-G* [2015] UKSC 21, [2015] AC 1787.

[188] Relying on the Freedom of Information Act 2000, ss 37, 40 and 41.

[189] *Evans v Information Commissioner (Correspondence with Prince Charles in 2004 and 2005)* [2012] UKUT 313 (AAC).

[190] *Evans* (n 187).

[191] ibid, at [71] and [76]–[77].

acted unlawfully and reasoned that the minister had a high burden of justification to meet before he could rely on the veto.[192]

The decision in *Evans* is controversial and critics argue that it amounted to a re-writing of the legislation.[193] While the design of a freedom of information law is best left to the legislature, the Supreme Court's decision can be defended as the court has an important role to play in interpreting that law. There is a strong case for judicial intervention to limit the discretion to use the veto, given that ministers have a vested interest in using that power to shield government from criticism and scrutiny. The ruling in *Evans* is important for newsgathering in strengthening rights of access to information and weakening the potential for the veto to narrow the flow of information. However, the ruling does not eliminate the veto. In a review of the Act, the Independent Commission on Freedom of Information concluded that the Attorney-General would be on stronger ground issuing the veto after a decision of the Information Commissioner (as opposed to a Tribunal decision) because that would overturn a decision of a regulatory body, rather than a judicial panel.[194] More broadly, the Commission called on the Act to be amended to make clear that the veto can be used when the executive takes a different view of where the public interest lies.[195] So far that recommendation has not been followed. To legislate for such a broad veto would give the government powers to control information that could undermine the value of the Act as a tool for political accountability.

iii. Practical Limits and Costs of Freedom of Information

The Freedom of Information Act will not be the primary tool for most journalists. Reporters working in Westminster will want answers fast and will have their own sources to investigate stories. A right to request information and receive a response within 14 days is unlikely to do much for the ordinary rough and tumble of day-to-day political reporting.[196] However, the Act is helpful for stories that are not time sensitive and for some longer-term reports. The Act does not replace the traditional methods of newsgathering, but supplements these methods with a new channel of information.

Despite these benefits for the media, there are legitimate concerns about freedom of information. Critics of the Act argue that it has unintended consequences, such as discouraging systems of record keeping.[197] However, a study on the first 10 years of the Act found that such a fear that had not been realised.[198] The Act nonetheless

---

[192] ibid, Lord Mance at [130].

[193] R Ekins and C Forsyth, *Judging the Public Interest: The Rule of Law vs. the Rule of Courts* (London, Policy Exchange, 2015).

[194] Independent Commission on Freedom of Information (n 185) 39. See also Lord Neuberger in *Evans* (n 187) at [83].

[195] Independent Commission on Freedom of Information (n 185) 38. In its response to that proposal, the government declined to make a change to the legislation at this stage, see Matt Hancock MP, HC Deb, 1 March 2016, vol 606, col 27WS.

[196] See B Worthy and R Hazell, 'Disruptive, Dynamic and Democratic? Ten Years of FOI in the UK' (2017) 70 *Parliamentary Affairs* 22.

[197] J Powell, *The New Machiavelli* (London, Bodley Head, 2010) 197–98.

[198] Worthy and Hazell (n 196).

imposes a considerable financial and administrative burden on public authorities. Some have questioned whether the costs of the Act are justified by the benefits. One criticism is that the Act does not lead to a more informed public, but has generated stories aiming at fairly easy targets, such as the expenditure of public bodies. A review of the early days of the legislation in 2006 reported a number of requests that were not 'in the spirit of the Act', such as requesting the amount spent on *Ferrero Rocher* chocolates in embassies or the statistics for people reported to have had sex with sheep in Wales.[199] In 2014, a list of 'bizarre' uses of the Act included a request to Wigan council to disclose emergency measures in the event of a dragon attack.[200] However, the legislation already has a guard against such misuse, as those requests that lack any serious purpose or are disproportionately burdensome can be refused as vexatious.[201]

Of greater concern are those stories that relate to issues of legitimate public concern and generate outrage, but provide little context for the issue. The danger is that the Act is used to single out outcomes that attract attention without looking at the reasons for the decisions or seeking to understand the system that produced the outcomes in question. Moreover, transparency often feeds a culture of political cynicism. The disclosure of information will prompt more questions and some will be quick to see foul play and abuse of power, even where the evidence is limited. Given these ways that information can be presented and interpreted, the potential of freedom of information to create an informed public is often overstated.[202] However, transparency remains preferable to secrecy and public ignorance, and the Act is used for research on matters of general interest and not just the lazier types of story. While there are a number of costs generated by the Act, it at least keeps the door open to serious journalism and in-depth research.

The right to access information may be constrained by practical considerations. If the public authority asserts an exemption, many requesters will give up rather than take matters to the Information Commissioner. While the terms of the Act attempt to create a tilt in favour of the applicant, in many areas the public body is a repeat player that has the experience, knowledge and resources to know how to fend off requests. While the individual requester may thereby find himself or herself at a disadvantage, the professional journalist will also be a repeat player and better placed to challenge any refusal to disclose by a public authority.

The costs and burdens of the Freedom of Information Act, not to mention the potential to embarrass public bodies, make it vulnerable to attack from government. Given that freedom of information is now generally accepted as a key part of a modern democracy, simple abolition of the statute is unlikely. Instead it is more likely to suffer collateral attacks through seemingly technical measures. These can arise through a number of methods such as tweaking the exemptions in the statute, imposing costs on the person making the request, or cutting the budget of the Information

---

[199] Frontier Economics, *Independent Review of the impact of the Freedom of Information Act: A Report prepared for the Department for Constitutional Affairs* (October 2006) 31.
[200] 'Dragon attacks, pet exorcisms and meteor showers: The 10 most bizarre FoI requests sent to local councils' *Independent* (16 August 2014).
[201] *IC v Dransfield* [2012] UKUT 440 (AAC) at [28]–[39].
[202] See Worthy and Hazell (n 196).

Commissioner to enforce the Act.[203] Another line of attack that was once proposed was to change the way the cost threshold of a request is calculated, so that more requests could be turned down.[204] It is important that the machinery for such account-ability, to the media or public, should not be diluted or subject to political tinkering. Seemingly minor amendments to freedom of information need to be carefully scruti-nised. The effectiveness of the Act can lie in these details, which provide a less obvious channel to limit rights to information.

VI. A Public Interest Defence

So far, the discussion has looked at the ways the law can protect certain aspects of journalistic research, and also at positive obligations that can aid the newsgathering process. More generally, there are a range of different laws and regulations that govern newsgathering, including those discussed in earlier chapters. There are various other laws that seem far removed from the usual media activities, which can also limit the gathering of information. For example, the offence of bribery can prevent journal-ists from making payments to officials to secure information.[205] Phone and computer hacking are both criminal offences.[206]

While the need for such limits on media intrusion is obvious, there is a risk that such laws could criminalise activities undertaken in the course of serious investigative journalism. A common example used in discussion is of a journalist offering a bribe to an official simply to see whether that person is corrupt or not.[207] Such an offer is a criminal offence, but the argument runs that such methods are sometimes the only way of securing evidence of corruption. A similar point can be made about phone hacking, as there might be extreme cases where such a method is the only way to check an allegation of serious wrongdoing.[208] A sting operation might use some illegal meth-ods, in so far as it requires deception to gain access to various institutions and people.

---

[203] While the Independent Commission on Freedom of Information (n 185), proposed some changes to certain exemptions and removing the right to a re-hearing before a tribunal, it rejected calls for a fee to be imposed and emphasised the need for the Information Commissioner to be adequately funded.

[204] See *Draft Freedom of Information and Data Protection (Appropriate Limit and Fees) Regulations 2007*, Department of Constitutional Affairs Consultation Paper (14 December 2007), though the changes were not implemented.

[205] G Millar and A Scott, *Newsgathering: Law, Regulation, and the Public Interest* (Oxford, Oxford University Press, 2016) 141–45, and Ch 7 for a number of controls on payments to witnesses.

[206] See, for example, the Computer Misuse Act 1990, s 2 and the Investigatory Powers Act 2016, s 3. The Data Protection Act 2018 provides for an offence of unlawfully obtaining personal data, which includes a public interest defence.

[207] *The Sun* uncovered corruption within Redbridge Magistrates' Court, revealing that a court official had accepted payments for speeding fines and for penalties not to be recorded. In order to establish the cor-ruption, it arranged for the official to be paid, 'Court in the Act' *The Sun* (4 August 2011).

[208] See J Robinson, 'Subterfuge can be in public interest' *The Guardian* (7 December 2011), reporting David Leigh's evidence to the Leveson Inquiry.

In many areas of criminal law, there is no public interest defence for the media to rely on. That much is unsurprising, as many of the laws will have been enacted to deal with specific problems and the application to journalistic activity may not been considered by the legislature. A recurring debate in media law is whether a general public interest defence for journalists should be enacted to fill this gap.

The complexity of the law is also advanced as an argument for a public interest defence. With so many laws regulating journalistic activity, editors may struggle to make a clear decision whether a particular method is unlawful or not.[209] The potential to fall foul of any of a wide range of laws may discourage the journalist from under-taking the more difficult and controversial lines of investigation. Ignorance of the law is no defence, but it is desirable to avoid a complex system that makes compliance too onerous. Under this argument, a general public interest defence would offer a simple framework enabling the journalist to make an informed decision before using a par-ticular newsgathering technique.

There are, however, a number of problems with a general public interest defence. First, it would provide special protection to act contrary to the legal standards that bind everyone else. An immunity for a particular actor would therefore run counter to the rule of law. There are dangers that the press could abuse such a defence as cover to engage in very intrusive methods that snoop on people's private lives. Aside from deliberate abuse, Leveson LJ argued that even where the unlawful act was part of a genuine public interest investigation, the journalist may incidentally discover facts relating to a person's private life that are of no public interest.[210] For example, read-ing a person's private emails may reveal information that is of public interest and that which is purely private. That concern could be partly addressed by restricting the publication of such data and requiring the media to dispose of any incidental informa-tion acquired in the process. Even with such a control, the potential for the media to stumble on personal details may still be a significant intrusion into a person's privacy and such costs should not be dismissed.

There are also questions about the scope of a public interest defence. There are some actions that seem impossible to justify by reference to the interest in media free-dom, such as an assault or burglary, even if it produced a valuable story. Accordingly, a defence could be narrowed to exclude such extreme cases. There is also a ques-tion of whether the same defence would apply to crimes of publication and those of newsgathering. The public interest of a publication can be assessed by looking at the content of the story and its value to the audience. As noted when discussing journal-ists' sources, the public interest can be harder to assess at the newsgathering stage, as there is no finished product to judge. Instead, a number of factors are likely to be relied on as a proxy for determining the public interest at this earlier stage, such as the con-duct and belief of the journalist. Consequently, the formulation of a defence would need to differentiate the issues relevant to the public interest in the publication, and the public interest in newsgathering.

If the public interest in newsgathering is assessed by looking at the conduct and reasonable belief of the journalist, then there are difficult questions in setting the

---

[209] See House of Lords Select Committee on Communications, *The Future of Investigative Journalism* (HL 2011–12, 256) at [82]–[85].
[210] Leveson (n 1) 1490–91.

standards to be met to establish the defence. When considering such a defence, Leveson LJ noted that it would be difficult to test claims that the journalist reasonably believed he or she was acting in the public interest at the newsgathering stage, as he or she would be able to claim that an anonymous source had provided a tip-off.[211] Leveson's concern is not insurmountable and similar issues can arise in assessing the reasonable belief standard in relation to defamation law. Accordingly, the court could look at a range of factors in addition to the good faith of the journalist, such as whether certain professional standards were fulfilled.

A further problem with a general public interest defence is that it may be difficult to draft in a way that is appropriate for all the relevant criminal offences. When looking at liability in relation to publication, the earlier chapters have shown that the public interest will be assessed in different ways according to the legal issue, type of activity and interests at stake. The public interest defences in defamation and privacy law operate very differently on account of the different nature of the rights. Similar differences in approach are found in relation to various areas of criminal law. Under s 5 of the Contempt of Court Act 1981, the protection applies where the prejudice to proceedings is incidental to a good faith discussion of matters in the public interest. By contrast, s 4 of the Obscene Publications Act 1959 provides a defence where publication is justified in the public good, in order to protect works of art and learning. The formulation differs as the appropriate balance struck varies according to the offence in question.

A similar point is likely to arise when looking at newsgathering. In some examples, the newsgathering activity infringes a legal right or causes some harm, but the journalist claims that harm is justified in the public interest. When a person's email is hacked to reveal important information, a breach of privacy rights takes place, but the argument runs that the intrusion should be tolerated. In other examples, the claim is that the public interest negates the very harm that the offence aims to guard against. Along these lines, a bribe paid to demonstrate that a public official is susceptible to corruption (and where that does not amount to entrapment) may be justified as serving the underlying aim of the law by detecting the commission of bribery offences. The two examples highlight another contrast in the reasons for breaking the law. In some cases, the law is broken to acquire a specific piece of information that is already held (as with the email hack). In others cases, the law may be broken by the journalist to stage an event that forms the basis of the story, for example where fraudulent means are used to gain access to stage a sting operation. The newsgathering activity is not the only variable, and where the legal interest at stake is particularly important, then the public interest may require a higher threshold.

None of these points defeat the case for a public interest defence, but they show that a general standard which applies across multiple criminal offences will have to accommodate a variety of circumstances. As a result, the presence of the defence itself would be unlikely to provide much certainty to journalists and will amount to a more general balancing exercise. In practice, a court would be likely to develop various sub-rules to guide the balancing process in the different situations. Given these issues, it may be

---

[211] ibid.

preferable to have a specific public interest defence for a particular criminal offence or group of offences (such as those relating to the payment of public officers)[212] that sets out the necessary requirements and factors, rather than to attempt to provide a generic defence to apply across the board.

Finally, there is also a question whether such a defence is necessary or not. The activities of the press are already given some protection from police investigation under PACE and other related provisions. The investigation of a journalist faces more hurdles and may make it harder for the police to collect evidence. Journalists are also protected through police discretion and prosecution policy, which makes proceedings in relation to a genuine public interest story less likely. While the *Telegraph* gained access to data on MPs' expenses via a leak, the Metropolitan Police stated that it would not investigate the legality of the disclosure, given that it found a prosecution was unlikely in light of the public interest in knowing about the abuse of the expenses system.[213] Even where a prosecution is pursued, there are still other safeguards, such as the potential for a jury to acquit and for the court to find an abuse of process.[214]

The informal safeguards of prosecution policy or appealing to the jury do not provide protection for every case. Where the action of a journalist is popular, though technically illegal, the informal safeguards will be strongest. That explains why cases such as the MPs' expenses leaks were not pursued. Prosecutors have relatively few incentives for heavy-handed use of prosecution powers and will normally be reluctant to antagonise the media and prompt a public backlash. The difficulty arises where the journalist works on an unpopular cause. If a journalist reveals details of unethical behaviour in a military operation, the journalist may be condemned by some parts of the public for undermining national interests. In such a case, the jury may be less inclined to acquit and the prosecutors may find there is public support for a prosecution. There is, therefore, a case for a type of public interest defence, though it is more easily drafted as a series of separate defences for specific offences or groups of offences (where possible), for the reasons given above. The difficulty lies in framing a defence in a way that does not put the journalist above the law and is not open to abuse, and which offers an appropriate formulation to accommodate various types of criminal offence.

VII. Conclusion

The protection of newsgathering is primarily concerned with the processes that take place prior to publication. At those stages, the focus is not on the finished media

---

[212] Such a grouping of offences could include bribery, inducing misconduct in public office and inducing a breach of official secrecy laws.
[213] 'Met chief: we won't pursue Telegraph' *The Daily Telegraph* (20 May 2009).
[214] Leveson Report (n 1) 1494.

product that is finally disseminated to the public, but on the methods of acquiring the raw materials that may be used to produce content. The area poses some significant challenges, as it is not simply a matter of asking whether the material in question is in the public interest (as in privacy law). Sometimes a journalist will have to investigate matters and receive information which turn out not to contribute to a debate of general interest. The journalist will need to look into those issues before deciding not to publish the content. That process of investigation still requires protection, even when it does not lead to a fruitful outcome. Along these lines a journalist should not be forced to disclose a source solely because the content of the information lacks a public interest. This does not mean the protection is unqualified, but the standard for the public interest is looser at this earlier newsgathering stage. That explains why the courts often look for other factors, such as the purpose of the source or the record of the journalist, to indicate the presence or absence of this looser type of public interest argument.

The difficulty in ascertaining the public interest can also arise in the context of the Freedom of Information Act 2000. The issue is slightly different, in so far as information provided under the Act can be made public, so the public interest of the audience in receiving the information has to be considered. At the same time, the information provided under the Act is raw data, rather than a final article intended for public consumption. So again, the public interest at stake is slightly different from that seen in defamation and privacy law. The question with regard to government data and information is whether it can be useful for the recipient as a form of research material. Concerns are sometimes expressed that the data will be misunderstood, misinterpreted or misused. The court has rightly dismissed such concerns, and in so doing shows how a stronger role is now assigned to the public to interpret events for themselves. Of course, there are strong arguments that the media and the public have a responsibility not to misuse the data, but that does not detract from the public interest in allowing access.

The discussion has also shown that the protection of newsgathering seeks to provide the media with a space of restricted state oversight, and freedom from certain legal obligations. That can be seen in the protection of sources in relation to court orders, the protection of journalistic material from police raids and the protection from surveillance. A general public interest defence for criminal offences and other areas of liability would go even further in developing a protected sphere for the media. As was argued, designing a general defence may face a number of challenges, in so far as the meaning of the public interest can change significantly depending on the context and the offence in question.

A key question is who should be able to benefit from the protection of newsgathering? If the protection is seen as carving a space for the media in line with the separation of powers view of media independence, then the protection should be understood in institutional terms. Under this view, the media is a specialised set of institutions with the knowledge and skills to conduct investigations and hold power to account. However, the current law has sought to cast the protection in functional terms. Sources are protected in relation to 'publications' and the Police and Criminal Evidence Act protects 'journalistic material'. How this functional definition should apply is not obvious. It cannot mean that any material held for the purpose of a publication of any type (ranging from blog posts, tweets or social media messages) should benefit from special privileges.

Despite being cast in functional terms, the protection will tend to protect media institutions in practice. In relation to sources, when balancing the interest in disclosure with the interest in media freedom, the court has looked at the record of the journalist in meeting standards of responsible journalism. In relation to the protection of journalistic material, the issue has yet to be fully tested, and the provision tends to be relied on by those in established media institutions. In so far as such protection offers a genuine exception from the normal legal processes, then a relatively limited range of actors should normally be expected to benefit. Without such a limit, the protection would cease to be a privilege and would come under competing pressure to give way to other factors. However, there is increasing pressure on this approach from the decisions of the ECHR stating that the protection of newsgathering should extend beyond the traditional media to include NGOs and other organisations. There is considerable force in the argument that protection should not be offered exclusively to traditional media formats. However, for the reasons given earlier, such protection should be extended with some caution and only to those who perform functions and follow processes analogous to media activities.

The issue is a little different with freedom of information. While legislation granting access to government data is an important element of newsgathering, freedom of information was primarily enacted to enhance transparency in government. As such, it changed the relationship between citizen and state, and seeks to empower individual citizens with access to data. The Act is obviously beneficial to the media, but can be relied on by anyone.

The chapter has looked at the need for secrecy and confidence in relation to newsgathering, and for transparency in relation to government. The media demands a degree of privacy for itself on the basis that its processes will otherwise be chilled, but tends to dismiss claims that government decisions need shielding from publicity for fear of chilling frank discussion. Despite the seeming contradiction in demanding secrecy and transparency, the two views can be reconciled by looking at the function of each institution and division of labour within the political system. The government is supposed to be scrutinised, while the media is supposed to conduct the scrutiny. It is hoped that both media confidentiality and government transparency will ultimately result in a better-informed public and increased government accountability.

The discussion has also shown how the threats to newsgathering have evolved, and the method of protection consequently needs to develop. Traditionally, the protection of newsgathering has come from shielding the physical space of the journalist. Under this approach, the courts limited police access to notebooks or to the offices of a media organisation. In *Entick v Carrington*, Lord Camden was protective of a writer's home and famously stated that an Englishman's papers were among his 'dearest property'.[215] In the digital era, this remains important, but the need for protection goes beyond the protection of physical property. The use of digital surveillance and the capacity of digital communications to be monitored renders the newsgathering process vulnerable even if there is no intrusion on physical space. The authorities may not need to seize notebooks if they can simply obtain the journalist's communication data and see who

[215] *Entick v Carrington* (1765)19 Howell's State Trials 1029.

has been spoken to. For this reason, the protections afforded to newsgathering need to keep pace with technology and methods of surveillance. This shows that underlying this area is not a concern simply with journalists' ethics in keeping promises, but in securing a space that preserves the process of acquiring and analysing data, which will in the long term produce the types of content that lie at the heart of media freedom.

Much of this book has been concerned with the abuse of media power and finding ways to make that power accountable. This chapter has, however, looked at the privileges afforded to the media and looked at measures that could entrench media power. The two points are not contradictory and can fit together. In so far as the media does benefit from special privileges that shield it from some of the ordinary mechanisms of legal accountability, then it strengthens calls for the media to be subject to some other systems of accountability to prevent the abuse of power. The need for certain channels of media regulation may represent a trade off in which the media enjoys certain privileges, but is subject to some specific obligations. Those special regulatory rules that apply to the media will be the focus of the following chapter.

6

Media Regulation

I. Introduction

The role of regulation is another recurring topic of debate in media law. The question of whether the newspaper industry should be regulated and, if so, by what method has been addressed by Royal Commissions and parliamentary inquiries on a number of occasions.[1] The Leveson Report is a notable example from recent years, and its proposals to reform newspaper regulation were a source of controversy.[2] By contrast, the broadcast media is subject to a system of statutory regulation that is generally accepted, although there are frequent debates about moves to further de-regulate the sector. At its heart, these debates revolve around the question of whether special rules and controls should be applicable to the media, and what impact such systems have on media freedom. Media regulation touches on many of the themes discussed in earlier chapters. Chapter 4 looked at the regulation of cinema and video under the British Board of Film Classification (BBFC). The laws of privacy and defamation are complemented by provisions in the regulatory codes of practice governing the broadcast and print media. Regulation permeates every area of media law, but this chapter will look at the issues concerning the design of regulation, rather than the specific rules governing particular media activities. The chapter will consider whether the media needs to be regulated and, if so, who should regulate it, what regulation should do and what methods of regulation should be employed.

Before beginning this discussion, it is first important to explain what is meant by media regulation. Many things 'regulate' the conduct of the media in the sense of

---

[1] Royal Commission on the Press 1947–1949, *Report* (Cmd 7700, 1949); Royal Commission on the Press 1961–1962, *Report* (Cmnd 1811, 1962); Royal Commission on the Press, *Final Report* (Cmnd 6810, 1977); D Calcutt, *Report of the Committee on Privacy and Related Matters* (Cm 1102, 1990); House of Commons Culture, Media and Sport Committee, *Privacy and media intrusion* (HC 2002–03, 458); House of Commons Culture, Media and Sport Committee, *Self-regulation of the press* (HC 2006–07, 375); House of Commons Culture, Media and Sport Committee, *Press standards, privacy and libel* (HC 2009–2010, 362).

[2] Leveson LJ, *An Inquiry into the Culture, Practice and Ethics of the Press: Report* (HC 780, 2012) (Leveson Report).

applying some form of pressure to shape and steer behaviour. The general laws that apply to everyone can be said to regulate the media, as can the demands of audiences and a range of other cultural pressures. This chapter will look at media regulation in two senses. The first is the narrow sense, meaning a system of media-specific rules that are established and enforced by a specialist body to govern media content and the conduct of staff. The second sense of the term regulation that will be considered is broader, referring to the way that the design and ownership of media institutions, along with the structure of the market, influence the way the media behaves. The ownership model of the media and whether it seeks to make a profit, for example, will regulate the conduct of the journalists working within the institution. Those pressures are themselves an object of media regulation, through special rules on media ownership and plurality.

In this chapter, no single type of regulation will be advocated as a magic bullet to eradicate the various ills laid at the door of the media. No regulatory method is perfect and each brings its own flaws and dangers. The discussion here will identify the key issues and debates, but the preference will be for a pluralistic approach, in which different tools of regulation can be employed in various settings and sectors. A system of regulation that achieves a balance among the various tools will not be perfect either, but allows for the flaws and weaknesses of one approach to be offset by the strengths of the other.

II. Regulating Content and Conduct

This section will look at the role of regulation governing the conduct of the media and the content it produces. It will look at the rationale for such regulation, the function of a regulator, the legitimacy of the system and the design of the regulatory institutions. After that, the discussion will highlight some of the key differences between the broadcast media and the press. Before looking at these matters, it is useful to outline some key features of the current UK regulatory system.

A. A Brief Sketch of UK Media Regulation

In the UK, the system of media regulation is a patchwork of different bodies covering different types of activity and format. A longstanding feature in the UK is the sharp contrast drawn between the broadcast and print media. The broadcast media has been subject to various forms of state regulation since its early days. Under the current system, broadcasters are subject to content regulations including provisions on fairness, offence and political impartiality. Some broadcasters are also subject to more far-reaching 'public service' obligations. A statutory regulator, called Ofcom, which also has responsibility for regulating telecommunications and postal services, oversees the broadcast regulations.[3]

By contrast, the newspaper industry has traditionally been subject to self-regulation, which has long been seen as a key element of its independence from government. The regulation of the press tends to be narrower in focus than the broadcast regulations. For example, the content controls in the press regulations protect certain personal rights and interests, such as privacy, but do not include the broader public service obligations that are applied to certain broadcasters. The press has been subject to a series of self-regulatory bodies. First, the General Council of the Press was established in 1953 and was reformed and renamed the Press Council in 1974, which in turn was replaced with the Press Complaints Commission (PCC) in 1991. Each replacement body sought to address the failures of the predecessor. The PCC was long criticised for failing to curb the rise of intrusive journalism, which was highlighted by the Leveson Report in the aftermath of the phone-hacking scandal. Leveson proposed a system of 'independent self-regulation' in which a state body would certify self-regulatory arrangements that meet certain standards.[4] The Leveson proposals were not fully implemented, but something similar was partially introduced through a Royal Charter. Since then, the system of press regulation has remained in a state of flux. Several newspapers remain members of a self-regulatory body called the Independent Press Standards Organisation (IPSO), which operates outside the Royal Charter system. A separate self-regulatory body operates within the Royal Charter framework, called the Independent Monitor for the Press (IMPRESS), although that has yet to have any major national newspapers subscribing to it. Several national newspapers are not subscribed to any regulatory body. At the time of writing, the press and campaigners for stronger regulation are in a political standoff, and it remains to be seen which side will prevail.

There are other elements of media regulation. Advertising is regulated through a system of 'co-regulation'. Cinema is regulated by a self-regulatory body, which also performs some statutory functions. There is also a role for the Information Commissioner in regulating certain aspects of media activities and digital communications that fall within data protection law.[5] A small number of media related organisations that have registered as charities are also under the jurisdiction of the Charities Commission. The internet is not subject to a general regulator, but some activities online are regulated. Advertisements on the internet, smart phones and tablets are subject to the Advertising Standards Authority. Video on-demand services are subject to a minimum level of regulation by Ofcom. The role of the Internet Watch Foundation and other channels of internet regulation are discussed further in Chapter 7. While debates about media regulation are largely dominated by the contrast between broadcast and print, the picture is more complex and involves a number of bodies. The discussion that follows does not attempt to give a comprehensive account of all media regulation, but will refer to various examples when considering the debates and key themes.

---

[3] Established under the Communications Act 2003. In 2017, Ofcom was granted new powers to regulate the BBC, in addition to its existing powers relating to the other channels. See the Royal Charter for the continuance of the British Broadcasting Corporation (December 2016, Cm 9365) cl 44 and the Communications Act 2003, s 198.

[4] Leveson Report (n 2).

[5] See Ch 2 on privacy.

B. Why Regulate the Media

The first issue is to identify the reasons for regulating the media. A starting point is the idea of 'market failure', which is a common rationale for regulating many industries. The argument is that certain outcomes are unlikely to be produced if the market is left to its own devices, and regulation is necessary to constrain the market and steer companies towards a desirable outcome. However, such a rationale begs the question of what the market is failing to do and what outcomes the media is expected to secure. Some of the goals can be explained in economic terms. For example, where there is a natural monopoly in a particular market, the dominant company has fewer incentives to be responsive to consumers and has the potential to abuse its power and entrench its dominant position.[6] The case for regulation is then cast as a way to address the economic problems, either by fragmenting ownership or imposing controls on the behaviour of the company. Another reason for regulation is to address various technical issues, such as determining who has access to certain channels of media distribution or allocating space on the broadcast spectrum. These, however, are limited goals for media regulation and many of the things the media is expected to do are not related to economic or technical issues.

The types of media regulation considered in this chapter are concerned with what can be broadly described as the public interest.[7] Under this view, the point of regulation is not simply to protect consumers and promote competition, but to ensure that the media performs the important functions that are necessary to a democratic society.[8] This means regulating to protect individuals that are subject to media attention, to avoid broader social harms and to promote certain professional practices. Some regulations also seek to encourage the media to produce information that is in the public interest and valuable to the audience. In some respects, the rationale for media regulation mirrors the justification for media freedom, in so far as it is about promoting the democratic functions of the media and curbing the abuse of media power.[9]

The rationale for regulation in serving the public interest does not mean that regulation is automatically compatible with media freedom. Whatever the intention behind the regulations, the public interest is often best served by leaving the media alone. There is also the question of whether regulatory controls are needed over and above the ordinary law. Even where there is a strong case for intervention, regulation poses a number of risks. For example, a specific regulatory rule may be framed in a way that has the effect of inhibiting news reporting and other valuable content. There are also risks of the regulatory power being abused or of the regulator's judgement being skewed by external pressures. The basic rationale for regulation can be easily stated in the abstract; the challenge lies in identifying the specific functions of regulation and the way to secure the integrity of the regulatory institutions, which will be considered in turn.

---

[6] See R Baldwin, M Cave and M Lodge, *Understanding Regulation: Theory, Strategy, and Practice*, 2nd edn (Oxford University Press, 2012) 15–22 for a range of market failure arguments for regulation.

[7] T Prosser, *The Regulatory Enterprise* (Oxford, Oxford University Press, 2010) 14–18 and M Feintuck and M Varney, *Media Regulation, Public Interest and the Law*, 2nd edn (Edinburgh, Edinburgh University Press, 2006) Ch 3, stressing the role of regulation in promoting democratic citizenship.

[8] Prosser, ibid, 15–17, refers to the role of regulation in promoting 'social solidarity'.

[9] See Feintuck and Varney (n 7) 15 and 275.

C. What is a Media Regulator Expected to Do?

There are many different models and functions of regulation, which vary across industries and sectors of an industry. This section will outline some of the key functions that can be performed by a media regulator, including standard setting, complaints handling, policy making, monitoring compliance and promoting professional education.[10] While these provide possible functions for a regulatory body, that does not mean any regulator should do all of these things.

i. Setting Standards for the Media

A regulator will normally be expected to set out rules for the media to follow, which it can then enforce.[11] In particular, a media regulator will be expected to set standards or draft a code of practice governing media content and the newsgathering process. In broadcasting, this function is provided for in the Ofcom Broadcasting Code (2017) and for newspapers in the Editors' Code of Practice ('Editors' Code'). In some areas, the standards will overlap with legal controls, such as regulatory provisions on respecting privacy. However, a regulatory body has more scope to provide guidance on ethical matters and good practice, which would be harder to frame as a general legal obligation or right.[12] For example, Ofcom's Broadcasting Code requires television and radio to report news with 'due accuracy'.[13] The Editors' Code requires newspapers to 'take care not to publish inaccurate, misleading or distorted information or images'.[14] Both duties are qualified, in so far as accuracy must only be 'due' for broadcasting and the newspapers need only take care. Neither therefore imposes an absolute standard of correctness. However, both are important in allowing the version of events being presented in the media to be challenged even where no legal right is at stake.

A regulatory code can also contain provisions for ethical practices, such as preventing reporting that perpetuates prejudice and discrimination. For example, the Broadcasting Code provides that television and radio should apply 'generally accepted standards' to content, which means not causing offence through 'offensive language, violence, sex, sexual violence, humiliation, distress, violation of human dignity, discriminatory treatment or language (for example on the grounds of age, disability, gender reassignment, pregnancy and maternity, race, religion or belief, sex and sexual orientation, and marriage and civil partnership)' unless justified by the context.[15] The Editors' Code provides that newspapers 'must avoid prejudicial or pejorative reference to an individual's, race, colour, religion, sex, gender identity, sexual orientation or to any physical or mental illness or disability'.[16] Again, both clauses have qualifications.

---

[10] See Leveson Report (n 2) 1651–54 on some core functions for a press regulator, which are discussed in this section.

[11] ibid, 1651 on the need for a statement of ethical standards.

[12] Baldwin, Cave and Lodge, *Understanding Regulation* (n 6) 131.

[13] The Ofcom Broadcasting Code (April 2017), section 5, www.ofcom.org.uk (last accessed 26 January 2018). The provision is legally required under the Communications Act 2003, s 319.

[14] Editors' Code of Practice, cl 1, www.editorscode.org.uk (last accessed 26 January 2018).

[15] The Ofcom Broadcasting Code (n 13) section 2.3.

[16] Editors' Code of Practice, cl 12.

However, the important point is that such obligations go over and above the general hate speech laws and impose on the media standards that are not demanded of individual speakers and other publishers.

The codes of practice also regulate the process of newsgathering, with provisions covering practices such as door-stepping, subterfuge and chequebook journalism. The codes may also enshrine certain professional standards, for example in requiring journalists to respect confidential sources.[17] The provisions of the various codes are not static and continue to evolve with professional ethics. The requirements set out in the codes also tend to be qualified by contextual factors and are often vague in nature. The trade-off is that regulation can cover questions of ethics that go beyond the normal legal controls, but allow those standards to be interpreted flexibly.

In formulating the various codes and in setting standards, a regulator can provide a forum for deliberation and for listening to the views of various interested parties about what is expected of the media.[18] As an example, the BBFC consults on audience expectations when setting new guidelines for film classification. Ofcom also engages in considerable consultation exercises both in relation to the Broadcasting Code and on policy matters. The term 'deliberation' often invokes high expectations about the level of inclusiveness in the process and the standard of reasoning employed by participants. The process of consultation should not be idealised. Those groups or interests that have the strongest incentives or resources to participate can dominate consultation exercises. Another line of criticism is that a regulator is not a neutral facilitator of deliberation, but will have a view on the preferred outcome that will shape the way issues are presented in the consultation, which can skew the process.[19] Even with these limits, the process of consultation and standard setting is still a valuable occasion for a broad conversation about acceptable ethical standards.

ii. Complaints Handling and Adjudication

If there is a professional code of conduct governing the media, then another role for the regulator is to handle any breaches of those standards. The most obvious way to deal with such breaches is through a complaints-handling process. A regulator can have different strategies for dealing with complaints. For example, the complainant may be advised to use the media company's internal complaints mechanism first. If that does not provide a satisfactory resolution, the regulator can first deal with the complaint informally by approaching the media company and seek a solution to be agreed between the parties. Such an informal mechanism has been one the primary strengths of the system of self-regulation of the press.

The regulator will also have a process for making formal adjudications for complaints where an informal resolution cannot be reached. While formal, that process is less complex than the courts. In many cases a regulatory adjudicator will hear formal complaints on paper without examination of witnesses, and will collect evidence

---

[17] The Ofcom Broadcasting Code (n 13) section 7.7; Editors' Code of Practice, cl 14.
[18] P Lunt and S Livingstone, *Media Regulation* (London, SAGE, 2012) 10.
[19] See discussion in Lunt and Livingstone, ibid, 77–81 and 93 fn 38.

through correspondence and telephone calls. In some cases, there are overlaps between the provisions of a regulatory code and a legal cause of action, so the individual will have a choice of where to take the complaint. Most obviously, a person suffering an invasion of privacy can make a claim before the courts in misuse of private information or can go the relevant media regulator. A complaint to the regulator offers some advantages to the complainant. The process does not require legal representation and is less time consuming than litigation. An individual may not be able to afford an application for a privacy injunction, but a complaint to a regulator is free of charge.

The system of regulatory adjudication has costs and benefits. While cheaper and normally quicker than the courts, the regulator will also lack the strong evidential procedures used by the court and will lack the time and resources to make detailed findings of fact in most cases. For example, the Editors' Code of Practice used by the newspaper regulator IPSO provides that the press 'must take care not to publish inaccurate, misleading or distorted information or images'.[20] In some cases, it will be clear whether a story is misleading or not. However, the issue is not always so straightforward where, for example, the meaning of the story is ambiguous or the facts are complex. In such cases, the newspaper regulator will look at the process undertaken by the journalist, such as whether the complainant was contacted for comment, and whether proper records and notes were kept.[21] However, this will not be comparable to the extensive findings on the meaning of the statement, its factual basis and the journalist's conduct made in defamation cases. While these factors can be seen as an advantage in providing an efficient resolution, such limits can have implications for the quality of decisions in some cases.

When adjudicating on a complaint, the regulator will often consider questions relating to the professional judgment of the reporter or editor. For example, the Ofcom Code provides that broadcasts can include offensive content if justified by the context. The application of the standard requires the scrutiny of certain editorial decisions, such as the type of offensive content that is appropriate in a particular setting. Similarly, clause 5 of the newspapers' Editors' Code requires an assessment of whether a report of a suicide contained 'excessive detail'. While a court could look into such matters, there might be concerns about judges second-guessing editorial choices.[22] A regulator may be better placed to assess professional conduct on account of its expertise in the field.

While comparisons with the courts are made, regulatory complaints handling processes do not aim to provide a direct alternative to legal controls. Even where legal and regulatory provisions overlap, for example with privacy, the regulatory provision may have a different formulation as to when privacy is protected. A regulatory body will also have different remedies available, which may be less heavy handed than legal sanctions, but allow for more creative and constructive solutions to complaints. More broadly, viewing a regulator as a low-cost court overlooks its other functions and characterises it as the sort of 'command and control' system that is often subject

---

[20] Editors' Code of Practice, cl 1.
[21] See Editors Code of Practice Committee, *The Editor's Codebook* (2018) 12–16.
[22] *Campbell v Mirror Group Newspapers Ltd* [2004] UKHL 22, [2004] 2 AC 406 at [59].

to criticism.[23] Instead, the complaints handling process can be seen as providing an important forum where editorial decisions can be contested before an independent body. The point of such a process is not simply to punish, deter or remedy certain behaviour, but has separate value as a channel of accountability where the media has to explain its decisions. It can be a place where the media institution is confronted with the effects of its conduct and required to reflect upon its practices.

While the function of adjudicating on a professional code of practice does not aim to replicate or substitute the judicial protection of legal rights, a regulator can also facilitate a separate alternative dispute resolution (ADR) scheme in relation to legal actions. For example, an arbitration service is a type of ADR that allows legal claims to be heard outside of the court and subject to a binding decision. One approach is for the regulator to approve a number of independent ADR service providers, which the regulated bodies are required to offer in the event of a complaint. Another approach is for the regulator to play a more direct role in providing its own system of ADR. Along these lines, under the Royal Charter that implemented elements of the Leveson proposals for press regulation, recognised self-regulatory bodies should offer an arbitration service, to allow for an affordable channel to hear disputes relating to legal rights.

iii. Monitoring Functions

A regulator can have a role in monitoring the industry. Such monitoring can help promote compliance with the professional the codes of conduct. The scale of media activity means that the regulator cannot oversee all media conduct to check compliance, and it is more efficient for this function to be delegated to individuals, who can bring a potential violation to the regulator's attention via a complaint. The task can also be delegated to media professionals, if the regulator operates a system for lapses in ethical standards to be reported anonymously (such as a whistleblower's hotline).[24] That does not mean a regulator must be limited to responding to complaints or tip-offs,[25] and a regulator can be empowered to take the initiative to investigate or at least undertake periodic reviews of media conduct. For example, if there is widespread concern that detailed newspaper reports of suicides are encouraging people to copy what they read, the regulator could conduct or commission research on such reporting. The monitoring function can also be connected to the broader policy-making or advisory functions of the regulator. The regulator can review various areas of media activity to assess how well the current regulations are working, make improvements to its own regulations or advise government on areas where new laws or powers may be necessary. For example, the broadcast regulator Ofcom is under a statutory duty to conduct periodic reviews of public service broadcasting and media ownership rules.[26]

---

[23] Baldwin, Cave and Lodge, *Understanding Regulation* (n 6) 106–11.

[24] For example, under the Royal Charter scheme for press regulation, the provision of a whistleblowers' hotline is part of the criteria for recognition.

[25] A criticism of the old Press Complaints Commission was that it was not proactive enough and would only wait until there was a complaint.

[26] Communications Act 2003, s 264 and s 391.

iv. *Policy-making and Implementation*

A media regulator may have roles relating to policy-making and policy implementation. The function of drawing up a code of conduct discussed earlier is an element of this role. The regulator may also be charged with drawing up policies to deal with more technical issues, or be asked to advise government on changes to policy that are necessary to meet certain objectives. Similarly, a regulator can play a role in implementing government policy. The broadcast regulator Ofcom performs several important roles in relation to media policy. For example, Ofcom is sometimes asked to assess the public interest implications of a media merger.[27] As seen in Chapter 4, the BBFC performs some statutory functions in relation to the classification of DVDs and in overseeing the age verification systems on adult websites.

The presence of official policy making and implementation functions will change the nature of the regulator. A regulator that has some official input into government policy is not confined to matters of professional practice that are internal to the industry. A greater level of expertise will be required from its staff, which will have implications for the composition of the body, to be discussed later. Where an official policy function is performed, there will normally need to be some form of statutory authorisation and channel of accountability to government or the public. In addition, care needs to be taken to ensure that the policy-related roles do not conflict with any other functions expected of the regulator.

v. *Professional Development and Education*

A regulator can offer certain training services, for example being able to educate the profession on matters of ethics or on how to comply with the professional standards. Most regulators will have some channels of outreach to publicise its work and ensure that people are better informed about what it does. At its most basic level, a regulator can hold meetings with the profession or provide advice on how to meet professional obligations.[28] A regulator can go further and possibly have some input into professional education events. This could take the form of sponsoring continuing education for those working within the profession. Alternatively, the regulator could liaise with journalism schools, to make sure that the syllabus covers the right ground. As a comparison, the Solicitors Regulation Authority oversees the educational and training requirements necessary to secure entry into the legal profession.[29] There are bodies that accredit journalism courses in the UK to make sure the right areas are covered.[30] While those accreditors are separate from the main media regulators, the oversight of professional education should be understood as part of a system of regulation and

---

[27] See Enterprise Act 2002, s 44A.

[28] For example, the newspaper regulator IPSO sometimes publishes advisory notices on specific issues.

[29] The legal profession is not directly comparable, as it has formal requirements for entry, while journalism does not.

[30] The National Council for the Training of Journalists and the Broadcast Journalism Training Council currently perform this task.

may prove to be a more effective way of shaping behaviour and promoting ethical conduct than the imposition of sanctions once things have already gone wrong.

vi. Meta Regulation

A regulator will not always regulate the industry directly, but may engage in 'meta-regulation' in which the regulatory body oversees the self-regulatory practices of a media company to make sure that it fulfils certain standards and criteria.[31] For example, a regulatory body may require a newspaper or broadcaster to have its own internal complaints-handling process or ombudsman, which is sufficiently independent of the editorial department. Under such a process, the regulator does not handle the complaints directly, but ensures the media company is well equipped to deal with the complaints fairly. The regulator may also require media companies to have a 'conscience clause' in employment contracts, so that journalists are not compelled to work on certain types of story and can make their own call on certain ethical issues. Along these lines, the regulator offers a kitemarking service for the media, for example by approving a media company's internal system for securing professional and ethical conduct. An approach based on meta-regulation, rather than direct regulation, therefore gives the industry a degree of trust in finding the best ways to put regulatory goals into operation.[32]

Meta-regulation can also take place by overseeing other regulators. Along these lines, certain industries may have multiple regulators in relation to different sectors. A central 'meta-regulator' may be charged with examining the operations of each regulator and ensuring that each complies with certain minimal standards. Such a system is partially in operation in relation to the newspaper industry following the post-Leveson Royal Charter, which allows for the certification of multiple regulators. Meta-regulation is an approach that prefers regulatory tasks to be devolved down as far as possible, with the central regulatory system simply aiming to ensure that certain benchmarks have been met. Such methods offer the hope of greater cooperation from the industry and internalisation of the standards, than with a system where standards are externally imposed. There can, however, be a cost in terms of a lack of uniformity among the various regulatory bodies once the minimum standards are attained.

vii. Defending Media Freedom

A media regulator should respect media freedom.[33] When it is adjudicating on a complaint, drafting a code or developing policy, the regulator should take into account the impact on media freedom. For example, when applying the Ofcom Code of Practice,

---

[31] For discussion, see M Coglianese and E Mendelson, 'Meta-regulation and self-regulation' in R Baldwin, M Cave, and M Lodge, *The Oxford Handbook of Regulation* (Oxford, Oxford University Press, 2010).

[32] See discussion in Baldwin, Cave and Lodge, *Understanding Regulation* (n 6) 152.

[33] See discussion in Leveson Report (n 2) 1653.

the regulator gives a degree of leeway to the broadcaster to respect the professional judgement of the editor. The leeway is provided not because the regulator lacks expertise, but rather because it recognises the dangers of micro-managing editorial decisions with the benefit of hindsight and accepts that a range of decisions are normally open to an editor. The regulator also needs to consider whether its decisions would be likely to inhibit the functions of the media in the future. Such respect for media freedom is uncontroversial, and where the regulator is a public authority such respect will be mandated under the Human Rights Act 1998. There is, however, a difference between respecting media freedom in regulatory decisions and becoming an advocate for the interests of the media. The risk of the two becoming blurred can arise in particular with a self-regulatory body that is financed and established by the very companies that it is supposed to regulate. For example, when the Human Rights Act was being enacted, the then head of the old Press Complaints Commission lobbied to avoid an indirect privacy law, which was seen as an action more appropriate for an interest group rather than a regulatory body.[34] A regulator will need to express a view on various policy issues, but it should do so in its capacity as an expert. A regulator is unlikely to be effective in acting as a check on the media if, at the same time, it acts as the industry's advocate in public. To avoid such a risk, a regulatory body needs to be separate from any institutions representing the interests of the media.

viii. Taking Stock

A regulator can perform a broad range of functions. The discussion has not sought to assess how well these functions are currently performed in the UK, but has provided a basis on which the goals of regulation can be evaluated. The reader may be forgiven for thinking that a regulator should perform all of these tasks. Simply that a wide range of functions is possible does not mean that a maximum number of functions should be imposed on a regulatory body. The performance of one function may have an impact on the way the regulator performs its other tasks. For example, Ofcom is under a duty to protect the interests of both citizens and consumers. However, some critics argue that in the event of a conflict between the two, Ofcom tends to prioritise the consumer interest and market over the interests of democratic citizenship.[35] One possible reason is that Ofcom has significant responsibilities as an economic regulator, which arguably leads it to view the public interest in economic terms. That background might also lead the regulator to prefer a view of regulation as addressing 'market failures', which sees regulation as an interference that is to be minimised as far as possible.[36] Similarly, an official role in advising on policy matters may be in tension with the independence of the regulator from government (just as the courts are separated from the legislature and executive). While these are matters for debate, it shows that there are costs in piling up functions on to an amalgamated super-regulator. The multiple functions can have an impact on the overall outlook of the regulator that shapes its performance of

---

[34] See Leveson Report (n 2) at 1262–70.
[35] Lunt and Livingstone (n 18) 39 and 62.
[36] Prosser (n 7) 4–6.

various tasks, and sometimes there is a case for allocating different tasks to different bodies.

D. Legitimacy, Media Freedom and Regulatory Failures

The previous section set out the key functions that a media regulator might be expected to perform. To execute these functions effectively and with authority, the regulator needs to enjoy a degree of legitimacy. What this requires depends on what is meant by legitimacy and how it relates to the particular regulatory function. To clarify some of these issues, Julia Black draws a distinction between legitimacy as a normative issue focusing on when a regulator '*should* be regarded as legitimate', and empirical legitimacy, which looks at whether the regulator *has* credibility and *is* accepted as legitimate in practice.[37] Starting with the normative question of when a regulator should enjoy legitimacy, Baldwin, Cave and Lodge provide criteria including a democratic mandate, accountability, procedural fairness, expertise and efficiency.[38] The list is not exhaustive and independence would be an obvious quality to add for the legitimacy of a media regulator. The emphasis given to the different criteria will vary according to the function of the regulator. For example, if a regulator performs an official role in policy design and implementation, then a democratic mandate will be more important. Such a mandate will be less pressing if a regulator is merely charged with enforcing the industry's own professional codes. Designing a system that meets the criteria can be challenging, particularly as some factors can be in tension with others.[39] For example, the democratic mandate and accountability of the regulator may constrain the ability of the regulator to perform its functions independently and according to its expert judgement.[40] Procedures offering a rigorous standard of fairness for the parties may impose costs in terms of efficiency. While there is no simple formula for normative legitimacy, the criteria is useful in assessing the design of the regulator and the functions it is expected to perform.

Empirical legitimacy looks at whether the regulator enjoys respect and authority in practice. This poses a number of challenges, as different groups and constituencies may have different ideas about whether a regulator is credible and acceptable.[41] The point has long been noted in debates about newspaper regulation, where a regulator has to 'command the confidence of a split constituency', which includes the industry that it regulates, the government and Parliament, and the public as a whole.[42] However, that poses a difficulty of design, as each of these constituencies may see competing qualities as necessary for legitimacy. The public is most likely to favour a system of

---

[37] See J Black, 'Constructing and contesting legitimacy and accountability in polycentric regulatory regimes' (2008) 2 *Regulation and Governance* 137, 145–46.

[38] Baldwin, Cave and Lodge, *Understanding Regulation* (n 6) 26–31. See also Feintuck and Varney (n 7) 170–76 on the importance of accountability and constraints on regulatory discretion.

[39] Black, 'Constructing and contesting legitimacy and accountability in polycentric regulatory regimes' (n 37) 153.

[40] ibid.

[41] ibid.

[42] House of Commons, Culture, Media and Sport Committee, *Privacy and media intrusion* (n 1) at [52].

regulation that is able to impose sanctions where necessary and is independent of the industry. By contrast, the media companies are likely to favour a regulator that understands the pressures and practices of the industry. This does not mean that any particular constituency has the right to veto any regulatory arrangement that it does not like, but the likelihood of a regulator being accepted is an important factor to take into account when designing a system.

A further issue for the legitimacy of media regulation is the compatibly of the system with the right to media freedom. On this question, opinion will divide according to the understanding of that right. Many arguments expressing outright hostility to any form of state or legislative input into the regulation of the media often rest on a formal understanding of media freedom as the absence of state interference. The formal understanding of media freedom was rejected in Chapter 1 and is not reflected in the domestic law or in the European Convention on Human Rights (ECHR) jurisprudence. Under the dominant approach in the current law, any interference with media freedom is to be permitted only where necessary and proportionate to a legitimate aim. This means media freedom is not a total barrier to state involvement in regulation, but does mean that regulatory institutions and rules require close scrutiny.

While there is a need to approach the design of media regulation systems with care, this does not mean that regulation is always a restriction on the exercise of media freedom. As discussed in Chapter 1, media freedom is not just about guarding against state action, but also about protecting the media from extraneous pressures from private actors. Media regulation can guard against this by inculcating journalists with a strong sense of professionalism that provides a counter to pressure from proprietors, the market and government.[43] Such a sense of professionalism may train the journalist to be wary of spin and not to become too close to officials. In so far as media regulation supports such professionalism, then it can promote the exercise of independent journalism. The regulation does not make the journalist free, in the sense of being able to do whatever he or she wants, but allows the profession to enjoy autonomy in the sense of operating according to its own internal values. That is a controversial and contested view about the nature of journalism, but it shows how regulation, if done correctly, can promote media freedom.

Even where regulation is legitimate and compatible with media freedom, there is a more basic question of whether it works. In their work on regulation, Baldwin, Cave and Lodge note that regulators can fail for a wide range of reasons, including external pressures from government and industry, lack of cooperation and limited information about the field.[44] Other shortcomings may lie inside the regulatory body, such as limited resources and powers. The people appointed to the regulatory body may have an agenda that is not aligned with the goals of the regulation and instead become 'captured' by the interests of the industry that they are supposed to regulate.[45]

---

[43] For example, when considering the public interest implications of a media merger, the Competition Commission (as it was then named) thought the professional culture at ITV would prevent BSkyB's holding having an adverse effect on plurality, see *Competition Commission, Acquisition by BSkyB Group of 17.9 Per Cent of the Shares in ITV plc: Final Report* (14 December 2007) at [41].

[44] Baldwin, Cave and Lodge, *Understanding Regulation* (n 6) Ch 5.

[45] For a classic text on regulatory capture, see G Stigler, 'The Theory of Economic Regulation' (1971) 2 *The Bell Journal of Economics and Management Science* 3.

Another possible failure is that regulatory rules may not promote the desired behaviour and may instead produce unintended consequences that undermine the regulatory goals. For example, if a regulator restricts the ability of the media to engage in certain types of intrusive reporting or disclose private information, then the professional media may leave such activities to various internet sources or bloggers to gather the information. That would provide an informal delegation of such reporting, in which the website researches and breaks a story, and then the mainstream media would follow up and carry the information. Those websites and online sources will be unregulated, offering no channel of accountability. In another example, the rules requiring adult websites to have an online verification system could inadvertently help to make some sites more profitable, if it means that entering credit card details is mandatory to access the site and makes it much easier for the site to charge visitors.[46] Neither of the examples defeats the case for the regulation in question, but the consequences may turn out to be very different from the goal of the rule.

Such shortcomings are a hazard in all types of regulation and there is wide body of literature on the methods of designing and assessing regulatory institutions to minimise these risks. In much of the literature there have been efforts to escape the limits of traditional 'command and control' techniques that set rules and impose a sanction for breach.[47] For example, the well-known 'nudge' techniques seek to utilise the strategic framing of information to encourage individual choices that are in line with regulatory goals.[48] The traditional forms of 'command and control' regulation are still important, and complaints handling remains a central function for a media regulator. However, that is only part of the picture, and many regulatory tools now supplement the traditional techniques.

No system of regulation is an unqualified success. All come with their flaws and problems. Even a well-respected regulator will make decisions that many regard as disappointing. The difficulty lies in determining whether such disappointments are simply part of the give and take of any regulatory system, or whether it reflects some deeper systemic problem. Such issues will be open to interpretation and will be difficult to identify. If we cannot easily distinguish bad judgment from broader systemic bias simply by looking at the outcome of a regulatory decision, then the system will be judged by its procedures and the integrity of its institutions. For that reason, it is particularly important to design and structure the regulator in a way that maximises legitimacy and minimises the risk of a systemic problem. If these risks are not addressed at the level of design, then the regulator may find everything it does being written off as biased towards a particular constituency. Without the right procedure and institutions, the regulator will be viewed with suspicion. With this in mind, the following sections will look at the way a regulator is designed and consider whether certain types of practice or structure are more likely to be successful, secure legitimacy and avoid the problems of regulatory failure.

---

[46] Digital Economy Act 2017.

[47] For example, see I Ayres and J Braithwaite, *Responsive Regulation: Transcending the Deregulation Debate* (Oxford, Oxford University Press, 1992), locating traditional techniques within a broader 'enforcement pyramid'.

[48] C Sunstein and R Thaler, *Nudge* (New Haven, CT, Yale University Press, 2008); C Camerer, S Issacharoff, G Loewenstein, T O'Donoghue, and M Rabin, 'Regulation for conservatives' (2003) 151 *University of Pennsylvania Law Review* 1211.

E. Designing a Regulator

Having looked at the possible functions and qualities of a media regulator, the next set of issues relates to the design of the regulator. The discussion will begin by looking at the distinction between self-regulation and state regulation of the media. After that, three specific issues of design will be considered. The first is the establishment of the media regulator, which includes questions about the regulator's source of power and whether the industry should be subject to the regulation on a mandatory or voluntary basis. A second issue of design concerns the management and staffing of the regulatory body, including who should sit on the regulatory body, who should appoint those people and who should provide funding to the body. On that theme, a central issue is whether the regulatory body should be composed of representatives of relevant interests or by experts. The third major theme for design is what powers should be available to the regulator. The questions under this theme include whether the regulator should have the power to impose penalties for a breach of professional standards. The answers to all these questions will depend on what function the media regulator is expected to perform and what element of legitimacy is being emphasised.

i. Self-regulation, State Regulation and Other Models

A useful starting point when considering regulatory design is to distinguish between state regulation and self-regulation. As will be seen, the distinction is something of a simplification and there are many ways to arrange a regulatory system. However, the distinction does capture one of the key fault lines in media law. In a system of state regulation, the regulatory body is established by statute, prerogative or other government power, has formal powers of investigation and sanction, and its jurisdiction is compulsory for the whole industry. In a non-media context, the presence of a statute conferring regulatory power is a sign of legitimacy in so far as the regulator has been approved by Parliament and will normally provide a channel of accountability.[49] In the case of the media, this argument is often turned on its head, with the statutory regulator being viewed with suspicion as potentially being subject to government direction.

Despite the concern about state regulation, Ofcom—a statutory corporation—regulates the broadcast media. The regulator is independent from government in the sense that it is not a government department. However, it was created under the Communications Act 2003 to amalgamate the functions of a number of earlier regulators and covers a broad range of areas including telecommunications, postal services, video on-demand services, as well as television and radio. Having been established after a period of general deregulation in the industry and scepticism about the effectiveness of traditional regulatory approaches, Ofcom was set up with a lighter touch in mind. A product of the Blair government, Ofcom is committed to the principles of 'better regulation'—meaning that it aims to be transparent, accountable and consistent, and intervene only when a measure is proportionate and targeted.[50] Among its

---

[49] Baldwin, Cave and Lodge, *Understanding Regulation* (n 6) 27–28.
[50] Communications Act 2003, s 3(3)(a).

various functions, Ofcom regulates the content of the broadcast media and is required to establish a Content Board,[51] which advises and oversees the operation of the broadcast standards including the Broadcasting Code, production quotas and public service broadcasting. Ofcom has various policy-related roles, which include conducting research and advising government. For example, Ofcom provides periodic reviews of public service broadcasting and of media plurality, and investigates the impact of media mergers on plurality.

Under a system of self-regulation, the industry itself is responsible for establishing and maintaining the regulatory regime.[52] There are a number of advantages for such an approach. Self-regulatory systems will generally be cheaper for the public, in so far as the industry picks up the costs. The industry has experience of the field being regulated, so will be able to develop a system that draws on that knowledge. If the industry recognises the self-regulatory body as one of its own, then that body is more likely to gain acceptance from those being regulated.[53] In relation to media freedom, self-regulation has the added benefit of keeping the state away from the affairs of the newspaper or broadcaster and thereby reduces the risk of interference.[54]

Criticisms of self-regulation often focus on the lack of independence from the regulated industry. If a self-regulatory body is dependent on the industry for funding, appointed by the industry and requires industry consent, then the fear is that the body will merely serve the interests of the industry. There are also problems of accountability.[55] If members of the public are unhappy with the decisions of the self-regulatory body, there may be little they can do, other than to demand a more independent system of regulation.[56] At its worst, self-regulation may be seen to be little more than an effort to stave off demands for stronger forms of regulation.

In some areas, there has been a move against 'pure' systems of self-regulation, in which an industry is wholly responsible for governing its own affairs.[57] For example, the scandal surrounding the abuse of MPs' expenses in 2009 led to disillusionment with the parliamentary system of self-regulation and MPs are now subject to independent scrutiny of their expenses claims under a statutory body.[58] While the legal profession traditionally regulated itself, in 2007 a statutory body, the Legal Services Board, was established to oversee the 'approved regulators' of the legal profession.[59] More

---

[51] ibid, s 12.

[52] The term self-regulation is open to different interpretations, but for these purposes it is used to refer to a division between state and non-state actors. For discussion see J Black, 'Decentring Regulation: Understanding the Role of Regulation and Self-Regulation in a "Post-Regulatory" World' (2001) 54 *Current Legal Problems* 103.

[53] Lunt and Livingstone (n 18) 25.

[54] The point has been repeated on many occasions, for example see the House of Commons Culture, Media and Sport Committee, *Privacy and media intrusion* (n 1) at [52], 'the industry has to regulate itself; otherwise the door is open to Government influence, censorship, even control'.

[55] Livingstone and Lunt point out the dangers of self-regulatory bodies being seen as 'self-interested bodies, unaccountable and ineffective in terms of enforcement and redress, unknown by and often unresponsive to ordinary people', Lunt and Livingstone (n 18) 25.

[56] Though see J Black, 'Constitutionalising Self-Regulation' (1996) 59 *Modern Law Review* 24, discussing judicial review as a mechanism of accountability.

[57] Commenting on the experience in Australia see R Finkelstein and R Tiffen, 'When Does Press Self-Regulation Work?' (2015) 38 *Melbourne University Law Review* 944, 950.

[58] Parliamentary Standards Act 2009.

[59] Under the regime, legal professional bodies are required to establish a separate regulatory arm, thereby dividing the functions of representing and regulating the profession.

broadly, the preference for self-regulation often rests on a sharp division between the state and private sector, which has become increasingly blurred in recent decades given the greater role for private bodies in carrying out public functions.[60] The blurring of public and private means that the media acts as a watchdog of both state and private sectors, and thus needs independence from both. Self-regulation may not provide a sufficient guard against the private power wielded by the industry. In any event, even seemingly pure forms of self-regulation are not wholly independent of the state, in so far as state regulation often lurks in the background as an alternative if the system fails to work.[61]

The scepticism about self-regulation can be seen in two areas of media law. The first relates to the BBC, which had been largely self-regulatory until 2017.[62] For example, between 2007 and 2017, the BBC Trust regulated the BBC. While the Trust was separate from the day-to-day management of the BBC, it was found to lack the expertise and independence to hold the organisation to account, had too few powers and thereby failed to be a credible regulator.[63] Disillusionment followed a number of high profile controversies at the BBC, including the response to the Jimmy Savile scandal and various payoffs to senior staff. Under the latest BBC Charter, the statutory body Ofcom regulates the BBC, which ends the broadcaster's period of self-regulation.

The second area is press regulation. While self-regulation has been the traditional approach for newspapers in many western democracies,[64] this system has come under considerable criticism in the UK. The PCC was established in 1991 following the publication of Calcutt Report.[65] Throughout its existence, the Commission was subject to the criticism that it lacked independence from the newspaper industry and was a mere public relations effort. Critics argued that it did the minimum possible to promote press ethics and failed to take a proactive stance. In particular, the PCC lost credibility for publishing a report that dismissed claims about widespread phone hacking within the newspaper industry in 2009, and subsequently withdrew that report.[66] More broadly, self-regulation under the PCC did little to deter phone-hacking or grossly intrusive stories about people's personal lives. While the aftermath of the phone-hacking scandal led to the demise of the PCC, self-regulation of the press has not died (yet) and a number of newspapers subscribe to the self-regulatory body, the Independent Press Standards Organisations (IPSO). The future of press self-regulation is part of an ongoing political battle.

Between the extremes of self-regulation and state regulation lie a number of other approaches that entail a mixture of the two.[67] Along these lines some self-regulatory

---

[60] Black, 'Decentring Regulation' (n 52) 112.

[61] I Bartle and P Vass, 'Self Regulation and the Regulatory State' (2007) 85 *Public Administration* 885, 895.

[62] Even though it is created by prerogative powers and to some degree accountable for its actions, the BBC was self-regulatory in the sense that decision-making was not overseen by a specialist external body.

[63] House of Commons Culture Media Sport Committee, *BBC Charter Review* (HC 2015–16, 398) at [24]–[25].

[64] D Hallin and P Mancini, *Comparing Media Systems* (Cambridge, Cambridge University Press, 2004). See also L Fielden, 'A Royal Charter for the Press: Lessons from Overseas' (2013) 5 *Journal of Media Law* 172.

[65] Calcutt (1990) (n 1).

[66] See Leveson Report (n 2) 1574.

[67] For discussion see Bartle and Vass (n 61) 895.

bodies perform statutory functions, such as the BBFC.[68] Another example is the Advertising Standards Authority, which is a self-regulatory body applying its own standards code. However, in regulating the broadcast media, the ASA applies a separate code and its responsibility for broadcast advertising is pursuant to a contract with Ofcom. The regulation of advertising on television and radio is therefore made under a system of 'co-regulation' between a self-regulatory body and statutory regulator.

In an attempt to steer a way through the weaknesses of self-regulation while avoiding the dangers of state regulation, the Leveson Report in 2012 proposed a system of 'independent self-regulation' for the press. Under the proposal, newspapers would be subject to a self-regulatory body, but that body would be subject to a form of recognition from a government established public body (a type of 'meta-regulation' referred to earlier). The Leveson proposals were not fully implemented and instead the government established a system under a Royal Charter.[69] The Charter provided for the creation of a Press Recognition Panel (PRP) to 'recognise' self-regulatory bodies that fulfil criteria for independence and effectiveness.[70] The criteria requires the self-regulatory body to be independent of the industry and the state, to provide a professional code for journalists, an arbitration service and have effective sanctions. The system is not state regulation, as the industry is regulated by its own body. However, for that regulator to be 'recognised', its systems need to be approved by the state body. The involvement of the state is therefore at one step removed.

The extent to which the Charter scheme avoids the hazards of either self or state regulation is the subject of controversy. Critics argue that the PRP could pressure the self-regulatory body to take a stronger stance on certain issues, such as privacy. Such claims are overstated. The structure under the Charter generates a risk of political pressure, but that risk is relatively remote given that the PRP can only decide to certify or not certify a body and cannot do much to influence specific applications of any regulation.

The debate about state or self-regulation represents a key fault line in British media law, albeit a line that is not as bright as sometimes assumed. For the remaining part of this section, three specific issues of design will be considered: the source of regulatory power; the management and composition of the regulator; and the sanctions available.

ii. Establishing the Regulator and its Source of Power

A key question in the design of media regulation is the regulator's source of power. This issue normally follows the divide between self-regulation and state regulation. In the system of self-regulation, the industry will normally set out the regulator's terms of reference and scope of its jurisdiction. In many cases, the source of the regulator's authority will come from a contract with the regulated bodies, as found with

---

[68] For example, under the Video Recordings Act 1984, s 4. For discussion see Ch 7.

[69] Royal Charter on Self-Regulation of the Press (2013).

[70] Leveson proposed that Ofcom would certify self-regulatory bodies by applying statutory criteria. The proposal was not directly implemented and the government declared that to rely on a statute in such an area posed a risk to press freedom and would open the door to future tinkering. For criticism of the argument see E Barendt, 'Statutory Underpinning: A Threat to Press Freedom?' (2013) 5 *Journal of Media Law* 189.

the current system of self-regulation of the press. By contrast, the state regulator will normally be established by statute or prerogative. The government or Parliament will then establish the terms of the regulatory body. As a result, the system may be seen as imposed on the industry, but it will at least have some democratic authority and its functions will reflect public policy goals. Again, there are hybrids between the two models. For example, the BBFC is an industry body, but is required under the Video Recordings Act 1984 to make 'adequate arrangements' for an appeals procedure, in relation to its classification decisions for video and DVD.[71] The requirement led to the establishment of the Video Appeals Committee (VAC), which is not a statutory body and is independent of government, but was created in response to a statutory requirement.

Closely related to the source of power is the question whether membership of the regulatory system is voluntary or mandatory. In many self-regulatory systems membership is voluntary, which fits with the source of power being based on contract.[72] While a voluntary system will reinforce the need of the regulatory body to win the confidence of the industry, that leaves it vulnerable to pressure from the industry that can opt out of the system. For example, the old Press Complaints Commission was a voluntary body and its weak position was highlighted when *Northern and Shell* (the *Express* newspaper group) withdrew from the self-regulatory system, leaving its titles unregulated. At the time of writing, there are several national newspapers (*The Guardian, Financial Times* and *Independent*) that do not belong to a self-regulatory body. In systems of state regulation, participation will normally be mandatory. For example, anyone holding a broadcast licence in the UK is subject to the regulations applied by Ofcom. Compulsory authority under law is not limited to regulators created by statute, as both the BBFC and ASA are industry bodies, but exercise statutory functions that have mandatory authority. For example, all retailers of DVDs have to comply with the BBFC's classification decisions.

The system for press regulation under the Royal Charter sits somewhere between the two models. Under the Charter scheme, membership of a recognised body is voluntary, but two main incentives were envisaged to encourage newspapers to join such a regulator. The first incentive provides that if a body is a member of an approved regulator, then it will be protected from exemplary damages in various media law claims.[73] The impact of that provision is likely to be limited, as exemplary damages are awarded only in extreme cases.[74] This provision thereby protects the media from what is a remote risk at best. The second incentive is more significant and relates to legal costs, but has not been brought into force at the time of writing. Under the incentive, if a newspaper is not a member of an approved self-regulatory body, then it may be liable to pay the claimant's costs in a media law action even if it wins its case.[75] The thinking behind the provision rests on the requirement under the Royal Charter that, in order to be recognised, the self-regulatory body must offer an arbitration scheme

---

[71]   Video Recordings Act 1984, s 4(3).

[72]   See *R v Disciplinary Committee of the Jockey Club, ex p Aga Khan* [1993] 1 WLR 909 for an example of contractual authority in relation to sports regulation.

[73]   Crime and Courts Act 2013, s 34.

[74]   ibid, referring to 'deliberate or reckless disregard of an outrageous nature for the claimant's rights'.

[75]   Crime and Courts Act 2013, s 40 refers to actions in libel, slander, breach of confidence, misuse of private information, malicious falsehood and harassment.

to deal with certain legal claims against the newspaper. Consequently, the argument runs that if the newspaper had been a member of a recognised regulator, then the case could have been resolved out of court under the lower cost arbitration scheme. If that arbitration scheme is not used because the newspaper has not joined the recognised regulator, then the newspaper bears responsibility for driving up the legal costs and should pay for those costs even if it wins its case. The provision is often presented in public discussion as a punitive measure on the press. However, it can partly be explained as an attempt to keep down legal costs by encouraging the use of alternative dispute resolution.[76] That goal is reflected in the fact that if the newspaper *is* a member of a recognised regulator and a claimant takes it to court without going through the arbitration scheme, then under the incentive the court would not order costs against the newspaper even if it loses the claim. As stated, the costs incentive has not been brought into force, and in early 2018 the government expressed its intention to repeal s 40 (which will leave the provision on exemplary damages as the sole incentive).

There are many other ways in which membership of recognised regulators could be incentivised. The media benefits from various privileges, such as access to certain courts, exemption from election spending laws and exemption from VAT. Any of these could have been made conditional on membership of a recognised self-regulatory body. However, the Charter system focused on the costs and damages regime, and reflects the central role of an arbitration scheme providing an alternative to the courts. Had the costs provision been brought into force, it would have provided a powerful incentive to join a recognised regulatory body. While the Charter scheme will remain in place, at present it looks likely that most national newspapers will continue to operate outside of that scheme.

If a system is mandatory or if there are incentives to join it, then there needs to be some definition of the field subject to regulation. In other words, there has to be a definition of a journalist or media company that is to be regulated. The Crime and Courts Act 2013 attempts to address this issue for the Royal Charter scheme by providing that the incentives apply to 'relevant publishers', which refers to those publishing 'news-related material' 'in the course of a business', which are 'written by different authors' and subject 'to editorial control'. The provision does not apply to those that merely host material.[77] Schedule 15 to the Act provides a number of exceptions, including special interest titles and 'micro-businesses' that employ fewer than 10 employees and have a turnover of less than £2 million per year. A micro-business is not subject to the incentives if: (a) it is a 'multi-author blog'; or (b) the publication of news-related content is incidental to the main activities of the business. The provision generates difficult questions of application, such as what constitutes a 'blog' for the purposes of the section. The exception seeks to carve out a space for those speakers that are not seen as the functional equivalent of the mass media.

The provisions have been criticised on the grounds that the definition of a relevant publisher is too broad and could potentially expand beyond newspapers to publications by certain NGOs, charities and political organisations.[78] The provision has yet

---

[76] It is only part of the rationale, in so far as a costs regime could be used to incentivise participation in an arbitration scheme without requiring membership of a self-regulatory body.

[77] Crime and Courts Act 2013, s 41(3).

[78] H Anthony, *Who Joins the Regulator* (English PEN, November 2014).

to be tested and much will depend on how terms such as 'special interest title' or the 'incidental' inclusion of news are interpreted. The issue highlights the problems of line-drawing and the risk of a regulatory regime being under- or over-inclusive in trying to define a media sector. The issue can be found in other areas of media regulation, such as defining a video on-demand service that falls under Ofcom's jurisdiction, and it is hoped that the tests will be refined through interpretation.

iii. Management and Composition

A key issue in the management of a regulatory body is the power to appoint its members, which is central to showing its independence. If a regulator is packed with people sympathetic to a particular interest, then that can undermine the functioning of the body. Unsurprisingly, the source of the regulator's powers tends to influence the way people are appointed. For example, the government has some input into the composition of the statutory regulator Ofcom. The Secretary of State for Digital, Culture, Media and Sport appoints the Chairman and non-executive members of the Board of Ofcom. The Chairman and non-executive members appoint the executive members of the Board, with the Secretary of State approving the appointment of the Chief Executive. Such government input is important if the regulator is going to play a significant role in policy making. The government input into appointments takes place only at the higher level, while Ofcom appoints most of its staff. By contrast, the government has no input into appointments of the self-regulatory bodies under the press regulation scheme envisaged by the Royal Charter. The Charter does, however, provide that the regulator needs to be independent of industry and government. In relation to IPSO, which operates outside the Charter scheme, there have been concerns that representatives of the newspaper industry have too much say in the appointments to the self-regulatory body and its key committees.[79] Despite the criticism, an external review of IPSO found no evidence that the appointments process has led to any undue influence on the regulator.[80] There is always the potential for suspicion about regulator appointments, given the difficulties in detecting the presence of bias resulting from an appointment (by either government or industry). It is therefore important for a regulator to have a transparent appointments procedure in place that inspires confidence and minimises the risks.

A body making the appointments to a regulator will not have a free hand and will be constrained by the criteria for its decisions. Those criteria should reflect the functions of the regulatory body and play a central role in defining the nature of the regulatory system. A contrast can be drawn between regulatory bodies that are composed of technical experts and those that are representative of the relevant groups (including members of the industry and the public).[81] Both models offer different types of legitimacy for a regulator. In practice, a regulator will want to have an element of

---

[79] The views of the Regulatory Funding Company, a body composed of people from the newspaper industry, must be taken into account when appointing industry members to the IPSO Board and the Complaints Committee. IPSO Articles of Association, 22.5 and 27.4.

[80] See J Pilling, *The External IPSO Review* (2016).

[81] See Prosser (n 7) 5–6.

both, but the appropriateness of either model will depend on the particular task being undertaken. Given its broad remit and policy-related function, Ofcom is composed of many experts in the field of communications. Such a staff is necessary for Ofcom to perform technically complex functions, to apply standards consistently and act in a principled and transparent manner.[82] While there are strong arguments for an expert staff, one criticism of this model is that it attempts to 'depoliticise' important policy issues into matters of technical competence.[83] There is force in the criticism, as the policy questions addressed by Ofcom such as media ownership or the future of public service broadcasters raise important political choices that are not simply about technical measurements and the application of complex formulas. However, even if a matter cannot be de-politicised, there are good reasons for keeping the application of certain policy questions, such as media ownership, away from elected politicians, as will be argued later.

Ofcom is not solely an expert regulator and provides some scope for representation too. The Ofcom Content Board, which is responsible for the Broadcasting Code, is composed of representatives from the nations and includes a majority of part-time members.[84] Such questions of broadcasting standards are not matters of technical expertise, but are often questions of value on which people will disagree. The legitimacy of a Content Board will lie in its ability to broadly represent contemporary standards. However, for much of Ofcom's other work, representation from various constituency groups is brought in externally.[85] The views of the industry and public are received through consultation exercises and opinion research, reflecting the role of the regulator as a forum for discussion.

The main newspaper self-regulatory body, IPSO, is very different. As it is primarily concerned with handling complaints under the Code of Practice, there is a much smaller staff than Ofcom. It cannot be compared with Ofcom as a whole and it is more appropriately compared with the Content Board of Ofcom. Given its function in applying the Editors' Code, there is less need for technical expertise about economic analysis or media market trends. The necessary expertise comes from a mixture of people from within and outside the industry. Of the 12 people sitting on IPSO's Board, seven are independent (not currently employed in the industry), while five are from the industry. While the industry presence raises questions of independence, some representation is important so that the people sitting on the regulatory body have knowledge of the regulated field.[86] Such knowledge will be valuable when the regulator has to assess the application of journalistic standards and professional ethics.

In addition to the questions of composition, another key issue for the management and operation of the regulator is its source of funding. If the regulator is funded by the very bodies that it is supposed to regulate, then there are dangers that controlling the purse strings can provide a channel to influence the regulator and prevent it from making decisions that go against the interests of the industry. Similarly, if the funding

---

[82] For discussion of expert regulators see Lunt and Livingstone (n 18) 21.
[83] ibid, 89.
[84] Communications Act 2003, ss 12 and 13.
[85] Prosser (n 7) 174.
[86] Baldwin, Cave and Lodge, *Understanding Regulation* (n 6) 139.

comes from the state, then there is a danger that it can be used to pressure the regulator on issues where the government has a vested interest. The sources of funding do not always follow the divide on self and state regulation. For example, Ofcom is a statutory regulator but is funded through fees and charges on the industry and through government grants. While a regulator needs to be independent of both government and industry, these are the most obvious sources of funds. What is important is to ensure that the funding is structured in a way that limits the opportunity for pressure. For example, the funding should be fixed for a period of time, so that the regulator is not subject to short-term pressures in relation to its decisions. Another safeguard is to have fees fixed by the regulator according to established criteria, or for an independent third party to either set or approve the fee in order to avoid funding decisions becoming a process of bargaining.

The independence of a regulator from the state or industry in its constitution and composition is important, but captures just one dimension of the issue. The public goals of the regulator can be compromised through informal and indirect influences. For example, the ongoing relationship between the regulator and regulated industries can be a factor that leads the regulator to become more sympathetic with the perspective of the industry.[87] The regulator may also lack the information held by the industry, and members of the public may lack the resources and the coordination to put forward a view challenging the industry perspective. Even if the institutional design of a regulator looks sufficiently independent on paper, there can still be significant practical challenges to its independence through such informal pressures.

iv. Sanctions

The final issue of design concerns the power of the regulator to impose sanctions on media bodies. If a regulator is to have a system for adjudicating on complaints, then there will need to be effective sanctions in the event of a finding against a media body. These questions are common to all regulators, and many have a full range of sanctions ranging from an informal reprimand and declaration, to powers to impose fines or recommend a financial remedy.[88] In professions such as law and medicine, gross misconduct can lead to the person being struck off by the regulator and unable to practise.

The wide range of sanctions that are available can be illustrated by Ofcom's enforcement of the Broadcasting Code. At one end of the spectrum, where a breach of the Code is found, the regulator publishes the report of its findings in the Broadcast Bulletin. That sanction relies on the power of publicity and is normally sufficient to provide notice of the breach and to vindicate the complainant. However, in the case of more serious breaches or repeated violations, the regulator has a number of more

---

[87] See discussion in J Kwak, 'Cultural Capital and the Financial Crisis' in D Carpenter and D Moss (eds), *Preventing Regulatory Capture* (Cambridge, Cambridge University Press, 2014).

[88] For example, the Financial Services Ombudsman, while not a regulator, can include a compensatory award in a determination upholding a complaint, see Financial Services and Markets Act 2000, s 404B. The corresponding regulatory body, the Financial Conduct Authority can impose fines, as well as stronger sanctions that prohibit individuals from carrying on certain services, see for example s 66.

formal sanctions at its disposal, such as a direction not to repeat a programme, to broadcast a correction or impose a fine.[89] In the most serious cases the regulator can shorten or revoke the licence of a privately-owned broadcaster.[90] While the more serious sanctions are not frequently invoked, the potential usage gives the regulator considerable credibility.[91]

The available sanctions have been a significant sticking point in relation to newspaper regulation. The primary remedy available to newspaper regulators has been the power to order publication of an adjudication and a correction, which again relies on the power of publicity. While IPSO's terms provide that such a correction must be made with 'due prominence', there is considerable debate about what that requires. Some critics argue that such publicity does not always match the prominence of the original article and may do little to reverse any damage done.[92] The lack of any further formal powers was a longstanding criticism of the old Press Complaints Commission. The criteria for recognition under the Royal Charter requires a self-regulatory body to have the power to impose a fine, which marks a significant change in the system of press regulation. Outside of the Charter system, IPSO can impose financial penalties, but only where the regulator has launched an investigation, which normally requires a higher threshold, such as evidence of serious and systemic breaches.[93] So far, that power has not been used and critics argue that the threshold for using that power is so high that it will be used rarely, if at all.

The powers of the regulator can lead to further demands about the design of the institution and its processes. If a regulator can impose formal and more severe sanctions on a media body, then the demands for procedural fairness will become stronger. Stronger sanctions mean that the regulator will need to have more rigorous processes to allow evidence to be tested and for the conclusions to be challenged. Along these lines, the self-regulatory body IPSO requires a more formal process, including an opportunity for an oral hearing, before a fine is imposed.[94]

The presence of significant sanctions is important in steering conduct and signalling the authority of the regulator. However, the severity of the sanctions awarded and frequency of use is not the primary indicator of the effectiveness of a regulator. Strong penalties do not guarantee an equally strong deterrent effect. If the commercial or professional incentives all reward certain types of unethical behaviour, then sanctions are unlikely to secure compliance with the professional standards. A need to issue the

---

[89] For example, the Discovery Channel was fined £100,000 for showing graphic scenes of a murder in a programme before the watershed, see *Decision by Ofcom: Discovery Communications Europe Limited* (16 July 2014). See *Ofcom Penalty Guidelines* (3 December 2015) for the factors considered when imposing a fine.

[90] In 2010, Ofcom revoked the licence of four adult channels that had broadcast sexual content, some equivalent to R18 certificate material, at pre-watershed times, see Ofcom press release, 'Ofcom revokes four adult channel licences' (26 November 2010). The Iranian broadcaster Press TV had its licence revoked as the domestic licensee did not have editorial control over the channel's content (which was being run in Iran). See www.ofcom.org.uk/__data/assets/pdf_file/0031/67198/press-tv-revocation.pdf (last accessed 26 January 2018), and 'Ofcom pulls plug on Iranian TV channel' *The Guardian* (21 January 2012).

[91] The range fits with Ayres and Braithewaite's pyramid model, see *Responsive Regulation* (n 47) and Feintuck and Varney (n 7) 190.

[92] For example, see Hacked Off, *The Failure of IPSO* (September 2015) 29.

[93] See IPSO, Financial Sanctions Guidance.

[94] IPSO Regulations, cl 67.

strongest penalties and use a 'stick' may show that the regulator is failing to inculcate the professional standards within the industry. Where a provision in a professional code is vague or primarily aspirational, then to impose a strict sanction may be disproportionate and may do little to deter future breaches (in so far as the requirements of the provision are unclear). The publication of an adjudication may be more constructive in relation to such problems, in making clear what the requirements of the code of practice are and providing a steer to the media. A focus on the severity of sanctions may also reflect a 'command and control' account of regulation, but it can neglect other methods. As noted earlier, professional education may have a better return than formal punishment in changing behaviour. Other publicity measures can also play a significant role. Requirements for a newspaper to publish the number of complaints received and those upheld may have a reputational effect that generates an incentive for compliance.[95] Sanctions are important, but have to be considered alongside other factors such as the purpose of the regulation, the broader incentives within the media institution and the professional culture.

F. Broadcast Regulation

i. Public Service and Broadcast Standards

So far, the discussion has shown how the broadcast media and press are subject to different regulatory bodies with different powers and functions. The difference between the two sectors also lies in the substance of the regulations. Some basic provisions mark out the broadcast media as something very different from the press. For example, to hold a broadcast licence, a person must be 'fit and proper'.[96] When applying this provision, Ofcom can look at a company's record of compliance with broadcasting regulations and at the conduct of the person or company more generally. Applying the fit and proper test in 1998, the regulator removed radio licences from Owen Oyston's control after he was convicted of rape.[97] More recently, Ofcom concluded that James Murdoch's conduct in relation to the phone-hacking scandal 'fell short of the standard to be expected' in his role as a non-executive director of Sky, but did not render the company unfit to hold a licence.[98] The test underlines the idea that a broadcast licence is a privilege for which there is some public responsibility. Another distinguishing feature of the broadcast media is that a minister can require licence holders to broadcast

---

[95] IPSO requires its members to submit an annual statement including brief details of the processes used by the newspaper to comply with Editors' Code and also the training of staff. The statement also includes details of complaints determined by the IPSO Complaints Committee and steps taken to comply with an adverse IPSO ruling. See Pilling (n 80) at [122]–[126].

[96] Broadcasting Act 1990, s 3 and Broadcasting Act 1996, s 3.

[97] See Radio Authority News Release, 'Radio Authority Agrees Transfers of Control of Licences Held by Owen Oyston' (9 April 1998).

[98] Ofcom, *Decision under section 3(3) of the Broadcasting Act 1990 and section 3(3) of the Broadcasting Act 1996: Licences held by British Sky Broadcasting Limited* (2012). In 2017, the same regulator conducted a similar investigation, this time in light of 21st Century Fox's proposed purchase of Sky, see Ofcom, *Decision under section 3(3) of the Broadcasting Act 1990 and section 3(3) of the Broadcasting Act 1996: Licences held by British Sky Broadcasting Limited* (2017).

an announcement.[99] The Secretary of State can also give broadcasters a direction to 'not broadcast or otherwise distribute any matter, or class of matter, specified in the direction, whether at a time or times so specified or at any time'.[100] The provision thereby gives the government a broad tool to act as a censor and restrain the content carried on television or radio. The presence of such a power underlines that broadcasters are not simply like a private speaker, but are at times considered a type of public utility.

The minister's power of direction and the 'fit and proper' test are significant in their presence, but are rarely invoked.[101] More central to the operations of the broadcast media are certain 'public service obligations', which apply to the BBC, Channel Four, S4C, ITV and Channel Five. The obligations have the purposes of 'informing our understanding of the world', 'stimulating knowledge and learning', 'reflecting UK cultural identity' and 'representing diversity and alternative viewpoints'.[102] These terms sound like lofty aspirations but to give them a more concrete application, the public service broadcasters are subject to obligations including quotas for independent and original productions,[103] conditions for securing the inclusion of high-quality news programmes[104] and regional programming.[105]

At a time when the media landscape is changing there are a number of debates about the future of public service broadcasting. Some critics argue that rules requiring the production of certain content are no longer necessary, given the vast array of websites and online video that cater to every niche. Another line of criticism is that the state-funded broadcaster spends too much time on mass appeal entertainment, which can be provided by the commercial broadcasters. These lines of argument add up to a view that the commercial media should be de-regulated and left to provide mass appeal content, and that the publicly-funded media should be limited to those types of content that the market cannot support. That view, however, misses the central aim of public service broadcasting to bring together a national audience and ensure that people are made aware of diverse content. That means the public service media needs to produce content that has mass appeal, while at the same time including more specialist content. It is also important to remember that the content carried on other outlets may be influenced by what is pioneered on the public service media. The commercial media entities do not work in isolation and may borrow formats or styles for their content. The public service media has its own distinctive role to play in the media system, but that is not achieved simply by filling a gap left by others.

Aside from the public service requirements, all licensed broadcasters are subject to the Ofcom Code, which has significant differences from the codes applicable to newspapers. For example, the broadcaster is under an obligation not to cause 'undue

---

[99] Broadcasting: An Agreement Between Her Majesty's Secretary of State for Culture, Media and Sport and the British Broadcasting Corporation (Cm 9366, 2016) cl 67; Communications Act 2003, s 336.

[100] ibid.

[101] But see *R v Secretary of State for the Home Department, ex p Brind* [1991] 1 AC 696.

[102] Ofcom, *Public Service in a Connected Society: Ofcom's Third Review of Public Service Broadcasting Review* (December 2014) at 10.

[103] Communications Act 2003, ss 277–278.

[104] ibid, s 279.

[105] ibid, ss 285–289.

offence', while an equivalent provision is not to be found in the code for newspapers. The most striking difference relates to political coverage. Newspapers in the UK are free to promote whatever political view they like and be biased in coverage, subject to certain rules on accuracy. Newspapers frequently engage in political campaigns and advocacy in elections. By contrast, all television and radio licence holders in the UK are required to show 'due impartiality' in the news and coverage of matters of political controversy.[106] This means that the owner or editor cannot use the broadcast media as a political instrument, at least not by engaging in overt advocacy. Paid political advertising on the broadcasting media is also completely prohibited at all times.[107]

There are a number of challenges facing the impartiality rules. First of all, most people would agree that it is difficult for any political coverage to be truly impartial. There will always be biases and assumptions that shape the way events are covered. Selecting stories based on news values will still come down to matters of judgement, namely what we find to be newsworthy.[108] However, this does not mean that the standard should be written off. While impartiality is difficult to attain, there is value in journalists aspiring to be impartial (while acknowledging the limits of the concept), rather than openly pursuing personal preferences. The rules only require impartiality in so far as it is 'due'. That qualification means that broadcasters are not to be subject to unrealistic expectations of perfect balance that are micro-managed by the regulator. In practice, journalists seeking to be impartial will attempt to include a range of views, taking into account the level of support for each viewpoint.[109]

A second line of criticism is that impartiality rules go against the current media trends. People are exposed to a wider range of openly partisan and potentially biased sources from some internet publications and social media. These trends are changing audience expectations, so that more politically 'attached' content is now accepted. If the broadcasters are to compete with such content, then they too may need to take a brash approach to gain attention. However, the rules do not prevent the broadcast of controversial and polemical content, and authored content relating to politics is permitted as long as this is offset by different views in the overall coverage. Instead, the rules seek to prevent the broadcaster's coverage *as a whole* being skewed to advance a particular view, or for the broadcaster itself to editorialise. Within those constraints there is much scope for politically attached commentary.

At a time where there is a cacophony of diverse views being aired with greater force and political attachment, there is a need for some impartial sources to ensure that people have the information necessary to evaluate and make sense of the various views being disseminated. The trends in media content may make impartiality more important than ever. The biggest challenge comes in deciding who should be required to be impartial and, as the following sections will show, it is harder to justify singling out one type of media for special regulation.

---

[106] The Ofcom Broadcasting Code (n 13), section 5.
[107] Communications Act 2003, s 321(2); *Animal Defenders International v UK*, App no 48876/08 (2013) 57 EHRR 21.
[108] T Gibbons, *Regulating the Media*, 2nd edn (London, Sweet and Maxwell, 1998) 103.
[109] Lord Annan (Chairman), *Report of the Committee on the Future of Broadcasting* (Cmnd 6753, 1977) at [17.10].

ii. Video On-demand

Audio-visual content is no longer restricted to those holding a broadcast licence. Content that is identical in style to that found on television can be distributed through the digital media. While that content is not subject to the full broadcast regime, certain regulations are applied to video on-demand services that have a principal purpose of providing TV-like programmes to the public.[110] A video on-demand service that is based within the jurisdiction is required to notify Ofcom before commencing the service. The services are also subject to a number of minimal standards relating to advertising, the protection of children and the prohibition of content inciting hatred.[111] The rules do not apply to user-generated content posted by individuals for 'non-economic' purposes.[112] Ofcom states that the goal of the regulations is to create a level playing field and that it is unfair for digital services to have a competitive advantage over television.[113] This approach treats the existing broadcast regulations as a given and assumes that some regulations must be applied to similar services online. There is much to commend this view, in so far as it avoids sleepwalking into deregulation. However, it does not engage with the broader debate about *why* certain media formats are regulated in a particular way.

The goal of promoting a level playing field means that the regulations only apply to those on-demand programmes that are in competition with television programmes. However, there are difficulties in determining what types of service are sufficiently comparable to television to fall within the regulations. Newspaper websites often contain audio-visual content, which raises the question of whether it should be regulated by the newspaper self-regulator or by Ofcom. When faced with this question in relation to the video section of *The Sun* newspaper's website, Ofcom looked at the website as a whole and its main purpose.[114] Ofcom concluded that it fell outside the regulations as the audio-visual element was ancillary to the main purpose of the website. In another decision, Ofcom found short videos posted by the BBC on YouTube to promote its television programmes were sufficiently different from television in 'form and content' to fall outside the regulations.[115] The test will be challenging when applied to other types of content. Some adult video on-demand services will have little in common with or comparable to mainstream television services.[116] As more content is viewed online, the

---

[110] See Communications Act 2003, Part 4A, s 368A: the criteria for a video-on-demand service is that 'its principal purpose is the provision of programmes the form and content of which are comparable to the form and content of programmes normally included in television programme services'.

[111] ibid.

[112] Ofcom, *Who Needs to Notify* (18 December 2015).

[113] The Audiovisual Media Services Directive, on which the provisions are based, sought to create a level playing field between television and those providing similar content through non-broadcast digital platforms. See Directive 2010/13/EU of the European Parliament and of the Council of 10 March 2010 on the coordination of certain provisions laid down by law, regulation or administrative action in Member States concerning the provision of audiovisual media services [2010] OJ L 95, Recital 10.

[114] Ofcom, *Appeal by News Group Newspapers Ltd Against a Notice of Determination by ATVOD that the Provider of the Service 'Sun Video' has Contravened s 368BA of the Communications Act 2003* (2011).

[115] Ofcom, *Appeal by BBC Worldwide Ltd Against a Notice of Determination of ATVOD that the Provider of the Service 'Top Gear YouTube' has Contravened Sections 368BA and 368D(3)(ZA) of the Communications Act 2003* (2013).

[116] See Ofcom Broadcast and On-Demand Bulletin, *Appeal by Pandora Blake about the service 'Dreams of Spanking'* (6 June 2016).

current test might have a limited shelf-life, as 'television' may stop being a useful point of reference to decide what services to regulate.

In addition to difficulties in identifying television on-demand, there are problems of jurisdiction. The regulations only apply when the person or company with editorial responsibility for the content is within the jurisdiction of the UK.[117] At the time of writing, the regulations do not apply to Netflix, which is based overseas, while Amazon Prime is subject to the regulations, as a UK-based subsidiary has responsibility for the service within the jurisdiction. The absence of Netflix means that one of the biggest rivals to the broadcast media is not subject to the domestic regulations, leaving the potential for gaps in the framework where the regulator in the country of origin does not apply the same standards.[118]

iii. A Mixed System of Regulation

The contrast between broadcast and press regulation should now be clear. The press has jealously guarded the system of self-regulation and declared any form of state input to be a step on the path to censorship. By contrast, the broadcast media has been subject to statutory regulation, including more stringent provisions for public service content and impartiality rules. The question then arises why this distinction is drawn between the two types of media. Why are such radically different approaches generally accepted? If the case for statutory regulation can be made for broadcasters, then why not for the press? If the statutory regulation is a type of censorship, then why allow it for the broadcast media? These questions have long posed a puzzle in media law and the changes in the media landscape make it more challenging.

In his study of broadcasting law, Eric Barendt has explored several possible reasons for the distinction. One explanation is that the difference between the broadcast and print media is historical.[119] Ideas of press freedom developed in an era when government censorship was thought to pose the biggest threat to the newspapers. As explained in Chapter 1, the 'whig' history recounts freedom of press being hard won following the lapse of press licensing in 1694 and further struggles throughout the eighteenth and nineteenth centuries.[120] Whatever the merit of the historical account, it has had a lasting legacy in the way the press thinks about its relationship with the state. By contrast, the broadcast media came of age at a time when state regulation was in the ascendency. Various industries were nationalised and subject to significant regulation. Moreover, broadcasting was initially limited to a state monopoly, so its regulation was akin to that of a public utility. The early days of broadcasting in turn went on to shape audience expectations and helped to explain why similar obligations were imposed on the small number of private broadcasters.[121] The historical

---

[117] Communications Act 2003, s 368A.

[118] Netflix is currently subject to equivalent regulations in Dutch law, which are required by the EU. However, the specific standards applied in other EU countries may differ from those applied in the UK. For more general discussion of the challenges posed by on-demand services to broadcast regulations see Ofcom, *Public Service Broadcasting in the Internet Age, Ofcom's Third Review of Public Service Broadcasting* (July 2015) 29.

[119] E Barendt, *Broadcasting Law* (Oxford, Oxford University Press, 1993) 3–10, discussing the general arguments for the distinction.

[120] For a critical account of the 'whig history' see J Curran and J Seaton, *Power Without Responsibility*, 7th edn (London, Routledge, 2009) Part 1. See also the discussion in Ch 1 of this volume.

[121] Barendt (n 119) 9.

difference provides a convincing *explanation* of the two regulatory regimes, but it does not provide a principled *justification* for its continuation.

Another line of argument is to distinguish broadcast and print media with reference to the technology. The scarcity of space initially available on the broadcast spectrum meant only a limited number of bodies could broadcast. A broadcasting licence was therefore a privilege that was thought to warrant regulation.[122] When commercial broadcasting was introduced into the UK, a single commercial channel was divided into a small number of regional franchises, the award of which was reportedly said by *Scottish Television* founder and newspaper owner Roy Thomson to be a 'licence to print money'. In the early days of public service broadcasting, the underlying idea was that the obligations were in exchange for the allocation of spectrum space. A similar argument ran that the airwaves are a public resource and therefore the state has the right to regulate it to ensure public goals are served.[123]

These factors do not explain why the current model of regulation was adopted. In conditions of scarcity, there are a number of options about how to distribute a resource. For example, the resource could be auctioned off to the highest bidder.[124] As Curran points out, the scarcity argument's reliance on technology masks the underlying ideological factors that influenced the policy.[125] The decision to subject broadcasters to content regulations seems to reflect a view that communicative power secured through a broadcast licence should be distributed in a way that serves democratic goals.[126] While the concern about communicative power remains forceful, the argument that this power is a result of spectrum scarcity is increasingly shaky given the multiple channels on digital broadcasting, satellite and cable. A broadcasting licence, while still limited, is not as scarce as it once was. Now, it is recognised that these benefits have declined in value and a place on the spectrum is not a guarantee of success.[127]

Another argument is that the broadcast media is subject to special regulation due to the distinctive and powerful nature of broadcasting. Sometimes that power is seen to lie in the audio-visual format, which is often said to have greater impact on the audience.[128] The power can also be seen in the broadcasters' ability to 'push' content to the audience in the privacy of their own homes.[129] The argument runs that broadcasters may be subject to regulation, for example on offensiveness (or at least provide warnings) so that people do not encounter unwanted content in the home. Even if that argument was convincing, the distinctive power of the broadcast media in this respect has faded. Newspaper websites send content directly into a person's home, including audio-visual content. Audiences also have more control over what they watch on television and greater potential to filter out unwanted content. The power of the media

---

[122] See Ofcom, *Public Service in a Connected Society* (n 102) 10, on the 'compact'.

[123] *Red Lion Broadcasting Co v FCC* 395 US 367 (1969).

[124] Barendt (n 119) 5.

[125] J Curran, *Media and Power* (London, Routledge, 2002) 197–98.

[126] Though Seaton argues that the state's interest at the time had more to with security concerns, J Seaton, *'Pinkoes and traitors': the BBC and the nation, 1974–1987* (London, Profile Books, 2015) 285–86.

[127] See Ofcom, *Public Service Broadcasting in the Internet Age* (n 118) 25.

[128] Though as Barendt points out, that alone does not explain why it must be singled out for special regulation (n 119) 7.

[129] See *R (on the application of Prolife Alliance) v British Broadcasting Corpn* [2003] UKHL 23, [2004] 1 AC 185 at [20] and [123].

provides a rationale for regulation, explaining why there are rules concerning harmful content, political coverage, privacy and so on. However, the power is no longer distinctive to broadcasters as a result of the format or form in which the content is delivered.

While the dual system of regulation is widely accepted and is expected by the audience, critics see it as a 'solution in search of a problem'.[130] The most convincing case for the dual system is that the two regulatory regimes complement one another and offset each other's weaknesses.[131] The print media is subject to fewer state controls and can provide coverage that is overtly politically attached. However, if the sole output of all media were the polemic and polarised views associated with certain parts of the press, then democratic debate would be poorly served. People might retreat into their 'echo chambers' and merely hear the views that they want to hear. In any event, if all media coverage was polemical and overtly partisan, people may have little basis to assess the various competing views.

The broadcast media is ideally a place where competing views come together.[132] The professional culture developed in the broadcast media is suited to mediating the public conversation, alerting audiences to the key differences of opinion and various issues. The various views expressed in the press can come face-to-face with each other on television and radio before a national audience.[133] While the press is often polarised and opinionated, the broadcasters aim to be impartial and provide a forum to make sense of the debates. This is, of course, an idealised picture, but it is one that shows how the two different regulatory regimes are complementary. Neither is ideal for regulating all types of media, but a combination of each allows for the two to balance one another.

As a rough division, the two regulatory regimes seem to make sense given the historical division.[134] There is, however, no reason for the division between broadcast and print to continue indefinitely. Consequently, there is a question of which digital media entities should in future be subject to public service style regulations that have been applied to broadcasters and which entities should be subject to the less comprehensive newspaper regulations.

One obvious approach is to say that those media entities that are currently regulated offline, such as print newspapers or broadcasters, should be subject to the same regulations in their online content too. Accordingly, the press self-regulatory body, IPSO, can adjudicate on content posted on a newspaper website. There is also a strong case for maintaining and strengthening the role of the existing public service broadcasters online (for example, by securing the prominence of their content in the various guides and platforms).[135]

---

[130] A Cronauer, 'The Fairness Doctrine: A Solution in Search of A Problem' (1994) 47 *Federal Communications Law Journal* 51, commenting on equivalent rules that once regulated US broadcasters.

[131] L Bollinger, 'Freedom of the Press and Public Access: Toward a Theory of Partial Regulation of the Mass Media' 75 *Michigan Law Review* 1 (1976), and Curran, *Media and Power* (n 125) Ch 8.

[132] Curran, *Media and Power* (n 125) 245.

[133] The workings of this model rest on the assumption that the main newspapers include a sufficiently diverse range of viewpoints. Whether that is attained in practice will depend on the particular media market, and emphasises the importance of media plurality.

[134] Barendt (n 119).

[135] Ofcom, *Public Service Broadcasting in the Internet Age* (n 118) 28.

The difficulty with that approach is that it still treats the distinction between broadcast and print as significant in determining how the digital media should be regulated. Having a separate print edition is no longer a defining feature of a newspaper. The *Independent* is recognised as a newspaper, but since 2016 has ceased in its print edition and is only available in digital formats. In 2016, *BBC3* was taken off the broadcast spectrum and is available only online, for example through the iPlayer. The two services are therefore available online only, but one is seen as a newspaper and the other as a broadcaster. More broadly, newspaper websites contain broadcast-like content and broadcaster websites provide written articles. There are good reasons for the current plural system of regulation, but this does not need to be divided according to whether the media body has a print edition or holds a broadcast licence. The regulatory system could be divided up in many different ways in the future, with the digital equivalent of the broadcast media subject to lighter touch regulations and digital newspapers having some public service obligations or being subject to parts of the Ofcom Code.[136]

One way to divide the regulatory system is to apply public services obligations only to those media entities that receive a state subsidy. If this approach is followed, then the BBC will be the main entity subject to public service regulations. However, the approach could be developed whereby the state provides support for forums and content outside of the BBC to serve public goals. For example, in 2004 Ofcom put forward proposals to establish a 'public service publisher' to promote and distribute public service content online that would operate separately from the BBC.[137] An approach that focuses solely on public funding, however, would lead to the deregulation of non-subsidised private sector broadcasters (or the digital equivalent), even where they hold considerable power. To address this, some public service style obligations could apply to private non-subsidised bodies that enjoy a large market share or dominant position (regardless of whether comparable to print or broadcast). The imposition of such regulations could be one of the tools used to regulate media plurality, discussed below.

The appropriate division of regulatory regimes is not an easy task and provokes controversy. However, the question will become more pressing as the media becomes increasingly converged and the number of online media entities with no offline counterpart play in an increasingly important role. Most obviously, there are newer players providing broadcast-style content, such as Netflix and Amazon, that have built a mass audience. While these services initially provided an online library for existing television and film content, the companies have invested in original productions. The most high-profile examples include drama and comedy programmes, but there is also some investment in documentaries. While those services have yet to invest in news, that could change. What is important is that the design of any regulatory system focus on the activity of the company rather than the particular format or platform being used.

The changes discussed above also mean that the system of regulation is not limited to two main regimes of regulation, and other systems are developing in relation to

---

[136] Barendt, *Freedom of Speech*, 2nd end (Oxford, Oxford University Press, 2005) 450.

[137] See Ofcom, *OFCOM Review of Public Service Broadcasting, Phase 3*—Competition for Quality (2005) Ch 5.

newer types of media activity. In particular, there is increasing debate about whether digital intermediaries should be subject to some form of regulation. This is not the same as broadcast regulation, but may entail types of public service obligations, such as rules about the takedown of content, for transparency in their decisions and fair terms of access for speakers. While such a system will be discussed in Chapter 7, for the present purpose the point is that intermediaries are emerging as a third sector for media regulation that is distinct from the regimes traditionally applied to print and broadcast.

G. Summary

It is hard to generalise about media regulations, as there are many things a regulator can do and many ways to organise a regulatory system. The discussion has not attempted to evaluate any particular institution, but has outlined the main considerations to take into account in the design and assessment of regulatory systems. The discussion has also shown that effective regulation need not be a violation of media freedom, but can even enhance that freedom in the right circumstances. The appropriate goals and methods depend on the specific context, and the function ideally performed by the media sector. The previous section argued that no one model of regulation is appropriate for the media as a whole. Instead, the ideal is for a plural system of regulation that allows the best qualities of the media to come out in the aggregate of the mixed system. The mix has traditionally rested on a division between print and broadcast. The big question for the future lies in deciding how that mix of regulatory systems should be applied in the changing media landscape.

III. Media Ownership and Concentration

Regulation is not solely a matter of rules relating to content or the process of newsgathering. Market conditions, the level of media concentration and the ownership model influence the functioning of the media. These factors can be said to 'regulate' the media by generating pressures on and incentives for media professionals. For example, the pressures and priorities in a media market that is concentrated in the hands of a dominant 'press baron' may work differently from a more competitive market. Similarly, for-profit media will have different incentives from the state-owned media. The structural processes that 'regulate' the behaviour of the media can themselves be the object of legal regulation.[138] Formal media regulations can target these

---

[138] See Black, 'Decentring Regulation' (n 52) 114, stating that government can create 'the conditions in which firms, markets, etc. steer themselves, but in the direction that governments want them to go'.

structures and ownership models to channel the various pressures that will be most conducive to the media's democratic functions. Two areas of regulation in this broad sense will be considered in relation to such structural controls: the first is media plurality and concentration; the second is the model of ownership, comparing the corporate, not-for-profit and state-owned models. Regulation that focuses on the structural aspects of the media is often seen to raise fewer media freedom issues, in so far as the regulator does not judge specific media content. However, the discussion will show that this area raises difficult questions of its own.

A. Media Concentration and Plurality

The issue of ownership touches on the central role of media law in constraining communicative power. The earlier chapters have looked at the relationship between media freedom and media power, and the role of laws such as privacy and defamation in addressing the abuse of that power. Regulation of ownership addresses the same broad problems of power, but takes a very different method by targeting the *distribution* of communicative resources. Two types of argument are commonly advanced to justify controls on media concentration.[139] The first is negative, in so far as it focuses on the danger of concentrated media ownership, namely that concentrated power is prone to abuse and that very large media companies may wield too much political power. The second argument can be cast in more positive terms, namely that greater pluralism will promote more diverse content and make media institutions more representative.

Starting with the negative part of the argument to limit media concentration, the basic point is obvious: that limiting the amount of media any person can own will curb the accumulation of communicative power and corresponding political influence. However, an initial question is whether the concern is with the *abuse* of power or the mere *existence* of excessive concentrations of media power. If the focus is on the abuse of media power, then one might argue that various laws—such as defamation, privacy and contempt of court—constrain such abuses and that further controls are not necessary. One response is that if a media company wields considerable communicative power, people may be wary of antagonising that company and less willing to enforce the media laws against it for fear of negative consequences. A very powerful organisation may feel able to breach ethical and legal standards with impunity. That seems plausible in some cases, though there has been no shortage of people willing to bring legal actions against large media companies.

Another argument is that there are some abuses of media power that are not legally prohibited, such as publishing non-defamatory untrue stories. The media laws only constrain the more blatant abuses of media power. The hope may be that any potential abuse of power is best checked by allowing rival media outlets to challenge one another. In a highly-concentrated market, there may be fewer opportunities for

---

[139] Ofcom, *Report to the Secretary of State on the operation of the media ownership rules listed under section 391 of the Communications Act 2003* (2015) 9. This section draws on the discussion in J Rowbottom, *Democracy Distorted* (Cambridge, Cambridge University Press, 2010) 186–89.

abuses and falsities to be checked, given that there are fewer rivals. More broadly, the abuse of power is more likely to cause significant damage if the media body is very powerful. The argument runs that the fragmentation of media ownership can in some circumstances reduce the risk of media power being abused and causing serious harm.

While these points seem convincing, the consequences of concentration on media behaviour cannot be generalised across the board. Companies in a highly competitive media market may feel greater pressure to cut professional corners or engage in sensationalist intrusive reporting in a bid to maintain a large audience. The fragmentation of power alone does not ensure higher ethical standards, as there are many other variables at play that will determine how the media will behave. However, the arguments above provide good reasons to stop any person controlling large sections of the media, even if such limits do not guarantee high standards of conduct.

The central negative argument for curbing media concentration concerns the *existence* of significant concentrations of media power and not simply the abuse of that power. The ideal in a democracy is political equality, in which people have roughly equal opportunities to influence collective decisions. Even if a dominant media body proves to be very responsible, political equality provides a good reason to avoid placing excessive communicative power in the hands of one person or company. For example, if a newspaper seeks to advocate a particular political position, that activity does not break any rules or necessarily deviate from journalistic standards, but can still cause problems for a democracy if it comes to dominate the debate and prevents other views being heard. This argument does not require a completely equal distribution of communicative resources, which would be to destroy the mass media and simply result in a large number of individual speakers.[140] The goal is to keep media concentration within reasonable limits and at a level that is thought to be most consistent with democratic goals. Any levels of media power within those limits should still be subject to the constraints and accountability in media law and regulation.

The positive case for promoting plurality is often expressed as a hope that a diversely owned media is more likely, in the aggregate, to provide distinctive perspectives on events and serve the audience with diverse viewpoints. While the argument has an intuitive appeal, it should not be taken at face value and diverse content does not follow automatically from diverse ownership of outlets. Three reasons illustrate why diverse media ownership may not have such an effect. The first is that even if there are multiple media outlets, diversity may be undermined if they get their stories from similar sources. Competing newspapers get some of their content from the same wire services, and different television stations may contract with the same production companies for content.[141] For example, Channel 4, Channel 5 and ITV contract with ITN for news production. While each media outlet may retain editorial control of such content under the terms of its contract, the external agency or production company still has a role in the selection and interpretation of events being covered. Moreover, if competition among rival outlets promotes cost cutting, then that in turn may lead to a

---

[140] C Edwin Baker, *Media Concentration and Democracy* (Cambridge, Cambridge University Press, 2012) 11.
[141] See Rowbottom, *Democracy Distorted* (n 139) 188; House of Lords Communication Committee, *Media Plurality* (HL 2013–14, 120) at [57]–[63].

reliance on similar external sources to get cheap content. Plurality in the *production* of media content is important in addition to plural outlets and publishers.[142]

A second reason why diverse media ownership may not result in diverse content is that each media company may be subject to the same pressures, whether from advertisers or in chasing similar audiences, to produce content that is largely similar in nature.[143] For example, if two middle-of-the-road newspapers are corporately owned and aim for the same type of audience, then they are likely to be competing for similar advertising revenues. While the content may have differences, there is a chance it will be similar in tone and likely to cover the same types of story—the familiar mixture of political outrage, celebrity gossip and human interest. Again, financial pressures and cost cutting may lead the media to stick to such tried and tested formulas to maintain that audience.

A third reason why a diversely owned media does not automatically produce diverse content relates to personnel. Journalists working on rival papers may share the same professional values, may have trained in similar places and previously worked on the same titles.[144] There is often a flow of staff from one media company to another. In such circumstances, the type of content among the media is unlikely to be radically different. Diversity of content therefore depends on a whole range of factors and not just the number of media entities. However, the avoidance of excessive concentration is normally a necessary step, even if it is not sufficient.

The positive case can be cast in different terms. Baker has argued that a more fragmented media is more likely to be representative of the whole population, so that every significant group in society has an outlet where its views can be expressed in its own terms.[145] Limiting the concentration of the media may be thought to make that outcome more likely, but will not by itself ensure that the media is representative.[146] For the reasons already mentioned, a diversely owned media may simply reflect a professional class or set of commercial interests. Further regulatory measures would be necessary to ensure that each group has its own outlet to represent its view or interests.

When looking at the consequences of media concentration, there is a counterintuitive argument that a larger media entity in a concentrated market can actually perform a better public service. A media body that is not under intense financial pressure may be in a stronger position to invest in more creative content or types of content that do not reap an immediate financial return. The large media body may also be in a better position to stand up to government and hold it to account. Again, this explains why the goal is not the maximum fragmentation of the media. While media law seeks to constrain media power, the democratic functions depend on the media wielding some power.

The discussion has shown the complexity underlying media plurality policies. The fragmentation and diverse ownership of the media alone is not an unqualified good that will produce beneficial consequences. Nor can the presence of significant concentrations of media power be completely eliminated. Media plurality has to be

---

[142] House of Lords Communication Committee, ibid, at [63].
[143] C Edwin Baker, *Media, Markets and Democracy* (Oxford, Oxford University Press, 2002) 178.
[144] ibid, and L Hitchens, *Broadcasting Pluralism and Diversity* (Oxford, Hart, 2006) 135.
[145] See Baker, *Media Concentration and Democracy* (n 140) 11.
[146] Rowbottom, *Democracy Distorted* (n 139) 186–87.

assessed in its context and in conjunction with the other goals of media policy. For example, the policy may look not only at diverse ownership, but also consider whether the media is commercial or not-for-profit, how it is regulated and so on. Media plurality regulation is not a substitute for other measures regulating the content and conduct of the media, but is just one tool in the overall framework of media law. Plurality goals need to be pursued with an awareness of the limits of the strategy.

Having set out the relevant issues related to the goals of ownership controls, the following section will look at the various issues and choices to be made when designing a media plurality policy.

i. Designing Media Ownership and Plurality Policies

There are several choices to be made when designing a policy to regulate levels of media ownership. The first is whether to have a system that is based on *fixed rules* about how much media a person or company can own, or whether the control should be based on the *discretion* of a regulator. One example of a fixed rule limiting media ownership in the UK is the '20/20 rule', in which a newspaper company with a 20 per cent market share cannot buy more than a 20 per cent share in a company holding an ITV licence.[147] Some commentators argue for greater use of fixed rules, calling for a cap on the total market share that can be held by any company.[148] Such rules provide a level of predictability. If a control on ownership depends on an exercise of discretion, then the decision is vulnerable to lobbying by media companies. By contrast, a fixed limit that can be applied automatically once a threshold is reached will limit the opportunities for the media company to influence the application of the rule.[149] However, a bright line rule of this sort focuses on specific metrics without looking at the context or likely effects.[150] If a cap on market share is fixed, then it will block any mergers above the threshold regardless of any beneficial effects, but would not prevent mergers below that threshold, even if it has a negative effect on plurality. The primary approach taken in the UK has been to regulate ownership through a discretionary power, which will be outlined below.

Another question in the design of a media ownership and plurality policy is whether controls should be imposed at a specific stage, such as a merger, or whether there should be a continuing review of media ownership that facilitates intervention at any time. A proposed merger of a media company provides a convenient moment to assess the issues because it marks a turning point where there will be a clear change in ownership that can be compared with the existing levels of plurality. A control at the merger stage also offers advantages in remedy. A merger can be blocked or permitted subject to conditions. By contrast, if a media company is found to have too big a share of the

---

[147] Communications Act 2003, Sch 14.

[148] See discussion in the House of Lords Communications Committee, *Media Plurality* (n 141) at [102]–[122].

[149] Rowbottom, *Democracy Distorted* (n 139) 192. See also J Rowbottom 'Politicians, the Press and Lobbying' (2013) *Journal of Media Law* 253.

[150] House of Lords Communications Committee, *Media Plurality* (n 141) at [146]–[147] on the risks of focusing on a single metric.

market simply because it has grown in size, then the most obvious remedy will be to order divesture or impose 'behavioural controls' on the company. However, as these controls are imposed on assets that the company already holds, the remedy appears more drastic in nature.

At the time of writing, the main control employed in the UK is a discretionary power at the merger stage. If a merger involving a newspaper or broadcaster meets a certain threshold,[151] the Secretary of State has a power to make a 'public interest intervention', in which Ofcom will make an initial investigation into the impact of the merger. Once Ofcom reports on the investigation, the Secretary of State then decides whether to refer the merger to the Competition and Markets Authority for a full assessment of the public interest. If the Competition and Markets Authority concludes that the merger would be contrary to the public interest, then the Secretary of State has the power to impose a remedy, which can include the blocking of the merger or imposing conditions on the takeover. The investigations are focused on the impact of the merger on certain public interest considerations, which include plurality of ownership and the effects on media standards.

The experience in the UK has highlighted some of the problems with discretionary controls and with controls at the merger stage. The discretionary power is particularly controversial as it involves a politician deciding when to trigger the public interest investigation and what action should follow. Even though the minister must follow published guidance in making a decision and is legally required to have regard to the Competition and Markets Authority report when deciding on remedies,[152] the involvement of a politician in the process has been the cause of considerable suspicion. The suspicion can arise where the minister is seen to be sympathetic or hostile to a particular proprietor. When the News Corporation sought to buy a bigger stake in *BSkyB* in 2010, the then Business Secretary, Vince Cable, was caught by journalists making statements that he had 'declared war on Mr Murdoch' and consequently had to transfer his responsibility for any public interest intervention. The decision was then handed to the Culture Secretary, Jeremy Hunt, whose role also provoked controversy after it emerged that the minister's special adviser had been in regular contact with a News Corporation lobbyist.[153] The bid was subsequently dropped in the aftermath of the phone-hacking scandal. When reviewing the episode in his report on media ethics, Leveson LJ stated that the contact with the lobbyist had generated a 'perception of bias'.[154] The decisions made by ministers are not always predictable or aligned with a particular political outlook,[155] but the role of a minister can generate controversy, given the political benefits that can flow from certain distributions of

---

[151] Under s 23 of the Enterprise Act 2002 the power to intervene arises: where the annual turnover of the enterprise being taken over exceeds £70 million; and/or where the merger meets a share of supply threshold. Where these conditions are not met, the Secretary of State can still intervene in 'special merger situations' where one of the companies meets a share of supply threshold for newspapers or broadcasters, s 59.

[152] Enterprise Act 2002, s 55(3) and s 66(7).

[153] See Lunt and Livingstone (n 18) on the controversy, 73–74.

[154] Leveson Report (n 2) 1407.

[155] In 2017, some commentators were surprised by Karen Bradley's decision to refer a proposed merger between Sky and 20th Century Fox to the Competition and Markets Authority on broadcasting standards grounds, as well as plurality grounds, Karen Bradley, HC Deb 12 September 2017, vol 628, col 653.

communicative power and the risk of the discretion being used to secure good relations with a particular media company. Consequently, there have been calls for the decision to be fully handed over to Ofcom, or at the very least to have a strong assumption that the Secretary of State will follow the regulator's advice.[156]

The system also shows the limits of controls at the merger stage. If plurality is examined at the time of a media merger, then the status quo is likely to be taken as a benchmark and the regulator will ask if the plurality of the media will be reduced if the merger takes places. That does not examine how the media system should be ideally working and what steps can be taken to get there. Merger controls provide no solution where a media entity simply grows bigger and gains a larger share of the market. Consequently, the House of Lords Communications Committee has called for a five-year periodic review of media plurality, so that areas of concern can be identified and remedies imposed in some cases.[157]

A further question in designing a plurality policy is what should happen if a regulator finds that media ownership is too concentrated. As has been mentioned, where the control applies at the merger stage, one option is to simply block the merger from going ahead. Where there is a continuous review of plurality, then the remedy can be to require the divestment of media holdings. Both of these remedies are the most extreme responses that simply limits the share of media resources that can be held. In other cases, the response may be to allow the continued ownership of the media holdings or to allow a merger to go ahead, but only subject to certain conditions or behavioural constraints. Such conditions can include safeguards to prevent the owner having too much influence on the content of the title. For example, some mergers have been permitted on the condition that editorial independence is guaranteed and that an independent board of directors oversees editorial appointments.[158]

While such measures look convincing on paper, the history of such undertakings of editorial independence is often less promising and suggests difficulties in terms of enforceability and in preventing proprietorial influence. For example, a requirement for an independent board to approve editorial appointments is unlikely to be effective if the board itself is not sufficiently independent of the proprietor.[159] While the direct dismissal of an editor might be difficult where approval from a board is necessary, the proprietor can sideline the editor in such a way as to make his or her position untenable. More broadly, the former *Times* editor Harold Evans wrote that independent directors are 'outsiders' that are 'incapable of monitoring the daily turmoil of a newspaper'.[160] There are also problems in determining exactly when a breach of the condition has taken place, as opposed to merely undermining the spirit of the

---

[156] Leveson Report (n 2) 1476.

[157] House of Lords Communications Committee, *Media Plurality* (n 141) at [196]–[222].

[158] A famous example is Rupert Murdoch's acquisition of *The Times* and *The Sunday Times*, which was approved without a referral to the competition authorities, subject to conditions including that editorial appointments be approved by an independent board of directors of the newspaper and that the editor would enjoy independence in directing the political commentary of the paper.

[159] In evidence to the House of Lords Communications Committee, Andrew Neil described the Independent Board at *The Times* and *The Sunday Times* as 'a bunch of establishment worthies and Murdoch policemen', House of Lords Communications Committee, *The ownership of the news* (HL 2007–08, 122-II) 344.

[160] H Evans, *My Paper Chase* (London, Little Brown, 2009) 441.

obligation, and what remedy can be imposed if the condition has been flouted. Such safeguards have value and should not be dismissed, but will have limited capacity to hold a determined proprietor in check.

An alternative remedy that could be developed is the imposition of behavioural controls, that are similar to certain public service style obligations, on the largest media organisations. For example, a large media organisation that endorses a particular electoral outcome could be required to carry messages from other candidates or parties. A media body that dominates a particular city could be expected to provide access to certain types of message, such as columns from candidates for the council or mayor in the run-up to an election. A large organisation could also be required to show a certain commitment to and investment in investigative reporting, professional standards and a channel of accountability. Earlier, it was noted that the differences between print and television are becoming less significant and that there are questions about the future targets of public service regulation. An approach that identifies the dominant and most powerful media organisations could provide one strategy for identifying which media should be subject to some public service obligations.[161] However, such a strategy is not currently pursued and it would require a major change in regulatory culture before a company outside of the broadcast sector takes on any such obligations.

ii. Defining Plurality

So far, the choices in designing a framework for regulating plurality and ownership levels have been examined, but not the standards for evaluating a distribution of ownership. One approach to this question is to look at the levels of concentration and the power held by the various media owners. Another approach is to look more broadly at the effects of the distribution of media ownership, which asks whether a change in control will have a detrimental impact on the ideal functions of the media. The current regulations on media mergers have elements of both. The statutory criteria for the public interest test provides that newspaper mergers should be assessed with reference to the impact on the accurate presentation of news, the free expression of opinion in the newspaper and the plurality of views in papers in that market. Consequently, this approach does not directly refer to the number of companies controlling newspapers, but instead looks at the effect of the merger on the content and culture of the newspaper. When the merger involves a broadcaster, then the number of people controlling media enterprises for that audience can be taken into account, along with the owner's commitment to broadcasting standards and the diversity of content. The controls imposed on the merger stage are therefore not exclusively concerned with plurality, but also look at the impact of the merger on standards and diversity.

Under the current media mergers regime, much is left to the regulators and Secretary of State to decide how these standards should be applied, which is largely determined

---

[161] See J Rowbottom, 'Media Freedom and Political Debate in the Digital Era' (2006) 69 *Modern Law Review* 489.

on a case-by-case approach. Given the uncertainties in these standards, Craufurd Smith and Tambini conclude that the vagueness of the current public interest test is 'patently unsatisfactory'.[162] In some cases, the standards may seem intuitive. Most people know a powerful media baron when they see one. However, to justify intervention there will normally need to be some evidence showing either that a merger will have a particular effect on the quality of content, the diversity of views, or the level of plurality. To show that a merger will have a detrimental effect on broadcast standards or the free expression of opinion in the press, the regulator will need to look at the past conduct of the company seeking to make the acquisition. This assumes that a regulator can identify when any proprietorial influence is inappropriate. Where an owner has a track record of bullying staff or there are failures to meet professional standards, such evidence may be found. However, it will be hard for a regulator to detect the subtler effects that a change in ownership can have on content and quality.[163]

Assessing the appropriate levels of media plurality (in terms of the amount of media owned by any person) is also a challenging task. First, there is a need to decide whether to assess plurality within a particular type of media (such as newspapers or broadcasters) or whether to look at the market as a whole across all platforms. Given that some media bodies play to a national audience while performing the distinct function associated with its particular sector, there will be good reasons to assess plurality at both levels in some cases.

Once the market is defined, there is the question of how to measure media plurality. The earlier discussion noted that plurality cannot be determined simply by looking at the number of media entities or controlling companies within the relevant market. Looking solely at the number of owners fails to take into account the differences in communicative power.[164] An alternative approach looks beyond the number of controllers and also considers the reach of the media entity and its share of the relevant market. However, that information also has limits and does not assess the impact of the media on those people that it reaches, which might be a key factor in determining its power. That data does not tell us whether the audience is served by plurality in terms of the various types of ownership model (such the balance between corporate and not-for-profit media organisations), among other contextual factors. If a standard for pluralism is devised using only those factors that are most easily quantifiable (such as source diversity or market share), then the danger is that various other subtle elements that are central to understanding the distribution of media power will be overlooked.[165] Even when the level of ownership can be measured, there is also the difficult question of when the ideal levels of media ownership have been exceeded. There is no point in trying to measure the levels of concentration or plurality if there is no basis for deciding what level is beneficial or harmful to a democracy.

---

[162] R Craufurd Smith and D Tambini, 'Measuring Media Plurality in the United Kingdom: Policy Choices and Regulatory Challenges' (2012) 4 *Journal of Media Law* 35, 49.

[163] Though regulators do take into account the potential for more subtle effects, see Competition and Markets Authority, *Anticipated Acquisition by 21st Century Fox, Inc of Sky Plc: Provisional Findings Report* (23 January 2018).

[164] See discussion in Baker, *Media Concentration and Democracy* (n 140) 82.

[165] K Karppinen, *Rethinking Media Pluralism* (New York, Fordham University Press, 2013) 185.

The temptation is to develop ever more complex standards for measuring pluralism.[166] For example, Ofcom has put forward criteria for assessing plurality that looks at the availability of media sources, the reach of each source, the impact of the source on the audience and contextual factors such as internal governance processes and editorial freedom.[167] The regulator can use such contextual information to assess the effects of the transaction, in terms of the diversity of views available or on the media company's political influence, to determine whether the level of plurality is sufficient.[168] There is much to be said for this sophisticated approach, but the strategy is not without problems. For example, the question of impact raises the difficult issue of measuring the effects of the media on the audience. Ofcom uses consumer survey research to determine the impact of a media source on the audience, asking the respondent about its importance and perceived impartiality. While there may not be a better method to assess impact, there are doubts about the accuracy of surveys and the reliability of the answers provided by respondents.[169] Moreover, a high impact on the audience is not always a reflection of excessive media power. If a media company has impact due to its high-quality output, that may provide an example of the responsible use of media power. However, it will be difficult to identify when impact is due to quality and when it is based on a structural advantage in the marketplace.

A more fundamental problem is the complexity of a multifaceted assessment, which means the formula for assessing plurality is less prescriptive and more open to competing interpretations. For example, decisions have to be made as to the selection of the relevant measurements and the weight assigned to each. As the formula becomes more complex, the decision-maker or regulator has discretion in deciding how to interpret the data. Such a complex approach is therefore not well suited to a system of fixed rules that seeks to maximise certainty.[170] An alternative is to take a mixed approach, in which the more simple (albeit incomplete) measurements such as availability and reach are used to trigger presumptions about plurality, but can be rebutted by evidence from the more complex forms of measurements that show whether the level of concentration is serving the audience's needs.[171] Such an approach would combine the benefits of fixed rules with the flexibility (and the shortcomings) of discretion.[172]

Approaching the issue from a different angle, Kari Karppinen warns that to rely on empirical data to determine levels of pluralism is to treat the matter as one of technical expertise, which masks the underlying questions of political judgement. The measurements for assessing pluralism and the weight assigned to each factor entail a value judgement. For example, those who argue that the number of sources or outlets is the most important element in plurality will tend to have greater faith in the workings of the market, on the basis that as long as people have choice among outlets, then the concerns about media concentration are addressed. Those who are concerned with media power will tend to argue for more sophisticated measurements of plurality that

---

[166] A 2009 study designed an inventory of 166 indicators to assess risks to media pluralism, see discussion in Centre for Media Pluralism and Media Freedom, *Monitoring Media Pluralism in Europe* (2014).

[167] Ofcom, *Measurement framework for media plurality* (November 2015).

[168] See *Anticipated Acquisition by 21st Century Fox, Inc of Sky Plc* (n 163).

[169] Craufurd Smith and Tambini (n 162) 50–51.

[170] ibid, 55–56.

[171] ibid 56.

[172] ibid 63.

attempt to assess the impact on the audience. The danger with the empirical approach to media plurality is that it renders the underlying political choices less transparent. Masking these issues in technical language and the veneer of scientific precision can shield the decision-maker from public debate and accountability.[173]

The discussion has shown a dilemma in tackling media plurality. On the one hand, there is a concern about the use of discretion on a politically-charged question of how communicative power should be distributed. Regulatory decisions on the distribution of the media cannot be taken on gut instinct alone. However, there are many problems with relying solely on empirical data to assess plurality, not least because such an approach may avoid important questions of value judgement. A balance needs to be struck between the two, which recognises the importance of empirical data, in so far as it provides a way of structuring discretion and tries to limit the scope for guesswork. However, it is important to be aware of the limits of such data and understand that empirical indicators are often devised and used in the service of political goals, rather than substituting politics.

B. Ownership Models

The level of concentration is just one element of media plurality. Another important issue is the model of ownership, which refers to the financing and institutional organisation of the media. The model of ownership generates various pressures that 'regulate' the media. For example, the sources that finance content production and its distribution, and the channels of internal accountability impose some discipline on the media body and can influence its output. The point should not be underestimated, as the internal culture of a media body may have a much bigger impact on what gets published than the laws controlling media content. For example, the investigative reporting output of a newspaper or broadcaster will often depend on the priorities for resources and whether the media entity is willing to support its staff in taking risks. What follows is an overview of the main ownership models and the types of pressure that they typically generate. This relies on a number of generalisations, to which there are no doubt exceptions, but provides an account of the key issues and areas of risk.

The first type of ownership is the classic model of the dominant proprietor.[174] This model refers back to the 'golden age' of the press barons, such as Lord Northcliffe and Lord Beaverbrook. Under this model, the company is owned by a dominant figure who will have considerable say in the direction of coverage. In some cases, the proprietor may be willing to finance the newspaper out of his own personal wealth and provide a type of subsidy for favoured types of reporting. Elements of this model can be seen today with Rupert Murdoch and the Barclay Brothers. Along these lines, Rupert Murdoch has been described as the editor-in-chief of *The Sun*.[175] More recent examples show how media ownership can become the pet project of a person who has acquired extreme wealth in other walks of life. Amazon's founder Jeff Bezos bought

---

[173] Karppinen (n 165) Ch 7.
[174] See J Turnstall, *Newspaper Power* (Oxford, Oxford University Press, 1996) Ch 5.
[175] See evidence given by Andrew Neil to the House of Lords Communications Committee (n 159) 339.

the *Washington Post* in 2013 and the wealthy Russian Evgeny Lebedev bought the *Independent* in 2010 and the *Evening Standard* in 2009. It is possibly the most worrying funding model in democratic terms, in so far as the media can become the political instrument of a very wealthy person or family.

It is important to understand the way that proprietorial power operates and avoid crude accounts of the control exercised by an owner. A media company is a complex institution with many individuals—and a few fragile egos—collaborating on its products. The media owner or controller is not the single author of the content produced by the newspaper or broadcaster. The scale of the enterprise means the media owner cannot know of every story or article being reported. The influence of the media owner is also constrained by the professional culture. Journalists that are committed to certain professional practices will exercise expert judgement in deciding what is newsworthy and what angle to promote, instead of taking instruction from on high.[176] However, the potential for influence depends on the style of management and arrangements within an institution. A strong proprietor will make senior appointments that are largely sympathetic to his own agenda and will reward those that are loyal. The views and interests of the proprietor may also be widely known on a few key issues, so that staff know which stories to pursue and which lines to take without any instruction from a proprietor. It is, however, difficult to generalise about owners. In some cases, the proprietor may take an arm's length stance in relation to editorial decisions. Defenders of this model argue that the proprietor is at least committed to investing in journalism. However, even the wealthiest of patrons is unlikely to unconditionally bankroll a media institution that makes a perpetual loss without making some intervention in the organisation.

A second funding model is corporate ownership. The modern day media barons mentioned above normally work within a system of corporate ownership, but the proprietor has effective control over the shares or over the company. In the case of a shareholder-owned company, then the main goal will be to return a profit to shareholders. In some cases, this model will also have a dominant chief executive or editor that holds considerable personal influence over the newspaper.[177] This model will generate a pressure for the media to attract the most profitable audiences and advertisers. The key interests of the company (for example its other investments) may be sufficiently internalised among its staff to influence content without direction. Some safeguards can be imposed to prevent this pressure directly impacting on specific journalistic decisions. In particular, many institutions will create a separation between commercial and editorial departments. However, whether such an institutional separation is effective is another question. Political journalist Peter Oborne resigned from *The Daily Telegraph* in 2015, claiming that the newspaper had not published an investigation into HSBC in order to protect the newspaper's commercial interests.[178] Whatever institutional separation is in place, an editor may feel reluctant to produce

---

[176] See Competition Commission, *Acquisition of BSkyB Group Plc of 17.9% of the Shares in ITV Plc* (December 2007) at [5.65]–[5.70].

[177] Turnstall (n 174).

[178] P Oborne, 'Why I have resigned from the Daily Telegraph' opendemocacy.net (17 February 2015) www.opendemocracy.net/ourkingdom/peter-oborne/why-i-have-resigned-from-telegraph (last accessed 26 January 2018). For the newspaper's response see 'The Daily Telegraph's promise to our readers' *The Daily Telegraph* (20 February 2015).

content that will alienate a leading advertiser or undermine the interests of a company under common ownership.

Even where specific journalistic decisions are not influenced by direct advertiser pressure, those working in the commercial media need to make general editorial choices that keep the entity profitable. In deciding how to use its resources, there may be little incentive to produce those types of investigative journalism that are expensive, but which are likely to attract a small audience at best. The market may make the media responsive to consumers, but that does not always serve the needs of citizens in a democracy.

The shareholder company, driven by profit, is not the only model of corporate ownership. Some media organisations may be owned by a company that is committed to journalistic goals over and above any commercial goals. Along these lines, the Scott Trust is a company that owns the Guardian Media Group and is committed to upholding the financial and editorial independence of *The Guardian* newspaper. The Scott Trust is responsible for appointing the editor-in-chief and does not distribute dividends to its shareholders. The goal of the arrangement is to make the commercial activities of the company serve the needs of its journalism, rather than vice versa. Despite this institutional arrangement, there will still be strong incentives to maintain a profit, and the journalism cannot be oblivious to the market pressures. Even where the company prioritises journalistic goals, it will still need to attract audiences, advertisers and sponsors.

There is a significant not-for-profit media sector in the UK that is not subject to such market pressures. For example, the Bureau of Investigative Journalism was established in 2010 and has produced a number of significant news stories that have been reported in the mainstream media. The organisation is funded through donations and philanthropic support. However, fundraising itself can generate pressures to produce the types of story that are likely to attract financial backers. For example, a media body that depends on a wealthy philanthropist may find itself under external pressures in relation to its agenda and coverage. More broadly, relying on a wealthy patron to bankroll journalism is hardly consistent with ideals of democratic equality. The criticism runs that by supporting non-profit media, the wealthy person can help to determine which types of media entity, which styles of journalism and forms of media activity will be rewarded. This is not the case for all non-profit media, as some receive small donations or grants from foundations. However, the model leaves open the potential for the wealthy to influence the political system via the media. Moreover, there is no guarantee that a wealthy patron will direct money to the journalistic activities where it is most needed.

There have been suggestions that the non-profit sector could be supported if journalism is treated as a charitable goal. Charitable status would provide a limited form of subsidy to certain media organisations, largely in the form of tax breaks, on the condition that public goals are pursued. The discussion above provides one reason for caution, in so far as indirect state support could, in some cases, work to amplify the political influence of wealthy patrons that choose to donate to certain media charities. The amplification arises because the value of the private donation would be increased by the available tax breaks. While that is true for all charities, the point is more sensitive in the case of the media, where some of the activities are aiming to influence public opinion.

There is also a question of whether charitable status is the most appropriate way to support the not-for-profit sector. To qualify as a charity, an organisation must be established to pursue certain purposes for the public benefit.[179] The charitable purposes listed in the Charities Act 2011 do not include journalism. Despite this, there are a small number of media organisations that have registered as charities serving one of the current charitable purposes. For example, Full Fact is an independent organisation committed to fact checking and is registered as a charity serving the purpose of education.[180] While there is scope for some media organisations to register along such lines, many will struggle to show that charitable purposes are being pursued.[181] A further difficulty is that a charitable organisation cannot exist to pursue political goals and can only engage in political activities that are incidental to its charitable goals. There are good reasons for this rule, as the charities are given benefits to serve goals that have been identified in legislation, rather than to campaign to influence what goals should be adopted by Parliament.[182] Accordingly, the charity exists to pursue those goals that are agreed to be worthwhile and of public benefit, while political debate addresses the prior question of deciding what goals are worthy and deserve state support. Granting charitable status to media organisations that engage in political advocacy could risk confusing these two matters.

The restriction on political activities, while in place for good reason, is in tension with some elements of media activity.[183] The media will often want to speak out on certain political issues or campaign for policy changes. A serious investigative report or watchdog journalism will often relate to a matter of political controversy. The experience with think tanks in the UK shows the difficulty in determining when a charity established for educational purposes crosses the line into political advocacy.[184]

Instead of accommodating the media in charity law, there may be merit in developing a special tax status for not-for-profit media organisations. Such a measure would have to come with safeguards to prevent the abuse of resources. For example, the not-for-profit media body could be subject to certain impartiality type rules (which is not the same as limiting political activity to where it is incidental to other purposes). At the very least, to obtain tax benefits a not-for-profit media entity may be expected to guarantee certain professional standards and accountability mechanisms. As with state support more generally, the issue is how such requirements can be developed to prevent the misuse of the tax benefits, while maintaining sufficient independence from the state. The approach is not without problems, but offers a possible alternative to reliance on charities law to provide indirect state support.

[179] Charities Act 2011, ss 1–3.
[180] Charity Commission of England and Wales: *Full Fact Application for Registration Decision of the Commission* (17 September 2014).
[181] See discussion in R Picard, V Belair-Gagnon and S Ranchordas, 'The impact of charity and tax law/regulation on not-for-profit news organizations' (Reuters Institute for the Study of Journalism and the Yale Law School Information Society Project, 2016).
[182] *National Anti-Vivisection Society v IRC* [1948] AC 31. For discussion see *Hanchett-Stamford v A-G* [2008] EWHC 330 (Ch) at [15]–[17]; *McGovern v A-G* [1982] Ch 321, 331.
[183] See discussion in the House of Lords Communications Committee, *The Future of Investigative Journalism* (HL 2010–12, 25) at [190]–[202].
[184] See Public Administration Select Committee, *The Role of the Charity Commission and 'Public Benefit': Post-legislative scrutiny of the Charities Act 2006* (HC 2013–14, 2013) [146]–[156].

The final model for media financing and organisation is public ownership. The state-owned media may be shielded from the pressures of the market and wealthy patrons, but has the potential to be influenced by government unless safeguards are in place. Throughout Europe, during the twentieth century there was a tradition for broadcasters to be publicly owned. In some countries, the publicly-owned broadcasters had relatively little independence from the government and were seen to function as the mouthpiece of the state.[185] In the UK, the dominant publicly-owned media organisation, the BBC, is a broadcaster that pursues certain public service goals, as opposed to a 'state broadcaster' that acts as the government's messenger. The distance from government is underlined by the fact it is governed by the BBC Board, and its Executive Committee (chaired by the Director General) is responsible for managing its operations. Under that structure, the BBC is not run directly by government or by people appointed to represent the government. As a public body, the BBC is subject to a number of additional channels of regulation. For example, it is subject to a 'public value' test in relation to new services and is subject to a level of transparency.[186]

The BBC's relationship with government has often been tense, whether over content critical of government or over its management and funding. The presence of tension and mutual accountability is important in any system of checks and balances. What is crucial is to ensure than neither institution has dominance over the other. The risk for the BBC lies in the existence of several channels for government to apply pressure. In particular, the BBC is established by Royal Charter, is publicly financed and government makes some key appointments.

The BBC's Charter determines the terms on which the broadcaster operates and is renewed periodically, with the current Charter in place for 11 years. Given the high stakes involved when negotiating a new Charter with government, the process of renewal can be a period of considerable strain for the BBC. If the broadcaster gives the government a difficult time or undermines the government's strategic goals in its coverage, then the government may look on the BBC's demands less favourably during the process. For example, the criticism of the government's case for the war in Iraq that led to the Hutton Report provided an awkward background for the Charter renewal negotiations for 2006. In 2016, the renewal took place against the background of the BBC's handling of the Jimmy Savile scandal and broader questions about whether the BBC's role should be to produce mainstream content that competes with the commercial channels. The pressure related to the Charter negotiations by no means reduces the BBC to a mouthpiece of government, but the broadcaster has to consider possible repercussions before taking any action that might antagonise the government.

The financing of the publicly-owned media can also provide a source of pressure. In the case of the BBC, the pressure is to some degree limited by the licence fee, which means the broadcaster does not have to make a case for its funding out of general tax revenues and compete with other areas of government activity. Moreover, the level of

---

[185] For example, in France the De Gaulle ministry used its control over television to give 'vastly disproportionate' airtime to government politicians while excluding or distorting opposing views. See R Kuhn, *The Media in France* (London, Routledge, 1995) 109. See also Hallin and Mancini (n 64) 30 on the 'government model' of ownership.

[186] For example, in July 2017, the BBC published salary details of its 'stars' who earn more than £150,000.

the licence fee is settled every five years to provide some stability.[187] At various times in its history, there have been suggestions in government to change the funding arrangement and abolish the licence.[188] Sometimes the proposal has been to finance the BBC out of general government funds, while at other times calls have been made to finance the broadcaster through commercial activities.[189] While such demands have not been made by recent governments, there are more indirect ways for the current financing arrangements to be challenged. A recurring debate concerns the 'top-slicing' of the licence fee so that the money is shared with other media organisations.[190] Whatever the merits of the proposal, it carries the threat of reducing the BBC's resources.

Finally, the government appoints the Chairman of the BBC Board and four of the non-executive members (representing the regions). On some occasions, there have been suggestions of politically-motivated appointments by the government.[191] In particular, Marmaduke Hussey was regarded as a well-connected Conservative when appointed Chairman of the BBC in 1986. Surprisingly, Mrs Thatcher is reported to have consulted Rupert Murdoch on the suitability of Mr Hussey's appointment.[192] More generally, the appointments may be seen to go to insiders and establishment figures that enjoy good relations with the government. Gavin Davies was seen to be well connected with 'New Labour' when appointed as Chairman in 2001. Before her appointment as Chair of the BBC Trust by the Cameron government in 2014, Rona Fairhead had served as a member of Cabinet Office board. After leaving the BBC she was appointed as a government minister by Theresa May in 2017. The power of appointment is a possible route for government to steer the direction of the BBC, or at least generate a perception of influence. However, there are some safeguards. For example, the Chair of the BBC must be subject to a parliamentary hearing prior to his or her appointment.[193] More generally, the structure and separation of power within the BBC, along with the size of the organisation, provides some limit on the scope for a single appointment to influence the broadcaster.

The BBC provides only one model for the state-owned media. Channel Four provides a very different model, as a state-owned company established by statute. The non-executive members of the Board of Channel Four are appointed by Ofcom, but in agreement with the Secretary of State for Digital, Culture, Media and Sport. The statutory goals for Channel Four include 'innovation, experiment and creativity in the form and content of programmes', appealing 'to the tastes and interests of a culturally diverse society' and to exhibit 'a distinctive character'.[194] Channel Four is commercially funded, rather than financed through taxation or a licence fee, and will

---

[187] The BBC Charter (n 3) cl 43.

[188] See Seaton, '*Pinkoes and traitors*' (n 126) 29, 44 and 48.

[189] The Peacock Committee was asked to look into alternatives for funding, but rejected proposals for commercial funding to replace the licence fee, A Peacock, *Report of the Committee on Financing the BBC* (Cmnd 9824, 1986) Ch 9. See Seaton, '*Pinkoes and traitors*' (n 126) 317–19.

[190] See discussion in T Gibbons and P Humphreys, *Audiovisual Regulation under Pressure* (Abingdon, Routledge, 2012) 93.

[191] Feintuck and Varney (n 7) 176.

[192] Seaton, '*Pinkoes and traitors*' (n 126) 320.

[193] BBC Charter (n 3), cl 22(5).

[194] Communications Act 2003, s 265.

therefore be subject to some commercial pressures. However, the company is not simply aiming to maximise its return to shareholders. Instead, it finances its own activities and uses its profits to pursue its statutory remit.

The BBC and Channel Four provide the main examples of publicly owned media in the UK, but there are other examples. Some local authorities produce their own newspaper-like publications to inform citizens about their activities. Such publications have been referred to by critics as 'town hall Pravdas' on the grounds that the local authority has editorial control and uses public resources to promote its political position. In recent years, the central government has sought to limit the use of local authority funds for such communications, and has statutory powers to direct local government bodies to comply with a code of practice on publicity.[195] However, some local authorities defend the regular newsletters as a way to communicate with citizens, and argue that the central government's clamp down amounts to a top-down attempt to censor opposing views. The controversy highlights the challenges in distinguishing legitimate government publicity from self-serving propaganda, as well as the problems in allowing the central government to draw the line between the two.

More broadly, state support for the media need not come solely through ownership. In some systems, the privately-owned media receives public subsidies to help maintain content that the market does not support. Such a system has been implemented in Scandinavia, though no direct equivalent is to be found for newspapers in the UK. However, a form of subsidy for local news is now provided by the BBC, in which the broadcaster spends up to £8 million per year on certain news resources to be shared with local providers and to pay for 'local democracy reporters' to work in the offices of local titles and scrutinise local government.[196] Other types of state subsidy may be provided in the form of government-backed grants to certain content producers, for example to finance artistic projects. Public subsidies to media organisations enable content to be produced free from certain market pressures, but at the same time it is important to ensure that the media receiving any funds remains independent of the state. The risks posed through state funds will depend on the type of subsidy, how it is awarded and any conditions attached to the funds.

The discussion has shown that each model of media funding and organisation comes with its own set of pressures and shortcomings. None is perfect. However, the ideal is to have a system in which there is a mixture of ownership models.[197] While there are benefits in having some state-supported media entities, a state monopoly in any sector would violate Article 10 of the ECHR.[198] In a system with mixed ownership models (as with the mixed system of regulation discussed earlier), the strengths of one sector will offset the weaknesses of another. Consequently, when looking at media plurality, it is important to think not only in terms of diverse ownership, but also diverse ownership models.

---

[195] Local Government Act 1986, ss 4A–4B (inserted by the Local Audit and Accountability Act 2014, s 39).
[196] The 'Local News Partnership' was set up following the agreement of the 2016 BBC Charter.
[197] See Curran, *Media and Power* (n 125) 239–47.
[198] *Informationsverein Lentia v Austria*, App no 13914/88 (1994) 17 EHRR 93.

IV. Conclusion

The debate about press regulation has been marked by politics between the industry and interest groups. Some sections of the newspaper industry seem to fight to keep self-regulation to the bare minimum necessary to stave off demands for stricter regulations. Critics of the press often give the impression that self-regulation outside of the Charter scheme can do little right. However, it is important to maintain some level of realism about what regulation can achieve and also the risks it poses. This chapter has sought to outline various features of regulatory systems and the key fault lines in debates, which can be used to evaluate the various forms of media regulation.

The discussion has shown that while media regulation overlaps with many of the issues discussed in previous chapters—such as privacy and newsgathering—the techniques used are different from the legal controls. Some media regulators rely primarily on correction and declaratory rulings, rather than awarding compensation. Media regulation goes beyond legal rights and serves a broader range of goals. The regulatory codes aim to promote professional standards through provisions on accuracy and discriminatory reporting. The system of regulation ideally plays a function in providing a space for the media to explain its actions and for the public to engage in a conversation about what the media is expected to do.

There are a number of regulatory strategies that can be employed and the appropriateness of each will depend on the goal being pursued. However, each strategy comes with its own set of problems. The traditional content regulations raise difficult questions about what those content standards should be, who should set them, and how compliance is monitored and enforced. The debate in the UK has often focused on state versus self-regulation. While that raises important issues, some problems are common to both. They both apply controls on the media after the event, relying on some channel of monitoring. The regulation also faces an uphill struggle in using a 'stick' to constrain the types of conduct that may be incentivised by certain market pressures. These standards-based methods of regulation are necessary, but are always going to have limited effectiveness. Moreover, there are risks that regulation will reinforce the position of the dominant players in the market and also for regulators to have sympathies with those being regulated. Given these limits, media bodies arguably have less to fear from regulation and those calling for stronger regulation will likely be disappointed by the results.

The rationale for regulation mirrors the justification for media freedom. Both refer to concerns about the abuse of media power and the need for media institutions to remain autonomous. For this reason, systems of regulation can be compatible with media freedom, but that does not mean any regulatory system is permissible. Much depends on the specific system of regulation and the context in which it is introduced. The discussion in this chapter looked at the criteria and factors that should be used to evaluate whether regulation is necessary, proportionate and consistent with media freedom. The need for regulation also fits with other parts of media law. In earlier chapters, a number of privileges and protections for the media have been discussed, such as defences to certain actions and the protection of newsgathering. The trade-off for such protection is the need for alternative channels of accountability, which is provided by regulatory bodies.

There is a clear division in the regulations applied to the press and television. The discussion showed how the impartiality rules apply only to broadcasters, while the press is free to be partisan. Both systems have their advantages and disadvantages. The politically-attached press allows for campaigning and partisan journalism, around which various groups or sections of society can mobilise. The impartiality rules mean the broadcast media provides a forum where different views can come together and be subjected to scrutiny. The justification for the dual regime seems to be based on a view of regulatory pluralism, in which the advantages of one offsets the disadvantages of the other and vice versa. There is, however, a question about how this regulatory pluralism will continue into the digital era when media becomes more converged and the differences between print and broadcast become less pronounced. Moreover, media regulation is not just about two sectors. Chapter 7 will discuss large online intermediaries as a type of media organisation that faces demands for regulation.

Media regulation is not simply about the control of content. The regulation of media ownership and plurality aims to limit media power and increase the chances of more voices being heard, by dispersing the control of the media. Just as important as media plurality, is the plurality of different funding and organisation models. The way a media institution is arranged will establish a set of pressures and a process of working that is a type of regulation in itself. The corporate media will be subject to a set of commercial pressures. By contrast, the not-for-profit sector will be subject to pressures to meet fundraising goals and its own objectives. The state-owned media will be subject to its internal pressures, generated by its accountability mechanism, and some longer-term external pressures to the public and government that provides its funds. The point is not to say that one is superior, but rather to say that plurality of ownership models is an important regulatory strategy for creating a diverse media.

In conclusion, there needs to be a plurality of regulatory strategies. There is a role for the more traditional content standards regulations that impose sanctions, but that takes place in a system where there are controls on plurality and for diverse funding models. More broadly, the professional development of journalism, with an emphasis on training and education, may do more to promote ethics than any amount of punitive sanctions. None should be seen as a silver bullet, but each has a role in promoting a media that is professional, accountable and serves the needs of the audience.

7

The Digital Media

I. Introduction

Digital communications have radically transformed the way the media works. Over two decades ago Justice Stevens in the US Supreme Court famously commented that the internet lacks the scarcity associated with broadcasting and allows any person with a connection to become 'a town crier with a voice that resonates farther than it could from any soapbox'.[1] Justice Stevens' comments capture the optimism of the earlier days of digital communications, but he was still speaking at a time when some basic technical skills were required to set up a website. The advent of social media and platforms for user-generated content has made the chance to communicate even easier.

Reflecting these changes, the European Court of Human Rights has stated that

> the Internet has now become one of the principal means by which individuals exercise their right to freedom of expression and information, providing as it does essential tools for participation in activities and discussions concerning political issues and issues of general interest.[2]

A right to internet access has now been recognised under the Article 10 jurisprudence, so an attempt to restrict access or block content will require a higher threshold for justification.[3] The Strasbourg Court has also noted the 'public service value' of the internet and called for policies to end the 'digital divide' (referring to the division between those that have access to the digital media and those that do not).[4] While it is common to hear statements about the empowering and democratising effects of the digital communications, the reality is more complex. As the discussion will show, it is hard to generalise about the internet or digital communications and there is as much variety in the types of speech found in the online world as there is in the offline world.

The impact of digital communications in relation to specific areas of media law has been considered in the earlier chapters. This chapter will consider some of the issues

---

[1] *Reno v ACLU* 521 US 844 (1996), 870.
[2] *Yildirim v Turkey*, App no 3111/10 (18 December 2012) ECHR at [54].
[3] ibid.
[4] *Kalda v Estonia*, App no 17429/10 (2016) 42 BHRC 145. See also Recommendation CM/Rec (2016) 5[1] of the Committee of Ministers to Member States on Internet freedom (13 April 2016).

raised by the digital media at a more general level and will cover three core themes. The first theme concerns the basic problems in applying media law to digital content. The challenges involve fundamental issues of what constitutes a publication for the purposes of media law, whether a publisher can be identified and whether there is anything that can be done where a publisher is outside of the jurisdiction.

The second core theme is to look at the role of user-generated content. Many of the media laws discussed in earlier chapters can attach liability to content posted and shared by users. In this chapter, it will be argued that the way those laws apply to the digital media means that there is potential for the law to regulate the casual conversations that people have online, as opposed to more formally prepared statements. It will be argued that such communications by private individuals should not be subject to the principles of media freedom that were developed for powerful mass media institutions. Instead, Article 10 should be applied in a way that takes into account the context of the communication and accommodates the freedom to engage in casual conversations and make spontaneous (and sometimes regrettable) comments.

The third core theme in this chapter is the role of digital intermediaries. Some intermediaries are the new media elites and gatekeepers that provide platforms for speakers, organise information and facilitate mass communication. The big players have attained a level of power and dominance on an international scale much greater than that enjoyed by the so-called 'big media' in the twentieth century. The question, then, is what relationship these organisations have with media law? Should the intermediary be legally responsible for the content it hosts or facilitates and be subject to the responsibilities that are expected of media organisations? The large technology companies have had much past success in persuading policy makers to treat intermediary services as distinct from the media, and to provide a level of protection from legal liability. While it is true to say that the large intermediaries are not the same as a newspaper or broadcaster, they play an important role in the media system. Just as the previous chapter saw the different regulatory systems for different media sectors, there is a case for recognising certain intermediary functions as occupying their own media sector. Steps are already being taken in this direction with a number of intermediary responsibilities being expected and incentivised. Such responsibilities are an important method of holding the newer powerful institutions to account.

II. Liability for Publications

This section will examine some of the general difficulties in applying well-established media laws to the digital media. Given that liability in many areas of media law attaches to the act of publication, the first basic question is what constitutes a publication on the digital media. In many cases, the answer will be obvious. Uploading content and making it available to the world at large is an act of publication analogous to printing an article or broadcasting a programme. However, some activities do not have a clear analogy in the offline world, such as linking, sharing and liking content. A second difficulty lies in determining *when* publication takes place, given that digital content is continuously available. A third issue is *where* publication takes place when content is available internationally and which laws it should be subject to. Finally, even if these questions can be answered, then another challenge can arise in identifying the publisher, given the potential for anonymity that is often a feature in digital communications.

A. Publications and Links

A broad definition of a publication is applied in many areas of media law, which can potentially impose liability on various links in the chain of distribution. The first challenge is how far the broad definition should reach into the different types of digital communication. One very common form of communication is the provision of hyperlinks to other websites. Hyperlinks can provide a way for writers to direct readers to sources for their content. People on the social media use hyperlinks to share content and direct friends to material worthy of attention. Hyperlinks can help others navigate the mass of content online and enable people to discover material that will be of interest. A key question is whether by linking something, a person should be treated as a publisher and held responsible for the linked content?

The issue was considered by the Canadian Supreme Court in the defamation case *Crookes v Newton* and the different judgments in that decision reflect the contrasting approaches that can be taken.[5] The first approach is to provide special protection for the use of hyperlinks. Along these lines, Abella J ruled that a hyperlink alone 'should never be seen as "publication" of the content to which it refers', as the person providing the link has no control over the content of the webpage.[6] Such an approach treats the link as analogous to a mere reference or footnote, which notes the existence of the content. On Abella J's view, liability should only arise when a person goes beyond the provision of a hyperlink and instead uses the reference 'in a manner that *in itself* conveys defamatory meaning'.[7] That approach provides internet users with a level of certainty when engaged in hyper-linking and prevents the law regulating everyday exchanges between individuals that provide a key way for information to circulate on the internet.[8] However, it could also over-protect those users that deliberately circulate hyperlinks to promote defamatory content and leave the claimant without a remedy.

To guard against abuse, the special protection can be modified so that it does not apply where a person linking content adopts or endorses the statement in the linked location, which was the approach taken by McLachlin J in *Crookes*.[9] That would be

---

[5] *Crookes v Newton* [2011] SCC 47.
[6] ibid. The opinion was limited to hyperlinks and did not decide on other types of automatic link [43].
[7] ibid at [40].
[8] ibid at [36].
[9] McLachlin J in *Crookes* ibid. See also the dissent in *Mouvement raelien suisse v Switzerland*, App no 16354/06 (2013) 56 EHRR 14.

similar to treating the link as a form of reportage, in which the speaker merely informs people about what others are saying, but expects a level of detachment from the linker.[10] However, it could also be open to abuse, as people may link content without endorsing it, but do so with the purpose of knowingly causing harm. The circulation of a link to a defamatory statement or private information is obvious example.

An alternative approach is to avoid a general rule and look at the context of the communication to decide how the hyperlink should be treated.[11] Along these lines, in *Crookes*, Deschamps J thought the traditional common law approach to publication provided sufficient flexibility to deal with digital communications. That approach would allow the courts to look at the extent to which a person assumed responsibility for the linked content in a particular case. While there would be no bright line rule, the lack of any endorsement would still be a significant factor in deciding whether a link amounts to a publication in a defamation case. That approach may cause some uncertainty for online speakers, but it allows the court to look at the context of the statement to determine whether the linker should be held responsible for the content. While the status of hyperlinks in defamation has not been decided in England and Wales, this approach seems the most likely to be taken.[12] Even where a hyperlink does amount to a publication under this approach, it does not mean the linker will be liable. Further protection can be provided by the various defences available and a hyperlink may not reach a threshold of harm that is required to impose liability.[13] In relation to defamation, the reforms of 2013 also provide some protection for people that link to content and are not the 'author, editor or publisher'.[14]

Whether a link should attract liability will also depend on the particular legal claim. As noted, the issue of endorsement of content is relevant in a defamation claim. In the case of privacy law, a link to an intrusive story or photograph may well be seen as a fresh invasion of the individual's rights. The question in such cases does not turn on whether the linker sought to endorse the content, but whether the person knew or ought to have known that the information was private. A person may also be held responsible for linked content for reasons other than legal liability. For example, a public authority may refuse to display a poster on its property or website that includes links to extremist content even where there is no endorsement and the content is lawful.[15] In such a case, the decision of the public authority does not make the person liable for a link, but the presence of the link is relevant to the public body's decision whether to grant access to the display area.

These questions show how our understanding of a publication is evolving with the new technology. Applying the existing law in the digital context is not a simple matter,

---

[10] See discussion in Ch 2.

[11] *Crookes* (n 5) at [59].

[12] N Moreham and M Warby (eds), *Tugendhat and Christie: The Law of Privacy and the Media* (Oxford, Oxford University Press, 2016) 776. See also *Islam Expo Ltd v The Spectator (1828) Ltd* [2010] EWHC 2011 (QB).

[13] See the protection offered under the Defamation Act 2013, s 1. In relation to criminal law, see the Crown Prosecution Service, 'Guidelines on Prosecuting Cases Involving Communications Sent via Social Media' (updated version, 2016), www.cps.gov.uk/legal-guidance/guidelines-prosecuting-cases-involving-communications-sent-social-media (accessed 26 January 2018).

[14] Defamation Act 2013, s 10. See M Collins, *Collins on Defamation* (Oxford, Oxford University Press, 2014) 102–103.

[15] *Mouvement raelien suisse v Switzerland* (n 9).

and there are some activities that do not have a straightforward analogy in the offline world. While there are good reasons for not adopting a rigid rule to protect a form of communication, courts should normally be cautious before attaching liability to a mere reference. Where such forms of communication do amount to a publication, it is important to develop safeguards and defences in the relevant law to prevent a chilling effect on everyday communications and disproportionate applications of the law.

B. When Does Publication Take Place?

Once something is found to constitute a publication, a further question is *when* the act of publication takes place. The date of a publication is significant for certain areas of media law. Private law claims have a limitation period that runs from the date of publication. Statutory contempt of court applies to publications while proceedings are active. While the publication date is relatively straightforward with print formats, there have been some unusual cases. The case of *Duke of Brunswick* concerned a defamatory article published about the claimant in 1830.[16] Seventeen years later, the Duke got one of his agents to buy a copy from the offices of a newspaper and obtain another copy from the British Museum. The provision of a fresh copy to the Duke's agent was deemed to constitute a fresh publication to a third party, re-triggering the limitation period for defamation law. Even without the changes to the law under the Defamation Act 2013 (discussed below), such a claim would still fail nowadays as an abuse of process, especially as the publication was at the request of the claimant.[17] However, the case provided a basic rule that each communication of information gives rise to a new cause of action (known as the multiple publication rule). In relation to the digital media, the rule has been interpreted to mean that every time a webpage is accessed, there is a fresh publication.

A multiple publication rule can raise a number of problems. In particular, the rule can provide a route around the limitation period and a publisher can become liable for content that was initially published long ago, but which remains available on a website. In addition to the uncertainty of such a position, the defendant may also be at a disadvantage in defending a claim where there has been a long lapse of time since the initial publication. After a long period of time, a publisher may no longer have any notes or records relevant to the publication.[18]

The multiple publication rule was abolished for defamation law in 2013 and replaced with a 'single publication rule'. Under that rule, the limitation period runs from the date of the *first* publication. A later publication of the same statement by the same person will trigger a fresh cause of action only if it is 'materially different' from the first publication.[19] While that is more protective of defendants, the new rule

---

[16] *Duke of Brunswick v Harmer* (1849) 14 QB 185.

[17] *Jameel v Dow Jones* [2005] EWCA Civ 75, [2005] QB 946 at [56].

[18] *Times Newspapers Ltd v United Kingdom*, App no 821/03 (2010) 50 EHRR 46. The European Court of Human Rights found that liability in defamation for a later internet publication is not necessarily in breach of Art 10, but could be so if there was a major lapse of time between the first publication and the internet publication.

[19] Defamation Act 2013, s 8(4).

could be harsh on some individuals that are defamed. For example, imagine that a person is defamed on a website, but chooses to turn a blind eye to an article with a small audience in the belief that litigation is more likely to generate adverse publicity. However, if, several years later, a spike in traffic causes the article to have a high readership, the limitation period may prevent the individual from taking action against the initial author. That will depend on whether the publication being viewed online is identical or 'materially different' to the first publication. In answering this question, the court can consider the prominence given to the statement and the extent of any subsequent publication.[20] So if the spike in traffic is a result of the initial publisher giving the statement a more prominent place on the website, then that could be a fresh publication.[21] However, if the content becomes widely viewed through no fault of the initial publisher, the claimant could be left without a remedy.[22] The single publication rule therefore strikes a balance that offers greater protection for publishers.

While a single publication rule now applies in defamation law, the multiple publication rule is still used in some other areas of media law. That approach reflects the different balance struck with other causes of action where the concerns about the multiple publication rule are less pressing. In privacy cases, publication on the internet can be a continuous infringement of privacy rights, and the claimant will normally seek removal of the content rather than damages. The defendant does not need to prove the truth of the statement and will be at less of a disadvantage due to the lapse of time. If the rule is applied to contempt of court, then publishers can become liable for old articles in an online archive that were initially lawful, but are connected to proceedings that have subsequently become active.[23] While that can generate a level of uncertainty, the rule may be less troubling in that area given the presence of other safeguards for publishers, the low risk of prosecution and the importance of fair trial rights. The appropriateness of treating the moment of uploading content or accessing content as the relevant publication date will therefore depend on the particular legal interest at stake and the potential hardship to publishers.

C. International Publications

In addition to questions of *when* publication takes place, there is also the issue of *where* digital content is published. Digital communications may be uploaded and hosted in one country, but available worldwide. Sometimes the process of production can involve multiple jurisdictions, with research and information gathering taking place in one country, the content being uploaded in a second country, and the publication hosted in a third country. While this feature brings many benefits, it raises the question of which law should govern a particular communication. For example, if a person uploads a message in Australia, should the message be subject to the law of England

---

[20] ibid, s 8(5).

[21] See Explanatory Notes to the Defamation Act 2013.

[22] Although an action may be brought against those people that re-publish by sharing the content and thereby make it more prominent. The Defamation Act 2013, s 8(6) also preserves the court's discretion to exclude the limitation period, which could be used to avoid such consequences for the claimant.

[23] See *HM Advocate v Beggs (No 2)* 2002 SLT 139.

and Wales if the content is accessed and read within the territory? If a publisher can be liable in any country where the content is viewed, then that can impose a considerable burden on the media. Such an approach risks reducing content on the internet to the standards of the most restrictive regimes. Conversely, the rules should not be too limited, otherwise the laws could easily be avoided by locating outside of the jurisdiction.

The challenge with international publications is that different countries have different rules and values, and protect different interests. There are some obvious exceptions where a consensus can be found. Most countries have shared standards in prohibiting images of child abuse, and there is considerable cooperation among nations in relation to that problem. However, this will not be the case in most areas. As Alex Mills notes, a central difficulty is that disputes arise between parties that are not part of the same political community.[24] The media laws in any single country, whether in private law, criminal law or regulation, reflect a particular balance between free speech and other interests.[25] For example, some religious countries may still have blasphemy laws, which were abolished in the UK. To explore these risks and the ways these issues are managed, the following sections will look at the approach to international publications in criminal law, private law and media regulation.

i. Criminal Law

Under international law, there are a number of grounds on which a state can assert jurisdiction. While the criminal law will obviously apply to conduct within the relevant territory, it is not necessary for the entirety of the offence to take place in the country. Under the principle named 'objective territoriality', jurisdiction can be asserted where criminal conduct is initiated outside the territory and completed within it.[26] 'Subjective territoriality' can be asserted in the reverse situation, where the offence is initiated within the territory and completed outside.[27] Aside from territoriality, states can assert jurisdiction in relation to criminal conduct taking place entirely overseas by non-nationals, that has an effect within the territory (known as the 'effects doctrine').[28] Jurisdiction can also be asserted over the conduct of British nationals outside of the territory, for example in the extra-territorial provisions of the Official Secrets Act 1989.[29] In most media law cases, it will not be necessary to rely on the broader doctrines as the domestic criminal law can bring much internet activity within the principle of territoriality.[30]

---

[24] A Mills, 'The law applicable to cross-border defamation on social media: whose law governs free speech in 'Facebookistan'?' (2015) 7 *Journal of Media Law* 1.

[25] ibid.

[26] R O'Keefe, *International Criminal Law* (Oxford, Oxford University Press, 2015) 10.

[27] ibid.

[28] O'Keefe, ibid, distinguishes this principle from objective territoriality, 15–16. D Rowland, U Kohl, A Charlesworth, *Information Technology Law*, 5th edn (Abingdon, Routledge, 2017) 29, take the two principles together.

[29] See s 15. There are also very limited powers to criminalise the conduct of non-nationals outside the territory, for example see discussion in Rowland, Kohl and Charlesworth, ibid, 44–45.

[30] O'Keefe (n 26) and Rowland, Kohl and Charlesworth, ibid, 29.

Two approaches can be taken in the criminal law to treat internet publications as taking place within the territory. The first asks whether 'a substantial measure of the activities constituting a crime takes place within the jurisdiction' and, if so, whether the court should not hear the case for reasons of 'international comity'.[31] This approach was followed in *Sheppard*, where the defendant was liable under the Public Order Act 1986 for publishing racially inflammatory material on the internet, including a pamphlet titled 'Tales from the Holohoax', that was hosted on servers in California.[32] The court found the publication to be subject to the domestic criminal law as the material had been produced, uploaded and aimed at people within the territory by two individuals that resided in England. The fact that the publication was hosted on a server overseas did not take the actions outside of jurisdiction, as a substantial measure of the offence took place in England and Wales.

Another approach is to ask whether the criminal act was completed (the last act in the ingredients of the offence) within the territory. In internet publication offences, the last act will normally be the accessing of the material on the viewer's screen. That approach was followed in *Perrin*, in which a French national residing in London published content that was hosted in the USA. No evidence was supplied to suggest that the material had been prepared or uploaded in England and Wales. The Court of Appeal nonetheless found that publication under the Obscene Publications Act 1959 takes place when a webpage is accessed in England and Wales, as publication for the purposes of that statute relates to the transmission of data.[33] The court accepted the prosecutor's argument that there was no need to show 'that the major steps in relation to publication were taken within the jurisdiction of the court'.[34] Any other approach, it was found, would make it easier for people to evade the law by simply taking the major steps to publish outside the jurisdiction.[35] Gillespie comments that the decision in *Perrin* 'undoubtedly widens the territorial application of the criminal law', and argues that it could lead to foreign publishers being arrested when entering the UK.[36] The concern is that the criminal law could in theory regulate those international publishers with a more remote connection with the country.

The approaches taken to territoriality in *Sheppard* and *Perrin* can overlap. If accessibility within England and Wales is sufficient for the purposes of jurisdiction in relation to internet publications, then the court in *Sheppard* could arguably have sidestepped the 'substantial measure' test and found publication to have taken place within jurisdiction once accessed here.[37] Neither case provokes a sense of injustice given that the

---

[31] See *R v Rogers* [2014] EWCA Crim 1680, [2015] 1 WLR 1017; *R v Smith (Wallace Duncan) (No 4)* [2004] EWCA Crim 631, [2004] QB 1418.

[32] *R v Sheppard* [2010] EWCA Crim 65, [2010] 1 WLR 2779. For discussion, see M Dyson, '*R v Sheppard (Simon Guy)*: public order on the internet' (2010) *Archbold Review* 6.

[33] In *R v Waddon* [2000] All ER (D) 502 (CA) the court also found that publication occurs when content is uploaded within the jurisdiction.

[34] *R v Perrin* [2002] EWCA Crim 747 at [51].

[35] ibid.

[36] A Gillespie, *Child Pornography: Law and Policy* (Abingdon, Routledge, 2011) 158. Rowland, Kohl and Charlesworth (n 28) 31 discuss the German case *Toben* (2000), in which a German-born Australian was arrested while on holiday in Germany after publishing anti-Semitic content in Australia.

[37] See D Ormerod, 'R. v Sheppard (Simon Guy): jurisdiction—publishing racially inflammatory material' [2010] *Criminal Law Review* 720, 722.

defendants were based within the territory. It is also notable that in *Sheppard*, the court took into account the various connections with England and Wales to explain why the matter was appropriate for the domestic courts.[38] Such considerations are important to prevent an overly expansive application of the domestic law to foreign publications. In theory, the approaches taken by the court provide flexibility to prevent the evasion of the law through digital publication outside of the territory. However, even if the letter of the law can regulate such cross-border conduct, in practice the reach of the criminal law is curbed by the limits on investigation and enforcement outside of the territory.

ii. *International Publications and Private Law*

In relation to private law claims such as defamation and privacy, the domestic law will normally apply if the publication and the consequent harm occur within the jurisdiction.[39] With internet content, publication occurs where the content is accessed. If the claimant wishes to complain about the publication of an article overseas and consequent damage suffered overseas, then there are more complex questions about which law should govern those publications in a hearing in England and Wales.[40] However, assuming that the domestic law does apply, there is also a question of whether the court has jurisdiction to hear the claim if the publisher is based outside of the territory. In such cases, permission is normally required to serve a claim. In relation to a tort claim, permission can be granted if there is a good arguable case that damage was sustained within the jurisdiction.[41] The court will also consider whether England and Wales is the most appropriate place to hear the claim. Separate rules apply when the defendant is based in an EU country or a party to the Lugano Convention. While EU law has previously allowed claims to be brought in the country where the 'harmful event' took place (such as the place where the content was distributed and where the claimant was known), later case law has been more restrictive on the choice of forum in relation to claims for rectification or an injunction to protect personality rights.[42]

The broad scope for publication to take place within jurisdiction gives rise to a potential problem of forum shopping, in which the claimant can choose where to bring a claim and select the country with the most favourable laws. The point can be illustrated by the decision in *Berezovsky v Forbes*, in which a claimant based in Russia brought a defamation action against an American magazine in the London courts, on account of approximately 2,000 copies sold within the jurisdiction.[43] While the court

---

[38] Rowland, Kohl and Charlesworth (n 28) 38.

[39] See A Collins (ed), *Dicey, Morris and Collins on the Conflict of Laws*, 15th edn (London, Sweet and Maxwell, 2012) at [35-107].

[40] In relation to defamation claims, the claimant has to show that the action would succeed in both the domestic law and the law of the jurisdiction where the tort took place, Private International Law (Miscellaneous Provisions) Act 1995, s 13. For the rules in disputes across EU member states see *eDate Advertising GmbH v X*, (C-509/09) [2012] QB 654.

[41] Civil Procedure Rules 1998, Practice Direction 6B, at [3.1].

[42] 'Recast Brussels Regulation', Regulation (EU) 1215/2012 [2012] OJ L 351, Art 7(2). See *Shevill Presse Alliance SA* (C-68/93) [1995] 2 AC 18 for the traditional rule. For the more recent development, see *Bolagsupplysningen OÜ v Svensk Handel AB* (C-194/16) [2018] EMLR 8.

[43] *Berezovsky v Forbes* [2000] UKHL 25, [2000] 1 WLR 1004. 800,000 copies were sold in the USA.

has discretion not to hear a case if it is not the most appropriate forum,[44] the House of Lords found that it was appropriate to hear the claim in London on account of the claimant's reputation in England and Wales, where some of his family lived and where he was a frequent visitor. In a powerful dissent, Lord Hoffmann warned that 'the English court should not be an international libel tribunal for a dispute between foreigners which had no connection with this country'.[45] The argument provides an important warning. While such a libel claim only compensates for damage occurring within England and Wales, a judicial decision can still have a far-reaching impact. For example, the remedies awarded by the English court could lead to the removal of content from the internet.[46] Moreover, the court's ruling has a declaratory effect in vindicating reputation. Accordingly, a favourable ruling in one jurisdiction can be used to contest and rebut allegations repeated in other jurisdictions. While *Berezovsky* concerned a printed publication, the risk of forum shopping is increased in relation to digital media content that is published across multiple jurisdictions.

In addition to the discretion not to hear the case, a defamation claim can also be struck out if it amounts to an abuse of process, for example where the claimant has suffered a relatively minor injury to reputation within the jurisdiction.[47] The Defamation Act 2013 creates a further safeguard, providing that the court does not have jurisdiction to hear a defamation case against a person domiciled outside the UK, EU or party to the Lugano Convention, unless England and Wales is 'clearly the most appropriate place in which to bring an action in respect of the statement'.[48] While the court previously had a discretion not to hear a claim, the statute creates a stronger presumption that goes to the jurisdiction of the court.[49] While this guards against the danger of forum shopping, the rule might also result in some hardship to claimants with an international reputation and impose a high threshold.[50] Alternative rules are no less problematic. A rule limiting claims to the jurisdiction of the claimant would potentially subject internet publishers to the laws of countries they have little connection with, while limiting claims to the defendant's place of residence would impose too many barriers for a claimant and encourage publishers to locate their activities in the place with the most favourable laws.[51] The difficulty lies in formulating rules that minimise the risk of strategic behaviour by either party.

In theory, the same problem of forum shopping can arise in relation to other causes of action. However, there are practical limits that reduce the risk of the abuse. In many cases, it will be obvious which law should govern the dispute, given the location of the

---

[44] Under the doctrine of forum non conveniens, which applies in cases not governed by the Brussels and Lugano Conventions.

[45] *Berezovsky v Forbes* [2000] UKHL 25, [2000] 1 WLR 1004 at 1025, agreeing with comments of the first instance judge.

[46] Mills (n 24) 18–19.

[47] *Jameel* (n 17).

[48] Defamation Act 2013, s 9(2).

[49] *Huda v Wells* [2017] EWHC 2553 (QB) at [21].

[50] For example, by denying a claim where the person has an equally strong connection with England and a number of other countries where publication takes places, so that England is not clearly the most appropriate place. Mills (n 24) 5. *Ahuja v Politika Novine I Magazini DOO* [2015] EWHC 3380 (QB), [2016] 1 WLR 1414 at [71].

[51] Mills, ibid, 22.

claimant and place of the harm.[52] In some cases, the remedies offered by the domestic court may offer little benefit to the would-be forum shopper. There are fewer incentives for a forum shopper based overseas to strategically seek an injunction restraining a foreign media company from revealing private information, given that damages are traditionally lower in privacy claims and an injunction to restrict publication in England and Wales will not restrain publication overseas. Given these limits, the problems of forum shopping should not be overstated, but it is important to be alert to the risks of the choice of forum being based solely on strategic concerns.

iii. International Media and Domestic Regulation

Finally, problems of jurisdiction arise in relation to media regulation. If media content is widely available within the UK, then there is a question whether a publisher should be subject to the domestic regulatory system. Different rules apply in the various media sectors. In relation to video on-demand, the regulations applied by Ofcom only cover services based within the jurisdiction.[53] That means that popular services such as Netflix that are based overseas are not subject to the domestic regulations, while Amazon Prime is subject to the controls due its delivery via a UK subsidiary.

The Royal Charter scheme for newspaper regulation raises the question of whether an international news website that is widely read within the jurisdiction is a 'relevant publisher' for the purposes of the (partially implemented) incentives to join a regulatory body.[54] That will depend on whether it is reasonable to expect a foreign publication to join the regulator,[55] which will be determined by looking at the scale of activity in the UK, whether the content targets an audience in the UK and the size of that audience. There are also questions about whether content published on a British newspaper website, but prepared overseas and targeted at a foreign audience, should be subject to the domestic regulatory rules. At the time of writing, the newspaper self-regulatory body, IPSO, is considering its approach to such an issue in relation to the Editors' Code.[56]

Even where it is clear that an international publication should be subject to domestic regulations, there are difficult questions about how the standards should be applied. Any body holding a broadcast licence in the UK is subject to the Ofcom Broadcasting Code. Some licences are granted to channels that have parent companies in other countries and show content initially made for a foreign audience. In such circumstances, the UK regulations can be applied with some flexibility to take into account

---

[52] In *Dow Jones v Gutnick* [2002] HCA 56 the High Court of Australia stated in relation to defamation claims that in most cases 'identifying the person about whom material is to be published will readily identify the defamation law to which that person may resort'.

[53] See Ch 6.

[54] Crime and Courts Act 2013, ss 34, 35 and 40.

[55] ibid, providing for the incentives not to be applied where there are good reasons why the publisher did not join the regulator.

[56] For example, in one case a British newspaper website argued that the press self-regulatory body had no jurisdiction to handle a complaint about a story written for its website about a US citizen based on events in the USA, written and edited by journalists in the USA, see *Miscavige v Mail Online*, IPSO ruling (23 June 2016). At the time of writing IPSO is consulting on rules governing its jurisdiction in relation to international publications, IPSO, *IPSO consultation on jurisdiction and global digital publishers* (July 2017).

the programme, channel and audience expectation.[57] A repeat of a US political talk show aimed primarily at an American audience may have greater leeway in relation to impartiality rules than a programme focused on domestic political issues. However, international channels are not exempt from the regulations and the broadcast of programmes made for countries with different audience expectations and values can put the system of content regulation under strain.[58] Those problems are likely to increase if domestic regulations are imposed on digital content that is produced for international consumption.

iv. Enforcement Problems

Even where the claimant establishes a legal wrong in the domestic court against a person based overseas, there can be problems in enforcing a court order. In particular, problems can arise where an order is inconsistent with the principles of other legal systems. In the US, the SPEECH Act of 2010 prevents US courts from enforcing foreign defamation judgments unless the ruling provides as much protection for speech as under the First Amendment. That measure specifically aimed to prevent English libel rulings being enforced in the USA. More broadly, there are practical hurdles in enforcing a judgment overseas, depending on where the speaker is and what international agreements are in place. Even where enforcement is possible, there will be challenges in terms of costs, time and logistics that may put off all but the most well-resourced and determined litigants. This section began by noting the risks of a system generating liability in multiple jurisdictions. However, whatever the theory about the domestic law and international publications, the practical constraints mean the risks for international publishers are not as high as it may initially seem.

D. Anonymity

A further issue relating to digital communications concerns the identity of the publisher. Anonymity is often seen to be an advantage of digital communications in so far as people feel free to speak out in an environment that is to some degree shielded from social consequences. This can be particularly important in facilitating whistleblowing and exposing wrongdoing. This feature can also be seen as a disadvantage, particularly in so far as it allows people to engage in unlawful activities or abuse without repercussions. Anonymity is sometimes blamed for the hostile culture associated with debate on the internet.[59]

There is no right to speak anonymously in the domestic law. Accordingly, a blogger will not normally be able to demand an injunction to prevent his or her identity being disclosed.[60] Nor does the law generally require people to reveal their identities

---

[57] See discussion in Ofcom, *Broadcast Bulletin* 311 (22 August 2016) on the decision on *Fox Extra* (broadcast on *Fox News*), and *Broadcast Bulletin* 341 (17 November 2017) on the decision on *Hannity* (broadcast on *Fox News*).

[58] ibid.

[59] For discussion see E Barendt, *Anonymous Speech* (Oxford, Hart, 2016).

[60] *Author of a Blog v Times Newspapers Ltd* [2009] EWHC 1358 (QB), [2009] EMLR 22.

when publishing on the internet. The permissibility of anonymous speech is something which is left to the digital platform and service provider to decide for itself. Some internet firms have their own internal rules that require the disclosure of a real name, most obviously Facebook.[61] While such policies might help to maintain civility and allow any unlawful conduct to be traced, Barendt notes that the intermediaries also have an economic incentive for such policies as a means of gathering the personal data of real people, for example in providing a targeted advertising service.[62] The policies are also controversial in so far as they might discourage the use of the service to engage in debate and mobilisation in areas where there are significant risks associated with political opposition.[63] The policy does not stop a person from using alternative social media services that do not require the user's real name, but the leading social networks may be an important tool for mobilising large numbers of people.

The difficulty with anonymous speech is the potential for legal rights and interests to be harmed without knowing who to bring an action against. Two strategies to deal with this problem can be contrasted. The first is to require the host to reveal the identity of the anonymous speaker, for example through a court order.[64] The success of that strategy assumes that the host has information that will reveal the identity of the author and that the host cannot rely on the statutory protection of confidential sources.[65] The second strategy is to make the host responsible for the content posted by the user, which will be discussed further in relation to intermediary liability.[66] That strategy can be used where the speaker remains anonymous, while providing a focus for a person's complaint. The strategies can be mixed, so that a host is liable only when it is not possible to locate the initial author.

The Defamation Act 2013 follows a mixed approach and provides a defence under s 5 for operators of websites that host user-generated content. On receiving a complaint about defamatory content, the website operator should contact the person posting the content with the details. If the operator does not know or cannot contact the original poster, then the message must be removed within two working days of receiving the notice.[67] Where the poster can be contacted by the operator and receives notice of the complaint, a response must be provided within five days to indicate whether he or she wishes the content to be removed. If the poster fails to respond or does not provide the information required, then the website operator must remove the content to keep the defence. If the poster does not wish the content to be removed, then he or she should provide a name and address to the website operator, indicating whether he or she agrees for these details to be forwarded to the complainant. If those details are forwarded to the complainant, then the website operator drops out of the picture and the complainant's action should be pursued against the

---

[61] See Barendt, *Anonymous Speech* (n 59).

[62] ibid.

[63] People seeking to engage in such activities can register in breach of the policy under a false name, but will risk having the account closed on discovery.

[64] See *Norwich Pharmacal Co v Customs and Excise Commissioners* [1974] AC 133.

[65] Contempt of Court Act 1981, s 10.

[66] *Delfi AS v Estonia*, App no 64569/09 (2016) 62 EHRR 6 and discussion in Barendt, *Anonymous Speech* (n 59).

[67] The Defamation (Operators of Websites) Regulations 2013, SI 2013/3028.

poster directly.[68] However, if the poster responds, but does not consent to the name and address being shared, then the complainant may need a court order to compel the website operator to disclose that information.

The approach under the Defamation Act 2013 seeks to deal with the issues of anonymous speech by placing primary responsibility on the original poster. The website operator will be liable only where there is a failure to follow the process. Where the poster wants to remain anonymous, the system places the final say at the discretion of the court when deciding whether to order the website operator to disclose the identity under a *Norwich Pharmacal* order.[69] While there is much sense in this framework, there are some criticisms that can be made of the provision. A defamed person may go through the process of getting the poster's details, only to find that it is not worth pursuing legal proceedings, for example where the author has no resources or where the author is based outside of the jurisdiction. Secondly, given the burdens, in terms of sending and receiving valid notices within the required timeframe, the website operator may simply to prefer to remove the content when receiving notice and avoid the process. However, s 5 does at least give website operators greater protection where they do not wish to take things down automatically. The example with defamation law shows the difficult issues in deciding where the costs of free expression should fall while not leaving legal interests unduly unprotected.

E. Taking Stock

This section has examined a number of issues that are often faced in applying laws regulating publication on the digital media. The challenges include defining a publication, deciding when and where it takes place, and identifying the publisher. In addressing many of these issues, the appropriate response cannot be generalised and different approaches will be taken depending on the legal interest at stake. Having explored some of the questions of definition, the following section will show that when applied to the digital media, the scope of the law and types of activity being regulated can fundamentally change.

III. User-generated Content

A. Expanding the Coverage of Media Law

The digital media allows anyone with an internet connection to become a publisher. The communications scholar Manuel Castells describes the digital media as facilitating

---

[68] If the complainant wins a subsequent ruling, then the court can order the operator of a website to remove the statement, Defamation Act 2013, s 13.
[69] *Norwich Pharmacal* (n 64).

a shift from mass media to mass self-communication.[70] While the traditional mass media followed a 'one-to-many' model, the digital media is seen to provide a model of 'many-to-many' communications. In particular, user-generated content and the social media give the average person more opportunities than ever before to publish, republish and share content with their networks and the world at large.

The vast opportunities to publish content on the digital media means that more people than ever are now subject to media laws. In theory, many media laws have always applied to non-media speech and have not been limited to a defined group of media institutions or to mass communications.[71] In practice the laws of defamation, privacy, contempt of court and so on, were unlikely to restrict the flow of everyday conversation. When words were merely spoken, the communication was heard by those in the near vicinity, but was not carried further and may not have been remembered by the listeners. Casual conversations in the offline world were thereby unlikely to be subject to a criminal prosecution or private law claim. As a result, the various media laws, while of general application, were typically concerned with speech that was recorded or had a large audience, of which newspapers and broadcasters were the prime examples.

The position is changing with digital communications, where casual conversations among individuals on some services are recorded, made available to the public (or sections of the public) and open to search.[72] As a result, the content can more easily be brought before potential litigants or prosecutors and the digital footprint provides concrete evidence of what has been said. Consequently, there is greater opportunity for media laws to be enforced against individual speakers.

In addition to this trend, individual speakers are not just subject to media laws, but also a range of other controls that attach to non-media speech. For example, s 4A of the Public Order Act 1986, which was initially enacted to control disturbances in public places, has been applied to digital messages that are threatening, abusive or insulting and intended to cause harassment, alarm or distress.[73] Statutes that were enacted to deal with poison pen letters and nuisance phone calls are now being interpreted to regulate grossly offensive digital messages to the world at large.[74] Similarly, the Protection from Harassment Act 1997 has been applied to the digital media. While there are good reasons to enact broadly worded 'catch all' offences, the scope of such criminal laws can apply to a lot of online content, in theory at least. Controls that were enacted to combat different types of activity and expression in different settings now overlap and can apply to the same content disseminated over the digital media. The users of digital communications now find themselves subject not only to the laws that newspaper editors traditionally worried about, but also to laws relating to public order, to telephone messages and the post.

---

[70] M Castells, *Communication Power* (Oxford, Oxford University Press, 2009).

[71] For example, see *Huth v Huth* [1915] 3 KB 32 in relation to a letter.

[72] Though this depends on the service in question, as some services allow the visibility of the communication to expire.

[73] *S v DPP* [2008] EWHC 438 (Admin), [2008] 1 WLR 2847.

[74] Malicious Communications Act 1988 and the Communications Act 2003, s 127.

The old laws are also being interpreted in new ways that increase the likelihood of the law regulating more informal conversations. The possible liability for linking content discussed earlier provides one example. The Obscene Publications Act 1959 has been interpreted to apply to messages sent between consenting adults on an internet relay chat.[75] In *Kordowski*, Tugendhat J held that posting information on a prominent website will amount to a course of conduct for the purposes of the Protection from Harassment Act 1997, as it was reasonable to infer that alarm and distress would be suffered on at least two occasions.[76] These examples show that it is not simply a matter of 'what is illegal offline is illegal online'. Instead, the existing laws take on a new life and scope when applied to the digital media.

B. Media Freedom, Freedom of Expression and the Digital Media

The fact that many media laws now apply to a vast number of online speakers may at first sight seem unproblematic. On this view, if media law is about protecting certain interests, then those laws should offer protection no matter where the communication comes from. There is an argument that the accessibility, searchability and durability of digital messages can increase the level of harm caused by such communications.[77] A nasty remark about a person made on the spur of the moment may turn up when people search online for that person. There is no case for allowing people to use digital communications without restraint or regard to any consequent harm or injury. However, the responsibilities and liabilities appropriate for user-generated expression may differ from those used to constrain the mass media. Much of media law is about constraining the communicative power of professional institutions and making that power accountable. Such concerns about power will be less pressing in relation to the digital speech of individuals.

To illustrate this point, a distinction can be drawn between speech that is 'low level' and 'high level'.[78] 'Low level' speech refers to the types of expression that are open to anyone with a broadband connection, likely to command a small audience, often spontaneous and that do not generally make a claim to be an authoritative statement. The term 'low level' is not used to say anything about the quality of the speech, instead it can be thought of as speech at the 'street level'. Consequently, there can be 'low level' speech among individuals that is of high quality and value to the audience, as well as speech that is of low value.

At the other end of the spectrum are 'high level' speakers, meaning those speaking on a stage to a large audience, with content that is carefully prepared, checked and packaged. Again, the terminology says nothing about the value of the content. There can be 'high level' speech that is of little value to democratic decision-making, such as

---

[75] *R v GS* [2012] EWCA Crim 398, [2012] 1 WLR 3368.

[76] *Law Society v Kordowski* [2011] EWHC 3185 (QB), [2014] EMLR 2 at [64].

[77] See danah boyd, *It's Complicated* (New Haven, Yale University Press, 2014) 10–14. See *Editorial Board of Pravoye Delo and Shtekel v Ukraine*, App no 33014/05 (2014) 58 EHRR 28 at [63].

[78] J Rowbottom, 'To Rant, Vent and Converse: Protecting Low Level Digital Speech' (2012) 71 *Cambridge Law Journal* 355.

a mass-market magazine that publishes only celebrity gossip. The two levels of speech are not rigid categories and operate on a continuum with much in between.

The rationale for media freedom that was outlined in Chapter 1 is primarily focused on the 'high level' speakers that tend to be professional institutions that hold significant communicative power. That account justified media freedom in terms of its service to the interests of the audience. One goal for media law under this view is to encourage the production of high-quality information that is thought to inform the public and hold power to account. In taking such an approach, the courts are often dismissive of any free speech interests concerning gratuitous insults, obscene content and hate speech.[79] Accordingly, the defences designed to protect media freedom rights tend to be framed to cover speech that is of value to the audience. As the previous chapters have shown, some defences are subject to conditions that certain standards are met by publishers, such as the content contributing to a discussion of general interest, or fulfilling the professional ethics and practices expected of media institutions. That approach makes good sense for media institutions that regularly command a wide audience, and was defended in Chapter 1. However, there are dangers in applying the same standards to all speakers on the digital media.

The first concern is that when applying public interest tests and defences to individual speakers, there is a risk of overlooking the different ways that individual low-level content can serve the audience interest. That risk is present where those tests and defences were devised to accommodate the rights of media institutions. When looking at the traditional high level media, the content tends to be judged as a finished product.[80] A newspaper article or television programme goes through a process of research, production and editing before it goes public. By contrast, many low level communications on the digital media can be seen as works in progress rather than finished products. The digital media can allow for collaboration among users, for example in examining primary materials and raw data released under a freedom of information request.[81] The digital media can enable raw data to be analysed, checked and refined transparently in an open process. In such a case, raw data can be posted on a digital forum and each member of a network can comment on what has been found, express possible conclusions and invite feedback from others. The public interest of such content should not be judged in isolation, but should be viewed as a contribution to an ongoing debate that is subject to revision. Consequently, the value of such low level communications should not be judged by the standards applied to a finished product in the professional media.

The second issue is more fundamental, namely that low level speech tends to be an exercise of individual freedom of expression. The right to freedom of expression is not just about serving the interests of the audience, but also the interests of the speaker. Consequently, even where there is no arguable public interest in a communication, there are good reasons for protecting the casual comments of a low level speaker. There is some value in allowing people to have the breathing space to make

---

[79] *Campbell v Mirror Group Newspapers Ltd* [2004] UKHL 22, [2004] AC 457 at [148].

[80] J Rowbottom, 'In the Shadow of the Big Media: Freedom of Expression, Participation and the Production of Knowledge Online' (2014) *Public Law* 491, 503.

[81] Y Benkler, *The Wealth of Networks* (New Haven, Yale University Press, 2006) 232.

errors of judgement and to say things that some people find offensive. When a person comments online on a newspaper website or social media, the speaker may think of it as the equivalent to a contribution to a conversation, rather than a publication. In *Smith v ADVFN plc*, Eady J compared statements posted on an online bulletin board to casual conversations 'which people simply note before moving on; they are often uninhibited, casual and ill thought out; those who participate know this and expect a certain amount of repartee or "give and take"'.[82] The online speaker may publish a spontaneous comment without much research or reflection. Words are exchanged as part of a process of give and take, in which people learn by expressing views and hearing others. A person may make an offensive remark, but the social response to that comment should educate the person about the boundaries of taste and civility. A standard that protects expression rights primarily where there is a contribution to a matter of general interest is unlikely to capture this dimension of communicative freedom.

There are several ways that the Article 10 jurisprudence and domestic laws can be adapted to accommodate some protection for the low level speaker. One strategy is to interpret existing laws so that a higher threshold of harm is required before a low level speaker is subject to liability. In *Magyar Tartalomszolgaltatok Egyesulete v Hungary* (*MTE*), the European Court of Human Rights stated that in applying Article 10, 'regard must be had to the specificities of the style of communication on certain Internet portals', in particular that 'a low register of style' is common and that it reduces the impact of the speech.[83] In other words, people react differently when someone is called a Nazi (or some other insult) in the user comments section of a newspaper webpage than when the same allegation is made in a report in the main content of a newspaper.[84] To some extent, this is recognised in the defamation cases, in which casual comments on a digital forum are unlikely to meet the threshold of seriousness required for a claim.[85] Similarly, the CPS prosecution guidelines in relation to offences on the social media require a high threshold of harm to justify the prosecution of grossly offensive communications that do not target specific individuals.[86]

Another way to accommodate the low level speaker is to vary the duties and responsibilities expected under Article 10 according to the context in which the expression takes place. Along these lines, an individual commenting on a political story on the social media is not expected to undertake extensive research or call a politician for comment prior to publication.[87] In *Delfi v Estonia*, the Grand Chamber recognised that a higher standard of care is to be expected of professional media outlets.[88] Along these lines, the duties and responsibilities expected of small scale self-communication should differ from the professional processes associated with the established media.

---

[82] *Smith v ADVFN plc* [2008] EWHC 1797 (QB) at [14].

[83] *Magyar Tartalomszolgaltatok Egyesulete v Hungary*, App no 22947/13 (2016) 42 BHRC 52 at [77].

[84] See *R (on the application of Gaunt) v OFCOM* [2011] EWCA Civ 692, [2011] 1 WLR 2355.

[85] In *Smith v ADVFN plc* (n 82), Eady J stated that such communications would be more likely to be treated as mere abuse. See also *Clift v Clarke* [2011] EWHC 1164 (QB). The position is now supported by the Defamation Act 2013, s 1.

[86] Crown Prosecution Service, 'Guidelines on prosecuting cases involving communications sent via social media' (n 13).

[87] See Ch 2.

[88] *Delfi* (n 66). See also Recommendation CM/Rec (2011)7 of the Committee of Ministers to Member States on a new notion of media (adopted on 21 September 2011).

There are difficulties in designing a system that respects these issues, but which does not simply provide a licence for people to abuse the freedom and interfere with the rights of others. It is important to recognise that the digital media can be used in many ways that are harmful to others, which should be taken seriously. However, the new communicative environment may require a slightly difference balance to be struck between Article 10 and competing interests. Such a response may entail more proportionate sanctions and alternative strategies such as intermediary responsibility. While often problematic for reasons that will be discussed later, such methods provide a better solution for dealing with some of the harms associated with digital speech than an attempt to impose liability for publication offences on large numbers of internet users.

C. Media Privileges and Citizen Journalists

While the discussion has focused on the protection found under Article 10, a further issue is whether those engaging in mass self-communication should be able to take advantage of the privileges afforded to media freedom. The courts have recognised that non-media actors can perform the watchdog role.[89] Armchair monitors can scrutinise and audit various official documents. For this reason, there are obvious arguments for extending some of the benefits of media freedom. For example, there is no reason to limit freedom of information rights to accredited journalists or media institutions.

However, there may be areas where the protection of media freedom rests on some level of professionalism and expertise. For example, there are reasons why certain family law proceedings and related court documents are not open to any member of the public, but can only be accessed by accredited members of the media. As was argued in Chapter 3, even if these privileges are opened up to some digital speakers outside traditional media institutions, they should only be offered to those that meet high standards of responsibility and professionalism. Similarly, the protection of confidential sources, discussed in Chapter 5, is about guarding the rights of those who gather information on a regular basis and respect professional ethics, and such protection should not be offered to any person that publishes. That provides a trade-off, in which lower standards are expected in the preparation of 'low level' digital speech, but some of the privileges may not be available.

The arguments above do not call for an overhaul of the Article 10 jurisprudence. While the principles that focus on journalistic responsibility and the public interest have served the court well, there is a need to continue to adapt those principles to the wider range of speech that can be found in digital communications. This means continuing to move beyond the traditional paradigms and beyond thinking solely in terms of the mass media. The discussion shows that as more types of speech converge on the digital media, it becomes important for the jurisprudence to differentiate between media freedom and freedom of expression. Steps have already been taken in that direction, and the existing principles under Article 10 have sufficient flexibility to allow such adaptation with the trends in communication.

---

[89] *Animal Defenders International v United Kingdom*, App no 48876/08 (2013) 57 EHRR 21 at [103].

D. Interacting Sectors

The discussion has shown that rather than treating the digital media as a unified sector to be judged by the same standards, it is composed of multiple sectors for which there are different expectations. Some types of communication on the digital media are like professional broadcasts, some perform a similar function to the print media, while a person's posts, blogs and live messages are normally a form of individual freedom of speech. In addition, there is also a sector of digital intermediaries, a newer form of digital media that will be considered later in this chapter. For present purposes, the important point is that the digital media has not ended the traditional model of the one-to-many mass media. Instead, the various models of communication co-exist.

The various sectors do not function in isolation. User-generated content, amateur websites and international media interact with the traditional media. For example, members of the public use the digital media to provide feedback to the traditional media bodies. Some user-generated content provides a source for the mass media, which is sometimes quoted, or provides a lead to be investigated. More broadly, the content on the digital media can influence the style and types of content in traditional newspapers and broadcasts. Audiences may come to have slightly different expectations as a result of what they see online. For example, broadcasters might seek to produce short, punchy sections on a television programme with the aim of the content going viral. Similarly, online headlines in some newspapers have followed the 'clickbait' style developed in certain digital publications. The influence, however, is not simply in one direction. The norms expected of the professional media have an influence on other sectors of the digital media and shape audience expectations. Those providing news and comment on the digital media often have to present the content in a style similar to that used in the traditional media, so that it is recognisable as a news product.

Traditional media outlets now have to compete for attention with the user-generated content, blogs, entertainment sites and other sources found on the digital media and compete for advertising revenues with the giant intermediaries. In light of this competition, the argument is sometimes made that media laws need to be scaled back to allow for free competition. The argument runs that if newspapers cannot report on celebrity gossip as a result of a privacy injunction or a regulatory provision, the audience for that content will simply move online to unregulated media. Similarly, the rules requiring impartiality may stop broadcasters making polemical editorials that are more likely to grab attention and which can be found all over the internet.

This line of argument leads to a race to the bottom of minimal controls. Such arguments have been rejected in the context of privacy law, with the court recognising that special considerations apply to the mass media.[90] Simply that a person's rights can be infringed by websites based overseas is not in itself a justification for large domestic publishers to further infringe those rights. Similarly, the calls for deregulation made on the same basis should be resisted. As the earlier sections and chapters have suggested,

---

[90] *PJS v News Group Newspapers Ltd* [2016] UKSC 26, [2016] AC 1081.

part of the solution is to 'level up' and apply media laws and regulations to those 'high level' speakers that are the functional digital equivalent of the traditional mass media. In any event, it is not clear that deregulation would improve the position of the professional media. Being subject to certain regulations, channels of accountability and professional standards can serve as a 'badge of honour' to show that the source is trustworthy and thereby help to maintain its audience and authority.

E. Audience Responsibility

The final area in which digital communication changes the activities regulated by media law concerns the responsibilities of the audience. Media laws typically focus on publications and other acts in the process of gathering and disseminating information. However, some laws take a different approach and target the final stage in the chain of communication, the audience. In the chapter on censorship, it was shown how the viewing of indecent images of children on a screen constitutes the 'making' of a fresh image for the purpose of criminal liability. It is also an offence to possess certain types of extreme pornography.[91] The imposition of liability on the audience is sometimes justified in practical terms given the problems in enforcing domestic laws where publishers are based overseas. If the publisher based overseas cannot be controlled, the audience within the jurisdiction can. Targeting the audience is not, however, limited to these pornography offences. There are also controls on the possession of information that is likely to be useful to a person committing or preparing an act of terrorism.[92] The government has announced an intention to strengthen that law in relation to the viewing of such content.[93] Copyright holders have sought to bring actions against some internet users that have downloaded illegal copies of music or films, although that strategy does not seem to have been pursued rigorously.[94] The rationale for audience-based controls could be extended to apply to other content, such as revenge pornography or gross invasions of privacy. That would signal a shift away from the publication offence.

These developments raise an important ethical question of what responsibilities are expected of the audience in the digital era. It is argued here that legal controls on the audience should be limited to the most extreme problems, such as child abuse images. The reason is that a member of the audience will often have a lower level of culpability in relation to the harms caused by the content. The recipient of the content may also lack knowledge of the illegality of the material, may view it inadvertently, or view it for any number of reasons. The more controls that are imposed on the audience, the greater the need to track individual viewing habits to enforce the law and the closer

---

[91] Criminal Justice and Immigration Act 2008, s 63.
[92] Terrorism Act 2000, s 58.
[93] Home Office, 'Law tightened to target terrorists' use of the internet' 3 October 2017.
[94] See 'The £350 bill for a download' *The Guardian* (17 July 2010). More recently, ISPs have sent alerts to account holders in relation to a breach of copyright via the account, but such notifications do not amount to a threat of legal action.

we get to something that looks like the monitoring of thoughts. It may sound far-fetched to even be contemplating this type of control. However, as such methods have already been developed and employed in relation to the more extreme content, there is a chance that demands will be made to extend similar measures to address other problems. It is argued here that the responsibilities of the audience and recipients of content are, in most cases, best understood in ethical rather than legal terms.

IV. Digital Intermediaries

While much of the discussion has focused on traditional media at the high level and individual speakers at the low level, the discussion that follows will focus on a different type of actor in the digital media: intermediaries. An intermediary is a term used to describe a body standing between the speaker and audience, providing a link between the two. A newsagent is an intermediary between a newspaper and reader. A broadcast network connects the programme maker and viewer. When the term is applied to the digital media, it refers to a broad range of services that provide the infrastructure for communications, including broadband providers, search engines, social networks and other publishing platforms. The question to be considered here is whether those providing such services should be subject to professional and legal responsibilities to protect certain interests and advance the goals of media freedom.

In Chapter 1, it was argued that one of the functions of the media in the digital era is to provide a platform for speakers and play a role in curating the content online, allowing users to navigate the mass of sources. The digital intermediaries are crucial to both these functions, for example in providing services that allow users to publish content easily and share it, as well as enabling people to search for information or be directed to relevant content. While the intermediaries were initially viewed as technology companies, it is important to recognise that such services are now a sector of the media that complements the traditional media institutions. As a media sector, intermediaries are increasingly expected to fulfil an evolving set of standards. These standards and rules determine the extent to which general media laws should be applicable to a digital intermediary, and also develop a separate body of rules that is a distinct system of intermediary regulation.

There are many reasons why people might want to hold an intermediary responsible in relation to content on the digital media. While the original publisher of the content might be unknown, outside the jurisdiction or have few resources, a large intermediary will be easy to find and have deeper pockets. Consequently, the intermediary may be the most visible point in the chain of publication. There are also efficiency reasons for targeting the intermediary.[95] For example, if content that infringes privacy rights

---

[95] See *Google Spain SL v Agencia Española de Protección de Datos (AEPD) and González* (C-131/12) [2014] QB 1022 at [84].

spreads on the internet via a social network, it will be far easier for the claimant to attempt to choke off the flow of information from a gatekeeper than to bring individual actions against every person who has re-posted the content. The latter strategy is likely to resemble a game of 'whack a mole', in which new re-posts will continuously reappear. Finally, by providing and profiting from the infrastructure for mass digital communications, the intermediary bears some of the responsibility for any harms that result from the use of its services.

Pursuing an intermediary may be attractive for all these reasons, but there are a number of challenges.[96] The intermediary may be a large, complex organisation with only a subsidiary based within the jurisdiction.[97] Consequently, proceedings may need to be taken against a company based overseas, which can raise problems of jurisdiction and enforcement. Despite the obvious advantages, pursuing an intermediary is not always the easy option.

In considering these issues, the discussion will first look at the status of an intermediary as a publisher of content for ordinary media law liability and at the possible defences available. The chapter will then look at specific controls, both legal and informal, that are specific to digital intermediaries. Finally, the discussion will look at some of the duties and responsibilities that can be expected of intermediaries.

A. Intermediary Liability as Publishers

This section will consider whether an intermediary should be treated like a publisher for the purposes of media law, and exposed to the legal obligations facing traditional media companies. There are different approaches that can be taken in response to this question. One extreme is to exempt the intermediary from the usual media law responsibilities. Along these lines, in the US, s 230 of the Communications Decency Act 1996 provides that intermediaries are not to be treated as speakers or publishers in relation to material 'provided by another information content provider'.[98] Aside from some exceptions, such as copyright and federal criminal law, the provision gives a largely unconditional level of protection that shields intermediaries regardless of their knowledge of any unlawful content.[99] An alternative strategy at the other extreme is to treat the intermediary as a publisher that is subject to all the media law liabilities of the person originating the content. A third strategy is to develop a conditional regime

---

[96] See Moreham and Warby (n 12) 803 for discussion.

[97] In *Metropolitan International Schools Ltd (t/a Skillstrain and/or Train2Game) v Designtechnica Corpn (t/a Digital Trends)* [2009] EWHC 1765 (QB), [2011] 1 WLR 1743, the court found that Google UK was not an appropriate defendant, as it was dedicated to marketing rather than controlling the workings of the search engine. In *Mosley v Google* [2015] EWHC 59 (QB), [2015] 2 CMLR 22 the action against the UK subsidiary was discontinued. In *Google Spain v Agencia Española de Protección de Datos (AEPD)* (n 95), the CJEU allowed the action to be pursued against the Spanish subsidiary for the purposes of data protection law, at [60].

[98] 'No provider or user of an interactive computer service shall be treated as the publisher or speaker of any information provided by another information content provider'.

[99] An exception is provided for intellectual property law, which is governed by the US Digital Millennium Copyright Act 1998.

that imposes liability only where the intermediary has failed to meet distinct conditions and responsibilities.

The approach taken in the UK is to treat certain intermediaries as a publisher in
relation to particular activities, but with conditional defences shielding it from the full
level of liability that is imposed on the media (thereby following the third approach
above). To explain this approach, the discussion will first look at when an intermediary
is a publisher, and the following section will look at the conditional defences. These
questions have been most frequently tested in defamation law. That is unsurprising,
given that libel is a strict liability tort, so if a claimant can establish that an intermediary is a publisher at common law, then it will have done much to make a prima facie
claim and the burden will shift to the intermediary to establish a defence. However,
it is important to note that the Defamation Act 2013 may now offer considerable
protection to some intermediaries, given that s 10 provides that the court does not
have jurisdiction to hear a claim 'against a person who was not the author, editor
or publisher of the statement' unless it is 'not reasonably practicable' to bring the
action against one of those people.[100] That is not an immunity for intermediaries.
For example, where a website takes some responsibility for the content it hosts, then
it may be deemed to be an editor and thereby fall outside the protection of s 10.[101]
Even where it performs no such function, an intermediary may still be the target for
liability, depending on how the 'reasonably practicable' requirement is interpreted.
Consequently, the question of whether certain intermediaries can be a publisher at
common law is still important in defamation. More broadly, the question is worth
examining to illustrate the general issues at stake, which can be relevant to various
other causes of action and legal controls.

It is hard to generalise about the status of intermediaries as publishers at common
law, given the range of different services offered by the various companies. The main
approach taken in England and Wales has been to look at the activity of the intermediary to determine whether it assumed responsibility for the content or at least
had some level of 'knowing involvement in the process of publication of the relevant
words'.[102] Applying this approach in *Bunt v Tilley*, telecommunications companies
were not deemed to publish the content sent through their broadband services, as they
lacked the necessary level of knowing involvement. In another case, Google was found
not to be a publisher at common law in relation to snippets of text from other websites
in its search results. Eady J emphasised the lack of human input from Google into an
individual listing, and found that it cannot be taken to have 'authorised or caused the
snippet to appear'.[103]

The position of an intermediary hosting material is different to a broadband provider or search engine, given its potential to moderate and remove content. An early
case took a relatively strict approach in treating a host as a publisher regardless of

---

[100] Defamation Act 2013, s 10(2) provides that the terms '"author", "editor" and "publisher" have the
same meaning as in section 1 of the Defamation Act 1996'.
[101] See *Brett Wilson LLP v Persons Unknown* [2015] EWHC 2628 (QB), [2016] 4 WLR 69.
[102] *Bunt v Tilley* [2006] EWHC 407 (QB), [2007] 1 WLR 1243 at [23].
[103] *Metropolitan International Schools* (n 97) at [51]–[53].

whether it had knowledge of the content.[104] However, the leading approach is to require that a host knew or ought to have known of the content in order to be a publisher. In *Tamiz*, the court found that prior to notification about the defamatory content, it was doubtful that Google's Blogger hosting service was even a secondary publisher (such as a distributor).[105] By contrast, *after* the hosting service received a complaint about the defamatory posts, it was at least arguable that it was a publisher for the period in which the content remained available. This approach blurs the question of whether the defendant was sufficiently involved in the process to be considered a publisher, with the question of whether the publisher has sufficient knowledge to be deserving of liability (which has been traditionally considered at the defence stage for secondary publishers). By requiring an assumption of responsibility or some level of knowledge, the approach appears to soften the strict liability of defamation law and builds more limits into the ingredients of the cause of action.[106]

The focus on the assumption of responsibility or active role of the intermediary can generate undesired incentives. If a company seeks to behave in a way that is responsible, moderates content and is in a position to remove it, then there will be a bigger risk that it will have assumed responsibility and taken a less passive role. Consequently, the standard could actually provide intermediaries with an incentive not to take steps to limit the harm in relation to the activities they facilitate.

It is worth noting that the intermediary often argues that it is not a publisher when the question relates to liability. However, if special privileges are open to publishers, then the intermediary sometimes characterises itself as a publisher analogous to the media. In *Totalise*, a website that hosted user comments sought to benefit from the protection of s 10 of the Contempt of Court Act 1981, which is open only to those taking responsibility for what is posted and exerting some editorial control.[107] More broadly, in the USA, companies operating search engines have argued that search results are protected as 'speech' under the First Amendment.[108] Sometimes the intermediary may be seen as trying to have it both ways, as having the rights of a publisher without having the corresponding liability.[109]

The difficulty in answering these questions lies in the fact that the intermediary plays a distinctive role in the system of communication, so direct comparisons with traditional publishers are not always helpful. For example, while Eady J looked at the lack of human input in a search result as a sign of a passive role,[110] such a lack of human decisions in the individual cases may simply reflect the different ways that an intermediary implements its choice for ranking content through its algorithm. Lack of human input alone should not absolve the intermediary from responsibility, as choices

---

[104] *Godfrey v Demon* [2001] QB 201.

[105] *Tamiz v Google* [2013] EWCA Civ 68, [2013] 1 WLR 2151 at [26].

[106] See A Mullis and R Parkes (eds), *Gatley on Libel and Slander*, 15th edn (London, Sweet and Maxwell, 2013) at [6.29] commenting on *Tamiz*. For criticism of this approach, see *Oriental Press Group Ltd v Fevaworks Solutions* [2014] EMLR 11 on the basis that such matters are more appropriately dealt with at the defence stage.

[107] *Totalise plc v Motley Fool Ltd* [2001] EMLR 29. See discussion in Ch 5.

[108] *Jian Zhang v Baidu.com Inc*, 10 F Supp 3d 433, 435 (SDNY 2014); *S Louis Martin v Google*, Case No CGC-14-539972 (Superior Court of California, 2014).

[109] See F Pasquale, *Black Box Society* (Cambridge Mass, Harvard University Press, 2015) 77.

[110] See *Metropolitan International Schools Ltd* (n 97) at [50]–[53].

by humans lie behind the design of the automated process. Rather than relying on technical similarity and equivalent methods to traditional publishers, such questions are best assessed by looking at the particular service and the type of editorial function performed that promotes the visibility of the content.

B. Intermediary Defences

Various areas of law have defences limiting intermediary liability. Defamation law and contempt of court provide for defences of innocent dissemination and publication, which were developed to protect distributors and can now protect certain intermediary activities.[111] Some areas of law also have specific defences for intermediaries. The system of 'notice and notice' under s 5 of the Defamation Act 2013 provides one example. Another example is the scheme discussed in Chapter 4 for the police to provide notice of terrorist propaganda and for intermediaries to take the content down to avoid liability for disseminating material encouraging or inducing acts of terrorism under the Terrorism Act 2006.

A more general set of defences is available under the Electronic Commerce (EC Directive) Regulations 2002 to intermediaries that provide 'information society services' that act as a conduit, cache or host.[112] The regulations offer protection against criminal sanctions and liability for damages, but not against an injunction. The conditions for each defence under the 2002 Regulations differ according to the type of activity undertaken by the intermediary. A mere conduit is afforded a defence that does not depend on whether the service provider had any knowledge of an unlawful use. However, as *Bunt* showed, those acting as conduits are unlikely to assume the responsibility necessary to be prima facie liable as publishers.

Another defence under the 2002 Regulations is provided for caching services, which are defined as services providing 'automatic, intermediate and temporary storage that is for the sole purpose of making more efficient onward transmission of the information to other recipients of the service upon their request'.[113] For example, some search engines provide links to cached websites in order to allow people to have access to the content even if the website is down (say, due to technical problems). Again, such conduct is detached from the process of production, so the defence helps to ensure that companies are not deterred from providing this service. However, the defence is subject to conditions. For example, to benefit from the defence, the intermediary should not modify the content. Accordingly, Eady J expressed the view that Google's

---

[111] Defamation Act 1996, s 1 and under the common law, *Vizetelly v Mudie's Select Library Ltd* [1900] 2 QB 170. See also the Contempt of Court Act 1981, s 3 and the Obscene Publications Act 1959, s 2(5). Though the approach taken in *Tamiz* (n 105) considers questions of knowledge when deciding whether the defendant was a publisher.

[112] Electronic Commerce (EC Directive) Regulations 2002, SI 2002/2013, reg 3(2) provides that the 'Regulations shall not apply in relation to any Act passed on or after the date these Regulations are made or in exercise of a power to legislate after that date'. Consequently, separate regulations with similar effect have been enacted to cover certain subsequent laws. For example, see The Electronic Commerce Directive (Terrorism Act 2006) Regulations 2007, SI 2007/1550.

[113] ibid, reg 18.

snippet view is unlikely to be protected by this regulation, as the production of a selected part of the text could constitute modification.[114] The defence also requires that the intermediary remove or disable access to the information stored:

> upon obtaining actual knowledge of the fact that the information at the initial source of the transmission has been removed from the network, or access to it has been disabled, or that a court or an administrative authority has ordered such removal or disablement.[115]

This helps to ensure that information that has been taken down in other places to prevent harm or an infringement of individual rights does not remain available through caching.

Most important for present purposes are the protections afforded to hosting services under the 2002 Regulations, which are defined as 'the storage of information provided by a recipient of the service'.[116] A service that stores or hosts content has greater chance of being a publisher, and is likely to be the subject of media law litigation. The defence is subject to the condition that the service provider does not have 'actual knowledge of unlawful activity or information' and, in relation to claims for damages, 'is not aware of facts or circumstances from which it would have been apparent to the service provider that the activity or information was unlawful'.[117] Where there is such knowledge or awareness, the intermediary is expected to 'remove or to disable access to the information'.[118]

This begs the question of what level of knowledge is necessary for the host to lose the defence under the 2002 Regulations. Showing a mere prima facie breach of legal rights sets the threshold too low and will result in many lawful comments being taken down upon complaint. The intermediary therefore has to have enough information to know the content is unlawful. However, the intermediary is not always in the position to calculate whether the content is lawful or whether a defence is likely to succeed. In *Davison v Habeeb*, Parkes J stated that when faced with a claim that a comment is defamatory and a defence to that claim, the intermediary cannot be expected to assess the two arguments and will be given the benefit of the doubt.[119] To lose the defence, the illegality must be clear rather than merely arguable, which gives stronger protection to the intermediary. Consequently, even where the host has sufficient knowledge *of the content* to count as a publisher in defamation law, it may not have sufficient knowledge *of the unlawful nature* to lose the defence. However, in some cases, knowledge of the facts and circumstances will be sufficient to show that the intermediary *should* have known that unlawful content was being hosted.[120] A large intermediary will be expected to have sufficient legal knowledge to be able to recognise

---

[114] *Metropolitan International Schools Ltd* (n 106) at [92].
[115] Electronic Commerce (EC Directive) Regulations 2002, reg 18.
[116] ibid, reg 10.
[117] ibid, reg 19(a)(i).
[118] ibid, reg 19(a)(ii).
[119] *Davison v Habeeb* [2011] EWHC 3031 (QB), [2012] 3 CMLR 6 at [68]. The court left open the possibility that sufficient knowledge would be found where 'a complaint was sufficiently precise and well substantiated, and where there was no attempt by the author of the defamatory material to defend what had been written'.
[120] See, for example, *L'Oreal v Ebay* (C-324/09) [2011] ETMR 52, [120] and [124].

a clear illegality from certain facts.[121] Moreover, to defeat the defence the claimant does not have to give the intermediary a clear legal categorisation for the complaint, but needs to provide enough to show the substance of the claim.[122]

The conditions for the defences encourage a system whereby the intermediary takes action when there is sufficient knowledge. The approach thereby requires the intermediary to fulfil certain standards to benefit from the defence, first in making an assessment of the merits of the complaint and, where appropriate, removing the content. As such, the approach can be compared with the strategy found throughout media law, where media bodies have defences subject to professional requirements. Obviously, the professional requirements demanded of an intermediary are very different from those demanded of a journalist, as the intermediary is not expected to take steps of verification, and so on. However, the conditional nature of the defences are broadly analogous. The debate is whether the right standards are being set for the intermediaries, which will be considered further below.

C. Intermediary Laws and Regulations

Aside from the general media laws, intermediaries can be subject to a separate set of measures that directly regulate their activities and processes. This approach avoids having to make difficult analogies with the traditional media or shoehorning an intermediary into a framework designed with the press and broadcasters in mind. Several examples, will be discussed here. The first will be the 'right to be forgotten' as an example of a legal control. The discussion will then look at voluntary cooperation with the government and the intermediary's own internal policies.

i. Right to Erasure

The responsibilities of certain intermediaries have been developed through the 'right to be forgotten'. This right seeks to address the concern that information on the digital media relating to a person can build up and follow that person for the rest of their life. Before the ubiquity of the digital media and search engines, people could to some degree escape an embarrassing incident or decide to start afresh by moving location. With the digital media, information about a person can be accessed in any place and is easy to discover by typing a person's name into a search engine. An individual's past can thereby follow the person through their digital profile. Jonathan Zittrain once warned that the scrutiny of past statements and conduct facilitated by the digital media poses the risk that people will become guarded in everything they say, like a politician staying on message in a press conference.[123] As a solution, Zittrain suggested a

---

[121] *J20 v Facebook Ireland Ltd* [2016] NIQB 98 at [75]. While the defendant's appeal was allowed in part on the facts in *JR20 v Facebook Ireland Ltd* [2017] NICA 48, the general principle remains.

[122] *CG v Facebook* [2016] NICA 54, [2017] 2 CMLR 29 at [69].

[123] J Zittrain, *The Future of the Internet and How to Stop It* (New Haven, Yale University Press, 2008) 212.

system of 'reputational bankruptcy' for those that want a fresh start and to escape the trail of data, which would allow individuals 'to express a choice to deemphasize if not entirely delete old information that has been generated about them'.[124] That approach aims to allow a person to re-start their digital profile from scratch, removing information that puts the individual both in a positive and negative light.

A system of 'reputational bankruptcy' has not been adopted, but a more selective right to edit the flow of information about oneself was established with the so-called 'right to be forgotten'. That right was crafted by the Court of Justice of the European Union (CJEU) through its interpretation of data protection law in the *Google Spain* decision.[125] The claimant had been named in a newspaper in 1999 as subject to proceedings to recover social security debts. He was concerned that references to this episode continued to be prominent in Google search results for his name. In an important decision, the CJEU decided that when acting as a search engine, Google is a controller of information under data protection law, as it determines the purposes and means of the processing of the data to provide a search facility.[126] As a controller, the search engine is required to remove web pages containing certain information relating to a person from the list of results following a search based on that person's name.[127] The right is not limited to information that is harmful to the complainant, but applies to information relating to the individual that is 'inadequate, irrelevant or no longer relevant, or excessive in relation to the purposes of the processing at issue carried out by the operator of the search engine'.[128]

The ruling did not require the information to be removed from the host site (whether hosted by a media site or not), as the decision was focused on the activities of search engines. That focus reflects the power of search services, particularly Google, in organising information. The Court noted the special role of search engines, which play 'a decisive role' in making data available, allowing users to build up a 'more or less detailed profile of the data subject'.[129] The Court recognised that the balance between free speech and competing rights may be struck in a different way with a search engine than with the traditional media, given that information included in search results can have a greater impact on privacy than the presence of the same information on the original publisher's website.[130]

The *Google Spain* decision is consolidated by the 2016 EU General Data Protection Regulation which overhauls EU data protection laws and includes a 'right to erasure' under Article 17.[131] Under Article 17, data controllers are under an obligation to erase personal data 'without undue delay' where that data meets one of a number

---

[124]   ibid, 228–29. See also the discussion of the problem in V Mayer-Schonberger, *Delete: The Virtue of Forgetting in the Digital Age* (Princeton, Princeton University Press, 2009).

[125]   *Google Spain v Agencia Española de Protección de Datos* (n 95).

[126]   See Ch 2.

[127]   *Google Spain v Agencia Española de Protección de Datos* (n 95), at [88].

[128]   ibid, at [94].

[129]   ibid, at [36]–[37].

[130]   ibid, at [86].

[131]   Regulation (EU) 2016/679 of the European Parliament and of the Council of 27 April 2016 on the protection of natural persons with regard to the processing of personal data and on the free movement of such data, and repealing Directive 95/46/EC, [2016] OJ L 119 (General Data Protection Regulation), Art 3. See also the Data Protection Act 2018.

of conditions.[132] Where the controller makes the personal data public, it is under an obligation to take reasonable steps to inform other processors that erasure has been requested. The right to erasure is not limited to search engines and can extend to other data controllers. It remains to be seen how this will extend to social media platforms and other hosts of content.[133]

The right to erasure is not absolute and Article 17 provides an exception where processing is necessary for the right to freedom of expression and freedom of information.[134] This means that when applying the right, a balance will be struck looking at the nature of the information, the impact on private life and the interest of the public in receiving the information.[135] For example, if a public figure sought to remove details of an embarrassing scandal from search results, that request could be rejected by a search engine on the basis of a legitimate public interest in accessing the content.

One line of criticism of the right to erasure is that it places an undue burden on the search engine to assess the complaint.[136] Claims about the costs of compliance are unlikely to trigger much sympathy in relation to companies such as Google. While there might a point about smaller search facilities, these are less likely to be subject to as many right to erasure requests.

A more convincing concern is that the right to erasure requires a private body to determine whether the information triggers the right and whether freedom of expression needs protecting. Critics argue that the right represents a form of private censorship in which a technology company decides what information can be accessed. In terms of safeguards, if an individual complainant is unhappy with the rejection of a 'right to erasure' request, then he or she can bring a claim before the courts or take the complaint to the Information Commissioner for breach of data protection law. A formal regulator thereby provides some oversight of the process. However, the author or publisher of the content that is removed from the search results does not have a corresponding legal right to challenge the decision to de-list content.[137] A decision to de-list upon receiving a complaint is therefore a safer option for the search engine, as there is no opportunity for that decision to be challenged before the regulator.

In the aftermath of the *Google Spain* decision, the European Union's Working Party on Data Protection advised that search engines should not as a general practice notify webmasters when a site has been removed from search results, as such notification can violate data protection rights (for example by revealing that an individual has made a request for information to be de-listed).[138] Notification of webmasters also raises a

---

[132] The conditions include where the data is no longer necessary for the purpose for which it was collected, where the individual objects to the processing (and there are no legitimate grounds for the processing), or where the data is unlawfully processed.

[133] See discussion in D Keller, 'The Right Tools: Europe's Intermediary Liability Laws and the 2016 General Data Protection Regulation' *Berkeley Technology Law Journal* (forthcoming).

[134] See also *Google Spain v Agencia Española de Protección de Datos* (n 95) at [81] and [97].

[135] ibid.

[136] See House of Lords European Union Committee, *Data Protection law: a 'right to be forgotten'?* (HL 2014–15, 40).

[137] The publisher only has an opportunity to request a review of the decision to delist under Google's policy.

[138] Article 29 Data Protection Working Party, *Guidelines on the Implementation of the Court of Justice of the European Union Judgment on "Google Spain and Inc v Agencia Espanola de Proteccion de Datos (AEPD)*

risk that a publisher will republish the information on a different site. For the right to be effective, the transparency of the complaint may need to be restricted. However, that lack of communication can limit the search engine's ability to evaluate matters of public interest and increase the scope for errors to be made.[139] For these reasons, the Working Party accepted that notification prior to a de-listing decision may be legitimate in difficult cases, but stated that proper safeguards need to be in place.[140] Google's current policy is to notify webmasters when a request has been made, but only to disclose the URL in question and not the individual complainant.[141] In many cases, however, the identity of complainant will be obvious from the URL. To provide a further safeguard, an undertaking could be sought from webmasters that the information and the fact of a request will not be further published.[142]

The right to erasure is not the only form of direct regulation and other avenues could be developed to regulate the activities of digital intermediaries. Given that the organisation of information, as opposed to the creation of original content, lies at the heart of the business of the big tech firms, it is likely that data protection law will play a prominent role in developing intermediary responsibility.

ii. Informal Regulation and Voluntary Cooperation

Intermediaries do not act only where there is an immediate threat of liability or regulatory sanction. Rather than seeking to legislate, the government has a strong preference for cooperating with the industry. This is likely to be more efficient and flexible for government and the industry. Standards elaborated in informal arrangements can be changed through mutual agreement, rather than through formal amendment. The intermediaries are also likely to prefer a method that avoids legal liability or formal regulation, so long as it does not undermine their business goals. By cooperating with government and developing its own self-regulatory systems, the industry may pursue a strategy to promote good public relations, customer service and stave off threats of more formal regulation. The willingness to enter into voluntary schemes varies according to the company, with some being proactive in taking action to prevent certain content being disseminated, while others wait for an official complaint or notification.[143] However, where an informal system is in place, it may lack the constitutional safeguards for free speech and privacy.

and Mario Costeja Gonzalez" C-131/12 (2014) at [23]. See D Erdos, 'Communicating Responsibilities: The Spanish DPA targets Google's Notification Practices when Delisting Personal Information' *Inforrm* (21 March 2017) at https://inforrm.wordpress.com/2017/03/21/communicating-responsibilities-the-spanish-dpa-targets-googles-notification-practices-when-delisting-personal-information-david-erdos (accessed 26 January 2018).

[139] See Erdos, ibid.
[140] Article 29 Data Protection Working Party (n 138).
[141] See https://support.google.com/transparencyreport/answer/7347822?hl=en (last accessed 26 January 2018).
[142] Erdos (n 138).
[143] House of Commons, Home Affairs Select Committee, *Radicalisation: the counter-narrative and identifying the tipping point* (HC 2016–2017, 135) at [35].

Two areas provide obvious examples of voluntary cooperation. The first concerns the laws prohibiting the making and possession of indecent images of children and the second relates to terrorism. The discussion in Chapter 4 noted the ever-stricter laws targeting both publisher and recipient in relation to indecent images of children. As part of the industry response to this problem, a self-regulatory body, the Internet Watch Foundation (IWF), was established in 1996.[144] The IWF provides a system in which indecent images of children can be reported to the self-regulatory body. Since 2014, the IWF has taken on a role in proactively searching for illegal content. If the content is hosted in the UK, the IWF will pass on the details to the police and will issue a takedown notice to the company hosting the content. If the content is hosted outside the UK, then it will report the content via a system under international agreements or to Interpol.

While the various authorities take steps to remove the content, the IWF provides information to intermediaries to enable content to be automatically blocked or removed. The information that the IWF supplies to intermediaries includes a list of URLs, an automated image recognition service to locate photos already identified as illegal, keywords associated with illegal activity, and virtual currency wallets associated with the distribution of illegal images.[145] The services rely on various technologies to process the information. For example, *Cleanfeed* is a technology developed by BT for its broadband services to automatically block websites appearing of the IWF's list. As the controls relate to illegal material, customers cannot opt out of the filters being applied to the service. According to the IWF website, over 1,000 webpages are assessed each week under the scheme.[146]

The IWF is not a government body, but it does not operate in isolation from the state. The system depends on a degree of legal protection for its activities. A defence is available for the 'making' of an indecent image of a child when necessary for the prevention, detection or investigation of crimes.[147] Such a defence ensures that the IWF staff do not commit an offence when receiving, storing and searching for illegal content as part of their regulatory function. The IWF system of notice and takedown is in practice workable through an understanding with the police and Crown Prosecution Service.[148] In addition, the IWF also has a connection with public bodies through its funding, some of which comes from the EU.[149] More broadly, compliance with the system by the intermediary is largely incentivised by the E-Commerce Regulations, which require a system of notice and takedown to avoid liability.[150] If the system of industry regulation were not in place, then direct legal controls would no doubt be imposed.[151] Against this background, the IWF rightly accepts that it is a public body and thus subject to the Human Rights Act 1998.[152]

---

[144] For discussion see E Laidlaw, *Regulating Speech in Cyberspace* (Cambridge, Cambridge University Press, 2015) Ch 4.

[145] See www.iwf.org.uk/what-we-do/how-we-assess-and-remove-content (accessed 26 January 2018).

[146] ibid.

[147] Protection of Children Act 1978, s 1B.

[148] Memorandum of Understanding Between Crown Prosecution (CPS) and the Association of Chief Police Officers (ACPO) concerning s 46 of the Sexual Offences Act 2003.

[149] Most of its funding comes from subscriptions and donations from the industry.

[150] Laidlaw (n 144) 129.

[151] ibid, 129.

[152] ibid, 166.

The IWF staff makes its own determination on the legality of the material reported or detected.[153] This is seen by critics as a form of private censorship, in which a private organisation decides what content should be inaccessible to the public. The IWF promotes some transparency by encouraging companies to provide a 'splash page' explaining why the material has been blocked.[154] As a safeguard, there is also a process to complain to the IWF about a decision to block, and to ask for the content to be reassessed. The process is usually conducted on paper, and can involve a reference to a police agency for assessment.[155] According to its 2015 Annual Report, the IWF received no complaints from content owners about inclusion on the URL list and no complaints about takedown notices (though it is easy to see why a person may be reluctant to draw attention to their publications or attempts to access potentially unlawful material).[156] Beyond the complaints process, a person unhappy with a decision can pursue judicial review proceedings, which are costly and in which the courts are likely to treat the decisions of an expert self-regulatory body with a degree of respect. While there are some criticisms of the processes employed, there is little of evidence that people are unhappy with the decisions being made by the IWF on a day-to-day basis.

The IWF is sometimes seen to provide a template that could be followed for content relating to terrorism.[157] As noted, while there are formal powers for government to provide notices to ensure the takedown of terrorist-related material, these are often unnecessary because the intermediaries normally cooperate with the authorities in countering terrorism voluntarily.[158] Under this informal system, the intermediary receives a request from the Counter Terrorism Internet Referral Unit (CTIRU) that asks for the removal of certain content identified as illegal, but without threatening liability.[159] With the terrorist material, a police officer at CTIRU makes the determination before approaching the intermediary. While the decision is made by a public official, that is not the same as a decision made at a contested hearing and can raise concerns about a prior restraint being imposed by administrative discretion. Between February 2010 and November 2017, over 290,000 items of terrorist-related content were reported to have been removed from the internet through this process.[160]

While the IWF and CTIRU have critics, it important to remember the value of the work in tackling serious problems. For all the concerns about prior restraints and censorship, there is a strong argument that it is preferable to stop people accessing content in the first place than to prosecute those people after the content has been accessed. Furthermore, in the case of indecent images of children or violent acts of terrorism, the rights of any individuals depicted in any real images are better protected if people are prevented from viewing the content. There are no doubt improvements that could

---

[153] See www.iwf.org.uk/what-we-do/who-we-are (accessed 26 January 2018).

[154] Internet Watch Foundation, *Annual Report 2015*, 21.

[155] Laidlaw (n 144) 162.

[156] Internet Watch Foundation, *Annual Report 2015*, 36.

[157] House of Commons, Home Affairs Select Committee, *Radicalisation: the counter-narrative and identifying the tipping point* (HC 2016–17, 135) at [37]–[39].

[158] Home Office, *Memorandum to the Home Affairs Committee: Post-Legislative Scrutiny of Terrorism Act 2006* (2011, Cm 8186) at [8.1.10].

[159] See https://lumendatabase.org/notices/11530201#, from Scotland Yard to Wordpress (last accessed 26 January 2018).

[160] Ben Wallace MP, 6 November 2017, Written Answer 110378.

be made, for example in increasing the level of transparency of the informal controls and allowing for greater accountability. However, building safeguards in this area is difficult, because the pressure is to look for ways to speed up the process of removal rather than to impose procedures for contestation that could slow it down.[161] There are also limits to the transparency that can be offered given the nature of the content that the IWF and CTIRU are dealing with. For example, if a suspected terrorist or member of a paedophile network is notified that their content has been removed or blocked, then that could provide a cue to relocate the material or tip the person off that they are under surveillance.[162]

The non-legal systems discussed above are relatively formalised arrangements with expectations on both sides. There are, however, more informal and ad hoc arrangements that can be developed to deal with various issues. For example, there are concerns about an 'invisible handshake' between government and intermediaries, where the latter remove content without a formalised agreement, but with some governmental pressure or encouragement.[163] Such measures are hard to detect or know about, but are another potential type of control.

All the various voluntary controls exist against a background of legal liability or potential liability. The legal environment makes a big difference to how the intermediaries respond to certain issues and complaints.[164] If legal obligations are stricter, then the informal system is more likely to be tilted in favour of the complainant and less likely to strike a balance with competing rights and interests.[165] In most cases, the intermediary will know that if it does not cooperate voluntarily, then there is scope for a legal action to be brought or for new laws to be introduced. The media laws therefore provide an underlying backstop that sets the incentives for co-operation. The legal context and relations with government are therefore significant in understanding the workings of a self-regulatory system.

iii. Internal Controls

In addition to the legal and voluntary controls, the various intermediaries have their own terms of use, which regulate the content that can be distributed on its services. For example, some social networks have rules on nudity or hate speech, even where such content does not violate the law. An intermediary needs to have terms and conditions governing user behaviour if it is to act with the level of responsibility expected. A central question is how these standards are formulated and applied in practice. Problems emerge if rules are changed without notice, for example with privacy defaults being altered overnight.

---

[161] Home Affairs Select Committee, *Radicalisation* (n 157) at [29].

[162] See D Anderson, *A Question of Trust: Report of the Investigatory Powers Review* (2015).

[163] See Y Benkler, 'A Free Irresponsible Press: Wikileaks and the Battle over the Soul of the Networked Fourth Estate' (2011) 46 *Harvard Civil Rights-Civil Liberties Law Review* 311, 314–15. For the trend more generally, see M Birnhack and N Elkin-Koren 'The Invisible Handshake: The Reemergence of the State in the Digital Environment' (2003) 8 *Virginia Journal of Law and Technology* 1.

[164] R MacKinnon, E Hickok, A Bar and H Lim, *Fostering Freedom Online: The Role of Internet Intermediaries* (Paris, UNESCO, 2014) 10.

[165] ibid, 11 and 129.

The terms are part of the contract the users agree to when signing up to a particular service. However, there are questions about whether that consent is meaningful or not, as many users are unlikely to go through each of the terms before clicking the 'agree' button. In any event, the individual user has little scope to negotiate the terms of agreement. While the user is not compelled to use a particular service, in practice a person may have little choice when certain large social networks are dominant. If all one's friends are connected via a particular service, the person either agrees to its terms or faces a form of social exclusion. Describing these provisions as contractual terms can underplay their significance. For example, the social network Facebook has, at the time of writing, over two billion monthly active users. Its terms of service govern the way people interact online. In terms of practical impact, its decisions can have a bigger impact on what is heard than a domestic law.[166]

These powers may be regulated in a number of ways. The intermediary is constrained by contract law, and will be regulated by implied terms and rules on the imposition of unfair contract terms. However, these provisions tend to focus on the rights of the user as a consumer, rather than to uphold freedom of expression and values associated with media law. Data protection law provides a control on the processing of personal data by the intermediary. Consequently, the Information Commissioner has the potential to become an important regulator of the intermediary sector. Within these constraints, there is still much discretion for the intermediary to determine the rules of its service. The control of terms and conditions is a significant source of intermediary power, which can set the terms on which people interact, and determines how information will be prioritised. Critics argue that there is greater need for transparency, consultation and appeal rights governing its internal processes and in setting the terms of service. Such channels of accountability need to be developed as part of a system of duties and responsibilities for intermediaries, which will be discussed in the following section.

D. Duties and Responsibilities of an Intermediary

Whether looking at a defence for intermediaries, direct regulations or voluntary systems, there are some evolving responsibilities expected of a large professional intermediary that apply in all these settings. Many of these matters relate not to specific rights, but are general procedures that can be employed in relation to a range of issues. The section here will consider some of the leading examples, in particular notice and takedown, fair procedures, record keeping, monitoring users and content, and fairness and neutrality rules.[167] Some of these have already been referred to in the earlier discussion, and the following discussion will look at various duties and responsibilities more generally to identify the benefits and risks.[168]

---

[166] See Mills (n 24).

[167] See J Riordan, *The Liability of Internet Intermediaries* (Oxford, Oxford University Press, 2016) 20–21 and 63–66 for discussion.

[168] The discussion will focus on the core responsibilities in relation to intermediary services. In practice, matters are more complex where a company acts as an intermediary and also produces its own media content.

i. Notice and Takedown

Notice and takedown policies are the most established element of intermediary responsibility, in which intermediaries take steps to remove material that is unlawful, breaches terms of service or infringes certain rights once they have knowledge of it. The intermediary defences under the E-Commerce Regulations 2002 referred to above incentivise a system of notice and takedown by making liability depend on knowledge. A system of notice and takedown can also be required under statute. A well-known example is the regime of notice and takedown liability applied to claims based on copyright in the USA, in which the intermediary is expected to take down content 'expeditiously' after receiving notice of a breach.[169] The Terrorism Act 2006 provides a formal system of notice and takedown, whereby the intermediary may be committing an offence if it does not comply with a formal notice from a police constable.[170] Alternatively, the system of notice and takedown may be implemented under a system of self-regulation or voluntary cooperation, as was found with the IWF.

In a notice and takedown system, the regulator or intermediary can be alerted to the content in a number of different ways. In many cases, notice will come from those people that have their rights arguably infringed, for example in defamation and copyright law. In other cases, the notice may come from members of the public that become alert to the unlawful content, such as the system for the anonymous reporting of indecent images of children to the IWF. In other cases, the government may notify the intermediary, as is the case with the provisions of the Terrorism Act 2006.

The earlier discussion of intermediary liability noted that a system of notice and takedown can be criticised as a form of private censorship, in which a company decides what content should remain accessible. In particular, the intermediary may have an incentive to take content down. When receiving a complaint that content is unlawful, the intermediary faces a choice. It can remove the content quickly to avoid the risk of liability and thereby make the problem go away. Alternatively, it can make its own assessment of whether the material is lawful or not, and decide to run the risk of legal challenges if it rejects the complaint. The former is the path of least resistance for the company, which may have little interest in defending the speech in court. The intermediary may also lack the information to defend certain claims, such as the truth of the content in a defamation claim.[171] Consequently, there is a danger that the regime creates a system in which an aggressively worded complaint leads to a quick removal of the content. That creates a type of complainer's veto.

The problem should not be overstated. The legal incentives to take content down have to be considered alongside the company's business model and economic pressures. A company that is in the business of hosting and organising information does not want a reputation for taking down information at a mere complaint and there may be commercial reasons for resisting takedown requests. Some of the internet giants

---

[169] Digital Millennium Copyright Act 1998.
[170] Terrorism Act 2006, s 3.
[171] See the discussion earlier on the level of knowledge required to defeat an intermediary defence, which seeks to guard against this risk.

are willing to challenge notices and are not over-zealous in removing content.[172] The legal pressures discussed above thus act as a counterweight to the commercial pressure to keep content up. However, it is important to recognise that a system of notice and takedown poses a risk of privatised censorship, even if in practice this varies according to the company.

ii. Filtering and Blocking

Once an intermediary has knowledge of harmful or illegal content, then in some circumstances, the intermediary will be able to take down the content. However, some services such as broadband providers do not host content and thereby cannot remove the material. Even when a host service can remove content, there are still risks that the content will be published elsewhere. To deal with this, intermediaries will often rely on automated technology to block or filter content. While early versions of blocking and filtering methods tended rely on the presence of certain words or phrases to detect content, the approaches are increasingly sophisticated. For example, *PhotoDNA* is a piece of software developed by Microsoft that can identify a 'fingerprint' of known images of child abuse. The service therefore gives intermediaries a way to detect, block or remove unlawful images and provides a strategy to prevent such images being accessed, re-posted and shared.

Blocking and filtering is widely used in a number of contexts that have already been discussed. The system operated by the IWF provides one example. In addition to illegal content, there are moves to encourage the voluntary use of filters in relation to certain adult material. The government expressed support for measures by the leading broadband providers to require customers to make an 'unavoidable choice' whether to use a parental filter.[173] The plan has been implemented in some cases by presenting customers with a screen asking them to choose whether to have the filters on or not. The page is normally pre-ticked to have the filters on and the user must make a choice in order to continue using the service. This service includes blocking categories ranging from pornography, drug use, hacking and suicide, although the user can choose to customise the filters to exclude certain categories and allow access to others. Under this approach, the use of blocking and filtering is seen to be part of the intermediaries' responsibility to protect children.

Some forms of blocking are also mandated by court order.[174] Section 97A(1) of the Copyright, Designs and Patents Act 1988 gives the High Court power to grant an injunction 'against a service provider, where that service provider has actual knowledge of another person using their service to infringe copyright'. As noted earlier, the E-Commerce Regulations 2002 only provide protection in relation to criminal liability and actions for damages, but not injunctions. Consequently, in *Newzbin2*, a film company was awarded an injunction against a broadband provider to require the use

---

[172] Professor Andrew Murray writes that the system has 'functioned extremely smoothly', A Murray, *Information Technology Law*, 3rd edn (Oxford, Oxford University Press, 2016) 199.

[173] See Ofcom, *Report on Internet Safety Measures* (2015). The policy was implemented following an agreement with the Prime Minister, David Cameron, in 2013.

[174] In relation to pornographic material, see also the Digital Economy Act 2017, s 23.

of *Cleanfeed* technology to block an anonymous site hosted overseas that breached copyright by providing links to unauthorised copies of films.[175]

An order requiring blocking raises Article 10 issues and can constitute a form of prior restraint.[176] The European Court of Human Rights has ruled that the basis for blocking orders needs to be clearly set out in law, that any orders should be narrowly tailored, and there should normally be a process to appeal against any limits on access to content.[177] The order should avoid curbing access to lawful sites. So, a decision to block all of YouTube or other mass hosting platforms simply to stop people accessing a handful of illegal pages is likely to be a disproportionate response.[178] By contrast the blocking order in *Newzbin2* was permissible because the site was largely used to obtain material that was in breach of copyright.[179] If a site is used exclusively to provide access to unlawful content, then there will be fewer objections to its being blocked.

In *Newzbin2*, the court found that the blocking order was proportionate, as the ISPs would not have to develop any new technology to meet the order.[180] The reason was that the *Cleanfeed* technology had already been developed to block indecent images of children and could be put to a new use. The reasoning highlights how once those automated technologies have been developed, one cannot easily make a case that such obligations are too costly or complex to be undertaken in another area.[181] The example reinforces the point in Chapter 4 that the law of obscenity can provide a laboratory for censorship, as there is very little resistance to the methods being used in that context. Technologies or regulatory solutions developed to deal with one type of problem can be treated as an 'off the peg solution' to deal with other types of legal wrong. That is something that should be considered when developing new technologies, even where the use in the particular case is widely accepted.

There are limits to what the technology can achieve. Blocking is a blunt mechanism that can be over- and under-inclusive. If the technology uses automated systems, then some feature of the content, such as the words used, will trigger the blocking. If this is the case, the system is likely to be subject to a number of false alarms or may miss content. On one occasion, when broadband providers blocked an IP address in response to a copyright complaint from the football Premier League, the measure inadvertently blocked access to the *Radio Times* website, which was hosted at the same IP address.[182] Clearly there is a need for a process to allow such errors to be reported and quickly corrected.

Blocking will be most effective in preventing people inadvertently accessing illegal content when browsing the internet. However, there are routes around the blocking software that will be available to those with a little technical knowledge. Virtual private

---

[175] *Twentieth Century Fox v BT* [2011] EWHC 1981 (Ch), [2012] 1 All ER 806 (known as *Newzbin2*).
[176] *Yildirim v Turkey* (n 2).
[177] ibid.
[178] ibid. See also *Cengiz v Turkey*, App nos 48226/10 and 14027/11 (1 December 2015).
[179] *Twentieth Century Fox v BT* (n 175) [186].
[180] ibid, [177] and [200].
[181] In *Mosley v Google* (n 97) the court considered the existing use of technology such as *PhotoDNA* to evaluate the burden on an intermediary in relation to an order to block access to private images.
[182] *Cartier International AG v British Sky Broadcasting* [2014] EWHC 3354 (Ch), [2015] 1 All ER 949 at [67].

networks (VPN) allow people to connect to the internet via an encrypted service, so can prevent the user's identity, messages and viewing habits being collected. The use of a VPN can also be used to bypass geographical restrictions imposed by a service provider, as it will not know which country the service is being accessed from.[183] A similar result can be achieved using The Onion Router (TOR), which encrypts communications on the digital media, allowing people's viewing habits to remain anonymous and also allowing webpages to be published anonymously (known as hidden services). Both TOR and VPN prevent service providers knowing which sites and material the user is accessing, so the blocks and filters will not be able to restrict the user accessing any specific content. While it might be possible to block or prohibit the use of such encrypted services outright, that would restrict much lawful behaviour and would be regarded as too broad. Those services can be useful for a number of activities, such as dissenters in authoritarian regimes escaping detection or allowing newspapers to receive whistleblowers' tipoffs anonymously.[184] Many employers and organisations also frequently use VPNs as a means of additional security. The difficulty is that the tools providing a route around the blocks can be used for both legitimate and unlawful purposes. Blocking and filtering play an important role in the system of intermediary responsibility, but there are limits to what it can achieve and there need to be safeguards to ensure errors are corrected and that decisions can be challenged, which will be discussed below.[185]

iii. Transparency and Contestation

In relation to decisions to block, filter or take down, there are often concerns about due process. If the measure is court ordered, then at least that decision takes place following a formal hearing. However, where the action is taken by the intermediary independently or following a complaint, there is no requirement for a hearing in advance. The challenge is that harmful content on the digital media spreads fast, but the process of justice is slow. If a formal process of adjudication is required to determine whether a statement is true or false, indecent or incites terrorism, by the time the issue is resolved the harm has already occurred. To prevent the harm requires a quick decision to be made without a full hearing on the facts. However, that quick process raises the problem of prior restraints mentioned earlier, along with the limited procedural rights.

While a court or tribunal hearing cannot determine complaints prior to removal due to issues of scale and time, large intermediary companies can be expected to provide a process of appeal in relation to certain decisions.[186] Such a system will not be possible in every case, for reasons noted earlier. If a person is engaging in malicious or criminal activities, notifying the publisher may simply facilitate further evasion of the

---

[183] For example, the right to be forgotten can be bypassed if the search engine does not know that the service is being accessed from Europe via a VPN.

[184] See discussion in Ofcom, *Ofcom report on internet safety measures* (16 December 2015) 17.

[185] See also Recommendation CM/Rec(2008)6 of the Committee of Ministers to member states on measures to promote the respect for freedom of expression and information with regard to Internet filters (26 March 2008).

[186] See discussion in MacKinnon, Hickok, Bar and Lim, 'Fostering Freedom Online' (n 164) 182.

controls. In the case of the right to erasure, notifying webmasters of a removal request could also amount to a breach of a privacy and data protection rights. In the absence of such concerns, some scope for challenge may be an important safeguard against the abuse and over-use of systems of notice and takedown, filtering, blocking and other intermediary decisions.

While an intermediary cannot offer a full hearing for every decision relating to content, it is reasonable to ask for some level of transparency and accountability. If such decisions are now a key aspect in the governance of digital communications, then transparency in decision making may be seen as a counterpart to open government and justice. More generally, the intermediary can provide some level of transparency to explain how its services work.[187] Transparency can arise at several levels. First, intermediary companies can be transparent in the policy that underpins the controls imposed. Such disclosure can include the grounds on which content will be blocked or taken down, or explaining in general terms the basis on which information is ranked. Secondly, transparency can be provided in giving data on the numbers of webpages that have been taken down, blocked, delisted, or deliberately moved down the rankings. That list gives people the chance to see the big picture and the general trends. A third level of transparency is in notifying the person whose site has been the subject of the intermediary decision. As noted earlier, there are instances when such notification is not appropriate, where it would undermine the interest protected by the decision.

Finally, there is the need for transparency to the internet users that find a website to be blocked, removed or de-listed. In *Cartier International AG v British Sky Broadcasting* an order to block sites violating trade mark rights required that users seeking to visit the site in question be told that the blocking was due to a court order and be provided with details of how to apply to have the order discharged.[188] With the parental filters implemented by broadband companies, the consumer is usually informed that a page has been blocked as a result of a filter, and there is a channel for any over blocking or mis-categorisation of websites to be reported to the intermediary. Similarly, the IWF system normally carries a splash page explaining why content has been blocked. Again, there are limits and in some cases it will not be appropriate to tell users that a page has been blocked, for example where it might alert people to the fact that a particular site contains sensitive information relating to national security. However, some level of transparency is important in providing a basis to evaluate and challenge intermediary decisions, depending on the legal interest at stake.

iv. Data and Record Keeping

Digital intermediaries have the potential to acquire considerable data about users, both posting content and viewing it. Much of the business model of such companies focuses on the acquisition of data, which provides the basis for services such as

---

[187] For example, Recommendation CM/Rec (2012)3 of the Committee of Ministers to Member States on the protection of human rights with regard to search engines (4 April 2012). On the issues of transparency and due process, see also Pasquale (n 109).

[188] *Cartier International AG v British Sky Broadcasting* (n 182) at [264]. The order was upheld by the Court of Appeal [2016] EWCA Civ 658, [2017] 1 All ER 700.

advertising. The acquisition of data can also help improve the services of the intermediary, for example in knowing the sorts of content the user is likely to be interested in. The data held by the intermediary can also help to strengthen security for certain services. Where the service is the provision of an email facility, then the provider will track the user's IP address or machines used to log into the device as a guard against unauthorised access. There are many types of responsibility that are developing to regulate the use of the data and records held by the intermediary, as can be seen with data protection law.

More specifically, there may be expectations and responsibilities that require the intermediary to keep certain data and make it available to others in some cases. Data protection laws require companies to keep records of processing activities, which facilitates a level of transparency, for example when a person makes a subject-access request.[189] Keeping records can help to identify those users that violate certain rights, at least where a court order requires the production of the data. A 'notice and notice' process, such as the defence under the Defamation Act 2013 s 5 discussed earlier, assumes that a website operator has sufficient records to trace a poster. Another example is the Digital Economy Act 2010, which sets out a scheme (not yet brought into force) for internet service providers to notify users that a complaint has been made about their use of the service to violate copyright and to keep a list of those users who have been subject to a higher number of complaints.[190]

The role of record keeping as a responsibility for an intermediary can be a source of controversy. The appropriateness of such a responsibility will partly depend on the type of service being provided. If a service hosts user content and makes it available to world at large, there will often be an expectation (subject to exceptions) for the host to provide some means to trace or contact the relevant author. If no means to trace the author is provided, then there is a stronger case for making the intermediary responsible. However, in some cases the need for record keeping may give way to interests in privacy and anonymity. There are some services where the meaningful records that can be expected of the intermediary are necessarily limited, such as services offering encryption as a means to ensure security. Similarly, a service that allows for anonymous reporting for whistleblowers would not be expected to keep records revealing the identity of the complainant, and should not be obliged to share that information even where it is held. Where record keeping is appropriate, the obligations on the intermediary need to be subject to limits and with safeguards in place to prevent unauthorised and unnecessary sharing.

The more far-reaching record-keeping obligations can raise a risk of surveillance. This issue can be particularly intrusive when looking at data that could reveal people's reading habits. For example, the Investigatory Powers Act 2016 allows the government to issue a notice requiring telecommunications companies to retain communications data for up to 12 months.[191] This means that broadband providers can be required

[189] General Data Protection Regulation (n 131) Art 30.
[190] Communications Act 2003, ss 124A–124R, as inserted by the Digital Economy Act 2010. The plans under the Digital Economy Act 2010 have not been implemented, and the industries have set up their own system for public education and email alerts to notify broadband account holders when a connection is being used to infringe copyright. See https://get-it-right.org/faq.html#q1 (last accessed 26 January 2018).
[191] Investigatory Powers Act 2016, s 87.

to keep records, including the various websites visited by a person. Such measures go beyond combatting the harms caused by expression and allow for much broader monitoring of behaviour. That can be valuable when investigating terrorist activity or organised crime, but raises pressing issues in relation to privacy. There are also difficult questions about who has access to the records and on what basis. Surveillance of this kind can potentially undermine the confidentiality of journalist's sources (for example, if the telephone numbers called by a journalist can be discovered).[192] More broadly, a system that monitors people's reading habits is more likely to create an environment that inhibits the free expression of ideas.[193] While safeguards can be imposed to regulate the disclosure of such information and government access to the database, there are questions as to how secure such systems are. The intermediary's database could be hacked and information disclosed that way. Consequently, some users will opt to use encrypted services that avoid record keeping and offer greater protection from detection. To some, not providing the infrastructure for such complete data retention and monitoring in the first place is the only reliable safeguard against abuse.

v. *Monitoring Obligations*

The challenge of a system of notice and takedown, erasure, or blocking is that the intermediary needs to know what content to take down, what to block and so on.[194] For this, the intermediary will rely on some form of notification. As noted earlier, the notice normally comes from a complaint from the public or an official body. There is a question of whether intermediaries should be more proactive in seeking out unlawful content. A duty to search for illegal or harmful content might, however, come into conflict with a provision of the European Directive on E-Commerce, which provides that EU member states shall not impose a general obligation to monitor content on service providers.[195] That provision led the CJEU to conclude that a requirement to filter content to prevent copyright infringements on peer-to-peer networks would be in breach of the Directive as it would require the company to monitor all of its users' activity.[196] The rule only applies to *general* monitoring obligations, for example in requiring the company to check the usage of the service to detect unlawful content. However, this does not preclude *specific* monitoring obligations that are more clearly defined, such as the blocking of a specific website through automated means and that does not require a detailed examination of user's data.[197]

---

[192] See Ch 5.

[193] N Richards, *Intellectual Privacy* (Oxford, Oxford University Press, 2015).

[194] See the discussion of intermediary liability and defences above on the issues surrounding the specificity of the knowledge required.

[195] Directive 2000/31/EC of the European Parliament and of the Council of 8 June 2000 on certain legal aspects of information society services, in particular electronic commerce, in the Internal Market, [2000] OJ L 178, Art 15.

[196] *Scarlet Extended SA v Societe Belge des Auteurs, Compositeurs et Editeurs SCRL (SABAM)* (C-70/10) [2011] ECR I-11959 at [36]–[48].

[197] *Twentieth Century Fox v BT* (n 175) [162].

Monitoring obligations are often criticised for the burdens imposed on the intermediary. Along these lines, the intermediary may struggle to stay on top of the proliferation of illegal material shared on social networks. There may be closed groups that are harder to monitor and unlawful material can be buried among other lawful content. To impose such monitoring burdens may discourage the provision of a service in the first place. To give a simple example, if an internet forum host has to monitor comments made by users, the host may simply find it more efficient to close down the forum. However, this may change in future, as technology makes detecting certain illegal content more efficient. The question is not just whether monitoring is too burdensome, but whether it is desirable for a private company to take on the role of policing content.

While EU law restricts monitoring obligations, that provision is not incorporated into domestic law through legislation and so could be more vulnerable to change post-Brexit. If so, there would still remain the question of whether such an obligation is compatible with the ECHR. However, the position under Article 10 is not so clear. In *Delfi v Estonia*, a news portal hosted an article claiming that a ferry company had destroyed a planned ice road, which prompted a number of user comments that were threatening and offensive.[198] The hosting company had a notice and takedown policy, as well its own internal rules prohibiting illegal, insulting and threatening messages. The messages were removed on the same day that the complaint was received, although that was six weeks after the initial publication. The domestic court therefore found the notice and takedown provision to be inadequate and found the company to be liable. The Supreme Court of Estonia reasoned that the news portal had an economic interest in the comments, in so far as user-generated content attracts traffic, and also had control over what messages could be hosted. The company argued that to meet this standard, it would have to disable discussion forums or employ an 'army of highly trained moderators'.[199]

In a highly controversial decision, the European Court of Human Rights found that the liability of Delfi did not violate Article 10. The Court first noted the difference between an intermediary and a traditional publisher, and found that the duties and responsibilities relating to each should vary according to the nature of the activity.[200] However, a key factor for the Court was that the news portal was a part of the professional media, which had a wide readership and was often a place for controversial discussion, and could therefore be distinguished from other internet forums.[201] On this view, the consequences of publishing unlawful comments were foreseeable to a professional publisher. While an action could have been brought against the author of the comments, the Court concluded that an action against the portal was not disproportionate, given the difficulties in locating anonymous authors and that the news portal did not make it easier to discover the identities of those posting the relevant statements.

---

[198] *Delfi* (n 66).
[199] ibid, [72].
[200] ibid, [113].
[201] ibid, [116].

The ruling attracted considerable criticism and a powerful dissent. At the heart of the criticism is a concern that the European Court of Human Rights is allowing liability to be imposed where the intermediary does not have 'actual knowledge' of the unlawful content.[202] By finding that the usual notice and takedown provisions are not enough, the worry is that the intermediary will have to engage in a system of monitoring to avoid liability.

The decision in *Delfi* does not impose any obligation to monitor; it merely states that in some circumstances such obligations will not violate Article 10. Individual states can therefore limit liability or provide further defences if they wish to do so. The ruling was also based on the fact that the platform in *Delfi* produced content and encouraged users to comment, which will not be true of all social media platforms.[203] *Delfi* can also be explained as an exceptional case, where it was dealing with forms of hate speech that do not benefit from strong Article 10 protection.[204]

The decision in *Delfi* can be contrasted with *MTE v Hungary*, where the European Court of Human Rights found that the liability of two news portals for user comments injuring a company's reputation violated Article 10.[205] Both portals in that case had a moderation policy and had removed the content on receiving notice. The case was distinguished from *Delfi*, where the expression was hate speech, which meant the comments had to be taken down with some urgency. By contrast, in *MTE* the message was not clearly unlawful and a different balance was struck. The Court stated that intermediaries should be treated in the same way as the press and found that to punish the intermediary would be akin to punishing a journalist for carrying the comments of others in an interview.[206] That connects the role of the intermediary with principle of *Jersild v Denmark*, which allows the media to report on views that are held by others.[207] Moreover, the Court warned of requiring intermediaries to show 'excessive and impracticable forethought' in knowing when harmful and unlawful comments are likely to be made. While the Court distinguished *Delfi* on the facts, the tone of the ruling certainly stands in contrast with the earlier decision. In particular, the Court was particularly alert to the dangers of closing down spaces for discussion and the risks of over-filtering.

The concerns that monitoring responsibilities could promote private censorship are well founded. However, there are good reasons to be cautious about demanding that Article 10 requires an 'actual knowledge' standard in all cases. The problem in *Delfi* was not the presence of a monitoring obligation, but that the domestic court set the bar too low to trigger such responsibilities. The initial article did not pose a higher risk of prompting threatening messages than any other news item. Simply that a news article touched on a controversial topic cannot be a reason for requiring additional

---

[202] See Judge Sajo's dissent in *Delfi*.

[203] ibid, [116]; *Tamiz v United Kingdom*, App no 3877/14 (19 September 2017) at [88].

[204] Though the dissenters in *Delfi* argued that the content was labelled hate speech without full examination. See Murray (n 172) 209.

[205] *Magyar Tartalomszolgaltatok Egyesulete* (n 83).

[206] ibid.

[207] *Jersild v Denmark*, App no 15890/8 (1995) 19 EHRR 1. The discussion in earlier chapters has argued that while such direct analogies with traditional media are not always helpful, the provision of a platform is a type of media function.

obligations. However, in some instances, a host for comments might be expected to take some preventive measures. For example, if the media reports an alleged rape, then the newspaper can be expected to disable comments if there are concerns that members of the public will post content that prejudices a fair trial or names the victim. In such cases, the professional media can be expected to think through the risks generated by the initial publication.

vi. Fairness and Neutrality

Another responsibility that can be expected of intermediaries is to act fairly among various speakers. This function is particularly important in relation to the larger intermediaries that perform a gatekeeping role and provide a platform for speakers. The algorithm used by a search engine or social media site may determine which content is most likely to get attention. Moreover, the intermediary may have special arrangements that prioritise the content of certain established news sites. While newspapers and broadcasters have defended their editorial discretion, they are now to some degree dependent on the editorial choices of the intermediary.

Debates on fair access have often focused on the issue of net neutrality, imposing rules that prevent certain intermediaries, such as broadband providers, from offering different tiers of service for different content providers.[208] For example, if the larger well-financed media companies can afford access to a faster service, which prioritises visits to their content above other internet traffic, then that might entrench the company's position and visibility. While important, the issue of 'net neutrality' only goes so far in ensuing fairness and does not level the playing field among speakers more generally.

There are concerns about fairness in relation to the more general decisions made by intermediaries. Many intermediaries provide services that organise masses of material on the internet, the most obvious examples being search engines or feeds on a social network. Such services by definition have to discriminate against some content and prioritise certain messages above others. As such, the services cannot be neutral in relation to the content.

The point is sometimes made that such decisions are done by algorithm and are automated, and therefore less prone to manipulation, inconsistency and personal bias than decisions of a human editor. However, even where the process is automated and 'non-human', there is scope for bias to emerge in the way the algorithm has been designed. The algorithm designer has to make a choice about what factors should give a page or content greater prominence on the service. This could have a number of effects. An emphasis on what the user has previously looked at might lead that user to exist in a 'bubble', hearing messages that reflect existing interests rather than diverse views.[209] Another side effect might be the 'rich get richer' dynamic, in which popular sources of content are given a higher ranking and thereby remain more popular.[210]

---

[208] For a classic argument, see T Wu, 'Network Neutrality, Broadband Discrimination' (2003) 2 *Journal of Telecommunications & High Technology Law* 141.

[209] See E Pariser, *The Filter Bubble: What The Internet Is Hiding From You* (London, Viking, 2011).

[210] M Hindman, *The Myth of Digital Democracy* (Princeton, Princeton University Press, 2009).

Approaching the issue from a different angle, the algorithm may fail to discriminate enough and do little to stop blatant falsities from being widely circulated.

A challenge lies in devising systems in which the intermediary can be held accountable for the algorithmic decision. One type of accountability can come through the processes for transparency and challenging decisions that were discussed earlier. More broadly, intermediaries could be subject to positive obligations to develop the algorithm or selection with certain goals in mind. One option is to arrange the algorithm in a way that ensures that people are confronted with diverse opinions and sources. Such an approach could be seen as the development of an equivalent to certain broadcast-style regulations, but devised to fit with the activities of the larger intermediary. The effects of the decisions by algorithm have received considerable attention in the wake of concerns about fake news. The infrastructure of digital media has made it particularly easy for falsities to circulate and gain attention, so the intermediaries cannot simply wash their hands of the problem. For example, pressure is being applied to stop identified fake news and extremist websites receiving advertising from the main internet companies. In addition to the choices made via an algorithm, some intermediaries are also engaging human fact checkers to identify false news stories. Once a falsity is found, then it could be blocked, taken down, pushed lower down the rankings or simply flagged to the reader.

However, there is an uneasiness about a company or even court engaging in either engineering or human evaluation to decide what quality of information is reliable and deserves to be circulated, save in the clearest examples of harmful content. That uneasiness also reveals a tension that runs throughout media law when looking editorial responsibility more generally. On the one hand, responsibility is demanded of the intermediary, but at the same time there is a fear that such responsibility entrusts the intermediary with a significant degree of power, which can be misused.

V. Conclusion

The changes brought about by digital communications have had an incredible impact on all areas of media law. The discussion has shown how the increased opportunities for expression have had an empowering effect for many, but have also increased the opportunities for harmful speech to be widely circulated. The changes also mean more people are now potentially brought within the scope of media law and subject to its controls. Media laws are no longer just the concern of the newspaper editor or broadcaster, but can apply to anyone making content available to a wide audience.

This chapter has shown the complexities in attempting to apply the pre-existing media laws and techniques of control to online communications. Some types of online activity do not have a clear analogy with publications in the offline world, as noted in the discussion of hyperlinking. In addition, there are challenges in determining when publication takes place and when it is appropriate for the content published internationally to be subject to domestic law. While the general rule is that publication takes place when the content is accessed within the jurisdiction, the rules are developing and special rules have been enacted in defamation law to limit the reach of that tort in relation to internet publications.

The growth of the digital media raises some fundamental questions about the future direction of media law. The digital media can be used to infringe rights to privacy and reputation, circulate obscene content, undermine national security, jeopardise court proceedings, circulate falsities, stir up hatred and division, and a multitude of other problems. In tackling these issues, there are several actors in the chain of publication that can be targeted, from the initial publisher, to intermediaries and the reader. An initial instinct is to say that the originator of the content should be held primarily responsible. In many cases, that will be an appropriate response. A person that posts revenge pornography, for example, should be held responsible for their actions. However, the initial speaker is sometimes the low-hanging fruit for prosecutors and litigators. Assuming the individual speaker on the social media lacks significant resources, a threatening letter from a lawyer or approach from the police is likely is to get the desired apology, retraction or removal, even when such a response is not warranted.

In other cases, imposing liability on speakers may be disproportionate. A person may make an insulting or offensive remark, but that alone should not provide a basis for criminal liability or private law damages. Such liability could have a chilling effect on the general flow of conversation online. People should be free to make mistakes, which sometimes overstep the mark and cause offence, without repercussions that involve criminal liability, lengthy litigation or crippling legal costs. Earlier it was argued that the Article 10 jurisprudence should develop in order to offer some protection for 'low level' speakers in line with individual freedom of expression. This does not mean that speakers should be immune from liability, but that legal sanctions should be reserved for the most serious types of case.

While informal conversations require some protection, there is good reason to ensure that such content does not remain available in perpetuity. A defamatory remark should not follow a person for the rest of their life whenever their name is typed into a search engine. In this context, action from the intermediary in removing the content or making it less prominent can provide a more proportionate response to deal with the harms. Intermediary responsibility represents a balance in which the initial poster is not subjected to punishment, but nor is the person affected by the comments left without any remedy.

Intermediary responsibility is, however, the source of controversy. While the technology companies often argue that they are not responsible for content and merely facilitate communication, such companies make important choices that perform a type of editorial function. While an algorithm provides an automated way to edit results, it is a reflection of a company's policy about how to prioritise content. Decisions about an algorithm are crucial in determining what sort of information is most likely to come to the public's attention. This may not operate like an ordinary editorial policy, but its function is powerful and has serious consequences.

The previous chapter examined the different regulatory approaches applied to the broadcast and print media, and argued that the dual system of regulation was beneficial by providing complementary approaches to the media. In the earlier days of the internet, there were debates about where the digital media should fit within that system and whether the appropriate regulatory model was broadcast or print. It is now clear that some parts of the digital media are similar to newspapers, while others are closer to broadcasters, though the differences are becoming less significant. However, in some cases there is no obvious comparator. Rather than making strained analogies with the traditional media, the distinct function of the intermediary in the system of communication needs to be recognised. The role of intermediaries should be viewed as providing an additional sector of the media to complement the distinct functions and expectations of other media sectors. The intermediary provides a platform for different viewpoints and speakers. The intermediary allows people to access what others have said and aims to be responsive to the requests and behaviour of the user. The intermediary nonetheless determines the terms on which people communicate. As such, it should be subject to a set of specific duties and responsibilities appropriate to those functions. These duties and responsibilities are still evolving, and are coming to form a distinct area of media law.

The duties and responsibilities discussed earlier aim to show the types of standard being expected from the intermediary. The point has not been to strongly endorse any particular model, but to explore the possibilities. Each type of responsibility raises potential problems. Not least there are concerns about private censorship, prior restraint and a lack of due process in relation to removing, blocking or filtering content. The role of record keeping is controversial, in so far as it undermines the potential for anonymity and raises dangers about the monitoring of behaviour. The challenge is therefore to develop these duties and responsibilities in a way that provides exceptions and safeguards to deal with these concerns.

It is hard to generalise about the digital media, given the range of different types of speaker, publisher and intermediary. Some perform the functions of traditional media bodies, others will perform newer functions, while others are individuals exercising expression rights. In relation to those digital publishers that perform a traditional media function, it remains important to uphold media standards and ethics online. The professional media can set a standard that influences content by non-media speakers, provide a focus for discussion and help to make sense of the vast quantities of information. However, the different types of communications and actors are subject to differing expectations, standards and responsibilities. The plural model for media regulation discussed in the previous chapter remains important in relation to the digital media. The ideal for media law is to facilitate and support a system of diverse types of activity, in which the range of communications collectively serve the needs of the public in a democratic society.

8

Conclusion

The preface asked whether there was any unity to media law, or whether it was simply a collection of diverse laws that happen to regulate publications. The previous chapters have shown that there are various common questions and approaches across the different parts of media law. The discussion started with an account of media freedom, which sees the performance of certain democratic functions as a condition for the legitimation of the media's communicative power. The subsequent chapters showed how various areas of law have sought to strike a balance in carving out a space for the democratic functions (for example through various defences or limits on liability), while assigning certain responsibilities to the media to prevent the abuse of power. The discussion has outlined some of the challenges for the current law and debates about the way that balance is struck. This conclusion will draw on the earlier discussion and note some of the common issues and broad trends that lie at the heart of media law. First, the way that media law reflects a changing role for public opinion in a democratic society will be discussed. The various methods by which the media is constrained and controlled will then be examined. The discussion will then look at the common methodology that is increasingly employed in various parts of media law. The way the law approaches the effects of the media on the audience will be considered. Finally, this conclusion will look at the issue of media power. While there are exceptions to the trends identified here, the discussion sets out the general direction of travel for media law.

I. The Changing Role of Public Opinion

In Chapter 1, it was argued that the understanding of media freedom is a product of the political and social culture. Accordingly, the changes in media law reflect a change in the role of public opinion in British democracy. The discussion in earlier chapters has shown how various media laws have adapted to the contemporary culture that demands greater transparency in public life and subjects more areas of life to public discussion. The evolution can be illustrated by changes in relation to the disclosure of wrongdoing. Traditionally, in some areas of law there was a view that a suspected wrongdoing should be reported to the appropriate authority or institution, and that the matter was not something the public had a strong interest in knowing. In defamation law, the defence of qualified privilege rarely attached to publications to the world at large.[1] There was no duty to inform the public on allegations of serious wrongdoing and instead communications to the police or investigators tended to be privileged. In line with this view, confidential sources for the police were protected, but not those of journalists.[2] Similarly, the old law of contempt of court could constrain 'trial by media' in which public opinion prejudged a determination of the court.[3] The approach was informed by a division of labour, in which the assessment of the allegation of wrongdoing was assigned to formal institutions of investigation and adjudication. The public were free to scrutinise the work of the police and courts, but were expected not to make an assessment of an allegation that would usurp the function of the formal institutions.

The division of labour remains in place, in so far as formal institutions take primary responsibility for certain tasks. However, the role for public opinion has changed and the public are sometimes entitled to know about certain allegations and claims, and to form their own view. In *Theakston*, Ouseley J stated in relation to privacy law:

> The free press is not confined to the role of a confidential police force; it is entitled to communicate directly with the public for the public to reach its own conclusion.[4]

In *ERK*, Nicol J stated that 'the police have a vital role in the investigation of crime, but that is not their monopoly' and that the watchdog function of the press includes the investigation of such matters.[5] The current law of contempt of court therefore does not aim to prevent the public forming an opinion on such matters, but is concerned with protecting the legal process from prejudicial media coverage. While reports of a police investigation are subject to the law of defamation, the public interest defence allows for some allegations to be made to the world at large even when the defendant cannot prove the truth of the statement.[6] Journalists' sources are now offered stronger, albeit qualified, protection. The change is not complete and there are still areas where a person is required to report misconduct to the official institutions, such as allegations made by whistleblowers about the security services.[7] Government secrecy remains an area for controversy, with critics calling for a public interest defence to permit a 'right to go public' as a last resort.

The division of labour between public opinion and the official institutions provides just one example of a broader trend, in which audiences are trusted to receive content that was previously restricted. In defamation law, the private right to a good name is partially qualified by the need to secure the flow of information where it serves the

---

[1] *Blackshaw v Lord* [1984] QB 1 (CA).

[2] *A-G v Clough* [1963] 1 QB 773 and *D v National Society for the Prevention of Cruelty to Children (NSPCC)* [1978] AC 171.

[3] *A-G v Times Newspapers Ltd* [1974] AC 273 (HL).

[4] *Theakson v MGN Ltd* [2002] EWHC 137 (QB), [2002] EMLR 22 at [69].

[5] *ERY v Associated Newspapers Ltd* [2016] EWHC 2760 (QB), [2017] EMLR 9.

[6] *Flood v Times Newspapers Ltd* [2012] UKSC 11, [2012] 2 AC 273.

[7] *R v Shayler* [2002] UKHL 11, [2003] 1 AC 247.

public interest. In relation to obscenity law, a wider range of content is freely available and less reliance is placed on moralistic arguments. The changing role of public opinion can also be seen in rights of access to government information. Traditionally, Britain had a reputation for state secrecy, and official information was released at the discretion of the government. The Freedom of Information Act 2000 marked a significant change, in which the presumption favours transparency and in which the public are entitled to raw data that has not been processed and framed by government. Accordingly, the risk that the public might misinterpret data is not a reason for withholding it under an exemption in the Act.[8] Similarly, the courts have found that such a risk of misinterpretation is not a reason to restrict reporting of certain family proceedings,[9] or to impose an anonymity order.[10] The move to a political culture that demands greater transparency has been underway for a long period, and the various changes in media law reflect a gradual consolidation of this position.

The role of the public continues to evolve and the demands of transparency and accountability are not the same as those advanced by reformers 30 years ago. While there has long been talk of the media serving the audience, the way the audience is expected to use information has changed. The role of the media was once thought to serve the public by offering a selection and interpretation of events that would enable citizens to participate in a democracy through formal democratic processes such as elections. Today, broader arguments are advanced that envisage an additional role for the citizen, as a producer and processor of information, as well as a recipient. In a more chaotic and fragmented political system, individuals are not expected to take information on trust from the media and will seek to interpret events for themselves. That can be seen in recent years with an increasing mistrust of experts (by some people at least) and the renewed interest in forms of direct democracy.

Chapter 1 noted several implications of these changes for the traditional media institutions. The first is that the changes can enhance the power of the media. If official sources of information and formal political institutions are less trusted, then the media may fill the vacuum as an authoritative voice. Despite the talk of citizen empowerment, people still rely on other bodies to gather and process information. At the same time, the authority of media institutions is itself under challenge. There are various outlets on the digital media that offer an alternative to the traditional news organisations. The rise in various alternative sources of news has generated considerable concern in recent years, especially over increasing levels of political polarisation and the circulation of fake news. The public may misunderstand the published information and draw the wrong conclusions. Reputations and privacy rights may be unduly injured in such a culture. The reliance on unofficial watchdogs, interest groups and other monitoring bodies can make people vulnerable to manipulation, and some organisations may frame the information to suit their own strategic interests.

The declining levels of trust and challenge to the authority of traditional news organisations also leads to calls for a change in the relationship between citizens and the media, particularly with demands for the media to be subject to systems of public

---

[8] *Department of Education and Skills (DfES) v Information Commissioner and the Evening Standard* (Information Tribunal, 19 February 2007).

[9] *Re B* [2007] EWHC 1622 (Fam), [2008] 1 FLR 482.

[10] *Khuja v Times Newspapers Ltd* [2017] UKSC 49, [2017] 3 WLR 351.

accountability. A call for accountability normally points to a level of transparency and public scrutiny. Accordingly, the public are not expected to take the media at face value and, when confidentiality is not required, it is reasonable to expect journalists to be as transparent as possible in relation to sources. However, such transparency cannot be the main channel for media accountability, as news organisations have traditionally demanded a level of secrecy and freedom from scrutiny in relation to their own processes. The protection afforded to journalists' sources and journalistic material reflects the fact that the media cannot conduct its research in full view of the public. Instead of relying on transparency, accountability can come from systems of regulation that rebalance the relationship with the public by allowing some aspects of media coverage to be challenged and holding journalists to certain ethical standards. Such forms of accountability may be important to maintain the authority of the media and legitimate its various privileges.

Finally, it would be a mistake to conclude that the changes in culture point to a progression towards greater freedom. Some of the traditional restrictions on media freedom may be under attack and to some degree curbed, but new restrictions grow in their place to respond to problems arising in contemporary culture. For example, privacy law has become increasingly important in marking the boundaries of those areas of life that should not be subject to public scrutiny. Accordingly, an allegation that a person is under investigation may be less likely to be prosecuted as a contempt, but may in certain circumstances be an infringement of privacy rights. Data protection law provides a newer means to protect individuals in relation to the processing of information (even where not private), which puts a limit on the effects of the more transparent culture. The rationales for controlling pornographic content have largely moved away from overtly moralistic arguments, but the controls are still present and tend to rest on the protection of individual rights, equality and dignity. In addition, there are newer types of control through the growth of digital surveillance and also the filtering of content on the internet. The central point is not that the media is necessarily more free, but that the framework in which controls are justified and challenged has shifted in line with the contemporary culture.

II. Media Law, Information Flows and Informal Controls

The previous chapters have looked at various laws that impose liability on publications. A description of the letter of the law, taken at face value, can sometimes give the impression of a highly restrictive system. The discussion in earlier chapters has shown that in many areas the reality is quite different. The number of prosecutions under the Official Secrets Act, the Obscene Publications Act and the Contempt of Court Act are relatively low. In some areas, low usage reflects a long-term trend, while in others a decline in enforcement has occurred in more recent years.

The low usage may partly reflect a reluctance to enforce these provisions strictly, in the knowledge that heavy-handed prosecutions can be counterproductive and cause a backlash, in addition to the general risks of litigation. The law of defamation and privacy, enforced by private parties, produces a higher number of reported cases. However, there are still many actions that are not brought due to the potential claimants' limited time and money, as well as the possibility for litigation to generate unwanted publicity.

It is important to understand how the significance of the law often lies outside the courtroom. In many cases, it is unnecessary to rely on a publication offence or tort, as there are various alternatives. Most obviously, in some areas there are regulatory bodies that provide a control on parts of the media. The statutory body Ofcom can provide a route for complaints about inaccuracy, unfair coverage and offensive content on television and radio. The work of the British Board of Film Classification means there is less need to rely on obscenity-related laws in relation to cinema, DVD and video on-demand. The Defence and Security Media Advisory Committee also provides guidance to the media, and has offered some protection for security related information without relying on the Official Secrets Act. The Internet Watch Foundation is a voluntary body that helps digital intermediaries to prevent indecent images being accessed by users. These are just several examples of the alternative systems in place.

Another alternative to legal controls can be found in the informal measures that have been discussed in many of the chapters. The government will seek to cultivate journalists or selectively release information, rather than resort to secrecy laws. The courts no longer rely on the offence of scandalising the courts, and the senior parts of the judiciary employ techniques of public relations and transparency to maintain authority. The trend is consistent with the earlier observation about the central role for public opinion in contemporary culture. Governments and other powerful institutions are less likely to put information out of reach of the public, but will instead attempt to manage public opinion. Accordingly, public relations methods can be used to deflect criticism or steer public debate in particular directions. While these methods may seem less objectionable than censorship, such approaches are not without problems and are not easily subject to legal challenge.[11]

The use of informal measures is not limited to government. Many private actors will engage in methods of reputation management, rather than initiate private law proceedings. Such techniques include the production of alternative content that will gain a higher ranking on search engines, alongside complaints to the relevant bodies and publishers. While avoiding the high costs of a defamation claim, such methods of reputation management are less transparent and can still influence which publications are likely to gain attention.

The discussion has shown that what happens in the courts provides a limited picture of how the law operates, and the law must be understood as an element in a broader

---

[11] J Rowbottom, 'Government Speech and Public Opinion: Democracy by the Bootstraps' (2017) 25 *Journal of Political Philosophy* 22.

system of controls. However, the standards found in media law provide the backbone for the informal controls and shape the negotiations between the various parties. The potential for liability can incentivise the participation in voluntary schemes of regulation. The implicit threat of an Official Secrets Act 1989 prosecution (or even a search) gives force to an informal request not to publish something. The law of defamation still provides the basis for many threatening letters relating to publications. The legal standards will also shape the actions of regulatory and self-regulatory institutions. The film classification authorities are expected not to certify films that fall foul of the law. The Internet Watch Foundation seeks to prevent access to material deemed illegal. The law sets the basic standards and expectations of the media. The formal and informal controls are closely related. Even when not widely enforced, the traditional publication offences play a significant role in influencing the other parts of the system of media control.

The targets for control are also changing, moving beyond the traditional focus on the publisher to other parts in the chain of communication.[12] To some degree it was always possible to target distributors, but the strategy is becoming more attractive in relation to the digital media, given the difficulties in identifying a publisher or enforcing the law where a publisher is based outside of the jurisdiction. Targeting the digital intermediary will often provide the most efficient means to ensure that content is not accessed, as opposed to going after multiple publishers based in different jurisdictions. Intermediary responsibility provokes a number of concerns about the potential for private censorship. When faced with a takedown request, the intermediary has to conduct its own assessment of material and it may not be in a position to assess the free speech issues. While these are important concerns, there is a move to recognise that intermediaries are performing a type of media function. As a result, a distinct set of principles, outlined in Chapter 7, is emerging, governing the duties and responsibilities expected of the digital intermediary.

The focus of legal attention sometimes moves to actors further down the chain of communication—the audience receiving the content. This move can be most clearly seen in offences attaching liability to the possession of indecent images of children, extreme pornography and certain types of terrorism-related content. The trend can also be seen in relation to contempt of court, where greater emphasis is placed on the responsibility of the juror not to seek out material or engage in research that could undermine the administration of justice. Chapter 7 argued that such liability on the viewer should be approached with care. A variation of this theme is the targeting of sources of information, rather than the publisher. Given the difficulties in enforcing the law in relation to the digital media and in controlling the flow of illegal content online, the government has an incentive to maximise the deterrent on the escape of information in the first place. More cynically, the focus on different parts of the chain of communication is backed by strategic considerations, as an individual viewer, possessor or leaker of information is less likely to have the resources to make a robust legal defence and will lack the means of communication to generate a publicity backlash.

---

[12] See J Balkin, 'Old School/New School Speech Regulation' (2014) 127 *Harvard Law Review* 2296.

These changes mean that even where publishers appear to enjoy greater freedom than before, it is important to look at the other points in the chain of communication when assessing media freedom.

III. The Methodology of Balancing in Media Law

The discussion in the preceding chapters has shown the adoption of a common methodology in many areas of law to strike a balance between media freedom and other competing interests. The methodology can be explained through the influence of the European Convention on Human Rights on the diverse legal doctrines. Most obviously, in misuse of private information the court strikes a balance between Articles 8 and 10. Similar balancing exercises apply when the court exercises its discretion to impose or discharge reporting restrictions, or whether to order the disclosure of a source. Such considerations are also taken into account when applying the public interest test under the Freedom of Information Act 2000. In defamation law, the public interest defence invites the court to examine the conduct of the defendant in making a fact-sensitive assessment. There are exceptions, for example s 1 of the Official Secrets Act 1989 applies a bright line rule that certain categories of information are not to be disclosed. Any moves to reform secrecy laws and adopt a public interest defence would invite the court to adopt a balancing test in line with other areas of law.

The broad methodology may be the same, but the specific nature of the interest at stake will vary according to the legal issue (along with the procedures and standards of proof) and type of media activity. With publication torts or offences, the question tends to focus on whether there is an interest in disseminating information to the world at large, for example in looking at whether it contributes to a matter of general interest. In Chapter 5, it was noted that when the media activity relates to the newsgathering process, the public interest is not simply what people are entitled to know about, but whether further research could reveal a matter that is in the public interest. While there are differences in the interests being balanced in these areas, each takes the same underlying concept of media freedom as a starting point.

The methodology of Article 10 tends to steer courts towards a case-by-case approach. While this makes decisions context sensitive, the approach generates greater uncertainty for potential litigants. A body of cases may build up over a period of time to provide greater guidance, but as the case law in areas such as privacy shows, these tend to merely indicate what factors will be given greater weight and which less. The case-by-case approach provides considerable discretion for the judges hearing the full evidence. The presence of such uncertainty can sometimes generate a chilling effect and lead to seemingly inconsistent decisions. That, however, is the inevitable consequence of a system that avoids bright line rules and seeks to make fact-sensitive determinations to do justice to the individual case.

IV. Media Effects

Many areas of media law raise the question of whether content has any effect on its audience. Most obviously, this question arises where some harm is thought to be caused by a publication, and there are demands for restrictions to be supported by evidence of causal link. In some cases, the government has sought to address this question directly and commissioned reviews of the evidence of links between viewing content and the beliefs or conduct of the audience.[13] However, such research raises difficult and contested empirical issues, and tends to divide opinion rather than generate support. Moreover, the discussion in Chapter 1 noted how the effects of the media can be subtle and do not represent a simplistic model of propaganda brainwashing people into holding certain beliefs. While it is appropriate for policymakers to examine the research on media effects when devising the general rules, they should do so with an awareness of the limits of the evidence and research. To demand a proven causal link between viewing content and certain harms would set an impossibly high threshold that is unlikely to be met.

There would be difficulties if the court were to enter into such debates about media effects when the applying a legal provision on the facts of a case and resolving a specific dispute. Some of the legal tests applied by the court nonetheless refer to the effect of the media on the audience. In defamation, a publication is assessed with reference to the effect it would have on a person's reputation in the eyes of right-thinking people. In obscenity law, the court asks whether the publication would tend to deprave and corrupt the likely reader. In contempt, the court considers whether a media publication would influence a juror. In many areas, the court treats the link between the content and its effect on the audience as a question of fact to be determined by the reasonable person. The susceptibility to media influence then depends on the qualities that the court assigns to the audience members. On some questions, the court will assume the audience is relatively robust and able to withstand media pressure.[14] On other questions, the court may see the audience as vulnerable to media influence.[15] In applying such tests, however, the court will often reason backwards, forming a conclusion about the content and then assuming a particular effect. For example, if a publication transgresses contemporary standards on sexual images, then the effect on the reader will be assumed in obscenity law. If a defamatory allegation against a person is particularly serious, then its effect on the reader and resulting harm can be assumed

---

[13] For example, see C Thomas, *Are Juries Fair* (Ministry of Justice, 2010) and C Itzin, A Taket and L Kelly, *The evidence of harm to adults relating to exposure to extreme pornographic material: rapid evidence assessment* (Ministry of Justice Research Series, 2007).

[14] See *A-G v Guardian Newspapers Ltd* [1999] EMLR 904.

[15] See *R (on the application of Animal Defenders International) v Secretary of State for Culture, Media and Sport* [2008] UKHL 15, [2008] 1 AC 1312, although that decision concerned the compatibility of a legislative provision with Art 10.

to follow. By taking these steps, the court (understandably) avoids the more difficult questions relating the effects of the media when applying the law.

V. Media Power

This book started with an account of media freedom that focused on communicative power and the subsequent chapters have explained many parts of media law as a means to curb the abuse of that power and hold powerful institutions to account. For some years, there has been considerable talk about the declining power of the media. Elite media organisations no longer hold a monopoly in the ability to communicate with a mass audience, and media power is coming under considerable challenge from the digital communications. Despite these significant changes, there are still a set of media organisations that are the main providers of news, documentaries, entertainment and sport. The digital media has not levelled communicative power, and there are some players that are building a global audience. There are some newer companies, such as Netflix and Amazon, that challenge the position of traditional television companies as producers of blockbuster mass appeal programmes. There are also the newer forms of media power held by the digital intermediaries that help to determine which material is most likely to be seen. For a person working in the newspaper industry, recent years may reflect a seeming decline in power, given falling revenues and cuts to budgets for journalism. However, that might have as much to do with a shift in power rather than its equalisation.

While digital communications have not equalised or eliminated media power, the changes have made the operation of media law more complex. The discussion has shown how it is often difficult to apply various laws to digital communications, due to issues of anonymity and jurisdiction. The boundaries between the different formats for communications are also breaking down. Individuals can make videos available to the world at large. Where regulations are applied to the digital media, there can be difficulties in identifying those publishers that really are the functional equivalent of the traditional media. For example, the extent to which audio visual content on the digital media should be treated as a type of broadcast has been a live issue in debates about regulation.

The changes show that media law is no longer just the law for reporters, newspaper editors or TV producers. It is an area that governs a complex landscape for mass communications, which includes various different types of actor. However, many of the traditional media laws were designed with a particular model of the media in mind, and thus may not be appropriate to apply to the many digital conversations taking place on social media. That does not mean those conversations should be free from all legal controls, but that they should not be expected to meet the duties and responsibilities required of a professional organisation. While there is a trend for saying that the protection for the media should be available to all publishers performing a similar function, there is a danger that such an approach can conflate issues of media freedom and freedom of expression (and under-value the latter where it is at stake). The challenge for media law is in adapting to this environment and ensuring that the different roles played by the various actors can be accommodated. At the same time, conversational speakers on social media should not benefit from all the privileges provided to the professional media, such as the protection of journalistic material or access to certain courts. That represents a trade-off in which individual freedom of speech is not subject to the same level of responsibility, but does not enjoy all the legal benefits on offer to the media.

It is hoped that this book has outlined the interests and justifications underlying media laws, and also various methods of meeting those goals. The discussion has shown the potential risks to media freedom in the various legal and informal controls. As the law has developed, much has been done to accommodate the freedom of the media to inform, scrutinise and provide a platform. Although as the old problems are tamed, new ones appear, and this makes the protection of media freedom a constant task. While recognising the importance of media freedom in democracy, it is also important to recognise it as a powerful actor in its own right, whose authority is under challenge in the contemporary culture. The account of media freedom given in this book is conditional and demands a level of accountability from the media, but it is also one that requires the legal protection of a space to enable the media to perform its vital function in a democratic society.

Index